HOMICIDE
A Forensic Psychology
CASEBOOK

HOMICIDE
A Forensic Psychology
CASEBOOK

Edited by

Joan Swart
Eisner Institute for Professional Studies
Encino, California, USA

Lee Mellor
Concordia University
Montreal, Canada

CRC Press is an imprint of the
Taylor & Francis Group, an **informa** business

CRC Press
Taylor & Francis Group
6000 Broken Sound Parkway NW, Suite 300
Boca Raton, FL 33487-2742

© 2017 by Taylor & Francis Group, LLC
CRC Press is an imprint of Taylor & Francis Group, an Informa business

No claim to original U.S. Government works

Printed on acid-free paper
Version Date: 20160322

International Standard Book Number-13: 978-1-4987-3152-2 (Hardback)

This book contains information obtained from authentic and highly regarded sources. Reasonable efforts have been made to publish reliable data and information, but the author and publisher cannot assume responsibility for the validity of all materials or the consequences of their use. The authors and publishers have attempted to trace the copyright holders of all material reproduced in this publication and apologize to copyright holders if permission to publish in this form has not been obtained. If any copyright material has not been acknowledged please write and let us know so we may rectify in any future reprint.

Except as permitted under U.S. Copyright Law, no part of this book may be reprinted, reproduced, transmitted, or utilized in any form by any electronic, mechanical, or other means, now known or hereafter invented, including photocopying, microfilming, and recording, or in any information storage or retrieval system, without written permission from the publishers.

For permission to photocopy or use material electronically from this work, please access www.copyright.com (http://www.copyright.com/) or contact the Copyright Clearance Center, Inc. (CCC), 222 Rosewood Drive, Danvers, MA 01923, 978-750-8400. CCC is a not-for-profit organization that provides licenses and registration for a variety of users. For organizations that have been granted a photocopy license by the CCC, a separate system of payment has been arranged.

Trademark Notice: Product or corporate names may be trademarks or registered trademarks, and are used only for identification and explanation without intent to infringe.

Library of Congress Cataloging-in-Publication Data

Names: Swart, Joan, editor. | Mellor, Lee, 1982- editor.
Title: Homicide : a forensic psychology casebook / editors, Joan Swart and
Lee Mellor.
Other titles: Homicide (CRC Press)
Description: Boca Raton, FL : CRC Press, 2017. | Includes bibliographical
references and index.
Identifiers: LCCN 2016007288 | ISBN 9781498731522 (alk. paper)
Subjects: LCSH: Homicide--Psychological aspects. | Criminal psychology. |
Psychology, Forensic.
Classification: LCC HV6515 .H636 2017 | DDC 614/.15--dc23
LC record available at http://lccn.loc.gov/2016007288

Visit the Taylor & Francis Web site at
http://www.taylorandfrancis.com

and the CRC Press Web site at
http://www.crcpress.com

Printed and bound in the United States of America by Publishers Graphics,
LLC on sustainably sourced paper.

To my friend and mentor, Jack Apsche: Your memories will forever remain in the hearts and minds of those your kindness touched.

—Joan Swart

This book is dedicated to my grandmother, Dorothea, across the ocean but always in my heart.

—Lee Mellor

In memory of the victims of homicide:

What though the radiance which was once so bright be now for ever taken from my sight,
Though nothing can bring back the hour
Of splendor in the grass, of glory in the flower.
We will grieve not, rather find
Strength in what remains behind.

—William Wordsworth (1837)

Contents

Foreword	ix
Acknowledgments	xi
Editors	xiii
Contributors	xv

1	Introduction *Lee Mellor*	1

Section I Reactive and Belief-Oriented Offenders

2	Reactive Aggressive Offenders *Joan Swart*	15
3	Domestic Homicide *Michelle Wright and Nicola Manning*	35
4	Disgruntled and Revenge Killers *Joan Swart*	55
5	Hate Crimes in America and the Slavery Paradigm *Allan L. Branson*	71

Section II Sexual Homicide Offenders

6	An Introduction to Sexual Homicides *Lee Mellor*	83
7	Necrophilic Homicide Offenders *Lee Mellor*	97

8 Sexually Sadistic Homicide Offenders — 125
Lee Mellor

Section III Personality and Mentally-Disordered Homicide Offenders

9 Psychopathic Homicide Offenders — 165
Lee Mellor, Katherine Ramsland, and Michel Funicelli

10 Psychotic Homicide Offenders — 187
Michael H. Stone

Section IV Homicide Offenders in Special Populations

11 Battered Women Homicide Offenders — 207
Joan Swart and Lenore E. A. Walker

12 Child and Adolescent Homicide Offenders — 235
Joan Swart

13 Intellectually Disabled Offenders — 257
Joan Swart

14 Intrapsychic Motivations in Stranger Homicides Involving Gay or Bisexual Males — 275
Dallas S. Drake

Section V Epilogue: Investigative Considerations

15 Cold Case Homicides: Challenges and Opportunities — 299
Michael Arntfield and Kenneth L. Mains

16 Piecing It Together: Using Crime Scene Reconstruction and Behavioral Profiling to Elucidate Homicide and Offender Characteristics — 315
Laura G. Pettler and Joan Swart

Index — 331

Foreword

When I started teaching forensic psychology 20 years ago, students who took the course were often surprised at the diversity of topics that were discussed. To offer a course in forensic psychology was a rather new endeavor (at least in my department) and even my colleagues looked at the topic with raised eyebrows.

Twenty years later, forensic psychology has become one of the most sought courses in the department. However, students registered for the course out of mere curiosity and as a break from their heavy science courses; today, they register out of interest, looking at this topic as a potentially career-orienting course. Most of the students are already familiar with many of the topics to be covered and delve into the course wanting to know more about this fascinating field. If anything, knowing more about criminal behaviors has become a timely topic, and more importantly, a topic rooted in scientific knowledge.

There is no doubt that this, rather amazing, change over the years has been fueled by a parallel enthusiasm for "forensics" in the media. Whether it is through films, series, documentaries, or the potentialities provided by the Internet, students and the lay public have acquired through the years a familiarity with the field, which was inexistent a few years back. What is portrayed in the media however, represents, at best, a mix of facts and fictions difficult to disentangle.

Of all the topics covered in an undergraduate forensic course, homicide is often the most popular and paradoxically the most apprehended one, most likely because it represents the ultimate criminal offense; the taking of one's life in all cultures remains a social and personal taboo. Homicides confront people in their understanding of life and death, trying to instill meaning in what is too often an incomprehensible act. As the present book demonstrates, homicide is indeed an extremely complicated, tortuous behavior that often escapes common comprehension. From manslaughter to sexually sadistic murders, from domestic violence to child and youth murderers, the panoply of homicidal behaviors raises important social, political, cultural, and personal questions. No matter how Sherlock Holmes or Hercule Poirot seems to magically weave their way out of inextricable cases, the understanding of homicidal behavior required to investigate a crime or to simply learn about its underpinnings demands a close, often intimate, venture into the biosocial–psychological makings of the homicidal brain.

Joan Swart and Lee Mellor's book is a welcome addition to this field and will be, I am convinced, an inescapable reference in years to come for the student, researcher, or investigator of homicide. Within its covers, it proposes an interesting mix of science, informed "intuitions," and practicality that will promote new ideas and understanding about homicide. As the authors remind us in the Introduction, homicide is an area where all shades of gray are permitted.

There are many aspects of this book that make it unique. First, the book surveys, disentangles, and regroups different types and situations of homicides to better differentiate their social, cultural, psychological, and biological specificity. Second, the addition of topics that have been relatively less explored, thus less understood, is an important aspect of this book. The chapters on the necrophilic offender and the sexually sadistic offender, to name two of them, are opening the field to new ways of conceptualizing, investigating, and understanding these offenders. Third, the authors demonstrate quite convincingly that cold cases can be useful in better conceptualizing and investigating the criminal mind. It is an ambitious book but the editors and authors have responded to the challenge in an informative and creative way.

To explore in-depth homicidal behaviors in all their permutations is also a sober reminder that while they can be studied and theorized in the comfort of a university office and laboratory, field investigators have to walk the path, embedding themselves in a reality that is likely to shake the foundation of their humanity. By providing detailed case studies, guides to interrogative interviews, and an intellectual foundation for behaviors that often escape rationality, front-line actors can acquire a deeper understanding of the homicidal mind.

For a teacher and researcher, this book offers a myriad of opportunities to explore new questions about homicides. It provides the reader with a useful topological map of the factors at play in homicide, a better grasp of the importance of the interrelations between the offender and his/her victims, and opens the door to look for similarities and differences between homicides and other violent criminal offenses such as physical and sexual assaults.

As Alexander Pope wrote in *An Essay on Criticism* (1711), "A little learning is a dangerous thing; drink deep, or taste not the Pierian spring." Pope's warning is particularly warranted when one considers homicide. This book allows us to delve deeply into the intricate relations between offenders and victims, and points the way to new theoretical and practical approaches to the multifaceted field of homicide.

Jean-Roch Laurence, PhD
Professor
Department of Psychology
Concordia University
Montréal, Québec, Canada

Acknowledgments

I would like to thank two of my colleagues and dear friends from Concordia University's psychology department, Dr. Jean-Roch Laurence for providing his wonderful Foreword to this volume, and Jessica Akerman for her kindness and astuteness in helping me review and correct the proofs. It is an honor to know and work with you, and I look forward to our future collaborations.

—**Lee Mellor**

Editors

Dr. Joan Swart received her doctorate in forensic psychology at the Eisner Institute for Professional Studies, Encino, CA, an MS (forensic psychology specialization) at Walden University in Minnesota, MN, and also holds an MBA. Joan served on the editorial board of the APA's *International Journal of Behavioral Consultation and Therapy* and is a behavioral science consulting member of the American Investigative Society of Cold Cases, and editor-in-chief of the *Journal of Cold Case Review*. She has published several books, book chapters, and articles in peer-reviewed journals, including a book published by Springer titled *Treating Adolescents with Family-Based Mindfulness*.

Lee Mellor is a PhD candidate (ABD) and lecturer at Montreal's Concordia University where he examines the role of paraphilia and identity in acts of violence, and their implications for linkage analysis and criminal profiling. He is the author of *Cold North Killers: Canadian Serial Murder* and *Rampage: Canadian Mass Murder and Spree Killing*, along with two chapters "Original Gangsta" and "Killing for Slender Man" in *The Criminal Humanities: An Introduction*, and four chapters in the forthcoming *Understanding Necrophilia*, of which he is also a lead editor. Mellor is the chair of the academic consulting committee for the American Investigative Society of Cold Cases and has appeared on the Discovery Channel program *Deadly Women*.

Contributors

Dr. Michael Arntfield is an associate professor in the Department of English and Writing Studies at Western University, Canada, where he specializes in literary criminology and forensic writing. He is also a previous visiting Fulbright Chair at Vanderbilt University, USA, specializing in law and literature, is a fellow with the Center for Research in Forensic Semiotics at the University of Toronto (Canada), and is a coeditor of Peter Lang's *Criminal Humanities and Forensic Semiotics* collection. A former police officer with over 15 years of experience across myriad areas of investigative and analytical specialization, he sits on both the law enforcement and academic committees of the American Investigative Society of Cold Cases and regularly serves as an investigative consultant for government, industry, and media.

Dr. Allan L. Branson is an adjunct criminal justice professor at Chestnut Hill College and Temple University, a Philadelphia Police lieutenant, and an academy instructor. Dr. Branson holds a bachelor's degree in communications from Temple University, a master's degree in criminal justice from St. Joseph's University, and a PhD in criminology from the University of Leicester. He maintains a position as an associate tutor with that institution's criminal justice graduate students. His research focuses on issues regarding race and crime, as well as the historic interpersonal and political discourse that influences communications and the criminal justice process.

Dallas S. Drake, BS, is a criminologist, author, and educator. He currently serves as the principal researcher at the Center for Homicide Research, Minneapolis, Minnesota. Drake received his bachelor of science degree in sociology in law, crime, and deviance from the University of Minnesota, graduating magna cum laude. His research encompasses deviant homicides, missing victim homicides, arson-associated homicides, church shootings, dismemberment homicide, and homicidal contagion. In 2004, his book chapter on GLBT homicide was published in an edited volume by Marcel Dekker, an imprint of Taylor & Francis. During the course of his research, Drake has performed case reviews on active and cold-case homicides, and was a consultant on the "Last Call Killer" case in New York and New Jersey. He is the recipient of the Homicide Research Working Group's 2013 Carolyn Rebecca Block Award for his practitioner-based research.

Michel Funicelli, MS, is an active police officer with the Royal Canadian Mounted Police with 30 years of service spread over postings in British Columbia and Quebec, with assignments in patrol, and in investigative units such as major crime, jewelry anti-smuggling, drug section, and organized crime. His master's degree in psychology dealt with identifying a personality and competency profile of police interrogators in Canada. Currently, he is a PhD candidate in psychology at Concordia University with research interests in investigative interviewing, detection of deception and memory, and psychopathy.

Kenneth L. Mains, BS, is a United States Marine Corps veteran and detective. Detective Mains uses a unique and particular combination of forensic science, criminal investigation, forensic psychology, victimology, crime reconstruction, crime scene assessment, and criminal profiling to solve cases. After investigating several cold-case homicides, detective Mains founded the American Investigative Society of Cold Cases (AISOCC) in 2013 to assist law enforcement members and victims' families in solving the plethora of unsolved cold cases. Mains has investigated, assisted, and reviewed several hundred missing persons, unsolved homicides, and cold cases. Additionally, detective Mains investigated public and political corruption and criminal organizations such as the Blood and Crips street gangs as well as the American Mafia or La Costa Nostra. He holds a bachelor of science (BS) degree in criminal justice from Lock Haven University and has taken a master's degree coursework in forensic criminology with an emphasis on criminal profiling.

Nicola Manning, MSc, is a registered forensic psychologist (Health and Care Professions Council), chartered psychologist (British Psychological Society), and senior lecturer in Forensic Psychology at Manchester Metropolitan University. She has worked as a forensic practitioner for over 15 years in secure psychiatric services and as an expert witness for the UK courts. She has experience in both developing and delivering a range of forensic treatment approaches, including group-based treatment for male violent offenders. She has carried out numerous assessments of male and female perpetrators of domestic abuse and has a strong background in risk assessment and forensic case formulation.

Dr. Laura G. Pettler is the CEO of Laura Pettler & Associates (LPA) and is the head of the LPA International Forensics Institute. Her practice is focused on crime scene staging, forensic criminology, intimate partner homicide, cold-case investigation, and crime scene reconstruction, and is the inventor of *The Kaleidoscope System*. Along with her dissertation, *Crime Scene Behaviors of Crime Scene Stagers*, she continues to conduct staging research and authored the world's first staging book, *Crime Scene Staging Dynamics in Homicide Cases*. In addition to her AISOCC vice presidency, Dr. Pettler served AISOCC as its first director of development and as one of its original Honorary Review Board members. Additionally, Dr. Pettler is a member of the IAI's Crime Scene Investigation Subcommittee, is the former chair of the Bloodstain Pattern Subcommittee, and a former member of the FDIAI's Forensic Medicine Subcommittee.

Dr. Katherine Ramsland teaches forensic psychology and criminal justice at DeSales University in Pennsylvania. She has published over 1000 articles, stories, and reviews, and 58 books, including *The Mind of a Murderer, Forensic Science of CSI, Inside the Minds of Serial Killers,* and *The Murder Game*. Her book, *Psychopath*, was a #1 bestseller on the *Wall Street Journal*'s list. She presents workshops to law enforcement, psychologists, coroners, judges, and attorneys, and has consulted for several television series, including *CSI* and *Bones*. She also writes a regular blog for *Psychology Today* called "Shadow Boxing" and consults for numerous crime documentary production companies.

Dr. Michael H. Stone is a professor of clinical psychiatry at Columbia University. His areas of specialty are psychoanalysis, personality disorders, and forensic psychiatry. He is the author or editor of 11 books and the author of over 250 articles and chapters. He serves as the host of the Discovery Channel YV program *Most Evil* for which he interviews serial killers, mass murderers, and other "high-profile" men and women convicted of serious violent crimes, some of whom exhibit various paraphilias.

Dr. Lenore E. A. Walker, EcID, is a professor at Nova South-eastern University Center for Psychological Studies and coordinator of the Clinical Forensic Psychology Concentration for doctoral students training to be clinical psychologists. She currently has an independent practice of forensic psychology and is executive director of the Domestic Violence Institute with affiliate centers around the world. Dr. Walker specializes in work with victims of interpersonal violence, particularly battered women and abused children. Dr. Walker has authored numerous professional articles and 20 books, including *The Battered Woman* (1979), *The Battered Woman Syndrome* (1984/2000), *Terrifying Love: Why Battered Women Kill and How Society Responds* (1989), and *Abused Women and Survivor Therapy* (1994). In addition, she wrote *Introduction to Forensic Psychology* (2004) with coauthor David Shapiro and *A First Responder's Guide to Abnormal Psychology* (2007) with coauthor William Dorfman. The fourth edition of *The Battered Woman Syndrome* will be available later in 2016.

Dr. Michelle Wright is a chartered psychologist (British Psychological Society) and senior lecturer in Forensic Psychology at Manchester Metropolitan University. She has a PhD, MPhil, and MSc degree in investigative psychology from the University of Liverpool. She has extensive experience of working with senior investigating officers in the United Kingdom and currently leads on research for the National Policing Homicide Working Group. Her research focuses on furthering the understanding of homicide, homicide offender decision-making, and criminal investigation processes to inform policing policy and practice.

1 Introduction

Lee Mellor

Contents

Glossary of Notable Terms 2
References 11

Homicide, the killing of one person by another, encompasses murder and manslaughter, lawful slayings during wartime, executions, euthanasia, and justifiable homicide. To write exhaustively about homicide would, therefore, necessitate several lengthy volumes, with each chapter spread fecklessly thin like jam over too much toast. For this reason, in *Homicide: A Forensic Psychology Casebook*, we have focused chiefly on unlawful homicide, extending to cases in which the legality of the killing has been subject to much debate and scrutiny. Thus, you will find homicide perpetrators such as George Zimmerman—controversially acquitted of the 2012 manslaughter of Trayvon Martin—alongside the likes of serial murderer Paul Bernardo and rampage killer Elliot Rodger. Where certain types of homicides are better accounted for by sociological and historical analysis than forensic psychology, we have given salience to the more useful academic lens, which incorporates a multitude of theoretical and applied perspectives.

Understandably, there are a great many factors that influence, motivate, or facilitate homicide, including biological factors such as psychopathy (see Chapter 9), psychosis (see Chapter 10), being a child (see Chapter 12), and being intellectually disabled (see Chapter 13). At other times, the spatial and social relationship between killer and victims play the crucial factor, as in domestic (see Chapter 3), disgruntled (see Chapter 4), lesbian, gay, bisexual, and transgender (LGBT) (see Chapter 14), and racially motivated (see Chapter 5) homicides. In other instances, the murder or acts of violence associated with it actually serve to sexually gratify the offender. Here, sexually sadistic (see Chapter 8) and necrophilic (see Chapter 7) homicides have been discussed at some length.

The variations of homicide in this volume are not mutually exclusive, in fact, many homicides show dynamic motivational interplay. As the sociologists Katz (1988) and Athens (1997) remind us, even premeditated homicide must play out in a series of immediate visceral moments, with the perpetrator reacting and adapting to unanticipated factors—an unexpected knock on the door, powerful resistance on the part of the victim, or a jamming pistol. Filmmaker Alfred Hitchcock's *Dial M for Murder* illustrates this wonderfully, as does Dostoevsky's *Crime and Punishment*, a classic of nineteenth century Russian literature.

In *Crime and Punishment*, the protagonist, Raskolnikov, decides to murder and rob an elderly and wealthy pawnbroker, Alyona Ivanovna. Though he plans the offense meticulously, upon actually perpetrating the killing, Raskolnikov finds himself encountering numerous contingencies—both physical and psychological—that affect how he commits the crime. Ms Ivanovna seems* more suspicious about answering her door than he assumed she would be. When she finally opens it a crack, Raskolnikov unintentionally reacts to her perceived caution by pulling the door forcefully toward him, almost causing her to fall into the street. Words tumble out of his mouth when he speaks to her, and when she asks him why he is so pale, he realizes that his nervousness is manifesting externally. After murdering Ms Ivanovna with an ax and looting her purse and cupboards, he returns to the room where her dead body lies, only to discover her half sister, Lizaveta, standing there aghast. Raskolnikov reacts by splitting Lizaveta's head open with the ax, but the gravity of this unforeseen event causes him to lose his cool. Next, visitors pound on the locked door to the shop, and he overhears that they are suspicious and about to notify the authorities. Raskolnikov beats a hasty retreat although the double homicide continues to gnaw at him for the duration of the novel. Homicide, like most things in life, is best summarized by paraphrasing the Scottish poet Robert Burns "the best-laid schemes of mice and men go awry and leave us with nothing but grief and pain for promised joy."

Generally, violence is conceptualized as being *instrumental* or *reactive* in nature, with *instrumental* violence being premeditated and goal oriented, and *reactive*—as the word itself implies—denoting impulsive violence, often driven by emotion and/or situational necessity (see Chapter 2). Some academics have assigned certain types of crimes to either the *instrumental* or *reactive* categories, with robbery or theft falling under *instrumental* and sex crimes under *reactive*. Unfortunately, this is both a misguided and simplistic approach. A rapist may stalk and prepare to attack a specific victim for days or months with the goal being to commit a sexual offense. In contrast, a robbery could hypothetically occur when a gambler in dire financial straits asks somebody who owes him money to pay him back, only to become unexpectedly enraged when the borrower laughingly replies, "you're never getting that back." In the heat of the moment, the gambler finds himself reacting by angrily and forcibly seizing the borrower's wallet. Thus, rather than saying that a type of crime is intrinsically *instrumental* or *reactive*, it is more fruitful to assess specific crimes on an individual basis. In the case of *Crime and Punishment*, Raskolnikov's murder of Alyona Ivanovna was *instrumental*, while his slaying of Lizaveta was *reactive*, as is often the case in double homicides. The killer must murder an *incidental* victim—another person who just happens to be there—to cover up the homicide of his *intended* victim.

Some of the keener psychologists and criminologists have therefore recognized the existence of *instrumental/reactive* and *reactive/instrumental* violent offenses—crimes that begin as instrumental but become reactive and vice versa. Mixed crimes can also incorporate numerous types of homicide from each chapter. David Parker Ray, for instance, was a psychopathic sexual sadist whose purported murders also fall into the cold cases category. Biological factors will, more often than not, take precedence in such instances. For example, a psychopathic domestic killer should be interviewed as one would interview a psychopath as this disorder constitutes the very core of his being.

All this to say that though the homicide types and associated phenomena such as paraphilia or the *instrumental–reactive* dichotomy are heavily couched in terminology, and the academic writing style has a clinical tone to it, the reader is urged to never let their understanding of homicides become too abstract. Ultimately, *how* something happened is just as important as *why* it happened, because one cannot fully understand one without the other. Having made this clarification, some idiosyncratic or reappearing terms have been listed below to offer the reader quick reference.

Glossary of Notable Terms

Adaptive functioning: An individual's ability to manage the day-to-day demands of life independently.

Adjustment disorders: A group of physical and psychological symptoms that emerge in the wake of a stressful or traumatic experience, which the individual struggles to cope with.

Affective violence: A response to a perceived imminent threat preceded by high levels of autonomic (sympathetic) arousal of emotions such as anger and/or fear.

Anger excitation: A type of rape in which the "rapist is sexually stimulated and/or gratified by the victim's response to the infliction of physical or emotional pain" (Hazelwood, 1995, p. 164).

---

* One of the more ingenious aspects of *Crime and Punishment* is its emphasis on Raskolnikov's mental state and his subjective perceptions. It is entirely possible that Alyona Ivanovna was not acting unordinary, but that Raskolnikov's paranoia resulted in him misinterpreting her as doing so.

Anthropophagy: More commonly known as cannibalism, is sexual arousal from the consumption of human flesh.

Antisocial behavior: Acts of aggression directed at others which may be covert or overt.

Antisocial personality disorder: A *Diagnostic and Statistical Manual of Mental Disorders* (DSM) Cluster B personality disorder characterized by a chronic impaired moral sense, history of disregarding or violating the rights of others, deception, and impulsivity.

Anxiety: Feelings of worry over events that have not yet happened, which can result in problems sleeping and concentrating, restlessness, physical tension, and nervous behavior.

Asperger syndrome: An autism spectrum disorder in which linguistic and cognitive development remains relatively unimpaired.

Asphyxiaphilia: Sexual arousal from the act of asphyxiating somebody, although this can also take the masochistic form of autoerotic asphyxiation (more details below).

Attention deficit hyperactive disorder (ADHD): A behavioral disorder characterized by hyperactivity, difficulty in concentrating, and impulsive behavior.

Autism spectrum disorders: A range of neurodevelopmental disorders which entail difficulties in communicating and socializing, fixation on esoteric interests or behaviors, and cognitive delays.

Autoerotic asphyxiation: When an individual intentionally restricts the flow of oxygen to their brain to achieve or heighten their sexual arousal.

Battered woman syndrome (BWS): "A combination of posttraumatic stress symptomatology, including re-experiencing a traumatic event (i.e., battering episode), numbing of responsiveness, and hyper-arousal, in addition to a variable combination of several other factors. These additional factors include, but are not limited to, disrupted interpersonal relationships, difficulties with body image, somatic concerns, as well as sexual and intimacy problems" (Walker et al., 2008, p. 42).

Bondage/domination sadomasochism (BDSM): An umbrella term for bondage and discipline, dominance and submission, and sadomasochism. BDSM differs from sexual sadism in that it is always consensual.

Behavioral profiling: Also referred to as criminal profiling, see "Profiling."

Biastophilia: A paraphilic preference for rape over consensual intercourse.

Bipolar disorder: A mental disorder characterized by alternating extremes of mania and depression.

Borderline personality disorder: A DSM Cluster B personality disorder characterized by unstable self-image and interpersonal relationships, impulsivity, anger, idealization and devaluation of others, and a marked fear of abandonment.

Callous–unemotional: Traits marked by affective and empathic deficiencies.

Catatonia: Abnormalities in an individual's movement, particularly restricted motion, which arise from mental disturbance.

Coercive control: "A malevolent course of conduct that subordinates women to an alien will by violating their physical integrity (domestic violence), denying them respect and autonomy (intimidation), depriving them of social connectedness (isolation), and appropriating or denying them access to the resources required for personhood and citizenship (control)" (Stark, 2007, p. 15).

Cognitive dissonance: Psychological discomfort arising from holding two or more contradictory ideas at the same time.

Comorbidity: The presence of two or more chronic diseases or conditions in a person.

Compliant victims of the sexual sadist: Spouses or romantic partners of a sexual sadist who, due to psychological conditioning, aid the sexual sadist in activities that are against their own interest, such as criminal acts or enduring pain.

Compulsive: The inability to resist acting on an urge, particularly against one's own wishes.

Conduct disorder: A childhood or adolescent psychological disorder, often a precursor to antisocial personality disorder, in which the rights of others and social norms are repeatedly violated.

Contingent paraphilia: A paraphilia which is only sexually desired by an individual when it is part of a greater overall fantasy scenario. If removed from this, it ceases to sexually interest the individual.

Crime analysis: The analytical study of specific elements of a criminal event that includes the breaking apart of individual structures for individual study of specific components that lead to the determination of relevant interrelationships of the whole.

Crime scene reconstruction: "Determination of the actions and events surrounding the commission of a crime" (Chisum and Turvey, 2011, p. 652).

Decapitation: The act of excising a person's head.

Dehumanization: Occurs when members of a society are desensitized to the value of life in general or aimed at specific groups, which results in murder, torture, rape, deprivation, pillage, etc.; also see "Depersonalization."

Defensive mutilation: Nonparaphilic mutilation, perpetrated to conceal a homicide.

Delusional disorder: A psychotic disorder in which patients experience one or more delusions—beliefs that are not susceptible to change even when faced with overwhelming evidence to the contrary; however, these are unaccompanied by thought or mood disorder, hallucinations, or flattened affect.

Dementia: A chronic disorder of impaired memory and reasoning, and marked changes in personality resulting from disease or injury to the brain.

Depersonalization: Occurs at an individual's personal level as the act of psychologically removing a person's humanity, typically so that one may hurt them without compunction.

Dependency: The state of being or the degree to which a person relies on another person.

Dependent personality disorder: A DSM Cluster C personality disorder characterized by a chronic and pathological reliance on others to look after one materially and emotionally.

Depression: Feelings of chronic and overwhelming hopelessness and helplessness—sometimes manifesting as sadness, anger, apathy, and irritability—which result in a substantial loss of the joy of life.

Derivative paraphilia: A derivative paraphilia develops during masturbation when a previously nonsexualized component of a paraphilic fantasy becomes sexualized through orgasmic conditioning.

Diagnostic and Statistical Manual of Mental Disorders: An official publication by the American Psychiatric Association that offers standard criteria for the classification and diagnosis of mental disorders; currently in its fifth edition (DSM-5).

Diminished capacity/responsibility: A defense by excuse in which defendants admit to having broken the law, but claim that due to "diminished" mental functioning they are not fully criminally liable.

Disembowel: See "Evisceration."

Disfigurement: The act of mutilating one or more body parts to make them look unattractive and/or to express a message (e.g., cutting a smile into a person's face).

Disgruntled/revenge killers: A person who seeks revenge for real or imagined wrongs at the hands of coworkers, employers, family, friends, or any other identifiable or stereotyped person.

Disinhibitors: That which serve to lower one's inhibitions.

Dismemberment: The act of excising a person's limbs. Sometimes this definition extends to their digits.

Dissociation: "A disruption of and/or discontinuity in the normal integration of consciousness, memory, identity, emotion, perception, body representation, motor control, and behavior" (American Psychiatric Association, 2013, p. 291).

Domestic abuse: "Any incident or pattern of incidents of controlling, coercive, threatening behavior, violence or abuse between those aged 16 or over who are, or have been, intimate partners or family members regardless of gender or sexuality. The abuse can encompass, but is not limited to: psychological, physical, sexual, financial, emotional" (Home Office, 2013).

Dysphoria: A state of extreme dissatisfaction or unease, often accompanied by anxiety or depression.

Egodystonic: Behaviors and thoughts which are in conflict with one's ideal self-image.

Egosyntonic: Behaviors and thoughts which are in keeping with one's ideal self-image.

Embitterment: A state of mood distinct from depression, hopelessness, and anger, but may share some of these features.

Empathy: The ability to understand or feel what another living being is experiencing.

Erotophonophilia: Sexual arousal from the act of killing another human being.

Etiology: Causation or origination of a psychological phenomenon.

Evisceration: The act of cutting open and removing one or more of a person's internal organs.

Excision: The act of cutting an anatomical part away from the human body.

Expressive/transformative behavior: Behavior preceding, during, or after a crime which is communicative—often through language or symbols. Through this process, the offender seeks to negotiate their individual identity.

Familicide: A murder, frequently followed by suicide, in which an adult kills more than one member of their own family.

Fetish: Abnormally high levels of sexual arousal from a specific object, whether anatomical (hair, breasts) or nonanatomical (balloons, shoes).

Filicide: The murder of children by their parent(s), stepparent(s), or another parental figure.

Foreign object penetration: The insertion of nonanatomical parts into the orifice of another human being.

Frotteurism: Sexual arousal from rubbing one's body against another person's without their consent or sometimes knowledge (as in a crowded subway situation).

Genuine necrophilia: When an individual fantasizes about sex with a corpse, sometimes acting out these desires.

Hallucinations: A false sensory perception of phenomena which is not represented by objective external stimuli.

Hate crime: A crime, typically violent, perpetrated against a person because of their actual or perceived membership in a stigmatized social group.

Hematolagnia: Sexual arousal from blood.

Histrionic personality disorder: A DSM Cluster B personality disorder characterized by extroversion, attention seeking, flirtatiousness, a strong need for approval, and egocentrism.

Hyperactive: Having an abnormally high level of activity.

Hypersexual: An extreme fixation on sexual desire and activity.

Hypoactive: Having an abnormally low level of activity.

Hyposexual: An extreme poverty of sexual desire and activity.

Incision: A stabbing or cutting wound.

Instrumental violence: Premeditated goal-oriented violence.

Intellectual disability: "A disorder with onset during the developmental period that includes both intellectual and adaptive functioning deficits in conceptual, social, and practical domains" (American Psychiatric Association, 2013, p. 33).

Intermittent explosive disorder: A disorder of recurrent, problematic, reactive (i.e., affective or impulsive), and aggressive behavior.

Intimate partner homicide (IPH): The killing of an intimate partner.

Intimate partner violence (IPV): Nonhomicidal violence directed against an intimate partner.

Justifiable homicide: A homicide which prevents harm to innocents or the perpetrator, and therefore is not considered as egregious as other forms of homicide.

Kleptomania: A recurrent inability to resist the desire to steal without profiting or meeting an important need.

Learned helplessness: Failure to escape or avoid a hostile situation due to the repeated infliction of prior negative stimuli such as physical and emotional abuse.

Legal insanity: A defense by excuse that the defendant is not responsible for their actions due to an episodic or persistent mental illness; legal definitions across jurisdictions are varied, but many enshrine the M'Naghten rules, namely, that a defendant should not be held responsible for his actions only if, as a result of his mental disease or defect, he did not know that his act would be wrong; or did not understand the nature and quality of his actions.

Lovemap: "A developmental representation or template in the mind and in the brain depicting the idealized lover and the idealized program of sexual and erotic activity projected in imagery or actually engaged in with that lover" (Money, 1986/2011, Kindle Location 5386).

Mania: Extreme excitement and euphoria resulting from mental illness.

Manic depression: Previous term for bipolar disorder.

Manslaughter: The killing of a human being without malice.

Mass murder: The murder of four or more people in one incident at a single location.

Modus operandi: The strategy that an offender uses to commit a crime. As the modus operandi does not gratify the offender in itself, it is much more likely to change than ritual behavior.

Murder: The unlawful killing of another human being with malice.

Murder by proxy: The targeting of victims that represent the perpetrator's primary target.

Mutilation: A physical injury which adversely affects the appearance or functioning of a body part.

Mutilophilia: Sexual arousal from the act of mutilation in itself, regardless if it is perpetrated on a living person or a corpse.

Narcissistic personality disorder: A DSM Cluster B personality disorder characterized by grandiosity, impaired empathy, unstable self-image, attention seeking, and a sense of entitlement.

Necrocoitolagnia: Sexual arousal from penile–vaginal penetration involving a corpse (Mellor, 2016a).

Necroexteriolagnia: Sexual arousal from pleasuring oneself in the vicinity of, or on the exterior of a corpse (Mellor, 2016a).

Necrofellatiolagnia: Sexual arousal from oral–penile penetration involving a corpse (Mellor, 2016a).

Necrofetishism: "Having a fetish for dead bodies" (Hickey, 2013, p. 158).

Necromutilophilia: Sexual arousal derived from the mutilation of corpses (Mellor, 2016b).

Necropenetrolagnia: Sexual arousal from penetrating a corpse with the phallus, or arranging a corpse so that their phallus penetrates one's orifice(s) (Mellor, 2016a).

Necrophilia: Sexual arousal from the corpse as an object in itself, and not necessarily any specific act perpetrated on it.

Necrornopositophilia: Sexual gratification derived from posing and/or decorating a corpse.

Necrosadism: Archaic term for "necromutilophilia."

Negative emotionality: A personality variable in which low self-concept and the onset of negative emotions such as depression or anxiety occur.

Obsessive–compulsive disorder (OCD): A mental disorder in which an individual repeatedly and ritualistically does an action such as washing one's hands, even when it is clearly unnecessary or irrational to do so, to the point of adversely affecting their lives.

Obsessive–compulsive personality disorder: A DSM Cluster C personality disorder characterized by rigidity, perfectionism, an obsession with procedure to the detriment of achieving goals, and an obsessive need for control.

Odaxelagnia: Sexual arousal from biting.

Oppositional defiant disorder (ODD): A disorder in children marked by argumentativeness, defiance, and anger.

Original paraphilia: The first paraphilia or fetish that an individual develops.

Ornophilia: Sexual arousal from dressing or decorating another living human being.

Overkill: Wounds extending into the postmortem period which are in excess of what is needed to kill the victim. This is distinct from acts of mutilophilia or necromutilophilia.

Paranoia: A thought process characterized by the irrational belief that one is being persecuted or that somebody is "out to get you."

Paranoid personality disorder: A DSM Cluster A personality disorder characterized by chronic and general distrust, hypersensitivity, and the belief that the world is a hostile place which is out to get them.

Paraphilia: "Any intense and persistent sexual interest other than sexual interest in genital stimulation or preparatory fondling with phenotypically normal, physically mature, and consenting human partners" (American Psychiatric Association, 2013, p. 685).

Paraphilic disorder: A paraphilia that either causes distress to the person who has it, or infringes on the rights of others.

Paraphilic pathways: This term refers to the ways in which paraphilias may evolve or spawn thematic or derivative paraphilias in the fantasy process.

Parricide: The killing of a parent or parents.

Partialist postmortem sex acts (PPSAs): When an offender excises a piece of the cadaver (head, foot, etc.) and either penetrates the disembodied part with his penis, rubs it against his genitals, or uses it as masturbatory stimulus.

Pedophilia: Sexual attraction to prepubescent children.

Placophilia: "Sexual arousal related to cemetery memorials (e.g., tombstones, grave markers)."

Posing: The positioning and/or ornamentation of a body postmortem.

Postpartum depression: Clinical depression, often thought to have a hormonal basis, occurring after childbirth accompanied by anxiety, hyposexuality, reduced energy, and disturbed sleeping and eating patterns.

Posttraumatic embitterment disorder (PTED): A type of adjustment disorder that is precipitated by a single, exceptional negative life event.

Posttraumatic stress disorder (PTSD): A mental illness that develops as a result of one or more traumatic events. Characteristics include hyperarousal, frightening flashbacks, and emotional numbness.

Precipitants: Short-term and acute triggers that act as catalysts for maladaptive behavior.

Predatory violence: See "Instrumental violence," also referred to as proactive violence or aggression.

Predisposers: Long-term and stable preconditions that become incorporated into the personality of the killer.

Proactive aggression: See "Instrumental violence."

Profile: "A projective process of looking for probabilities related to the type of unknown individual who may commit this type of offense… the focus is upon the offender's implied and probable behaviors, mental health status, character issues, motivations, and sexual paraphilia. Within this paradigm, the acquired data may infer information about the perpetrator's age, race, work, education, hobbies, and so on. Again, the profiler is concentrated upon the individual through the psychological continuum seeking individualized identity factors" (Walter et al., 2015, pp. 152–163).

Psychological torture: When an offender employs techniques which do not physically harm the victim, purely to make his victims suffer (i.e., are not part of his modus operandi). This can include instilling fear in them; intentionally disorienting them by placing a bag over their head, giving them psychotropic drugs with the intent to frighten them, etc.; or encouraging the victim's hope before maliciously revealing this to be a trick.

Pseudonecrophilia: Sexual acts with a corpse perpetrated by an individual who does not sexually fantasize about corpses.

Psychopathology: The scientific study of mental disorders; also refers to the manifestation of behaviors and experiences which may be indicative of mental illness or psychological impairment.

Psychopathy: A personality disorder marked by significantly diminished empathy, antisocial behavior, interpersonal exploitation, and impulsivity.

Primary: Psychopathy with strong factor 1 traits, associated with genetic causation.

Secondary: Psychopathy with strong factor 2 traits, associated with environmental causation.

Psychosis: A psychological condition in which there is a loss of contact with reality. This may include hallucinations, delusions, thought disorder, catatonia, etc.

Psychotherapy: The treatment of mental health issues by speaking with a professional.

Pygmalionism: The fetishism of dolls, mannequins, or statues.

Pyromania: Obsessive fire starting.

Pyrophilia: Sexual arousal from fire.

Reactive violence: Violence that is not premeditated, but arises as an unexpected emotional response to an insult, threat, or perceived insult or threat.

Recidivism: The likelihood that an individual will relapse into committing criminal behavior.

Ritual: Nonmodus operandi, often paraphilic, elements of a homicide which remain relatively static in their fundamental character.

Sarxenthymiophilia: Sexual arousal to pieces or parts of the human body that have been taken from the corpse.

Schizoaffective: A persistent psychotic disorder with major mood episodes.

Schizoid personality disorder: A DSM Cluster A personality disorder characterized by asociality, apathy, and immersion in a complex internal fantasy world.

Schizophrenia, paranoid: The most common type of schizophrenia, paranoid schizophrenia involves persecutory delusions which are frequently accompanied by hallucinations.

Schizotypal personality disorder: A DSM Cluster A personality disorder characterized by asociality, bizarre beliefs, and behaviors.

Scripting: When an offender instructs his victims to repeat specific phrases which are usually integral to his sexual fantasy.

Serial murder: The murder of two or more individuals in separate incidents. Some advocate that there must be a "cooling-off period" between these murders, though what constitutes a "cooling-off period" is itself a matter of contention. We advocate replacing this with a "return to routine" in which the offender resumes his typical life behavior for a period of time before committing subsequent murders.

Sexual masochism: Sexual arousal from being humiliated or having pain inflicted upon one's self.

Sexual sadism: Sexual arousal from observing a human in pain or humiliation.

Sexual torture: The nonconsensual use of painful or uncomfortable sexual penetration to torture one's victim.

Shame attack: When one who identifies as heterosexual, experiences cognitive dissonance after engaging in a homosexual act and seeks to resolve this by inflicting violence on the homosexual partner.

Signature: This term is alternately used to describe individual ritual behaviors and the combination of modus operandi and ritual behaviors.

Somnophilia: The sexual attraction to sleeping or unconscious people.

Souvenirs: Possessions of a victim, often of little monetary value, taken by a perpetrator for him to remember the crime and/or victim.

Staging: A deliberate rearrangement of the crime scene to hide evidence or misdirect investigators.

Stressor: A negative event or anticipated negative event which causes an individual to experience stress.

Strokes: A term proposed to describe individual behaviors in Keppel & Birnes' definition of signature.

Substance use disorder (SUD): A condition in which the use of one or more intoxicating substances leads to marked impairment or distress.

Surrogate enactment: The acting out of paraphilic fantasies on nonhuman objects, when a human is the desired object in the paraphilic fantasy.

Suspectology: An approach that is applied to help identify the primary suspect in a homicide investigation.

Taphophilia: Sexual arousal from funerals which by some definitions can also extend to being sexually aroused by cemeteries and tombstones.

Thanatohierophilia: Sacred and/or religious artifacts associated specifically with death or funerary practices are eroticized.

Thanatophilia: Sexual attraction to death as a concept, rather than corpses or only corpses (Mellor, 2016a).

Thematic paraphilia: A paraphilia which has developed along the same thematic principle (e.g., stillness) as a previous paraphilia.

Thought disorder: Disorganized thinking, usually symptomatic of another mental illness.

Trauma events: Occurrences after birth which destabilize the individual emotionally and regarding identity. These can also include organic damage which leads to impulsivity or affective deficits.

Trophies: A victim's body parts taken and used for the offender's sexual arousal (see "Partialist postmortem sex acts").

Undoing: Symbolic crime scene behaviors, perpetrated by an offender to reduce his negative feelings about the murder (e.g., bandaging the victim's wounds, covering the victim's face).

Vampirism: Sexual arousal from tasting or ingesting human blood.

Victimology: The analytical study of the victim, from the victim's daily routine to their most personal and private matters.

Vincilagnia: Sexual arousal from acts of bondage and restraint.

Visceralagnia: Sexual arousal from viewing and/or touching internal organs.

Voyeurism: Sexual arousal from clandestinely observing another person without their consent, often when they are in a state of undress or engaging in sex acts.

Zoosadism: Sexual arousal from observing an animal in pain.

References

American Psychiatric Association. 2013. *Diagnostic and Statistical Manual of Mental Disorders* (5th ed.). Arlington, VA: American Psychiatric Association.

Athens, L. 1997. *Violent Criminal Acts and Actors Revisited*. Urbana, Chicago, and Springfield, IL: University of Illinois Press.

Chisum, W. J. and Turvey, B. E. 2011. *Crime Reconstruction* (2nd ed.). San Diego, CA: Academic Press.

Hazelwood, R. R. 1995. Analyzing the rape and profiling the offender. In: R. R. Hazelwood and A. Wolbert (Eds.), *Practical Aspects of Rape Investigation: A Multidisciplinary Approach*. Boca Raton, FL: CRC Press, pp. 97–122.

Hickey, E. 2013. *Serial Murderers and Their Victims* (6th ed.). Belmont, CA: Wadsworth.

Home Office. 2013. *Domestic Violence and Abuse New Definition*. Retrieved from http://bit.ly/1J4g8KB.

Katz, J. 1988. *The Seductions of Crime*. New York, NY: Basic Books.

Mellor, L. 2016a.* Wider shades of pale: Expanding the necrophilic behavioral spectrum. In: L. Mellor, A. Aggrawal, and E. W. Hickey (Eds.), *Understanding Necrophilia: A Global Multidisciplinary Approach*. San Diego, CA: Cognella.

Mellor, L. 2016b.* Mincing words: Refining the language of mutilation. In: L. Mellor, A. Aggrawal, and E. W. Hickey (Eds.), *Understanding Necrophilia: A Global Multidisciplinary Approach*. San Diego, CA: Cognella.

Money, J. 2011. *Lovemaps: Sexual/Erotic Health and Pathology, Paraphilia, and Gender Transposition in Childhood, Adolescence, and Maturity*. Buffalo, NY: Prometheus Books. Kindle Edition. Originally published in 1986.

Stark, E. 2007. *Coercive Control: How Men Entrap Women in Personal Life*. New York, NY: Oxford University Press.

Walker, L. E., Duros, R., and Tome, A. 2008. Battered woman syndrome. In: B. Cutler (Ed.), *Encyclopedia of Psychology and Law*. Thousand Oaks, CA: Sage, pp. 40–44. DOI: 10.4135/9781412959537.n17.

Walter, R., Stein, S. L., and Adcock, J. M. 2015. Suspectology: The development of suspects using pre-, peri-, and post-offense behaviors. In: J. M. Adcock and S. L. Stein (Eds.), *Cold Cases: Evaluation Models with Follow-Up Strategies for Investigators* (2nd ed.). Boca Raton, FL: CRC Press, pp. 151–176.

---

* These essays are also available in Mellor, L. (in press). *Necrophilia: Theoretical Perspectives for the New Millennium*. Toronto, Canada: Grinning Man Press.

I
Reactive and Belief-Oriented Offenders

Reactive Aggressive Offenders

Joan Swart

Contents

Introduction 15
  What Is the Extent of the Problem? 16
Reactive versus Proactive Aggression 16
  Characteristics of Reactive and Proactive Aggression 16
  Neurobiology of Aggression 17
  Co-Occurring Proactive and Reactive Aggression 18
Reactive Aggression and Mental Illness 18
  Intermittent Explosive Disorder 19
  Comorbid Conditions 20
  Reactive Aggression and Homicide-Suicide 20
The Legal and Forensic Aspects of Reactive Aggression 22
  IED as Legal Defense 22
  Heat of Passion 24
  Impact of Comorbid Conditions on Criminal Responsibility 25
  Questioning a Reactive Aggressive Suspect or Defendant 26
    Interviewing an Angry Suspect 26
    Cross-Examining a Reactive Aggressive Defendant 28
Treatment of Pathological Reactive Aggression 28
  Cognitive Behavioral Therapy 28
  Mindfulness 29
  Pharmacology 30
Conclusions 30
References 30

Introduction

A reactive aggressive tendency is associated with a developmental perspective and other externalizing problems such as disruptiveness, noncompliance, hyperactivity, and impulsivity during childhood and adolescence. Reactive aggression is rooted in hostile attribution biases and normative beliefs, which are cognitions and beliefs about expectations and appraisals of the self and others in social relations. Adolescent reactive aggression is linked to poor psychosocial adjustment, antisocial behavior, negative emotionality, and substance abuse in early adulthood. Some outcomes are intermittent explosive disorder (IED) and romantic relational aggression, which are often factors in homicides by reactive aggressive type perpetrators.

In this chapter, in addition to the underlying developmental, behavioral, and clinical theories, pointers will be offered for investigators who work on a case that may involve reactive aggressive homicide behavior. These professionals examine the organization of the crime scene, the relationship between victim and offender, situational aspects, and mental health (including personality and risk) features that could be considered in identifying, investigating, and interviewing the perpetrator. Points to contemplate during the trial will also be explored, including the effect of provoking the suspect during cross-examination on the stand, possible mitigating and risk factors, likelihood of reoffending, prognosis for rehabilitation, and responding to claims of insanity, incompetence, or reduced culpability.

What Is the Extent of the Problem?

The majority of homicides not involving gangs or organized crime are quick and straightforward to solve, although America's homicide clearance rate has declined from around 90% in 1965 to about 63% in 2012 (FBI, 2012) for other reasons. These are mostly blamed on limited resources and manpower, as well as higher standards for charging someone (Geberth, 2015). According to a study by Wellford and Cronin (2000), the declining homicide clearance rate could also be due to an increase in homicides where there is no preexisting social relationship between the victim and offender. Such stranger-to-stranger homicides have likely become more prevalent due to more activity in illegal drug trades and other organized crimes, which is also a deterrent for witnesses to come forward—another possible contribution to lower clearance rates.

However, what continues to make many homicides easier to solve is that almost 80% of homicides in the United States are still committed by an acquaintance of the victim, and slightly less (71%) involve a single offender and single victim (Swart, 2013). An overwhelming percentage of offenders are male (90%), with 78% male victims. Two-thirds of the known causes of a homicide event are precipitated by an argument or physical brawl (Swart, 2013). Note that these statistics only reflect the cases where the victim and offender(s), and their situation and relationship have been identified. According to the FBI Uniform Crime Reports, the identity of the offender(s) is unknown in about 30% of homicide cases in the United States.

Therefore, the majority of homicides are preceded by events that involve an impromptu fight between male acquaintances. But most often, even with many stranger-to-stranger homicides, there is a lack of premeditation to commit murder. The act is committed in an unplanned and disorganized way with weapons of convenience. Many times, angry perpetrators give little thought to conceal their crimes. There are also often witnesses present with a spur-of-the-moment reaction. Typically, such behavior is governed by an innate tendency to reactive aggression triggered by an external situation that creates emotional conflict or instability within the offender. In this sense, reactive aggression is contrasted with proactive or instrumental aggression, although there may be a level of overlap with any given individual.

Reactive versus Proactive Aggression

Proactive or instrumental aggression is distinguished from reactive aggression by being "cold-blooded," deliberate, and goal-driven while reactive aggression is typified by "hot blood," impulsivity, and uncontrollable rage. In a legal context, the difference has also been associated with the distinction between murder (committed with malice aforethought) and manslaughter (enacted in the heat of passion in response to being provoked) in criminal law as a reflection of the instrumental/reactive aggression dichotomy (Fontaine, 2007). However, such a parallel becomes less clear when a higher provocation interpretational bias is linked with reactive aggression, thereby rendering the reasonable person standard more difficult to interpret. Such bias makes the person more prone to interpret ambiguous situations as substantially provocative (Fontaine, 2007). In the first two steps of social information processing, a person perceives and organizes various aspects and features of a stimulus before interpreting the meaning of the social cue, whereby attributions are made as to "causality and the stimulus actor's intent, social style, and affect" (p. 247). Only then are preferred outcomes of the situation clarified, alternative ways of responding considered and evaluated, leading to the selection of behavior for enactment.

Characteristics of Reactive and Proactive Aggression

The problem is that reactive aggression is most often linked to hostile world schemata (i.e., the belief that the world is a hostile and dangerous place). This hostile attribution bias contains aggressive scripts that include "normative beliefs about the appropriateness and legitimacy of aggression and about the situational cues that prompt an aggressive response" (Krahé, 2013, p. 267). A hostile person has characteristics that include suspiciousness, cynicism, resentfulness, jealousy, and bitterness. Hostility, anger, and aggression are linked

Table 2.1 Characteristics of Reactive and Proactive Aggression

Reactive Aggression	Proactive Aggression
Insecure attachment	Lack of mentalization and affective responsiveness
Lack of prosocial orientation	Antisocial orientation
Rejected aggressiveness	Accepted aggressiveness
Goal blocking and frustration proneness	Reinforcement contingencies (instrumental goals)
Negative, unexpected, uncontrollable life events	Adaptive attempts to control negative life events
Emotionally driven	Intellectually driven
Negative self-attribution	Negative constructs with regard to others
Lower on callous-unemotional traits	Lack of empathy
Emotion regulation problems	Less emotionally reactive
Delayed guilt and remorse	Absence of guilt and remorse
High fearfulness	Low levels of fear in threatening situations
Punishment decision linked to perceived provocation	Poor responsiveness to punishment cues
High levels of anxious and depressive symptoms	Low levels of anxiety
Negative reaction to rejection and others' negative emotions	Ambivalence about disapproval
Specific provocation present	Provocation may not be present
High risk of internalizing disorder	Associated with adult psychopathic features and antisocial behavior
Moderated by positive parent and peer relationships	Stronger association with delinquent peers and negative role models
Associated with alcohol and binge drinking in adolescence	Increased substance use in early adulthood
Self-control issues	Need to control others
Developmental progression less severe and persistent	Developmental progression more severe and persistent
High emotional reactivity	Blunted negative affect
Frustration driven	Sensation seeking
Hostile attribution bias; belief about effectiveness of aggression to reduce aversive treatment	Biased outcome expectations related to tangible awards
Based on frustration–anger model	Based on social learning model

Source: Swart, J., Bass, C. K., and Apsche, J. A. 2015. *Treating Adolescents with Family-Based Mindfulness.* New York, NY: Springer, pp. 243–272.

but there are small conceptual distinctions: anger pertains to emotion and aggression to behavior, while hostility is a cognitive attitude that is enduring as the underlying framework that generates anger and aggression (Guyll and Madon, 2003). As such, reactive aggression is committed in response to a perceived insult or threat and is fueled by intense emotion rather than to achieve a goal. Such an outburst is typically accompanied by the sense of a loss of control and physiological hyperarousal (Brosbe, 2011). Also, some other typical differences between reactive and proactive aggression are described in Table 2.1.

Neurobiology of Aggression

Neurobiological and developmental studies suggest different bases of these differences between those with reactive aggression compared to those with proactive aggression. Reactive aggression is regulated by brain regions associated with impulsiveness (i.e., limbic systems) while proactive aggression involves higher cortical systems with low levels of physiological arousal (LaPrairie et al., 2011). Limbic structures, which include the amygdala, hippocampal formation, septal area, prefrontal cortex, and anterior cingulate gyrus serve important modulating functions, and excitatory neurotransmitters modulate rage behavior (Siegel et al., 2007). If the threat or frustration is experienced as sufficiently intense, an aggressive reaction becomes relatively automatic as a motor response driven by the amygdala, hypothalamus, and the periaqueductal gray (PAG), and is maladaptive when appropriate reinforcement values do not exist to modulate the reaction.

There are also various neurochemical systems implicated in reactive aggression, of which the role of serotonin, dopamine, and gamma-aminobutyric acid (GABA) is perhaps best understood (Blair, 2013). Polymorphisms of these chemicals are linked to increased amygdala responsiveness to perceived threats. According to Shiina (2015), some hormones are also involved in the regulation of aggressive behavior, in particular an imbalance between testosterone and cortisol at the subcortical level, while the neuropeptides vasopressin and oxytocin mediate impulsivity. Genetic factors have also been implicated in the tendency to reactive aggression, specifically a mutation in the monoamine oxidase A (MAOA) gene that prevents metabolizing of serotonin and norepinephrine. This MAOA gene variation is thought to be associated with impulsivity rather than antisocial behavior itself. Furthermore, maltreated children with this MAOA genotype are more likely to develop antisocial behavior than those who were not maltreated. As LaPrairie et al. explained (2011): "Early adverse perinatal experiences, in combination with predisposing genetic factors, combine with unstable family environments to substantially increase the vulnerability for a trajectory of delinquent and aggressive behavior throughout the lifespan; however, these outcomes are both complex and multidimensional." (p. 242). According to Haller (2014), the cognitive/emotional mechanism of aggression is twofold. First, the functional particularities of the brain anatomy determine the probability of being aggressive. Second, adverse developmental conditions negatively affect brain development, which introduces dysfunctional and hostile schemata, disrupts moral judgment, the ability to recognize the intentions of social actors, and emotional responses under pressure. "These adversely affect the choice of lifestyle, which alone or in combination with brain deficits increase the likelihood that the neurobehavioral mechanism...[of reactive aggression]...is activated under particular conditions." (p. 160).

Co-Occurring Proactive and Reactive Aggression

Although conceptually distinctive, reactive and proactive aggressions often co-occur in one individual. Despite this prevalence, the mechanisms and its impact have received surprisingly little attention in research, which continue to focus on the dichotomy between reactive and proactive aggression (Chan et al., 2013). Reactively aggressive persons are typically more inattentive, impulsive, anxious, depressed, and excitable than their proactively aggressive or nonaggressive peers, and tend to have fewer friends overall, probably because they feel rejected, socially isolated, and victimized by parents and peers. However, there is a sizable mixed subtype of proactive–reactive aggressors that is difficult to define (Vitaro et al., 2002). The results of the study by Vitaro et al. suggest that about 10% of children are proactive–reactive, which is about the same as those who are reactive or proactive aggressors combined (Figure 2.1).

It further seems that the dimensional stability of the subtypes remains relatively unchanged at these ages, and although comparable numbers are not available into and during later adulthood, it appears as if reactive aggression tends to abate with age while proactive types are more fixed (Swart et al., 2015). Furthermore, with social skills development, parental skills training, hostile attribution interpretation training, anger management, and emotion regulation therapy, reactive aggression is reduced, but proactive aggression is much more resistant to interventions (Barker et al., 2010). Therefore, it is important to identify and distinguish between reactive and proactive aggression from an early age to apply the most appropriate intervention and improve the prediction of later adjustment problems.

Reactive Aggression and Mental Illness

Reactive aggression is not a mental health disorder per se, but can be a symptomatic response to a wide variety of underlying psychological problems. It is associated, mostly as a derivative but also in a causal sense, with depression, anxiety, emotional instability, poor self-esteem, and beliefs of injustice, hopelessness, and persecution. As such, reactive aggression is often a part of recognized disorders, which include major depression, generalized anxiety disorder, post-traumatic stress disorder (PTSD), and antisocial personality disorder. The highest prevalence of comorbidity is found with alcohol use disorders. Although reactive aggression is most commonly found in people without a clinical diagnosis, instances of higher frequency and/or severity are likely part of a more extensive psychopathology that may be suggestive of intermittent explosive disorder (IED).

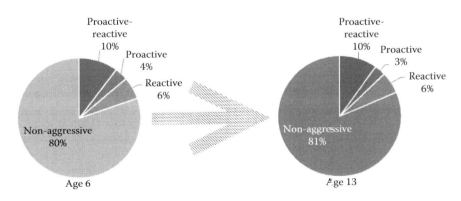

Figure 2.1 Children in reactive and proactive aggression subgroups.

Intermittent Explosive Disorder

An official disorder of impulsive aggression has been included in the first edition of the *Diagnostic and Statistical Manual of Mental Disorders*, or DSM, in 1952 (Coccaro, 2012). In the third edition, published in 1980, it became known as "Intermittent Explosive Disorder," a term that is still used in the current revision, the DSM-5 (American Psychiatric Association [APA], 2013). The criteria were relaxed from the previous version to include verbal aggression and nondestructive/noninjurious physical aggression in addition to destructive/injurious physical aggression. The condition is grouped with other disruptive, impulse control, and conduct disorders: oppositional defiance disorder, conduct disorder, pyromania, and kleptomania.

IED represents a disorder of recurrent, problematic, reactive (i.e., affective or impulsive), and aggressive behavior. Over the lifetime, it affects about 5%–6% of individuals in the United States, which is much higher than that of the weighted average of non-U.S. countries for which data is available (1.6%) (Coccaro et al., 2014). It is most prevalent among individuals between 35 and 40 years, compared with individuals older than 50 years, and in individuals with a high school education or less (APA, 2013). The onset of recurrent, problematic, and impulsive aggressive behavior problems is most common in late childhood or early adolescence. It is chronic and persistent and can be linked to attention deficit hyperactivity disorder (ADHD), conduct disorder, and oppositional defiant disorder when younger. Twin studies have shown that impulsive aggression has a substantial genetic influence, and is associated with serotonergic abnormalities, specifically in areas of the limbic system and orbitofrontal cortex. The amygdala—the brain area responsible for emotional reaction—of a person with IED responds quicker and more intense to anger stimuli. The DMS-5 criteria for the diagnosis of IED are described in Table 2.2.

The strongest correlates of IED are trait aggression and anger (Coccaro et al., 2014). Only a modest proportion of IED individuals display clinically significant features of psychopathy, such as lack of empathy, callousness, manipulative, grandiosity, superficial charm, and emotional shallowness, which are generally associated with proactive aggression. Although antisocial personality disorder and borderline personality disorder may also present impulsive anger outbursts, its level and intensity are typically lower than with IED.

In the homicidal sense, IED is most often linked to incidents of lethal physical altercations, domestic violence, road rage, school and workplace shootings, and other mass murders. According to Schreiber et al., (2011), the first outburst often occurs in early adolescence and the people with IED have an average of 43 lifetime attacks resulting in about $1,400 in property damage each. Although a large majority (81%) of people with IED report significant psychosocial impairment due to IED and consider their behavior distressing and problematic, only a minority—less than 30%—ever seek and receive treatment (Schreiber et al., 2011).

As IED is a behavioral disorder, it can technically only be diagnosed by means of reported or observed behavior over time. However, it is also possible to better characterize the symptoms and underlying mechanisms of IED by measuring individual criteria such as impulsivity, romantic relational aggression, and

Table 2.2 DSM-5 Diagnostic Criteria of Intermittent Explosive Disorder

1. Recurrent behavioral outbursts representing a failure to control aggressive impulses as manifested by either of the following:
    a. Verbal aggression (e.g., temper tantrums, tirades, verbal arguments, or fights) or physical aggression toward property, animals, or other individuals, occurring twice weekly, on average, for a period of 3 months. The physical aggression does not result in damage or destruction of property and does not result in physical injury to animals or other individuals.
    b. Three behavioral outbursts involving damage or destruction of property and/or physical assault involving physical injury against animals or other individuals occurring within a 12-month period.
2. The magnitude of aggressiveness expressed during the recurrent outbursts is grossly out of proportion to the provocation or to any precipitating psychosocial stressors.
3. The recurrent aggressive outbursts are not premeditated (i.e., they are impulsive and/or anger-based) and are not committed to achieve some tangible objective (e.g., money, power, intimidation).
4. The recurrent aggressive outbursts cause either marked distress in the individual or impairment in occupational or interpersonal functioning, or are associated with financial or legal consequences.
5. Chronological age is at least 6 years (or equivalent developmental level).
6. The recurrent aggressive outbursts are not better explained by another mental disorder (e.g., major depressive disorder, bipolar disorder, disruptive mood dysregulation disorder, a psychotic disorder, antisocial personality disorder, borderline personality disorder) and are not attributable to another medical condition (e.g., head trauma, Alzheimer's disease) or to the physiological effects of a substance (e.g., a drug of abuse, a medication). For children, aged 6–18 years, aggressive behavior that occurs as part of an adjustment disorder should not be considered for this diagnosis.

Source: American Psychiatric Association. 2013. *Diagnostic and Statistical Manual of Mental Disorders* (5th ed.). Arlington, VA: American Psychiatric Association.

victimization. The psychological test measures that have been found to predict IED, the best in terms of effect sizes are the aggression score on the Life History of Aggression (LHA) scale and Barratt Impulsiveness Scale (BIS-11) (Coccaro, 2012).

The *LHA* is an 11-item scale that was developed to assess trait aggressive behavior based on an interview. Three subscales are used. The first is the Aggression subscale that includes temper tantrums, physical fights, verbal aggression, physical assaults on people (or animals), and assaults on property. The second is the Self-Directed Aggression subscale that quantifies self-injurious and suicide attempts. The third is the Consequences/Antisocial Behavior subscale that denotes school disciplinary problems, problems with supervisors at work, antisocial behavior not involving the police, and antisocial behavior involving the police. Each item is rated on a 5-point Likert scale based on the number of occurrences of the behavior since adolescence, from 0 (no event) to 5 (so many events that they cannot be counted).

The *BIS-11* is a 34-item self-report questionnaire developed to assess impulsive behavior, taking into account the multifactorial nature of the construct (e.g., "I don't pay attention," "I say things without thinking," "I act on impulse"). Each item is scored on a 4-point Likert scale: 1 (rarely/never), 2 (occasionally), 3 (often), and 4 (almost always/always). Items are then summed to yield a total impulsivity score.

The Buss–Perry Aggression Questionnaire (BPAQ) is another test instrument that is useful to explore different dimensions of aggression and is discussed in more detail later. In addition to diagnostic value, these measurements are useful to define the nature, type, and level of aggression that is problematic, which enables a more effectively targeted intervention strategy.

Comorbid Conditions

In essence, reactive aggression is an externalized expression of internal distress as a coping mechanism to relieve a buildup of pressure such as frustration and despair. The trait most often coexists with mood disorders (e.g., depression, dysphoria, bipolar disorder, and anxiety) (Bubier and Drabick, 2009; Sher and Rice, 2015) and disruptive behavioral disorders (e.g., ADHD, conduct disorder, and oppositional defiant disorder) (Bubier and Drabick, 2009). Other factors are persecutory ideation (e.g., paranoid schizophrenia, delusional disorder) (Felthouse, 2008) and personality disorders (e.g., antisocial personality disorder, borderline personality disorder, and Paranoid Personality Disorder) (Lobbestael et al., 2015). Reactive aggression is significantly exacerbated by problematic alcohol use (Liu et al., 2013). According to Kay (2008), dementia with behavioral disturbance and PTSD can also present with impulsive aggression.

A large majority (82%–96%) of patients diagnosed with IED—a disorder categorized in the *Diagnostic and Statistical Manual of Mental Disorders* (DSM-5) under the "Disruptive, Impulse-Control, and Conduct Disorders" category—have at least one comorbid DSM-IV Axis I disorder. These include anxiety disorder (48%–78%), mood disorder (37%–93%), and substance use disorder (35%–60%) (Kay, 2008). Occurrences of reactive aggression often worsen during periods of depression, mania, or alcohol use (Kay, 2008). Incidences of migraines are also linked to aggression. Impulsive aggression appears to have a bidirectional association with depression, anxiety, and substance use as it is both a risk factor and outcome of these conditions.

It is especially the effect of frequent and hazardous alcohol use that is associated with incidents of reactive aggression that lead to homicide. In addition to any co-occurring disorder, alcohol may further increase affective impulsivity, thereby raising the risk of violence and homicidal behavior. Sher and Rice (2015) argued that it is especially true for individuals with schizophrenia, which presents a twofold risk for homicide that increases to eightfold with substance use compared to the general population. A sizable percentage—about one-third—of individuals with schizophrenia have alcohol use problems, which increases the concern with this population and the potential for violence and homicide. Aggressive tendencies are more pronounced if accompanied by paranoid or persecutory thinking and antisocial tendencies (Hodgins, 2008; Fazel et al., 2009).

Reactive Aggression and Homicide-Suicide

The association between reactive aggression and suicidality has been well established (Conner et al., 2003). This has also been extended to homicide-suicide behavior that is often found in domestic and mass homicide offenders, including school and workplace shooters. Prolonged experiences of embitterment and related feelings—sometimes referred to as post-traumatic embitterment disorder, or PTED—are common in these individuals. They have deep feeling and fear of rejection, believe they always will be outsiders, and have a very poor and unstable sense of self-worth. However, they may otherwise appear to be normally functioning with minimal or no diagnosable psychopathology (Conner and Weisman, 2011). Acute embitterment can be seen as a trait negativity that involves "a feeling of having been let down, of injustice and helplessness together with the urge to fight back and the inability to define a proper goal" (Linden et al., 2007, p. 160). According to Conner and Weisman (2011), five of the six most common emotions experienced by PTED patients are aggression related, namely injustice, anger, rage, embitterment, and revenge. The sixth emotion is a feeling of helplessness (Linden et al., 2007).

One measure that can be used to determine the presence and level of embitterment is the Hostility Scale of the BPAQ. The BPAQ explores three dimensions of aggression in 29 items ranked along a 5-point Likert scale ranging from "extremely uncharacteristic of me" to "extremely characteristic of me": cognitive (hostility), affective (anger), and behavioral (physical and verbal). Questions such as "I wonder why sometimes I feel so bitter about things," "At times I feel I have gotten a raw deal out of life," and "Other people always seem to get the breaks" are explored (Buss and Perry, 1992). Although the link between embitterment and suicidal behavior has not yet been well researched, the Hostility Scale has been shown to distinguish suicidal individuals from nonsuicidal subjects (Conner and Weisman, 2011).

The role of embitterment in reactive aggression behavior that leads to homicide-suicide has even been studied less. However, many descriptive reports of homicide-suicide scenarios strongly suggest such a link—the following is the most common homicide-suicide scenario that implies a proneness to reactive aggression, depression, and embitterment:

> …a male perpetrator who kills his long-time female partner and then himself (and more rarely others are also killed); he has a mood disorder, personality disorder(s), history of aggression, and/or a history of suicidal behavior; and he perceives a threat to the relationship (often infidelity – real or imagined) and/or the relationship is dissolved against his wishes. (Conner and Weisman, 2011, p. 242).

The same chronic embitterment, beliefs of injustice, and reactive disorders are found in many mass murderers, including school and workplace shooters, who often have a suicide plan, or at least no escape strategy. Therefore, the co-occurrence of internalized distress (e.g., embitterment and depression) and trait aggression seems to be a potent combination leading to acts of homicide-suicide and other self-destructive acts, especially in the presence of a trigger (e.g., financial, social, psychological, and relational stressors), that threaten the ideal self-concept of a person.

Case Study: The Thurston School Shooter, Kip Kinkel

On May 21, 1998, 15-year-old Kipland "Kip" Kinkel parked his mother's Ford Explorer two blocks from Thurston High School in Springfield, Oregon where he was a freshman. Entering the cafeteria with a rifle, two handguns, and two hunting knives concealed under a long trench coat, Kinkel opened fire, killing two students—Ben Walker, age 16, and Mikael Nickolauson, age 17—wounding 25 more. The previous evening, Kinkel had shot and killed his parents, Bill and Faith Kinkel, in their home, after he apparently overheard his father enquiring on the phone about sending him to boot camp. Kinkel pleaded guilty to four counts of murder and 26 counts of attempted murder and was sentenced to 111 years in prison (Moeller, 2001). In court testimony, psychiatrists described Kinkel as a paranoid schizophrenia who had been hearing commanding and derogatory voices since he was 12-years-old and harbored delusions of a paranoid nature, including that a plague was imminent, China was about to invade America, and the government implanted a computer chip in his brain.

Although Kinkel did not meet the criteria for conduct disorder, he had serious behavioral problems too, which were likely linked to the frustration, shame, anger, and fear he felt as a result of his schizophrenia. He had a history of abusing and torturing animals (Gullone, 2012), uncontrollable rage, shoplifting, and vandalism. In school, Kinkel was suspended twice for kicking another boy in the head after the boy pushed him and throwing a pencil at another student. The day before the shooting, he was suspended again, this time for purchasing a stolen semi-automatic pistol from a student. He was also depressed, suicidal, and had dyslexia (Finley, 2011). He openly discussed his desire to kill others, and his family on both sides of the tree had a history of severe mental illness, including schizophrenia, which meant that Kinkel had a significant genetic loading for major psychological problems (Langman, 2015).

Kinkel reportedly was "hyperactive, insecure, extremely sensitive, and likely to have temper tantrums from his earliest years" (p. 41). His explosive temper intimidated others and he reacted with fury when someone dared to disparage him. Like many other mass murderers, it seems that Kinkel's hidden frustrations festered until a final experience of rejection triggered the sudden, deadly acts of violence.

According to Langman (2009), Kinkel was neither an abused child nor a psychopath—the other two typologies of typical rampage school shooters, schizophrenic being the third type. It can also be added that his apparent idea was to commit suicide at the school—he had bullets taped to his chest for that purpose. When he was unexpectedly tackled and restrained by fellow students while reloading, he begged to be shot. Afterward, at the police station, Kinkel attacked an officer with a knife, again in the hope of being shot and killed. His journal evidenced his deep bitterness, despair, hopelessness, disappointment, and rejection from others, and his wishes to die.

The Legal and Forensic Aspects of Reactive Aggression

Unless directly associated with a severe debilitating mental disorder at the time of a criminal act, reactive aggression does not meet the standard for legal insanity as it does not affect the offender's ability to know right from wrong. However, in certain circumstances, it could be offered as a mitigating factor, especially when sufficient provocation existed. Knowledge of reactive aggressive tendencies of a suspect or defendant could also guide techniques in custodial interrogation and court cross-examination settings to achieve appropriate legal outcomes.

IED as Legal Defense

The characteristics and diagnosis of IED have already been discussed. Here, we look at its presentation as a mitigating factor in a homicide trial. As an officially recognized condition characterized by the failure to resist or control aggressive impulses, IED understandably has an appeal as an instrument of legal defense. The problem with offering claims of IED in this context is that it is precisely defined as involving several discrete episodes of failure to resist aggressive impulses. These outbursts had to result in serious acts of assault or destruction of property. Furthermore, the degree of aggressiveness expressed during the episodes had to be grossly out of proportion to any precipitating psychosocial stressors. The burden is on the defense to prove such a relatively complex construct, which is a difficult task, especially as it is defined exclusively as a dysfunctional behavior pattern. This alone excludes it as an actual base of an insanity defense under the premise that a defendant cannot be held accountable for criminal conduct when he or she did not understand the nature of the criminal act, or did not understand that it was morally or legally wrong due to a mental disease or defect. All but a few U.S. states have disallowed the irresistible impulse or control prong after *United States v. John W. Hinckley, Jr*, 672 F.2d 115 (D.C. Cir. 1982). As such, there are no legal grounds to question the person's capacity to inhibit violent behavior or the underlying roots of such behavior, which is the typical claim in IED. It is more often used as a rationale for diminished responsibility and heat-of-passion arguments, in particular, in the context of the effect of coexisting mental health disorders and provocation. The distinction between conditions recognized as mental health disorders and those recognized by law for the purpose of mitigation or diminished responsibility has to remain as clear as possible with the acknowledgment of well-established rules. After all, the "presence of a recognized medical conditions is a necessary, but not always a sufficient, condition to raise the issue of diminished responsibility" (Ormerod and Laird, 2014, p. 582). Therefore, although a medical condition can be a requirement for a diminished responsibility plea, it also has to "accommodate future developments in diagnostic practice and encourage defenses to be grounded in a valid medical diagnosis linked to the accepted classificatory systems which together encompass the recognized physical, psychiatric, and psychological conditions" (p. 582). In practice, this means that the legal defense team of a homicide offender has to clearly establish IED according to official diagnostic criteria and link it directly to the homicidal act according to reasonable man principles.

Case Study: The Angry Husband, Jon Douglas Hall

According to *Hall* 8 S.W.3d 593 (1999) at pp. 596–599: Jon Hall and his wife, Billie Jo Hall, who had two daughters, Jennifer and Cynthia, from a previous relationship had two more daughters, Stephanie and Jessica, in the time of their marriage. The youngest, Jessica, suffered from cerebral palsy. In 1994, the victim and the petitioner began having marital problems and were living separately. On the night of July 29, 1994, Jon went to the victim's house to discuss reconciliation and pay child support. He disconnected the telephone line at the utility box on the outside wall of the house before entering. When Billie answered the door, Jon pushed his way into the room where she and the children were watching television. He told the girls to go to bed. When they did not immediately obey his order, he tipped over the chair in which the victim was sitting. Jon and Billie went back into her bedroom. The children, who had gone to their bedrooms, could hear "[t]hings slamming around" and their parents yelling at each other. When the children tried to enter the room, they found the door blocked. The three oldest children, Jennifer, Cynthia, and Stephanie, persisted in their efforts to get into the room and finally succeeded. They attempted to stop their dad from hurting their mother. Cynthia jumped on Jon's back and bit him. This did not stop his attack. When Billie told the children to go to a neighbor's house, Jon told them that if they went for help, "he was going to kill Mama." He also told Billie, a college student at the time that she would never live to graduate. Cynthia and Stephanie tried to use the telephone to call for help, but they discovered the telephones would not work. At that point, they went to a neighbor's house where they called 9-1-1. Jennifer, the oldest child, was the last to leave the house, carrying her sister Jessica. Before she left, she saw her mother and Jon leave the bedroom and go outside. She watched the petitioner drag her mother, "kicking and screaming," to the small pool in the back yard.

When the first officer, Chief Jerry Bingham, arrived on the scene, he found the victim's body floating face down in the water. Another officer, Agent Brian Byrd, arrived and found the main bedroom in disarray with bloodstains on the bed, countertop, and a wedding dress. The telephones in the house were off their hooks. A trail of drag marks and bloodstains led from the master bedroom, out the front door, over the driveway, past the sandbox, and down to the pool in the back yard. The victim's t-shirt was lying beside the pool. Clumps of grass ripped from the ground floated in the blood-tinged water of the pool. Outside the front door of the house, the telephone junction box was opened, and the telephone line was disconnected.

The primary cause of death was asphyxia resulting from a combination of manual strangulation and drowning. There was bruising on the left and right sides of the victim's neck, hemorrhaging in the neck muscles around the hyoid bone in the neck and bleeding in the thyroid gland, which indicated that extensive compression had been applied to the neck. Water found in both the victim's stomach and in her bloodstream provided evidence that supported drowning as a contributing cause of death.

Before dying, the victim sustained at least eighty-three separate wounds, including several blows to the head, a fractured nose, multiple lacerations, and bruises and abrasions to the chest, abdomen, genitals, arms, legs, and back. Abrasions on the victim's back were consistent with having been dragged across pavement. The injuries to her arms, legs, and hands were described as defensive wounds, and those to the face, neck, and head as "intentional target wounds."

In a confession to a fellow prisoner, Jon Hall claimed that she rejected his plea for reconciliation and demanded that he leave. As a result, he lost his temper and began to strike her until he panicked, threw her in the swimming pool. He then reentered the house, took the car keys, and drove away in the victim's minivan. He admitted that he was depressed and had been drinking since earlier that day. He explained that he disconnected the telephone line because when he and his wife argued in the past, she had called the police.

At the trial, a psychiatrist Dr. Lynn Donna Zager testified on the defendant's behalf and diagnosed him as depressed and suffering from alcohol dependence. She also noted personality characteristics of paranoia and dependency, all of which were compounded at the time by various stressors, including a sick child, loss of employment with the resulting financial problems, his impending divorce, and the terminal illness of a brother. She believed that he acted in an impulsive rather than premeditated manner. His father, an alcoholic, physically and verbally abused his wife until he died of a heart attack in 1974 when Jon was 10 years old. He denied that Jon was his son and constantly snubbed him. The jury did not find sufficient mitigating factors and convicted and sentenced Hall to death.

During a postconviction hearing on appeal, Hall's lawyers presented an expert witness who testified Hall had IED. This was supported by evidence of low serotonin levels in his brain and characteristics consistent with the disorder, which the defense claimed rendered him unable to form the requisite intent for the alleged crime, and to mitigate his culpability for sentencing. The prosecution rebutted, arguing that it is impossible to measure the serotonin levels in the synapses where it operates. Also, there was no consensus on what constitutes normal levels of serotonin anyway; in addition, many medical, neurological, and psychiatric conditions have been linked to altered serotoninergic levels (Bernet et al., 2007).

Other expert testimony offered that the defendant had difficulty controlling his emotions in emotionally charged situations. His responses tended to be unmodulated. He has a low self-esteem. There was evidence of internal anger. He may have trouble understanding people and perceiving them in accurate ways. A valid diagnosis of IED is only made after other mental disorders that might account for episodes of aggressive behavior have been ruled out. Forensic experts for the defense argued that IED and adjustment disorder resulted in a rage reaction during which he was unable to premeditate this crime or control his actions and oblivious that his conduct was reasonably certain to cause his wife's death. They conceded that there was a very high co-occurrence of being an alcoholic and having IED, in that alcohol reduces impulse control further in people who already had trait impulsivity.

Dr. Caruso also testified that the defendant met criteria for several personality disorders, including narcissistic personality disorder, borderline personality disorder, and antisocial personality disorder. Furthermore, the significant stressors that the defendant experienced at the time contributed to a state of serious impairment. However, ultimately, his appeal failed and his conviction and death sentence were affirmed based on three major aspects. First, he did not present evidence of his psychiatric condition at the first trial. Second, measures that he took before the murder, such as disconnecting the phone lines outside the house on his arrival, suggested a measure of premeditation. Third, the court did not find the claims of IED convincing in that there was a consistent pattern that could be directly related to his homicidal behavior and that there was such deficiency that he could not control his behavior at the time.

Heat of Passion

A killing that would otherwise be murder is reduced to voluntary manslaughter if the defendant killed someone because of a sudden quarrel or in the heat of passion. The requirements for such a claim are:

1. The defendant was provoked.

2. As a result of the provocation, the defendant acted rashly and under the influence of intense emotion that obscured (his/her) reasoning or judgment.

3. The provocation would have caused a person of average disposition to act rashly and without due deliberation, that is, from passion rather than from judgment.

No specific emotion such as anger or rage is required, but it has to be sufficiently intense to cause the offender to react without pause to deliberate or reflect. It can be "any violent, intense, high-wrought or enthusiastic emotion." (*People v. Breverman* (1998) 19 Cal.4th 142, 163–164 [77 Cal.Rptr.2d 870, 960 P.2d 1094].) There must have been an extreme provocation that had a direct and immediate influence on the resulting behavior, which must be such that a reasonable person, faced with the same degree of provocation, would react in the same way. Sufficiency of provocation has been established in the following cases: In *People v. Breverman*, sufficient evidence of provocation existed where a mob of young men trespassed onto the defendant's yard and attacked his car with weapons. (*People v. Breverman* (1998) 19 Cal.4th 142, 163–164 [77 Cal.Rptr.2d 870, 960 P.2d 1094].) Provocation has also been found sufficient based on the murder of a family member (*People v. Brooks* (1986) 185 Cal.App.3d 687, 694 [230 Cal.Rptr. 86]); a sudden and violent quarrel (*People v. Elmore* (1914) 167 Cal. 205, 211 [139 P. 989]); verbal taunts by an unfaithful wife (*People v. Berry* (1976) 18 Cal.3d 509, 515 [134 Cal.Rptr. 415, 556 P.2d 777]); and the infidelity of a lover (*People v. Borchers* (1958) 50 Cal.2d 321, 328–329 [325 P.2d 97]).

In the following cases, provocation has been found inadequate as a matter of law:

- Evidence of name calling, smirking, or staring and looking stone-faced (*People v. Lucas* (1997) 55 Cal.App.4th 721,739 [64 Cal.Rptr.2d 282]);

- Insulting words or gestures (*People v. Odell David Dixon* (1961) 192 Cal.App.2d 88, 91 [13 Cal.Rptr. 277]);

- Refusing to have sex in exchange for drugs (*People v. Michael Sims Dixon* (1995) 32 Cal.App.4th 1547, 1555–1556 [38 Cal.Rptr.2d 859]);

- A victim's resistance against a rape attempt (*People v. Rich* (1988) 45 Cal.3d 1036, 1112 [248 Cal. Rptr. 510, 775 P.2d 960]);

- The desire for revenge (*People v. Fenenbock* (1996) 46 Cal.App.4th 1688, 1704 [54 Cal.Rptr.2d 608]); and

- A long history of criticism, reproach, and ridicule where the defendant had not seen the victims for over two weeks before the killings (*People v. Kanawyer* (2003) 113 Cal.App.4th 1233, 1246–1247 [7 Cal.Rptr.3d 401]).

Also, the Supreme Court has suggested that mere vandalism of an automobile is an insufficient provocation to satisfy a heat-of-passion defense (See *People v. Breverman* (1998) 19 Cal.4th 142, 164, fn. 11 [77 Cal. Rptr.2d 870, 960 P.2d 1094]; *In re Christian S.* (1994) 7 Cal.4th 768, 779, fn. 3 [30 Cal.Rptr.2d 33, 872, P.2d 574]). Evidence of a defendant's violent temperament, or other "extraordinary character and environmental deficiencies" (*People v. Steele* (2002) 27 Cal.4th 1230, 1253 [120 Cal.Rptr.2d 432, 47 P.3d 225]), constitutes a subjective standard that does not satisfy the requirements of a heat-of-passion argument either.

Impact of Comorbid Conditions on Criminal Responsibility

It is universally agreed that in appropriate cases, persons suffering from serious mental disorders that directly affected their actions should be relieved in part or whole of the consequences of their criminal conduct. As reactive aggression is not an accepted mental disorder but a psychological trait that is most often part of recognized syndromes or disorders, it frequently forms part of a larger inquiry of psychopathology. As illustrated, even IED, officially codified in the two classification systems that are widely used globally, is not readily accepted as an excuse defense. These diagnostic systems are the American Psychiatric Association's *Diagnostic and Statistical Manual of Mental Disorders* (DSM-5) and the World Health Organization's 10th revision of the *International Statistical Classification of Diseases and Related Health Problems* (ICD-10).

A person who commits a criminal offense is criminally responsible if it is done with intention, recklessness, or negligence. A person acts intentionally when he or she acts purposefully or knowingly. A person acts recklessly when he or she takes a risk that is objectively unjustifiable with regard to the circumstances known to the person, despite being aware that such a risk exists. A person acts negligently when he or she, unaware of any risk, takes a risk that is objectively unjustifiable with regard to the circumstances known to the person. In criminal law, the burden is on the defendant to present proof of diminished responsibility (or diminished capacity). This is a potential defense by excuse by which the defendant argues that although he or she broke the law, they should not be held fully criminally liable for doing so, as their mental functions were "diminished" or impaired. If accepted, these mitigating factors may lead to reduced charges or lesser sentences. As such, a "diminished capacity" plea differs from a "not guilty by reason of insanity" decision in that it does not absolve the defendant of all criminal responsibility. In the example of murder and manslaughter, diminished capacity states that a certain defendant is incapable of intending to cause death, and, therefore, must have at most caused such a death recklessly, reducing the charge to manslaughter.

As a partial defense of excuse, diminished responsibility has been claimed in murder cases based on lack of impulse control, abnormalities of the mind (e.g., delusions, hallucinations, suicidality, jealousy, premenstrual tension, depression), or brain injuries that resulted in gross impairment of judgment and emotional responses. Such abnormalities must be caused by an inside source. External factors causing the abnormality such as alcohol or drugs cannot be taken into account. Therefore, the effect of the alcohol or drugs upon a defendant's actions does not constitute a valid claim of diminished responsibility, since abnormality of mind induced by alcohol or drugs is not (generally speaking) due to inherent causes.

The question becomes then whether the combined effect of the other inherent abnormalities amounted to such abnormality of mind that it substantially impaired the defendant's mental responsibility, where "substantially impaired" means that the requisite impairment need not be total, but must be more than "trivial or minimal." Therefore, for alcohol dependency to amount to an abnormality, it must have at the time of the crime reached a level at which the brain had been sufficiently damaged by repeated insult from intoxicants so that there was gross impairment of judgment and emotional responses. Giving in to a craving is not an involuntary act, even if it is very difficult to control or avoid.

Therefore, claims of diminished responsibility rest on four components. First, there must be the presence of an abnormality of mental functioning. Second, such abnormality must be a recognized medical condition. Third, the condition had to substantially impair a defendant's ability to understand the nature of the conduct, form a rational judgment, or exercise self-control. The fourth requirement is that the particular abnormality must be directly relevant to provide an explanation for the criminal act (Loughnan, 2012). A thorough psychopathological profile and diagnosis, which includes behavioral observations and history, medical and mental health records, and family background, is required to establish a well-supported claim of diminished capacity. The most difficult aspect is usually to prove a direct connection between known mental difficulties and the criminal act, especially if arguments solely rest on volitional aspects and conditions that courts and juries are not that familiar with. Therefore, to be valid in a defense involving diminished capacity to negate mens rea, evidence has to be consistent and structured along accepted scientific principles to illustrate the presence of a recognized mental defect, as well as how it directly contributed to the criminal act.

Questioning a Reactive Aggressive Suspect or Defendant

Many things can cause a suspect or defendant to become angry, especially if they have an elevated tendency to react impulsively and lack emotional regulation. When a questioner becomes aware of such a possibility, they can use it to their advantage to elicit information from the other person. Someone who is uncontrollably angry is more likely to leak information unintentionally through words or behavior. It can also provide a window on the person's inner thoughts and fantasies that he would have wanted to keep hidden. This is commonly referred to as "leakage" in criminal profiling terms.

Interviewing an Angry Suspect

If a suspect is inclined to a reactive type of aggression, he is less likely to use anger as a tool to manipulate the interviewer, but they will probably have unsuccessful attempts to contain their feelings if they feel unjustly accused, blamed, or disrespected. In such a situation, the interviewer actually has a lot of power to guide the tone of the interview. Depending on the mood at each specific moment and the specific objective of the interview (e.g., information, confession, plea), the interviewer should adapt his strategy accordingly. He should also take into account any signs or knowledge of a mental disorder, both when inquiring about the suspect's behavior during the criminal act and at that moment in the interview. Remember that many symptoms of mental illness, such as hallucinations, dissociation, and mania, are not present all the time. Therefore, the fact that the suspect appears "normal" during the interview does not necessarily mean that he was in the same state of mind during the criminal act.

Returning to the topic of a reactive aggressive suspect: One can assume that the person is emotionally unstable, prone to depression and anxiety, and views the world as hostile and unjust, and themselves as hopeless and unfairly treated. Many share this typical profile, and, as a result, they often harbor a deep anger and resentment too, which boils over uncontrollably when their inner feelings become unbearable. Basically, the interviewer has a choice to make: He can intentionally cause the suspect to become angry, or make a concerted effort to calm the suspect down if he is already agitated or ensure that he remains calm. Aggressive interviewing techniques are not the preferred approach for this type of suspect as the anger will likely often surface, escalate quickly, and become unmanageable and counterproductive.

If the suspect is not an antisocial personality with cunning and manipulative features, he is not likely to attempt deception, or at least not at a sophisticated level. Even if there is such a suspicion, it is best to keep the situation calm by maintaining a nonjudgmental and fair approach to encourage the suspect to talk. In an uncomfortable and stressful situation, the reactive aggressive person is likely to experience even higher levels of anxiety and paranoia than usual. Building rapport in this context is very important (Vanderhallen and Vervaeke, 2014), which helps the communication flow and keeps the suspect emotionally stable. The objective should be to build a narrative around the criminal event with consistent information, which is best achieved with an equanimous foundation.

Accusatory interviews generally generate stronger feelings of inconvenience and distress than interviews conducted in an information-gathering style, especially for reactive aggressive suspects who are already emotionally unsettled. A neutral or agreeable style also encourages good rapport that has been shown to enhance the cooperation of suspects, which resulted in more accurate and detailed information (Vanderhallen and Vervaeke, 2014). Furthermore, by humanizing an interview (e.g., showing empathy, respect, and personalizing the interaction), recall memory is enhanced and revelations and true confessions are more likely.

In building a rapport, eliciting accurate information, and considering possible deception in responses, it is extremely helpful to plan and adapt an interviewing approach based on the personality dimension of the suspect. Reactive aggressive types are likely to have one of four general personality profiles: antisocial, borderline, inadequate, and paranoid. The following tips and guidelines are proposed by Ackley et al. (2010) to interview the different personalities.

Antisocial dimension:

- Remain calm, sincere, and friendly in tone and demeanor.
- Be prepared and know the facts of the case and history of the suspect.
- Maintain an open and attentive body language.
- Emphasize the immediacy and seriousness of the situation, but convey hope and face-saving options.

- Stay away from emotionally based bonding; emphasize benefits for the suspect instead.
- Treat the suspect with respect.
- Maintain objectivity.
- Be attentive to attempts to manipulate the interaction or exploit your vulnerabilities.
- Do not be aggressive, confrontational, authoritative, or defensive.
- Remember that an antisocial personality can also feel guilt and shame, especially if he has acted impulsively or under the influence of substances.

Borderline dimension: The borderline personality is typically unstable with volatile mood shifts that include intense anger. They constantly fear abandonment and go to great lengths to avoid it. They are impulsive, anxious, have unstable relationships and views of themselves and others, and may engage in self-injurious or suicidal behaviors.

- Be understanding, calm, and reassuring.
- Lead the conversation in an open and nonjudgmental way.
- Be patient and do not react to any instability or intense emotions from the suspect.
- Express empathy and interest without being condescending or false.
- Do not be confrontational or dismissive.
- Be careful of transference issues where you may feel the need to protect the suspect.

Inadequate dimension: This person has feelings of inadequacy, is typically easily overwhelmed, impulsive, and unable to delay gratification; they have poor defined (or no) long-term goals and a deficient conception of consequence. They are often easily influenced, overly dependent, and exhibit poor judgment. This person is young, or likely comes across as childlike.

- Portray empathy and understanding by being comforting and nurturing.
- Be patient and provide guidance and reassurance within reason.
- Do not be confrontational, dismissive, or too direct.
- Inquire about their feelings and express an understanding of the role that it likely played in their behavior.
- Adjust your inquiries to their abilities.

Paranoid dimension: The paranoid person has a pervasive view of the world as hostile and a permanent sense of distrust and suspicion. They believe others are untrustworthy, malicious, and deceptive. As a result, they are constantly hypervigilant and interpret minimal or ambiguous cues as hostile. They have a serious demeanor and act in aggressive ways to manage the perceived threats. They perceive social information in extremes (e.g., criticism, aggression, confrontation). They rationalize and justify their behaviors in the context of their beliefs of threat and injustice.

- Manage their expectations by outlining the interviewing process from the outset and explain your role and objectives.
- Be professional, open, and straightforward.
- Be brief and careful of being ambiguous and leaving room for misinterpretation.

- Be patient, tolerant, and considerate of their worldviews, and avoid challenging any directly.

- Respect their need for boundaries and do not become defensive, emotional, or aggressive.

- Come across as confident, but not arrogant or condescending.

- Do not try and relate emotionally (e.g., empathy, friendliness, supportive).

It is in the best interest of the interviewer to keep the interviewee calm and controlled. If a suspect becomes angry for whatever reason—probably a defensive reaction, attempt to manipulate the interviewer or response to a perceived cue—the best tactic is to defuse the situation by physically shifting and facing away while still maintaining the same distance from the suspect. Keep gestures away from him and assert your position as a neutral party, not an opponent (Zulawski and Wicklander, 2002). Remain objective and not defensive or return aggression. Question the underlying reasons for the anger without judgment.

Cross-Examining a Reactive Aggressive Defendant

The same basic principles apply during cross-examination in the courtroom compared to a custodial investigative interview, but the objectives are slightly different, primarily because of the importance of the jury's opinion and interpretation of the counselor and defendant. It may not be the primary concern if the defendant becomes angry on the stand, but a counselor does not want to be seen as overly as aggressive, arrogant, intimidating, and humiliating the defendant, which may generate sympathy from the jury. Utilize the personality dimensions previously mentioned to guide the questioning and predict likely outcomes. Be confident and repetitious, but maintain a respectful line.

If you are the defendant's counsel, also utilize the same profiles to coach the defendant to remain calm and in control. They should expect aggressive tactics from the opposing counsel, but refrain from reacting in an angry or confrontational way, which will not be to the defendant's advantage. For a reactive aggressive person, this may be challenging, but with good preparation it is possible. Use objections to create a short relief and disrupt the questioner's strategy. Advance preparation and practice is key; make sure to understand the beliefs and attitudes of the defendant and, if required, get treatment for the defendant to stabilize any serious psychological issues, which will help his ability to remain calm and stable during the trial, which is in the defense team's best interest.

Treatment of Pathological Reactive Aggression

There are several treatments available for impulse control disorders, more specifically anger and aggression issues such as IED. The majority of these are based on cognitive behavioral theory and principles, where the underlying dysfunctional belief system and habitual thinking of a person are addressed while training skills and behavioral techniques are applied to prevent or redirect maladaptive behavior. Mindfulness practices are also used to help a person relax, cope with stress, and become aware of and manage negative thoughts. Pharmacological options are used as a stand-alone or adjunct treatment to psychotherapy.

Cognitive Behavioral Therapy

The cognitive behavioral therapy (CBT) treatment for many impulse control disorders is often composed of seven steps:

1. *Conduct an assessment and provide education*: A thorough clinical assessment helps to identify the nature and risk of aggressive behavior and it's underlying psychological and situational aspects. It also provides an opportunity to build an alliance with the client, formulate goals and values, and clarify expectations and commitment.

2. *Develop stress reduction skills*: There is a variety of different techniques that can be used to relieve feelings of tension and anxiety that often precede aggressive behavior. A few examples are progressive muscle relaxation, visualization, cue-controlled relaxation, and special place imagery. Typically, these techniques utilize thoughts, words, or images to bring about a more relaxed state.

3. *Challenge distressing thoughts*: Cognitive coping skills are applied to identify, challenge, and restructure dysfunctional and illogical thoughts, which often lead to unpleasant emotions and impulsive

behaviors. Attention is brought to these automatic negative thoughts with the use of a daily thought record to identify problematic patterns and formulate better alternatives.

4. *Prevent damaging behaviors*: A situational analysis is completed to examine the events and situations that happen just before and after a person engages in impulsive behavior. This is especially important in identifying the triggers and consequences of problematic behavior to anticipate when similar situations may occur and what interventions may be most appropriate (e.g., avoidance, alternative response, stress reduction, delay gratification).

5. *Develop emotion regulation and distress tolerance skills*: Emotion regulation skills help people identify their emotions more clearly and easily and help them cope with their painful emotions instead of getting overwhelmed by them (e.g., attentional deployment, cognitive change, response modulation). Distress tolerance skills can help a person cope with sudden, overwhelming emotions in a healthier way so that the pain does not lead to long-term suffering. These skills include distraction techniques, self-soothing techniques, and learning to accept emotions.

6. *Develop problem-specific coping skills*: In addition to relaxation and cognitive coping skills, these usually involve social, communication, and interpersonal effectiveness skills to help establish and/or improve relationships that may be at the core (or mercy) of aggressive tendencies.

7. *Prevent relapse*: When a person becomes able to control impulsive behaviors, coping skills and strategies that have been effective are maintained and monitored. Adjustments are made where necessary and recurring problems accepted and dealt with in the same way as before in the process.

A randomized-controlled trial with 45 adult IED participants who received a 12-week CBT treatment program demonstrated reductions in aggression, anger, hostile thinking, and depressive symptoms, while improving anger control (McCloskey et al., 2008). Large effect sizes imply significant treatment changes, which were also maintained at 3-month follow-up. As the only clinical study known to specifically focus on the treatment of IED with CBT, this research provides initial support for the efficacy of CBT in this application.

Mindfulness

Mindfulness training is provided as a stand-alone technique to improve well-being and reduce distress, or is integrated with a psychotherapy approach, most often CBT, to achieve a more specific psychological outcome or symptom reduction. It is outside the scope to explore the origins and detailed principles of this eastern-oriented philosophy. But, in short, mindfulness is a state of mind that is best described as "paying attention in a particular way: on purpose, in the present moment, and nonjudgmentally" (Kabat-Zinn, 1994, p. 4). An alternative description is: "bringing one's complete attention to the present experience on a moment-to-moment basis" (Baer, 2003, p. 125). Mindfulness exercises are done individually or in a group and involve focused breathing, visualization, and guided meditation—usually focused on a specific topic or quality such as loving-kindness, relaxation, values, thoughts, etc. Several research studies have outlined the effects of mindfulness training on aggressive behavior and underlying facets. Heppner et al. (2008) reported that mindfulness could be linked to lower levels of ego involvement and hostile attribution bias, which decreased hostility and aggressive behavior. Participants also responded less aggressively when receiving social rejection feedback.

Another aspect that is linked to feelings of anger and aggressive behavior is rumination or the excessive-compulsive focused attention on the symptoms of one's distress, and on its possible causes and consequences, as opposed to its solutions. Research supported the idea that mindfulness reduces rumination, by partially mediating the causal link between mindfulness and hostility, anger, and verbal aggression (Borders et al., 2010). Improvement of mindfulness is especially effective for reducing anxiety, depression, and stress (Khoury et al., 2013), and to improve emotional balance and relationship issues (Sedlmeier et al., 2012)—all of which are precipitators of aggressive behavior.

However, although mindfulness has a wide range of psychological and health benefits, it is not a panacea for all problems, especially those that could interfere with engagement and acceptance. Serious substance dependence, bereavement, psychosis, severe depression, and some personality disorders (e.g., antisocial personality disorder, borderline personality disorder, and narcissistic personality disorder) could cause resistance to the mindful experience. In these cases, it would often be more appropriate to address the most serious concerns first and achieve more balanced emotionality and openness with psychotherapy and pharmacological treatment before introducing mindfulness training. Nevertheless, in general, there are tremendous possibilities to apply mindfulness as an intervention for reactive aggression and its associated problems.

Pharmacology

Antidepressants, such as fluoxetine (Prozac), fluvoxamine (Luvox), sertraline (Zoloft), and venlafaxine (Effexor), have often been used to treat IED. Because impulsive behaviors have been associated with low levels of the serotonin and with blunted serotonergic response, drugs targeting serotonin neurotransmission are also used. As individuals with reactive aggression also often experience elevated rates of mood instability, mood stabilizers may be effective in controlling symptoms of internal distress that lead to problematic externalized behavior. In one of four known studies of drug treatment for IED, a 12-week, randomized, double-blind study with 116 IED patients, administration of divalproex sodium failed to have a significant influence on their aggression (Hollander et al., 2003). Similarly, a study assessing levetiracetam for IED did not show any improvements in measures of impulsive aggression (Mattes, 2008). The remaining three studies reported more success. A double-blind, randomized, placebo-controlled trial of fluoxetine in 100 participants with IED produced a sustained reduction in aggression and irritability as early as the second week of treatment. Full or partial remission of impulsive aggressive behaviors occurred in almost half (46%) of those treated with fluoxetine (Coccaro et al., 2009). In another, smaller treatment study where oxcarbazepine was administered to 24 participants, improvements in IED symptom severity, specifically measures of impulsive aggression, were found (Mattes, 2005). Although some of these studies have shown promise, the paucity of treatment research for IED remains a concern with significant potential for further work, especially given the widespread and severe consequences that IED and reactive aggression have on individuals and societies.

Conclusions

It is clear from this discussion that reactive aggression is a distinctive type of behavior pattern, but it does not represent a straightforward psychopathology. At typical levels it is highly prevalent in most populations, and even as an impulse control disorder, a sizable number of individuals are afflicted. It is highly comorbid with other mental health conditions, including depression, anxiety, antisocial and other personality disorders, paranoid thinking, and alcohol abuse. Such complex psychopathology further increases the risk of violent behavior, including homicide, suicide, and homicide-suicide significantly. The majority of homicides involve a physical altercation between male acquaintances with alcohol involved, which is suggestive of reactive aggression that is triggered by revenge, despair, fear, or anger, in response to a perceived hurt, slight, or violation that is often exacerbated by hostile attribution bias and poor social information processing.

References

Ackley, C. N., Mack, S. M., Beyer, K., and Erdberg, P. 2010. *Investigative and Forensic Interviewing: A Personality-Focused Approach*. Boca Raton, FL: Taylor & Francis.

American Psychiatric Association. 2013. *Diagnostic and Statistical Manual of Mental Disorders* (5th ed.). Arlington, VA: American Psychiatric Association.

Baer, R. A. 2003. Mindfulness training as a clinical intervention: A conceptual and empirical review. *Clinical Psychology: Science and Practice*, 10(2), 125–143. DOI: 10.1093/clipsy/bpg015.

Barker, E. D., Vitaro, F., Lacourse, E., Fontaine, N. M. G., Carbonneau, R., and Tremblay, R. E. 2010. Testing the developmental distinctiveness of male proactive and reactive aggression with a nested longitudinal experimental intervention. *Aggressive Behavior*, 36(2), 127–140. DOI: 10.1002/ab.20337.

Bernet, W., Vnencak-Jnes, C. L., Farahany, N., and Montgomery, S. A. 2007. Bad nature, bad nurture, and testimony regarding MAOA and SLC6A4 genotyping at murder trials. *Journal of Forensic Sciences*, 52(6), 1362–1371. DOI: 10.1111/j.1556-4029.2007.00562.x.

Blair, R. J. R. 2013. The neurobiology of aggression. In: D. S. Charney, P. Sklar, J. D. Buxbaum, and E. J. Nestler (Eds.), *Neurobiology of Mental Illness* (4th ed.). New York, NY: Springer, pp. 1103–1111.

Borders, A., Earleywine, M., and Jajodia, A. 2010. Could mindfulness decrease anger, hostility, and aggression by decreasing rumination? *Aggressive Behavior*, 36(1), 28–44. DOI: 10.1002/ab.20327.

Brosbe, M. H. 2011. Hostile aggression. In: S. Goldstein and J. A. Naglieri (Eds.), *Encyclopedia of Child Behavior and Development*. New York, NY: Springer, pp. 757–758.

Bubier, J. L. and Drabick, D. A. G. 2009. Co-occurring anxiety and disruptive behavior disorders: The roles of anxious symptoms, reactive aggression, and shared risk processes. *Clinical Psychology Review*, 29(7), 658–669. DOI: 10.1016/j.cpr.2009.08.005.

Buss, A. H. and Perry, M. P. 1992. The aggression questionnaire. *Journal of Personality and Social Psychology*, 63(3), 452–459. DOI: 10.1037/0022-3514.63.3.452.

Chan, J. Y., Fung, A. L., and Gerstein, L. H. 2013. Correlates of pure and co-occurring proactive and reactive aggressors in Hong Kong. *Psychology in the Schools*, 50(2), 181–192. DOI: 10.1002/pits.21665.

Coccaro, E. F. 2012. Intermittent explosive disorder as a disorder of impulsive aggression for DSM-5. *American Journal of Psychiatry*, 169(6), 577–588.

Coccaro, E. F., Lee, R. J., and Kavoussi, R. J. 2009. A double-blind, randomized, placebo-controlled trial of fluoxetine in patients with intermittent explosive disorder. *Journal of Clinical Psychiatry*, 70(5), 653–662. DOI: 10.4088/JCP.08m04150.

Coccaro, E. F., Lee, R. J., and McCloskey, M. S. 2014. Relationship between psychopathy, aggression, anger, impulsivity, and intermittent explosive disorder. *Aggressive Behavior*, 40(6), 526–536. DOI: 10.1002/ab.21536.

Conner, K. R., Duberstein, P. R., Conwell, Y., and Caine, E. D. 2003. Reactive aggression and suicide: Theory and evidence. *Aggression and Violent Behavior*, 8(4), 413–432. DOI: 10.1016/S1359-1789(02)00067-8.

Conner, K. R. and Weisman, R. L. 2011. Embitterment in suicide and homicide-suicide. In: L. Linden and A. Maercker (Eds.), *Embitterment*. New York, NY: Springer, pp. 240–247.

Fazel, S., Gulati, G., Linsell, L., Geddes, J. R., and Grann, M. 2009. Schizophrenia and violence: Systematic review and meta-analysis. *PLoS Medicine*, 6(8), 1–15. DOI: 10.1371/journal.pmed.1000120.

Federal Bureau of Investigation (FBI). 2012. *Uniform Crime Reports: Crime in the United States 2012*. Retrieved from https://goo.gl/IxdlQi.

Felthouse, A. R. 2008. Schizophrenia and impulsive aggression: A heuristic inquiry with forensic and clinical implications. *Behavioral Sciences & the Law*, 26(6), 735–758. DOI: 10.1002/bsl.846.

Finley, L. L. 2011. *Encyclopedia of School Crime and Violence*. Santa Barbara, CA: ABC-CLIO.

Fontaine, R. G. 2007. Disentangling the psychology and law of instrumental and reactive subtypes of aggression. *Psychology, Public Policy, and Law*, 13(2), 143–165. DOI: 10.1037/1076-8971.13.2.143.

Geberth, V. J. 2015. *Practical Homicide Investigation: Tactics, Procedures, and Forensic Techniques* (5th ed.). Boca Raton, FL: CRC Press.

Gullone, E. 2012. *Animal Cruelty, Antisocial Behavior, and Aggression: More than a Link*. New York, NY: Palgrave McMillan.

Guyll, M. and Madon, S. 2003. Trait hostility: The breadth and specificity of schema effects. *Personality and Individual Differences*, 34(4), 681–693. DOI: 10.1016/S0191-8869(02)00054-5.

Haller, J. 2014. *Neurobiological Bases of Abnormal Aggression and Violent Behavior*. New York, NY: Springer.

Heppner, W. L., Kernis, M. H., Lakey, C. E., Campbell, W. K., Goldman, B. M., Davis, P. J., and Cascio, E. V. 2008. Mindfulness as a means of reducing aggressive behavior: Dispositional and situational evidence. *Aggressive Behavior*, 34(5), 486–496. DOI: 10.1002/ab.20258.

Hodgins, S. 2008. Violent behavior among people with schizophrenia: A framework for investigations of causes, effective treatment, and prevention. *Philosophical Transactions of the Royal Society B*, 363, 2505–2518. DOI: 10.1098/rstb.2008.0034.

Hollander, E., Tracy, K. A., Swann, A. C., Coccaro, E. F., McElroy, S. L., Wozniak, P., and Nemeroff, C. B. 2003. Divalproex in the treatment of impulsive aggression: Efficacy in cluster B personality disorders. *Neuropsychopharmacology*, 28(6), 1186–1197. DOI: 10.1038/sj.npp.1300153.

In re Christian S. 1994. 7 Cal.4th 768, 779, fn. 3 [30 Cal.Rptr.2d 33, 872, P.2d 574].

Kabat-Zinn, J. 1994. *Wherever You Go, There You Are: Mindfulness Meditation in Everyday Life*. New York, NY: Hyperion.

Kay, J. 2008. Intermittent explosive disorder. *Psychiatry*, 11(5), 2–10. Retrieved from http://goo.gl/FMfyFc.

Khoury, B., Lecomte, T., Fortin, G., Masse, M., Therien, P., Bouchard, V., and Hofmann, S. G. 2013. Mindfulness-based therapy: A comprehensive meta-analysis. *Clinical Psychology Review*, 33(6), 763–771. DOI: 10.1016/j.cpr.2013.05.005.

Krahé, B. 2013. *The Social Psychology of Aggression* (2nd ed.). New York, NY: Psychology Press.

Langman, P. 2009. Rampage school shooters: A typology. *Aggression and Violent Behavior*, *14*(1), 79–96. DOI: 10.1016/j.avb.2008.10.003.

Langman, P. 2015. *School Shooters: Understanding High School, College, and Adult Perpetrators*. Lanham, MD: Rowman & Littlefield.

LaPrairie, J. L., Schechter, J. C., Robinson, B. A., and Brennan, P. A. 2011. Perinatal risk factors in the development of aggression and violence. In: R. Huber, D. L. Bannasch, and P. Brennan, (Eds.), *Aggression*. San Diego, CA: Academic Press, pp. 215–253.

Linden, M., Baumann, K., Rotter, M., and Schippan, B. 2007. The psychopathology of posttraumatic embitterment disorders. *Psychopathology*, *40*(3), 159–165. DOI: 10.1159/000100005.

Liu, J., Lewis, G., and Evans, L. 2013. Understanding aggressive behavior across the life span. *Journal of Psychiatric and Mental Health Nursing*, *20*(2), 156–168. DOI: 10.1111/j.1365-2850.2012.01902.x.

Lobbestael, J., Cima, M., and Lemmens, A. 2015. The relationship between personality disorder traits and reactive versus proactive motivation for aggression. *Psychiatry Research*, *229*(1–2), 155–160. DOI: 10.1016/j.psychres.2015.07.052.

Loughnan, A. 2012. Differences of degree and differences of kind: Diminished responsibility. In: *Manifest Madness: Mental Capacity in the Criminal Law*. New York, NY: Oxford University Press, pp. 226–258.

Mattes, J. A. 2005. Oxcarbazepine in patients with impulsive aggression: A double-blind, placebo-controlled trial. *Journal of Clinical Psychopharmacology*, *25*(6), 575–579.

Mattes, J. A. 2008. Levetiracetam in patients with impulsive aggression: A double-blind, placebo-controlled trial. *Journal of Clinical Psychiatry*, *69*(2), 310–315.

McCloskey, M. S., Noblett, K. L., Deffenbacher, J. L., Gollan, J. K., and Coccaro, E. F. 2008. Cognitive behavioral therapy for intermittent explosive disorder: A pilot randomized clinical trial. *Journal of Consulting and Clinical Psychology*, *76*(5), 876–886. DOI: 10.1037/0022-006X.76.5.876.

Moeller, T. G. 2001. *Youth Aggression and Violence: A Psychological Approach*. New York, NY: Psychology Press.

Ormerod, D. and Laird, K. 2014. *Smith and Hogan's Text, Cases, and Materials on Criminal Law* (11th ed.). New York, NY: Oxford University Press.

People v. Berry 1976. 18 Cal.3d 509, 515 [134 Cal.Rptr. 415, 556 P.2d 777].

People v. Borchers 1958. 50 Cal.2d 321, 328–329 [325 P.2d 97].

People v. Breverman 1998. 19 Cal.4th 142, 164, fn. 11 [77 Cal.Rptr.2d 870, 960 P.2d 1094].

People v. Brooks 1986. 185 Cal.App.3d 687, 694 [230 Cal.Rptr. 86].

People v. Elmore 1914. 167 Cal. 205, 211 [139 P. 989].

People v. Fenenbock 1996. 46 Cal.App.4th 1688, 1704 [54 Cal.Rptr.2d 608].

People v. Kanawyer 2003. 113 Cal.App.4th 1233, 1246–1247 [7 Cal.Rptr.3d 401].

People v. Lucas 1997. 55 Cal.App.4th 721,739 [64 Cal.Rptr.2d 282].

People v. Michael Sims Dixon 1995. 32 Cal.App.4th 1547, 1555–1556 [38 Cal.Rptr.2d 859].

People v. Odell David Dixon 1961. 192 Cal.App.2d 88, 91 [13 Cal.Rptr. 277].

People v. Rich 1988. 45 Cal.3d 1036, 1112 [248 Cal.Rptr. 510, 775 P.2d 960].

People v. Steele 2002. 27 Cal.4th 1230, 1253 [120 Cal.Rptr.2d 432, 47 P.3d 225].

Schreiber, L., Odlaug, B. L., and Grant, J. E. 2011. Impulse control disorders: Updated review of clinical characteristics and pharmacological treatment. *Frontiers in Psychiatry*, *2*(1), 1–11. DOI: 10.3389/fpsyt.2011.00001.

Sedlmeier, P., Eberth, J., Schwarz, M., Zimmermann, D., Haarig, F., Jaeger, S., and Kunze, S. 2012. The psychological effects of meditation: A meta-analysis. *Psychological Bulletin*, *138*(6), 1139–1171. DOI: 10.1037/a0028168.

Sher, L. and Rice, T. 2015. Prevention of homicidal behavior in men with psychiatric disorders. *The World of Biological Psychiatry*, *16*(4), 212–229. DOI: 10.3109/15622975.2015.1028998.

Shiina, A. 2015. Neurobiological basis of reactive aggression: A review. *International Journal of Forensic Science & Pathology*, *3*(3), 94–98.

Siegel, A., Bhatt, S., Bhatt, R., and Zalcman, S. S. 2007. The neurobiological bases for development of treatments of aggressive disorders. *Current Neuropharmacology*, *5*, 135–147.

State v. Hall 8 S.W.3d 593 (Tenn. 1999).

Swart, J. 2013. *Homicide in Armed Conflict: A Psychological Perspective*. Detroit, MI: Lilit Publishing.

Swart, J., Bass, C. K., and Apsche, J. A. 2015. Treating externalizing disorders: FMDT for adolescents with aggressive behavior. In: *Treating Adolescents with Family-Based Mindfulness*. New York, NY: Springer, pp. 243–272.

United States v. John W. Hinckley, Jr, 672 F.2d 115 (D.C. Cir. 1982).

Vanderhallen, M. and Vervaeke, G. 2014. Between investigator and suspect: The role of the working alliance in investigative interviewing. In: R. Bull (Ed.), *Investigative Interviewing*. New York, NY: Springer, pp. 63–90.

Vitaro, F., Brendgen, M., and Tremblay, R. E. 2002. Reactively and proactively aggressive children: Antecedent and subsequent characteristics. *Journal of Child Psychology and Psychiatry, 43*(4), 495–505.

Wellford, C. and Cronin, J. 2000. Clearing up homicide clearance rates. *National Institute of Justice Journal*, 2–7. Retrieved from https://www.ncjrs.gov/pdffiles1/jr000243b.pdf.

Zulawski, D. E. and Wicklander, D. E. 2002. *Practical Aspects of Interview and Interrogation* (2nd ed.). Boca Raton, FL: CRC Press.

3 Domestic Homicide

Michelle Wright and Nicola Manning

Contents

Introduction 35
Nature of Domestic Abuse 36
    Power and Control 36
    Coercive Control 36
From IPV Typologies to a Dimensional Approach 40
    Pathways to IPV 40
Understanding Domestic Homicide 40
    Cognitions of Men Who Are Violent toward Women 41
    Role of Emotion 41
Risk Factors for Domestic Homicide 42
Familicide 43
Role of Forensic Psychology in the Assessment of IPV Perpetrators 45
    IPV Risk Assessment 46
    At-the-Scene Risk Assessments 46
    IPV Risk Assessments for Other Purposes 46
    IPV Victim Risk Appraisal 47
    Predicting Risk versus Predicting Severity/Potential Lethality 48
Conclusion 49
Recommendations for Advancing Understanding of Domestic Homicide 49
    Learning the Lessons 49
    Offender Focused 50
    Victim Focused 50
    Practice Focused 50
References 51

Introduction

Domestic homicide is a broad category that includes all homicides that occur in a domestic context, the most common of which is the killing of an intimate partner, intimate partner homicide (IPH). IPH is also the "type" of homicide most likely to be followed by a self-destructive act, with the offender attempting to, or actually succeeding in taking their own life following the killing (Liem and Roberts, 2009). This chapter focuses on male-perpetrated IPH, the killing of a female by her current or ex-partner. The killing of male intimate partners is detailed in Chapter 11. Domestic mass murders, familicides, are also covered within the current chapter. Familicides are defined as the "deliberate killing within a relatively short period of time of a current or former spouse or intimate partner and one or more of their children" (Websdale, 2010, p. 1). The majority of familicides are perpetrated by males and have been referred to as intimate partner collateral murders (Dobash and Dobash, 2015).

To understand the causes, characteristics, and situational contexts in which domestic homicides occur, it is necessary to draw upon the extensive body of literature on intimate partner violence (IPV). This is because interpersonal relationship dynamics and how IPV perpetrators think about, feel, and behave toward their female partner sets the scene for developing an understanding how and why a minority of IPV perpetrators' abusive behavior escalates and results in a lethal violent act.

In comparison to IPV, the empirical research base for IPH is relatively small; however, the existing IPH literature identifies the nature and characteristics of IPH offenders and the circumstances in which they kill. Developing an understanding of IPH offender decision making prior to, during, and after the killing is crucial for informing IPV risk assessments and the development of effective offender interventions.

Nature of Domestic Abuse

On average, 30% of women who have been in a relationship report experiencing some form of physical or sexual violence by their intimate partner (World Health Organization, 2013). In the Crime Survey of England and Wales (2015), 28% of women and 15% of men reported experiencing domestic abuse since the age of 16. With a reluctance to report domestic abuse incidents, official statistics are likely to underestimate the true prevalence of domestic abuse (Websdale, 1999; Westmarland, 2015).

Domestic abuse is defined as "any incident or pattern of incidents of controlling, coercive, threatening behavior, violence or abuse between those aged 16 or over who are, or have been, intimate partners or family members regardless of gender or sexuality. The abuse can encompass, but is not limited to: psychological, physical, sexual, financial, emotional" (Home Office, 2013). This definition covers the range of abuse a victim may experience and makes no distinction between IPV and familial violence. The situational context in which domestic abuse occurs is also important as the privacy of the family home enables violence to escalate to lethal levels (Websdale, 1999).

Researchers have advocated the need to differentiate between different types of abuse (Johnson, 1995, 2008; Pence and Sadusky, 2009) and characteristics of IPV perpetrators (Gondolf, 1988; Holtzworth-Munroe and Stuart, 1994; Dutton, 1998) to identify risk factors for future partner violence and inform the development of perpetrator behavior change programs.

Power and Control

The dynamics of abusive relationships and the cycle of abuse (Walker, 1989) provide a starting point for understanding domestic homicide. Developed from the lived experience of domestic abuse victims, the Duluth Power and Control Wheel encapsulates the multifaceted nature of domestic abuse (see Figure 3.1). At the core is power and control, with eight control tactics that domestic abusers use to exert power and control. The use of the term "tactics" is important because it emphasizes the instrumental nature of abusive behavior.

The Duluth model adopts a gender-based approach to domestic violence with the Power and Control Wheel used to educate men arrested for domestic violence and mandated by the courts to attend a domestic violence program. Practitioners who work with victims of domestic abuse also use the model to illustrate the range of behaviors that constitute abuse (Pence and Paymar, 1993). The model is, however, not without its critics. Dutton and Corvo (2007) refer to the model as a "data impervious paradigm" criticizing the patriarchal view on which it is based, its development from a small and unrepresentative sample, and its lack of focus on perpetrator characteristics. Based on an archival analysis of domestic homicides and familicides, Websdale (2010) suggests that it should be termed the "powerless and out of control wheel" because an actual or perceived loss of power and control more accurately captures the experiences of those who inflict lethal violence.

Coercive Control

Stark (2007) proposes an alternative model of abuse which focuses on the viewpoint and experiences of survivors of domestic abuse. Stark (2007) details the personal entrapment of women resulting from coercive control. Coercive control is defined as "a malevolent course of conduct that subordinates women to an alien will by violating their physical integrity (domestic violence), denying them respect and autonomy (intimidation), depriving them of social connectedness (isolation), and appropriating or denying them access to the resources required for personhood and citizenship (control)" (Stark, 2007, p. 15).

Nature of Domestic Abuse 37

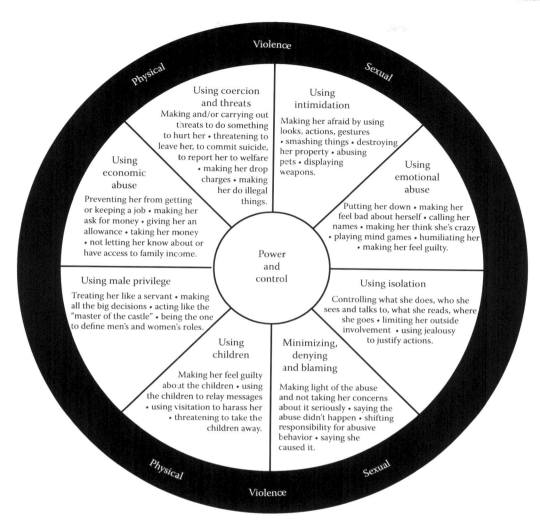

Figure 3.1 The Duluth Power and Control Wheel. (Domestic Abuse Intervention Project. 2011. *The Duluth Model*. Retrieved from http://www.theduluthmodel.org/training/wheels.html.)

Stark (2007) reports how coercive control is marginal in mainstream thinking on domestic abuse. However, as a result of campaigning by women's support groups and charity organizations in the United Kingdom, a new offence "Controlling or Coercive Behavior in an Intimate or Family Relationship" was introduced in England and Wales on December 29, 2015 under Section 76 of the Serious Crime Act 2015 (Home Office, 2015; CPS, 2015).

The three core facets of coercive control are intimidation, isolation, and control. Control involves microregulation by the abuser of the victim's everyday behavior such as what clothes they wear, who they see, how they carry out household tasks, what food to eat, and monitoring of activities such as phone calls and who they are with when they are not together. In the digital era, technology softwares, such as spyware and tracking devices, make monitoring of a partner's movements easier for abusers (Westmarland, 2015). The control and regulation of their everyday life has a traumatic effect on the victim both physically with them experiencing anxiety, panic, and fear and psychologically as their sense of self is eroded and they become isolated from family and friends.

Both Websdale (1999, 2010) and Stark (2007) detail the agency of domestic abuse victims in terms of how they negotiate the abusive relationship as part of their safety strategy. It is the fear they experience that keeps them within an abusive relationship and feeling unable or unwilling to leave because they consider it to be safer to stay than to leave. Victims fear that if they were to leave their abusive partner, there would be serious consequences. This is extremely important for intervention work with victims/survivors of domestic abuse and assessment of risk because research has shown that victims are accurate in their view of the level of risk of future harm to them (Bowen, 2011). As will be discussed when considering the risk factors for IPH, separation is a key risk factor for lethal violence.

Coercive control has been found to be more consistent in abuse than violence (Stark, 2007). Built up over time, controlling behavior has an enduring and cumulative effect on the victim. Coercive control and verbal threats have been found to be more positively correlated with homicide than violence alone and should therefore be taken extremely seriously (Monckton-Smith et al., 2014). The murder of Kelly-Anne Bates is detailed as an example of how coercive controlling behavior can escalate to lethal violence.

Case Study: The Murder of Kelly-Anne Bates

BACKGROUND AND OFFENCE DETAILS

On April 16, 1996, 17-year-old Kelly-Anne Bates was found having been brutally murdered by her boyfriend James Smith, aged 48, at the home they shared in Gorton, Manchester, United Kingdom. They had been in a relationship for 3 years and had been living together for 5 months. Kelly-Anne had met Smith when she was babysitting for his friends who lived on a nearby housing estate to where she lived with her mum, dad, and two younger brothers. Smith befriended her by offering to walk her home in the evening after she had been babysitting. A grooming process commenced with Smith encouraging Kelly-Anne to keep their relationship a secret from her parents. Her parents did not find out about the relationship until Kelly-Anne was 16.

Over a period of months, her parents noticed a change in Kelly-Anne's behavior. She began to stay out late or not return home, resulting in her parents phoning around and visiting her friends. When they failed in their efforts to locate her, they called the police asking for their assistance. Being 16, the police informed them there was little they could do. Her parents also became extremely concerned when Kelly-Anne came home with physical injuries, the first time a badly beaten face and the second time with a bite mark on her hand. When asked how she had received these injuries, Kelly-Anne on the first occasion said she had been attacked in the street by a group of girls and on the second occasion dismissed the bite mark on her hand as the result of an accident.

On November 30, 1995, Kelly-Anne left the family home and moved in with Smith. By December, she had resigned from her part-time administrative job at a local mailing company. From this point, contact with her family was limited to phone calls. The last phone call to her mother was on March 10, 1996. Her parents had become extremely concerned about the lack of contact in the weeks prior to her murder. In the month before she was killed, a mother's day card, birthday card for her father, and wedding anniversary card to her parents were sent, purportedly from Kelly-Anne, but handwritten by Smith.

During this time, Smith was keeping Kelly-Anne as a prisoner in his two-bedroomed semidetached house. He had withheld food and water and tied her up by her hair to a radiator in the bedroom. Smith subjected Kelly-Anne to a prolonged and extremely violent attack, torturing her over a period of 3 weeks using a range of sharp instruments as well as his fists. A postmortem revealed that she had 150 separate injury sites. She had scalding to her buttocks and left leg; burns on her thigh caused by the application of a hot iron; a fractured arm; multiple stab wounds caused by knives, forks, and scissors; stab wounds inside her mouth; crush injuries to both hands; both her knee caps had been smashed; mutilation of her ears, nose, eyebrows, mouth, lips, and genitalia; wounds caused by a spade and pruning shears. She had been partially scalped; both her eyes had been gouged out and there were stab wounds to her empty eye sockets. The cause of death was drowning after Smith had beaten Kelly-Anne around the head with a showerhead in the bathroom. The Home Office Pathologist, William Lawler, who examined Kelly-Anne's body, described her injuries as "the worst he had seen on a murder victim" with so many injuries at different points of healing.

DISCOVERY OF THE CRIME

Smith attended the local police station, informing the police that Kelly-Anne had drowned in the bath. He gave an account of an accidental death. PC Tracy Turner testified at the murder trial that Smith had told her: "I've killed her. I know I have." and told another officer: "I know I'm going away. I know there is no point. I'm going to get found out anyway." When police attended Smith's home address, Kelly-Anne's emaciated six-and-a-half stone body was found naked on the floor of the bedroom, covered with blankets. Her blood was found in every room of the house. Smith was immediately charged with Kelly-Anne's murder. He denied that he had done anything to Kelly-Anne that she had not specifically asked him to do.

When police visited Kelly-Anne's parents to notify them of her death, Kelly-Anne's mother recalls stating, "He's killed her. I knew he would." Kelly-Anne's parents provided a detailed account of changes in Kelly-Anne's behavior during her relationship with Smith. When she moved in with Smith, contact with her family became infrequent, from visits to their home address to phone contact to no contact at all in the weeks prior to her murder. Her parents had become increasingly concerned about the lack of contact.

TRIAL AND SENTENCING

Smith denied murder on the grounds of diminished responsibility. At the opening of the trial, Prosecuting Counsel, QC Peter Openshaw, said Smith had kept Kelly-Anne as a prisoner in a house where she was tied up, starved, and tortured. "It was as if he deliberately disfigured her, causing her the utmost pain, distress and degradation. Injuries to her neck suggested she had been held with a ligature. The injuries were not the result of one sudden eruption of violence, they must have been caused over a long period. The injuries were so extensive and so terrible that the defendant must have deliberately and systematically tortured the girl." The psychiatrist who gave evidence described Smith as an adult sadist who will always be a danger to women.

It was also revealed during the trial that the day before Smith had attended the police station he had spoken to a minister of a religious group he belonged to. During this conversation, Smith had complained that "his girlfriend and her lying was making him mad" and that "he could well understand why men killed their women." Smith gave evidence at his murder trial and claimed that Kelly-Anne "would put me through hell winding me up." He also claimed that Kelly-Anne had "taunted him" about his dead mother and had "a bad habit of hurting herself to make it look worse on me." When asked to account for the extensive injuries to Kelly-Anne's body, he said that she had challenged him to cause her harm. He provided an explanation for how some of the injuries had been caused which was extremely distressing for Kelly-Anne's family who attended the trial. The jury took 55 minutes to reach a verdict. Smith was found guilty of Kelly-Anne's murder on November 19, 1997 and was sentenced to life imprisonment with a minimum tariff of 20 years. Due to the level of violence inflicted on Kelly-Anne by Smith and the detail of the physical injuries and crime scene photographs shown to the jury during the trial, the jury at Manchester Crown Court were offered and all accepted counselling.

BACKGROUND AND PERSONAL CHARACTERISTICS

At the time of the killing, Smith was unemployed. He was described by acquaintances as fastidious, house-proud, and well groomed; he was a teetotaler and nonsmoker. Details of his previous relationship history were outlined at the trial with two of his ex-partners testifying about the abuse they experienced while in a relationship with him. In 1980, his marriage had ended after 10 years due to his violence toward his wife. In 1980–1982, Smith had an affair with a 20-year-old whom he subjected to severe beatings while she was pregnant with his child and attempted to drown her while she was bathing. The victim escaped the relationship, and in 1982, Smith began a statutory rape relationship with a 15-year-old, who was also a victim of his violence. In one attack, Smith attempted to drown her by holding her head under water in the kitchen sink. There was a clear pattern of violence against women. Interestingly, as he had got older, each of his partners was the same age. The accounts from each of his ex-partners were similar in terms of the injuries received and the escalation in his violence was clearly evident. In the words of Kelly-Anne's father, "he was a time bomb waiting to go off." Smith had not come to the attention of the police for these previous IPV offences or any other crime. He had no previous criminal record, reprimands, or warnings on the Police National Computer (PNC). The murder of Kelly-Anne was his first recorded criminal offence.

KEY ASPECTS OF THE CASE

The murder of Kelly-Anne Bates illustrates the nature of coercive control and the escalation of violent behavior within an intimate partner relationship. From the outset, Smith groomed Kelly-Anne, he manipulated and controlled her behavior by making her keep their relationship secret from her family, lying about his age and name when their relationship finally became known to her family. The age difference was a crucial factor. Kelly-Anne's parents describe how she associated with older people but they were very uncomfortable and unhappy that her boyfriend was of a similar age as her father. Kelly-Anne's mother took an instant disliking to Smith after coming home from work and finding him walking down the staircase in their family home. She recalls how: "As soon as I saw Smith the hairs on the back of my neck went up. I tried everything I could to get Kelly-Anne away from him."

Kelly-Anne's parents were so concerned about their daughter's relationship that they sought advice from the police and social services; however, they were unable to intervene because Kelly-Anne was over 16 (the age of consent in the United Kingdom). The danger signs were there for her parents to see: his age, his lies about his age and name, his controlling behavior which included washing her clothes, buying her toiletries, and persistent phone calls to the family home checking up on her when they were not together. Kelly-Anne's parents noticed a change in her personality and demeanor; she began to lose weight, had stopped bathing, and taking care of her appearance. When Kelly-Anne and Smith briefly split up, he would pursue her until she returned to him and on one occasion he threatened to kill himself. Kelly-Anne's mother describes how "he had her in his clutches and we couldn't save her." Isolating Kelly-Anne from her family occurred quickly once she had moved in with him. At this point, he had total control over her. While the level of violence in this IPH is extreme, Smith's known preoffence behavior, isolating Kelly-Anne from her family, is an extremely common coercive control tactic seen in many domestic homicide cases. The fact that Smith had not previously come to police attention for violence against women highlights the difficulty of identifying and preventing IPH.

From IPV Typologies to a Dimensional Approach

The Duluth model previously outlined illustrates the range of abusive behavior and coercive control tactics employed by abusers. In developing an understanding of IPV, researchers have identified different forms of violence perpetrated by offenders with differing characteristics, highlighting the heterogeneity of IPV (Dixon and Browne, 2003).

Pathways to IPV

Day and Bowen (2015) advocate the need for a dimensional rather than typological approach to understanding IPV, highlighting issues with the development of perpetrator behavior change programs based on IPV typologies. Day and Bowen (2015) focus on the offence process and pathways to IPV and propose a self-regulation model of coercive controlling IPV. This model consists of nine phases: developmental/predisposing factors, triggering life events, desire for power and control, goals around power and control in relationships, strategy selection and systematic planning (approach-explicit pathway), victim contact and gain compliance, physical violence, evaluation involving rationalization and justification.

Day and Bowen's (2015) model provides a useful starting point for understanding the cognitions and decision-making processes of coercive controlling IPV perpetrators who are considered to be the highest risk. The model represents a move away from a typological approach to develop a more holistic understanding of pathways to IPV, the offence process, and the cognitions of IPV perpetrators.

Focusing on the cognitions of IPV perpetrators, Anderson and Bushman's (2002) general aggression model (GAM) provides a useful theoretical framework for understanding how cognitive processes mediate violent behavior. The GAM details how individuals interpret, perceive, interact, and respond to situations is guided by their preexisting stored knowledge and experience, their active internal cognitive structures referred to as schemas or scripts. Anderson and Bushman (2002) theorize that aggression is the result of the convergence of both personological (schemas) and situational factors. Personological factors include thoughts and feelings that influence and shape how an individual reacts to a specific situation. Anderson and Huesmann (2003) suggest "The right situation can provoke most people to behave aggressively, but some people are much more likely to aggress than others" (Anderson and Huesmann, 2003, p. 299). This is interesting to consider in the context of IPV and the fact that there is potential for any IPV incident to result in homicide. Not all IPV perpetrators will kill their intimate partner but the potential for them to do so must be recognized, with the assessment of dangerousness and lethality vital for saving lives.

Understanding Domestic Homicide

Homicide is rare in context of the vast number of domestic abuse incidents that are reported to the police. Campbell et al. (2007) report that for every homicide, there are nine near fatal incidents. In 2012, one in every two female homicide victims was killed by their partner or family member and one in twenty of all men was killed in such circumstances, thereby highlighting the gendered nature of domestic homicide (UN Women, 2015). In a global study of the prevalence of IPH, Stöckl et al. (2013) found that an intimate partner committed one in seven (13.5%) homicides.

While there has been a reduction in the number of males killed by their female intimate partners over the years, the number of females killed by their male partners has remained relatively stable (Campbell et al., 2007). With Stark (2007, p. 7) commenting how "the prevalence of violence against women has not changed significantly in thirty years." The key reasons for the reduction in males killed in a domestic context are the support and interventions provided for female domestic abuse victims (Campbell et al., 2007). In England and Wales, the murder of females in an intimate partner relationship continues to constitute a significant proportion of all females who are murdered (Dobash and Dobash, 2015), with two women a week killed by their partner or ex-partner (Office for National Statistics, 2015).

Cognitions of Men Who Are Violent toward Women

IPH perpetrators have been found to minimize, defend by externalizing blame, or deny they are responsible for their lethal violent actions. A common retort to why they killed their current or former intimate partner is "she made me do it" (Dobash and Dobash, 2015). Smith's explanation for how Kelly-Anne received her injuries is a prime example of this. Victim blaming is an example of how IPH offenders externalize problems and have an external locus of control.

Typologies of IPV perpetrators have identified differences in attitudes toward women and violence (Holtzworth-Munroe and Stuart, 1994). Family-only IPV perpetrators who commit violence solely within a family context displayed no hostile attitudes toward women or attitudes supportive of violence. Dysphoric-borderline IPV perpetrators who committed a higher frequency of IPV were found to have hostile attitudes toward women and attitudes supportive of violence. The generally violent/antisocial perpetrators who were the most violent committing violent acts against their partner and others outside of a domestic context viewed violence as permissible and justified and expressed negative attitudes toward women. Eckhardt et al. (2012) found similar results using an implicit association test (IAT) to examine implicit attitudes of IPV males toward gender and violence. IPV males showed more positive implicit attitudes toward violence and a more rapid association between women and violence.

Wider research on violent offenders has revealed how the "decision" to resort to violence or, in relatively rare instances, to kill is dependent upon how offenders perceive, interpret, and react both cognitively and affectively to elements of the micro-situation, which is guided by their schemas, scripts, and implicit theories (Brookman and Wright, in press).

Normative attitudes and beliefs influence how violent offenders process information (Anderson and Bushman, 2002) and, it is argued, increase the likelihood of aggressive or violent behavior (Huesmann, 1988; Bowes and McMurran, 2013). Such cognitive biases, attitudes, and beliefs are theorized as stemming from maladaptive schemas also referred to as "hostile world schemas" (Seagar, 2005) developed from direct and observational learning and experience in which antagonistic behavior serves a functional purpose (Anderson and Huesmann, 2003).

The way in which violent offenders interpret and respond to perceived threats or hostility is an area of growing research interest. The implicit theories of violent offenders has been studied extensively (Ward, 2000; Beech et al., 2005; Gilchrist, 2009; Weldon and Gilchrist, 2012; Pornari et al., 2013). How martially violent males appraise situations and interpret events has been explored by Holtzworth-Munroe and Hutchinson (1993). Drawing upon the social information processing model of reactive and proactive aggression (Dodge and Coie, 1987), married violent males were more likely than two comparison groups (nonviolent and married distressed and nonviolent and nondistressed) to attribute negative and hostile intentions, have selfish motivation, and blame their wives. Many IPV perpetrators have been found to have social information processing skill deficits and use aggression and/or violence as a means of resolving problems and conflict. These cognitions have developed as a result of their childhood experiences (Dodge et al., 1995; Dutton, 1999).

Role of Emotion

Related to the externalizing of attributions for one's own behavior is shame-proneness (Dutton et al., 1995) which is also related to anger arousal (Dutton, 1995), and are identified characteristics of men who abuse their intimate partner. Lewis (1971) first noted the link between shame and anger in clinical casework. Gilligan's (1996) work on shame and humiliation also illustrates how humiliation can elicit violence and even homicide. Gilligan (1996) found that homicide and violent offenders identified being "disrespected" or "ridiculed" as a key trigger for their violence as it engendered feelings of shame and humiliation. Gilligan (1996) like Luckenbill (1977) and Athens (1997) explains how violence often stems from violent offenders' motivation to "save face."

Websdale (2010) explores IPV through the lens of human emotion, focusing specifically on the role of shame and humiliation. He also considers societal and cultural norms that result in men being encouraged from an early age not to express their emotion because it is perceived as a weakness to do so. As a result of early childhood experiences and socialization processes, some males learn to use violence as a way to solve problems. Further research is needed to build upon the pioneering research of Websdale (2010) in unravelling the role that emotion plays in the commission of violent acts against an intimate partner and family members.

Risk Factors for Domestic Homicide

In Websdale's (1999) study of domestic homicide in Florida, men committed 106 of the 132 IPHs (80%), 103 of the 141 family homicides (73%), all 15 of the love triangle killings, and 39 of the 44 suicides (88%). In approximately three-quarters of cases, intimate partners were either separated, estranged, or divorced at the time of the killing. Many of the male perpetrators had criminal histories of violence and 102 engaged "in a regime of domestic terrorism to attempt to keep women in a subordinate position, usually taking the form of women battering that long preceded the fatal episode" (p. 205). Websdale (1999) posits that examination of situational antecedents will assist in identifying IPV cases at higher risk of lethality.

One of the only studies to use a control sample to identify risk factors for female IPH is that by Campbell et al. (2003). They examined 220 cases of IPH and 343 domestic abuse cases from 11 cities in the United States. The risk factors identified were previous violence to the victim, estrangement, forced sex, threats to kill, and threats made with a firearm. In 80% of the IPH cases, the perpetrator was drinking at time of the killing, two-thirds were intoxicated and a quarter had consumed alcohol and drugs. This is a significant finding because alcohol and substance misuse are disinhibitors that influence an individual's self-control. Access to firearms and use of illicit drugs were strongly associated with IPH (Campbell et al., 2003), and the risk is more than doubled if the victim had a child living with them who was not the biological child of the abuser.

In a review of 22 empirical studies on spousal homicide perpetrators, Aldridge and Browne (2003) identified nine risk factors for spousal homicide:

1. Witness of family violence and/or victim of family violence (static)

2. Married versus *de facto* relationship (dynamic)

3. Age disparity (static)—higher risk identified when the male is 10 years older than the female

4. Drug and alcohol abuse (dynamic)

5. Sexual jealousy (dynamic)

6. Separation/threat of separation/length of separation (dynamic)

7. Stalking (dynamic)

8. Personality disorder (static)

9. Previous domestic violence (static)

Across all studies on the characteristics and risk of IPH, the most dangerous time for a victim in a domestic abuse relationship is when the victim is planning to leave or after they have left (Websdale, 1999; Aldridge and Browne, 2003; Campbell et al., 2003, 2007; Dobash and Dobash, 2015). Separation or threat of separation is therefore a high-risk "trigger" for homicide.

Stalking has also consistently been found to be associated with IPH (McFarlane et al., 1999), with victims who reported being spied on or followed twice as likely to be killed. Stalking behavior was reported in 49% of attempted homicide and homicide cases where the victim had not reported physical abuse. In cases where threats were made to harm the children if the partner left or did not return, there was a ninefold increase in the likelihood of the victim being killed.

Based on data gathered from the largest UK murder study, Dobash et al. (2004) compared the characteristics of 106 men who had murdered an intimate partner with 424 male–male murderers. Differences were found between the two groups with those that had killed an intimate partner considered more "ordinary," they had a conventional upbringing, were high school educated, and in employment at the time of the murder. The IPH perpetrators did, however, have a history of relationships that had broken down, and used violence against a previous female partner. These findings are comparable to U.S. research by Adams (2007) who found that IPH perpetrators had more conventional backgrounds when compared to domestic abusers and males convicted of attempted murder. One-third of perpetrators in Adam's (2007) study had at least one previous conviction with 16% defined as career criminals. Of the IPH perpetrators, 48% had completed high school, 87% were employed in a blue-collar role, and 13% were employed in a white-collar occupation at the time of the killing.

The notion that IPH perpetrators are less criminogenic than IPV is an interesting finding and one which also relates to the fact that between 24% (Dobash and Dobash, 2015) and 55% (Thornton, 2011) of IPH perpetrators in the United Kingdom had no recorded contact with the police prior to killing their current or former intimate partner.

Familicide

Research on familicides in the United States (Websdale, 2010) and the United Kingdom (Yardley et al., 2013) suggests an increase in the number of these types of domestic homicides over the last 20 years. While rarer in occurrence than IPH, familicides share similar dynamics, with familicide perpetrators use of violence as an attempt to gain power, with the majority often linked to male conflict with a female partner, which has led to them being referred to as "intimate partner collateral murders" (Dobash and Dobash, 2015). Defined as "annihilators of the nuclear family," familicides differ from IPH in that they "represent a quantum leap that reaches back into the past and forward into the future, destroying a lineage and eliminating new blood. It is not only the number of victims the familicidal hearts claim that marks the gravity of the transgression. Rather, its seriousness stems from the undoing of romantic attachments and sets of interdependencies emblematic of modern freedom of choice in intimate life" (Websdale, 2010, p. 259).

Websdale (2010) conducted an archival analysis, exploring the emotional styles of 211 individuals who had committed familicide and describes an emotional continuum from the livid coercive heart to the civil reputable heart. The livid coercive familicide perpetrator acts out of humiliated fury. They were more likely to be of working class status, with a previous history of domestic abuse. The livid coercive was desperate to hold on to their partner and nuclear family. Male livid coercive hearts had the role of sole provider and female livid coercive hearts as wives and mothers. The civil reputable familicide perpetrator killed out of a sense of rescue or mercy. Civil reputable hearts were respectable and well-controlled individuals. They were more likely to be middle class, have no prior history of abuse and be despondent or depressed. The civil reputable perpetrator tended to be experiencing life changes that they considered insurmountable such as financial difficulties, illness or the breakdown of their relationship with their female partner.

The majority of familicidal perpetrators experienced shame at failing to live up to societies standards with "the diminution or evaporation of a feeling of power central to the understanding the familicide" (Websdale, 2010, p. 264). In shining a spotlight on the role of emotion in the perpetration of familicide, Websdale (2010) encourages researchers and practitioners to acknowledge and delve further into the role emotion plays in these types of killings.

The familicide committed by John List is presented as an example of a civil reputable perpetrator.

Case Study: Familicide Committed by John List

OFFENCE DETAILS

On November 9, 1971, John Emil List, aged 46 years, shot and killed five of his family members at their family home, Breeze Knolls, a 19-room Victorian house in Westfield, New Jersey. His wife, Helen List, aged 46, with whom he had been married for 20 years was killed first via a shot to the back of the head as she sat drinking coffee in the Kitchen just after 9 a.m. after their children had left for school. On killing his wife, List then went upstairs to the attic room where he shot his mother, Alma List, aged 84, once above her left eye. List cleaned up both crime scenes before his children returned home from school. He also carried out a number of chores; attending the post office to arrange for mail delivery to be stopped and visited the bank to cash his mother's saving bonds. He then returned home and ate lunch. As each of his teenage children, Patricia aged 16, John aged 15, and Frederick aged 13, arrived home individually from school, he shot each of them in the hallway. All died from a single gunshot, with the exception of List's final victim his youngest son, Frederick, who was shot over 10 times in the chest and face.

Following the killings, List moved the bodies of his wife and three children into the ballroom of the house, where he laid them out side by side on sleeping bags and placed a towel over each of their faces. His mother's body was left in the attic because he found her "too heavy to move." That evening List wrote a series of letters, one of which was a "confession letter" to the local pastor, one titled "to the finder" detailing the scene at the house, one to his ex-employer explaining his ideas on how they could recruit new clients, and letters to his relatives. List also cut himself out of all the family photographs he could find in the house. This was a clearly calculated act aimed at ensuring that when the murders were discovered, the police would have no recent photograph of him that they could use in their media appeal to apprehend him. List then ate dinner and slept that evening at the house. In the morning, he set classical music to play from the intercom system, turned all the lights on in the house and left.

DISCOVERY OF THE CRIME

This familicide was not discovered until December 7, 1971, 29 days after the murder. Neighbors had noticed the lights on at the house and that some of these had begun to burn out; however, it was not until they saw two people on the driveway of Breeze Knolls that they called the police to report trespassers. The trespassers were Patricia's drama teachers who had become suspicious and concerned about Patricia's length of absence from drama classes. Patricia had not long before reported to one of her drama teachers her concern that her father may kill her and the rest of the family. The police arrived at the property, forced entry, and discovered the scene of carnage.

The police search of the house recovered the "confession letter," which List had left on his desk to the pastor at the local Lutheran church. In this letter, List wrote that he had seen too much evil in the world and had killed his family to save their souls. He also explained how he had "got down and prayed after each one." List's car was found parked at Kennedy International Airport, but police could find no evidence that he had boarded a flight. List evaded law enforcement efforts to apprehend him for 17 years, 6 months, and 23 days.

While living as a fugitive, List assumed a new identity as Robert Peter Clark. In 1972, he settled in Denver and worked for 6 years at a paper box manufacturing company outside of Denver. He met Delores Miller, aged 48, at a Lutheran congregation, and they married in 1985. List had numerous jobs during their marriage and in 1988 secured a job as an accountant in Richmond, Virginia where they moved in February 1988.

Law enforcement had not given up on their efforts to apprehend List; almost 18 years later, details of the case and the wanted John List was aired on the Americas Most Wanted Show on May 21, 1989. The broadcast included an aged progression clay bust of List. Following the broadcast, the police received over 200 calls, one of which was from List's former neighbor in Denver who recognized the likeness of the clay bust to "Robert Clark" and had called police. Eleven days after the show was broadcast, List was arrested on June 1, 1989 at his workplace in Richmond, Virginia. List denied his true identity until February 16, 1990 when faced with irrefutable fingerprint evidence from his military records.

TRIAL AND SENTENCING

At the trial for the murders, List gave an account of his financial difficulties, that his wife had health issues, alcoholism, and was suffering from syphilis. A psychiatric evaluation of List concluded that he had an obsessive-compulsive personality disorder. The psychiatrist for the prosecution concluded that List was suffering only from a midlife crisis as evidenced by the years he had enjoyed living under an alias following the killings. The jury rejected the defense's case of diminished capacity and List was convicted of five counts of first-degree murder on April 12, 1990. He was sentenced to five life terms in prison on May 1, 1990. List attempted to appeal the conviction on two grounds. First, that he had been suffering posttraumatic stress disorder (PTSD) from his military duty during World War II and the Korean War; and second, that the details contained in the confession letter should not have been admissible at the trial because this detailed private correspondence with his pastor. His appeal was rejected.

POSTCONVICTION ACCOUNT

In 2002, List was interviewed in prison by ABC news reporter Connie Chung. This was the first time List had spoken publicly about killing his family. During the interview, he expressed some remorse as he stated: "I wish I had never done what I did." More, interestingly, however, was the rationale he gave both for his violent acts and why he did not take his own life. List explained how he feared his family would be torn apart by financial difficulties and that they would lose their family home and "drift away from their Christian beliefs." List told Chung: "So eventually, I got to the point where I felt that I could kill them, hopefully, they would go to heaven and then maybe I would have a chance to later confess my sins to God and get forgiveness." When asked why he did not take his own life, he expressed his belief: "that if you kill yourself, you won't go to heaven" and he hoped to be reunited with his family in heaven. List died in prison on March 21, 2008, aged 82, from complications caused by pneumonia.

BACKGROUND AND PERSONAL CHARACTERISTICS

List was born in Bay City, Michigan on September 17, 1925; he was the only child of Alma and John Frederick List. His mother was domineering and overprotective and his father authoritarian. List attended the University of Michigan graduating with a bachelor's degree in business administration and a master's degree in accounting. List served time in the army during World War II and the Korean War. He met his wife Helen in 1950 while on active military service in Virginia and they married on December 1, 1951 in Baltimore. In 1965, they moved to the affluent area of Westfield where they attended church each week. The family was described as reclusive, with List controlling the family's social life. His employment history showed that he had difficulty in maintaining a job. List was a devout Lutheran and described by his neighbors as quiet and aloof.

KEY ASPECTS OF THE CASE

At the time of the killing, List was unemployed and experiencing financial difficulties, owing $11,000 in mortgage arrears. He had lost his job as an accountant and had kept his unemployment a secret from his family for months, leaving each day and spending time at the local train station. To make ends meet, he had been taking money from his mother's bank account. List's wife had tertiary syphilis and consumed excessive amounts of alcohol and List suspected that his daughter had been experimenting with cannabis. This combination of financial and domestic stressors led List to fear that he was losing control of his family. His strongly religious beliefs appear influential in his decision to kill his family so that they could go to a better place, heaven. List justified his actions with the rationale that "by killing them they would die Christians." List resembles Websdale's (2010) "civil reputable" familicide perpetrator. He meticulously planned the killings and his actions are an example of controlled and instrumental violence within a domestic context. Prior to the killing, List carried out target practice with the firearms that he later used to kill his five family members. His behavior during the commission of the offence and post-offence was methodical; a single gunshot to the head, the cleaning of the scene, and arrangement of the bodies. Post-offence he displayed numerous examples of detection avoidance behavior; first by planning a cover story to explain the children's absence from school and their part-time jobs and then eerily cutting himself from family photographs to hinder police attempts to apprehend him.

Role of Forensic Psychology in the Assessment of IPV Perpetrators

The role of forensic psychology in the assessment of IPV perpetrators is broad. The most obvious role involves an assessment of the perpetrator either prior to, or following conviction. Prior to conviction, assessment often involves exploring the individual circumstances of the offence and whether any mitigating factors were present that could influence how the case is handled at court. Following conviction, assessment tends to focus more on the personal circumstances and psychological profile of the perpetrator to assist the court to make decisions about the most appropriate disposal outcome. This could include decisions about whether the perpetrator requires certain monitoring or treatment conditions, or whether a prison sentence or a court order for treatment in a psychiatric hospital or mental health service is warranted.

The evidence base that forensic psychologists draw upon to carry out an IPV perpetrator assessment is built on the work of forensic psychology researchers worldwide. Forensic psychologists have a key role both behind the scenes, in providing the research evidence for forensic practice, and directly, by conducting risk assessments, and developing formulations and intervention plans to assist the courts and other criminal justice agencies in dealing with IPV perpetrators. Semistructured risk assessments, such as the Spousal Assault Risk Assessment (SARA) (Kropp et al., 1995) and Brief Spousal Assault Form for the Evaluation of Risk (B-SAFER) (Kropp et al., 2005) used by forensic psychologists and law enforcement officials have been developed from forensic psychological research. In the United Kingdom, psychological and criminological research has also led to the development of risk assessment tools for police first responders, such as the Domestic Abuse, Stalking and Honor-Based Violence (DASH) Risk Identification, Assessment and Management Model (Richards, 2009), Merseyside Risk Identification Tool (MeRIT) (Nixon, 2009), and Domestic Abuse and Stalking Reference Tool (DART) (Monckton-Smith, 2014).

IPV Risk Assessment

The development of IPV risk assessments has followed a pattern similar to that for other violent crimes, with outdated and unreliable forms of unstructured clinical judgment being replaced by actuarial and structured professional judgment approaches (see, for example, the HCR-20 version 3, Douglas et al., 2013). Actuarial-type assessments employ a scoring system based on the number of relevant risk factors present in a case and use this to compare individuals to a norms-based reference group. An example is the Ontario Domestic Assault Risk Assessment (ODARA) (Hilton et al., 2004) which combines 13 specific domestic violence risk factors, with general risk factors for offending behavior, to assist police officers in reaching decisions about whether to detain a suspect and the support required for victims.

Structured professional judgment approaches, such as the SARA (Kropp et al., 1995) and B-SAFER (Kropp et al., 2005) assessments, provide guidelines on key risk factors, reflecting current theoretical and empirical knowledge about IPV, that should be evaluated to form a comprehensive spousal assault assessment. Structured professional judgment assessments tend to focus on more dynamic and changeable factors, with the aim of generating management and prevention strategies appropriate to the risk factors identified. The SARA consists of 20 risk factors, split across 4 broad domains (criminal history, psychosocial adjustment, spousal assault history, and alleged (current) offence). The B-SAFER is a shortened version of the SARA. Research exploring the reliability of risk assessments based on actuarial and structured professional judgment approaches suggests that both are effective in predicting recidivism (Au et al., 2008). The choice as to whether to use an actuarial or structured judgment approach is therefore best determined by the nature of the assessment required and the assessment context.

At-the-Scene Risk Assessments

Assessments used at the scene of a domestic incident, by attending police officers, tend to, quite rightly, employ an actuarial approach, which requires police response officers to identify the presence or absence of a range of risk factors and score these to make an overall determination about risk level. In the United Kingdom, DASH and MeRIT are examples of such assessments. Research suggests that, in such circumstances, the response officer will make a judgment about risk based on the number of risk factors present, with a greater number of risk factors indicating higher risk. The substantial literature for the development of violence risk assessments supports that, to some degree, the more risk factors that are present, the higher the general level of risk (Belfrage and Strand, 2012). However, research also purports that the presence of a single risk factor, if that factor is assessed as having had a substantial influence on past behavior, could be sufficient to provide an assessment of high risk of recidivism (Kropp et al., 2005; Douglas et al., 2013). The existing literature on IPV risk assessment and potential lethality in IPV cases, in particular, seems particularly prone to this phenomenon. A risk assessment profile suggesting low or moderate risk overall, for example, is likely to be significantly elevated if the victim decides to leave the offender and especially if the victim becomes pregnant with someone else's child (Garcia et al., 2007). The complexity of this part of the risk assessment process tends to be somewhat missed in at-the-scene assessments carried out by first response police officers. However, the nature of at-the-scene risk assessments means that an actuarial-type approach allows for a broad range of information to be gathered, largely through interviewing the victim, in a short space of time.

The scoring system used in actuarial risk assessments is quick and straightforward and allows the responding officer to make a structured decision about the level of intervention required at that time, without requiring an in-depth knowledge of the theoretical and empirical knowledge base for IPV. It is, however, essential that the first responding officers tasked with carrying out such risk assessments receive adequate training in how to use the risk assessment tools and have a good understanding of the characteristics and dynamics of domestic abuse.

IPV Risk Assessments for Other Purposes

For forensic psychologists completing a risk assessment for other purposes, such as a court assessment or for treatment/management planning, the information gained through an actuarial assessment is less useful. Actuarial assessments in this context are an excellent way of capturing a generalized risk of recidivism but do not provide the rich information that is gained through a structured professional judgment approach.

Assessments such as the SARA or B-SAFER allow for rich and detailed information to be gathered, from multiple sources, providing a comprehensive account of the circumstances specific to the offender and the victim (Kropp et al., 2005). Unlike actuarial approaches, assessments such as the SARA or B-SAFER should never be used other than for research purposes as a scoring system because they have not been designed for this purpose (Kropp et al., 1995, 2005).

The training for these risk assessments requires the practitioner to gather relevant information and then analyze its relevance in relation to the available research evidence base. The IPV evidence base tells us, for example, that a history of mental disorder increases the risk of recidivism, but exactly how an offender's past history of mental disorder influences their behavior is ascertained using the clinical skill of the assessing practitioner, usually by determining a pattern of symptoms and behaviors. An expanding evidence base makes this task even more challenging for the forensic practitioner, highlighting the importance of continued professional development and keeping abreast of the latest research evidence relevant to the specific IPV risk markers in each case. Taking the mental health risk marker already mentioned as an example, most IPV risk assessments ask the assessing practitioner to explore the presence or absence of this risk factor. However, further investigation of the available evidence base might suggest, for example, that a female victim's experience of depression increases the risk of their male partner's violence, but the male perpetrator's own depressive symptoms are not robustly predictive of violence toward women (Kim et al., 2008). Capaldi et al. (2012) suggest that the association between depression and risk of IPV is not robust and that depression may be a stronger risk factor in assessments of women perpetrators than in men. Similarly, Ehrensaft et al. (2006) found that after controlling for social economic status, race, sex, and age, cluster A personality difficulties (such as those referred to in DSM-IV-TR as paranoid, schizoid, and schizotypal) and cluster B personality difficulties (histrionic, narcissistic, and borderline) in early adulthood predict later perpetration of IPV. With cluster C personality difficulties (avoidant, depressive, and obsessive-compulsive) found to decrease the risk of IPV in individuals who had experienced childhood abuse and adolescent conduct disorder. Such examples of complicated interactions between risk markers are not limited to issues of mental disorder. Alcohol and drug misuse provides another complicated example (Capaldi et al., 2012). For example, while a range of research has suggested an association between alcohol use and increased risk of IPV and IPH (Garcia et al., 2007), other research suggests a more complicated relationship. Alcohol use was found by Caetano et al. (2005), for example, not to significantly predict recurrence of male-perpetrated IPV, but that both male and female volume of alcohol intake significantly predicted recurrence of female violence toward men. In this study however, volume of alcohol intake (five or more drinks per occasion) rather than frequency of alcohol use (three or more times a week) was found to be important.

The preparation of a comprehensive and individual risk assessment is essential in any assessment for use as part of a legal trial or in developing intervention plans. In such circumstances, the development of a working formulation of the perpetrator's behavior is key. This way, the practitioner is able to gain a full understanding of the distal and proximal factors that led to the offence, whether the offender shows a pattern of behavior and the role of maintaining factors, including, somewhat controversially, but nevertheless essential, victim characteristics. By understanding the specific personal and situational factors that increase the risk of IPV and by setting this in the context of current research on IPV, the practitioner is able to determine and recommend areas for intervention. While practitioners from a range of disciplines have the requisite skill to conduct such assessments, the broad understanding forensic psychologists have of offending behavior and how this is applied to the assessment process make forensic psychologists particularly suited to carry out complex, structured professional judgment assessments, such as those required when developing intervention plans for IPV perpetrators.

IPV Victim Risk Appraisal

There is emerging evidence that suggests that one invaluable and reliable piece of risk information is often missed from structured risk assessment guides. Assessment approaches such as SARA and B-SAFER are generally performed by forensic practitioners based on perpetrator information. However, Hanson et al. (2007) suggest that women's appraisals of their own risk level are almost as accurate in predicting recidivism and dangerousness as specific IPV risk assessment tools, including actuarial and structured professional judgment approaches. Evidence demonstrating the validity of victim appraisals of their own risk adds further support to obtaining intimate partner reports (Bowen, 2011). Particular attention should therefore be given to how "safe" a victim feels. Conversely, both empirical evidence and forensic clinical experience suggest that it is usually inadvisable to place much weight on the perpetrator's own estimation of their risk level, and that such an approach is likely to result in a dangerous underestimation of the potential for recidivism and future dangerous behavior (Kropp, 2008). In addition, practitioners need to remain mindful of the potential impact of coercive control in IPV cases. Some victims, as a result of their partner's coercively controlling behavior, may minimize or justify their partner's violence (Kropp, 2008). In such situations, both victim and perpetrator appraisals are likely to be unreliable, necessitating the practitioner to rely solely on an objective approach to risk assessment, using a structured tool and reference to the IPV research evidence base.

Predicting Risk versus Predicting Severity/Potential Lethality

Most available structured IPV risk assessments show good reliability and validity in predicting recidivism (Au et al., 2008; Bowen, 2011; Belfrage and Strand, 2012; Dayan et al., 2013; Storey et al., 2014); however, accuracy in assessing potential severity or lethality in a given case is often a key weakness of IPV risk assessments. In the United Kingdom, the actuarial system of risk assessment previously described is used to determine which cases require police intervention, such as a Multi-Agency Risk Assessment Conference (MARAC), and which do not. However, as already outlined, the risk assessment literature does not fully support the notion that a larger number of risk factors (in actuarial terms, a higher score) unequivocally indicate a higher level of risk of recidivism. The support for this in relation to lethality is even less convincing. So how can a practitioner know whether a particular case will result in a low, moderate, or severe and potentially fatal level of violence? As already outlined, IPH and near-fatal violence is infrequent in comparison to incidents of IPV (Echeburua et al., 2008). In the United Kingdom, it has been found that a number of IPH that were classified as standard or medium risk on the basis of at-the-scene, actuarial-type assessment have resulted in fatal offences (Monckton-Smith et al., 2014). Do such false-negative evaluations indicate a flaw in the structure of the risk assessment system, the experience of the assessing practitioner, or the system of intervention? Certainly, in the United Kingdom, victim protective systems such as MARAC are only put in place for those cases designated high risk and with good reason. Storey et al. (2014), for example, demonstrate that risk management recommendations are associated with decreased recidivism in high-risk perpetrators, but increased risk in low-risk perpetrators. Belfrage and Strand (2012) demonstrate that recidivism rates of IPV offenders are high across all risk groups, except high-risk offenders. This finding can be explained by the fact that interventions are routinely put in place for high-risk offenders, suggesting that police interventions are effective at reducing IPV in these cases leading to low rates of recidivism in this group of offenders. However, what about offenders and victims that are assessed as being at standard or medium levels of risk? In the United Kingdom, IPV victims assessed as of standard or medium level of risk are most often given information about community services and helplines. There is little work carried out directly by the police to monitor and safeguard such victims, and ongoing monitoring of such cases by the police is rare. The categorical system of intervention described seems at odds with a system of assessment that offers a dimensional classification of risk. Logic would suggest that a graded approach to intervention should be offered, tailored to the risk level of each case. Perhaps then, cases that were initially assessed as being standard or medium risk could continue to be monitored through low-level police interventions. This could include implementing routine checks with the victim via telephone calls, for example, in the weeks following an IPV incident, thereby allowing the victim's appraisal of the level of risk to be used to inform decisions about the need for reassessment by specialist officers. This way, potential changes that could indicate an increased risk of lethal violence could be more easily detected. Such changes, however, would place even more pressure on an already stretched and somewhat under-resourced police service.

The research evidence base for predicting potential lethality in IPV cases, as with any other area of forensic practice, is constantly developing. With the structured professional judgment approach, it is extremely important that the assessing practitioner incorporates contemporary research on the role of specific risk markers, as outlined earlier. When assessing potential lethality, for example, an emerging evidence base suggests that particular risk markers for IPH include a pattern of IPV, the victim threatening to, or actually leaving the perpetrator, the victim leaving the abuser for another partner, stalking occurring alongside IPV, availability of potentially lethal weapons, and alcohol and/or drug misuse by the perpetrator (Sheehan et al., 2015).

The study by Sheehan et al. (2015) suggests that a combination of a high number of IPV risk factors such as those measured on actuarial or structured risk assessments and the presence of acute risk factors indicates an increased risk of lethality. The acute risk factors identified by Sheehan et al. (2015) were a loss of sense of control for the perpetrator triggered by a change in circumstances such as child custody or threats to leave, a dramatic change in the perpetrator's behavior such as an escalation in severe violence, and barriers to help for the victim, such as the isolation created by the perpetrator, but also failings in the criminal justice system, such as the limitations of court orders. The study by Sheehan et al. (2015) emphasizes the importance of gathering information from family members and friends of IPV victims to understand offender behavior prior to killing their intimate partner.

Despite increased knowledge about risk factors for IPH, there remains a crossover between risk factors that predict general recidivism and those that predict severity and potential lethality. This makes risk assessment for potential lethality extremely complex and challenging. It could be argued that risk assessments of IPV are not specific enough about which factors predict recidivism and which predict severity and how to determine which factors predict recidivism in general or potential severity of violence in each individual case. In addition, the training provided to UK police first responders, those officers most likely to complete IPV risk assessments and to determine potential future risk level, has been criticized for being somewhat inadequate due to the complexity of IPV (HMIC, 2014). The criticisms of both the specificity of available risk assessments and the training provided to first response officers suggest that a multifaceted approach is required to improve the identification of which IPV cases might be most likely to result in homicide. The IPV literature reviewed in this chapter highlights the need for practitioners involved in IPV risk assessment to fully understand the nature and dynamics of domestic abuse and identify coercively controlling behavior as a key risk factor for potential lethality (Stark, 2007).

Regardless of the context of the IPV risk assessment or the expertise of the practitioner conducting the assessment, it is vital that those conducting risk assessments have a broad understanding of IPV and, ideally, should have experience of working with both perpetrators and victims. Comprehensive risk assessment training is key and continued appraisal of the relevant research evidence base is essential. The potential dangerousness of all IPV perpetrators has been illustrated in this chapter. A risk assessment can only ever be as comprehensive and robust as the information on which it is based and this includes the knowledge the practitioner has of the research evidence base. Little is more dangerous than a risk assessment based on inadequate information or a risk assessment that has been carried out by a practitioner who has an incomplete understanding of the complex and dynamic nature of IPV.

Conclusion

Assessing dangerousness and potential for lethality in domestic abuse cases is highly complex. There is a difference between the system of actuarial risk assessment and what existing research tells us about individual risk and lethality assessment. When assessing an individual case, the presence of a single risk factor may be enough to convey a high-risk rating and a high potential for lethality. This is case specific. Actuarial risk assessment entails generalization to groups and a higher score (i.e., more risk factors present) conveys a high-risk rating. This misses the subtlety of individual risk formulation that is often key to accurate risk assessment and lethality assessment in each case.

While incidences of physical violence are likely to have occurred prior to an IPH, the most frequent antecedent is coercive control (Stark, 2007). In reviewing the existing literature and case examples of IPH and familicide, it appears that perpetrators perceived or actual loss of power and control is a common trigger for these types of domestic homicide. Day and Bowen's (2015) self-regulation model of coercive controlling in IPV provides a useful theoretical framework for understanding and working with perpetrators identified as high risk (Day and Bowen, 2015). However, consideration must also be given to the role of event characteristics and situational factors in influencing cognition and emotion "in the moment" to develop an understanding of how personal and situational factors may combine to result in behavior which has a lethal outcome. As Websdale (2010, p. 36) explains: "emotion is the juice of human interaction," we, therefore, need to further understand the role of emotion in the perpetration of lethal violence within a domestic context.

Recommendations for Advancing Understanding of Domestic Homicide
Learning the Lessons
Accounts of victim experiences of violent intimate partner relationships are incorporated within fatality reviews in the United States (Websdale, 1999) and domestic homicide reviews (DHRs) in the United Kingdom (Home Office, 2011). The findings of fatality reviews and DHRs are of vital importance for identifying risk factors for IPH. However, to be effective, these findings need to be shared in a timely manner. In the United Kingdom, the Home Office has the responsibility for collating the findings from DHRs; unfortunately, however, little information has been shared with the police service since DHRs were introduced in 2011 under

Section 9 of the Domestic Violence, Crime and Victims Act 2004. To date, only a basic list of recommendations has been published (Home Office, 2013). Enhanced risk assessment training for police first responders is clearly needed, as a recent inspection by Her Majesty's Inspectorate of Constabulary (HMIC) rated only 8 out of the 43 police forces in England and Wales as providing a "good" service to domestic abuse victims (HMIC, 2014).

The review of the IPV, IPH, and risk assessment literature in this chapter highlights the issue of cases where no reports are made to the police regarding a male partner's abusive behavior. The police are unable to identify risk and work to prevent domestic homicide if they are not aware of ongoing abuse. This is particularly relevant for cases involving coercive control because there may be no or very little physical violence (Stark, 2007). Findings from fatality reviews and DHRs show that it is rare for a homicide to be committed without any precursor behaviors or risk indicators (Campbell et al., 2007; Mockton Smith et al., 2014). IPV perpetrators who exert control and power using psychological rather than physical tactics are considered the most dangerous (Stark, 2007; Day and Bowen, 2015). While IPV victims may be reluctant to report abuse to the police, current research suggests victims are likely to disclose information to family members and close friends (Sheehan et al., 2015). Education and awareness raising campaigns of reporting all domestic abuse can therefore help save lives.

Based on current IPV theory, research, and forensic psychological practice, recommendations are detailed below which are aimed at advancing understanding of domestic homicide.

Offender Focused

A dimensional rather than typological, gender-inclusive approach to understanding domestic abuse is necessary to ensure the development of intervention programs tailored to perpetrator's behavior to reduce recidivism.

- While the evidence base for distal and proximal factors of IPV is well established, the literature on IPH is relatively small. There is, therefore, a need for further empirical research examining IPH perpetrator characteristics, their actions, and decision making prior to, during, and after killing. To fully understand what "triggers" an individual to kill their intimate partner, perpetrators accounts of their thoughts, feelings, and actions need to be captured and analyzed. While it is acknowledged that many perpetrators tend to justify, rationalize, and minimize their offending behavior, their narratives are crucial for advancing our understanding of the role of personal and situational factors in the commission of IPH. Building on Athens's (1980) seminal work on violent actors and their actions will develop understanding of the cognitions of IPH perpetrators in terms of how they view and define the situation in which they engage in abusive and violent behavior. The findings of such research will have direct implications for risk assessment and violence intervention and prevention programs.

- Further empirical research is needed to build upon Websdale's (2010) proposition that emotion, particularly shame, is influential in propelling an individual to kill an intimate partner or family member.

Victim Focused

The lived experiences of IPV survivors and IPH victim's family and friends are vital for enhancing understanding of the interpersonal dynamics that lie at the heart of IPV.

- Fatality reviews and DHRs should be collaborative with family members and friends interviewed to ensure the victim's perspective is central to the review process.

Practice Focused

The lessons learned from fatality reviews and DHRs must be shared with relevant organizations in a timely manner for learning to be implemented in practice.

- With issues identified of domestic abuse cases assessed as standard or medium risk resulting in homicide, an evaluation of current risk assessment tools and practices is needed to establish effective policy and practice that saves lives.

- Forensic psychologists can play a key role in assisting the development of early intervention strategies, enhancing awareness, and educating the public of the need to report all incidents of domestic abuse to prevent future homicides.

References

Adams, D. 2007. *Why Do They Kill? Men Who Murder Their Intimate Partners*. Nashville, TN: Vanderbilt University Press.

Aldridge, M. L. and Browne, K. 2003. Perpetrators of spousal homicide: A review. *Trauma, Violence and Abuse*, 4, 265–276.

Anderson, C. A. and Bushman, B. J. 2002. Human aggression. *Annual Review of Psychology*, 53, 27–51.

Anderson, C. A. and Huesmann, L. R. 2003. Human aggression: A social cognitive view. In: M. A. Hogg and J. Cooper (Eds.), *The Sage Handbook of Social Psychology*. Thousand Oaks, CA: Sage Publications, pp. 296–323.

Athens, L. H. 1980. *Violent Criminal Acts and Actors: A Symbolic Interactionist Study*. London, UK: Routledge and Kegan Paul.

Athens, L. H. 1997. *Violent Criminal Acts and Actors Revisited*. Chicago: University of Illinois Press.

Au, A., Cheung, G., Kropp, R., Yuk-chung, C., Lam, G. L. T., and Sung, P. 2008. A preliminary validation of the Brief Spousal Assault Form for the Evaluation of Risk (B-SAFER) in Hong Kong. *Journal of Family Violence*, 23, 727–735.

Beech, A., Fisher, D., and Ward, T. 2005. Sexual murderers' implicit theories. *Journal of Interpersonal Violence*, 20 (11), 1366–1389.

Belfrage, H. and Strand, S. 2012. Measuring the outcome of structured spousal violence risk assessments using the B-SAFER: Risk in relation to recidivism and intervention. *Behavioral Sciences and the Law*, 30, 420–430.

Bowen, E. 2011. An overview of partner violence risk assessment and the potential role of female victim risk appraisals. *Aggression and Violent Behavior*, 16, 214–226.

Bowes, N. and McMurran, M. 2013. Cognitions supportive of violence and violent behavior. *Aggression and Violent Behavior*, 18, 660–665.

Brookman, F. and Wright, M. in press. "Deciding" to kill: Understanding homicide offenders' decision making. In: W. Bernasco, H. Elffers, and J.-L. Van Gelder (Eds.), *The Oxford Handbook of Offender Decision Making*. Oxford, UK: Oxford University Press.

Caetano, R., McGrath, C., Ramisetty-Mikler, S., and Field, C. A. 2005. Drinking, alcohol problems and the five-year recurrence and incidence of male to female and female to male partner violence. *Alcoholism: Clinical and Experimental Research*, 29(1), 98–106.

Campbell, J. C., Glass, N., Sharps, P. W., Laughon, K., and Bloom, T. 2007. Intimate partner homicide review and implications of research and policy. *Trauma Violence Abuse*, 8(3), 246–269.

Campbell, J. C., Webster, D., Koziol-McLain, J., Block, C. R., Campbell, D., Curry, M. A., and Laughon, K. 2003. Risk factors for femicide in abusive relationships: Results from a multi-site case control study. *American Journal of Public Health*, 93(7), 1089–1097.

Capaldi, D. M., Knoble, N. B., Shortt, J. W., and Kim, H. K. 2012. A systematic review of risk factors for intimate partner violence. *Partner Abuse*, 3(2), 231–280.

Crown Prosecution Service (CPS). 2015. *Controlling or Coercive Behavior in an Intimate or Family Relationship*. Retrieved from http://bit.ly/1Onp3sV.

Day, A. and Bowen, E. 2015. Offending competency and coercive control in intimate partner violence. *Aggression and Violent Behavior*, 20, 62–71.

Dayan, K., Fox, S., and Morag, M. 2013. Validation of spouse violence risk assessment inventory for police purposes. *Journal of Family Violence*, 28, 811–821.

Dixon, L. and Browne, K. 2003. The heterogeneity of spouse abuse: A review. *Aggression and Violent Behavior*, 8(1), 107–130.

Dobash, R. E. and Dobash, R. P. 2011. What were they thinking? Men who murder an intimate partner. *Violence against Women*, 17(1), 111–134.

Dobash, R. E. and Dobash, R. P. 2015. *When Men Murder Women*. Oxford, UK: Oxford University Press.

Dobash, R. E., Dobash, R. P., Cavanagh, K., and Lewis, R. 2004. Not an ordinary killer—Just an ordinary guy. When men murder an intimate woman partner. *Violence against Women*, 10(6), 577–605.

Dodge, K.A. and Coie, J. D. 1987. Social information processing factors in reactive and proactive aggression in children's peer groups. *Journal of Personality and Social Psychology*, 53, 1146–1158.

Dodge, K., Pettit, G. S., Bates, J. E., and Valente, E. 1995. Social information-processing patterns partially mediate the effect of early physical abuse on later conduct problems. *Journal of Abnormal Psychology*, 104(4), 632–643.

Domestic Abuse Intervention Project. 2011. The Duluth Model. Retrieved from http://www.theduluthmodel.org/training/wheels.html.

Douglas, K. S., Hart, S. D., Webster, C. D., and Belfrage H. 2013. *HCR-20 Version 3: Assessing Risk for Violence: User Guide*. Mental Health, Law and Policy Institute, Simon Fraser University.

Dutton, D. G. 1995. Male abusiveness in intimate relationships. *Clinical Psychology Review*, 15(6), 567–581.

Dutton, D. G. 1998. *The Abusive Personality: Violence and Control in Intimate Relationships*. New York, NY: Guilford Press.

Dutton, D. G. 1999. Traumatic origins of intimate rage. *Aggression and Violent Behavior*, 4(4), 431–447.

Dutton, D. G. and Corvo, K. 2007. The Duluth model: A data-impervious paradigm and a failed strategy. *Aggression and Violent Behavior*, 12, 658–667.

Dutton, D. G., Van Ginkel, C., and Starzomski, A. 1995. The role of shame and guilt in the intergenerational transmission of abusiveness. *Violence and Victims*, 10(2), 121–131.

Echeburua, E., Fernandez-Montalvo, J., de Corral, P., and Lopez-Goni, J. J. 2008. Assessing risk markers in intimate partner femicide and severe violence: A new assessment instrument. *Journal of Interpersonal Violence*, 24(6), 925–939.

Eckhardt, C. I., Samper, R., Suhr, L., and Holtzworth-Munroe, A. 2012. Implicit attitudes towards violence among male perpetrators of intimate partner violence: A preliminary investigation. *Journal of Interpersonal Violence*, 27, 471–491.

Ehrensaft, M. K., Cohen, P., and Johnson, J. G. 2006. Development of personality disorder symptoms and the risk for partner violence. *Journal of Abnormal Psychology*, 115(3), 474–483.

Garcia, L., Soria, C., and Hurwitz, E. L. 2007. Homicides and intimate partner violence: A literature review. *Trauma, Violence and Abuse*, 8(4), 370–383.

Gilchrist, E. 2009. Implicit thinking about implicit theories in intimate partner violence. *Psychology, Crime and Law*, 15(2–3), 131–145.

Gilligan, J. 1996. *Violence: Our Deadly Epidemic and Its Causes*. New York, NY: Vintage Books.

Gondolf, E. 1988. Who are those guys? Toward a behavioral typology of batterers. *Violence and Victims*, 3, 187–203.

Hanson, R. K., Helmus, L., and Bourgon, G. 2007. *The Validity of Risk Assessments for Intimate Partner Violence: A Meta-Analysis*. Ontario, CA: Public Safety Canada.

Hilton, N. Z., Harris, G. T., Rice, M. E., Lang, C., Corimer, C. A., and Lines K. J. 2004. A brief actuarial assessment for the prediction of wife assault recidivism: The Ontario domestic assault risk assessment. *Psychological Assessment*, 16(3), 267–275.

Her Majesty's Inspectorate of Constabulary (HMIC). 2014. *Everyone's Business. Improving the Response to Domestic Abuse*. Retrieved from http://bit.ly/1U4t1Vx.

Holtzworth-Munroe, A. and Hutchinson, G. 1993. Attributing negative intent to wife behavior: The attributions of maritally violent versus nonviolent men. *Journal of Abnormal Psychology*, 102(2), 206–211.

Holtzworth-Munroe, A. and Stuart, G. L. 1994. Typologies of male batterers: Three subtypes and the differences among them. *Psychological Bulletin*, 116(3), 476–497.

Home Office. 2013. *Domestic Homicide Reviews: Common Themes Identified as Lessons To Be Learned*. Retrieved from http://bit.ly/1RG5IDA.

Home Office. 2013. *Domestic Violence and Abuse New Definition*. Retrieved from http://bit.ly/1J4g8KB.

Home Office. 2015. *Controlling or Coercive Behavior in an Intimate or Family Relationship. Statutory Guidance Framework*. Retrieved from http://bit.ly/1YxaVSp.

Huesmann, L. R. 1988. An information processing model for the development of aggression. *Aggressive Behaviour*, 14, 13–24.

Johnson, M. 2008. *A Typology of Domestic Violence: Intimate Terrorism, Violent Resistance and Situational Couple Violence*. Boston, MA: University Press of New England.

Johnson, M. P. 1995. Patriarchal terrorism and common couple violence: Two forms of violence against women. *Journal of Marriage and the Family*, 57, 283–294.

Kim, H. K., Laurent H. K., Capaldi, D. M., and Feingold, A. 2008. Men's aggression toward women: A 10-year panel study. *Journal of Marriage and Family*, 70(5), 1169–1187.

Kropp, R. 2008. Intimate partner violence risk assessment and management. *Violence and Victims*, 23(2), 202–220.

Kropp P. R., Hart, S. D., and Belfrage, H. 2005. *Brief Spousal Assault Risk Assessment Form for the Evaluation of Risk (B-SAFER) User Manual*. Vancouver, BC: ProActive ReSolutions.

Kropp, P. R., Hart, S. D., Webster, C. D., and Eaves, D. 1995. *Manual for the Spousal Assault Risk Assessment (SARA)* (2nd ed.). Vancouver: The British Columbia Institute against Family Violence.

Lewis, H. B. 1971. *Shame and Guilt in Neurosis.* New York, NY: International Universities Press.

Liem, M. and Roberts, D. W. 2009. Intimate partner homicide by presence or absence of a self-destructive act. *Homicide Studies, 13*(4), 399–354.

Luckenbill, D. F. 1977. Criminal homicide as a situated transaction. *Social Problems, 25*(2), 176–186.

McFarlane, J. M., Campbell, J. C., Sachs, C. J., Ulrich, Y., and Xiao, X. 1999. Stalking and intimate partner femicide. *Homicide Studies, 3*(4), 300–316.

Monckton-Smith, J., Williams, A., and Mullane, F. 2014. *Domestic Abuse, Homicide and Gender.* Hampshire: Palgrave Macmillan.

Nixon, K. 2009. *The Development and Validation of a Domestic Abuse Risk Identification and Management Tool.* Unpublished PhD Thesis. University of Liverpool.

Office for National Statistics. 2015. *Chapter 2: Violent Crime and Sexual Offences—Homicide.* Retrieved from http://bit.ly/1Yxj5KC.

Pence, E. and Paymar, M. 1993. *Education Groups for Men Who Batter: The Duluth Model.* New York, NY: Springer.

Pence, E. and Sadusky, J. 2009. *Engage to Protect: Foundations for Supervised Visitation and Exchange. Recognizing and Understanding Battering.* Retrieved from http://bit.ly/1PkVs1W.

Pornari, C. D., Dixon, L., and Humphreys, G. W. 2013. Systematically identifying implicit theories in male and female intimate partner violence perpetrators. *Aggression and Violent Behavior, 18*, 496–505.

Richards, L. 2009. *DASH (2009) Saving Lives Through Early Risk Identification, Intervention and Prevention.* Retrieved from http://www.dashriskchecklist.co.uk/.

Seagar, J. A. 2005. Violent men: The Importance of impulsivity and cognitive schema. *Criminal Justice and Behavior, 32*, 26–49.

Sheehan, B. E., Murphy, S. B., Moynihan, M. M., Dudley-Fennessey, E., and Stapleton, J. G. 2015. Intimate partner homicide: New insights for understanding lethality and risks. *Violence against Women 21*(2), 269–288.

Stark, E. 2007. *Coercive Control: How Men Entrap Women in Personal Life.* New York, NY: Oxford University Press.

Stöckl, H., Devries, K., Rotstein, A., Abrahams, N., Campbell, J., Watts, C., and Moreno, C. G. 2013. The global prevalence of intimate partner homicide: A systematic review. *Lancet, 382*, 859–865.

Storey, J. E., Kropp, P. R., Hart, S. D., Belfrage, H., and Strand, S. 2014. Assessment and management of risk for intimate partner violence by police officers using the brief spousal assault form for the evaluation of risk. *Criminal Justice and Behavior, 41*(2), 256–271.

Thornton, S. 2011. *Predicting Serious Domestic Assaults and Murder in the Thames Valley.* Unpublished Masters Dissertation. University of Cambridge.

UN Women. 2015. *Facts and Figures: Ending Violence against Women.* Retrieved from http://bit.ly/1kBBx01.

Walker, L. E. 1989. Psychology and violence and against women. *American Psychologist, 44*, 695–702.

Ward, T. 2000. Sexual offenders' cognitive distortions as implicit theories. *Aggression and Violent Behavior, 5*, 491–507.

Websdale, N. 1999. *Understanding Domestic Homicide.* Boston, MA: Northeastern University Press.

Websdale, N. 2010. *Familicidal Hearts. The Emotional Styles of 211 Killers.* New York, NY: Oxford University Press.

Weldon, S. and Gilchrist, E. 2012. Implicit theories in intimate partner violence offenders. *Journal of Family Violence, 27*(8), 761–772.

Westmarland, N. 2015. *Violence against Women. Criminological Perspectives on Men's Violences.* New York, NY: Routledge.

World Health Organization (WHO). 2013. *Responding to Intimate Partner Violence and Sexual Violence against Women.* Retrieved from http://bit.ly/1wkpds6.

Yardley, E., Wilson, D., and Lynes, A. 2013. A taxonomy of male British family annihilators, 1980–2012. *The Howard Journal of Criminal Justice, 53*(2), 117–140.

Disgruntled and Revenge Killers

Joan Swart

Contents

Introduction 56
Theory of Revenge and Embitterment 56
Chronic Psychopathology Trajectory of Revenge Killers 58
    Mental Health and Social Problems 60
    A Female Revenge Killer with Signs of Chronic Psychopathology 60
    A Different Kind of Revenge: The Aurora Shooter 61
Psychology of Posttraumatic Embitterment-Type Revenge Killers 62
    Posttraumatic Embitterment Disorder 62
    Posttraumatic Embitterment Trajectory 63
        Dorner's Psychology 65
    A Female Posttraumatic Embitterment-Type Revenge Killer 66
Linguistic Analysis Comparison 67
Filicide as a Motive for Spousal Revenge 67
Interviewing and Defending Revenge Killers 68
Conclusions 69
References 69

A disgruntled and revenge killer is a person who seeks revenge for real or imagined wrongs at the hands of coworkers, employers, family, friends, or any other identifiable or stereotyped person. He or she may have harbored the need for vengeance for a long time, even since childhood, and victims may be the actual targets or represent the target in some way, such as resembling them physically, by culture, location, and so forth. Regarding criminal behavior, victim selection and preplanning is important, and may be accompanied by homicidal fantasies to help manage the distressing feelings. Revenge killers may also engage in stalking behaviors. The relationship with the victim or origin(s) of the hatred is important in understanding and managing these killers. Examples of disgruntled killers are ex-LAPD officer Christopher Dorner, who sought revenge against his fellow officers, and USCB college student Elliot Rodger, who went on a killing rampage to wreak revenge against women for rejecting him. These case studies, as well as those of Jennifer San Marco, a disgruntled former U.S. Postal Service employee; Amy Bishop, murderous university professor; and James Holmes, Aurora theater mass shooter, are used to propose two primary pathways of revenge killers: posttraumatic embitterment and chronic psychopathology.

Introduction

Disgruntled or revenge murders involve offenders killing persons at schools, workplaces, shopping malls, restaurants, or government agencies. They target specific people for real or imagined wrongs or those who represent them. They often have an obsession with guns and homicidal fantasies that are initially sufficient to offer them release from the pent-up feelings.

Two basic types of revenge killers are proposed, namely, the posttraumatic embittered offender and chronically disordered offender. One-time homicides, either with single or multiple victims, motivated by revenge, are relatively rare compared to heat-of-the-moment, or reactive-type murders. The revenge killer is driven by a deep, overwhelming anger associated with an obsessive attachment to the target of his feelings. Most victims of revenge killers are known to them (e.g., family members or coworkers) or are symbolic of an offending organization.

Disgruntled and revenge homicide offenders usually have had long-term mental health issues that involve paranoia, depression, anxiety, and anger, or had endured a traumatic event that derailed their life, which they viewed as an injustice. They are often unemployed at the time of the homicide or had experienced a trigger event shortly before. Most give preattack warnings and have access to legally obtained semiautomatic and other firearms. Many do not have an escape plan or attempt to escape. Almost half of revenge mass murders commit suicide or are killed by others during the commission of the crime.

Many times, individuals who have committed acts of revenge have thought about it for some time, slowly building the fantasy over weeks, months, and even years. Although their initial feelings of anger may subside, other setbacks later in life, such as being fired from work, failing an important exam, a broken relationship, romantic rejection, or losing custody of a child, trigger even more anger. Eventually, their need for revenge increases until breaking point. At this time, they are unable to handle the internal stress any further and urgently seek release from their emotional pain.

Revenge murderers commonly have weak egos and low self-esteem or a traumatic event threatened their perception of self-value. They believe that life and others have abandoned them, taking away the happiness, position, and approval that is rightfully theirs. They may have filed multiple grievances against an employer or company, had arguments with coworkers, teachers, and fellow students and became angry when disciplined.

Many disgruntled employees who kill have been dismissed from their jobs, abandoned studies, or placed on medical leave or disability before the murder (Holmes and Holmes, 2001). They may have had frequent psychiatric counseling and are known to authorities. The personal injustices that they believed they have suffered and are beyond their control accumulate until it reaches a breaking point.

As a result, they kill at home or go to their places of employment, study, or neighborhood establishments to avenge the wrongs that they perceive have been done to them. They target specific individuals who have caused them injustice, or others who may represent them. The principle characteristic that most share is paranoia. Their primary motivation is to right a wrong by punishing those responsible or call attention to the wrongs that have been done to them (Holmes and Holmes, 2001).

Theory of Revenge and Embitterment

The incubation period of a disgruntled and revenge killer is characterized by a series of perceived wrongs that induced increasing feelings of anger and resentment. Over time, beliefs about the benevolence of the world, being persecuted, and being the recipient of gross mistreatment and injustice are reinforced by a string of adversarial events, which are again brought on by antisocial and maladaptive personality characteristics and behavior. Alternatively, suffering a single devaluing event may cause embitterment and revenge. Anxiety, depressive feelings, social awkwardness, and withdrawal, fear of rejection and disapproval, and delusional beliefs are common instigators and reinforcers of the need for revenge.

Knoll (2010a, b) describes the revenge killer as someone with a "mortally wounded self-esteem" (p. 87) who develops revenge fantasies as an avenue of relief or as LaFarge (2006) called the desire for revenge as "a ubiquitous response to narcissistic injury" (p. 447). This ego survival instinct is an important component in the revenge killer's makeup, which he justifies in recovering a sense of self that he believes others have wrongfully harmed. As such, it is a reaction to intolerable feelings of humiliation and a loss of control and achievement that may be chronically personality-based or linked to a humiliating event. In the pathway to violence, revenge eventually becomes the final step to punish or correct the injustice that was done to him.

At first, the individual engages in revenge fantasies, which is sufficient for a while to relieve his or her feelings of powerlessness and figurative emasculation or devaluing. As these thoughts become increasingly intrusive and persistent, and the feelings of rage, hate, and paranoia grow, the need to act eventually becomes an omnipresent desire. As the vicious cycle devolves, all other strategies evaporate, even if viable (e.g., cognitive reframing, alternative careers). Planning and preparing for revenge in increasingly meticulous details provide temporary relief, which may even cause satisfaction at imagining the suffering of his targets and a feeling of accomplishment of his goals to punish and right the wrongs that were done to him.

But when these thoughts exceed his limits of rationality and morality, the road to destruction becomes inevitable. He then typically also starts to objectify his targets, convincing himself that they deserve revenge to further justify his plans and deflect blame. Many revenge killers of the chronic psychopathology type are fixed in a narcissistic-paranoid-schizoid frame of mind that developed from an adverse or over-indulged childhood, which ill-prepared them to deal with life's disappointments and rejections that they view as intentional and personal attacks. They typically have under-developed social skills, an impaired ability to trust others, and have an external locus of control, deflecting blame onto others. They also often have feelings of destructive envy where they are obsessed with other's possessions, status, and the way they are able to enjoy their lives.

Such beliefs and feelings are sometimes fueled by a desire to escape their predicament and pain, which may involve aversive self-awareness. As a result, the revenge killer's personality descends into hopelessness, irrationality, poor risk assessment, and lack of restraint. They increase their efforts to externalize their distress until it culminates in a violent attack. "At this point, the individual is unable or unwilling to re-emerge from his heroic fantasy of justified, honorable revenge" (Knoll, 2010a, p. 93). When the willingness to sacrifice his life settles, his fantasies turn to reality and he formulates and plans his final stance, many times leaking or communicating their intent before the attack (Knoll, 2010b). These communications or behaviors typically reveal varying levels of persecutory delusions, envy, and/or social and vocational failure.

Unlike serial and stranger killings, revenge killing usually does not pose a challenge to investigators. The perpetrator often dies at the scene or waits meekly to be apprehended, their compelling desire fulfilled. Although revenge can also take the form of serial murders, where the victims are the proxies of the perpetrator's revenge target, it is typically enacted in a single event. As many revenge killers, especially mass murderers, do not survive their crimes, limited data of their causes, pathways, and motivations are available. Even when they leave detailed writings and live to be arrested, explanations often consist of long ramblings spewing hate and accusations. The cases of Elliot Rodger, Christopher Dorner, and Jennifer San Marco are good examples of written accounts left after their deaths to provide clues to their planning, reasons, and state of mind.

As most revenge killers target specific victims, or at least those who represent the object of their reprisal, they mostly choose an efficient and predictable weapon that is easily available to them, which is a handgun or rifle, at least in America. According to Fox and Levin (2003), mass murderers infrequently attack strangers and the revenge subtype even less so. About 40% of mass murders are committed against family members and 40% against victims known to the perpetrator (e.g., coworkers).

Similarly, the majority of revenge killings, whether targeting a single victim or multiple victims, do not happen during a heated argument but are coldly calculated and planned, sometimes months and years in advance. All the case studies presented here are a testament to that fact. Two of the conditions of mass murders that Fox and Levin (2003) suggested are relevant to revenge killings, namely (p. 52):

1. Predisposers, long-term and stable preconditions that become incorporated into the personality of the killer

2. Precipitants, short-term and acute triggers, that is, catalysts

The category of "predisposers" implies the presence of a psychopathology of the perpetrator that renders him (or her) much more susceptible to chronic paranoid and persecutory beliefs, social rejection and isolation, and an inability to cope with disappointments. The second primary condition, "precipitants," is related to a traumatic incident that dramatically affects the individual's life, which was reasonably "normal," even high achieving, before the event. The ensuing embitterment permeates his or her activities and thoughts until the need for relief becomes unavoidable. A few differences between the two groups are suggested, illustrated by the case studies of Elliot Rodger, Jennifer San Marcos, and James Holmes, who are proposed as high psychopathology types, and Christopher Dorner and Amy Bishop, who are proposed as posttraumatic embittered types. Although the exclusivity of this distinction has not yet been empirically established, it is put forward as an avenue for future exploration. It is not proposed that the two types have no overlap, but that a set of characteristics is sufficiently different between the two to provide a more meaningful understanding and interpretation of their behavioral and cognitive trajectories.

Meloy et al. (2004) referred to a classification of mass murder among six dimensions, namely, (i) motivation, (ii) anticipated gains, (iii) victim selection, (iv) victim relationship, (v) traits, and (vi) spatial mobility. These aspects are also considered in the distinction between the high psychopathology and posttraumatic embitterment types.

Chronic Psychopathology Trajectory of Revenge Killers

These individuals fantasize about revenge for a long time before moving on to planning the assault. Many have had childhoods that either made them paranoid and distrustful or entitled to have others cater to their needs. Either way, their social skills, and resilience are lacking and they are ill-prepared to handle life's disappointments. From a young age, they have problems building personal relationships but it is most often rejection in a social and romantic sense that is devastating. Typically, the effects of a series of disappointments accumulate until they have to act to protect an already weak ego. Revenge killers with chronic psychopathology are often loners, have difficulty fitting in, and seem socially awkward. They eventually blame a specific person or type of person for their unhappiness, which develops into a fixed revenge fantasy.

Accordingly, they carefully select specific victims, while others are depersonalized as collateral damage. They may also commit "murder by proxy" where they target victims that represent their primary target. Katsavdakis et al. (2011) provided the following profile of a typical adult mass murderer driven by revenge:

> A significant number of men who are adult mass murderers have major mental disorders and often personality disorders, and over the course of time proceed on a "pathway to violence," nurturing a grievance, researching an attack, planning and preparing for such an attack, breaching whatever security stands in the way, and carrying out the killing. They often exhibit a pattern of fascination with war and weaponry and develop a "warrior mentality" that is characterized internally by grandiose and violent fantasies. These ruminations eventually coalesce into a desire and decision to commit a mass murder. A triggering event, however, often a humiliating loss in relationship or work, may start the clock and determine the time, place, and targets of the killing. Such perpetrators typically do not communicate a direct threat to the target(s) beforehand but may leak their intent to third parties (p. 813).

Their homicidal trajectory is typically more prolonged than the posttraumatic embitterment type, with an earlier onset, and they tend to act at a younger age. Sometimes their target develops into a more general hatred of society. They feel belittled and ridiculed by others around them. The mentally ill revenge killer usually annihilates their families, fellow students, and others who represent their nemesis. They are much younger than the average posttraumatic embitterment type (e.g., disgruntled employee), often still in their teens or early twenties. This type of revenge killer is typically a loner who abuses alcohol and drugs, has a history of abuse and victimization, and is preoccupied with violent fantasies (Meloy et al., 2001). About one-quarter of this group has a history of psychiatric hospitalization or treatment.

They are often socially awkward and have trouble establishing and maintaining romantic relationships. As a result, these individuals tend to be very depressed and anxious and often lack a specific individual target, which is different from the posttraumatic embitterment type. Instead, their acts are more symbolic in nature as they make a statement with violence against the behavior and values of others, often in the same age group. Although no single profile adequately fits this asocial group, chronic symptoms of personality disorder, childhood trauma, and psychosis are present in many cases that are characterized by a history of physical and emotional abuse, parental substance abuse issues, and a history of crime in the family.

They have a profound sense of being different, have trouble fitting in, and are very sensitive to rejection, criticism, and ridicule. They blame others that they are made to feel insignificant and worthless and want to exact revenge for their malaise. A social stressor usually sets this type of revenge killer in motion. Their motivation has been described as "ceremonial" as they typically desire to gain notoriety (Fast, 2008). Similar to the posttraumatic embitterment type, they can be described as suicidal with hostile intent (Rocque, 2012). They choose to release a tremendous amount of hostility in one final act. In 71% of the cases, rejection in the form of isolation, disconnect with society, persecution, and bullying are primary triggers for despair and rage.

Cumulative strain theory has been suggested as the most appropriate theoretical construct of younger, asocial revenge killers (Levin and Madfis, 2009). Chronic strains that originate from childhood generate frustrations that contribute to social isolation and a perceived lack of support that exacerbates the effect of any real or imagined short-term negative event. Such disappointments and failures become increasingly devastating, which initiates violent fantasies to relieve and cope with the strain.

Eventually, fantasies become inadequate to lessen their inner distress, and concrete plans are starting to materialize to regain a sense of self and control. The individual starts to conduct research on potential methods, targets, and locations; train and acquire the equipment needed, most often firearms. Frequently, they leak their plans to others, either unintentionally or in a conscious or subconscious effort to be stopped, which may present an opportunity to prevent a tragedy. One such example is Elliot Rodger.

Case Study: 2014 Isla Vista Killings, Elliot Rodger

On May 23, 2014, 22-year-old Elliot Rodger killed 6 people and injured 14 others in Isla Vista near the campus of the University of California, Santa Barbara (UCSB), before committing suicide. Rodger had been preparing for the attack for a long time. He started visiting a shooting range in September 2012 and saved $5000 from allowance given to him by his parents and grandmothers to buy firearms. He bought his first handgun, a Glock 34 pistol, in Goleta in December 2012. In his manifesto, he described it as "an efficient and highly accurate weapon" (Rodger, 2014, p. 113). The next year, in March 2013, he bought an SIG-Sauer P226 pistol in Burbank, and in February 2014 another SIG-Sauer P226 in Oxnard (Brown, 2014).

THE KILLING SPREE

Friday afternoon of May 23, 2014, Rodger stabbed to death his two roommates, Weihan Wang and Cheng Hong, and a friend, George Chen, one by one as they entered the apartment at separate times. Wang had 15 and Hong 25 stab wounds. Rodger stabbed Chen 94 times (Brown, 2014). This level of overkill is often associated with feelings of intense personal anger or rage toward the victim or hatred and envy projected toward a target group. After each murder, Rodger tried to clean up and concealed the bodies with blankets, towels, and clothing. Police found the bodies the next day after the shooting spree.

At 7:38 p.m., Rodger bought a triple vanilla latte at the Isla Vista Starbucks coffee shop and was seen sitting in his car in his apartment parking lot at about 8:30 p.m. He was working on his laptop, and at 9:18 p.m. he uploaded the "Retribution" video, and emailed his manifesto. From there, he drove to the Alpha Phi sorority house at Embarcadero del Norte and Segovia Road near the UCSB, which he referred to in his manifesto as the "hottest sorority house of UCSB." He wrote that he had planned to kill every woman inside. When nobody responded to his knocks on the front door, he shot at people nearby, killing two Delta Delta Delta sorority sisters and wounding a third.

Rodger returned to his car and drove to the Isla Vista Deli Mart where he shot and killed a student inside. He drove south on Embarcadero del Norte on the wrong side of the road, striking a pedestrian and continuing to fire at people on the sidewalk. He turned east on Del Playa Drive and made a U-turn. He exchanged fire with a sheriff's deputy who had responded to a 9-1-1 call, injuring two more pedestrians. He turned north on Camino del Sur, shot and injured three more people, and struck three more with his car. Turning east on Sabado Tarde, he struck another skateboarder and shot two more men. Near Acorn Park, he exchanged fire with three sheriff's deputies and was shot in the left hip.

With police in pursuit, Rodger turned south again on El Embarcadero and west on Del Playa. After striking a bicyclist, crashed on the north sidewalk just east of the intersection of Del Playa and Camino Pescadero. He committed suicide with a shot to the head. When the dust settled, 6 people were dead and 14 injured. At 9:33 p.m., only 15 minutes after posting his video and story online, Elliot Rodger's killing spree (and life) was over. Police recovered two knives, three handguns, six empty 10-round magazines, and 548 rounds of unspent ammunition, also in 10-round magazines or ammunition boxes, from his car.

BACKGROUND

Rodger was born in England on July 24, 1991, and moved to the United States with his parents when he was 5 years old. His father was a filmmaker and after a divorce in 1998, remarried a Moroccan actress. Rodger graduated from Independence Continuation High School in Lake Balboa in 2010. He moved from his mother's Calabasas, California apartment to the Capri Apartments in Isla Vista in June 2011 (Duke, 2014b). Of this time, he wrote:

> I was desperate to have the life I know I deserve; a life of being wanted by attractive girls, a life of sex and love. Other men are able to have such a life…so why not me? I deserve it! I am magnificent, no matter how much the world treated me otherwise. I am destined for great things (para. 7).

But he was deeply disappointed when he continued to experience the same rejection and injustice. He attended Santa Barbara City College until February 2012 when he dropped out of class, commenting that he did not want to see all those beautiful girls he could never have. "It completely ended all hope I had of living a desirable life in Santa Barbara. Violent revenge had been in the back of my mind ever since" (Duke, 2014b, para. 15). For a while, he pinned his last hope on becoming wealthy, thereby achieving "a form of happy, peaceful revenge." He continued to become enraged seeing happy people enjoying their lives. In August 2012, Rodger noted that he spent the whole month in his room visualizing the final outcome of winning the lottery jackpot.

In September 2012, when he did not win the Mega Millions $120 million jackpot, the "Day of Retribution" became his last option. He started firearm training and purchased his first handgun 2 months later. After that, his revenge plans started to consume his thoughts and life. After delays of his original timeline due to a broken leg and a cold, he chose May 24 as the date of his final retribution. "During the last few weeks of my life, I continued my daily adventures around town, trying to experience as much of the world as I could before I die," Rodger wrote in one of his last entries.

Mental Health and Social Problems

Rodgers had a history of mental health and social problems, seeing various therapists since the age of eight, although he was never formally diagnosed. He was prescribed antipsychotic medication used to treat schizophrenia and bipolar disorder and was informally diagnosed with Asperger syndrome, according to his mother (Duke, 2014a). He was bullied at school and the one friend that he had ended the friendship in 2012 (Rodger, 2014). He had a blog and YouTube account where he described his feelings of loneliness and rejection. After turning 18, he ceased all medication and mental health care, and increasingly isolated himself. In his manifesto, Rodger noted various scuffles and vengeful acts that he committed since 2011, many directed at girls who he thought rejected or ignored him.

He also referred to his "War on Women," that he deeply resented still being a virgin at age 22, and blamed his parent for his lack of wealth (Rodger, 2014; Duke, 2014a). In his final YouTube video, he stated:

> Well, this is my last video, it all has to come to this. Tomorrow is the day of retribution, the day in which I will have my revenge against humanity, against all of you. For the last eight years of my life, ever since I hit puberty, I've been forced to endure an existence of loneliness, rejection, and unfulfilled desires all because girls have never been attracted to me. Girls gave their affection, and sex and love to other men but never to me…[]…I don't know why you girls aren't attracted to me, but I will punish you all for it. It's an injustice, a crime… (Garvey, 2014, para 6)

It is clear that Elliot Rodger was intensely resentful that he could not attract girls, for which he blamed women in general. Some called him an entitled narcissist. He may have been overprotected and spoiled as a child, which fuels feelings of entitlement in later life. When those expectations do not materialize, the young person becomes deeply disillusioned. As he has grown to expect others to placate and provide his needs, he blames others when it does not happen. From a young age, he uses rage to get what he wants. Their worldview is that they are entitled to others doing their bidding and they take no responsibility for failures.

Such an indulged child often tries to assert his needs aggressively onto others, which reinforces experiences of rejection and disapproval. As with, Elliot Rodger, they are also often not socially adept. Instead of cultivating modesty and responding with sensitivity and empathy, they continue to assert their wishes in aggressive ways. They do not adapt to negative social feedback. Instead, their maladaptive beliefs are fueled further, making it even more difficult to deal with hardship and disappointment. They do not understand their peers' reactions and externalize blame. The cycle of feeling ostracized and humiliated intensifies, and, rather than changing their world view, some choose retribution as the last option to cope with his disappointment.

A Female Revenge Killer with Signs of Chronic Psychopathology

Disgruntled and revenge murders, especially on a mass scale, are very rare among female perpetrators. Jennifer San Marco and Amy Bishop are two of the handful of female mass murderers whose actions involved revenge motives. San Marco is proposed as a chronic psychopathology type, while Bishop, who appeared to have been a high achiever before a traumatic event derailed her life, is suggested as a posttraumatic embitterment type.

On January 30, 2006, 45-year-old former U.S. Postal Service worker shot and killed seven people in Goleta, California before committing suicide.

San Marco worked nights at the mail processing plant from 1997 but left in early 2003 on a mental disability retirement. Two years before, in February 2001, she was involuntarily hospitalized following a disturbance in which police removed her from the facility. She was sent to a Ventura psychiatric hospital for 3 days of assessment, but the outcome is not known.

In July 2003, she moved to Milan, small town in New Mexico, 70 miles west of Albuquerque, with a population of about 2200 people. It is here where authorities noticed her increasingly bizarre behavior. She was accused of harassing an office worker and appearing naked at a gas station. She was known for racist remarks and applied for a business license in 2004, planning to launch a publication titled "The Racist Press." She was also observed carrying on conversations and arguments with herself, family members who were not present, and an imaginary friend. She was not known for violent or threatening behavior.

San Marco left writings at her New Mexico home that alluded to a conspiracy involving the Goleta mail-sorting plant, a local medical facility, and the Santa Barbara County Sheriff's Department. She bought a 15-round, 9-mm Smith and Wesson model 915 and ammunition in August 2005 from pawn shops in the New Mexico towns of Grants and Gallup, respectively. A background check did not reveal any problems.

In the last week of January 2006, she flew from New Mexico to California before driving 2 hours to her old apartment complex. On Monday night, between 7:15 and 8:15 p.m., she snuck into a previous neighbor's home in Santa Barbara and killed 54-year-old Beverly Graham with two close-range shots to the head and face. The neighbor had complained about her loud music and noisy ramblings when she was still living there. Police found the body the next day. After killing Graham, San Marco drove to the mail-sorting plant. She entered the premises by driving through the gate behind another vehicle and gained entry to the building by taking an employee's identification card at gunpoint.

At 9:00 p.m., San Marco started shooting postal employees in the parking area outside the facility, firing six rounds that killed three women. She then entered the center. Once inside, she continued to fire, killing two more women and one male, reloading once before shooting herself to death. All of the victims at the mail-sorting plant were minorities: three were black, one was Chinese-American, one was Hispanic, and one was Filipino. It was possible that the killings were racially motivated and that she chose her victims, but it remains unconfirmed, although she mentioned at least two victims in her writings.

In retrospect, it seems that the revenge ideation of San Marco centered around her racist beliefs and the conspiracies that she believed were being plotted against her. She exhibited signs of psychosis for at least 3 years before the shooting, which became progressively worse. Kendra's law, legislation implemented in all but four other states to order treatment of mental health patients who are deemed a danger to themselves and others, does not apply in New Mexico. A modified version has been proposed, but lawmakers failed to pass the bill in time before the end of the 2015 Senate session.

In an analysis of the San Marcos case, Katsavdakis et al. (2011) concluded that her thinking became increasingly delusional, paranoid, and disorganized in New Mexico. In her newsletters, "The Racist Press," she emphasized the intrusive role of government and religion, stating that the Ku Klux Klan and the U.S. government worked in unison, and repeatedly linked the Rocky Horror Picture Show with the government. She also made references to sexual assault and incest.

The grievance of her dismissal by her employer of nearly 6 years was grossly magnified by her paranoid delusional beliefs (Katsavdakis et al., 2011). Her behavior before and during the attack suggests predatory violence rather than affective violence. Affective violence is defined as a response to a perceived imminent threat preceded by high levels of autonomic (sympathetic) arousal of emotions such as anger and/or fear (Meloy, 2006). It is also described as impulsive, reactive, and expressive. Predatory, or instrumental violence, on the other hand, is characterized by cognitive planning and the absence of emotion and threat at the time of the attack. In the case of San Marcos, a perceived need for self-preservation, associated with revenge against her previous employer and colleagues, was probably at the center of her plans for revenge. Although her victims were part of a target group, individual selection was opportunistic rather than targeted. San Marco's refusal to seek and comply with psychiatric treatment is also common among revenge killers.

A Different Kind of Revenge: The Aurora Shooter

James Holmes had homicidal thoughts too, but his fantasies of revenge seemed more existential, questioning his own value and those of others. He was diagnosed with schizotypal personality disorder, but deemed rational and therefore legally sane during the mass shooting at Aurora during which he shot and killed 12 people and wounded 70. Holmes believed that killing would add value to his life by absorbing his victims' life experiences, hopes, and dreams into his own (Holmes, 2012). He had been obsessed with killing for more than a decade and decided to act after a series of setbacks that included failing at school and breaking up with his girlfriend. He had been plagued by night terrors and depression since the age of 14. He was obsessed with his beliefs that he had many physical shortcomings and complained of fatigue, catatonia, insomnia, social awkwardness and isolation, hyperactivity and problems with his eyes, ears, nose, he wrote in his journal. However, his biggest problem was difficulty in forming thoughts into words. He had trouble communicating and felt uncomfortable in contact with others. As a result, he hated humanity.

Although not as straightforward a case of revenge as with Elliot Rodger, the mass shooting seemed to have been Holmes' attempt to recreate his persona, achieve relevance, meaning, and value by taking the lives of others (Holmes, 2012). For him, his life had no meaning at all. In his 35-page notebook that he sent to his psychiatrist days before the shooting, Holmes wrote that he had an "obsession to kill," and a "lifelong hatred for mankind." It was "my state of mind for the past 15 years" (Holmes, 2012, p. 26). In his meticulous plotting and planning, he compared different methods and locations of mass killings, including diagrams of the theater complex and estimated police response times. For him, killing others was the only alternative to suicide when he could not fix his "broken mind" by other means, including pursuing knowledge. "In order to rehabilitate the broken mind, my soul must be eviscerated," Holmes wrote. He argued that his recent relationship and work failures were expediting catalysts, but that the state of his mind since adolescence was the cause that finally moved him to do "one more battle to fight with life, to face death, embrace the longstanding hatred of mankind, and overcome all fear and certain death."

Psychology of Posttraumatic Embitterment-Type Revenge Killers

The posttraumatic embitterment type is proposed as the second group of revenge killers. They are typified by a single traumatic event that threatens their self-value and the justness and fairness of the world. Before the event, they were often high achievers and had no prominent psychopathology. They are, on average, older than the chronic psychopathology type.

Posttraumatic Embitterment Disorder

Posttraumatic embitterment disorder (PTED) is a type of adjustment disorder that is precipitated by a single, exceptional negative life event. Linden (2003) listed the core criteria of PTED as follows (p. 195):

1. A single exceptional negative life event precipitates the onset of the illness

2. The present negative state developed in the direct context of this event

3. The emotional response is embitterment and feelings of injustice

4. Repeated intrusive memories of the event

5. Emotional modulation is unimpaired, patients can even smile when engaged in thoughts of revenge

6. No obvious other mental disorder in the year before the event that can explain the reaction

The traumatic event does not have to conform to the DSM criteria as a life-threatening situation but affect an important element of a person's life sufficiently to cause psychological turmoil and significant impairment to premorbid functioning. Examples are the death of a loved one, divorce, or loss of a job. As a reactive disorder, PTED is often undiagnosed as the symptoms may appear to be subclinical.

Embitterment is a state of mood distinct from depression, hopelessness, and anger, but may share some of these features. PTED consists of persistent feelings of unfairly being let down, humiliated, and rejected. The embittered person feels revengeful but helpless. These contrasting feelings escalate often while the person tries multiple avenues to correct the wrong that was done to them. These may include complaints, appeals, advocating their case, and attempting to mobilize support. When these courses of action are exhausted, revenge fantasies often intensify until it compels the person to formulate specific plans for revenge, followed by preparation and execution. Such a process may take months or years until the attack is followed through.

Nearly all individuals that satisfy the criteria for PTED expressed feelings of injustice, rage, and restlessness (Linden et al., 2007). This is a highly unstable state of mind that cannot be placated or contained for a significant length of time before becoming untenable and in desperate need of release. Research has also established that the symptoms of PTED do not have a tendency to spontaneously remit as other adjustment disorders. This fact underscores the importance of identification and intervention efforts to manage the potential effects of PTED.

The event that triggers PTED causes the violation of a person's basic belief in a just and fair world. Such a belief in a just world construct is at the core of people's experience of reality and their sense of self-value (Linden and Maercker, 2011). If shattered, revenge becomes the mechanism underlying embitterment as the primitive "urge to fight back" (p. 42). The traumatic event is experienced as a violation of central values, which implies being victimized and helpless. In an important sense, revenge is a coping strategy to deal with these inner conflicts and threats to the ego.

Posttraumatic embitterment most often follows separation, divorce, loss of a job, or the death of a loved one for which someone else is blamed. The person typically feels that their whole life's accomplishments and hopes have been destroyed in one act of injustice and unfairness.

Posttraumatic Embitterment Trajectory

In such a situation, persons feel bitter about their loss and helpless to make a positive change. Their sense that their ego is under attack and that someone else has intentionally caused them harm initiate thoughts of revenge as a coping mechanism.

As a prominent posttraumatic embitterment type, the disgruntled employees target victims at their current or previous place of employment. Although disgruntled employees could also have serious psychopathology, a devastating experience at their work, which is usually a very important component of their lives and self-image, triggers embitterment. They have often been fired, disciplined, or given poor performance reviews. They blame their employer and coworkers for their distress, which is often related to perceptions of ridicule, discrimination, or unfair treatment. They lack opportunities to find suitable alternative employment and believe that killing their coworkers will draw attention to the injustices that they endured.

Fox and Levin (1994) pointed out that the average workplace murderer is 38 years old, about 9 years older than the average murderer. At that age, their job becomes more important and they typically have fewer alternative opportunities. This aspect is often made more pronounced by chronic or recent social isolation or rejection. At that point, they view their jobs as the only stable and meaningful factor in their lives. Although they may not have a criminal record or known for violent or erratic behavior, their frustrations have built up for a long time, making them feel increasingly worthless and insignificant. Although some revenge killers lash out at random victims when they eventually snap, most (84%) target specific victims or types that represent them.

Examples of posttraumatic embitterment revenge killers that are discussed in following sections include Christopher Dorner and Amy Bishop. Many of this type of revenge killers do not exhibit prominent thought disturbances before the traumatic event, although thought disturbances may be a result of the trauma. They experience great personal injustices that are beyond their control (Holmes and Holmes, 2001), and kill to retaliate for these losses of their jobs, reputation, and integrity (e.g., Dorner, Bishop).

Declercq and Audenaert (2011) had the opportunity to complete a comprehensive interview and analysis of a male mass murderer who shot and killed a salesman and four others at their home with the help of an accomplice. Their initial intention was only to rob them but scaring and exercising power over the victims "made up for years of fear and powerlessness" (p. 137). Although they were hesitant to commit murder, the accomplice got angry during a verbal exchange with the salesman and snapped, shooting him in the side of the head from a distance of about 20–30 cm, effectively executing him.

They were searching the house when another female family member arrived at the house with a friend. They locked the woman up in the basement with the other two that they have secluded there, and took the male friend to the garage where the offender shot him in the back of the neck. He went back to the basement and led the last arriving family member to the living room where he made her undress and lie down on the couch. As he considered women to be "whores," he wanted to humiliate her. The accomplice tried to rape her but was unsuccessful. The offender asked her to put a cushion over her face, after which he shot her twice in the face at point-blank range. He went back to the basement where the last two victims were still locked up and shot both fatally in the neck and head, again from a short distance. They stole some money, a revolver, and other items from the home and left in one of the victims' cars. They were apprehended the next day.

In the interview with Declercq and Audenaert (2011), the offender stated that he experienced severe frustration because of the perceived wrongs that he has suffered. He hated society and wanted to get even, which seemed rooted in the 7-year prison sentence that he previously received for a series of thefts. Similar to many other revenge killers, he had a blue-collar job and a long criminal history of shoplifting, theft, and breaking and entering. He always worked with one or more accomplice. He stole to provide for his family, a need that was made more urgent by a belief that he would die young.

As with many disgruntled and revenge killers, he held negative beliefs, including "the world is dangerous and malevolent" and "we are powerless victims" (p. 138). As such, he presented antisocial and borderline personality features. He blamed the jury for his first sentence, which he believed was a profound injustice and, therefore, wanted to harm civilians. He lost his wife and children because of the prison sentence and had a fixed belief that he will never find a romantic partner again, especially as he found himself "physically repulsive and worthless" (p. 139). He also believed that single women his age are "whores." When he was 12 years old, he was involved in a serious traffic accident that left his face scarred and his eyes asymmetrical. He felt ashamed and was ridiculed by other children because of his disfigurement.

He withdrew from social contact and felt deeply unhappy. When he was 15, he sustained an eye injury at school that caused permanent damage and the need to wear dark glasses constantly. As a result, he was mocked even more, and his self-esteem and attachments deteriorated further. Although he continued to crave affection and acceptance, he viewed others as unreliable and malevolent. Only when he was 20, he gathered enough courage to approach a 17-year-old girl, who, to his surprise, reciprocated his attraction. They married and had two children. Their relationship was sometimes tumultuous, marred by quarrels involving his jealousy and short temper that are common in borderline personality disorder.

Although this offender exhibited signs of an antisocial and borderline personality disorders since his teens, he had managed to establish and maintain a reasonably satisfying life, until he was sent to prison and lost his wife. This created posttraumatic embitterment that reinforced his already negative worldviews, which finally turned into revenge and homicidal ideation when he suspected his girlfriend of being unfaithful.

Such a precipitant is present in most disgruntled and revenge killings, which was the loss of a romantic relationship that he found soon after his release from prison. After only two months, they moved in together. The relationship quickly turned bad when she lost her job, her abuse of alcohol and pills worsened, and she began to go to a pub while he was at work, which triggered feelings of intense jealousy, hate, resentment, and revenge. The evening of the murders, she left him alone again to go to the pub. If she had stayed with him, he declared: "Then, all of it wouldn't have happened" (p. 139).

The offender was lonely, despondent, and isolated, which was a result of his insecure attachment style that frustrated his need of intimacy and contact with others. Attachment issues are very common among disgruntled and revenge killers, due to insecure, fearful, or angry styles. There is often associated dysphoric symptoms, accompanied by feelings of emptiness, unstable mood, low self-perception, brooding, indecisiveness, and diminished interest in activities that used to be pleasurable. These types of homicide offenders typically externalize blame and believe themselves to be the victim of their partner, boss, coworkers, the criminal justice system, and society in general.

There is also often an obsessive rumination about revenge that may involve grandiose fantasies of achieving authority, recognition, and omnipotence. In such cases, these egosyntonic fantasies fuel the offender's pathological narcissism and are often accompanied by a fascination with weapons and military paraphernalia. In some cases, including this one, however, the rumination is more egodystonic and compulsive. Its intrusiveness caused an immense internal pressure in the presence of a trigger that desperately needed a release, rather than the typical pseudocommando style of chronic hatred and fascination with weapons.

Disgruntled and revenge killings are generally of a predatory nature instead of an impulsive, emotionally charged reaction to a perceived threat (Declercq and Audenaert, 2011). It is, therefore, mostly "planned, purposeful, and lacks an emotional display" (p. 140). In this sense, the homicidal act is a response to protracted and conflict-ridden inner turmoil. It is the second part of a sequence of three phases: incubation, violence, and relief. In the incubation phase, emotional tension increases over time until it becomes unendurable. Dysphoria, withdrawal and isolation, egocentric thinking, and sometimes hallucinations and thought disorders are present. Ideation of murder and revenge temporarily relieves the inner distress. The brooding and distress become increasingly intense in the weeks or months before the killing and are often accompanied by somatic and physiological symptoms.

Initially, a conflict exists in the offender's mind and the homicidal thoughts are rejected. But, after a while, no measure relieves the pressure, and the compulsion takes over. In this case, the offender described his experience after the final trigger as follows: "Like an alcoholic needs alcohol to find relief, I felt I had to kill to find peace" (p. 141). After the murders, his headaches and stomach cramps disappeared, his feelings of hate against society dissipated, but he felt deep sorrow and regret afterward.

As this case has illustrated, the distinction between a chronic psychopathology revenge type and a posttraumatic embitterment type is not always clear-cut but depends on the specific mix of early-onset mental illness and effects of a traumatic event. In this case, his personality profile increased the risk of violence significantly, but it was the sense of injustice in his last relationship that tipped the scale. Such distinction is much clearer in the next two case descriptions, where a single event appeared to have compelled revenge from two offenders who have functioned well before the traumatic experience.

Case Study: California Cop Killer, Christopher Dorner

Christopher Dorner was born on June 4, 1979, and grew up in Southern California. He graduated from Cypress High School in 1997 and majored in political science at Southern Utah University in 2001. Dorner joined the United States Navy Reserve in 2002 and stayed until 2013 when he was honorably discharged as a lieutenant. During this time, he entered the Los Angeles Police Department in 2005, graduated from the academy in 2006, but was deployed by the Navy Reserve to Bahrain until July 2007.

He was paired with training officer Teresa Evans to complete his probationary training. Shortly afterward, on July 2007, Dorner and Evans responded to a complaint at the Doubletree Hotel in San Pedro that Christopher Gettler, a schizophrenic with severe dementia, was causing a disturbance. Gettler was arrested. Two weeks later, after a performance review, Dorner filed a report alleging that Evans had used excessive force against Gettler by kicking him in the face twice while handcuffed and lying on the ground. The 7-month investigation concluded that no such incident had taken place and Dorner had lied (Leonard et al., 2013). As a result, he was dismissed by the LAPD in 2008. Dorner's appeals failed and the appeals court found that his allegations were not credible.

In early February 2013, Dorner's killing spree started, which coincided with the publication of a detailed note on Facebook. This 11,000-word post became known as his "manifesto" and detailed his revenge plans, including the names of 40 law enforcement personnel whom he planned to kill (Mohan and Schaefer, 2013). He demanded a public admission by the LAPD that his dismissal was an act of retaliation for reporting excessive force based on racist motivations.

His killing spree began on February 3, 2013, with the murder of the daughter of the LAPD captain who was his defense counsel in the review board hearings, and her fiancé in a car parked outside their condominium complex. The next day, on February 4, he published his manifesto online, naming targets, his reasons for targeting them, and his objective, which was getting his name cleared. On February 7, 2013, around 1:00 a.m., two officers followed a pickup truck in Corona with a driver matching Dorner's description when the driver stopped and fired a shot at them, grazing the one officer. About 20 minutes later, two officers were ambushed in Riverside at a red traffic light. One officer died, and the other was critically injured but survived.

Another hour and 25 minutes later, around 3:00 a.m., a man matching Dorner's description tried to steal a boat in San Diego to go to Mexico. Hours later the same day, Dorner's burnout dark gray Nissan Titan truck was found on a remote trail near Big Bear Lake, about 100 miles east of Los Angeles. Despite an intensive manhunt, Dorner managed to evade capture. On February 10, authorities announced a $1 million award for information leading to his capture.

Two days later, San Bernardino County Sheriff's Department deputies responded to a report of a carjacking of a white Dodge truck at 12:22 p.m. Officers spotted the car and Dorner as the driver, chasing him to a cabin near Big Bear Lake where he opened fire on two officers, killing one. Dorner barricaded himself in the cabin. Police knocked down most walls using a demolition vehicle and shot pyrotechnic tear gas canisters into the structure, which set the cabin on fire. A single gunshot was heard from inside.

On February 13, police confirmed that human remains have been found inside the cabin, as well as a wallet that contained Dorner's driver's license. Dental records confirmed the identity of the remains as that of Dorner. He died from a single gunshot wound to the head, most likely self-inflicted.

Dorner's Psychology

Dorner needed and craved respect. His reputation meant everything to him. He viewed any personal sleight with deep and extreme anger and disappointment that did not subside with time but only confirmed his innermost fears of being marginalized and losing control. When he sensed betrayal from his fellow officers, including many whom he considered as friends, he was devastated. His job, colleagues, and the respect, well deserved, he believed, had been his life. This illusion was completely shattered during the protracted and unsuccessful disciplinary and appeals processes.

He felt abandoned and betrayed by those whom he trusted. He channeled these feelings into violent fantasies and plans, eventually formulating a well-defined plot that he published online. His "manifesto" named 40 targets. He rationalized his actions as "a necessary evil" to reclaim his name and bring about substantial change in the LAPD. He referred to reputation as "your life, your legacy, your journey, sacrifices, and everything you've worked hard for every day of your life as and adolescent, young adult, and adult." He blamed officers involved in the investigation of the complaint against Officer Evans of favoritism, racism, lying, and lacking integrity.

From his writing, it is clear that he had harbored resentment and anger over personal injustices for a very long time, noting incidences from first grade elementary school in Norwalk, California. From that day, he made a life decision not to tolerate injustice. He also noted his accomplishments and performance with extreme pride but felt that the "the system betrayed, slandered, and libeled" him. He stated that he had been denigrated a "whistleblower" and "bully" by officers who tried to cover-up lying, racism, victimization, and using excessive force against civilians, a culture that had not changed since the Rodney King beating more than two decades before. His calling in life had been finally crushed because he could not reconcile himself with their lack of values and ethos.

Dorner's manifesto revealed that he had suffered two concussions playing football, in 1996 and 1999. He had been diagnosed with severe depression in 2008. These are common characteristics of revenge killers. He also had no intention to survive the spree, which is another typical feature.

A Female Posttraumatic Embitterment-Type Revenge Killer

Amy Bishop is one more example of a posttraumatic embitterment revenge killer. The 44-year-old biology professor at the University of Alabama in Huntsville (UAH) killed three colleagues and injured three others in a shooting during a faculty meeting on February 12, 2010. In March 2009, Bishop had been denied tenure at the university. As per university policy, spring 2010 was to be her last semester there.

In the investigation, several previous violent incidents in which she had been implicated were reevaluated. In 1986, when she was 21, she shot and killed her brother in Braintree, Massachusetts with a shotgun. The incident has officially been ruled an accident. The case was only reexamined after the 2010 shooting and she was charged with first-degree murder in her brother's death on June 16, 2010.

In 1993, she was questioned, together with her husband, James Anderson, in a letter bomb incident directed toward her previous lab supervisor who had given her critical performance reviews that caused her to resign. Paul Rosenberg, a Harvard Medical School professor and physician at Children's Hospital Boston, received a package containing two pipe bombs that failed to explode. A witness called the investigation tip line, reporting that Anderson threatened to kill Rosenberg. The couple refused to cooperate with investigators and to take a polygraph test. The case was closed due to a lack of evidence.

In 2002, Bishop was charged with misdemeanor assault for punching a woman in the head during a dispute over the last booster seat at an International House of Pancakes in Peabody, Massachusetts. She received probation and the judge recommended that she attend anger management classes, but she never did.

Bishop joined the faculty of the Department of Biological Sciences at the University of Alabama in Huntsville as an assistant professor in 2003. She increasingly showed evidence that the smallest of incidents could set off disproportionate and occasionally violent reactions. According to colleagues, her behavior varied wildly between fury and rage, and empathy and scientific brilliance.

Bishop had authored three unpublished novels, believing that fiction writing would be her ticket out of academia. The novels reportedly "reveal a deep preoccupation with the concept of deliverance from sin." Colleagues described her as smart but abrasive in personal interactions, and out of touch with reality. She felt entitled to praise and often interrupted meetings with bizarre tangents, which earned her the label of "crazy." In 2009, students complained to administrators several times. After receiving multiple warnings that she needed to publish more to qualify, she was denied tenure in March 2009. Her appeal was unsuccessful and she became severely distressed at the likelihood of losing her job.

At 3:00 p.m. on February 12, 2010, Amy Bishop sat down at a conference table with 13 professors and staff in the Biology Department at a meeting on the third floor of the Shelby Center for Science and Technology (Keefe, 2013). For 50 minutes Bishop, who is normally outspoken, remained quiet. As the meeting was concluding, she stood up, pulled a 9-mm Ruger semi-automatic handgun from her handbag and shot the department chairperson, Gopi Podila, in the head. Blocking the door, she continued to shoot until the gun jammed. In less than a minute, three of her colleagues were dead and three more injured. She went downstairs, rinsed the gun in a ladies' room, and phoned her husband to let him know that she was done for the day. A sheriff's deputy apprehended her when she exited the building through the back.

Bishop's case attracted special attention as she did not fit the typical profile of a revenge killer. She was a female, high achiever, and appeared to have a stable marriage. She had no criminal record and no history of mental illness or substance abuse. According to a close friend of the Bishops, Amy was a narcissist with a deep desire to be reaffirmed. Bishop also claimed to have paranoid schizophrenia, that she experiences delusions, and was treated with Haldol, an antipsychotic drug. These claims could not be corroborated in court. A battery of psychiatric tests also proved inconclusive (Keefe, 2013). Bishop pleaded guilty to murder and was sentenced to life in prison without the possibility of parole for the shooting in Alabama. Although speculation remained rife that she intentionally killed her brother all those years ago, perhaps in a fit of anger aimed at her mother, Alabama authorities declined to extradite her to face the murder charge in Massachusetts (Keefe, 2013). As Massachusetts does not have the death penalty, it would not have much meaning, they argued.

Whether accidental or not, Bishop reportedly carried a deep sense of guilt about the death of her brother. She apparently projected some of this guilt into hard work, which had a primary role in her life. Despite some complaints, there were enough indications that she was gifted and innovative, although she was described as awkward in personal interactions and acted superior to her colleagues (Van Wormer, 2010). Being denied tenure must have been the ultimate traumatic experience for Bishop. The most likely result is the "end to one's career, to one's livelihood, sense of personal disgrace, loss of home, friendships, and community" (para. 7). It is made worse by the fact that Bishop had to face her "adversaries," those who rejected her, for another last year, and that the blow came after 5 years of apparent successful reviews of her work. The discussions leading up to the shooting were about teaching plans for the following year, which must have incensed and humiliated her further.

Linguistic Analysis Comparison

To further explore possible differences between the two suggested types of revenge killers (chronic psychopathology and posttraumatic embitterment), the manifestos of Dorner and Rodger were compared using linguistic analysis software. An analysis of Dorner's manifesto, using Linguistic Inquiry and Word Count software (LIWC), revealed much higher anger and resolve (cause) than the norm but lower tentativeness (see http://liwc.wpengine.com/how-it-works). Relativity regarding references to motion, space, and time is lower while much more focus was afforded to work and achievement aspects. Words related to assent were below the norm and references to death far above. Expressions of sadness were at the norm while exhibiting lower anxiety. Not surprisingly, the linguistic analysis suggests a person angry that his achievements at work have been thwarted and he expressed a resolve to enact revenge. More importantly, regarding linguistics, the threats are authentic and imminent.

Compared with the linguistic analysis of Dorner's manifesto, Rodger's manifesto is much more self-referential, mentions the past almost twice as much, refers to social aspects 30% less, and is more emotional in tone, especially expressing anxiety about three times as much, and sadness almost twice as much. Both indicated less tentativeness and more certainty than the norm, which is typical of suicide notes (Fernández-Cabana et al., 2015). These differences tally with the retrospective knowledge that Dorner targeted young people in general as they made him feel worthless and rejected while Dorner, from a more cognitive perspective, targeted specific officers who he believed had wronged him.

Filicide as a Motive for Spousal Revenge

Filicide, the murder of children by their parent(s), stepparent(s), or another parental figure, is rare compared to other circumstances. Already in 1969, Resnick described five types of filicide, of which spousal revenge is the rarest. The other four types are (i) altruistic, (ii) acutely psychotic, (iii) fatal maltreatment, and (iv) an unwanted child. Parents, mostly mothers, who kill their young children to make their spouse suffer, often have had stressors in their lives that may have included domestic abuse, infidelity, abandonment, traumatic breakup, and/or a child custody battle. Filicide only accounted for 2.3% of all murders committed in the United States in 2014 (Federal Bureau of Investigation [FBI], 2014), with the spousal revenge type accounting for only 2% of filicide cases in Resnick's study (Resnick, 1969). A large proportion of filicides are also murder-suicide with 16–29% of mothers and 40–60% of fathers who commit filicide also committing suicide (Friedman et al., 2005). This means that of the nearly 12,000 murders annually in the United States, about 275 are recorded as filicides and only a handful of these—five or six—cases can be associated with a primary revenge motive.

Such a case was recently heard in a Canadian court. Elain Campion of Toronto was charged with murder after drowning her two daughters, ages 3 and 19 months, in their bathtub in October 2006. Afterward, she dressed the girls in princess dresses and curled their hair before laying them out on the bed, hands folded. She videotaped the drowning and aftermath. At one point, she looked at the camera, and addressed her husband: "Here, are you happy now?," adding "The children are gone. How does that make you feel?" They were in the middle of a bitter custody battle at the time. She waited 33 hours before notifying authorities, claiming that she killed the children because they belonged to her and not her husband (Spargo, 2014). At trial, her defense team claimed that she genuinely believed she was saving them from her ex-husband and that, by murdering them, she was providing them with a safe haven where they could be happy together. The prosecution insisted that despite suffering from mental illness that included persecutory delusions, she knew what she was doing at the time of the killing, which she committed to take revenge on her abusive ex-husband (CTV News, 2010). The jury was unconvinced by the defense's claims and convicted her of two counts of first-degree murder. Her appeal was dismissed in early 2015, and her sentence to life in prison with no parole eligibility for 25 years affirmed.

In this case, it would seem that Campione's comorbid unspecified psychosis and other conditions were caused or exacerbated by an abusive marriage that culminated with her husband facing multiple counts of assault involving his wife and eldest daughter. Subsequently, revenge fantasies likely were triggered by the possibility of losing custody of her children to the subject of her distress. In divorce documents, Campione claimed that he threatened to tell everyone she was "crazy" and that she would never see her children again (Spargo, 2014). Her mental illness was not disputed as she had spent time in psychiatric hospitals and attempted suicide once before the murders. The defining factor was that there appeared to have been cognitive reasoning and planning with a revenge motive present, which, almost without fail, compels a jury to find a defendant criminally accountable for a deliberate act that they knew was wrong.

Interviewing and Defending Revenge Killers

Although many revenge killers do not survive their criminal acts, some are captured and charged. Both the chronic psychopathology and posttraumatic embitterment types of revenge killers usually rationalize their crimes when interviewed. They are usually very talkative and ramble on about their real or imagined victimization. They believe that others are responsible for ruining their lives by rejecting them, firing them, or denying them important needs. They felt wounded and cornered, lashed out from their pain and resentment as a result. Their anger shows and they are usually eager to talk about the wrongs their targets have done to them, thereby rationalizing their behavior and denying or minimizing responsibility. They say things like "They pushed me too far, and they had to pay." "Some people deserved to be killed." They felt so badly hurt that the only recourse they could see was murder. They are full of rage and despair, and it often still shows after the murder. They are also usually quite open about their deviant desires, long-term homicidal ideations, and preparations, including scoping out their targets and practicing the event. They rarely have remorse, believing that the people who were destroyed deserved it for what they have directly or indirectly done to the killer.

Many revenge killers have a diagnosable mental health disorder, but with complex motivations and psychopathology it is often difficult to generalize. They often have a mixture of psychotic disturbances, mood disorders, substance use disorders, and/or personality disorders. In the case of personality disorders, a combination of antisocial, paranoid, narcissistic, and schizoid traits is mostly found, which render such an offender self-centered with a lack of empathy for others, chronically indifferent to others, have an external locus of control and is detached from his emotional life. Despite their disordered profiles, very few revenge killers are found legally insane or incompetent to stand trial. There is a wide-spread popular belief that psychotic individuals are not able to plan in a meticulous and methodical manner. But a break with consensual reality, and viewing the world in an idiosyncratic and paranoid way does not mean that they cannot research appropriate weapons, purchase firearms and ammunition, stake-out their target location and victims, practice their plans, and tactically carry it out to the letter.

Delusions typically help strengthen their resolve by eliminating any ambivalence from their minds and contribute to their victim selection process and motivation to kill. Their typical paranoid beliefs are often rooted in the inadequate development of social perspectives and communication skills, thereby preventing realistic appraisals in their beliefs about the attitudes and motives of others. This deficiency in social reality testing makes the individual more vulnerable to inner drives and fantasies and culminates in a conviction that he "is the focus of a community of persons who are united in a conspiracy of some kind against him"

(Cameron, 1959, p. 53). This "paranoid pseudo-community" that may constitute actual and imagined opponents provides that delusional revenge killer with an explanation of his beliefs.

Despite the prevalence of psychotic disorders in revenge killers, in most U.S. states and elsewhere, the legal test of sanity requires the defense counsel to prove that the defendant, as a result of a severe mental disease or defect, was unable to appreciate the nature and quality or the wrongfulness of his acts. The burden of proof is either by clear and convincing evidence or preponderance of the evidence. In the large majority of cases, courts found revenge killers knew right from wrong when they murdered, although their mental illness influenced their decisions and actions. Therefore, they are deemed to meet the legal definition of sanity, but often escape the death penalty based on mental illness as a mitigating factor. As Dr. Jeffrey Metzner, a court-appointed psychiatrist in the James Holmes trial explained: "Having psychosis doesn't take away your capacity to make choices. It may increase your capacity to make bad choices. He acted on his delusions, and that's a reflection of the severity of his mental illness" (Associated Press, 2015, para. 9). Holmes and other cases such as Anders Breivik illustrated that executive functions can still operate efficiently in the psychotic realm, enabling the offender to appear normal, raise no alarms, and plan and prepare with great detail.

Conclusions

As is evident from the case studies previously described, most revenge killers share typical characteristics and symptoms. They often have a history of strange and unstable behavior, which may be accompanied by complaints and/or criminal charges of disturbances and acts of violence. They often ruminate about injustices that others have done to them, which increases in frequency and severity until it absorbs their whole life and affects their daily functioning. It is proposed that most revenge killers can be distinguished by two main types: those who have chronic and early-onset psychopathology, which may include personality disorders, mood disorders, and abuse-related disturbances; and those with posttraumatic embitterment disorder caused by a single traumatic event that changed their life and threatened their self-worth.

Both types of homicide are preplanned, often in meticulous detail over months or years. It is not the result of someone who "snaps" unexpected and without warning. With revenge killers, the old adage "revenge is a dish best served cold" holds true. A reliable distinction between different types will better facilitate early identification of at-risk individuals and inform the most appropriate treatment or other intervention.

References

Associated Press. 2015, July 28. Defense witnesses: Colorado theater shooter still loved. *Chicago Tribune*. Retrieved from http://trib.in/1OI3jo8.

Brown, B. 2014, May 23. Isla Vista mass murder: Investigative summary. *Los Angeles Times*. Retrieved from http://bit.ly/1NhdNvw.

Cameron, N. 1959. The paranoid pseudo-community revisited. *American Journal of Sociology*, 65(1), 52–58. DOI: 10.1086/222626.

CTV News. 2010, November 16. *Spousal Revenge Rare Motive for Killing Kids, Experts Say*. Retrieved from http://bit.ly/1laBKKX.

Declercq, F. and Audenaert, K. 2011. A case of mass murder: Personality disorder, psychopathology, and violence mode. *Aggression and Violent Behavior*, 16(2), 135–143. DOI: 10.1016/j.avb.2011.02.001.

Duke, A. 2014a, May 28. California killer's family struggled with money, court documents show. *CNN*. Retrieved from http://cnn.it/1lNzEAw.

Duke, A. 2014b, May 28. Timeline to "Retribution": Isla Vista attacks planned over years. *CNN*. Retrieved from http://cnn.it/1lkQJ4m.

Fast, J. 2008. *Ceremonial Violence: A Psychological Explanation of School Shootings*. New York, NY: The Overlook Press.

Federal Bureau of Investigation. 2014. *Crime in the United States: Uniform Crime Reports*. Retrieved from http://1.usa.gov/1XBbfPB.

Fernández-Cabana, M., Jiménez-Féliz, J., Alves-Pérez, M. T., Mateos, R., Rodriguez, I. G., and García-Caballero, A. 2015. Linguistic analysis of suicide notes in Spain. *European Journal of Psychiatry*, 29(2), 145–155. DOI: 10.4321/S0213-61632015000200006.

Fox, J. A. and Levin, J. 1994. *Overkill: Mass Murder and Serial Killing Exposed*. New York, NY: Plenum.

Fox, J. A. and Levin, J. 2003. Mass murder: An analysis of extreme violence. *Journal of Applied Psychoanalytic Studies*, 5(1), 47–64.

Friedman, S. H., Hrouda, D. R., Holde, C. E., Noffsinger, S. G., and Resnick, P. J. 2005. Filicide-suicide: Common factors in parents who kill their children and themselves. *The Journal of the American Academy of Psychiatry and the Law, 33*, 496–504.

Garvey, M. 2014, May 24. Transcript of the disturbing video "Elliot Rodger's Retribution." *Los Angeles Times*. Retrieved from http://lat.ms/1lKpwkw.

Holmes, J. 2012. Aurora Theater shooting trial documents. *Denver Post*. Retrieved from http://dpo.st/1NxPo75.

Holmes, R. M. and Holmes, S. T. 2001. Mass murder. In: *Murder in America*. Thousand Oaks, CA: Sage, pp. 53–78.

Katsavdakis, K. A., Meloy, J. R., and White, S. G. 2011. A female mass murder. *Journal of Forensic Sciences, 56*(3), 813–818. DOI: 10.1111/j.1556-4029.2010.01692.x.

Keefe, P. R. 2013, February 11. A loaded gun: A mass shooter's tragic past. *The New Yorker*. Retrieved from http://bit.ly/1sIrhmo.

Knoll, J. L. 2010a. The "pseudocommando" mass murderer: Part I, The psychology of revenge and obliteration. *Journal of the American Academy of Psychiatry and the Law, 38(1)*, 87–94.

Knoll, J. L. 2010b. The "pseudocommando" mass murderer: Part II, The language of revenge. *Journal of the American Academy of Psychiatry and the Law, 38*(2), 263–272.

LaFarge, L. 2006. The wish for revenge. *The Psychoanalytic Quarterly 75*(2), 447–475.

Leonard, J., Rubin, J., and Blankstein, A. 2013, February 11. Dorner manhunt: Conflicting testimony in ex-cop's firing case. *L. A. Now*. Retrieved from http://lat.ms/21fIdo9.

Levin, J. and Madfis, E. 2009. Mass murder at school and cumulative strain. *American Behavioral Scientist, 52*(9), 1227–1245. DOI: 10.1177/0002764209332543.

Linden, M. 2003. Posttraumatic embitterment disorder. *Psychotherapy and Psychosomatics, 72*(4), 195–202. DOI: 10.1159/000070783.

Linden, M., Baumann, K., Rotter, M., and Schippan, B. 2007. The psychopathology of posttraumatic embitterment disorders. *Psychopathology, 40*(3), 159–156. DOI: 10.1159/000100005.

Linden, M. and Maercker, A. (Eds.), 2011. *Embitterment: Societal, Psychological, and Clinical Perspectives*. New York, NY: Springer.

Meloy, J. R. 2006. Empirical basis and forensic application of affective and predatory violence. *Australian and New Zealand Journal of Psychiatry, 40*(6–7), 539–547. DOI: 10.1080/j.1440-1614.2006.01837.x.

Meloy, J. R., Hempel, A. G., Mohandie, K., Shiva, A. A., and Gray, T. 2001. Offender and offense characteristics of a nonrandom sample of adolescent mass murderers. *Journal of the American Academy of Child and Adolescent Psychiatry, 40*(6), 719–728.

Meloy, J. R., Hempel, A. G., Gray, B. T., Mohandie, K., Shiva, A., and Richards, T. C. 2004. A comparative analysis of North American adolescent and adult mass murderers. *Behavioral Sciences and the Law, 22*(3), 291–309. DOI: 10.1002/bsl.586.

Mohan, G. and Schaefer, S. 2013, February 7. Manhunt manifesto. *Los Angeles Times*. Retrieved from http://bit.ly/1fKnxjz.

Resnick, P. J. 1969. Child murder by parents: A psychiatric review of filicide. *American Journal of Psychiatry, 126*, 73–82.

Rocque, M. 2012. Exploring school rampage shootings: Research, theory, and policy. *The Social Science Journal, 49*(3), 304–313. DOI: 10.1016/j.soscij.2011.11.001.

Rodger, E. 2014. My twisted world: The story of Elliot Rodger. *New York Times*. Retrieved from http://nyti.ms/1nsvTgL.

Spargo, C. 2014, November 27. Mom who drowned her two daughters and then filmed as she put them in princess dresses and curl their hair to punish ex-husband appealing murder conviction. *Daily Mail*. Retrieved from http://dailym.ai/1QVSe6m.

Van Wormer, K. S. 2010. Amy Bishop and the trauma of tenure denial. *Psychology Today*. Retrieved from http://bit.ly/1Rasylx.

5 Hate Crimes in America and the Slavery Paradigm

Allan L. Branson

Contents

Slavery and Discourse Analysis..72
Evolving Otherness 73
"Hate Crimes" against African-Americans 74
Hate Speech and the Impact of Discourse, Race, and Otherness..75
Discussion and Why "We Want Our Country Back" 76
James Byrd, Trayvon Martin, and Telishment 77
    James Byrd, Jr. 78
    Trayvon Benjamin Martin...78
    Telishment 78
Conclusion...78
References 79

While other countries and peoples have experienced their own brand of hate crimes often in the aftermath of colonialism, war, and social upheaval, this chapter focuses on "hate crimes" in the United States utilizing its unique paradigm of chattel slavery. With that goal in mind, an initial examination of colonialism and slavery in America is helpful toward illuminating the social dynamics of hate crimes and groups targeted by them. To dismiss slavery as a significant contributor to the legislation of hate crimes in the United States is to deny American history and lack a clear understanding of its import, however tedious that may be. Slavery as an institution in the United States was not comparable to that of other New World countries. Laws regarding miscegenation, education, and public access developed in the United States maintained their social exclusion for hundreds of years, including much of the post emancipation era, leaving an indelible stigma on black Americans. African slaves in America were demonized, depicted, and legislated as subhuman beasts—childlike, yet deserving of fear, loathing, punishment, and worse. They were considered intellectually capable of only the most rudimentary tasks. The consequences of this situation were laws established in the foundling United States that required an institutionalized, socially accepted, dehumanization of black people in order to maintain the profitable status quo for dominant white society, both during and after slavery.

Examining the significance of slavery and the concepts of "others,"[*] nativism and political discourse that oft times continues to foment a legacy of division and acts of violence against a particular group is the intent of this article. It is further expected that in doing so, our contemporary view of hate crimes and the legislation

---

[*] Jewkes (2004/2011) states that "…Implicit in all these forms of intolerance is the notion of a despised 'other' as a means to maintaining an idealized self…people are frequently underpinned by powerful psychic notions of otherness which frequently find expression in a tendency to see crime perpetrated by non-white people as a product of their ethnicity…" (pp. 110–111).

enacted to address them will be enhanced. An analysis of the James Byrd lynching, Matthew Shepard murder, and the killing of Trayvon Martin seeks to illuminate the evolution of how we perceive and define hate crimes in the United States. Each crime is an example of America's past, its evolution, and rationalization of hate crimes.

Slavery and Discourse Analysis

It is a significant point to note that slavery was not the result of racism but rather the need for a cheap labor force to aid the development of a fledgling New World country's primarily agricultural-based economy. The aftermath of the slaves' emancipation led to a sort of nativism* against those former African slaves brought to this country who would attempt to assimilate into an already established predominant white immigrant culture. After their emancipation, their victimization continued. These acts of violence perpetrated against them were not only commonplace but also made easy due to constitutional laws that dehumanized them.† This process of dehumanization, as a means of social control deemed necessary, also assisted the perpetrators avoidance of the cognitive dissonance that they might experience as a result of their inhumane acts.‡ Furthermore, the consistent utilization of language as a tool of oppression, describing these Africans in diaspora as less than human (e.g., "niggers" and "coons"), was reinforced with such vigor by each successive generation that the pejoratives metastasized. Stereotyping creates an obvious narrowing of one's focus, limiting perspective in the face of facts to the contrary. Laws and social policies further ensured the disenfranchisement of blacks. From the post-Reconstruction period through World War II, the great migration of blacks from the South to the northern states changed the demography of both regions. Seeking a better life through employment, an upsurge of European immigration continued to "whiten" the United States, and took job opportunities away from blacks who had been trained more for an agricultural than industrial environment increased tensions. Immigration to the North provided the possibility of freedom from the oppressive post-Civil War South. Fearful of how demographic and legal changes might affect the white way of life, the American South saw an increase in lynchings of African-Americans.§ Garland, arguing against suggestions that lynchings were merely part of an American tradition of vigilantism devoid of racial overtones, states:

> Whatever these lynchings were—aggressive displays of racial control, political theaters of white supremacy, communal rituals of sovereign power—they were not simple vigilantism… (2005, p. 352).

The negative stereotypes and discourse about these former African slaves were created for a purpose (Liggio, 1976). They aided the slave's subjugators justify the brutal treatment of blacks, both before and after the Civil War. The forced labor economy was maintained by local, state, and federal laws that sanctioned punishments without trial, such as lynchings and castrations. Therefore, the history of mistrust between African-Americans and law enforcement, which will be discussed later, is in large part a result of slavery as a legislated institution. So brutal was the system of chattel slavery in the United States that the French historian Alex de Tocqueville¶ (ca. 1835–1840) suggested that America's greatest failing would be its history of slavery, whose potential backlash was not worth its costs, he declared it "…the most formidable of all the ills that threatened America…" (Adams and Sanders, 2003, p. 22).

In conjunction with slavery as a social institution, one cannot gain a full understanding of hate crimes in the United States without examining the accompanying discourse. Slavery's impact on American society's perspective was reflected in discourse of the founding fathers (e.g., Thomas Jefferson and Ben Franklin [Ibid]), who, through their disparaging writings regarding black Africans, simultaneously revealed the importance of chattel slavery to their New World economy. Even in the twentieth century, President Woodrow Wilson, a history scholar who had also served as president of Princeton University, endorsed D.W. Griffith's degrading

---

* A similar nativism was noted not only in Nazi Germany directed specifically at those of Jewish descent but also including all non-Aryans.
† Article 1, Section 2 of 1787 U.S. constitution deemed African slaves as three-fifths of a human.
‡ These actions by any oppressing group are not unusual in times of war and great social upheaval. Nazi Germany dehumanized the Jews depicting them as rats to ensure their extermination could be done with little empathy (Kellerman, 2001).
§ After Reconstruction and during the first four decades of the twentieth century, many whites feared that the Negro was "getting out of his place," threatening the white man's social status, which thus needed protection. Lynching was seen as the method to defend white domination and keep the Negroes from becoming "uppity." Therefore, lynching was more the expression of white Americans' fear of black social and economic advancement than of actual Negro crime. *Source*: http://www.yale.edu/ynhti/curriculum/units/1979/2/79.02.04.x.html
¶ cf. Alex de Tocqueville (circa 1835–1840) *On Democracy in America*.

film *Birth of a Nation*,[*] further justifying the social exclusion of blacks from the highest elected office in America. He wrote for the silent film:

> ...the white men were aroused by a mere instinct for self-preservation...at last there had sprung into existence a great Ku Klux Klan,[†] a veritable empire of the South, to protect the Southern country... (Lennig, 2004, p. 139).

These views are presented to illuminate the socially accepted beliefs about a group seen as inferiors, the despised others, rendered by the most prestigious members of the newly founded society from the country's inception into the twentieth century. The significance of the negative discourse (Philo, 2007) from the founding fathers of this fledgling nation not only set the tone for egregious acts of barbarism to beset African-Americans which cannot be emphasized enough but also acted as a psychological salve for the collective psyche for those who participated in them. The significance regarding the impact of racist rhetoric from political leaders will be revisited in the "Discussion" section.

Evolving Otherness

Hate crimes in the United States have historically and consistently been based on "race." And while colonialism and the institution of slavery may not have been defined as "hate crimes," the considerable evidence regarding continued acts of brutality perpetrated against those colonized people were crimes fueled by hate (Fanon, 1963; Alia and Bull, 2005). The crimes against African-Americans alone are too extensive to catalogue here. However, hate crimes based on the social construct of "race" are most familiar. What people determined to be the "race" of a targeted group in the United States and the subsequent intolerance for the same is part of American history (e.g., Native Americans, African-Americans, Asians, and Hispanics). Despite the fact that race is a social construct, factually argued by geneticists, one cannot eliminate its significance most often determined by skin color and hair texture (Thompson, 2006). These have been the traditional identifiers combined with nefarious intent of individuals that have led to the assaults and murders of individuals and or whole groups, seen as the "others." It should then come as no surprise that most often the perpetrators of these acts of violence and the victims often differ in appearance. Without any genetic testing of the targeted individual or groups, a determination is made by the perpetrator(s) of these crimes that their victims are the "others"—those people. We shall further explore the concept of otherness and its impact on hate crime legislation. Next we will examine broadening and evolving criteria required to define the "others."

Prior to the October 22, 2009 passing of the Matthew Shepard James Byrd Jr. Hate Crimes Act, signed into law by President Barack Obama, the legacy of chattel slavery ensured that the U.S. history was replete with race-based acts of violence and murder. Prior to that legislation, the 1964 Civil Rights Act[‡] demonstrations fueled by numerous acts of violence targeting African-Americans were thought to remedy crimes against that one particular group. Most significant of these heinous acts were the 1964 murders of "Freedom Riders" Schwerner, Chaney, and Goodman, which became a rallying point for the Civil Rights movement in the United States[§] and the creation of a law that sought to protect individuals from what was yet to be defined as hate crimes. Additionally, the murder of Viola Liuzzo the following year only emphasized the need for federal protection not only for individuals who were perceived as the "others" but also for those who would also befriend or attempt to aid members of a targeted group. Schwerner, Goodman, and Liuzzo were white Americans who sought to help oppressed blacks in the South. While blacks may have been viewed as the "others," the concept of race could no longer be considered the sole factor determining who might become the victim of a hate crime.

The murder of Matthew Shepard[¶] near Laramie, Wyoming that same year, however, was based on his sexuality. James Byrd was black, Matthew Shepard was white, and each individual's murder was based on

---

[*] *Birth of a Nation* promoted a racist philosophy toward African-Americans based on its content and the assumption that, as a popular art form, it had a mass audience (Gallagher, 1982).

[†] Calvin Coolidge, Warren Harding, and Harry Truman were alleged to be former members of the Klan before their ascent to the White House. Hugo Black, previously a U.S. senator, denounced his membership when he was appointed a U.S. Supreme Court Justice (cf. *The Ku Klux Klan in America, The Fiery Cross* [Wade, 1987]).

[‡] The 1964 Federal Civil Rights Act, 18 U.S.C. § 245.

[§] A landmark murder investigation (1964) of three Civil Rights workers—James Chaney, Michael Schwerner, and Andrew Goodman—in Mississippi was chronicled in the 1988 movie *Mississippi Burning*. The film portrays members of the FBI as zealous investigators, even as it reveals the truthful aspect that some local members of law enforcement engaged in the murders.

[¶] Matthew Shepard was tortured and murdered near Laramie, Wyoming and James Byrd Jr. dragged to his death until he was dismembered.

the perception by the perpetrators of the victim as being the "other." While there is no lack of documentation in American regarding the murder of African-Americans due to their race, it would be naive to assume that Matthew Shepard was the first gay man murdered because of his sexuality.[*] The manner and details regarding the murder of Matthew Shepard for his sexuality garnered national attention. His death became a tipping point regarding public aware gay rights, and a new type of hate crime as defined by Congress[†] and investigated by the Federal Bureau of Investigation (FBI).[‡]

How hate crimes in the United States are defined evolves in conjunction with not only the rights of individuals to exist in a free society but also their insistence to do so. *The Advocate*[§] noted that 21 transgender women were murdered in the United States by July 2015. Muslim college students, Deah Shaddy Barakat, his wife, Yusor Mohammad, and her sister, Razan Mohammad Abu-Salha, in North Carolina were recent multiple murders committed by a neighbor. By necessity, the definition of "hate crimes" has expanded to include these acts of aggression against transgender individuals as well as those of various religious groups. By way of explanation, Craig Hicks stated that he murdered the three Muslim students because he was his intent on enforcing the parking rules at his apartment complex. While hate crimes appear easy to recognize, they are like the concept of *modern racism* (McConohay, 1983), subtle and less overt. In the conclusion of this work, the concept of modern racism appears to merge with an earlier criminological theory to reveal a potentially greater historical injustice when contrasting the convictions of the 1998 murder of James Byrd and the 2012 not guilty verdict regarding the murder of Trayvon Martin.

"Hate Crimes" against African-Americans

It is not possible to list every act of violence perpetrated against African-Americans that might be deemed traumatic. Viewed by African-Americans within their historic and sociopolitical context, media presentations of these events can trigger feelings associated with intergenerational trauma (Degruy-Leary, 2005). Some of the events are categorized here.

New York Draft Riots 1863: An unaccounted number of African-Americans were killed in the streets by blue collar workers. Initially resentful of the military draft, they later directed their anger at blacks with whom they competed for jobs (cf. Martin Scorsese's [2002] *Gangs of New York*).

East St. Louis Riots 1917: Based on heightening tensions regarding job security, and taking place after black men and white women were seen fraternizing at a labor meeting, as many as 3000 whites rushed through the city attacking blacks. Numerous deaths, extensive injuries, and property damage occurred. Artist Jacob Lawrence's rendering of one of the largest race riots in American history is a well-known image featured at the Museum of Modern Art (MOMA) in New York City.[¶]

Tulsa Riots 1921: A white mob in Tulsa, Oklahoma invaded a prosperous black community known as the "Negro Wall Street of America," set fire to businesses and residences, and shot several residents. Death toll unknown (cf. Madigan [2001] *The Burning*).

Rosewood Massacre 1923: A self-sufficient black community in Levy County, Florida was destroyed by whites. Sixty years later, after much national recognition via John Singleton's (1997) movie *Rosewood*, descendants successfully sued the state for not protecting their ancestors.

Murder of Emmett Till 1955: A 14-year-old black male was beaten, shot in the head, one eye was gouged out, and he was flung into the river with a 70-pound engine attached to his neck with barbed wire for the crime of "reckless eyeballing" (staring at a white woman). Nobel Prize winner Toni Morrison's play *Dreaming Emmett* (1986) featured the case, but revised history. Novels, ballads, and poems about Till have also been created.

---

[*] Harvey Milk, an openly gay member of San Francisco's board of Supervisors was shot and killed by fellow supervisor Dan White in 1978.

[†] 18 U.S. Code § 249—Hate crime acts.

[‡] cf. https://www.fbi.gov/about-us/investigate/civilrights/hate_crimes

[§] cf. "These are the U.S. Trans Women killed in 2015." *Source*: http://www.advocate.com/transgender/2015/07/27/these-are-trans-women-killed-so-far-us-2015

[¶] *Source*: http://www.moma.org/collection/object.php?object_id=78545

16th Street Baptist Church Bombing 1963: Four young black girls attending Sunday school were killed by a bomb blast in Birmingham, Alabama. Members of the Ku Klux Klan committed the act as retribution for Civil Rights demands. The victims were, Addie Mae Collins (aged 14), Denise McNair (aged 11), Carole Robertson (aged 14), and Cynthia Wesley (aged 14). Spike Lee's film *4 Little Girls*, based on the murders, was nominated as "Best Documentary" during the 1997 Academy Award.

It is reasonable to suggest that the continuum of traumatic events experienced by any group (gay, transgender, Muslim, etc.) cemented by their historical social exclusion and despised "other" status might trigger frustration, anger, and feelings leading to antisocial behaviors. Additionally, these triggers could result from varied personal incidents, such as being closely watched and followed in a store by security personnel, trailed by a police car, or simply having a loan application rejected. Rodney King's 1991 beating in Los Angeles County by police, the sight of black citizens awaiting delayed government assistance after Hurricane Katrina in New Orleans, or reports of incidents such as the previously mentioned James Byrd's 1998 dragging death are all reminders of historic exclusion. These events constitute stressors that, within the trauma model, are capable of triggering a reaction. Such events have an immeasurable impact on the mental health of those who deemed as the "others" do not constitute the predominant culture in any given country (Grand, 2000).

Hate Speech and the Impact of Discourse, Race, and Otherness

The discourse of hate and resulting crimes in America are documented in some of the most notable speeches, novels, and films that commemorate these incidents. While some are fictional and the others face, they are part of the discourse of hate (e.g., *To Kill a Mocking Bird, A Time to Kill, Black Like Me, Mississippi Burning, In the Heat of the Night*, etc.). It is worth noting that within Faulkner's 1929 novel *The Sound and the Fury*,[*] the statement "The past is not dead it's not even the past…" is, within this work, suggestive of the constant presence of our history. In the same source, more graphically phrased, one of Faulkner's characters states, "…when people act like niggers, no matter who they are the only thing to do is treat them like a nigger…." (p. 1016). James Baldwin suggests that people are trapped in history and that history is trapped in them. These lauded American authors' statements are indicative of stereotyped perceptions regarding behaviors and our conditioned responses to them as well as a rationale for social exclusion from the "others." Young (2001) explains social exclusion as a social problem rather than an individual one:

> Firstly, it is multi-dimensional: social exclusion can involve not only social but economic, political, and spatial exclusion, as well as lack of access to specific desiderata such as information, medical provision, housing, policing, security, etc.…[It has also been noted that] These dimensions are seen to interrelate and reinforce each other: overall they involve exclusion in what are seen as the "normal" areas of participation of full citizenship…[†]

The concept that limited interpersonal associations, as well as negative media images, contribute to the perceptions of members of one particular group toward the other is supported by several studies (e.g., Ng and Lindsay, 1994; Dasgupta and Greenwald, 2001; Smith et al., 2004). Continued segregation through exclusionary neighborhood housing and schools still perpetuates opinions shaped through the media. Allport's (1954) suggested in his *group contact theory* that under certain circumstances, contact between members of different societal groups serves to reduce tensions, prejudices, and fears. We have recently witnessed acts of terrorism abroad, specifically in Paris where much of the same otherness has been depicted of its Muslim population over time. "Islamophobia" is as the word phobia suggests, an anxiety disorder or an irrational fear. It is interesting to note that acts of violence resulting in the death committed by alleged Christians in the United States (against synagogues, mosques, government institutions, etc.) are not perceived or responded to with the same outrage as similar acts done by Muslims. What is being suggested here is that the aforementioned historic dynamics of societal laws and political discourse can create an atmosphere of division that increases the likelihood of hate crimes within any country and in doing so also a cycle of violence. Whether the targets are a particular racial group, woman's medical facilities (e.g., Planned Parenthood), Christians, Muslims, or the LGBT community, world history suggests rhetoric marginalizing any group adds to the discourse of hate that can incite violence.

---

[*] William Faulkner (2006). *Novels, 1926–1929*. New York: Library of America.
[†] *Source*: http://www.oup.com/uk/orc/bin/0199249377/resources/synopses/ch14.doc

Discussion and Why "We Want Our Country Back"

There is some irony that a nation supposedly founded on principles of liberty and justice for all would engage in acts of brutality against other people based on the same intolerance from which those settlers fled. So one question is why does this brand of xenophobia persist to this day? One theoretical answer is *nativism*, a belief in the policy of protecting native-born people against an immigrant population. Yet that would hardly explain in retrospect the treatment of the Native Americans and certainly not the treatment of Africans under the yoke of chattel slavery, considering the treatment for both groups may be seen as attempted genocide. The United States has grown with its immigrant population from Europe, South America, Mexico, and other countries, and so have those groups been victims of racial discrimination. Yet no other group entering this land except those brought here under the auspices of slavery have experienced otherness in quite the same way.

The extreme example regarding the historical discourse of African-American otherness* in the United States has been used to segregate blacks from the mainstream, predominantly white, American society—in all but a few areas such as sports, entertainment, and penal institutions (Wacquant, 2001). U.S. segregation laws (1876–1965) prohibited interpersonal contact between blacks and whites, other than in work situations. For example, laws were enacted regarding miscegenation and racial interaction in the public sphere.

And while the limits of this article do not permit this writer to explore all events regarding the discrimination of all groups of people who have experienced racism, it might be illuminating to note that this same sociological paradigm exists for any group subjected to similar historic events previously discussed, specifically extreme acts of violence perpetrated by individuals who seek to rid them from their country or neighborhood.

The historic political rhetoric and discourse revisited here is significant. It is suggested that in an effort for those who wish to further a narrative of division, exclusion, and otherness, a continuum of negative images via print, photos, and film aids in that effort. It becomes even more powerful when advocated by respected members of the dominant culture (i.e., political leaders).

By way of example, prior to *Gone with the Wind* and its influential view of the Civil War South, D.W. Griffiths' (1915) *Birth of a Nation*, also known as *The Clansmen*,† was a wildly popular silent film. Blacks were portrayed as sexual beasts preying upon white women, as well as thieves and toe-picking, chicken-eating members of the U.S. Senate. These portrayals were meant to be public warnings of potential dangers should African-Americans gain equal rights. The filmmaker was quoted as saying:

> If it is right for historians to write history, then by similar and unanswerable reasons it is right for us to tell the truth of the historic past in motion pictures… (D.W. Griffith cited in Lennig, 2004, p. 1).

President Woodrow Wilson, a history scholar who had also served as president of Princeton University, endorsed D.W. Griffith's degrading film, further justifying the social exclusion of blacks from the highest elected office in America. He wrote for the silent film:

> …the white men were aroused by a mere instinct for self-preservation…at last there had sprung into existence a great Ku Klux Klan,‡ a veritable empire of the South, to protect the Southern country… (Ibid., p. 139).

The U.S. President's endorsement of the film came in the form of a statement he allegedly made after watching a screening. He also proclaimed, "It is like writing history with lightening, and my only regret is that it is all so terribly true" (Ibid., p. 122). Despite calls to ban the picture by the National Association for the Advancement of Colored People (NAACP), indicative of the members' fear of its potential negative impact, the movie premiered in New York on March 3, 1915. The following day, the editor of *The New York Age* telegraphed the city's mayor, stating:

---

* "Implicit in all these forms of intolerance is the notion of a despised 'other' as a means to maintaining an idealized self…media representations of immigrants, political refugees and British-born black and Asian people are frequently underpinned by powerful psychic notions of otherness which frequently find expression in a tendency to see crime perpetrated by non-white people as a product of their ethnicity" (Jewkes, 2004/2011, pp. 110–111).

† The Ku Klux Klan was conceived of as a fraternal organization, but it quickly became a terrorist group that engaged in intimidation and murder, specifically against blacks. The group's membership included legislators and law enforcement agents, which, in many instances, made members immune to prosecution. By 1921, the Ku Klux Klan had 3 million members, including 16 U.S. senators (cf. The History Channel [2005] *Ku Klux Klan: A Secret History* [A & E Home Video]).

‡ Calvin Coolidge, Warren Harding, and Harry Truman were alleged to be former members of the Klan before their ascent to the White House. Hugo Black, previously a U.S. senator, denounced his membership when he was appointed a U.S. Supreme Court Justice (cf. *The Ku Klux Klan in America, The Fiery Cross* [Wade, 1987]).

...the film appealed to baser passions and seeks to disrupt friendly relations existing between white and colored citizens of New York City (Ibid, p. 124).

Birth of a Nation promoted a racist philosophy toward African-Americans based on its content and the assumption that, as a popular art form, it had a mass audience. Calvin Coolidge, Warren Harding, and Harry Truman were alleged to be former members of the Klan before their ascent to the White House. Hugo Black, previously a U.S. senator, denounced his membership when he was appointed a U.S. Supreme Court Justice (cf. *The Ku Klux Klan in America, The Fiery Cross* [Wade, 1987]).

There is little doubt that these politicians' rhetoric gave comfort and aid to those who would seek to rid "their" country of those deemed as the others. Taken within this historical context, it should not be surprising to note that in a country with such a violent history regarding issues of race, under the watch of the twice elected African-American president there has been a 300% increase in the number of hate groups in the United States. The U.S. Secret Service, charged with protecting presidential nominees, as well as the president and his family, notes several unique events surrounding Obama's bid for the presidency and subsequent election. The first African-American president has received more death threats, prior to his election and afterward, than any other in American history. These facts are significant because they reveal that hundreds of years after slavery, there remain in the United States deeply embedded race-based perceptions of black males, regardless of their achievements. Despite the president's call for "change" in America, racist discourse is still part of its political landscape (e.g., images of the White House with watermelon patches on the front lawn harken back to nineteenth century stereotypes about blacks). On September 15, 2009, former president Jimmy Carter gave his opinion that "the intensely demonstrated animosity" directed at President Barack Obama is fueled by racism, based on the fact that he is a black man. It is not unreasonable to conclude that the "otherness" of blacks in American society remains a prominent fixture within its cultural landscape, despite President Obama's momentous victory (Wolfe, 2009).

Recent presidential candidates in 2015 have resurrected negative tropes regarding Mexican and Syrian immigrants. Based on the pollsters and the responses from their audiences, one may assume that they speak to a segment of the population who are in agreement with their ideals of walls, and databases to watch certain groups. It is precisely that rhetoric that can lead to hate crimes. If popular political leaders hold these negative opinions, their cause of discrimination, bias, and prejudice reinforces those ideals among their followers. History has revealed that over time, it has been the cumulative effect of movements created by people and their demonstrations that aid in raising the consciousness of most Americans regarding hate crimes. They have historically silenced the voices of division and discrimination even from the "bully pulpit."

James Byrd, Trayvon Martin, and Telishment

The impact of hate crimes targeting any particular group is trauma. This trauma is not limited to one generation of Jews, Muslims, Irish et al. (Kellerman, 2001). It affects those who have not yet been first-party recipients to the treatment. In that context, African-Americans make little distinction between hate crimes targeting them as defined by the FBI, perpetrated by individuals and organized hate juxtaposed to those resulting in death by members of law enforcement or vigilantes (e.g., Laquan McDonald in Chicago, Michael Brown in Missouri, Trayvon Martin in Florida, et al.). Gabbidon and Greene (2013) note that the killing of African-Americans by law enforcement can be traced to the earliest forms of policing in America known as "slave patrols." Historically, white law enforcement agents' strained relationship with African-Americans is, in part, due to those agencies being charged with maintaining the status quo. That status quo was segregation and discriminatory laws. To put it in perspective, the Supreme Court ruling against separate but equal education in *Brown v. the Board of Education* occurred in 1954. Therefore, recent incidents of brutality of blacks whether at the hands of police or a mass shooting in a black church in Charleston, South Carolina[*], are viewed as a continuum of not only discrimination but also a history of hate[†]-inspired crimes. Although hate crimes currently have a more broad definition and are no longer limited to the issue of race, this component still exists. The 1998 murder of James Byrd in Jasper, Texas is stark reminder of a traditional race-driven hate crime.

---

[*] Dylan Roof shot and killed nine African-Americans while attending church. His shooting was inspired after reading an article regarding the killing of Trayvon Martin and his racist belief that blacks were taking over. *Source*: http://www.cnn.com/2015/06/19/us/charleston-church-shooting-suspect/

[†] The Southern Poverty Law Center is an independent watch group whose primary mission is to track hate groups.

James Byrd, Jr.

On June 7, 1998, a 49-year-old black man in Jasper, Texas was murdered by Shawn Berry, Lawrence Russell Brewer, and John King. Byrd had accepted a ride home from the driver Shawn Berry, with whom he was familiar. Byrd was taken to a remote location, where he was beaten, had his throat slashed, urinated on, and then chained by his ankles and dragged by a pickup truck until his body broke apart. The remains were then gathered by the offenders and left on the grounds of a nearby black church. Brewer and King were known to have ties to white supremacist groups prior to their incarceration. Brewer received lethal injection in 2011, King is appealing his conviction, and Berry received life in prison. The offenders in this case were punished for a lynching that historically occurred too often and was not limited to the South. It appears to be a measure of required justice if not progress. Yet, when contrasted with the vigilante style killing of Trayvon Martin by George Zimmerman suggests something more than the death of an innocent black youth, it appears that neither justice nor progress has been made.

Trayvon Benjamin Martin

On February 26, 2012, George Zimmerman, a neighborhood watch captain in Sanford, Florida dialed 911 to report a suspicious person. That suspicious person was Trayvon Martin, wearing a hooded sweatshirt, and who moments earlier was captured on videotape purchasing candy and an ice tea drink at a 7-Eleven store. Although it was raining, Zimmerman stated to the 911 operator that the male appeared to be suspicious. He was advised not to approach the male who was walking back to his temporary residence. Zimmerman ignored this advice and an unarmed Trayvon Martin was shot and died as a result of this encounter. The voices pleading for help captured on the 911 tape could not be determined. The allegation of a prolonged struggle between Zimmerman and Martin failed to be supported via a DNA analysis of Trayvon's fingers. Trayvon Martin was shot in his chest and laid face down on the ground upon police arrival.

What these killings suggest is a continuum of black lives is easily extinguished in this country with little consequence. Furthermore, being found not guilty meant that Zimmerman was justified killing an unarmed young black male for the way he looked (at night, wearing a hoodie).* This rationale can justify violence against any group whose negative tropes are created by the dominant group in a society. It is the dehumanization of African-Americans, much like the toe-picking, chicken-eating legislators blacks were depicted as in D. W. Griffith's *The Birth of a Nation*, a black male at night with a hoodie is a threat. When one considers the number of black males killed post-Trayvon Martin's death, an argument can be made that being black alone (skin color) is enough of a reason to be killed. Ferguson Police Officer Darren Wilson stated that, Michael Brown looked "…like a demon…."† It is not unreasonable to suggest that harkening back to Allport's *group contact hypothesis* that any group of individuals who do not look like you may appear to be threatening if you have limited interpersonal or social contact with them.

Telishment

Illuminating a rationale for Zimmerman's not guilty verdict and the possibility of similar verdicts specifically regarding victims of "hate crimes" is John Rawls (1971) concept of telishment. In his notable work, *A Theory of Justice*, Rawls offers the concept of "telishment" as a sort of utilitarian justification for the punishment of an innocent. It is essentially an act committed for the greater good, the punishment of the innocent as a deterrent. Within the context of a hate crime, punishing the "others" is rationalized as an act for the greater good of society. Punishment so that those people, the despised others, would not dress that way, would not talk the way they do, would not engage in an alternative lifestyle or belief system (i.e., sexuality, religion, etc.) for the greater good of the dominant culture. And for all who transgress there will be punishment.

Conclusion

Laws regarding what we knew as hate crime have been and will continue to evolve. And because laws and definitions change so too will our understanding of them. Perhaps in the future, hate crimes will be adjudicated by international courts regarding victims of international terrorism. An argument can be made that the numerous murder of innocent civilians solely based on their religious practices constitutes a hate crime.

---

* cf. George Zimmerman's postings of Trayvon Martin's dead body and statements about Muslims, http://www.huffingtonpost.com/entry/george-zimmerman-tweets_5661ef01e4b079b2818e8fbd

† cf. Darren Wilson's testimony. *Source*: https://www.washingtonpost.com/news/morning-mix/wp/2014/11/25/why-darren-wilson-said-he-killed-michael-brown/

Additionally, might we also see what has previously been defined as "serial murders" fall into a new category? Beasley's (2004) discussing a postincarceration interview of Chester Elroy revealed that during his 2003 interview with Elroy Chester, a black serial killer and Death Row inmate in Texas stated that the reason he killed his victims was that he hated white people. This researcher also noted Derrick Todd Lee, the African-American convicted of the Louisiana serial murders, as well as Coral Watts primarily sought white victims. While we are only left to speculate who is to say that, these were not motivated by hate.

In fact, numerous black offenders have chosen primarily white victims (e.g., Derek Todd Lee, Coral Watts, and Kendall Francois), while the converse is also true regarding white serial murderers (e.g., Gary Ridgeway and Jeffrey Dahmer, among others, who killed nonwhites). As of this writing, few studies regarding specific black serial killers exist in general, and there is a lacuna of research based on interviews or a study of their victimology; such research might illuminate specific aspects of these murderers' psychologies and personal histories (Branson, 2016). A valid question within the context of intergenerational trauma is: Are crimes by African-Americans committed against whites' hate crimes?

It is important to consider the cycle of violence that can be created by hate crimes. Additionally, we cannot ignore the historic treatment or subsequent reactions of those who have felt marginalized and targeted by a dominant group or society. There is a natural inclination for those who are marginalized to want to become a part of something larger than themselves—to feel empowered by this inclusion to act for a noble cause. By way of example based on a pervasive theme of violence and revenge, it is worthy of note that some American blacks converted to Islam in the U.S. prisons. While initially this may have been for self-protection, it was the Nation of Islam (generally respected in the U.S. African-American communities) that was considered an extremist radical group when formed in the 1960s. They frequently equated "the white man" with the devil, due to slavery, continued repression, and social injustices. The resurgence of a radical Islamist (e.g., Al Qaeda and the Islamic State) seeking revenge against the United States provides another venue for poor urban blacks or others who feel disenfranchised from mainstream America, to become radicalized and direct their anger and vengeance against the dominant group's ideals and symbols of power. As we have seen, those participating actors are increasing in their diversity.

It is also important to understand the history of discrimination, social practices, and the laws that have led societies to view groups of people as the despised others. It requires little thought for the dominant culture in any society to dismiss the resultant backlash of violence from the "others" as a justification for why they are despised. It is more difficult to comprehend the antecedents of their violence.

References

Adams, F. D. and Sanders, B. 2003. *Alienable Rights: The Exclusion of African Americans in a White Man's Land*. New York, NY: Harper Collins, pp. 1619–2000.
Alia, V. and Bull, S. 2005. *Media and Ethnic Minorities*. Edinburgh: Edinburgh University Press.
Allport, G. W. 1954. *The Nature of Prejudice*. Cambridge, MA: Perseus Books.
Beasley, J. O. 2004. Supervisory Special Agent, assigned to the National Center for the Analysis of Violent Crime/Critical Incident Response Group, Stafford, VA. Personal communication, April 19, 2004.
Branson, A. 2016. *The Anonymity of African American Serial Killers: From Slavery to Prisons a Continuum of Negative Imagery*. CreateSpace Publishing.
Dasgupta, N. and Greenwald, A. G. 2001. On the malleability of automatic attitudes: Combating automatic prejudice with images of admired and disliked individuals. *Journal of Personality and Social Psychology*, 81(5), 800–814.
Degruy-Leary, J. 2005. *Post Traumatic Slave Syndrome*. Milwaukie, OR: Uptone Press.
Fanon, F. 1963. *The Wretched of the Earth*. New York, NY: Grove Press.
Gabbidon, S. L. and Greene, H. T. 2013. *Race and Crime* (3rd ed.). London, UK: Sage Publications.
Garland, D. 2005. Penal excess and surplus meaning: Public torture lynchings in 20th century America. *Law and Society Review*, 39(4), 793–833.
Grand, S. 2000. *The Reproduction of Evil: A Clinical and Cultural Perspective*. Hillsdale, NJ: The Analytic Press.
History Channel. 2005. *Ku Klux Klan: A Secret History* [video]. United States: A & E Home Video.
Jewkes, Y. 2004/2011. *Media and Crime*. London, UK: Sage Publications.
Kellerman, N. 2001. Transmission of Holocaust Trauma. *Psychiatry*, 64(3), 256–267.
Lennig, A. 2004 Myth and fact: The reception of *The Birth of a Nation*. Film History, 16, 117–141.
Liggio, L. P. 1976. English origins of early American racism. *Radical History Review*, 3(1), 1–36.

Madigan, T. 2001. *The Burning Massacre: Destruction and the Tulsa Race Riot of 1921.* New York, NY: St. Martin's Press.

Scorcher, N. and Cohen, L. J. 1997. Trauma in children of Holocaust survivors: Transgenerational effects. *American Journal of Orthopsychiatry, 67*(3), 493–500.

McConohay, J. 1983. Modern racism and modern discrimination, the effects of race, racial attitudes, and context on simulated hiring decisions. *Personality and Social Psychology Bulletin, 9*(4), 551–558.

Ng, W. and Lindsay, R. C. L. 1994. Cross-race facial recognition: Failure of the contact hypothesis. *Journal of Cross-Cultural Psychology, 25*, 217–232.

Philo, G. 2007. News content studies, media group methods and discourse analysis: A comparison of approaches. In: E. Devereux (Ed.), *Media Studies: Key Issues and Debates.* Thousand Oaks, CA: Sage, pp. 101–133.

Rawls, J. 1971. *A Theory of Justice.* Cambridge, MA: Harvard University Press.

Singleton, J. 1997. Rosewood. Warner Bros Picture, USA.

Smith, S. M., Stinson, V., and Prosser, M. A. 2004. Do they all look alike? An exploration of decision-making strategies in cross-race facial identifications. *Canadian Journal of Behavioural Science, 36*(2), 146–154.

Thompson, E. C. 2006. The problem of race as a social construct. *Anthropology News, 47*(2), 6–7.

Wacquant, L. 2001. Deadly symbiosis: When ghetto and prison meet and mesh. *Punishment and Society, 3*(1), 95–134.

Wade, W. C. 1987. *The Ku Klux Klan in America: The Fiery Cross.* New York, NY: Oxford University Press.

Wolfe, R. 2009. *Renegade: The Making of a President.* New York, NY: Random House.

Young, J. 2001. Crime and Social Exclusion. *The Oxford Handbook of Criminology.* Oxford, UK: Oxford University Press.

II
Sexual Homicide Offenders

An Introduction to Sexual Homicides

Lee Mellor

Contents

Etiology of Paraphilia 84
Criticism 89
Investigating Paraphilic Crime in General 90
Wound Interpretation and the Assessment of Paraphilia 91
Overlapping Paraphilic Crimes 92
Screening and Counselling for Investigators and Other Specialists 94
References 95

The following two chapters deal with homicides motivated by *paraphilia*: specifically, sexually sadism, and necrophilia. According to the DSM-5, "the term *paraphilia* denotes any intense and persistent sexual interest other than sexual interest in genital stimulation or preparatory fondling with phenotypically normal, physically mature, consenting human partners" (American Psychiatric Association, 2013, p. 685). As Moser (2013) keenly observes, *paraphilia*—which was coined by IF Krauss (Money, 1990)—is actually incorrect as it refers to unusual (*para*) love (*philia*), when it should be *paralagnia*, with "lagnia" referring to sexual desire. Mellor (2016a) acknowledges this, but points out that the term has become so entrenched in the psychological nomenclature that it would be unrealistic and confusing to attempt to change it at this point.

Abel et al. (1988) propose that an average paraphile has between 3 and 4 paraphilias. Similarly, Holmes (1991) cites 4–8 paraphilias, though he does not provide research to support this. Such statistics will likely inflate in accordance with the number of paraphilias identified and named by the academic and mental health communities. This raises several methodological and semantic issues; for instance, does a perpetrator with the necrophilia-spectrum paraphilias—*necrocoitolagnia, necromutilophilia, necrornopositophilia,* and *sarxenthymiophilia*—have four paraphilias, or are these merely all manifestations of a single paraphilia—*necrophilia*?

To cover every form of paraphilic homicide would necessitate an entirely separate and voluminous text in itself. *Sexual sadism* and *necrophilia* have been chosen because they (i) are easily identifiable from crime scene behavior, (ii) account for a large portion of paraphilic homicides, and (iii) are common in serial offenders, meaning that identifying, arresting, and successfully prosecuting these offenders is of critical importance.

Sexual sadism, *necrophilia*, and *erotophonophilia* (lust murder) are frequently conflated, with numerous researchers including necrophiles among studies of sexual sadists (MacCulloch et al., 1983), while many researchers associate *sexual sadism* and *necrophilia* with *erotophonophilia* (Gratzer and Bradford, 1995).

Researches show us that clinical treatment for individuals whose ultimate sexual gratification entails or necessitates extreme violence toward another person is generally not successful. As these offenders tend to target strangers, investigating their crimes is particularly challenging and often necessitates proactive strategies and specialized knowledge. Therefore, the treatment sections of these chapters are significantly smaller than their investigatory sections. The reader is strongly encouraged to review Chapter 9 on psychopathic homicides before continuing, as psychopaths comprise a large number of sexually sadistic murderers (Stone, 1998; Hare et al., 1999; Holt et al., 1999; Porter et al., 2000, 2003, 2009; Mokros et al., 2011), and seemingly half of necrophilic homicide offenders (see Chapter 7, but note the author encourages caution in using this statistical finding due to methodological limitations).

Chapters on *pedophilic* (sexual attraction to children) or *gerontophilic* (sexual attraction to the elderly) homicides have not been included in this section because, for the most part, these can be understood within the motivational framework of rape-slaying, sexual sadism, and necrophilia.

Etiology of Paraphilia

The renowned sexologist, John Money (2011), outlined a theory of paraphilia based upon *vandalized lovemaps*. Money observed that sexualization begins even before an infant is born, with sonograms showing erections in male fetuses. Male children are also known to become erect during breastfeeding and children as young as three and four have been observed grinding their pelvises together in sexual rehearsal play. Money argues that despite our society's taboos against such behavior, these are actually healthy ways to develop a *native lovemap*. In fact, it is the prohibition of early childhood sexuality through punishment which itself may vandalize the *lovemap*. Lovemaps are also vandalized when a child witnesses sexually sadistic behavior or becomes a partner in a pedophilic and/or incestuous relationship. The most vulnerable age for the defacing of a paraphilic lovemap is between 5 and 8 years of age, though Money notes that the human brain continues to develop throughout puberty, and that major trauma between age 8 and the peripubertal years can still greatly affect how a *lovemap* is consolidated.

Money goes on to explain how paraphilia results from this process:

> As in the case of any wound, a vandalized lovemap tries to heal itself. In the process it gets scarred, skewed, and misshapen. Some of its features get omitted, some get displaced, and some get replaced by substitutes that would not otherwise be included…Displacements and inclusions transform it into a paraphilic one. The paraphilic transformation seems at the time to be a satisfactory compromise. It disassociates lust from its vandalized place in the heterosexual lovemap, and relocates it. In the long run, however, the relocation proves to be a compromise that is too costly (Money, 2011, Kindle Locations 1057–1064).

Any change in the *lovemap* after puberty occurs through a process of decoding an already extant *lovemap* rather than encoding it. In cases where a juvenile has been subjected to sexual activity with a partner that is many years older than them, they may act out a *paraphilic lovemap* that mirrors this experience, but with themselves now in the role of the older participant. The 22 murders committed by South Africa's "Station Strangler," for instance, were highly reminiscent of the homosexual rape he had been subjected to in childhood at the hands of his brother. The coinciding of a neutral, traditionally nonsexual *act*, *object*, or *act-object* with feelings of genital arousal in a child may also lead to the formation of a *paraphilic lovemap*.

That almost all paraphiles are men (Money, 2011) is largely attributable to the emphasis males place on visual sexual stimulus compared to women, who favor tactility. Money (2011), though noting that there have been no cross-cultural studies to look at the sociological elements of this phenomenon, claims this preference is a biological reality determined in the prenatal stage of development. A male's *lovemap* is, therefore, constructed through the *acts*, *objects*, and *act-objects* (Mellor, 2016b) that he encounters visually through his social environment.

The first of several influential models examining sexual homicide was the Motivational Model of Sexual Homicide developed by Burgess et al. (1986) and later refined in Ressler et al. (1992) (Figure 6.1).

Ressler et al. (1992) proposed that the desire to commit sexual homicide begins with an *ineffective social environment* in which a child's concept of his primary caretakers and the way in which they interact with him develops in an unhealthy way. These caretakers may emotionally neglect or fail to protect the child, or fail to correct antisocial behavior on the part of the child by ignoring it, rationalizing it ("he's just a boy"), or normalizing it (e.g., physical abuse at home gives the child the impression that violence is not abnormal). As the manner with which one attaches to one's parents influences how one bonds with society in general, these children may carry schemata from their family environment into situations involving other people. The individual may be punished for antisocial behaviors by his teachers or the police, but the early influence of his

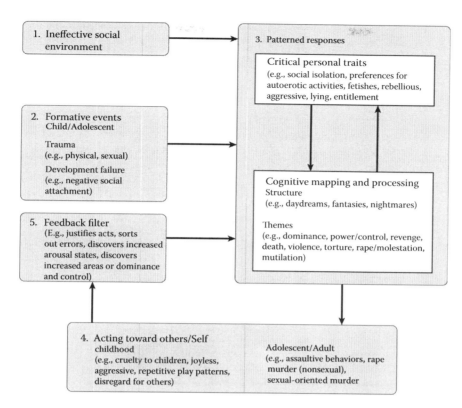

Figure 6.1 Motivational Model. (From Ressler, R., Burgess, A., and Douglas, J. 1992. *Sexual Homicide: Patterns and Motives*. New York, NY: The Free Press.)

ineffective social environment means that the punishment does not affect him experientially or cognitively in the long term.

Often linked to the *ineffective social environment* are the *formative events* which occur in childhood or adolescence. These include trauma such as the experiencing or witnessing of physical, emotional, or sexual abuse. Where another child might be removed from these traumatic situations, the emerging killer's *ineffective social environment* means that nobody is looking out for him. Such traumas will shape the thought patterns of the child, resulting in daydreams or fantasies, typically involving sexual and/or violent content. These dominance and control themes arise partially because the child has not been removed from the situation which leads him to feel helpless. He compensates by imagining scenarios in which he is in control. This is reflected in the way that a child plays, which is typically creative and carefree, but, in the case of the burgeoning sex murderer, is "conflicted and obsessive" (Ressler et al., 1992, p. 71). The aforementioned failure to bond with an adult caretaker can result in the underdevelopment of the child's emotional responses, such as a diminished capacity for empathy. Finally, if the child's caretakers are antisocial or engage in criminal behavior themselves, then the child is left with no positive role models.

Two important *patterned responses* to *ineffective social environmental* and *formative events* will arise. The first is the development of negative personality traits which impede the individual's ability to establish social relationships, which also affect their capacity for emotion. In the absence of a social life, this socially isolated individual becomes dependent on his fantasy world rather than actual human interaction. This obviously severely limits his ability to absorb and internalize social values. He deals with this by either completely withdrawing from human relationships or directing anger at society for having ostracized him. Fantasy becomes the only avenue through which he can relate to others, and of course these "others" are only symbolic replications of actual people. Unsurprisingly, this self-contained fantasy world is fertile ground for the development of auto-erotic activities and paraphilia, and becomes "the primary source of emotional arousal and that emotion is a confused mix of sex and aggression" (Ressler et al., 1992, p. 73).

The second patterned response is cognitive mapping and processing which arises and is sustained by the *ineffective social environment* and *formative events*. Cognitive mapping and processing structures the internal life of an individual by giving events meaning and links the individual to the social while preserving his psyche by minimizing personal fear and anxiety. Predictably, the cognitive mapping and processing of a lust murderer constantly obsesses on negative themes—manifesting as dreams, daydreams, fantasies, and thoughts—and comes to define the aspirations and motivations of the individual, which in this case is largely to commit acts of sexual violence. Due to living such a self-contained existence, the individual comes to view the outer world in black-and-white generalities, developing strong and inflexible preconceived notions as to cause, effect, and probability.

The violent and aggressive fantasies of sex murderers manifest outwardly during childhood in destructive activities such as arson, theft, vandalism, and cruelty to animals and others. When these expressions of antisocial rage are not followed by negative consequences for the child, due to either a lack of punishment or the child being immune to change as a result of punishment, they may escalate to more intense behaviors in adulthood such as sexual offenses and/or homicide. Such activities also frighten away would-be friends, which deepens the offender's isolation and means that his worldviews are never effectively challenged, leading to a sense of entitlement to act in an antisocial manner.

Once the sexual offense and/or homicide has been committed, the individual reflects on his actions through a *feedback filter*, at which point he justifies them, notes ways to improve similar acts in the future, and may alter the content of his *fantasies*. These then become a part of his *patterned responses* (Figure 6.2).

Where the Motivational Model examined sexual homicide, Hickey's (2013) Trauma-Control Model (see below) looked specifically at serial murder, though we argue it also works for a single incidence of sexual homicide.

Hickey (2013) does not consider *predispositional factors* a necessary component in the development of a serial killer; however he notes that they can exert a strong influence. He gives the examples of having an extra Y chromosome or alcohol use as possible predispositional factors, seemingly indicating that these might consist of endocrinological, neurobiological, and toxicological (via substance abuse) influences which can lead to increased natural aggression or impede impulse control.

Trauma event(s) are a prime mover in every serial killer's background, and are defined as occurrences after birth which destabilize the individual, presumably emotionally and in terms of identity, but also include organic damage which leads to impulsivity or affective deficits. They include neurological, social, interpersonal, and physical and sexual abuse traumas. Childhood trauma may adversely affect the individual's capacity to cope with stresses. Serial killers, Hickey claims, are most often subjected to the trauma of rejection at the hands of their parents and/or classmates and other influential figures. Abuse can also result in neurosis, fantasies of revenge, and a fixation on violent imagery.

Hickey proposes that, usually as a result of the trauma, *dissociation*—"a disruption of and/or discontinuity in the normal integration of consciousness, memory, identity, emotion, perception, body representation, motor control, and behavior" (American Psychiatric Association, 2013, p. 291)—may occur, which often includes the construction and adopting of a mask to conceal the individual's destabilized personality, instead, portraying a sense of composure and confidence.

Serial killers deal with rejection through violence, inflicting animal or domestic abuse, and the destruction or vandalism of material objects. Their trauma devastates their self-esteem, and leads them to have a skewed view of themselves and the world. As mentioned earlier, they will often develop *low self-esteem*

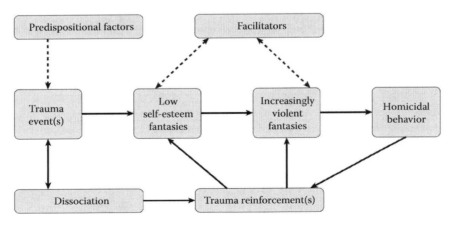

Figure 6.2 Trauma-Control Model. (From Hickey, E. 2013. *Serial Murderers and Their Victims* (6th ed.). Belmont, CA: Wadsworth.)

fantasies of control and dominance to compensate, which invariably become *increasingly violent fantasies.* These violent fantasies are ultimately realized in *homicidal behavior.*

Trauma reinforcement(s) stem from the reduced ability of the individual to cope due to the traumatic childhood events, and refer to stresses in the day-to-day life of the individual such as getting in a fight with his wife, or losing his job. These reactivate the *low self-esteem* and *increasingly violent fantasies.* Homicidal behavior itself can produce guilt, anxiety, and feelings of abnormality which may be traumatic.

Like *predispositional factors, facilitators* are not necessarily present in the development of a serial murderer, but they frequently are. They include substances like alcohol—involved in anywhere from 40% to 65% of homicides—and other drugs which disinhibit the individual and/or affect his moral decisions. Materials such as pornography or certain types of art might also lead to violent or sexually violent fantasies. Hickey (2013) highlights the role of pornography as an initial sexual stimulant during pubescent boys' masturbatory fantasies. He argues that pornography might distort the child's understanding of human sexuality.

Seeing strengths in both Burgess et al.'s and Hickey's models, Arrigo and Purcell (2001) created an Integrated Model (Figure 6.3) to explain paraphilia, with specific focus on *erotophonophilia* (lust murder) which they define as "the acting out of deviant behavior by means of brutally and sadistically killing the victim to achieve ultimate sexual satisfaction" (p. 7). The authors also drew from the research of MacCulloch et al. (1983) to extend their model further.

Arrigo and Purcell (2001), observing that the detrimental effect of dysfunctional childhood surroundings on attachments between children and parental figures is represented in both the *ineffective social environment* of the Motivational Model and the sociological aspects of the *predispositional factors* in the Trauma-Control Model, along with Hickey's (2013) emphasis on congenital biological determinants such as a male possessing an extra Y chromosome, have incorporated these into *formative development* in their Integrated Model. Similarly, trauma is emphasized as a key factor in the development of sexual violence, encompassed in the *formative events* of the Motivational Model and *trauma event(s)* of the Trauma-Control Model, which are also subsumed by the *formative development* stage of the Integrated Model.

Arrigo and Purcell (2001) show that in both preceding models, the result of trauma is that the child experiences *low self-esteem* due to feelings of helplessness or failure. This child compensates through *early fantasy development* of domination and control to cope with his anger. Violent fantasy becomes a substitute

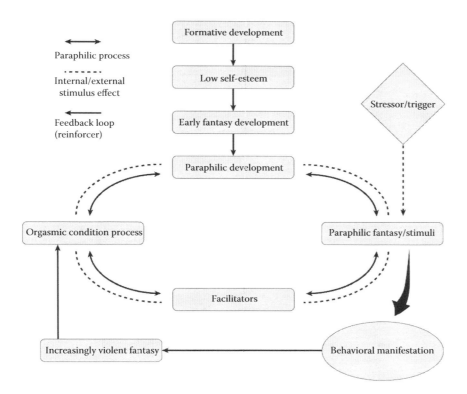

Figure 6.3 Integrated Model. (From Arrigo, B. and Purcell, C. 2001. *International Journal of Offender Therapy and Comparative Criminology, 45,* 6.)

for socializing with others, with the Motivational Model proposing that this accounts for negative personality traits and general misanthropy.

It is when these fantasies become sexualized that *paraphilic development* begins to occur. With their conceptualization of paraphilia as cyclical and generating a synergistic effect, Arrigo and Purcell (2001) introduced an element to the Integrated Model that is not represented in the Motivational or Trauma-Control models. They demonstrated that a paraphilia is sustained through *paraphilic fantasy and stimuli* (such as *acts* or *objects* or *act-objects*), and is reinforced through an *orgasmic conditioning process* in which the individual masturbates to climax while mentally visualizing certain stimulus, which then links those *acts*, *objects*, or *act-objects* in the fantasy process with positive gratification. The more time the individual spends on masturbatory conditioning to abnormal fantasy stimuli, the farther away from "normal" sexual behavior he drifts. Finally, Arrigo and Purcell (2001) included Hickey's *facilitators* in this *paraphilic process*, which seems logical when considering pornography, but less so with intoxicating substances, because according to the model these substances do not immediately disinhibit the offender from committing the physical expression of the paraphilic fantasy.

The *paraphilic process* can often be triggered by *stressors* which are in many ways tantamount to Hickey's *trauma reinforcements* in that they are experiences related to childhood or adolescent traumas which interfere with the individual's ability to cope adequately with day-to-day life. Sometimes *stressors* might actually trigger a *behavioral manifestation* of the *paraphilic process*, which is often sexual homicide. *Behavioral manifestations* may occur regardless of being triggered by a *stressor*, as a natural outcome of the *paraphilic process*. In their aftermath, the Integrated Model draws from the Motivational Model's *feedback filter* and Trauma-Control Model's eponymous *increasingly violent fantasy*, to examine how the violent content associated with the *orgasmic conditioning* escalates following a *behavioral manifestation*.

Each of the three preceding models emphasizes the importance of *fantasies*, especially violent ones, in the phenomenon of sexual homicide. They provide examples of the content of such fantasies—rape, torture, mutilation, dominance—however, none of these models explore the symbolic interplay and mutation implicit in fantasy itself in any kind of detail. For this reason, they can be thought of as *macro-etiologies* of paraphilic violence.

Complimentary to these macro-etiologies is Mellor's Thematic-Derivative Model of Sexual Progression (2016b), a *micro-etiological* model which can be used to trace the spawning and mutation of new paraphilias from older ones in a single individual (Figure 6.4). Mellor, taking a cue from Money (2011), notes that *objects* or *acts* or *act-object* pairings such as "stabbing (*act*) with a knife (*object*)" can enter a person's *fantasies* through three possible sources: (1) *stimulus introduction*—the *act*, *object*, or *act-object* becomes introduced to the person either tangibly, through media, or oral description, at which point the person may place importance

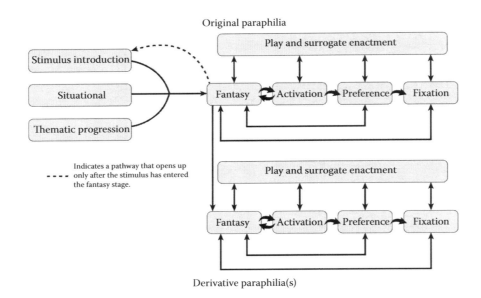

Figure 6.4 Thematic-Derivative Model of Sexual Progression. (From Mellor, L. 2016b. *Understanding Necrophilia: A Global Multidisciplinary Approach*. San Diego, CA: Cognella.)

on it or disregard it, (2) *situational*—the *act, object,* or *act-object* is subject to a sexual act perpetrated on a whim, and not part of the individual's fantasies at the time, and (3) *thematic*—the *act, object,* or *act-object* evolves from the *need* within a fantasy process rather than a visual fantasy. Mellor (2016b) describes how an offender's need for "stillness" can lead him from sexual arousal from mannequins to unconscious people to corpses. Another example is the *piqueristic* offender who escalates along the theme of "cutting" from stab wounds to *mutilophilic* evisceration (Mellor, 2016c). Orgasmic conditioning is incorporated in the *fantasy* stage of this model.

Money (2011) proposes that "the distinguishing mark of a paraphilia is the imagery of its lovemap, which appears as dream or fantasy and gets translated into practice" (Kindle Locations 1224–1226). Mellor (2016b) uses the term *fantasyscape* to describe the scenario in the imagination where the *lovemap* becomes animated, and occurs in space and sequentially.

Once *desired* in the *fantasy* process, the *act, object,* or *act-object* may, typically through orgasmic conditioning, become an *active* paraphilia. It may also be or eventually become the subject's *preferential* sexual desire, meaning that he would rather experience it sexually than anything else. Finally, it can be a *fixation*, where that particular sexual desire becomes so salient that the subject cannot be sexually satisfied unless experiencing it.

Mellor (2016b) observes how, at any of these four stages, the subject may engage in auto-erotic or cooperative sex play or act out his sexual desires on surrogate objects. For example, "BTK" Dennis Rader would dress as his victim and engage in auto-erotic asphyxiation and bondage to mirror his *vincilagnic* and *sexually sadistic* fantasies. He also gagged and bound female dolls using them as surrogate objects for human females (Mellor, 2016a).

Perhaps most importantly, Mellor (2016b) demonstrates how *derivative* paraphilias can be born in the fantasy process. Pedophile Westley Dodd would fantasize about sexually assaulting male children, but after reasoning that he would have to kill them to eliminate a witness; he began to find that he was increasingly more sexually aroused by fantasies of the painful murders than molestation. Thus, *erotophonophilia* and *sexual sadism* became *derivative* paraphilias of *pedophilia*, in that they were modus operandi acts in a *pedophilic* fantasy that became sexualized and eclipsed the dominant paraphilic behavior. The Dodd case is also a useful illustration of what Mellor (2016b) refers to as *contingent paraphilia*. Dodd was both a sexual sadist and pedophile, but there is no indication based on any of his behavior or testimony that he had sexually sadistic urges toward adults. Therefore, Dodd's *sexual sadism* is actually contingent on his *original paraphilia* of *pedophilia*, in that, without being joined with *pedophilia* in the fantasy process, his *sexual sadism* likely would not have existed.

Mellor asserts that the practical utility of his micro-etiological model is that it should, with further research, allow both clinicians and police investigators to retroactively trace the *paraphilic progression* in an individual in order to more effectively treat them and link them to earlier crimes. With enough data and a solid understanding of paraphilic spectrums, it would theoretically also be possible to predict the paraphilic expressions or escalations in a killer's future crimes.

Criticism

It would be problematically biased and partisan not to mention many of the valid criticisms that have been levied at the concept of paraphilia throughout the latter half of the twentieth and beginning of the twenty-first centuries. Chief among these criticisms is that paraphilias do not actually represent any kind of actual psychopathology and instead reflect subjective value judgements as to what sexual preferences an individual *should* have (Tallent, 1977; Silverstein, 1984; Suppe, 1984; Moser, 2013). A common example given of the dangers implicit in this is that homosexuality was listed as a mental disorder until the 7th printing of the DSM-II in 1974, when it was branded as a sexual orientation disturbance. By the DSM-III, it had been replaced by ego-dystonic homosexuality, which only specified homosexuality as a problem if it caused the subject to suffer from personal distress. Another, and somewhat complimentary criticism of paraphilias in the DSMs, is that there is a dearth of reliable evidence to actually underpin their existence as a medical condition (Schmidt, 1995; Schmidt et al., 1998; Moser, 2013).

Though we acknowledge the importance of these arguments and strongly encourage that these methodological and sociological aspects continue to be discussed, the fact that sexual preferences do serve to motivate certain homicides (*sexual sadism, necrophilia, biastophilia, picquerism, pedophilia*) is indisputable, and confirmed by the admissions of the perpetrators themselves. These sexual needs are observable as *ritual* crime scene behaviors, which are relatively static compared to *modus operandi* (Keppel and Birnes, 2009).

Investigating Paraphilic Crime in General

For this reason, it is important to understand the idiosyncrasies of some of these sexual preferences so that their perpetrators can be identified and apprehended in order to prevent further fatalities.

The most fundamentally important aspect of investigating paraphilic crime is to (1) identify the *signature* behavior, and (2) interpret it accurately. Definitions of the term *signature* vary. Many speak of signatures as individual behaviors in the plural, behaviors that are enacted for psychological reasons. So when Jeffrey Dahmer both mutilated and had sexual intercourse with his victims' bodies (Chapter 7), some would say that postmortem mutilation and postmortem intercourse represented two signatures. Keppel and Birnes (2009) take a different approach, looking at the *signature* as the sum total of *modus operandi* (dynamic) and *ritualistic* (psychologically gratifying, often paraphilic, acts that tend to be relatively static) behaviors at a crime scene. So, in their definition, Dahmer's signature would be luring young men back to his apartment, drugging their drinks, and then murder, followed by a variety of necrophilic behaviors extending to cannibalism. These rival definitions of *signature* might be respectfully dubbed the *microscopic* and *macroscopic* uses of signature. Mellor (2016c) suggests that if we are to use Keppel's *macroscopic* signature that we refer to the individual behaviors that comprise it as *strokes* as in the strokes of a pen as it forms a signature.

A partial list of the paraphilic *strokes* potentially observable at a crime scene is:

Stroke (Ante-Mortem)	Possible Corresponding Paraphilias
Biting	Odaxelagnia, sexual sadism, anthropophagy, vampirism
Body part taken	Sarxenthymiophilia, anthropophagy
Bondage	Vincilagnia
Cannibalism	Anthropophagy
Decapitation	Mutilophilia, sarxenthymiophilia, sexual sadism
Disfigurement	Mutilophilia, sexual sadism
Dismemberment	Mutilophilia, sexual sadism
Evisceration	Mutilophilia, visceralagnia
Excised body part (not taken)	Mutilophilia, sarxentyhmiophilia, sexual sadism
Forced oral copulation	Biastophilia, sexual sadism (if notably violent or following anal rape)
Foreign object insertion	Sexual sadism
Incised body part	Picquerism, mutilophilia, sexual sadism
Picqueristic incisions	Picquerism, sexual sadism
Rape (anal)	Sexual sadism, biastophilia
Rape (vaginal)	Biastophilia, sexual sadism
Torture (many forms)	Sexual sadism
Vampirism	Vampirism
Victim forced to wear specific clothing	Ornophilia, fetishism (of clothing object)
Victim nude	x
Victim partially undressed	x

Stroke (Postmortem)	Possible Corresponding Paraphilias
Biting	Odaxelagnia, anthropophagy, vampirism
Decapitation	Necromutilophilia, sarxentyhmiophilia, mutilophilia
Disfigurement	Necromutilophilia, mutilophilia
Dismemberment	Necromutilophilia, sarxenthymiophilia, mutilophilia
Evisceration	Necromutilophilia, visceralagnia, mutilophilia
Excised body part	Necromutilophilia, sarxentyhmiophilia, anthropophagy, mutilophilia
Forced oral copulation	Necrofellatiolagnia, necropenetrolagnia
Foreign object insertion	Necropenetrolagnia
Incised body part	Necromutilophilia, mutilophilia
Masturbation onto corpse	Necroexteriolagnia
Picqueristic incisions	Picquerism

Posing	Necrornopositophilia, fetishism (of clothing object if applicable)
Rape (anal)	Necosodomolagnia, necropenetrolagnia
Rape (vaginal)	Necropenetrolagnia, necrocoitolagnia

Wound Interpretation and the Assessment of Paraphilia

Having examined several forms of sexual homicide in this chapter, it is now important to learn how to distinguish between them. Before the offender is apprehended and interviewed, this is best understood by wound pattern analysis (Turvey, 2008). If necrophilic wounds are mistaken for sexually sadistic, or nonparaphilic wounds for paraphilic (and vice versa), then both the investigation and linkage analysis will be hindered significantly. To the naked eye, these differences may seem subtle, but become more apparent with an understanding of motivation. The motivation for mutilation, in particular, can be challenging to interpret. The following chart offers some guidance in this investigatory endeavor:

Nature of Wound	Associated Paraphilia
Series of deep incised wounds, not clustered, and occurring before death, sometimes extending beyond death.	Generally not indicative of paraphilia. Typically reflects either anger toward the victim, a loss of control over the victim, psychosis, or concern that the victim will not die. The latter can sometimes indicate an inexperienced murderer. If accompanied by sexual assault, this is likely a rape-slaying. See the case of Michael Satcher below.
Series of deep incised wounds, not clustered, only occurring after death.	Can indicate anger toward the victim, *expressive/transformative behavior*, or necrophilic behavior.
Series of shallow-clustered incised wounds; directed at breast, nipple, genitals, feet, or buttocks, and occurring before death.	This is picquerist behavior which is often, though not necessarily, comorbid with sexual sadism.
Body dismembered and parts concealed in space that is large enough to have fit a fully intact corpse. Dismemberment began while victim was alive.	Strong possibility of sexual sadism and/or mutilophilia.
Body dismembered and parts concealed in space that is large enough to have fit a fully intact corpse. Dismemberment began while victim was dead.	Strong possibility of necromutilophilic or mutilophilic behavior. However, consideration should be given as to how the offender transported the body. The body might have been dismembered postmortem to make it easier to transport unseen or without encumberance.
Body dismembered and parts concealed in a space or spaces that are too small to fit a fully intact corpse. Dismemberment began while victim was alive.	Strong possibility of sexual sadism and/or mutilophilia.
Body dismembered and parts concealed in a space or spaces that are too small to fit a fully intact corpse. Dismemberment began while victim was dead.	Likely defensive mutilation.
Body dismembered and parts scattered in a secluded area, but not displayed.	May be defensive mutilation. See the case of Paul Bernardo and Karla Homolka in Chapter 8. If dismemberment occurred prior to death, then there is a possible indication of sexual sadism.
Body dismembered with parts placed on open display or mailed to individuals.	This is often *expressive/transformative* behavior (Mellor, 2016b), although if the dismemberment occurred prior to death, then there is also a possible indication of sexual sadism.
Head and hands excised after death.	Though on rare occasions this can be necrophilic behavior, usually it is an attempt by the perpetrator to conceal the victim's identity by eliminating dental records and fingerprints. If the head and hands are found in the vicinity of the victim's corpse, this is a stronger indication of a mutilophilic or necromutilophilic motivation.
Bludgeoning or stabbing wounds, not clustered, and in excess of what is needed to kill the victim.	*Overkill*. Generally not indicative of paraphilia. Typically reflects either anger toward the victim, a loss of control over the victim, psychosis, or concern that the victim will not die. The latter can sometimes indicate an inexperienced murderer. If accompanied by sexual assault, this is likely a rape-slaying. See the case of Michael Satcher below.

Body part(s) excised and missing. Excision began while victim was still alive.	Strong possible indication of sexual sadism, mutilophilia, and sarxenthymiophilia. Anthropophagy, a possibility.
Body part(s) excised and missing. Excision began while victim was dead.	Indication of necromutilophilia and sarxenthymiophilia. Anthropophagy a possibility. Can also be defensive mutilation used by perpetrator to hide identifying marks on victim such as scars, tattoos, moles, or might also be an attempt to get rid of the offender's bite marks.
Body part(s) excised and located near body. Excision began while victim was alive.	Strong indication of mutilophilia and sexual sadism, small chance of sarxenthymiophilia.
Body part(s) excised and located near body. Excision began while victim was dead.	Indication of necromutilophilia or mutilophilia, small chance of sarxenthymiophilia. Can also be defensive mutilation used by perpetrator to hide identifying marks on victim such as scars, tattoos, moles, or might also be an attempt to get rid of the offender's bite marks.
Body part disfigured. Disfigurement began while victim was alive.	Strong indication of sexual sadism and mutilophilia.
Body part disfigured. Disfigurement began while victim was dead.	Strong indication of necromutilophilia, or potentially mutilophilia.

Overlapping Paraphilic Crimes

Not every sexual homicide necessarily entails paraphilia. One of the more common types is a rape-slaying, in which a sexual murderer kills to eliminate the only witness to a sexual assault or does so unintentionally during an attempted or successful sexual assault. Occasionally, an offender appears who is a rape-slayer/necrophile, rape-slayer/sex sadist, or sex sadist/necrophile (Fred West, Ted Bundy, Gerard Schaefer, Albert Fish). These should be thought less of as categories, and more like capsules for paraphilic psychological concepts. The traits of a sexual sadist—typically psychopathic—usually supercede those of the homicidal necrophile or rape-slayer; in other words, when there is crime scene evidence that a victim was tortured, murdered, and then subject to postmortem mutilation, posing, or necrophilic intercourse, the interviewer and prosecutor should expect a suspect to have more of the sex sadist's charming, psychopathic character. This could theoretically account for the statistical anomalies of Ted Bundy and Samuel Dixon—murderers who engaged in necrophilic behavior but scored 30 or higher on the Hare PCL-R (see Chapter 7)—their sexual sadism took precedence. An interesting and common combination is a type 5 sexual sadist who is also a type C homicidal necrophile. This 5C lust murderer is often a *mutilophile*, who Mellor (2016c) describes as an individual who has

> Sexual arousal stemming from acts of mutilation which go beyond simple incision (cuts, piercing, stab wounds), regardless of whether the mutilation occurs at the ante, peri, or postmortem stage. It does not include excision, if the act of excising is not sexually gratifying in itself, and its sole purpose is to obtain a body part for some other purpose. The mutilophile differs from the necromutilophile, in that extreme acts of mutilation such as dismemberment, evisceration, and/or decapitation are gratifying to him in themselves, whether perpetrated on a living or dead victim. This differs from the necromutilophile—who exists along the necrophilia-spectrum—and requires a corpse to achieve sexual pleasure from his acts of mutilation.

In past tabloids, this *mutilophilic* offender was called a "ripper," with Jack the Ripper and Andrei Chikatilo, perhaps representing some of the more interesting case studies of this type of offender.

Finally, the dynamism and responsiveness of human behavior almost always influence the events, acts, and emotions that occur during a sexual homicide. Not every paraphilic lovemap is expressed as competently or specifically as the offender wished. In fact, it may fall short in this regard on the majority of occasions. The psychopathic child-raping "Moors Murderer" Ian Brady talks about how this inability to perfectly realize the fantasy actually fuels the compulsion (Brady, 2001).

Michael Satcher's sexual murder of Anne Borghesani exemplifies how the offender's angered emotional state, the victim's resistance, and a determination to rape resulted in a particularly gruesome homicide. Or is there more to the story?

Case Study: Michael Satcher

The crimes of Michael Satcher are somewhat ambivalent in motivation. He operated outdoors along the Custis Trail—a four mile paved bicycle path which runs east from the Washington and Old Domain Railroad Trail to Rosslyn's Key Bridge in Arlington County, Virginia.

At 6:55 p.m., 25-year-old Dana Veldhuis* set out on her mountain bike from Georgetown in Washington DC to ride 10–15 minutes to her boyfriend's apartment in Rosslyn. Noting the absence of other pedestrians and cyclists on the trail, she rode over Key Bridge traversing the hilly terrain with some speed. As she approached a hill, a stocky Black male stepped out onto the path and knocked her from her bicycle. She flew into the grass near a ditch. Before she could recover, her attacker pounced on her back, using his weight to press her against the blacktop, and covered her eyes with his hands. Dana tried to speak to him, but every time she moved her head he pinched or pushed her face down. She informed him that her purse was on her bike and that it had money in it, but he seemed disinterested. When she ceased struggling, he began to pull her pants down. Fortunately, a male cyclist happened to ride by, spotted them, and rushed to the rescue. Seeing him, the attacker grabbed Dana's purse and fled. The cyclist checked Dana for serious injuries, then together they headed to a nearby apartment complex in Fort Georgetown to find help. There a tenant waved down a passing police cruiser.

The officer spoke with Dana Veldhuis and noted her description of the attacker as a clean-shaven short-haired Black male, 25–30, 5'9"–5'10" and in the vicinity of 195 lbs, clad in a navy blue zippered sweatsuit with light colored sneakers. He issued a BOLO ("Be On the Look-Out") for the suspect, and patrol cars began to search the neighborhood. Uniformed Arlington County Police began walking east along the bike path to catch the fleeing attacker, and a K-9 Unit was dispatched to try and pick up his trail.

Within 20 minutes of the first assault, a second young woman was attacked on the Custis Trail. Anne Elizabeth Borghesani had entered the path around the Fort Bennett apartments on North 215 Street, and was taking a 5-min shortcut to reach the metro rail station. Less than 100 yards from the site of the Veldhuis incident, by a concrete sound barrier which separated the trail from the Lee Highway, Borghesani was grabbed from behind by the collar. She began to scream, kick, bite, and scratch at her attacker, but he overpowered her. Dragged through the plants and trees at the side of the Air Force Association Building and down a fire stair, Borghesani's struggle came to an abrupt end when her attacker slammed her face repeatedly, and stabbed her 21 times in the chest, neck, and head with an awl. He then tore off Borghesani's panties and proceeded to rape her perimortem, potentially extending into the postmortem stage. When he was finished, he took her purse and two rings from her fingers. He also tore her earrings off through the lobes, leaving them beside her, and then fled the scene. At 8:30 p.m. he was seen by several residents of 21st Street apartments running into the forest in the direction of the Potomac River.

Anne Borghesani's bloody corpse was discovered at 8:25 the following morning by two friends who had gone looking for her when she failed to arrive for her own 23rd birthday party. Arlington County police detectives and forensic technicians began securing and processing the scene at 10:15 a.m.

The coroner attributed Borghesani's death to insanguination—literally drowning on blood. He also collected a semen sample and an African-American pubic hair from the Caucasian Borghesani's genital region. Veldhuis's and Borghesani's purses were found three days later by police searchers on a hillside near Scott Street Bridge which was often frequented by vagrants.

Anne Borghesani's killer struck again on the morning of August 18. Sherri Kerringer,* 42, was power walking along South Arlington's Washington and Old Dominion recreational trail when she was seized from behind and yanked into the trees. Her assailant was carrying some kind of blade, and told her to "come with me" as he pulled her further and further away from the trail. Terrified, Sherri urinated in her clothing. When she told him this and that she was very scared, he left. Sherri was unable to provide a physical description of him to police beyond the fact that his sleeve was red.

As was the case with his previous attacks, The Bike Path Killer would offend again on the same day. Two hours later, he seized 39-year-old jogger Tabitha Holt* from behind on the Washington and Old Dominion path, and put a blade to her throat. As he maneuvered her off the trail, Tabitha struck him repeatedly with a bag full of videotapes. They fell onto the ground, struggling. Tabitha shouted for help, and when her attacker noticed two joggers nearby, he took off. As the joggers helped Tabitha to the top of a hill next to the Park Lane condominiums, they met a witness. Ethel Rankin* had been arranging items

---
*A pseudonym.

in her car trunk when she was nearly bowled over by a Black male in a t-shirt and red sweat pants. Ethel's description of the man matched that of Tabitha's attacker. The two hurried to Ethel's apartment where they phoned the police to report the assault, and provided details of the attacker's appearance.

Responding to the call, motorcycle officer James Page of the Arlington County police was riding along the Barcroft Bike trail, when he passed a terrified looking female jogger being chased by a man who fit the suspect's description. Pulling his motorcycle to a halt, he detained the man on suspicion of assault and requested that he provide identification. The man handed him a driver's license which identified him as Michael Charles Satcher, a resident of Southeast Washington DC—an area notorious for violent crime and narcotics. Eventually, an opened lockblade knife was found concealed in a bundle in Satcher's hand. Ethel Rankin identified him on the spot as the man she had seen fleeing the area, and he was subsequently arrested, and charged with two counts of abduction and one count of malicious wounding. Hair, blood, and saliva samples were taken from Satcher and submitted to Northern Virginia Forensic Laboratory for analysis.

A search of the glove compartment of Satcher's 1984 Volkswagen Jetta revealed an awl. Though this was never conclusively linked to the murder of Anne Borghesani due to an absence of blood on the tool, the coroner testified that it was consistent with the dimensions of the wounds to Borghesani's body. The results of the laboratory testing indicated that the hair found in Borghesani's pubic hair did not belong to Satcher, but that his DNA matched her attacker's semen.

The trial of Michael Satcher began on July 17, 1991. On July 30, 1991 he was found guilty on all charges including capital murder. In the second stage of his bifurcated trial, the jury deliberated 3 hours before determining that Satcher would be put to death. On December 9, 1997, the state of Virginia executed Michael Satcher by lethal injection.

At the time of his arrest, Satcher had been a 22-year-old unmarried father of two children and a professional furniture mover. He had two previous convictions for possession of PCP.

Judging by the details of his known offences, Michael Satcher was either one of two types of offenders:

1. A *rape-slayer* who murdered out of frustration and in response to Anne Borghesani's fierce resistance, rather than to eliminate a witness. In this scenario, the violence Satcher had inflicted on Dana Veldhuis, Sherri Kerringer, and Tabitha Holt was simply to assure their cooperation. The Veldhuis attack seemed to indicate that once a victim was compliant, Satcher would sexually assault her. If murder had been the goal of his attacks, then Satcher would have killed Sherri Kerringer rather than abandoning her once she revealed that she had soiled herself.

2. A Category D *homicidal necrophile* who planned to murder all of the women and have sex with their corpses, but was only successful in doing so with Anne Borghesani.

The author interprets this case as a high anger *rape-slaying* which manifested in *overkill* and became a case of *pseudonecrophilia*. It is unlikely that any of the acts reflected Satcher's actual sexual fantasies.

Screening and Counselling for Investigators and Other Specialists

Cases involving extremely graphic incidences of homicide have a particularly high risk of trauma to the investigators and professionals involved in the processing or assessment of them. After watching a video in which David Parker Ray (Chapter 8) inserted a hot cattle prod into a screaming female victim's vagina until blood leaked from her orifices and she went limp, numerous seasoned FBI agents vomited. Among the viewers was Patricia Rust, who spent a total of four days inside Ray's "Toybox," tasked with drawing detailed sketches. Having received praise for her work from her boss on the morning of April 2, 1999, Rust went home and committed suicide (Fielder, 2003).

In 2013, Canadian forensic psychiatrist Dr. John Bradford, who had studied videotapes of the sexual tortures of Leslie Mahaffy and Kristen French at the hands of Paul Bernardo and Karla Homolka (Chapter 8), suffered a mental breakdown half an hour after viewing footage of Canadian serial killer Russell Williams' rape and murder of Marie-France Comeau and his repeated sexual assaults on Jessica Lloyd. Bradford was subsequently diagnosed with posttraumatic stress disorder. An article by the *Ottawa Citizen* quotes Bradford as saying "The Williams tapes brought back the Bernardo tapes. I had this video show going on and on and I couldn't sleep. I would stay up till 2 a.m. to avoid going to sleep and so it was worse the next day" (Cobb, October 11, 2013). Bradford had initially experienced symptoms 20 years earlier when viewing the Bernardo tapes, but these had dissipated after 6 months, so he had largely ignored them. Aside from the videotapes, Bradford had also spent approximately 100 hours interviewing Bernardo, and many hours with Williams. With the help of medication and counselling, Bradford's condition has reportedly improved significantly, though he now refuses to watch any video footage from cases involving graphic violence, notably turning down the high-profile Luka Magnotta case.

As successful police and mental health work in these areas necessitates emotional resilience and a certain level of objectivity, professionals might avoid seeking help for trauma as this could affect their career or because they are afraid to admit weakness to themselves or their colleagues. The examples of Rust and Bradford demonstrate the need for law enforcement and the mental health community to be proactive and insistent in finding help for professionals who have to deal with such abject materials. After the Green Ribbon Task Force reviewed the Bernardo sexual torture tapes on October 11, 1994, for instance, Inspector Vince Bevan arranged for each member of the task force to see a counsellor (Williams, 1996).

References

Abel, G. G., Becker, J. V., Cunningham-Rathner, J., Mittelman, M. S., and Rouleau, J. L. 1988. Multiple paraphilic diagnoses among sex offenders. *Bulletin of the American Academy of Psychiatry and the Law*, *16*, 153–168.

American Psychiatric Association. 2013. *Diagnostic and Statistical Manual of Mental Disorders* (5th ed.). Washington, DC: American Psychiatric Association.

Arrigo, B. and Purcell, C. 2001. Explaining paraphilias and lust murder: Toward an integrated model. *International Journal of Offender Therapy and Comparative Criminology*, *45*, 6.

Brady, I. 2001. *The Gates of Janus: Serial Murder and Its Analysis*. Port Townsend, WA: Feral House.

Burgess, A. W., Hartman, C. R., Ressler, R. K., Douglas, J. E., and McCormack, A. 1986. Sexual homicide—A motivational model. *Journal of Interpersonal Violence*, *1*(3), 251–272.

Cobb, C. 2013, October 11. "Tough forensic guy" John Bradford opens up about his PTSD. *Ottawa Citizen*. Retrieved from http://bit.ly/1zfiy2v.

Fielder, J. 2003. *Slow Death*. New York, NY: Pinnacle.

Gratzer, T. and Bradford, J. M. W. 1995. Offender and offense characteristics of sexual sadists: A comparative study. *Journal of Forensic Sciences*, *40*(3), 450–455.

Hare, R. D., Cooke, D. J., and Hart, S. D. 1999. Psychopathy and sadistic personality disorder. In: T. Millon, P. H. Blanney, and R. D. Davies (Eds.), *Oxford Textbook of Psychopathology*. New York, NY: Oxford University Press, pp. 555–584.

Hickey, E. 2013. *Serial Murderers and Their Victims* (6th ed.). Belmont, CA: Wadsworth.

Holmes, R. 1991. *Sex Crimes*. Newbury Park, CA: Sage.

Holt, S. E., Meloy, J. R., and Strack, S. 1999. Sadism and psychopathy in violent and sexually violent offenders. *Journal of the American Academy of Psychiatry and Law*, *27*(1), 23–32.

Keppel, R. and Birnes, W. 2009. *Serial Violence: Analysis of Modus Operandi and Signature Characteristics of Killers*. Boca Raton, FL: CRC Press.

MacCulloch, M., Snowden, P., Wood, P., and Mills, H. 1983. Sadistic fantasy, sadistic behavior, and offending. *British Journal of Psychiatry*, *143*, 20–29.

Mellor, L. 2016a.[*] Wider shades of pale. In: L. Mellor, A. Aggrawal, and E. W. Hickey (Eds.), *Understanding Necrophilia: A Global Multidisciplinary Approach*. San Diego, CA: Cognella.

Mellor, L. 2016b.[*] Necrophilia and the thematic-derivative model of sexual progression. In: L. Mellor, A. Aggrawal, and E. W. Hickey (Eds.), *Understanding Necrophilia: A Global Multidisciplinary Approach*. San Diego, CA: Cognella.

Mellor, L. 2016c.[*] Mincing words: Refining the language and interpretation of mutilation. In: L. Mellor, A. Aggrawal, and E. W. Hickey (Eds.), *Understanding Necrophilia: A Global Multidisciplinary Approach*. San Diego, CA: Cognella.

Mokros, A., Osterheider, M., Hucker, S. J., and Nitschke, J. 2011. Psychopathy and sexual sadism. *Law and Human Behavior*, *35*(3), 188–199.

Money, J. 1990. Forensic sexology: Paraphilic serial rape (biastrophilia) and lust murder (erotophonophilia). *American Journal of Psychotherapy*, *44*(1), 26–36.

---

[*] These essays are also available in Mellor, L. (in press). *Necrophilia: Theoretical Perspectives for the New Millennium*. Toronto, Canada: Grinning Man Press.

Money, J. 2011. *Lovemaps: Sexual/erotic Health and Pathology, Paraphilia, and Gender Transposition in Childhood, Adolescence, and Maturity.* Buffalo, NY: Prometheus Books. Kindle Edition.

Moser, C. 2013. Paraphilia: A critique of a confused concept. In: P. J. Kleinplatz (Ed.), *New Directions in Sex Therapy: Innovations and Alternatives.* Philadelphia, PA: Brunner-Routledge, pp. 91–108.

Porter, S., Fairweather, D., Drugge, J., Hervé, H., Birt, A., and Boer, D. P. 2000. Profiles of psychopathy in incarcerated sexual offenders. *Criminal Justice and Behavior, 27,* 216–233.

Porter, S., Ten Brinke, L., and Wilson, K. 2009. Crime profiles and conditional release performance of psychopathic and non-psychopathic sexual offenders. *Legal and Criminal Psychology, 14,* 109–118.

Porter, S., Woodworth, M., Earle, J., Drugge, J., and Boer, D. P. 2003. Characteristics of sexual homicide committed by psychopathic and nonpsychopathic offenders. *Law and Human Behavior, 27,* 459–470.

Ressler, R., Burgess, A., and Douglas, J. 1992. *Sexual Homicide: Patterns and Motives.* New York, NY: The Free Press.

Schmidt, C. W. 1995. Sexual psychopathology and DSM-IV. *Review of Psychiatry, 14,* 719–733.

Schmidt, C. W., Schiavi, R., Schover, L., Segraves, R. T., and Wise, T. N. 1998. DSM-IV sexual disorders: Final overview. In: T. A. Widiger, A. J. Frances, H. A. Pincus, R. Ross, M. B. First, W. Davis, and M. Kline (Eds.), *DSM-IV Sourcebook.* Vol. 4. Washington, DC: American Psychiatric Association, pp. 1087–1095.

Silverstein, C. 1984. The ethical and moral implications of sexual classification: A commentary. *Journal of Homosexuality, 9*(4), 29–38.

Stone, M. 1998. Sadistic personality in murderers. In: T. Millon, E. Simonsen, M. Birket-Smith, and R. D. Davis (Eds.), *Psychopathy: Antisocial, Criminal, and Violent Behavior.* New York, NY: Guilford Press, pp. 346–355.

Suppe, F. 1984. Classifying sexual disorders: The diagnostic and statistical manual of the American Psychiatric Association. *Journal of Homosexuality, 9*(4), 9–28.

Tallent, N. 1977. Sexual deviation as a diagnostic entity: A confused and sinister concept. *Bulletin of the Menninger Clinic, 41,* 40–60.

Turvey, B. 2008. *Criminal Profiling: An Introduction to Behavioral Evidence Analysis.* London, UK: Academic Press.

Williams, S. 1996. *Invisible Darkness.* Toronto, Canada: McArthur and Company.

7 Necrophilic Homicide Offenders

Lee Mellor

Contents

Introduction	97
Etiology (Specific to Necrophilia)	98
Features and Assessment of Necrophilia	100
Prevalence	100
Diagnosis	100
Typologies	100
Characteristics of Necrophilic Homicides and Their Perpetrators	109
Identifying and Investigating Necrophilic Homicides	110
Crime Scenes	110
Linkage Analysis and Offender Profiling	110
Placophilia	111
Pygmalionism/Agalmatophilia	111
Sarxenthymiophilia	111
Somnophilia	112
Taphophilia	112
Thanatohierophilia	112
Thanatophilia	112
Visceralagnia	112
Recommendations for Handling Cases of Necrophiles Who Kill	117
Interviewing	117
Building a Case against the Necrophile	118
Legal Aspects	118
Treatment	120
References	121

Introduction

The term *necrophilia* (ancient Greek for the "love" *philia* of "corpses" *nekros*) was coined by the Belgian alienist Joseph Guislain in the mid-nineteenth century after reading of the case of Parisian grave robber Sgt. Francois Bertrand who gratified himself sexually by mutilating and engaging in intercourse with the corpses of young women (Vronsky, 2016). Over the years, there has been much disagreement as to what constitutes the fundamental character of necrophilia.

In academic discourse, the term now problematically refers to (1) the love of corpses, (2) sexual arousal from corpses, (3) sexual acts carried out with a corpse, and (4) the love of death (Hucker and Stermac, 1992). This results in a jingle fallacy in which the same word is used to describe separate phenomena, and can lead to confusion or misunderstanding when discussing the topic. Mellor (2016a) defines necrophilia as sexual arousal from the corpse as an *object in itself*, and not necessarily any specific act perpetrated on it. This definition and understanding will be used for the purposes of this chapter. Though the general public usually conceptualizes necrophilia as genital contact with a corpse, in reality, there are a number of subparaphilias related to corpse fetishism which fall under the necrophilic umbrella including *necromutilophilia, necrornopositophilia,* and *sarxenthymiophilia* (Mellor, 2016a). These are outlined later in this chapter.

Due to the statistical rarity of known necrophilic cases and general unavailability of police and mental health files concerning the cases that exist, the phenomenon cannot be accurately studied using quantitative research, though attempts have been made (Rosman and Resnick, 1989). Though the works of Krafft-Ebing (1886/2011), Havelock Ellis (2004), Stekel (1929/2013), and deRiver (1949/2000) report numerous fascinating case studies for us to draw upon, their interpretations are outdated and many of the underlying premises have been refuted. The first comprehensive volumes of academic worth on the subject came with Aggrawal's *Necrophilia: Forensic and Medico-Legal Aspects* (2011), followed 5 years later by *Understanding Necrophilia: A Global Multidisciplinary* approach (Mellor et al., 2016d). Still, when compared with other violent paraphilias such as sexual sadism and pedophilia, necrophilia research has only just taken its baby steps.

Etiology (Specific to Necrophilia)

The hypotheses for a biological etiology of necrophilia have been summarized by Aggrawal (2011) and found wanting. Though there has been speculation regarding a genetic cause for necrophilia, no empirical evidence of a necrophilia gene has hitherto been discovered to exist. Similarly, several necrophiles have sustained head injuries, but there is a similar lack of conclusive support for brain trauma as an explanation. Naturally, psychoanalytic arguments are abundant, but ultimately speculative, so they will not be detailed here. Psychosis was only found to be present in 11% of the necrophiles in the study by Rosman and Resnick (1989). There are numerous examples of necrophiles who habitually abused alcohol or were intoxicated at the time of their offense, though this more likely reflects the role of alcohol and drugs as disinhibitors for paraphilic urges and not the origin of the paraphilias themselves. Sexual inadequacy does seem to be a common enough trait in necrophiles (Rosman and Resnick, 1989) and should be accepted as a foundational influence in the etiology of necrophilia which underpins the *passivity/inertia* allure (Mellor, 2016d).

Though Mellor (2016d) does not explain why some people become attracted to corpses and others do not, he has identified five "allures" of necrophilia which may coexist or exist independently. The most common is the *passivity/inertia* allure, whose attraction is that the corpse is motionless, and by extension, unrejecting, uncritical, and compliant. This can ease the necrophile's anxieties over his sexual performance or predilections, increase his sense of power over another "person," or both. Another allure is *corporeal/sensory*, where sexual stimulation arises from looking at, hearing (death rattle, postmortem gas releases), smelling, touching, or tasting a dead body—including its innards. The *spiritual/magical* allure is the eroticization of metaphysical ideas regarding death as a state or force, including mythical figures associated with it, such as Azazel or the Grim Reaper, while the *ritual/iconography* allure relates to sexualizing cultural symbols associated with death or funerary practices (e.g., coffins, tombstones, burial shrouds). The *reminiscent/identity* allure applies to a specific individual who the necrophile loved in life, with their attraction to that individual continuing into the postmortem stages.

One recent and appealing hypothesis pertaining to the etiology of necrophilia is that where normally functioning human beings experience activation in the amygdala, hippocampus, and mid-insula upon seeing faces that appear *almost* human (for more information see the "Uncanny Valley" in Mori, 1970/2012), necrophiles do not (Foell and Patrick, 2016). This brain activity would have the evolutionary function of making people uncomfortable around dead bodies, presumably in order to avoid disease (Vronsky, 2016). The hypothesized lack of similar brain activity in necrophiles explains their lack of aversion to corpses (Foell and Patrick, 2016). Naturally, this hypothesis needs to be verified by functional magnetic resonance imaging (fMRI)-based neurobiological research on necrophiles and control groups, but from a theoretical view, it seems promising.

HN Case Study 1: Samuel Dixon (Category B Necrophile)

Samuel Dixon was an African-American ordained minister and psychopathic conman who, beginning at the age of 59, murdered two adult males and two adult females over a period of 11 months. Dixon claimed his first victim, a homeless 22-year-old black woman, in May 2000. According to Dixon, he convinced the young lady (henceforth known as Victim 1) to accompany him home to his Los Angeles apartment intending to have consensual sexual relations with her. There, they showered together, and fondled each other before Dixon provided Victim 1 with alcohol, marijuana, and crack cocaine. They then had sexual intercourse multiple times over the next 2 days. When Victim 1 attempted to leave, Dixon punched her several times in the head to subdue her and bound her arms and legs behind her back with stereo wire so that her vagina and anus were accessible. He gagged her and threatened her with a butcher knife when she would not remain silent. Annoyed that she continued to struggle, Dixon drugged her with amitriptyline, and proceeded to rape her anally and vaginally on his bed for a period of 24 h. As Victim 1's body has never been recovered and Dixon denies intentionally murdering her, the cause of her death cannot be determined. However, after Dixon had sexually assaulted her continuously for almost a day, she somehow died. This did not deter Dixon from continuing to rape and sodomize Victim 1's corpse for an additional 24 h. He placed her body into a bathtub with lye and bleach to break it down, where it remained for more than a week.

During that time, a 37-year-old black female acquaintance (Victim 2) came to Dixon's apartment, where a near identical scenario transpired, from the frequency and duration of sexual activities to the narcotics used by Victim 2. Eventually, Victim 2 announced that she had to leave to take care of her children, at which point Dixon pinned her down, tied her hands and feet together in front of her body, gagged her, and drugged her with amitriptyline. He forcibly sodomized her for up to 48 h, and then murdered her either through strangulation, bludgeoning, or some combination of these two methods. As with Victim 1, he continued to have vaginal and anal intercourse with Victim 2's corpse for another 48 h before placing it in the bathtub beside Victim 1's.

Sometime within 2 weeks after murdering Victim 2, Dixon was approached by a 36-year-old Hispanic male (Victim 3) who allegedly offered to have sex with him in exchange for $15. The two returned to the apartment, where Dixon sodomized the man for 4 h. Knowing that Victim 3 would eventually have to leave, Dixon slipped some amitripyiline into his beer, and then drugged, bound, and gagged him. Victim 3 endured 2.5 days of anal rape before he too perished. Consistent with his previous habits, Dixon continued to sodomize Victim 3's corpse for 24–48 h. This time, he deviated in his body disposal methods, by placing the corpse in a garbage bag and transporting it in a shopping cart to a nearby park.

Nearly 9 months would pass before Dixon killed again. During that time, however, Dixon would release five male and three female potential victims from his clutches either because the sedatives he employed failed to work or because he allegedly wanted to see if he could control his sexually violent urges. Victim 4, a 46-year-old Caucasian male, approached Dixon in a San Diego bathhouse on April 28, 2001, and they had consensual anal sex. Later, they relocated to Victim 4's apartment for further sexual activities before parting ways during the day of Sunday, April 29. That evening, they reconvened at the apartment, and following several more hours of consensual anal sex, Victim 4 expressed his wish to go to sleep. Angered by this, Dixon forcibly raped him, tied his foot to the bed with wire, and attempted to bind his hands together with shoestrings. Victim 4 managed to resist this last gesture and began to cry out, so Dixon hurried to the kitchen, seized a rolling pin, and struck him twice in the head. Dixon then claimed that he had accidentally smothered Victim 4 to death by forcing large quantities of petroleum jelly into his nose and mouth to prevent him from making noise. Although Victim 4 was already dead, Dixon bound him in the same manner as Victim 2, in order to make anal penetration easier. In this case, no postmortem sex acts could occur, as the phone began to ring. Realizing that Victim 4's coworkers were likely wondering about his failure to show up for work, Dixon stuffed the body into a closet, and stole Victim 4's chequebook and car. Arrested and charged with autotheft on May 17, 2001, in Los Angeles, Dixon unexpectedly confessed his four murders to the authorities claiming that God was telling him to perpetrate them (Reavis, 2011; Hickey, 2015).

Features and Assessment of Necrophilia

Prevalence

Estimates of the prevalence of necrophilia in sexual homicide is estimated to range from 0.3% (Häkkänen-Nyholm et al., 2009) to around 7.6%* (Stein et al., 2010) or 7.9% (Schlesinger et al., 2010). Unfortunately, such numbers are dependent on differing definitions or understandings of what constitutes necrophilia. Though generally rare, in the realm of sexual homicide, necrophilia is present in such a significant proportion of crimes that it certainly merits study and understanding.

Diagnosis

Necrophilia is given as an example of an "other specified paraphilic disorder" in the *Diagnostic and Statistical Manual of Mental Disorders, Fifth Edition* (DSM-5). Regarding other specified paraphilic disorder:

> This category applies to presentations in which symptoms characteristic of a paraphilic disorder that cause clinically significant distress or impairment in social, occupational, or other important areas of functioning predominate but *do not meet the full criteria for any of the disorders in the paraphilic disorders diagnostic class* [emphasis added]. The other specified paraphilic disorder category is used in situations in which the clinician chooses to communicate the specific reason that the presentation does not meet the criteria for any specific paraphilic disorder. This is done by recording "other specified paraphilic disorder" followed by the specific reason… Examples of presentations that can be specified using the "other specified" designation include, but are not limited to, recurrent and intense sexual arousal… that has been present for at least 6 months and causes marked distress or impairment in social, occupational, or other important areas of functioning. Other specified paraphilic disorder can be specified as in remission and/or as occurring in a controlled environment (American Psychiatric Association, 2013, p. 705).

Though meeting the criteria for a paraphilic disorder, necrophilia is not specifically listed as such in the DSM-5 because of its statistical rarity when compared with other paraphilic disorders. However, if one is to consider a corpse an object (Segal, 1953) then necrophilia would actually be subsumed under fetishistic disorder. This has been reflected in Hickey's (2013) use of the term *necrofetishism* to denote "having a fetish for dead bodies" (p. 158), which is essentially synonymous with necrophilia (Rosman and Resnick, 1989). Even if a person does not participate in sexual activities with corpses, if their fantasies of doing so cause them personal distress, then they meet the criteria for paraphilic disorder. Such a predilection would be described as mere *necrophilic sexual interest* if unaccompanied by personal distress and confined solely to the world of fantasy.

Typologies

Since the study of abnormal sexuality began in earnest in the nineteenth century, numerous typologies of necrophilia have been proposed (Krafft-Ebing, 1886/2011; Wulffen, 1910; Jones, 1931; Hirschfield, 1956). The most influential was published by Rosman and Resnick (1989) who, drawing upon 88 cases from world literature and 34 unpublished case reports, dichotomized them into *genuine necrophiles*, who have a "persistent sexual attraction to corpses…manifested in…a series of necrophilic acts. [T]he corpse represents a fetishistic object" (p. 154)—and *pseudonecrophiles* who are transiently attracted to corpses, with dead bodies playing no role in their sexual fantasies. *Genuine necrophilia* is further subdivided into *regular necrophilia*, *necrophilic fantasies*, and *necrophilic homicide*. Rosman and Resnick noted that many homicides involving postmortem sexual acts are *pseudonecrophilic*.

These four types of necrophilic attachment are encompassed in Mellor's Thematic-Derivative Model of Sexual Progression, with *necrophilic fantasies* occupying the *fantasy* stage, *pseudonecrophilic* acts in the *situational* stage, and the other two stages of *genuine necrophilia* spread across three levels of attachment: *activation*, *preference*, and *fixation*.

In their typology of serial killers, Holmes and Holmes (2009) relegate necrophilia to three of their six categories of murderer. Perhaps the most popular and oft-cited typology of serial murder, the Holmes–Holmes Typology links crime scene behavior to a single motive. As seen in Table 7.1, necrophilia is associated with

---

* Though this is a lower number than Schlesinger et al.'s, it is drawn from a much larger sample and is therefore likely to be more reliable.

Table 7.1 Crime Scene Analysis of Suspected Serial Murder Cases

Crime Scene	Visionary	Mission	Comfort	Lust	Thrill	Power/Control
Characteristics						
Controlled	No	Yes	Yes	Yes	Yes	Yes
Crime Scene						
Overkill	Yes	No	No	Yes	No	No
Chaotic	Yes	No	No	No	No	No
Crime Scene						
Evidence of torture	No	No	No	Yes	Yes	Yes
Body moved	No	No	No	Yes	Yes	Yes
Specific victim	No	Yes	Yes	Yes	Yes	Yes
Weapon at the scene	Yes	No	Yes	No	No	No
Relational victim	No	No	Yes	No	No	No
Victim known	Yes	No	Yes	No	No	No
Aberrant sex	No	No	No	Yes	Yes	Yes
Weapon of torture	No	No	No	Yes	Yes	Yes
Strangles the victim	No	No	No	Yes	Yes	Yes
Penile penetration	?	Yes	Usually not	Yes	Yes	Yes
Object penetration	Yes	No	No	Yes	Yes	Yes
Necrophilia	Yes	No	No	Yes	No	Yes
Gender usually	Male	Male	Female	Male	Male	Male

Source: Holmes, R. and Holmes, S. 2009. *Profiling Violent Crimes: An Investigative Tool* (4th ed.). Thousand Oaks, CA: Sage. With permission.

the *visionary*, *hedonist lust*, and *power/control* types, while mutilation, which Holmes and Holmes problematically term "overkill" (Mellor, 2016b), is confined to only the first two of these categories.

The Holmes–Holmes typology was a revolutionary new way to approach types of serial murderers and remains a useful heuristic for students and investigators making their initial forays into the world of abnormal homicide. However, when attempting to apply it to the majority of serial murder cases, its shortcomings became apparent. One example is that the only category of offender that Holmes and Holmes (2009) claim leaves a chaotic crime scene is the *visionary* who "is propelled to kill by voices he hears or visions he sees" (p. 119). Yet some of the crime scenes of *nonvisionary* killers such as Braeden Nugent, Richard Ramirez, Levi Bellfield, Faryion Wardrip, and the Dnepropetrovsk Maniacs were also chaotic, sometimes more so than such prototypical *visionary* killers as Herbert Mullin and Joseph Kallinger. Another issue is that serial murderers rarely have a single motive, with power and control playing a large motivational role in the majority of such homicides. Holmes and Holmes have sought to reconcile this problem by proposing that certain offenders may be a hybrid of two types, such as *visionary/hedonist lust*, but doing so significantly lessens its usefulness for crime scene assessment and criminological categorization. For instance, Holmes and Holmes specify that a *hedonist lust* killer leaves a controlled crime scene and transports his victims' bodies to be dumped, while a *visionary*'s crime scene is chaotic with the body left where the murder occurred. As the controlled/chaotic crime scene and body transported/body left dichotomies exist in direct opposition to each other, the creation of a *visionary/hedonist lust* killer hybrid—the solution put forth by Holmes and Holmes—gives birth to parameters which are self-contradictory to the point where their typology loses its utility.

Furthermore, neither Holmes and Holmes's typology nor the two types of necrophilic murder proposed by Rosman and Resnick account for the many paraphilic comorbidities we see commonly associated with necrophilic murder.

By far, the most robust and detailed typology of necrophiles is Aggrawal's (2011) 10 classes in which homicidal necrophiles (HNs) occupy Class IX. Aggrawal's parameters for the classification of Class IX offenders include whether (1) the victim was tortured or mutilated while living, (2) the offender had sex with the victim(s) antemortem, (3) the offender mutilated the victim(s) postmortem, and (4) if sex acts were perpetrated on deceased victim(s) (Table 7.2).

Aggrawal's typology is commendable for both its pleasing simplicity and innovation, and is undoubtedly the best proposed to date. Unfortunately, it too has its shortcomings. As the torture and mutilation of living

Table 7.2 Various Subclasses within Class IX Necrophiles

Class	Victim Living	Victim Dead	Major Protagonists	Torture/ Mutilation Sex	Mutilation Sex (Examples)
IXa	No	No	Yes	No	Jack the Ripper, Ed Gein, Monster of Florence (*Il mostro di Firenze*), Frederick Baker
IXb	No	No	No	Yes	John Christie (1898–1953), Eli Ulayuk (1968–)
IXc	No	No	Yes	Yes	Joseph Vacher (1869–1898)
IXd	Sex (nonconsensual) *or* torture/mutilation		Sex *or* mutilation		Surendra Koli Gruyo (1970–)
IXe	Sex (nonconsensual)		Sex *and/or* mutilation (*Note*: This subclass would include those combinations that do not fall in subclass IXd and Ixf)		Jerry Brudos (sex during *and/or* torture/mutilation life; sex *and* after death—most typical behavior)
IXf	Yes	Yes	Yes	Yes	Ted Bundy, Jeffrey Dahmer

Source: Aggrawal, A. 2011. *Necrophilia: Forensic and Medico-Legal Aspects.* Boca Raton, FL: CRC Press. With permission.

victims (or lack thereof) constitutes a quarter of each of his six subclasses, the depths to which the more relevant postmortem activities can be explored are limited.

Aggrawal wisely includes mutilation of the corpse—a common co-occurrence in necrophilic murderers—but does not address the ends which the killer sought to achieve through these actions. British serial slayer Dennis Nilsen, for example, seems to have dismembered the bodies of his victims purely to facilitate their disposal. According to the "Kindly Killer" himself:

> In the end, when it was say two or three bodies under the floorboards, they began to accumulate. But come the summer it got hot and I knew it would be a smell problem. …And I thought "what would cause the smell more than the hot?" And I came to the conclusion it was the innards, the soft parts of the body, the organs and stuff like that. So on the weekend I would sort of pull up the floorboards—and *I found it totally unpleasant—I'd get blinding drunk so I could face it*, and start dissection on the kitchen floor. I got sick outside in the garden. (Morley and Clark, 1993)

Contrasting this with Japanese murderer Issei Sagawa's sexually charged description of his postmortem mutilation and cannibalization of Renée Hartevelt, the need for further distinction becomes increasingly evident:

> Her beautiful white body is before me. I've waited so long for this day and now it is here. …I wonder where I should bite first. I decide to bite the top of her butt. …I get a knife from the kitchen and stab it deeply into her skin. …Finally I find the red meat under the sallow fat. I scoop it out and put it in my mouth. I chew. It has no smell and no taste. I look into her eyes and say: "You are delicious." I cut her body and lift the meat to my mouth again and again. Then I take a photograph of her white corpse with its deep wounds. I have sex with her body. …I kiss her and tell her I love her. (King, 1996, p. 216)

Under Aggrawal's typology, both Nilsen and Sagawa would belong to subclass IXc because their nonconsensual sexual activities and mutilations were confined solely to the period after the victim's death. Yet, if we are to believe their accounts, Nilsen's butchery of the corpse was an unpleasant but necessary measure (*modus operandi*), while Sagawa's was a highly eroticized process (*ritual*). Clearly, if an offender's postmortem mutilation is undertaken sheerly as modus operandi, he should be differentiated from killers for whom the act is sexual. It is proposed that Nilsen's dismemberments were altogether irrelevant to the motivation for his murders, and that he would be better lumped in with the likes of serial killer John Christie than Issei Sagawa.

Finally, in Aggrawal's typology, Nilsen and Sagawa would theoretically occupy the same category as the "French Ripper" Joseph Vacher. Yet how do we reconcile Vacher's frenzied postmortem disfigurements and "love 'em and leave 'em" (for lack of a better term) necrophilic sexual penetration (Starr, 2010) with the lengthy periods of time Nilsen and Sagawa spent repeatedly violating their victims' corpses? To not demarcate between an offender who spends days or months committing sexual acts with the remains (Masters, 1985; King, 1996), and an offender who does so only momentarily, misses a crucial distinction.

With this in mind, a new typology of homicidal necrophilia is proposed below. In order to expand our focus on the postmortem aspects, antemortem acts have been eliminated. Maintaining the two would spawn such an overabundance of types that categorization would be useless. At its core, this typology of homicidal necrophilia is based on the interplay between two factors: *destructiveness* and *duration*.

Destructiveness refers to the propensity for paraphilic mutilation (*necromutilophilia*), *partialist postmortem sex acts*—or PPSAs (Mellor, 2016a,b)—and *cannibalism/vampirism* (Rosman and Resnick, 1989; Mellor, 2016a; Boon, 2016; Stone, 2016). PPSA is a term that refers to when an offender excises a piece of the cadaver (head, foot, etc.) and either penetrates the disembodied part with his penis, rubs it against his genitals, or uses it as masturbatory stimulus. For example, "Sunset Strip Slayer" Doug Clark decapitated one of his victims and fornicated with her head orally in the shower (Hickey, 2013). Often this is synonymous with what has been traditionally called "trophy" taking, in which "victim body parts [are] used for sexual arousal" (Hickey, 2013, p. 200). Trophies are distinct from "souvenirs" such as jewelry or identification (Hickey, 2013). Mellor (2016a) has argued that simply referring to "body parts" rather than "trophies" avoids unnecessary confusion. Cannibalism is the ingestion of a human victim's flesh, while vampirism is the imbibing of their blood (Hickey, 2006). In this case, it was deemed unnecessary to separate these into separate factors for reasons of simplicity, similarity in motive, and their frequent comorbidity. An HN who does not commit *destructive* paraphilic acts is considered *preservative*.

Duration determines whether an offender is labeled *cold* (continually revisiting or keeping a body for sex, even when it is rotting or skeletal) or *warm* (committing sexual acts once or twice on a fresh corpse before abandoning or disposing of it). An HN is deemed to be category A or B (cold), when he engages in sexual activities with a victim who has been deceased for approximately 2 or more hours in a temperate climate or comparable indoor environment. "Sexual activities" refer to any manifestation of penile or digital penetration, PPSAs, and acts of fondling, rubbing of the genitals against the corpse, or mutilation which result in sexual arousal.

This 2-h cutoff was determined by considering a number of factors related to the physical transformation of the body after death, the focus being on the *corporeal/sensory* necrophilic allure (Mellor, 2016d). Though, according to Snyder Sachs (2002), the temperature of a corpse becomes room temperature somewhere between 24 and 48 h, there are nevertheless significant visible changes to a body within a 2-h period, namely, rigor mortis—"a condition in which the muscles of the body become hardened as a result of chemical changes within the muscle fibers" (Fisher, 1980, p. 14)—and livor mortis, in which blood begins to settle in certain areas of the body, staining the flesh. Fisher (1980) notes that rigor mortis "usually becomes manifest within two to four hours and advances until approximately twelve hours" (p. 14), while "livor mortis formation begins immediately after death, but it may not be perceptible for as much as two hours. It is usually well developed within four hours and reaches a maximum between eight and twelve hours" (p. 17). Taking these factors into consideration, it has been determined that after approximately 2 h of death, the rigidity and appearance of the corpse is such that any HN who continues to be sexually aroused by it is doing so because, to some extent, he is either (a) attracted by the *corporeal/sensory* necrophilic allure (Mellor, 2016d) or (b) not repelled by these physical changes. This 2 h cutoff point is obviously an informed subjective judgment; however, it is one that unfortunately cannot be made in a way that is objective and quantifiable.

Though a dichotomy is drawn between "warm" and "cold" necrophilia at the 2 h point for the simple heuristic necessity of formulating a typology, there are a number of additional stages which occur naturally that should be considered. Four hours is the latest time period that rigor mortis becomes evident (Fisher, 1980), and simultaneously the earliest at which livor mortis becomes well developed.

Eight hours is the phase where livor mortis moves toward reaching maximum development (Fisher, 1980). At 12 h, rigor mortis ends and livor mortis reaches its maximum possible development (Fisher, 1980). Fisher (1980) notes that while putrefaction usually commences in 1 week when the corpse is left in the open air in a temperate climate, "it is not uncommon to see advanced decomposition within 12–18 h to the point that facial features are no longer recognizable" (p. 20). This is particularly true when there are external injuries to the corpse—a common quality in homicide—because it allows bacteria to enter the body. Taking all of this into consideration, it may be possible in the future to develop a gradient system based on 2 or 4 h intervals and consisting of a number of steps from respiratory death to full skeletonization, rather than the crude dichotomy made here.

Whereas popular typologies of serial killers (Holmes and Holmes, 2009), multiple murderers (Fox and Levin, 2005), and rapists (Groth, 1979) have centered on motive, the vast majority of necrophilic murderers in this study were driven by a perverse interplay of lust (paraphilia and fantasy), power (the desire to possess and control), and personal inadequacy. Therefore, following Aggrawal's lead, the categories in this typology

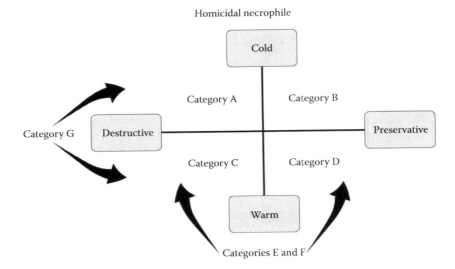

Figure 7.1 A new typology of homicidal necrophiles.

have not been primarily defined by motivation. Ultimately, eight categories were constructed, each based upon a constellation of behaviors observable in necrophilic offenders (Figure 7.1).

Categories A–D refer to homicidal necrophilia in the classic sense—the *active*, *preferential*, or *fixated* levels in the Thematic-Derivative model or Rosman and Resnick's *genuine* necrophilia (1989). The "Dabbler" (category E) engages in acts of *situational* postmortem sexual activity, but these do not become *desired* in his *sexual fantasyscape* (Mellor, 2016c), meaning that he tries them once or twice but they are of little interest and are nonparaphilic (Mellor, 2016c). In Rosman and Resnick's (1989) terms, such an offender is a *pseudonecrophile*. Catathymic (category F) HNs are a particularly peculiar group and merit further exploration. Schlesinger (2004) elaborates on Fredric Wertham's original concept of the "catathymic crisis," explaining:

> An individual with underlying emotionally charged conflicts develops a fixed idea that he must kill the future victim, and he does so after a protracted period of rumination. Catathymic homicides may also be sudden acts of violence, similarly induced by underlying conflicts that erupt with a trigger. In both forms, the chronic and the acute, a superficially integrated individual who is secretly struggling with feelings of inadequacy, particularly sexual inadequacy, resorts to violence when the potential victim challenges his sense of integrity, adequacy, or sexual competence. Thus, the violent act serves the purpose of freeing one's self from the source of threat to psychological stability. (p. 106)

As the murder tends to resolve the offender's inner conflicts, it is exceedingly rare that despite the underlying sexual motive for the crime a catathymic slayer kills again. This distinguishes him from the vast majority of compulsive HNs in this study. In the case of the catathymic HN, Schlesinger (2004) provides the example of an 18-year-old with the pseudonym "A. A." who strangled a young woman to death with a length of rubber hose before sodomizing her corpse. She had made sexual advances toward him one night at the gas station where he was employed, but when they attempted intercourse, he was unable to obtain an erection. When she mocked him, telling him to go home to his mother, he murdered her, stuffed her cadaver in the trunk of his car, and dumped it in a nearby field. Schlesinger does not detail exactly when the necrophilic sex act occurred, but does emphasize several important qualities. A. A. described (a) being in a dreamlike state during and immediately following the murder, (b) being so unsure that it had actually taken place that he returned to the field to see if the body was there, and (c) feeling an immense sense of relief after confessing. These are all experiences consistent with Schlesinger's (2004) understanding of catathymic homicide. Interestingly, all five catathymic HNs in Schlesinger's study committed murders of the acute variety.

Moving beyond catathymic HNs, the last two categories in this typology encompass offenders who do not engage in "traditional" postmortem sex acts, but whose behavior is widely believed to be a variation or permutation of necrophilia. Category G covers offenders who take pleasure purely in corpse mutilation, sometimes accompanied by masturbation—the exclusive necromutilophiles—and the category is indistinguishable from Aggrawal's Class IXa. The case of Robert Napper detailed in Michael Stone's Chapter on "Psychotic Homicide Offenders" exemplifies the Category G HN. Sexual cannibals and vampires constitute category H. Boon (2016) and Mellor (2016b) have proposed that cannibalism is an extension of necrophilia through the need to completely possess. And what is vampirism other than a partialist form of anthropophagy? Cannibals and vampires motivated purely by psychotic delusion, cultural practices, or religious rituals have been excluded from this typology, as necrophilia, when discussed here, is always a sexual act.

Sometimes an HN may have an attraction to *cold* corpses, but lacks the opportunity—due to unseen circumstances, lack of a private space, etc.—to spend more than 2 h participating in sexual acts with them. The case of Sean Vincent Gillis provides an example of an HN whose necrophilic behaviors were highly influenced by his living arrangement with his girlfriend. Had Gillis not been cohabiting at the time of his murders, it is possible that his home may have come to resemble that of Jeffrey Dahmer's, whose case we will examine later. Gillis was also a *destructive* HN, who was sexually aroused by postmortem mutilation, engaged in PPSAs with numerous excised body parts, and cannibalized nipples on several occasions. Gillis represents a case of a Category A HN who sometimes committed *warm* or *preservative* acts of necrophilia when circumstances did not permit otherwise.

HN Case Study 2: Sean Vincent Gillis (Category A: Cold/Destructive)

Sean Vincent Gillis was born June 24, 1962. In 1994, he met Terri Lemoine in Baton Rouge, Louisiana, and they set up home together the following year. Though affectionate, Sean admitted he was not at all interested in sex, which Terri did not really understand until they moved in together. She soon came to realize that Sean was addicted to internet pornography. When he showed her a website featuring dead naked women, she was horrified, but resigned herself to the fact that he loved his computer, and there was no point in getting upset about it.

What Terri did not know was that, in March 1994, Gillis had entered a room in a retirement home at 3 a.m., where 82-year-old Caucasian, Ann Bryan, lay sleeping. He mercilessly knifed and mutilated the defenseless woman, slashing her throat so deeply that she was almost decapitated, and slicing open her stomach so that her intestines and bowels were exposed. Her right breast was almost completely excised, and her genitals and face were also mutilated. In all, there were 47 stab wounds, inflicted postmortem, and Ann's body had been carefully arranged so that her genital area was exposed to the police who discovered her body. Despite the best efforts of law enforcement and rewards being offered by the family, the case eventually went cold.

Gillis would not kill again until 1999. In January of that year, Sean picked up Katherine Hall, a small 30-year-old black prostitute, and drove her to a deserted property where, after she performed oral sex on him, he suddenly cinched a nylon zip tie around her neck. Katherine managed to escape and ran from the car, so he chased after her, knocked her to the ground, and punched and stabbed her. Sean used a knife to slice through skin, muscle, and flesh, cutting through her left eye, breasts, stomach, and genitals—16 wounds in all before a final slash across her throat killed her. Having plenty of time and privacy now, Sean undressed Katherine and started to carve her up. He sliced a deep gash along her arm from shoulder to hand, slashed around one breast and cut open the other, stabbed her stomach and genitals eight times, and excised one of her eyes. Turning her body over, he plunged his knife into her left buttock, then dragged the blade in a deep path, stopping at her knee, and then sliced open her calf. Twenty-one of the wounds were inflicted postmortem. Katherine's murder would become another cold case.

That May, Sean noticed Hardee Moseley Schmidt, a 52-year-old Caucasian wife and mother from an affluent and respected Baton Rouge family, who was out for her usual early morning run. Having spotted her once before, he decided to attack driving right into her in his company car. While she lay stunned in the roadside ditch, he wrapped a nylon zip tie around her neck and tightened it until he was sure she was dead. Putting her body in the trunk of his vehicle, he drove off to an isolated area in a park and stripped off her clothes. He pulled down his pants and rubbed his penis over her body, including her vaginal area, finally raping her corpse and leaving his semen behind. Gillis placed the body in the trunk of his car as he went to pick up his girlfriend from work. The next morning, he drove to a rural area some distance away, then dragged the body into a swamp inhabited by alligators. Hardee's body was found the following day.

Gillis was now increasingly obsessed with death, dismemberment, and severed body parts. After dropping Terri off to start her night shift, he liked to drive around, picking up prostitutes, looking for the perfect victim. In November, he saw 36-year-old black prostitute Joyce Williams walking along, and became aroused by her legs. She got into his car, and they chatted and sang along to the radio. He headed out of town to an area of deserted fields in West Baton Rouge Parish. Joyce said she needed to urinate, and they both got out of the car. Gillis slipped a nylon zip tie around her neck and tightened it until she was dead. Then he placed her corpse in the car and took her to his house, where he laid it on the kitchen floor. He stroked her body, and decided he wanted to keep her legs. Using a sharp knife, he tried to cut through the muscle, but had to resort to using a hacksaw to remove the first leg. Trying to dismember the second leg, the hacksaw blade snapped off halfway through the femur. Next was her arm, but despite using a sharp knife at both elbow and wrist, and twisting it hard, the limb would not come free. So, he decided to try removing the head. He commented later that it was easy, just like cutting butter. He rinsed it off in the sink, and inserted his penis into the throat area, but it was uncomfortable, as something scraped his scrotum, so he put his penis in her mouth instead. Finally, he picked up the leg, and held the foot close to his face. In a frenzy of excitement now, he excised both nipples and ate them. Sated at last, he set to work, placing the body, the leg, and the head in separate garbage bags, and then put them all into a packing box while he scrubbed the kitchen floor. The packing box went into the trunk of his car, surrounded by other garbage, and he drove to collect Terri from work. While Terri slept in her bed, Gillis drove to a distant spot in Iberville Parish where he could drop the body parts into a river. It was not until the following January that two men walking in woods spotted a human leg and detectives then found other bones and a skull. Dental records identified the victim as Joyce Williams.

Sean Gillis claimed his fifth known victim in January 2000. He spied 52-year-old black prostitute Lillian Gorham Robinson strolling his favorite area of Baton Rouge and offered her money for oral sex. Driving to a secluded spot, he slipped the nylon zip tie around her neck, killing her, then drove her body to his house, and placed it in the kitchen. He did not have as much time as he would have liked, as Terri would soon be coming home, so he had to content himself by fondling the body, squeezing the breasts, and rubbing the genitals before placing his penis in the mouth. He later admitted that he wanted to mutilate the body with his saw, but there would be too much blood to clean up. So he put Lillian's body in his car and drove to a murky river, where he tossed her over the railings and into the water. The corpse was found by fishermen in March, many miles along from where she had been dumped.

Thirty-eight-year-old Caucasian prostitute, Marilyn Nevils, was picked up by Sean in October of that same year, agreeing to oral sex for $10. Driving her to a quiet spot in Lafayette parish, he waited until Marilyn had finished, then slipped the usual nylon zip tie around her neck. To his surprise, it would not lock, and Marilyn seized upon her chance to escape, kicking and hitting him, and smashing the windshield. She managed to get out of the car and ran off, followed by Sean, clutching a metal bar he had spotted along the way. He caught up with her and smashed the metal bar against her head repeatedly until she fell to the ground, zip tie still around her neck. Sean pulled it tight until she was dead, and then put her in the car, intending to take her to his house. However, he was so excited, he pulled over to ogle her naked body before continuing on his journey. Taking her corpse into the house, he was shocked to see warm urine spilling from the body, and decided he would shower with it. He tried to put his penis in the mouth, but a locked jaw stopped it, and he did not have time to cut the body up, so just held it close for a while, then wrapped it in packing paper and took it to the river. He left the naked body on the levee, where it would lie, undiscovered, for 11 days. Marilyn Nevils had not even been reported missing.

Three years would pass before Gillis committed another murder. In October 2003, he found Johnnie Mae Williams, a black female friend whose home he had once been to for Thanksgiving dinner, streetwalking to feed her drug habit. She readily got into his car. He drove to a grassy area behind a restaurant, where he punched her in the head and body, repeatedly. Frail from years of drug abuse and self-neglect, Johnnie Mae had no strength to fight back, and soon fell to the ground dead. Stripping her naked, Sean took out his knife and sliced along the back of her leg, cutting deeply into the muscles. He punched then mutilated her buttocks, making an incision that ran from her lower back into the crease between the buttocks, and then cut open the back of the other leg. He continued to cut and punch repeatedly, relishing the sight of the veins, muscles, and tissues of the legs. Next he sawed through both wrists, severing the hands and dropping them into a ziplock bag for his later enjoyment. Gathering up her clothing, which he placed in a box in the trunk, he sat the body in the front passenger seat, and then drove off to some woods. He dragged Johnnie's corpse to an embankment, over which he draped it, with arms tucked underneath and buttocks raised up into the air. Sean took photographs for his later pleasure, and returned to his car, where he removed the severed hands from the ziplock bag and rubbed them all over his body. A young boy riding his four-wheeler through the woods found the body.

In February 2004, following his usual pattern, Sean spotted Caucasian prostitute Donna Bennett Johnston, 43, walking unsteadily at 3 a.m., and agreed to pay her for oral sex. She got into his car and fell asleep as he drove around, looking for a secluded place to park. As he began to cinch the nylon zip tie around her neck, Donna woke up, jumped out of the car and took off running across the field. Sean gave chase, caught up with her, grabbed the end of the zip tie and pulled it tight until Donna was dead. The murder had occurred in the parish of East Baton Rouge. Putting the body in the trunk of his car, Sean drove off, knowing that the darkness would soon lift. He found a suitable place to park, and put the body on the ground before grabbing his tools. He removed Donna's clothing and discovered that she had been wearing a wig, which he removed, along with her dental plate. He sawed the arm at the elbow, forcing the blade through flesh, muscle, and bone until the limb fell off. Noticing a butterfly tattoo on the right thigh, he dug around it with his knife, removing the chunk of flesh and rolling it between his fingers before placing it carefully on the ground. He excised the right nipple, and then mutilated the left breast, slicing off the other nipple. He then cannibalized both nipples. Putting the body in the trunk, he carefully wrapped the tattooed flesh in a paper towel, and the severed arm in a cloth. He took photographs and fondled the mutilated breasts, the vagina, and the remains of the arm. Satisfied with his work, he put the body in the trunk and threw the dental plate and wig into the woods before driving off toward his home. Dragging Donna's mutilated corpse across the ground, he posed it with the buttocks pointing up in the air, severed arm tucked beneath the torso, and her jacket covering the face and right arm. He then stomped on her back, leaving behind a bloody shoeprint. Driving for miles, Sean got out of the car and threw the tattooed piece of flesh into a roadside ditch, then he drove some more miles, stopped, and threw the severed arm into a levee so that it would be washed away by the river. His final stop, near Baton Rouge, was to toss into a ditch the cloth that had been wrapped around the arm.

Following up on tire track evidence at the Johnson crime scene, police arrived at Gillis's door in April 2004. They took a deoxyribonucleic acid (DNA) sample and found that Gillis's DNA matched that of the killer of Katherine Hall, Johnnie Mae Williams, and Donna Bennett Johnson. Arrested on these three counts of murder and ritualistic acts, Gillis gleefully confessed to the other murders, going into great and lurid detail. From time to time, he would ask for a lawyer, only to return to talking immediately after.

On April 29, 2004, police searched the home Gillis shared with Terri Lemoine. Items expected to be found on the warrant included plastic tie wraps, cutting instruments, blood, hair, photographs, printed and electronic documents, fingerprints, CDs, DVDs, cameras, jewelry, clothing, and body parts. After searching the premises, the following items were bagged:

1. Fourteen condoms
2. A wooden club
3. Pocketknife with 2-inch blade
4. Machete
5. Two hacksaws missing their blades
6. Multipurpose tool
7. Two toolboxes
8. Two saws
9. An axe
10. A Maglite flashlight
11. A black and silver belt
12. A pair of black shoes
13. Eighteen books: *The Blooding, The Hillside Strangler, Son of Sam, An Unquiet Mind, Alone With the Devil, Cops & Robbers, Sudden Fury,* and *The Silence of the Lambs*
14. Four *Pocket Fox* magazines and eight *Playboy Playmate* magazines
15. Three photographs of Johnnie Mae Williams
16. A digital camera
17. Kodak memory stick
18. Three hard drives
19. Three computer towers
20. Photos and articles on Carrie Yoder, victim of convicted Baton Rouge serial killer Derrick Todd Lee

On subsequent searches of the home, they took away:

1. A bayonet with 14-inch blade
2. Three kitchen knives
3. A cooler

4. A scanner
5. Two pieces of shoe molding
6. Thirty-one VHS cassette tapes
7. Empty VHS case
8. Two pornographic videos
9. Two rolls of film
10. Photographs

Among the various folders of pornography, from "Asians" to "Old Fucks," on his computer, were the much more nefarious files "B&W Dead," "Beheadings and Hangings," "Best of Snuff," "Bondage," "Dead Webs," "Extra Dead," "Fake Dead," "Russian Necro World," and "Various Dead" distributed between the folders "Kinky" and "Macabre."

Gillis was indicted in East Baton Rouge Parish on June 10, 2004, for the first-degree murder of Donna Bennett Johnson. According to Louisiana State Law, a murder can only be first-degree if it is perpetrated alongside another felony offense, thus the murder charge was also accompanied by charges of second-degree kidnapping and armed robbery. July 15, 2005 saw Gillis indicted for the killing of Joyce Williams in the parish of West Baton Rouge.

An adamant opponent of capital punishment, Gillis's defense attorney managed to delay the trial until mid-2008. He also argued vociferously that (i) Gillis's confession should be excluded from his trials as he had twice asked for a lawyer and (ii) that Gillis had neither robbed nor kidnapped his victims. In West Baton Rouge, Judge Free ruled that the videotape of Gillis's confession would be allowed in his courtroom, while Judge Bonnie Parker, who was presiding over the trial in East Baton Rouge parish, excluded it.

The issue of robbery is particularly relevant to the legal prosecution of HNs because it centers around whether a human body part is an item that actually can be stolen. The decision of Judge Jackson was that because body parts have no monetary value, it is not "theft" to steal them from a dead body in Louisiana. Fortunately, for the prosecution, a belt taken from Johnson did qualify as theft, meaning that the death penalty they hoped for was still on the table. Prem Burns, the prosecutor in the Johnson case, also successfully filed a Prieur motion which would allow her to introduce the evidence that Gillis had killed Johnnie Mae Williams and Katherine Hall to the jury during the punishment phase of the trial, should Gillis be found guilty.

In August 2007, Gillis agreed to a Crosby Plea in West Baton Rouge Parish, which, in this case, entailed pleading guilty to the second-degree murder of Joyce Williams on the condition that he could appeal if the Louisiana Court of Appeal later ruled that his confession would be excluded as evidence from his trial. Gillis received a life sentence in prison without the possibility of parole.

On July 21, 2008, Sean Gillis stood trial for the first-degree murder, armed robbery, and kidnapping of Donna Bennett Johnson. Even without his confession, the evidence against him was so overwhelming that there was little chance of him being found innocent. After 3.5 h of deliberation, on July 25, the jury unanimously found him guilty of first-degree murder.

The next day, the sentencing portion of the trial commenced. For the first time, Prem Burns introduced the jurors to the fact that Sean Gillis had also been connected through DNA to the murders of Johnnie Mae Williams and Katherine Hall. At this phase, the defense's strategy was to show that Gillis suffered from any number of psychiatric disorders. They called forensic psychologist and neuropsychiatrist Thomas Reidy to prove that if Sean Gillis was spared capital punishment, that he was unlikely to violently reoffend in prison, basing his conclusions on static actuarial measures. Next, neuropsychologist Dr. Ruben Gur used quantitative analysis to explain that Gillis's amygdala, occipital lobe, corpuscallosum, and right hemisphere were all abnormal. He diagnosed Gillis as suffering from schizoaffective disorder. He proposed that Gillis's brain had congenital defects, but had also likely been further compromised by head injuries.

Finally, psychiatrist Dr. Dorothy Lewis took the stand, revealing that she had interviewed Gillis for 26 h. She ran down the history of psychosis on Gillis's paternal side of the family and the mood disturbance on his maternal side. Lewis said that Gillis had suffered numerous head injuries as a child, and that damage to his frontal lobe might also affect his amygdala. He had told her that he experienced migraines and seizures, had been sexually abused, believed that ants had infiltrated his brain, that he wanted to kill his female side "Goldilocks," and hallucinated. A Star Trek fanatic, he also referred to himself as "Admiral Sean Gillis." Dr. Lewis believed that Gillis was bipolar.

The prosecution called Dr. Donald Hoppe, a clinical psychologist, to rebut these claims. Hoppe noted that there had simply been too many diagnoses, and that in science it is desirable to seek parsimony. Hoppe proposed that Gillis had Asperger's syndrome, instead. A number of neurologists also testified that they had examined Gillis's brain and found no deviations of significance.

At 5:45 p.m., after 2 h and 45 min of deliberation, the jury announced that they were unable to reach a verdict, meaning that Sean Gillis was automatically sentenced to life imprisonment by Judge Jackson. On February 17, 2009, he pled guilty to the first-degree murder of Marilyn Nevils in Lafayette parish and received another life sentence (Mustafa and Israel, 2011).

Characteristics of Necrophilic Homicides and Their Perpetrators

Offenders who receive sexual gratification from acts perpetrated on their victims' corpses are a remarkably heterogeneous group. For the purposes of this chapter, biographical information and video footage of 14 HNs has been reviewed in order to determine their approximate scores on the Psychopathic Checklist-Revised. In a 15th case, the HN was scored as a psychopath by another clinician who had interviewed him and conducted a case file review. Readers who are not familiar with the construct of psychopathy are encouraged to read Chapter 9. All but one of these offenders met the criteria for a serial killer, and were drawn from the United Kingdom (3), United States (11), and the former Soviet Union (1). Their scores ranged from as low as 14.7 to the notably high score of 37. Eight of the 15 offenders (53.3%) did not meet the cutoff score of 30 points to qualify them as Hare psychopaths. Of the remaining seven (46.6%) who had scores of 30 or higher, only four could be considered actual necrophiles. The remaining four were all *dabblers* or *pseudonecrophiles* in Rosman and Resnick's terms. In fact, only one *dabbler* (25% of the total *dabblers*) did not qualify as a Hare psychopath from the sample of four. This seems to reflect Porter et al.'s (2000, 2009) findings that psychopaths are equal opportunity sex offenders (see Chapter 9: Psychopathic Homicide Offenders; Table 7.3).

Though biographical secondary sources have been used in academic publications by Rosman and Resnick (1989), Dietz et al. (1990), Stone (1998, 2016), Leyton (1985/1995), and Katz (1988), they are admittedly insufficient for completely reliable diagnoses, and the sample size of this study is not large enough to merit any definitive findings. Nevertheless, in the absence of other research, this exercise establishes a useful heuristic for those looking to interview offenders who have committed postmortem sexual offences. This tentative finding is that offenders who consistently perpetrate homicides involving necrophilous acts tend not to be psychopaths, at least, in Hare's conception of the term. However, offenders who commit postmortem sex acts with corpses once or very rarely over a series of homicides seem to have higher rates of psychopathy. To reiterate, these findings are preliminary and tenuous, and should therefore be applied with caution. It is hoped that its implications might provide an impetus for further, more stringent research.

Table 7.3 Psychopathic Checklist-Revised Scores in Homicidal Necrophiles

Name of Killer	Homicidal Necrophile Category	Total PCL-R Score	Facet 1 Score	Facet 2 Score	Facet 3 Score	Facet 4 Score	Nonaligned to Facet
Bundy, Ted	A	**33**	8	8	8	7	2
Chase, Richard	E	26.3	1	7	9	7[a]	1
Chikatilo, Andrei	C	14.7	3	6[a]	2	1	2
Christie, John	B	25.3	6	6[a]	7	3	2
Dahmer, Jeffrey	A	25	4	6	9	4	2
Dixie, Mark	E	**32.2**	8	6[a]	6	7[a]	2
Dixon, Samuel	B	**33**	?	?	?	?	?
Gillis, Sean	A	27	6	8	7	4	2
Kemper, Ed	A	22	5	6	4	6	1
Nelson, Earle	D	**32.6**	5	6[a]	9	9	2
Nilsen, Dennis	B	16	4	7	2	1	2
Ramirez, Richard	E	**36**	7	8	9	10	2
Ridgway, Gary	E	21.1	5	7	2	3[a]	3
Rolling, Danny	E or F	**34.7**	5	8	10	8[a]	2
Russell, George	E	37	8	8	10	9	2

[a] Facet in which one of the items was omitted according to the recommended procedure of the PCL-R because there was insufficient evidence to score it accurately.

For the most part, the psychopathic HNs found in this exercise were typically misogynistic sexual sadists who exhibited a predatory charm. Nearly all of them could be described as nomadic. The nonpsychopathic HNs seemed to lack interpersonal skills and tend toward introversion, insecurity, shyness, and solitude. This asocial quality may be tied to the nature of their paraphilia: the individual struggles to form or maintain relationships with sexual partners due to their social deficits and begins to fantasize about a partner who is anthropomorphic but does not possess the capacity to resist their sexual advances, reject or criticize them, or abandon them—a corpse.

Based upon the research of Money (2011), Rosman and Resnick (1989), and Hickey (2013), Mellor (2016e) has conceptualized this as the *passivity/inertia* allure of necrophilia, and proposes that it explains necrophilia's frequent comorbidity with *pygmalionism*—the fetishism of dolls, mannequins, or statues—and *somnophilia* which is the sexual attraction to sleeping or unconscious people. These three paraphilias are linked along the theme of stillness. The inverse may also be true, where the necrophile's obsession with fantasies of corpses or people as passive objects makes them disinterested in living persons, leading them to interact less with others. Thus, necrophiles do not acquire the interpersonal skills one gains from regular socializing. This social detachment may reflect schizoid or schizotypal personality disorders, or autism spectrum disorders (American Psychiatric Association, 2013).

Identifying and Investigating Necrophilic Homicides

Crime Scenes

A homicide investigator or criminal profiler should immediately entertain the notion that they have stumbled upon a necrophilic crime scene if there is evidence of postmortem sexual activity (obviously) or postmortem mutilation such as *decapitation, dismemberment, evisceration, disfigurement*, or the *excision* or elaborate *incision* of body parts (Mellor, 2016b).

Mellor (2016a) refers to PPSAs in which an excised body part is touched or held by the offender as the individual masturbates or spontaneously ejaculates, or comes into some degree of contact with his genitals. Body parts known to have been used for PPSAs by necrophilic offenders include heads (Ted Bundy, Doug Clark), breasts ("The Chicago Rippers"), feet (Jerry Brudos), arms and hands (Luka Magnotta, Lam Kor Wan), legs (Sean Gillis), hair (Danilo Restivo), viscera (Jeffrey Dahmer), and, potentially, fingers and toes (Fred West) and eyeballs (Charles Albright). Thus, when a body part has been *excised* from a corpse, investigators should entertain the possibility that a necrophilic offender is at work. Often the body part in question has been so fetishized that the offender will ritualistically remove it after every homicide. However, as we saw in the Gillis case, the same offender may also enact different mutilations with different victims at different times.

Linkage Analysis and Offender Profiling

Given their statistical rarity, the idea that (i) crimes involving postmortem sexual acts should be linked, (ii) crimes involving paraphilic postmortem mutilation should be linked, and (iii) crimes involving cannibalism or vampirism should be linked, is obvious. As the Gillis case demonstrates, however, it is also advisable for investigators to consider linking homicides in which the corpse has remained intact but postmortem sex acts have clearly occurred (preservative)—including penile and/or foreign object penetration of the mouth, vagina, anus, or open wounds, or masturbation onto a dead body or next to it—with murders where body parts have been excised or other postmortem mutilation has occurred (destructive), regardless of any forensic evidence of sexual activity. Gillis both committed PPSAs on several of his victims, and disfigured and eviscerated some while engaging in preservative postmortem sex with the bodies of others. As he dumped most of his victims' bodies where they were easily found, forensic evidence of both PPSAs and preservative necrophilic sex was detectable. An important rule of thumb is that the presence of the overarching paraphilia of necrophilia should always take precedence over the individual differences present in necrophilia-spectrum behaviors.

The table below outlines the discrepancies in victimology and necrophilic behaviors enacted by Sean Gillis on his first four victims. Police investigators in Baton Rouge during the time of the murders would have likely not linked crimes 1 and 3 to the same perpetrator, let alone to crimes 2 and 4. However, the necrophilia-spectrum signature behavior—rare in even the largest cities—is evident across all four cases (Table 7.4).

Below is a complete list of necrophilia-spectrum paraphilias which may be present in a single offender, meaning that the sexual activities associated with each paraphilia may be used to establish a link between killings. The names of the paraphilias are provided in italics, with their behavioral manifestations in parentheses.

Table 7.4 First Four Known Homicide Victims of Sean Vincent Gillis

Gillis Victim (Age/Race). All Victims Are Female	Date and Location Where Body Was Discovered	Necrophilic Behaviors Known to Police	Necrophilic Behaviors Unknown to Police
1. 82/w	1994/retirement home where murder took place	*Partially decapitated*; *Eviscerated*; Breast, face, and vagina *disfigured*. Body *posed*	N/A
2. 30/b	1999/victim transported to outdoor area where they were left after they were murdered	Breasts, arms, and legs *incised*. Eye *excised*. *Incisions* to genitals and stomach	N/A
3. 52/w	1999/body transported to outdoor area	Hit with offender's car. Postmortem vaginal intercourse	N/A
4. 36/b	1999/body transported to outdoor area	*Partially dismembered*. Legs *incised*. *Decapitated*. Nipples *excised*	Nipples cannibalized. PPSAs with severed head

Note: PPSAs, partialist postmortem sex acts.

Necropenetrolagnia (evidence of postmortem vaginal, oral, or anal penetration)

Sexual arousal from penetrating a corpse with the phallus, or arranging a corpse so that their phallus penetrates one's orifice(s) (Mellor, 2016a).

Necrocoitolagnia (a more specific subparaphilia of necropenetrolagnia, evidenced by postmortem vaginal penetration)

Sexual arousal from penile–vaginal penetration involving a corpse (Mellor, 2016a).

Necrofellatiolagnia (a more specific subparaphilia of necropenetrolagnia, evidenced by postmortem oral penetration)

Sexual arousal from oral–penile penetration involving a corpse (Mellor, 2016a).

Necrosodomolagnia (a more specific subparaphilia of necropenetrolagnia, evidenced by postmortem anal penetration)

Sexual arousal from penile–anal penetration involving a corpse (Mellor, 2016a).

Necroexteriolagnia (masturbation onto or within sight of a corpse)

Sexual arousal from pleasuring oneself in the vicinity of, or on the exterior of a corpse (Mellor, 2016a).

Anthropophagy (consumption of body parts) and *vampirism* (consumption of blood)

Anthropophagy "more commonly known as cannibalism, is sexual arousal from the consumption of human flesh" (Mellor, 2016a). Vampirism is sexual arousal from tasting or ingesting human blood. Both anthropophagy and vampirism have been linked to necrophilia by a number of researchers, historic and contemporary (Épaulard, 1901; Stekel, 1929/2013; Prins, 1985; Green McGowan, 2006; Heasman and Jones, 2006; Aggrawal, 2011; Mellor, 2016a; Boon, 2016; Stone, 2016).

Necromutilophilia (evidence of paraphilic postmortem mutilation)

Sexual arousal derived from the mutilation of corpses (Mellor, 2016b).

Necrornopositophilia (evidence of paraphilic posing or dressing of corpse)

"Sexual gratification derived from posing and/or decorating a corpse" (Mellor, 2016a). This may be difficult to discern from *expressive/transformative* (nonparaphilic) posing of the corpse—such as when serial killer Colin Ireland arranged two teddy bears in a "69" position on the body of a homosexual victim (Gekoski, 2000)—because *necrornopositophilic* posing always encompasses *expressive/transformative* psychological reinforcement to some degree. Rather than considering the sexual symbolism of posing or decorating a corpse, it is recommended that one should focus only on the direct sexual posing or dressing of the body itself (e.g., pantyhose is put on the corpse of a female victim, a female victim is found nude and posed so that her legs are intentionally splayed).

Placophilia

"Sexual arousal from tombstones and grave markers" (Arntfield, 2016).

Pygmalionism/Agalmatophilia

Sexual arousal from dolls or mannequins.

Sarxenthymiophilia

Sexual arousal to flesh souvenirs (Stone, 2016).

Somnophilia

"Sexual arousal while watching a person sleep" (Hickey, 2013, p. 192).

Taphophilia

"Sexual arousal from funerals...which by some definitions can also extend to being sexually aroused by cemeteries and tombstones" (Mellor, 2016a).

Thanatohierophilia

"Sacred and/or religious artifacts associated specifically with death or funerary practices are eroticized" (Mellor, 2016a).

Thanatophilia

Sexual attraction to death as a concept, rather than corpses or *only* corpses (Mellor, 2016a).

Visceralagnia

Sexual arousal from viewing and/or touching internal organs.

Though many HNs seem to share specific personality traits (introversion, timidity, inadequacy), these are not consistent enough across HNs as a whole to allow definite claims to be made about an offender based on their paraphilic activities alone. However, there are several antecedents that are overrepresented in the backgrounds of HNs that deserve mention. One comorbidity we have discussed is that of *somnophilia* along the theme of stillness. With this in mind, it is suggested that investigators look at any prior offences, homicidal or nonhomicidal, in the area where the HN is known to operate which involve (1) victims being watched or attacked as they sleep, (2) victims being knocked unconscious or drugged before being sexually assaulted, or (3) particularly unusual activities in cemeteries or at funeral services. The first two may be modus operandi elements which have been subsequently sexualized, or they may instead be paraphilic acts associated with the theme of stillness. HN Ted Bundy attacked several of his first and last victims while they were asleep in bed, and was known to club nearly all of his victims unconscious before raping them (Leyton, 1985/1995). Jeffrey Dahmer drugged and sexually assaulted a number of victims before and after he began his murder series in earnest (Hickey, 2013). In Canada, "Bedroom Strangler" Russell Johnson progressed from breaking into women's apartments to observe them while they slept, to sexually assaulting them in their beds, and then to acts of necrophilia (Mellor, 2012). British HN John Christie rendered his female victims unconscious with gas before raping their inert bodies (Gekoski, 2000). Later he would keep their corpses in an alcove to be used sexually.

Regarding the graveyards and funerals, HN Ed Gein was grave robbing for years prior to committing his first known murder. Similarly, "Green River Killer" Gary Ridgway—who routinely participated in acts of postmortem intercourse with his victims' bodies—admitted that he had considered grave robbing to obtain victims (E. Hickey, personal communication). Sean Gillis informed law enforcement that as a child "I spent a lot of time at my grandmother's, had a funeral home right across the street. And me and my cousin we would do morbid things like sleep in the coffins…" (Weller, 2014). Suspected necrophile John Wayne Gacy admitted to a similar activity while he was employed at a funeral home (Mellor, 2016e).

Occasionally, investigators might stumble upon the residence of a necrophile which contains a hoard of human anatomical parts. The case of Jeffrey Dahmer is perhaps most infamous of these. Dahmer engaged in sexual activities in funeral homes, though was never caught for these. His case is also remarkable due to the sheer number of necrophilia-spectrum paraphilias that he is known to have evidenced.

HN Case Study 3: Jeffrey Dahmer (Category A: Cold/Destructive)

At 11:30 p.m. on July 22, 1991 in Milwaukee, Wisconsin, a black male frantically waved down two policemen on North 25th Street. Identifying himself as Tracy Edwards, the 32-year-old man who had handcuffs dangling from his wrists, told them how he had escaped the clutches of a crazed white man. According to Edwards, the man had given him $100 and alcohol for the pleasure of his company, and invited him back to apartment 213 in the nearby Oxford Apartments. When he was distracted, the white man had suddenly pulled a knife, slapped handcuffs on him, and held him prisoner, forcing him to watch the movie *Exorcist II* in his smelly bedroom. Edwards had convinced the man to unlock his handcuffs to allow him to go to the bathroom, and once he was free, had struck him and fled the apartment.

When the officers were unable to use their own keys to remove the handcuffs from Edwards's wrist, they decided to drive him back to the apartment so that the abductor could use his key to unlock them. Approaching apartment 213, the police noticed a noxious stench surrounding the area. They knocked on the door which was opened by the tenant, a tall cooperative Caucasian named Jeffrey Lionel Dahmer. Though Dahmer agreed to retrieve the key, the officers entered the apartment with him to look around and observed Polaroids of mutilated corpses and disembodied parts in the bedroom. When it occurred to them that the photographs had been taken in the apartment, they wrestled Dahmer to the floor, and despite his resistance, managed to handcuff him.

Along with 83 photos of male corpses in various stages of mutilation, in Dahmer's apartment, officers from police squad 216 found a human head in the fridge and two plastic bags each containing a heart. A third bag packed with excised muscle was retrieved from the adjoining freezer. Inside a separate standing freezer were three additional heads and two plastic bags with the first holding a human torso and the second portions of flesh and internal organs. Two bleached skulls, a carved out genital region, and an aluminum kettle with two human hands were all discovered inside a hallway closet. A filing cabinet contained three green-painted skulls, a paper bag with mummified genitals, a second paper bag with a section of scalp, and a human skeleton. Inside a blue 57-gallon plastic drum were three decomposing human corpses. A complete human skeleton hung from the shower head and another box contained a disembodied human head (Masters, 1993; Hickey, 2013).

Over the next few days, technicians carefully removed biological and other evidence from the apartment. In the meantime, Dahmer had confessed to having committed 17 murders of young men and teenaged boys from 1978 to 1991, four of which had been slain within the past 3 weeks. Only three of Dahmer's victims had been white, while the rest consisted of blacks, Hispanics, and Asians. Later this would lead to accusations that both Dahmer and the Milwaukee police were racist. Dahmer would use the 57-gallon blue drum to dissolve his victims' body parts in muriatic acid, which he then poured into the drain or flushed down the toilet for disposal. Wishing to keep trophies of his victims so that they would never leave him, Dahmer boiled many of the body parts till the flesh separated, and collected the bones. Dahmer's plan was to construct an altar from human bones and skulls, illuminated by blue lights—which he had drawn a schematic of—so that he could sit in front of it in a large black chair meditating to gain power. He had purchased yellow contact lenses for the occasion and hoped to become like the character of The Emperor from the *Star Wars* Trilogy. He also admitted to eating portions of his victims so that they would always "be part" of him.

Thirty-one years earlier, on May 21, 1960, Jeffrey Lionel Dahmer had been born at Evangelical Deaconesses Hospital in Milwaukee, the first child of Lionel Herbert Dahmer and Joyce Annette Dahmer (née Flint). Lionel, a PhD student in chemistry, soon relocated his family to suburban Ohio. The first signs that anything was amiss came when Jeffrey had a double hernia operation at the age of 4. Following the procedure, he was in so much pain that he reportedly asked his mother whether the doctor had cut off his penis. Though some psychiatrists have speculated that this trauma may have laid the foundation for his subsequent paraphilias, this cannot be verified. Lionel has himself explained that following the operation, Jeff seemed to transform from a happy-go-lucky child to being withdrawn and silent.

It did not help matters that Lionel was often away from home studying well into the night, while Joyce was practically bedridden with depression, being hospitalized for a month following a nervous breakdown. Nevertheless, in 1966, the Dahmers moved once more to Doylestown and gave Jeff a younger brother, David. Lionel found gainful employment as an analytical chemist in Akron. Painfully shy and sick of hearing his parents argue, Jeffrey would spend most of his time alone in the woods behind his home. The unemotional and socially isolated youth retreated into a world of fantasy. When combined with his fascination about anatomy—an interest that was initially fostered by his well-meaning father with whom he collected animal bones in a metal pail, then deepening following his dissection of a fetal pig in biology class—Dahmer began to develop necrophilic desires at the age of 14. He would ride around on his bicycle collecting roadkill in a garbage bag, then eviscerating them in the woods so that he could play with their viscera. The forensic psychiatrist Park Dietz, who interviewed Dahmer at length, would later comment on this bizarre sexual development:

The best we could figure out as to how eventually some of the gross kinds of images that happened with the mutilation of the human corpse could become sexy to him were his thinking about dissection of animals while masturbating as an adolescent. He had done high school biology class dissections and also had collected some dead animals from the woods and kept their body parts. Now most kids who would have those experiences don't think about that as they masturbate, they instead think about a cute human. So that's a mistake (ABC News Productions, 2005).

Dahmer also built a pet cemetery complete with crosses, and began to keep specimens in jars.

In high school, Dahmer became increasingly aware that not only was he a perpetual outsider but also a homosexual—which was highly stigmatized in 1970s in Wisconsin. He began to drink heavily—Scotch or vodka—and was often seen staggering around the school. In a failed attempt to ingratiate himself to his classmates, he would play practical jokes such as faking seizures or anaphylactic reactions to food in public. With his parents making no progress in marriage counselling, combined with his own severe problems, the highly intelligent Dahmer's grades plummeted. At age 16, having read about a young man who had been killed in a motorcycle accident, Dahmer went to the funeral home to view the body in a coffin and became so aroused that he masturbated in the restroom. That same year, he lay in wait with a baseball bat for a man who jogged past his house every day, plotting to beat him unconscious and sexually assault him. Fortunately, for the jogger, on that day he did not pass by.

In the summer of 1978, when Dahmer was 18 and following his high school graduation, Lionel and Joyce finally called it quits. Joyce took Jeff's younger brother David and moved away, while Lionel went to live in a nearby motel. Feeling abandoned yet simultaneously free from his parents' watchful eyes, Dahmer picked up an attractive 18-year-old hitchhiker named Steven Hicks who was on his way to a concert at Chippewa Lake. The two went back to the Dahmer's residence where they drank alcoholic beverages and listened to music. However, when Hicks decided to leave, Dahmer smashed a 10-pound barbell into his head, and then strangled him to death. He spent the next 2 days mutilating and masturbating over Hicks's corpse, plunging his hands into his warm internal organs. Eventually, Dahmer disposed of the remains by carving the flesh away, and smashing the bones into shards with a sledgehammer and scattering them. What little remained, he transported in garbage bags to the local dump.

Unaware that his son had committed murder, but concerned about his alcoholism, Lionel Dahmer tried to take him to Alcoholics Anonymous (AA) and then helped him enroll in college. Jeff did not last long in either, and by December 1978, Lionel compelled him to join the army in order to bring structure to his life. Unsurprisingly, Dahmer became a field medic. Shipped to West Germany, he lasted nearly his full 3-year term in the military before his alcoholism got the better of him, resulting in an early discharge.

Returning to the United States, Dahmer was afraid to face his father, and delayed the process as long as possible by living in a Miami Beach motel and working at a sandwich shop. Finally unable to pay rent due to his drinking, he called up Lionel to ask him for money. Instead, he received a plane ticket back to Ohio and soon he was sent to live with his highly religious grandmother in West Allis, a suburb of Milwaukee. But attempts to cure Jeffrey of his drinking and homosexual tendencies through regular church attendance were unsuccessful. In August 1982, Dahmer was fined $50 for indecently exposing himself to two youths at the Wisconsin State Fair. Undeterred, in September of 1986 he was caught masturbating in front of two 12-year-olds on the banks of the Kinnickinnic River, charged with disorderly conduct, and placed on a year's probation.

Increasingly, compelled to perpetrate acts of necrophilia, Dahmer tried to resist by stealing a mannequin (see *pygmalionism* above) from a department store to use as a sex toy. However, he also began to lurk around funeral homes again, and once tried to exhume the body of a teenage male from a cemetery, thwarted only by the frozen ground. He also regularly frequented gay bath houses where he participated in homosexual sex with strangers. Yet, though Dahmer enjoyed sodomizing other men, he was not fond of being on the receiving end, and dealt with this by crushing Halcion pills into his partners' drinks to anally rape them when they were unconscious (see *somnophilia* above). Word got around about him being a rapist, and he was no longer welcome at a number of bathhouses.

On September 15, 1987 he met 24-year-old Steven Tuomi at a gay bar, and the two decided to go back to a room at the Ambassador Hotel together. Dahmer, who had been drinking heavily, claims that he awoke the next day to find Tuomi beaten to death beside him, and his own fists bloodied, but had no recollection of murdering him. Panicked, he was able to effectively dispose of the young man's body by hiding it at his grandmother's house, butchering it and concealing it.

The Tuomi murder was to mark a point of no return for Dahmer, who would then go on to murder victims in increasingly shorter intervals—James Doxtator, 14, on January 17, 1988 (sodomized and corpse dismembered, kept skull); and Richard Guerrero, 23, on March 24, 1988 (performed fellatio on the corpse, dismembered the corpse, kept skull).

When his grandmother finally tired of Dahmer's erratic behavior, she kicked him out of the house, and he moved to 808 North 24th Street. To pay the rent, he worked as a chocolate mixer at the Ambrosia Chocolate Factory. On September 26, 1988, Dahmer approached a 13-year-old Laotian boy, Somsack Sinthasomphone, and asked him to pose for pictures back at his apartment in exchange for $50. Once there, Dahmer attempted to drug the boy by secreting crushed Halcion tablets in his Irish Cream Liqueur, then kissed and licked his stomach and fondled his genitals. The boy did not go unconscious, and upon returning to his parents, reported the incident to the police. Dahmer was arrested for second-degree sexual assault and enticing a child for immoral purposes. Evaluated by several psychologists, he was determined to be "in significant psychological distress" and unquestionably "in need of long-term psychological treatment." Furthermore, Dahmer was diagnosed as having schizoid personality disorder with paranoid features. Dahmer would eventually plead guilty to the crime on January 30, 1989, and was sentenced to a year in the house of correction and 5 years' probation. During this time, he was allowed out on work release 6 days a week at the Ambrosia Chocolate Factory, as long as he returned to the house of correction following his shift. On March 25, 1989, he picked up 26-year-old Anthony Sears at a gay bar, murdered him, decapitated and flayed his corpse, and excised and kept his genitals for PPSAs. Sears was the first of Dahmer's many African-American victims.

After successfully writing a letter pleading for leniency, Dahmer was released from the Work House on March 2, 1990. He became a resident of the Oxford Apartments at 924 North 25th Street, apt # 213. With his own place at last, Dahmer escalated in his criminal behavior, claiming the lives of 12 additional males from 1990 to 1991:

Victim (Age/Race)	Date	Criminal Behavior
Raymond Smith (33/B)	May 20, 1990	Dismembered corpse. Skull-painted gray and kept. Bones used as ornaments
Eddie Smith (27/B)	June 24, 1990	Body defleshed. Attempted to keep skeleton and skull unsuccessfully
Ernest Miller (22/B)	September 1990	Eviscerated. Organs excised. Dismembered. Skeleton reassembled and painted and kept in wardrobe, intended to be later used in shrine. Limbs, muscle, and organs placed in freezer for consumption
David Thomas (23/B)	September 24, 1990	
Curtis Staughter (19/B)	February 17, 1991	Dismembered corpse. Skull kept
Errol Lindsey (19/B)	April 7, 1991	Necrofellatiolagnic sex. Dismembered corpse. Skull kept
Tony Hughes (31/B)	May 24, 1991	Dismembered corpse. Skull kept
Konerak Sinthasomphone (14/A)	May 27, 1991	Hole drilled in skull and acid injected in failed attempt to make sex zombie. Corpse dismembered
Matt Turner (20/B)	June 30, 1991	Corpse dismembered and left in apartment
Jeremiah Weinberger (23/B)	July 7, 1991	Failed sex zombie experiment. Corpse dismembered
Oliver Lacy (23/B)	July 15, 1991	Corpse dismembered with *necrosodomolagnic* acts in between. Heart kept in refrigerator for consumption. Skeleton intended to be used in Dahmer's shrine
Joseph Bradehoft (25/W)	July 19, 1991	Corpse dismembered partially. Head and torso kept in apartment

Dahmer would often drug his victims unconscious and cuddle them, putting his head on their chest so that he could hear their hearts beat. This went hand-in-hand with his *visceralagnia*. In several bizarre attempts to create a "living sex zombie," he also drilled and injected acid or hot water into his victims' brains, only to have them die.

Jeffrey Dahmer is perhaps the most extreme case of homicidal necrophilia yet to be discovered, as he harbored almost all of the known necrophilia-spectrum paraphilias: *necroexteriolagnia, necropenetrolagnia, necromutilophilia, sarxenthymiophilia, somnophilia, pygmalionism, visceralagnia, necrornopositophilia, anthropophagy,* and *vampirism.*

During his January 13, 1992, preliminary hearing, Dahmer pled guilty but insane. Given this plea, District Attorney Michael McCann's primary interest when vetting jurors was to ensure that they did not conflate the depravity and scale of Dahmer's murders with insanity. This would become the fundamental focus of the proceedings.

The trial of Jeffrey Dahmer began on January 30, 1992, presided over by Judge Laurence Gram. "This was not an evil man," Defense Attorney Gerald Boyle said in the conclusion of his opening statement, "this was a sick man." When Tracy Edwards took the stand, he described how after pulling the knife on him, Dahmer displayed rapid and severe mood changes, which Edwards referred to as Dahmer "going out of himself" (Masters, 1993, p. 182). Similarly, he testified that he thought that Dahmer was "a crazy guy" (Masters, 1993, p. 182).

Early February would see numerous mental health professionals take the stand. The Defense first called Dr. Fred Berlin, the Director of the Sexual Disorders Clinic at Johns Hopkins University, followed by Dr. Judith Becker, a professor of psychiatry and psychology and a specialist in the field of paraphilia. Both Berlin and Becker asserted that because Dahmer suffered from the paraphilic disorder of necrophilia, he lacked the capacity to keep himself from acting on his urges. A cross-examination of Dr. Becker by the prosecution asked her why, if Dahmer had uncontrollable paraphilic urges necessitating homicide, was he able to stop himself from murdering Somsak Sinthasomphone because he had to go to work, or release another victim because he had put up too much physical resistance. Rather than dwelling on paraphilia, psychiatrist Dr. Carl Wahlstrom said that Dahmer was psychotic and suffered from borderline personality disorder, only without hallucinations, and that he killed so that he would not be alone. Wahlstrom stated that Dahmer was delusional.

These Defense experts were followed by the testimonies of two court-appointed psychologists who had interviewed Dahmer: Dr. George Palermo and Dr. Samuel Friedman. Palermo had diagnosed Dahmer as a sexual sadist,* judging him to have been legally sane at the time of the killings. He confessed that he had expected to find a major psychiatric illness after 4 h of interviewing, but had not been able to do so. Strangely, Palermo also doubted Dahmer's accounts of necrophilia, cannibalism, his desire to build a shrine, and the notion that he killed so that he would not be lonely. For his part, Dr. Friedman disagreed with Palermo, and confirmed the necrophilia diagnosis. He acknowledged that Dahmer certainly had psychological problems and practically no personal insight, but ultimately concurred with Dr. Palermo that Dahmer had been legally sane.

Dr. Frederick Fosdal was the first witness to testify for the prosecution. In his view, Dahmer was not mentally ill, simply "odd." Where Palermo had asserted that Dahmer was a rageful man who sought to destroy his own ego-dystonic homosexuality by murdering other gay men, Fosdal testified that he believed Dahmer dispassionately killed only those who he liked. He said that though Dahmer was a necrophile, this was not his primary paraphilia. Rather, Dahmer preferred unconscious males (*somnophilia*). Fosdal testified that paraphilia in itself was not enough to interfere with Dahmer's capacity to conform to the law, it only could if it were accompanied by another mental disease, of which he had found none. Like Dahmer himself, Fosdal said Dahmer's shrine was not evidence of delusion, it was simply unusual.

The final prosecution witness was the eminent psychiatrist Dr. Park Dietz. His approach was a practical one: he highlighted that Dahmer had taken precautions to avoid being seen in the company of his victims, acquired pills to sedate them beforehand, and scheduled his killings on weekends. He painstakingly went over each of the 15 cases for which Dahmer was standing trial, illustrating why Dahmer had been legally sane during all of them. Like Dr. Berlin, Dietz agreed that Dahmer was a necrophile, but said that though a person cannot choose to have a sexual desire, they can choose whether or not to act on it. He agreed with Dahmer's defense team that his last two homicides had been so erratic they basically ensured he would be caught, but Dietz attributed this to his alcoholism, not the influence of any kind of mental disease. When asked whether Dahmer's altar of bones and skeletons from which he desired to draw power qualified him as delusional, Dietz split hairs, saying that it did not because Dahmer did not fully believe that it would work, merely suspected it might. This was superstition, not delusion.†

On February 15, the jury found Jeffrey Lionel Dahmer to have been legally sane on all counts in a 10-2 decision. Shortly after, Judge Gram sentenced Dahmer to a life sentence plus 10 years to run consecutively for the first two counts, and life without the possibility of parole for 70 years for the remaining 13. After his sentence was passed, Dahmer was permitted to speak aloud to the public, saying "I feel so bad for what I did to those poor families, and I understand their rightful hate. I have seen their tears, and if I could give my life right now to bring their loved ones back, I would do it. I am so very sorry."

---

* A shockingly inept diagnosis. For an understanding of the sexually sadistic homicidal offender and why Dahmer was not this type of offender, please see Chapter 8.
† For a critical evaluation of the concept of superstition and delusion being separate, see my "Killing For Slender Man" in Arntfield's *The Criminal Humanities: An Introduction*.

Following an approved request to be transferred to a less secure area of the prison, in August 1994, Dahmer and a fellow prisoner, Jesse Anderson, were beaten to death with a metal bar by psychotic inmate Christopher Scarver (Davis, 1995; Masters, 1993).

Recommendations for Handling Cases of Necrophiles Who Kill

Interviewing

Due to what seems to be their lower levels of psychopathy per capita compared to other lust murderers, the psychological makeups and personalities of necrophilic murderers tend to be more diverse than those of sexual sadists. Contrast, for example, the cooperative and docile postarrest manner of nonpsychopath HN Jeffrey Dahmer with psychopath HN Ted Bundy's evasive manipulation. For this reason, an analysis of crime scene behavior is of little use in determining an interview strategy. It is recommended that potential interviewers (1) speak with friends, family, or coworkers of the offender and/or (2) surveil the offender's social interactions, in order to gather information on their personality traits before the interview begins. Naturally, this is contingent on whether such information can be acquired without jeopardizing the investigation or lives. A more viable option is to glean information from the casual interactions of the offender with investigating or arresting officers or guards, before deciding upon an interrogation strategy. If the offender shows confidence and extroversion, an approach to interviewing consistent with a psychopathic offender (see Chapter 9) is recommended. In the event that the offender presents as meek and cooperative, an interview style that is patient, sympathetic, and establishes trust will likely achieve better results. Psychosis is also represented in 11% of necrophilic sex offenders (Rosman and Resnick, 1989), so it is advisable to always keep the offender's disability in mind and conduct the interview accordingly. This will limit the possibility of false confession and prevent or mitigate effective criticism from defense attorneys as to how the interview was conducted when the case goes to trial.

Naturally, due to the virtually unrivalled stigma attached to necrophilic offending, an HN interviewee is often very reluctant to discuss the sexual nature of their crimes (Harkins et al., 2010). Detective Patrick Kennedy, who established a commendable rapport with Jeffrey Dahmer, which not only resulted in a full confession but also extended to subsequently interviews. describes his methods below:

> The first thing he said to me is "you're not going to let anybody hit me anymore are you?" and I said, "No…no one's going to hit you no more. As a matter of fact, no one else is going to talk to you but me. …Before we get started I'm going to myself a cup of coffee. Would you like one? Would you like a cigarette?" And to that he said, "I would love both"… I put my hand out and I said… "My name is Pat… and I'm the one that's going to be talking to you about the head in the refrigerator." And at that point he said to me "I really don't think that it's in my best interest to talk to you about this.".… He started asking me "what'll happen if I don't talk to you?" So I went into a very blasé description of our booking process, and as I was describing it he was kind of nodding, and I could see that he was very familiar with the booking process. And then he said to me, he goes, Is there anyways I could get my own cell. And as soon as he said that, I knew he was familiar with the booking process… And I picked up that he was afraid of the bullpen. And I said "well," I said, "tonight is a very busy night, I think every cell is full and that bullpen is packed. So you can stay here and talk to me"—and already he saw that he had a cup of coffee going and the cigarettes—"or you can go [to the bullpen]." You wanna make [suspects] uncomfortable but not too uncomfortable so you're… close enough to get intimate if you want, but far enough away were they're not feeling threatened… I said "well we could talk about other things…" We did have a lengthy location about many things…We also had a long talk about religion. I being a Catholic and I spent five years in the seminary. I knew some stuff about Martin Luther and the Lutheran religion… and he was actually knowledgeable on it we talked about it and that sent us into a whole discussion about God and whether or not there was a God. From that discussion about God where we were talking about a higher power which he did believe there was a higher power. He didn't know if it was God or the Devil… that also got us into a discussion about alcoholism, because I noticed that he was drunk and a couple of times during the thing he would blurt out, you know, "I can't believe this has happened to me… I can't believe I'm sitting here, I can't believe I got caught." And I said "well what did you think?" He goes, "I just got drunk. I lost control. I just got drunk, otherwise I wouldn't be here." And he wasn't telling me what happened but he kept referring to alcohol… At that point I started telling him that probably the head in the refrigerator probably had something to do with alcohol. If in fact you are an alcoholic, alcoholism is a disease. And then he started making tacit admissions like "well, for what I've done there's no excuse…" Not saying what he'd done but little tacit admissions where I knew he was starting to crack a little bit. He was starting to come forward… I said "hey Jeff… our forensic guys are at your apartment and they're afraid…" And all of a sudden I saw the realization and he said "you're in my house, searching my house?" And I said "well if we're not, we're going to Jeff. Of course, there's a homicide. We're going to go through everything in that house." Three

hours and ten minutes in… he finally said "well, you're going to find out everything now so it's no sense. I might as well tell you… But Pat, when I tell you what I'm going tell you, first of all you'll probably hate me." I said "Jeff, I've seen a lot of evil stuff, right. There's nothing you can do that would freak me out, right." I said "I've talked to a lot of murderers… besides that I don't believe in judging. We had this discussion about God. I'm not here to judge you. That's not what I'm about. I'm here to solve this problem." And then he said "well, when I tell you this Pat, you'll be famous." He said "If I'm going to tell you about it I might as well start at the beginning…" And that's when he started telling me about his first homicide back in Bath, Ohio, 13 years previous when he was 18-years-old… He started talking about his second victim… And then we went into two or three other victims that he was talking about… From there we talked until about 10:30 the next morning and by then he had given me the basic rundown of fifteen victims… Before Jeff was put in a cell I had made a deal with him that he would not talk to a lawyer until he helped me identify all of the victims. As an investigator, when somebody is put back in a jail cell you can't just go and talk to them the next day. That's against their constitutional rights. The only way they can talk to you is if they request to talk to you. And this [the fact that Dahmer did] gives a little insight into the relationship that I built with Jeffrey and that he bought into this relationship as his means of salvation (Smith et al., 2013).

Seemingly, the more extreme the necrophilic homicide is (Jeffrey Dahmer, Edmund Kemper III, Dennis Nilsen, Ed Gein), the more likely it will be that the suspect will be cooperative if the approach to interviewing is right. An important caveat, however, is that none of the four aforementioned offenders meet the Hare Psychopathy Checklist-Revised (PCL-R) criteria to be considered a Hare psychopath. Those who do, such as Ted Bundy, are likely to be much more difficult to interview. See "Interviewing" a Psychopathic Homicidal Offender in Chapter 9.

Building a Case against the Necrophile

As seen in the Gillis and, especially, the Dahmer case, HNs who perpetrate postmortem sex acts in their own residences are among the easiest sex slayers to build a case against, as there is often ample biological evidence from their victims in plain sight. Cold-destructive HNs, warm-destructive HNs, exclusive necromutilophiles, and sexual cannibals/vampires often excise their victims' body parts and take them home for consumption or to use in PPSAs. Cold-destructive HNs, cold-preservative HNs, and sexual cannibals/vampires may even keep their victims' bodies in tact in their residences.

In cases in which the acts of necrophilic homicide are perpetrated elsewhere, such as outdoors or in the victim's own residence, investigators must rely on conventional methods of gathering forensic evidence as they would in any other homicide. In short, if one is to stumble into an HN's lair, then the case becomes a relatively easy one to build, but if not, the criminal activities of an HN do not provide any significant advantage or disadvantage to investigators, only in linkage analysis.

The Dahmer and Gillis cases also show that by the 1990s, *cold/destructive* necrophiles started to photograph their victims' corpses in various stages of mutilation. Photographs the HN took of their victim may be in hard copy or in digital storage devices such as computers, external hard drives, etc. They could be stashed away (Gillis), or literally hanging from the walls (Dahmer).

Also, the Internet facilitates and the easy distribution and accessibility of photographs of human corpses in all states, and as the Gillis case evidences, HNs may use this as pornography. We know that Gillis used images of death for sexual stimulation because he stored them in the same file folder as his pornography. Such images, in this context, are important behavioral evidence which can help to prove that the offender had longstanding necrophilic interests. This is particularly crucial in cases such as the Gillis case, where the offender dumped the bodies of his victims outdoors in different parishes. The necrophilic violence that is behaviorally manifested on the body can now be linked to the statistically rare phenomena of a suspect who masturbates to corpse pornography. Similarly, items such as mannequins, coffins, etc. might be indicative of the *necrophilia-spectrum* behaviors discussed above, and should be treated as important pieces of evidence.

The search warrant for Sean Gillis's property is an excellent reference resource for investigators looking to draft one of their own for an HN.

Legal Aspects

When investigators find bodies or anatomical parts, or photos/video footage of an offender having sex with the corpse in the possession of a Cold-Destructive (category A) or Sexual Cannibal/Vampire (Category H) HN, they should prepare for some kind of insanity defense. As the overwhelming physical evidence makes a traditional "not guilty" claim nearly indefensible, and given the popular (inaccurate) belief (Rosman and Resnick, 1989) that anybody who would commit sexual acts and/or cannibalism on a corpse surely *must* be mentally ill, a not guilty by reason of insanity (NGRI)-type plea becomes the most feasible option for many HNs. So often is this defense used by HNs that leading up to the *Commonwealth of Pennsylvania v. Gregory R. Graf*—currently underway at the time of this writing—prosecuting attorney John Morganelli worked pre-emptively to have an NGRI plea barred (http://www.pennlive.com/nation-world/2015/10/da_wants_to_bar_insanity_defen.html).

In the case of Gillis, the defense attempted successfully to circumvent the death penalty by presenting evidence that Gillis had a number of debilitating mental health problems. As the jurors could not reach a unanimous verdict, in the State of Louisiana, this meant that Gillis received the lighter sentence. Jeffrey Dahmer's plea of guilty but insane was also disputed among the jurors, but the rules governing sentencing in Wisconsin do not require a unanimous vote, therefore he was judged to have been sane. Other important reference cases include *State of Wisconsin v. Edward Theodore Gein* and *Regina v. Luka Rocco Magnotta*.

The case of Mark Dixie provides us with an example of another defense for the HN, one in which an offender admitted to the lesser crime of sexually abusing a dead body in order to explain away DNA evidence implicating him in a homicide. This strategy has also been used by homicidal rapists like "Abbotsford Killer" Terry Driver who claimed that he had found the dying body of Tanya Smith and sexually assaulted her, but had not actually been the attacker.

HN Case Study 4: Mark Dixie (Category E: Dabbler)

Eighteen-year-old Sally Anne Bowman was an attractive aspiring model and singer who lived in Croydon, South London, UK. On the night of Saturday, September 24, 2005, Sally had gone out with her sister and others to celebrate a friend's birthday at Lloyd's Bar in central Croydon. She was driven home at 2:30 a.m. on September 25 by her recently ex-boyfriend, Lewis Sprotson. Parked within a few yards of Sally's home on Bleinhem Road, the two began to argue. At approximately 4:15 a.m., Sally exited the vehicle and started toward her home, while Lewis drove off.

Around that time, a neighbor was awoken from her sleep by a gurgling sound and a scream. Looking out of the window she saw nothing, but checking 5 min later, she spotted an adult male pass by. The neighbor returned to bed. At 6:30 a.m., neighbor Ann Harding noticed what she thought were two mannequin legs sticking out from behind a nearby skip (Dumpster). Upon further investigation, she was shocked to find the partially nude body of Sally Anne Bowman. The police were summoned to the scene, and later it was determined that Sally Anne had been stabbed seven times—three of the blows having penetrated her body and coming out of the other side—with two to the stomach, and three to the neck severing her carotid artery and damaging her voice box. Her attacker had also bitten her four times on the neck and breast, and there were indications that he had engaged in vaginal intercourse with her after death. He had also inserted pieces of concrete into her orifices, and made off with her Prada handbag, white cardigan, bra, thong, and mobile phone. But he had left something that would prove to be his undoing: DNA evidence on Sally's body.

When police finally found Lewis Sprotson, he explained to them that he had not talked to Sally since last night as they had had an argument. Suspecting him of the murder, they arrested Lewis, took DNA samples, and questioned him for 4 days. However, when the results of the DNA comparison came back from the lab, it indicated that Lewis was not the killer, and furthermore, that whoever had murdered Sally Anne Bowman had also been responsible for an unsolved 2001 sexual assault in Purley to the south. During that attack, a woman had been in a phone booth, when an adult male had suddenly pushed himself inside and masturbated onto the floor. Police also learned that minutes before Sally Anne's attack, only blocks away, a woman on her cell phone had been approached by a man who had said "I'm sorry" before repeatedly hitting her. Fortunately for her, a taxi driver had scared him away, though he had snatched her cell phone away from her in the process.

E-fits of the man responsible for the Purley attacks and the assault on the other woman just minutes before Sally Anne Bowman's murder were formulated and circulated. Police began door to doors of 6000 addresses in South Croydon, looking at 4000 local men who resembled the e-fit. At one point, they set up a local DNA center and asked for volunteers to submit samples of their DNA so that they could be eliminated and a possible familial DNA link could be established. Though this narrowed down the pool of suspects significantly, after 6 months the investigation had come to a standstill.

Then, on June 27, 2006, the DNA from Bowman's murderer was found to match that of 37-year-old man Mark Dixie, who had been arrested following a World Cup bar brawl in Crawley days earlier.

Dixie was an alcoholic chef and drug abuser who led a nomadic lifestyle, living and working in Australia and Spain. Born on September 24, 1970 in Streatham, he had been raised by his mother and stepfather in southeast London. At the age of 16, he was charged with fondling a woman's breasts at knifepoint, though the case never made it to court. By 1988, he had been convicted on multiple counts of robbery and indecent assault, as well as indecent exposure, serving time in prison. Moving with his girlfriend to Australia in 1993, Dixie travelled from Sydney to Queensland to Melbourne to Perth. While in Western Australia, he broke into the apartment of a student on June 21, 1998, stabbed her eight times then sexually assaulted her, and also became a suspect in the unsolved Claremont Killings of two young women, and the disappearance of a third in suburban Perth. At the time, he was not considered for the apartment stabbing and rape. But, having overstayed his visa, Dixie was deported from Australia in 1999 following yet another sexual offence committed on New Year's Day.

Aside from his sex crimes, which included an ongoing history of violent attacks and indecent exposure, Dixie also had multiple convictions for theft and robbery, and had assaulted a police officer.

A year after the murder of Sally Anne Bowman, Dixie had served 6 months in jail for attacking and threatening a married mother.

The night of the Bowman murder had been Dixie's 35th birthday and he had been drinking heavily and using cocaine with friends in Croydon. He had been "upset" that Stacey, the 21-year-old girlfriend who had broken up with him 3 weeks earlier, had not called to wish him happy birthday. Dixie returned to his friends' flat, but when they went to bed, he went out in search of a victim.

During his 4-week trial at the Old Bailey in 2008, Mark Dixie was faced with the problem of explaining how his semen, which had been identified by DNA analysis, had come to be in Bowman's vagina. His strategy was to claim that he had not committed the murder, but instead had found Bowman lying in the street and decided to rape her. He claimed that initially he thought she had just passed out or fallen over, but during the sex act realized that she was dead. That the story was ludicrous was not helped by witnesses testifying to other sexual attacks that Dixie had perpetrated on them, or a home video he had taken 6 months after the Bowman slaying which showed him masturbating over her photograph in the newspaper. Unsurprisingly, after 3 h of deliberation, the jury of seven women and five men unanimously convicted Dixie of murdering Sally Anne Bowman. Sentenced to a minimum of 34 years in prison, Dixie was denounced by Judge Gerald Gordon: "I shall only say that what you did that night was so awful and repulsive that I do not propose to repeat it… Your consequent conduct shows you had not the slightest remorse for what you had done." He has since been linked to several more sexual attacks in the United Kingdom and Spain, and cleared of any involvement in the Claremont cases.

Mark Dixie displays strong psychopathic traits and would be categorized as a *Category E: Dabbler* under Mellor's typology (occupying the *situational* level of necrophilia on the Thematic-Derivative model of sexual progression), and IXb under Aggrawal's classification system. He does not sufficiently display enough evidence of necrophilic predilections to be considered a genuine necrophile, instead it is likely that his willingness to have sex with a dead body more accurately reflects his psychopathy (Balakrishnan, 2008; Broughall and Alderton, 2012; Stubley, n.d.; Gammell, 2008).

Treatment

The literature on clinical treatment of necrophilia as a paraphilic disorder is incredibly scant. Kunkle (2016) has noted the significant difficulties in treating patients with necrophilia owing to (1) evidence of the paraphilia that is either lacking or not reliable enough to make an initial diagnosis and (2) the reluctance of necrophiles to admit to their predilections (Harkins et al., 2010). Like many paraphilic disorders, necrophilia remains largely invisible until an individual is convicted of necrophilic activities. Furthermore, clinicians neither receive the training in criminal investigation nor is there adequate information exchange between mental health practitioners to assist clinicians in forming a diagnosis. Finally, the frequently lengthy duration between the time the offender commits a crime and their mental health assessment means that important files often go missing in the interim.

Should a patient with necrophilic sexual preferences come to the attention of a clinician, Brankley et al. (2016) propose cognitive behavioral therapy (CBT) as a course of treatment. They recognize that most clinicians are familiar with these techniques, but may be reluctant to apply them to necrophilia because the subject matter seems to demand some other alternative. This necessitates "case conceptualization," which is of particular use in complex and abnormal cases.

Case conceptualization consists of four stages:

1. Identifying the problem through assessment of file information, conducting semistructured interviews with the patient, and speaking with somebody close to them if possible. Brankley et al. (2016) propose beginning an interview with a necrophilic patient by asking open-ended questions; however, if this method is unsuccessful, the authors provide a list of specific questions which may be broached.

2. Identifying the mechanisms—that is the feelings, thoughts, behaviors, and physical sensations—which support these necrophilic desires. The cluster of mechanisms, *sexual arousal, sexual sadism*, or *intimacy aversion*, is most likely to relate to necrophilic behavior. Sexual arousal seems to be associated with Mellor's *corporeal/sensory* allure, while the *passivity/inertia* allure corresponds more to intimacy aversion. The authors propose that *intimacy aversion*-based necrophilia should not be treated for deviant arousal, as they are not so much sexually attracted to a corpse, as not repelled by it. This would seemingly apply to all *dabblers* and *catathymic* necrophiles.

3. Identifying the proximal precipitants of necrophilia in order to comprehend the cycles of offending and preventing a relapse from occurring. As each precipitant in the chain of necrophilic offending can potentially be seized upon as a chance to break the cycle, this is of the utmost importance.

4. Identifying the distal origins of necrophilia in the individual. One of CBT's strengths is that it helps the clinician to develop a multifactorial model of the patient's issue (Brankley et al., 2016). Building empathy, interpersonal skills, and addressing chronic loneliness and innate hostility in the necrophilic patient are necessary as these are aspects of the client's personality which arguably facilitate necrophilic desire.

The authors also recommend the Risk–Need–Responsivity (RNR) model for the treatment of necrophiles along with a modified permutation being developed by Abracen and Looman (in press) and Looman and Abracen (2013).

Possible psychopharmacological treatment exists in the form of selective serotonin reuptake inhibitors (SSRISs) which lowers the sex drive and assists clients in dealing with negative emotions, making them more inclined to participate in treatment programs. They caution against medication used for androgen deprivation therapy (ADT), and advocate its use only in cases where the client has been determined to have an uncontrolled variant of the cluster mechanisms of sexual sadism and sexual arousal.

A treatment that has been found useful for pedophilia and should theoretically work similarly for necrophiles is the combination of aversive therapies, in which stimuli related to the deviant sexual desire are paired with negative reinforcement such as nausea-inducing apomorphine, with masturbatory reconditioning where the patient is encouraged to masturbate to "normal" stimuli.

References

ABC News Productions. 2005. *Conversations with Killers*. USA: ABC News Productions.

Abracen, J. and Looman, J. (in press). *Treatment of High Risk Sexual Offenders: An Integrated Approach*. Oxford, UK: Wiley-Blackwell.

Aggrawal, A. 2011. *Necrophilia: Forensic and Medico-Legal Aspects*. Boca Raton, FL: CRC Press.

American Psychiatric Association. 2013. *The Diagnostic and Statistical Manual of Mental Disorders* (5th ed.). Washington, DC: American Psychiatric Association.

Arntfield, M. A. 2016. Necrophilia in literature, poetry, and narrative prose. In: L. Mellor, A. Aggrawal, and E. W. Hickey (Eds.), *Understanding Necrophilia: A Global Multidisciplinary Approach*. San Diego, CA: Cognella.

Balakrishnan, A. 2008, February 22. Ex-chef sentenced to 34 years for model's murder. Retrieved December 20, 2015, from http://www.theguardian.com/uk/2008/feb/22/ukcrime3

Boon, J. 2016. The aetiology and nature of necrophiliac offending. In: L. Mellor, A. Aggrawal, and E. W. Hickey (Eds.), *Understanding Necrophilia: A Global Multidisciplinary Approach*. San Diego, CA: Cognella.

Brankley, A., Goodwill, A., and Abracen, J. 2016. A cognitive-behavioural case conceptualization approach to the assessment and treatment of necrophilia. In: L. Mellor, A. Aggrawal, and E. W. Hickey (Eds.), *Understanding Necrophilia: A Global Multidisciplinary Approach*. San Diego, CA: Cognella.

Broughall, N. and Alderton, N. 2012. Sally Anne Bowman [Television series episode]. In: N. Broughall, (Ed.), *Crimes That Shook Britain*. Manchester, UK: Title Role Production.

Carlo, P. 1996. *The Night Stalker*. New York, NY: Pinnacle.

Davis, D. 1995. *The Jeffrey Dahmer Story: An American Nightmare*. New York, NY: St. Martin's Press.

DeRiver, J. P. 1949/2000. *The Sexual Criminal: A Psychoanalytic Study*. Burbank, CA: Bloat Books.

Dietz, P., Hazelwood, R., and Burgess, A. 1990. The sexually sadistic criminal and his offenses. *Journal of the American Academy of Psychiatry and the Law, 18*(2), 163–178.

Épaulard, A. 1901. *Vampirisme: Necrophilie, Necrosadisme, Necrophagie*. Lyon: Stork.

Fisher, R. S. 1980. Time of death and changes after death. In: W. U. Spitz and R. S. Fishers (Eds.), *Medicolegal Investigation of Death: Guidelines for the Application of Pathology to Crime Investigation*, pp. 12–38. Springfield, IL: Thomas.

Foell, J. and Patrick, C. 2016. A neuroscientific perspective on Morbid Paraphilias. In: L. Mellor, A. Aggrawal, and E. W. Hickey (Eds.), *Understanding Necrophilia: A Global Multidisciplinary Approach*. San Diego, CA: Cognella.

Fox, J. A. and Levin, J. 2005. *Extreme Killing: Understanding Serial and Mass Murder*. Thousand Oaks, CA: Sage.

Gammell, C. 2008, April 12. Mark Dixie: 20 Years of Sexual Violence. Retrieved December 20, 2015, from http://www.telegraph.co.uk/news/uknews/1579461/Mark-Dixie-20-years-of-sexual-violence.html

Gekoski, A. 2000. *Murder By Numbers*. London, UK: Andre Deutsch.

Groth, N. 1979. *Men Who Rape: The Psychology of the Offender*. New York, NY: Plenum Press.

Green McGowan, M. 2006. The spectrum of blood-drinking behaviors. In: E. W. Hickey (Ed.), *Sex Crimes and Paraphilia*, pp. 111–119. Upper Saddle River, NJ: Pearson.

Häkkänen-Nyholm, H., Repo-Tiihonen, E., Lindberg, N., Salenius, S., and Weizmann-Henelius, G. 2009. Finnish sexual homicides: Offence and offender characteristics. *Forensic Science International, 188*, 125–130. DOI: 10.1016/j.forsciint.2009.03.030.

Hare, R. D. 2003. *The Hare Psychopathy Checklist-Revised* (2nd ed). Toronto, ON: Multi Health Systems.

Harkins, L., Beech, A. R., and Goodwill, A. M. 2010. Examining the influence of denial, motivation, and risk on sexual recidivism. *Sexual Abuse: A Journal of Research and Treatment, 22*, 78–94. DOI: 10.1177/1079063209358106.

Ellis, H. 2004. *Studies in the Psychology of Sex*, Vol. 3, Project Gutenburg. E-Book.

Heasman, A. and Jones, E. 2006. Necrophilia. *Sex Crimes and Paraphilia*, pp. 273–280. In: E. W. Hickey (Ed.), Upper Saddle River, NJ: Pearson.

Hickey, E. 2006. *Sex Crime and Paraphilia*. Upper Saddle River, NJ: Pearson.

Hickey, E. 2013. *Serial Murderers and Their Victims* (6th ed.). Belmont, CA: Wadsworth.

Hickey, E. 2015. *Serial Murderers and Their Victims* (7th ed.). Belmont, CA: Wadsworth.

Hirschfield, M. 1956. *Sexual Anomalies*. New York, NY: Emerson.

Holmes, R. and Holmes, S. 2009. *Profiling Violent Crimes: An Investigative Tool* (4th ed.). Thousand Oaks, CA: Sage.

Horvath, I. 1984. Murder—No apparent motive. Documentary. United States: Rainbow.

Hucker, S. J. and Stermac, L. 1992. The evaluation and treatment of sexual violence, necrophilia, and asphyxiophilia. *Psychiatric Clinics of North America, 15*, 703–719.

Jones, E. 1931. On the nightmare. *International Psychoanalytic Library*, Vol. 20. London, UK: Hogarth.

Katz, J. 1988. *Seductions of Crime: Moral and Sensual Attractions in Doing Evil*. New York, NY: Basic Books.

Keppel, R. 2005. *The Riverman*. New York, NY: Pocket Books.

King, B. 1996. *Lustmord: The Writings and Artifacts of Murderers*. Burbank, California: Bloat Books.

Krafft-Ebing, R. 1886/2011. *Psychopathia Sexualis*. New York, NY: Arcade.

Kunkle, C. D. 2016. Enhancing the identification, assessment and diagnosis of necrophilia and other related paraphilic disorders. In: L. Mellor, A. Aggrawal, and E. W. Hickey (Eds.), *Understanding Necrophilia: A Global Multidisciplinary Approach*. San Diego, CA: Cognella.

Leyton, E. 1985/1995. *Hunting Humans: Rise of the Modern Multiple Murderer*. Toronto, ON: McLelland & Stewart.

Looman, J. and Abracen, J. 2013. The risk need responsivity model of offender rehabilitation: Is there really a need for a paradigm shift? *International Journal of Behavioral Consultation and Therapy, 8*, 32–39.

Lourie, R. 1993. *Hunting the Devil*. New York, NY: Grafton.
Masters, B. 1993. *The Shrine of Jeffrey Dahmer*. London, UK: Hodder & Stoughton.
Masters, B. 1995. *Killing for Company*. London, UK: Arrow.
Mellor, L. 2012. *Cold North Killers: Canadian Serial Murder*. Toronto, ON: Dundurn.
Mellor, L. 2016a.* Wider shades of pale: Expanding the necrophilic behavioural spectrum. In: L. Mellor, A. Aggrawal, and E. W. Hickey (Eds.), *Understanding Necrophilia: A Global Multidisciplinary Approach*. San Diego, CA: Cognella.
Mellor, L. 2016b.* Mincing words: Refining the language and interpretation of mutilation. In: L. Mellor, A. Aggrawal, and E. W. Hickey (Eds.), *Understanding Necrophilia: A Global Multidisciplinary Approach*. San Diego, CA: Cognella.
Mellor, L. 2016c.* Necrophilia-spectrum behaviour and the thematic-derivative model of sexual progression. In: L. Mellor, A. Aggrawal, and E. W. Hickey (Eds.), *Understanding Necrophilia: A Global Multidisciplinary Approach*. San Diego, CA: Cognella.
Mellor, L. 2016d.* The five allures of necrophilia. In: L. Mellor, A. Aggrawal, and E. W. Hickey (Eds.), *Understanding Necrophilia: A Global Multidisciplinary Approach*. San Diego, CA: Cognella.
Michaud, S. and Aynesworth, H. 1993. *The Only Living Witness*. New York, NY: Signet.
Money, J. 2011. *Lovemaps: Sexual/Erotic Health and Pathology, Paraphilia, and Gender Transposition in Childhood, Adolescence, and Maturity*. Buffalo, New York, NY: Prometheus Books. Kindle Edition.
Mori, M. 1970/2012. The uncanny valley. *IEEE Robotics & Automation Magazine, 19*(2), 98–100. DOI: 10.1109/MRA.2012.2192811.
Morley, M. and Clark, S. 1993. *Murder in Mind*. Television documentary. London, UK: Boxtree.
Mustafa, S. and Israel, S. 2011. *Dismembered*. New York, NY: Pinnacle.
Philpin, J. and Donnelly, J. 1994. *Beyond Murder*. New York, NY: Onyx.
Porter, S., Fairweather, D., Drugge, J., Hervé, H., Birt, A., and Boer, D. P. 2000. Profiles of psychopathy in incarcerated sexual offenders. *Criminal Justice and Behavior, 27*, 216–233.
Porter, S., ten Brinke, L., and Wilson, K. 2009. Crime profiles and conditional release performance of psychopathic and non-psychopathic sexual offenders. *Legal and Criminal Psychology, 14*, 109–118.
Prins, H. 1985. Vampirism: A clinical condition. *British Journal of Psychiatry, 146*, 666–668.
Reavis, J. 2011. Serial murder of four victims, of both genders and different ethnicities, by an ordained Baptist minister. *Case Reports in Psychiatry, 2011*, 1–9.
Rosman, J. P. and Resnick, P. J. 1989. Sexual attraction to corpses: A psychiatric review of necrophilia. *Bulletin of the American Academy of Psychiatry and the Law, 17*(2), 153–163.
Rory Enrique Conde v. State of Florida. No. SC00-789, 2003.
Rory Enrique Conde v. State of Florida. No. SC06-1998, 2010.
Rule, A. 1981. *The Stranger Beside Me*. New York, NY: Signet.
Schechter, H. 1998. *Bestial: The Savage Trail of a True American Monster*. New York, NY: Pocket Books.
Schlesinger, L. B. 2004. *Sexual Murder: Catathymic and Compulsive Homicides*. Boca Raton, FL: CRC Press.
Schlesinger, L. B., Kassen, M., Mesa, V. B., and Pinizzotto, A. J. 2010. Ritual and signature in serial sexual homicide. *Journal of the American Academy of Psychiatry and the Law, 38*, 239–246.
Segal, H. 1953. A necrophilic phantasy. *The International Journal of Psychoanalysis, 34*, 98–101.
Smith, C., Polterman, B., Turner, J., and Thompson, C. J. 2013. *The Dahmer Files*. Milwaukee, WI: IFC Films.
Snyder Sachs, J. 2002. *Corpse: Nature, Forensics, and the Struggle to Pinpoint Time of Death*. Cambridge, MA: Perseus Books.
Starr, D. 2010. *The Killer of Little Shepherds: A True Crime Story and the Birth of Forensic Science*. New York, NY: Vintage Books.
Stein, M. L., Schlesinger, L. B., and Pinizzotto, A. J. 2010. Necrophilia and sexual homicide. *Journal of Forensic Sciences, 55*, 443–446. DOI: 10.1111/j.1556-4029.2009.01282.x.
Stekel, W. 1929/2013. *Sadism and Masochism—The Psychology of Hatred and Cruelty*. Vol. II. Read Books Ltd. Kindle Edition.
Stone, M. 1998. Sadistic personality in murderers. In: T. Millon, E. Simonsen, M. Birket-Smith, R.D. Davis (Eds.), *The Psychopath: Antisocial, Criminal, and Violent Behavior*. New York, NY: Guilford Press, pp. 346–355.

---

* These essays also available in Mellor, L. (in press). *Necrophilia: Theoretical Perspectives for the New Millennium*. Toronto, Canada: Grinning Man Press.

Stone, M. 2016. Necrophilia, cannibalism, and other paraphilias among serial killers. In: L. Mellor, A. Aggrawal, and E. W. Hickey (Eds.), *Understanding Necrophilia: A Global Multidisciplinary Approach*. San Diego, CA: Cognella.

Stubley, P. n.d. Mark Dixie: The Killer on the Doorstep. Retrieved December 20, 2015, from http://www.courtnewsuk.co.uk/c_sex_killers/a_mark_dixie/crime_vaults

Vronsky, P. 2016. Necrophilia: A forensic historiography from ritual and romance and the case of François Bertrand the "Vampire of Montparnasse" to paraphilia and necrophobia in big history. In: L. Mellor, A. Aggrawal, and E. W. Hickey (Eds.), *Understanding Necrophilia: A Global Multidisciplinary Approach*. San Diego, CA: Cognella.

Weller, T. 2014. The Baton-Rouge Ripper. [Television series episode] In: T. Weller, (Ed.), *Born to Kill?* Plymouth, UK: Two Four Production Companies.

Wulffen, E. 1910. *Enzyklopädie der Modernen Kriminalistik*. Berlin: Langenscheidt.

Sexually Sadistic Homicide Offenders

Lee Mellor

Contents

Introduction 125
Features and Assessment of Sexual Sadism 127
    Prevalence 127
    Diagnosing Sexual Sadism 127
    Etiology 135
    Typology 136
        Destructive versus Preservative 137
        Prolonged versus Brief 137
        Elaborate versus Simple 137
        Category 1: Fred West: A Destructive/Prolonged/Elaborate (DPE) Sex Sadist 138
        Category 2: Robert Berdella: A Preservative/Prolonged/Elaborate (PPE) Sex Sadist 138
        Category 3: The Chicago Rippers: Destructive/Prolonged/Simple (DPS) Sex Sadists 138
        Category 4: Keith Hunter Jesperson: A Preservative/Prolonged/Simple (PPS) Sex Sadist 138
        Category 5: Andrei Chikatilo: A Destructive/Brief/Simple (DBS) Sex Sadist 138
        Category 6: Dennis Rader: A Preservative/Brief/Simple (PBS) Sex Sadist 139
        Categories 7 and 8: No Offenders Discovered: Preservative/Brief/Elaborate (PBE) and Destructive/Brief/Elaborate (DBE) Sex Sadists 139
Characteristics of Sexually Sadistic Homicides and Their Perpetrators 139
    Identifying and Investigating Sexually Sadistic Homicide Crime Scenes 140
    Linkage Analysis 149
Offender Profiling and Investigation Strategies 151
    Comorbid Paraphilias 153
Recommendations for Handling Cases of Sexual Sadists Who Kill 153
    Arresting, Charging, and Prosecuting the Sexual Sadist 153
    Interviewing 155
    Treatment 158
References 158

Introduction

Sadism was named after the Marquis de Sade, Donatien Alphonse François, an eighteenth-century aristocratic French writer and revolutionary who gained notoriety and was eventually jailed for penning scandalous erotica. In these tales, the typically female object of desire is subjected to acts of extreme violence and humiliation, with the stories often framed by François' prenihilist libertine philosophy. Though the term *sadism* soon became part of the French vernacular meaning "cruelty," it premiered in scientific literature when the German alienist Richard von Krafft-Ebing employed it in his *Psychopathia Sexualis*, describing *sadism* as

> [T]he experience of sexual pleasurable sensations (including orgasm) produced by acts of cruelty, bodily punishment afflicted on one's own person or when witnessed in others, be they animals or human beings. It may also consist of an innate desire to humiliate, hurt, wound or even destroy others in order thereby to create sexual pleasure in one's self (Krafft-Ebing, 1886/2011, p. 53).

Since the early work of Krafft-Ebing, the concept of sadism has been refined substantially.

Many of the activities in his definition have since been disaggregated into individual paraphilias such as *sexual masochism* (when inflicted on one's self) and *zoosadism* (sexual sadism involving animals). Several paraphilias (*picquerism, mutilophilia, necromutilophilia, pyrophilia*, etc.) represent destruction-related sexual pleasure in its different permutations and manifest in crime scene behavior (Mellor, 2016a).

In the DSM-III-R, sadistic personality disorder (SPD)—a nonsexual form of sadism relating mostly to dominance-associated personality traits—was listed as a Cluster B personality disorder (Table 8.1).

With the publication of DSM-IV, SPD was eliminated due to a lack of evidence to support it as a distinct personality disorder. It is important to emphasize that though SPD can include elements of sexual arousal, it is separate from *sexual sadism disorder*, which is strictly paraphilic. The diagnostic criteria for sexual sadism disorder are discussed in this chapter under the section "Features and Assessment of Sexual Sadism."

James Mitchell DeBardeleben, widely considered one of the most extreme sexual sadists encountered by law enforcement, once defined "sadism" as follows (with spelling and grammatical errors preserved):

> The wish to inflict pain on others is *not* the essence of sadism. One essential impulse: *to have complete mastery over another person*, to make him/her a helpless object of our will, to become the absolute ruler over her, you become her God, to do with her as one pleases. To humiliate her, to enslave her *are means to this end*; and the most important radical aim is to make her *suffer* since *there is no greater power over another person than that of inflicting pain on her* to force her to undergo suffering without her being able to defend herself. The pleasure in the complete domination over another person is the very essence of the Sadistic drive [emphasis in original] (Dietz et al., 1990, p. 165).

This emphasis on total domination of the victim had also been described in the previous writings of Karpman (1954), Brittain (1970), Fromm (1973), and MacCulloch et al. (1983). John Money (1990) has characterized sexual sadism as involving "an obsessive and compelling repetition of sexual thoughts, dreams or fantasies that may be translated into acts in which the mental or physical suffering of a victim is intensely sexually arousing" (p. 27).

For the purposes of this chapter, the definition of sexual sadism will be in accordance with that of the DSM-5's and that used by Dietz et al. (1990) "which is that only those crimes reflective of an enduring pattern of sexual arousal in response to sadistic imagery ought to be regarded as sexually sadistic offenses"

Table 8.1 DSM III-R Diagnostic Criteria for Sadistic Personality Disorder

1. A pervasive pattern of cruel, demeaning, and aggressive behavior, beginning by early adulthood, as indicated by the repeated occurrence of at least four of the following:
   a. Has used physical cruelty or violence for the purpose of establishing dominance in a relationship (not merely to achieve some noninterpersonal goal, such as striking someone in order to rob him or her)
   b. Humiliates or demeans people in the presence of others
   c. Has treated or disciplined someone under his or her control unusually harshly (e.g., a child, student, prisoner, or patient)
   d. Is amused by, or takes pleasure in, the psychological or physical suffering of others (including animals)
   e. Has lied for the purpose of harming or inflicting pain on others (not merely to achieve some other goal)
   f. Gets other people to do what he or she wants by frightening them (through intimidation or even terror)
   g. Restricts the autonomy of people with whom he or she has a close relationship (e.g., will not let spouse leave the house unaccompanied or permit teenage daughter to attend social functions)
   h. Is fascinated by violence, weapons, martial arts, injury, or torture
2. The behavior in A has not been directed toward only one person (e.g., spouse, one child) and has not been solely for the purpose of sexual arousal (as in sexual sadism)

Source: American Psychiatric Association. 1987. *Diagnostic and Statistical Manual of Mental Disorders: DSM-III-Revised* (3rd ed.), p. 371. Washington, DC: American Psychiatric Association.

(pp. 164–165). For activities such as paraphilic corpse mutilation, once oxymoronically labeled *necrosadism* but now reconceptualized as *necromutilophilia* (Mellor, 2016a), refer to Chapter 7 on necrophilic homicides.

Two studies form the bedrock of this chapter, that of Dietz et al. (1990) and Gratzer and Bradford (1995). The latter compared the characteristics of Dietz et al.'s sample of 30 sadistic sexual offenders to those of 29 nonsadistic sexual offenders and 28 sadistic offenders whose pathologies were less severe from the Royal Ottawa Hospital in Ontario, Canada.

The work of the Dietz, Hazelwood, and Warren research team on American sexual sadists seems to be restricted to sexual sadists in categories 1 and 2 (see Mellor's "Typology" below). This should always be taken into consideration when this research team is cited. Owing to spatial constraints and a lack of comparative research, this chapter does not devote sufficient attention to those homicidal sexual sadists (HSSs) in the latter six categories in this chapter; however, they have not been entirely overlooked (Gratzer and Bradford, 1995).

Features and Assessment of Sexual Sadism

Prevalence

The representation of sexual sadism disorder in the general population is extremely difficult to determine, as it is mostly assessed only in a forensic setting. Estimates based upon questionnaires (Kinsey et al., 1953; Hunt, 1974; Crepault and Couture, 1980) and the circulation of pornography with S&M themes (Gayford, 1978; Dietz and Evans, 1982) seem to indicate that anywhere between 5% and 20% of the male population have sexually sadistic tendencies. Krueger's (2010) research has found that less than 10% of incarcerated sex offenders in the United States are full-blown sexual sadists, and that the presence of this paraphilia ranges from 37% to 75% in those who have committed sexual homicides. Perhaps the most conservative estimate proposes that only 2–5% of sex offenders are sexual sadists (Kingston and Yates, 2008). An important caveat is that these statistics are dependent on the definition of sexual sadism being used in a given article at a given time (Kingston and Yates, 2008; Mellor, 2016c).

Diagnosing Sexual Sadism

The fifth edition of the *Diagnostic and Statistical Manual of Mental Disorders* classifies sexual sadism as a paraphilic disorder, and specifies that in order to diagnose an individual as suffering from sexual sadism, they must (1) derive "recurrent and intense sexual arousal from the physical or psychological suffering of another person, as manifested by fantasies, urges, or behaviors" (American Psychiatric Association, 2013, p. 695) over a period of 6 months or longer; and (2) have "acted on these sexual urges with a nonconsenting person, or the sexual urges or fantasies cause clinically significant distress or impairment in social, occupational, or other important areas of functioning" (American Psychiatric Association, 2013, p. 695).

After conducting a number of tests on both inmates previously diagnosed as sexually sadistic and *non*sexually sadistic using pre-DSM-5 diagnostic criteria, Marshall et al. (2002a) made some troubling but crucial discoveries. Namely, in phallometric studies, the inmates who had been diagnosed as *non*sexually sadistic showed higher rates of sexual arousal to stimuli that was hypothetically supposed to arouse a sexual sadist than the sexual sadists themselves. Then, in a follow-up experiment, after contacting 24 of the world's leading psychiatrists to diagnose patients with sexual sadism, they found that the experts' diagnoses were so inconsistent that the kappa was an astonishingly low .14 (Marshall et al., 2002b). Marshall and Hucker (2006a) note that a kappa of .9 is needed to make important decisions.

In an attempt to solve this dilemma, Marshall and Hucker (2006a) created an inventory of 17 items divided into four groups. Group 1 consists of the five heaviest weighted items that were determined by a group of experts to be essential in diagnosing sexual sadism. The subsequent items decrease in weight, with the lowest weightings given to items 16 and 17. The more weight that accumulates over the course of the assessment, the more likely the subject is to be a sexual sadist (Table 8.2).

As this inventory exists on a gradient rather than being categorical, and has not been supported by sufficient quantitative research, the exact amount of "weight" needed in order for us to say that a person has even the mildest form of sexual sadism is unclear. For instance, would somebody whose crimes evidence ritualism and who abducts a victim qualify?

To be fair, Marshall and Hucker proposed this as merely a starting point or incentive to formulate a new diagnostic approach to sexual sadism. It was born of sheer pragmatism, following the shocking revelations of their findings. Nevertheless, it is our belief that the problem lies not in the DSM-5 criteria, but more likely in the charlatanism of some mental health professionals who have little knowledge of the highly specialized field of paraphilia.

Table 8.2 Marshall and Hucker's "Items of the Sadistic Scale"

1. Offender is sexually aroused by sadistic acts
2. Offender exercises power/control/domination over victim
3. Offender humiliates or degrades the victim
4. Offender tortures victim or engages in acts of cruelty on victim
5. Offender mutilates sexual parts of the victim body
6. Offender has a history of choking consensual partners during sex
7. Offender engages in gratuitous violence toward the victim
8. Offender has a history of cruelty to other persons or animals
9. Offender gratuitously wounds victim
10. Offender attempts to, or succeeds in, strangling, choking, or otherwise asphyxiating victim
11. Offender keeps trophies (e.g., hair, underwear, ID) of victim
12. Offender keeps records (other than trophies) of offense
13. Offender carefully preplans offense
14. Offender mutilates nonsexual parts of the victims body
15. Offender engages in bondage with consensual partners during sex
16. Victim is abducted or confined
17. Evidence of ritualism

Source: Marshall, W. L. and Hucker, S. J. 2006a. Issues in the diagnosis of sexual sadism. *Sexual Offender Treatment*, *1*(2). Retrieved from http://www.sexual-offender-treatment.org/40.html

In a study of 100 male forensic patients, of whom 50 had been diagnosed with sexual sadism, Nitschke et al. (2009) made the following conclusions about Marshall and Hucker's "Items of the Sadistic Scale": (1) A diagnosis of sexual sadism could be made using a cut-off score of four items; (2) Items 1, 2, 3, 4, 5, 7, 11, 14, 16, and 17 stood out as being useful in identifying sexual sadism, with 1 (Offender is sexually aroused by sadistic acts), 2 (Offender exercises power/control/domination over victim), 3 (Offender humiliates or degrades the victim), and 7 (Offender engages in gratuitous violence toward the victim) being the most important discriminators; and (3) An 18th item—insertion of object into victim's bodily orifice—was also diagnostically useful; however, research by Gratzer and Bradford (1995) has actually found that foreign object insertion is not uniquely associated with sexual sadists.

An inventory by Proulx et al. (2006) consists of two categories (Scale A and Scale B). Under this system, an offender who evidences one behavior on Scale A and two behaviors on Scale B qualifies for a diagnosis of sexual sadism (Table 8.3).

Though the authors used this scale to diagnose 45% of the homicidal offenders and 25% of the rapists in their study as sexual sadists, they did not test for the scale's reliability (Healey et al., 2013). The fact that an offender could be diagnosed as a sexual sadist using a combination of "postmortem intercourse" and any two of the Scale B items stands out as immediately problematic. "Postmortem intercourse," when paired with "marks of violence on erogenous zones," and "burns inflicted *after the murder*" or "insertion of objects into body cavities" could instead reflect a homicidal necrophile (see Chapter 7) with *necromutilophilia* (Mellor, 2016a). Or if "postmortem intercourse" is paired with "insertion of objects into body cavities" and "burns inflicted *after the murder,*" this could simply reflect a necrophile who attempted to incinerate his victim's body to destroy evidence. Problematically, Scale B's "insertion of objects into body cavities" has been found to be unassociated with sexual sadism in one important study (Gratzer and Bradford, 1995). Finally, those scored as sadists using this inventory did not differ from nonsadists in their arousal to images of nonsexual violence. However, the sadists were more aroused by scenes of rape with humiliation and rape with physical violence than the nonsadists. This could indicate that they were simply aroused by rape (or even vaginal intercourse) and not turned off by the accompanying violence or humiliation, as "rape" is the common denominator.

Table 8.3 Sexual Sadism Indicators and Related Indicators in Proulx et al. (2006)

Scale A	Scale B
1. Presence of intense and recurring sexual fantasies	1. Marks of violence on erogenous zones (anus, vagina, breasts)
2. Torture of victim prior to death	2. Burns inflicted prior to or after the murder
3. Ritualized violence	3. Insertion of objects into body cavities
4. Postmortem intercourse	

With the prospect of facing stigma and/or formal institutional punishments, many sexual sadists are not "admitting individuals"—that is, they do not admit their paraphilic desires, even when convicted of violent crimes (Dietz et al., 1990; Marshall and Hucker, 2006a; Healey et al., 2013). The diagnostic criteria of the DSM-5 have been constructed to account for this. When an "admitting individual"—that is, a person who is transparent about his or her predilections—declares that they do not personally suffer as a result of their sexuality, nor has anybody else, and if their mental health and legal files corroborate that they have not hurt a nonconsenting person, then these individuals are considered to have "sadistic sexual interest" rather than "sexual sadism disorder." However, if there is evidence that the individual has been sexually stimulated by observing pain or humiliation that they have inflicted on another person, then they should be diagnosed with sexual sadism disorder.

In the DSM-5, sexual sadism is considered "recurrent" when either (i) the subject has been sexually aroused by the suffering of three or more victims on separate occasions, or (ii) the subject has been sexually aroused by the suffering of fewer than three victims in multiple instances. An example of the latter can be seen in the case of Cameron Hooker, who, along with his wife Janice, abducted Colleen Stan in 1977 and kept her imprisoned at their home in Red Brook, California until 1984. Hooker tortured Colleen for sexual satisfaction on a daily basis over the next seven years (McGuire and Norton, 1989).

It is important not to confuse sexual sadism with an interest in practicing BDSM (bondage, discipline, sadism, masochism), which is necessarily consensual and often involves sexual role playing. Participants take the roles of either a *top/dominant* (one who controls the sex act), *bottom/submissive* (one who is controlled), or a *switch* (one who changes between the two roles). Aspects of BDSM include bondage and discipline (B&D, B/D, BD), dominance and submission (D&s, D/s, Ds), and sadism and masochism (S&M, S/M, SM). In BDSM relationships, there is often a preestablished "safe word" which the *bottom/submissive* can utter to alert the *top/dominant* that they need to stop or tone down whatever act is occurring, because the *bottom/submissive* is uncomfortable with it.

Differential diagnoses with antisocial personality disorder, sexual masochism disorder, hypersexuality, and substance use disorder are common, as these mental health disorders are frequently comorbid with sexual sadism disorder.

Dietz et al. (1990) caution against diagnosing sexual sadism in an individual whose sexual behavior seems to be sadistic only when they are having a psychotic episode. Similarly, they note that too often clinicians are so puzzled by the bizarre nature of sexual sadism that they wrongly attribute it to psychotic features. Furthermore, Dietz et al. emphasize that, in order to properly diagnose sexual sadism, one must be prepared to ask detailed and often taboo questions about the interviewee's sexual fantasies and practices (e.g., "In this scenario, are you more sexually aroused by the victim's screams or the expression on their face?").

Where both the DSM-5 criteria and Marshall and Hucker's Sadistic Scale would have immediately revealed the presence of sexual sadism in the case of Paul Bernardo, the sexual sadism indicators of Proulx et al. (2006) would have excluded him from such a diagnosis as he did not usually attack his victims' erogenous zones or burn their bodies.

Case Study: Paul Bernardo and Karla Homolka

Paul Kenneth Bernardo was born on August 27, 1964 in Scarborough, Canada, the product of his mother Marilyn's extramarital affair with her former lover. His two older siblings, David and Debbie, were the legitimate offspring of Marilyn and Kenneth Bernardo. As a boy, Paul had a number of congenital defects, including a large black transient blood clot on the left side of his head and a webbing of skin which attached his tongue to his palate. The former faded within six weeks and the latter was fixed with corrective surgery when Paul was a toddler. Excerpts from Marilyn's diary describe him as "not the least bit affectionate... very selfish and stubborn" (Williams, 1996, p. 64).

The Bernardo household was a tumultuous environment in which to raise a child. Ken was physically and emotionally abusive toward his wife, which adversely affected her mental health. Combined with Marilyn's thyroid disorder, this led to her being unhygienic, reclusive, short-tempered, and emotionally unavailable for her children. Ken was also a window peeper who routinely sexually abused Paul's sister, sometimes while the family was gathered in the same room watching television. As Paul neared puberty, he too became a habitual voyeur, and in his teens began to collect violent pornography and videos featuring women urinating and defecating. A turning point in his development seems to have come in grade 10 when his mother Marilyn reportedly burst into his bedroom, angrily presented him with a photograph of his biological father, and informed him that he was "a bastard" and had better get used to it. From that moment on, she would frequently call him a "bastard child from hell" and other names revolving around the theme of his illegitimacy. He in turn responded by berating her as a "slut" or "slob."

Boyishly handsome and superficially charming, Paul Bernardo had a number of girlfriends throughout high school—sometimes sustaining several relationships at the same time—and began to pressure them into participating in sex acts involving bondage, asphyxiation, sodomy, and humiliation. Intelligent and ambitious, Paul was admitted to the University of Toronto, where he studied Economics and Commerce at the Scarborough campus. He continued to live with his mother and father in Scarborough's upper-middle-class Guildwood Village.

In May of 1987—the same year that he graduated from U of T—the 22-year-old Bernardo committed his first known offense in a series of at least 18 vicious sexual assaults and rapes on strangers in Scarborough, while living with his mother and father. Typically, these attacks involved the victim being subjected to a blitz assault while walking home from bus stops, suddenly beaten, threatened with a knife, strangled with a coaxial cable, then raped vaginally and anally before Bernardo forced them to perform oral sex on him, ejaculating into their mouths. He would ask them their names and details of their personal lives, make the victims refer to themselves as "sluts" or "cunts" (*scripting*), rub dirt into their hair, and threaten to kill them if they told the police.

That September, Bernardo began working in downtown Toronto at the Pricewaterhouse accounting firm. In October 1987, he met attractive 17-year-old Karla Homolka, a veterinarian's assistant from nearby St. Catharines while she was attending a convention at a Howard Johnson hotel. Within hours, the two were having sex in the hotel room that Homolka was sharing with her friend. From that moment on, they were boyfriend and girlfriend, with Paul driving out to stay with Karla at her family's home in St. Catharines every weekend. Karla was much more open to Paul's affinity for BDSM sex—in fact, when she presented him with handcuffs as a gift, she may have normalized his sadistic tendencies—with their oft-videotaped sex lives involving Karla roleplaying a schoolgirl.

Bernardo's name first came to the attention of police in January 1988 when one of his former girlfriends contacted Sergeant Kevin McNiff to discuss getting some money back from Bernardo which he owed her. As McNiff and the ex-girlfriend spent more time talking, she began to open up about Bernardo's sexually sadistic tendencies. Much to his credit, McNiff realized that Bernardo was a potential suspect in the Scarborough rapes. He forwarded a three-page report on Bernardo to the Scarborough Rapist Task Force which noted that Bernardo resided in Scarborough, that he was "manipulative and aggressive," was physically and emotionally abusive toward females, wished to hold a knife to his girlfriend's throat while they had sex, and carried a Stiletto blade. This report, like many others to come, was not followed up on due to a faulty case management system.

After a prolonged rape on May 26, 1990, a victim was able to provide details which led to a composite sketch of her attacker. It was a dead ringer for Bernardo. The image was circulated in fliers and news media around the Greater Toronto Area. With his strong likeness to the composite, multiple informants independently submitted Bernardo's name to the police. A bank teller had noted that Bernardo had changed his hair style after the composite had been circulated. One of Bernardo's friends and his wife actually came into the Sexual Assault Squad Office and said that Bernardo resembled the composite; was known to have sex with girls after they were drunk; hit females in front of them; spoke about raping girls; was sly, manipulative, and domineering; carried a knife; was into rough and abnormal sex; and had raped an unconscious woman in front of his friend.

Interviewed by police on November 20, 1990, Bernardo agreed to submit a blood sample for testing. He was classified as a "B Suspect": a "viable suspect who was not in the highest priority category" (Campbell, 1996, p. 31). For a myriad of reasons, it would be over two years before the Centre of Forensic Sciences processed the sample and identified Bernardo as "The Scarborough Rapist." By that time, at least three young females would be dead as a result of his actions, with many more raped.

The first was Karla Homolka's 15-year-old sister, Tammy. Bernardo frequently complained that because Karla had not been a virgin when they met Karla had somehow cheated him. He demanded that she give him Tammy's virginity as a Christmas gift. Karla acquiesced, and stole Halcion pills and halothane from the veterinary clinic where she worked. In the wee hours of the morning on December 24, 1990, while the rest of the Homolka family slept upstairs, Bernardo drugged Tammy by crushing and mixing Halcion pills into drinks which Karla served to her. Once Tammy was unconscious, Bernardo videotaped Karla removing her sister's tampon and performing cunnilingus on her. Then, while Karla ensured that Tammy remained unconscious by periodically smothering her with a halothane-soaked rag, Bernardo proceeded to vaginally and anally rape Tammy, videotaping the assault. Suddenly, Tammy began choking on her own vomit. Paul and Karla panicked, and attempted to hide evidence of the assault while simultaneously summoning emergency services. Paramedics arrived too late to save Tammy. Despite the presence of a 3 × 1.5-centimeter red burn mark on her face from the halothane, Tammy Homolka's death was ultimately ruled accidental, the result of her aspirating vomitus. Karla explained away the mark as being a "rug burn" from when they had dragged Tammy across the floor, but the pathologist attributed it to gastric juices. On numerous occasions after Tammy's death, Homolka would dress in a schoolgirl outfit and pretend to be Tammy while engaging in sex acts with Bernardo.

Now engaged to be married, in January 1991, the couple moved into a rented house at 57 Bayview Drive in Port Dalhousie, Ontario near St. Catharines. Despite their appearance of upward mobility, Bernardo had quit his prestigious job as a junior accountant at Pricewaterhouse and was now earning his income by cheating social services and smuggling cigarettes into Canada from the United States. Karla continued to work as a veterinarian's assistant. Soon after relocating, in April, Bernardo raped a woman jogging on Henley Island, less than a mile from his new home, displaying signature behavior that was consistent with the Scarborough rapes.

On June 6, Karla invited family friend Samantha Moss* over to 57 Bayview Drive while Paul was out. She drugged the girl using the same methods that she had used on her sister, and then called Paul on his cell phone, telling him to come home to receive his wedding present. When he arrived, they sexually assaulted Samantha and videotaped it.

Around 2 a.m. on June 14, 1991, while scouring a middle-class neighborhood in nearby Burlington, Ontario to steal license plates for his illegal border crossings, Bernardo encountered 14-year-old Leslie Mahaffy. Leslie had been locked out of her parents' home for missing her curfew. Bernardo chatted with her, and lured her into his vehicle with the promise of a cigarette. Once she was inside, he put a knife to her throat, blindfolded her, and drove her to his home in Port Dalhousie. There, Leslie was forced to urinate and masturbate in front of Bernardo while he videotaped. Over the next 24 hours, Bernardo and Homolka repeatedly sexually assaulted her. The majority of the sexual assault—which included Bernardo's signature bondage, scripting, beating, and anal intercourse followed by forced fellatio—was recorded on video camera by Bernardo or Homolka. Following Bernardo's instructions, Karla also performed cunnilingus on Mahaffy. Leslie was also forced to lick Bernardo's anus: a humiliation which Karla documented on the camera. At some point in that 24-hour period, Leslie was murdered. The version of events the jury would choose to believe was that Bernardo had strangled her to death with an electrical cord. Two days later, Bernardo dismembered Leslie Mahaffy's body with a power saw, encased her body parts in concrete, and dumped them in Lake Gibson with the help of Homolka. Leslie's remains were discovered on June 29—the same day that Bernardo and Homolka were wed in a lavish ceremony at Niagara-on-the-Lake. After returning from their Hawaiian honeymoon in August, they once again drugged and sexually assaulted Samantha Moss at 57 Bayview.

Their third and final known homicide victim was Kristen French, 15, abducted on April 16, 1992, while walking home from school in broad daylight in St. Catharines. Pulling their gold Nissan SX into the parking lot of Grace Lutheran Church, Homolka lured Kristen over to the car to ask her directions. Once she was close enough, Bernardo surprised Kristen by holding a knife to her throat, and forcing her into the car. Kristen was blindfolded and taken back to 57 Bayview where she was subjected to similar treatment as Leslie Mahaffy, though her ordeal lasted three days. Bernardo escalated the level of sadism in his violence, thrusting a wine bottle into Kristen's anus, urinating on her and attempting to defecate on her, and strangling her with an electrical cord while sodomizing her. In one instance, he placed a knife in the middle of the floor and dared her to pick it up and stab him with it, while in another, he demanded that Kristen say she hated her boyfriend: sophisticated forms of psychological torture. Kristen's last words captured on videotape to Bernardo were, "I don't know how your wife can stand being around you."

Meanwhile, the police had recovered Kristen's shoe, a strand of brown hair, and a torn piece of a map from the parking lot of Grace Lutheran Church. A witness had also come forward who had seen a struggle there, and was persuaded by the police that she could identify the car. She did so incorrectly, saying that it was an ivory or cream-colored Camaro or Firebird.

On April 19, Kristen French was murdered. The jury would later believe that Paul Bernardo had strangled her to death with an electrical cord. To rid the body of forensic evidence, Bernardo and Homolka bathed Kristen's corpse, burned her clothing, cut off her hair, and douched her vagina and anus. Shortly after, Bernardo and Homolka dumped Kristen's nude body down a leafy embankment in North Burlington, Ontario, where it was discovered on April 30.

---

* A pseudonym.

In January 1993, following significant escalation in Bernardo's abuse of Homolka, he finally went too far. While sodomizing Karla and strangling her with the same electrical cord he had used to kill Kristen French, Bernardo bashed her across the head with a flashlight. The impact slammed Karla's brain into the front of her skull producing twin black eyes, an effect known as "raccooning." With some effort, Homolka's family finally encouraged her to leave Bernardo, and she took refuge in her aunt and uncle's apartment.

More bad luck soon followed for Bernardo, when CFS labs finally matched his DNA to that of the Scarborough rapist and informed Toronto Metro Police. On February 8, Toronto Metro shared this information with the Niagara Police's Green Ribbon Task Force (GRT) who were charged with investigating the murders of Leslie Mahaffy and Kristen French. As the Toronto Metropolitan Police were planning to interview Karla Homolka, GRT head Investigator Vince Bevan requested that they ask her (i) what Paul Bernardo had been doing from June 15–29, 1991, and April 16–30, 1992; (ii) details of the jewelry Paul and Karla had in their possession, and (iii) about a Mickey Mouse watch, believed to have once belonged to Kristen French, that Karla had been wearing when she reported Bernardo's physical abuse in January.

The next evening, February 9, investigators from the Toronto Metropolitan Police arrived at the apartment of Karla's aunt and uncle to interview her, which they spent the next 5 hours doing. They informed her that Bernardo was a suspect in a series of sexual assaults. Her demeanor changed notably when they questioned her about the Mickey Mouse watch, which she said belonged to her sister, Lori. After Karla voiced some suspicions, they managed to obtain her fingerprints. As soon as the investigators left, Karla told her aunt and uncle that Paul Bernardo was the Scarborough rapist and that he had killed Leslie Mahaffy and Kristen French. She immediately contacted a lawyer, George Walker, and booked an appointment to consult with him two days later.

During their meeting, Karla confided in Walker that she and Bernardo had kidnapped and sexually assaulted Leslie Mahaffy and Kristen French, and that Bernardo had murdered them. She also told him about the drugging, rape, and accidental death of her sister, Tammy.

That night, Walker was approached by officers from the GRT who mentioned that they would entertain offering a deal to Karla Homolka in exchange for information on the homicides. Over the next week, Walker met with Inspector Bevan and director of the Crown Law Office, Murray Segal, to begin negotiating a plea bargain for Karla Homolka. The information that Homolka had disclosed qualified her to be convicted of first-degree murder; however, without her testimony, the GRT had no evidence with which to charge Bernardo or obtain a warrant to search 57 Bayview. On the other hand, the Toronto Metropolitan Police, who had DNA evidence linking Bernardo to the Scarborough rapes, were eager to arrest him. Bevan asked them to hold off. He needed time to prepare search warrants of 57 Bayview Drive, so instead of arresting Bernardo, they placed their suspect under surveillance.

Bevan and the prosecution had also become aware of an article by FBI profiler Roy Hazelwood, Janet Warren, and Park Dietz titled "Compliant Victims of the Sexual Sadist" soon to be published in *Australian Family Physician*. They decided that Karla was a so-called "compliant victim" and used this as a justification to forge ahead with their plea bargain (see "Assessing the Culpability and Agency of Accomplices" later in the chapter).

On February 17, Bevan became aware of a significant media leak which threatened to tip-off Bernardo about his impending arrest. The hand of the GRT head was now forced. They had to move quickly and without sufficient preparation. That same day, constables from the Metropolitan Toronto Police and GRT arrived at 57 Bayview Drive and arrested Paul Bernardo on four counts of sexual assault, and for the murders of Leslie Mahaffy and Kristen French.

Attempts to interview Bernardo using the 95/5 technique at Halton Regional Police Quarters were unsuccessful (see "Interviewing" below). Fortunately, it was not necessary to obtain a confession from him in light of the DNA evidence linking him to the Scarborough rapes, and Karla's testimony which implicated him in the murders. By the time the search of 57 Bayview was completed, they would not even really need Homolka.

Two days after Bernardo's arrest, search warrants were executed on 57 Bayview Drive. In total, the property would be scoured in a grid pattern for a period of 71 days by 16 identification officers. Among the evidences recovered from the property directly related to the crimes were

- A list of the Scarborough rapes in chronological order
- The 22nd edition of the *Compendium of Pharmaceuticals and Specialities* with Halcion and halothane highlighted

- Bloodstains from Leslie Mahaffy and Kristen French
- A 1:58-minute-long video hidden in a briefcase which showed Karla participating in Lesbian sex acts with two women—the first with a consenting participant in a hotel room, and the second with a seemingly unconscious female
- Audiotapes of Bernardo crying about how Karla had left him

Other items potentially indicative of a sexual sadist and paraphile included:

- A paper bag containing used panties
- A security guard uniform
- Numerous true crime books: *Across the Border*; *Bitter Blood*; *The Confessions of Henry Lee Lucas*; *A Deadly Silence*; *Devil Child*; *The I-5 Killer*; *In His Garden*; *In Broad Daylight*; *A Killing in the Family*; *Life with Billy*; *Lisa, Hedda and Joel*; *Masquerade*; *The Perfect Victim*; *Poisoned Blood*; *Small Sacrifices*; *The Ultimate Evil*; *The Violent Years of Maggie MacDonald*; and *Who Killed Cindy James?*

After two weeks of negotiation, on February 25, 1993, George Walker met with Murray Segal to finalize the plea bargain. They agreed to hand Karla two 10-year sentences to be served concurrently for the manslaughters of Leslie Mahaffy and Kristen French. However, before the plea bargain could be finalized, they would need Homolka's presentencing report. The next day, Karla Homolka signed the following plea resolution authorization (in Mellor, 2012):

> I, Karla Leanne Homolka, of 61 Dundonald St., St. Catharines, Ontario, do hereby authorize and instruct my counsel, George F. Walker, Q.C., to continue towards finalizing my plea bargain arrangement with Murray Segal, Esq., of the ministry of the Attorney General of Ontario.
>
> I understand that I must co-operate fully with the investigating officers, be truthful and frank in providing answers to all questions asked, and to provide full details of my knowledge and/or participation in the Mahaffy and French investigations and any others. That I will provide induced statements to the investigators at a time and place convenient to the officers.
>
> I do understand that I will be called upon to testify against my husband at his trials and I hereby agree to do so. *That this agreement is null and void if I commit perjury* [emphasis added]. I understand that I will enter a plea of guilty to 1 count manslaughter vis-a-vis, Mahaffy, and 1 count manslaughter, vis-a-vis, French and at least one other charge in relation to each victim. That I am to receive sentences totaling 10 years in custody.
>
> That the Crown will not seek an increase in the period before parole eligibility. That the Crown will write to the Parole Board, will include a record of my trial proceedings, will indicate my co-operation, remorse etc. and will indicate on behalf of the police and the Crown that they will leave the matter of when releases and/or parole should commence, up to the Parole Board without further comment. That my counsel and the Crown will go before the Justice beforehand to ensure the terms of the agreement are acceptable. That when charged I will go before a Provincial Court Judge, waive my preliminary hearings, be brought before a Justice, enter my pleas of "guilty" and be released pending sentencing. That the Attorney General's office will indicate to the Federal Correctional Authorities and Provincial Authorities that they are not opposed to the offender being transferred from a Federal to a Provincial Institution to serve my sentence.
>
> That I have had all my rights explained to me by my counsel and have been advised that I am free to contact another lawyer for another opinion but have advised my counsel that I fully understand and wish to proceed with the agreement forthwith.
>
> **DATED at the City of Niagara Falls this 26th day of February, 1993**
>
> **Witnessed by Karel and Dorothy Homolka**
>
> **Notarized by Geoffrey Hadfield**
>
> **Signed, Karla Leanne Bernardo**

On April 30, Walker and Segal met once again. Segal insisted that Karla Homolka would have to suffer additional consequences for the death of her sister, Tammy, which she had recently disclosed to them. They agreed to add two years—for a total of 12—but with no additional criminal charges.

On May 14, 1993, Karla Homolka's plea bargain with the prosecution was finalized. An important clause read: "They (the authorities) will provide no protection for a prosecution if it is discovered that she lied, including a prosecution for obstructing justice, public mischief, fabricating evidence, *perjury, inconsistent statements* [emphasis added] and/or false affidavits" (Williams, 1996, p. 470).

Four days later, Paul Bernardo was officially charged with two counts of first-degree murder, two counts of kidnapping, two counts of unlawful confinement, two counts of aggravated sexual assault, and indignity to a human body. At a subsequent bail hearing, three additional counts of sexual assault and buggery were added.

Videotaped police interviews with Karla Homolka soon began, and would last for four days. Homolka lied by either commission or omission in the following recollections:

1. When describing Paul's relationship with Samantha Moss, Karla neglected to recall the occasion on June 6, 1991, when she had invited Samantha to 57 Bayview while Bernardo was out, drugged Samantha unconscious, then telephoned Bernardo to tell him that she had a surprise "wedding present" waiting for him at home. They had then sexually assaulted Samantha and videotaped it.
2. She said that Paul and Samantha had been close, but that their relationship had ended when Samantha's mother interfered. This was contrary to Samantha's own statements which had already been obtained by police.
3. Karla did not tell them that she had facilitated Bernardo's rape of Tammy's friend, Natalie Black.* Karla also obfuscated the nature of the relationship between the two. Police had statements from Natalie Black which showed otherwise.

In all three of these instances, there were no repercussions for Karla's deceitfulness.

When the investigators enquired as to the videotape footage recovered from 57 Bayview of Karla engaging in lesbian acts with two women, Karla presumably realized that they had not found the three or more hours of footage which showed her and Bernardo sexually assaulting Leslie Mahaffy, Kristen French, and Tammy Homolka. Adjusting her strategy, she claimed falsely that she believed all of the footage was on a single videotape, but could not be sure as she had never watched it of her own volition. Bernardo, she said, had told her that he kept the tape in the insulation. Karla recounted the Mahaffy and French abductions, sexual assaults, and slayings, saying that she had been forced to go along with them, and that both girls had been strangled to death with a ligature by Bernardo.

Karla then learned that the police had found a videotape from which they had isolated a still frame of Karla taking an unconscious girl's limp hand and inserting it into her own vagina. There is little doubt that Karla knew this to be her teenage friend, Samantha, who she had drugged on two occasions and sexually assaulted with Bernardo. She had confided as much in her psychiatrist, Dr. Arndt. However, Karla had not mentioned this specific incident, and knew that it would destroy her credibility and jeopardize the plea bargain. So, when she was later shown the footage, she said that it must have been Kristen French or Leslie Mahaffy because the video had been shot in their bedroom at 57 Bayview.

On May 18, Karla waived her right to a preliminary trial and was remanded until June 7. Karla Homolka's trial began on June 28, 1993. The plea bargain was reviewed by the court, and on July 6, it was approved. Homolka was sentenced to 12 years in prison.

Once incarcerated and receiving treatment for her "posttraumatic stress disorder/battered woman syndrome," Homolka suddenly reported having dreams about a "forgotten" victim: Samantha Moss. She wrote to George Walker that they might have a "major problem" because she "forgot" to tell police of the sexual assaults committed on Moss in June and August of 1991. The victim, Homolka reported, had been drunk. Now the photograph that her interviewers had showed to her in June was jogging her memory, and she was worried that she might have also directly been involved in the sexual assault. Walker handed the letter to Murray Segal, and on December 6, 1993, police returned to show Homolka the 1 minute and 58 seconds of video footage from which they had originally taken the still photograph. Still, Homolka claimed that she could not identify the victim.

Paul Bernardo's murder trial began on May 4, 1994, with Karla Homolka taking the stand to testify against him. In defense attorney Carolyn MacDonald's cross-examination of Homolka, MacDonald questioned Karla about some claims she had made to Dr. Arndt that there was a video of a victim who had not been murdered, whose hand Karla had inserted into her vagina. Caught in a lie, Karla deflected the question by explaining that her memory had suffered tremendously as a result of the abuse. The prosecution, knowing fully well that she was being deceptive and hence breaking the terms of the plea bargain, did

---
* A pseudonym.

nothing. In fact, they even instructed their star witness on how to evade some of MacDonald's questions. To quote an expert on the case, "Karla's statements were never cross-referenced with other witnesses' statements, or, if they were, and the many discrepancies discovered, like the 1:58 videotape found in the house...they were simply ignored" (Williams, 2004, p. 239).

Bernardo's trial ground to a halt on September 12 when Ken Murray suddenly resigned as Bernardo's attorney, handing the case over to the formidable John Rosen. Having long deliberated on the matter, Murray revealed that on May 6, 1993—under Bernardo's instruction—he had gone to 57 Bayview Drive and removed six 8-mm videocassettes that were hidden behind a light fixture in the bathroom. Somehow the identification officers had missed them. Murray had subsequently reviewed the three and a half hours of footage on the videocassettes, and copied them onto VHS. These tapes, which showed Karla Homolka enthusiastically participating in a number of sexual acts and games with the captives, were turned over to Inspector Vince Bevan on September 22. Karla was notified by police that they had the tapes in their possession on September 27.

The GRT first viewed the tapes on October 11, 1994. The contents of the first tape included a brief scene in which Bernardo had filmed a young woman through her window without her knowing. It also contained footage of Leslie Mahaffy and Kristen French. Tape 2 showed the rapes, sexual assaults, and nonfatal violence against Mahaffy and French. There was also 18 minutes of additional footage of Karla Homolka drugging Samantha Moss with halothane as she sexually assaulted her. At this point, the plea bargain with Homolka should have unquestionably been null and void.

When Bernardo's trial was underway once again on May 1, 1995, the harrowing video tape footage left little doubt that he was a sexually sadistic psychopath who had abducted, repeatedly sexually assaulted, and tortured Leslie Mahaffy and Kristen French. The question was whether he had murdered them or whether Karla had. When Homolka took the witness stand on June 25 to testify against her former husband, John Rosen attempted to convince the jury that Karla had not been coerced, but had enjoyed the atrocities as much as Bernardo. Furthermore, he presented evidence from a pathologist's report to support his assertion that she had smothered Leslie Mahaffy to death, and murdered Kristen French with a rubber mallet. Though Rosen presented a compelling case, Homolka remained adamant in her account and surprisingly unflappable on the witness stand.

The jury began their deliberation on August 31, 1995, and by the next day had found Paul Kenneth Bernardo guilty on all counts. He would eventually be given the designation of "dangerous offender," which allows for life without the possibility of parole in Canada, but is usually reserved for violent individuals who have not been convicted of first-degree murder.

Karla Homolka was released from Sainte-Anne-des-Plaines prison in July 2005. She has since changed her name to "Leanne," married, and given birth to three children. In 2007, she moved to the Caribbean island of Guadeloupe with her husband and children. When her name last surfaced in 2014, she was once again living in Quebec, Canada.

Etiology

The renowned sexologist John Money (1990) proposed five possible etiological pathways for sexual sadism: *hereditary disposition* (genetic or chromosomal), *hormonal functioning* (impairment at prenatal, neonatal, or pubescent stages), *pathological relationships* (problems between a child and his caregivers during his formative years), *sexual abuse syndrome* (being traumatized by sexual abuse as a child), or a *syndrome overlap* as in a case when another personality disorder or mental illness contributes to the development of sexual sadism. As we have seen, many of these pathways were evident in the case of Paul Bernardo.

The neurobiological explanations for sexual sadism are numerous and varied. Money (1990) asserted that sexual sadism is a disease that ravages the center and pathways of the human brain related to sexual arousal. Specifically, it affects the limbic system—the amygdala, hippocampus, and hypothalamus—which have been linked to violence. Money proposes that due to brain malfunction, possibly the result of a tumor or head injury, the brain becomes conditioned to send messages related to sex and violence simultaneously. This is a paroxysmal process. One of the more convincing neurobiological explanations for sexual sadism which has statistical support is that it is somehow related to damage to the right temporal horn (Graber et al., 1982; Hucker et al., 1988; Langevin et al., 1988).

In reality, congenital and physical-damage-based origins of sexual sadism are likely only small pieces of a larger picture explained by the Motivational, Trauma-Control, Integrated, and Thematic-Derivative models.

Finally, a link between sexual sadism and psychopathy has long been established (Holt et al., 1999; Porter and Woodworth, 2006; Mokros et al., 2011). Recently, Robertson and Knight (2014) conducted two studies.

The first found that the interpersonal, lifestyle, and antisocial facets of the PCL-R have low-order positive correlations with sexual sadism,* while interpersonal, affective, and antisocial had low-order positive correlations with sadism in the second study. They thus concluded that total PCL-R score, the interpersonal facet, and antisocial facet were all related to sexual sadism.

Where as Dietz et al. (1990) found that the majority of sexual sadists in their study suffered from narcissistic personality disorder, Gratzer and Bradford (1995) discovered more evidence of antisocial personality disorder in their own sample, with their subjects evidencing more impulsive behavior which unsurprisingly correlated with defects in the frontal lobe. It is our contention that the sexual sadists selected for the study by Dietz et al. (1990) were likely *primary psychopaths* (see Chapter 9) whose affective deficits, grandiosity, and capacity for social predation are phenotypical of narcissism, while Gratzer and Bradford (1995) drew more from the ranks of *secondary psychopaths* (see Chapter 9) whose poor self-control mirrors antisocial personality disorder.

This provides some context for the typology of HSSs below. The HSSs in Dietz et al. (1990) belong exclusively to categories 1 and 2, with the Gratzer and Bradford (1995) HSSs mostly occupying categories 4–6.

Typology

The first to devise a classification system of sexual sadists was Krafft-Ebing (1886/2011), who formulated a rather rudimentary and, in hindsight, flawed eight-part typology consisting of (1) lust-killers, who associate murder with sexual stimulation, including *anthropophagy*; (2) *necrophiles* and corpse mutilators; (3) nonlethal wounders of females; (4) those who sexually assault females; (5) those who commit acts of symbolic sadism such as clandestinely snipping off women's hair; (6) sadistic fantasizers; (7) *zoosadists*; and (8) those who commit sadistic acts that do not fit into the aforementioned categories (e.g., flagellation of male children).

Of course, it is now known that not all those who kill for sexual pleasure or are sex offenders are sexual sadists (Kingston and Yates, 2008), that postmortem activities do not qualify somebody for sexual sadism (Mellor, 2016a), and that the cutting of women's hair—being generally painless—is more likely to reflect *trichophilia* (hair fetish).

For the purposes of this book, an eight-category typology of sexual sadists has been constructed, with two of these categories remaining hypothetical at present. The typology takes three parameters into consideration: (1) whether or not an offender inflicts ante- or peri-mortem destruction (i.e., mutilation) on his victim, (2) whether the period over which torture is inflicted is *brief* (1 hour $\geq$) or *prolonged* (1 hour <), and (3) whether the torture inflicted is *simple* or *elaborate* in nature.

The category that an offender falls into in this typology is based on his behaviors, not his fantasies. Indeed, it may be that he fantasizes about certain sexually sadistic acts, but has not perpetrated them. Serial child killer Westley Dodd, for example, was planning to bind his next victim to a torture board and mutilate him while he was still alive. Fortunately, Dodd was caught before he could inflict these horrors upon anyone. As he had not mutilated previous victims, he is classified as a category 4 HSS who was rapidly developing toward category 1 (Table 8.4).

Table 8.4 Mellor's Typology of Homicidal Sexual Sadists

Category	Destructive	Prolonged	Elaborate	Example
1[a]	Y	Y	Y	Fred West
2[a]	N	Y	Y	Robert Berdella
3	Y	Y	N	Chicago Rippers
4	N	Y	N	Keith Jesperson
5	Y	N	N	Andrei Chikatilo
6	N	N	N	Dennis Rader
7	*N*	*N*	*Y*	*N/A*
8	*Y*	*N*	*Y*	*N/A*

Note: Categories in *italics* may hypothetically exist, though our research has revealed no examples of offenders who exemplify the category.

[a] Categories that would be considered sexual sadists by the standards of Dietz, Hazelwood, and Warren in their numerous collaborative studies and articles on the phenomenon. Such offenders have been termed *complex sexual sadists*.

---

* Though it is apparent in this paper that the authors are discussing sexual sadists, they use the term "sadists" or "sadism," which can be confusing. It is recommended that future researchers be more specific.

Destructive versus Preservative

A *destructive* sexual sadist mutilates his victims while they are still alive. Mutilation does not refer to superficial stab wounds or biting used to torture the victim, or stab or slash wounds which were inflicted to hurt and/or kill a victim. Rather, mutilation refers specifically to incidences in which a body part is intentionally *disfigured* or has parts *excised*, or when the victim is *eviscerated*. If no such mutilations occur in the ante-mortem or peri-mortem stages, the offender is instead classified as a *preservative* sexual sadist.

Randy Steven Kraft was known to sometimes excise his victims' genitals while they were still alive (McDougal, 1991). Kraft is an example of a *destructive* sexual sadist. Billy Lee Chadd used shallow incisions to torture his victims and often killed them by stabbing them; however, as he did not mutilate them in the way specified above, he is considered a *preservative* sexual sadist (Hazelwood and Michaud, 2001).

Prolonged versus Brief

A *prolonged* sexual sadist intentionally tortures his victim either continuously or episodically over the course of approximately 1 hour or more, whereas a *brief* sexual sadist does so for a shorter period of time. Leonard Lake and Charles Ng kept sex slaves who they sadistically raped and abused for weeks if not longer, making them *prolonged* sexual sadists (Fox and Levin, 2005). This contrasts with Kendall Francois who would only torture his victims for minutes (*brief*), looking into their face as he raped, and manually strangled them to death (Fox and Levin, 2005).

Elaborate versus Simple

The elaborate–simple dichotomy is the most subjective of the three facets of sexual sadism. A useful heuristic is that if the offender falls into at least three of the four categories listed below, then he qualifies as *elaborate*. If not, he is *simple*.

1. Variation in torture methods

    An elaborate sexual sadist will typically inflict pain using four or more separate methods. For our purposes, all variations of intentionally painful sexual assault—including foreign object penetration—count as a single method: sexual torture. Thus, an offender who hurts his victims by forcefully vaginally raping them, sodomizing them, inserting a branch into their orifices, and beating them has only used two pain inflicted methods, because the vaginal rape, sodomy, and foreign object insertion are all grouped under the single offense of sexual torture. Similarly, methods that humiliate or degrade a victim such as urinating on them or rubbing their face in mud also count as a single method—humiliation/degradation. Interestingly, some researchers have actually proposed that humiliation may be more important in arousing the sexual sadist than acts of violence (Proulx et al., 1994). Psychological torture is not counted among these torture methods (but see below).

    Lawrence Bittaker sexually tortured his victims, tore their skin with pliers, beat them with a hammer, and strangled them with wire, showing high variation in torture methods (Fox and Levin, 2005).

2. Complex torture apparatus

    Complex torture apparatus refers to the use of instruments with moving parts (not including firearms) specifically constructed or purchased by the offender to inflict pain. Examples include pulley systems, motors, electrical devices, etc. Gary Heidnik suspended one of his victims from the ceiling using a system of chains to hurt her, and administered electric shocks to several others (Englade, 1988). Both of these qualify as complex torture apparatus.

3. Psychological torture

    Psychological torture occurs when the sexual sadist employs techniques that do not physically harm the victim, purely to make his victims suffer (i.e., are not part of his modus operandi). This can include instilling fear in them; intentionally disorienting them by placing a bag over their head; giving them psychotropic drugs with the intent to frighten them, etc.; or encouraging the victim's hope before maliciously revealing this to be a trick. For instance, Richard Cottingham was known to leave a pistol within his victims' reach. Seeing a chance to escape, they would pick the weapon up and point it at him, only to find that it was not loaded. This evidences Cottingham's use of psychological torture (Leith, 1983).

4. Record making

The sexual sadist documents the suffering of his victims using video cameras, photographs, audio recordings, sketches, etc. The taking of souvenirs or body parts does not qualify as record making. "Moors Murderer" Ian Brady tape recorded his fourth known victim begging for her life and later used it sexually arouse himself (Brady, 2001).

Category 1: Fred West: A Destructive/Prolonged/Elaborate (DPE) Sex Sadist
Aided by his wife Rosemary, British serial killer Fred West was known to abduct his young female victims for weeks at a time, suspending them from chains in his basement dungeon in Gloucester. There, he would subject them to various types of sexual assaults, completely cover their heads in duct tape so that they would have to breathe through plastic tubes inserted into their nostrils, *disfigure* their genitalia, and *excise* their digits, along with numerous other depraved acts. Like most sexually sadistic serial killers, the degree and extent of West's violence built up over a period of years, with DPE forms of torture representing the height of his fantasies and control. Typically, he would murder them by strangulation or stabbing (Wilson, 1998).

West is also believed to be a Category A homicidal necrophile (see Chapter 7).

Category 2: Robert Berdella: A Preservative/Prolonged/Elaborate (PPE) Sex Sadist
Antiques shop owner Bob Berdella drugged, restrained, and forcibly confined at least seven men, one who survived, in his Kansas City residence, subjecting them to tortures such as multiple and diverse sexual assaults, electrocution, injecting drain cleaner into their throats, pouring bleach into their eyes, and gouging their eyeballs over the course of days. When Berdella had finished abusing his victims, he generally suffocated them to death with a plastic bag. Berdella documented the process of torture by taking Polaroid© photographs, and recording his victims' reactions to torture in a written log. Unlike West, however, he did not mutilate his victims' bodies for paraphilic purposes when they were alive or dead (Jackman and Cole, 1992). The cases of Paul Bernardo and David Parker Ray discussed in this chapter are both examples of Category 2 HSSs.

Category 3: The Chicago Rippers: Destructive/Prolonged/Simple (DPS) Sex Sadists
The "Chicago Rippers" are referred to here as a group, rather than any one individual, as there is much debate over the respective level of involvement of their four members: Robin Gecht, Edward Spreitzer, Thomas, and Andrew Kokoraleis. Though the latter three were convicted of murder, they all independently claim that Gecht was their ringleader, and harbored the most intensely violent paraphilic urges. Between 1981 and 1982, the Rippers abducted at least 13 women, gang-raped them, *excised* their breasts while they were alive, and then murdered them by stabbing, shooting, or strangulation. Several victims survived and later identified the men (Newton, 2000).

Some of the rippers may arguably be Category C homicidal necrophiles (see Chapter 7), as they masturbated into the open wounds of their victims, and onto their severed breasts which they devoured.

Category 4: Keith Hunter Jesperson: A Preservative/Prolonged/Simple (PPS) Sex Sadist
Keith Hunter Jesperson was a Canadian-born American long-haul trucker who, after offering to give women at truck stops (often prostitutes) rides across the country, kept them forcibly confined in his sleeper cab. There he would repeatedly vaginally rape them, while strangling them unconscious with his bare hands, only to revive them and commence this brutal torture sometimes for hours. He referred to this practice as the "death game" and it would inevitably end with Jesperson fatally throttling his victim (Mellor, 2012).

Category 5: Andrei Chikatilo: A Destructive/Brief/Simple (DBS) Sex Sadist
In the former Soviet Union, pedophile Andrei Chikatilo realized that he could spontaneously ejaculate by watching a victim react to the pain and suffering that he was inflicting upon them. Generally, Chikatilo would stab them multiple times, achieving sexual climax sometimes without direct genital manipulation or at other times by simultaneous masturbation. Chikatilo would also frequently inflict ante-mortem or

peri-mortem mutilations on his victims such as biting out their tongues, *excising* or *disfiguring* their genitals, and *eviscerating* them (Lourie, 1993). Unsurprisingly, given the extent of his violence, none of his victims would survive for more than an hour.

He was also a Category C homicidal necrophile (see Chapter 7).

Category 6: Dennis Rader: A Preservative/Brief/Simple (PBS) Sex Sadist

Having been aroused by thoughts of binding (*vincilagnia*) and torturing females since he was a boy, Dennis Rader christened himself "BTK" (Bind, Torture, Kill). He would break into his victims' homes, gain control over them by threatening them with a firearm, tie them up, and then strangle or suffocate them in and out of consciousness for a short period before finally ending their lives. It is important to note that *vincilagnia* seemed to be Rader's dominant paraphilia, with *sexual sadism* taking a secondary position (State of Kansas v. Dennis Lynn Rader, 2005a,b).

Though the extent of his activities are unknown, it could also be argued that Rader was a homicidal necrophile (McClellan, 2010; Mellor, 2016c) occupying Category D or E (see Chapter 7).

Categories 7 and 8: No Offenders Discovered: Preservative/Brief/ Elaborate (PBE) and Destructive/Brief/Elaborate (DBE) Sex Sadists

As the nature of elaborate torture seems to be invariably perpetrated by offenders who wish to prolong the process, no PBE or DBE HSSs have been discovered during the course of this research. This does not mean that such offender may not be identified in the future, but as of this writing, their existence is purely hypothetical.

Characteristics of Sexually Sadistic Homicides and Their Perpetrators

Like necrophilia, there is no firm consensus as to what constitutes sexual sadism (Healey et al., 2013). As Marshall and Hucker (2006b) observe, apart from the criteria advocated in the DSM-5 and Dietz et al. (1990), some researchers attribute sexually sadistic pleasure to the infliction of pain (Power, 1976; MacCulloch et al., 1983; Ressler et al., 1992; Seto and Kuban, 1996), while others relate it to the feeling of possessing the victim and becoming dominant (Brittain, 1970; Fromm, 1973; Levin and Fox, 1985; Gratzer and Bradford, 1995; Giannangelo, 1996; Egger, 1998).

It is our opinion that sexual sadism is best understood as an eroticized communication process—a *sadistic cycle*—in which the perpetrator (1) *inflicts* negative stimulus, (2) watches his victim *react*, and (3) *experiences* an enhancement in self-concept. Given the definition of sexual sadism used in this chapter, it is necessary that Step 2 is sexualized, though any or all of the three steps in the cycle could theoretically sexually stimulate the HSS. This unites the various competing theories listed above into a holistic understanding of the phenomenon. Moreover, the model applies at both a macro- and microcosmic level. In the small picture, the cycle moves quickly—the sadist inflicts the snap of a whip, hears the victim scream and sees their body react, feels powerful and important, and inflicts another snap of the whip. He may be in a sustained state of sexual arousal throughout the turning of the cycle, regardless of which stage of the process is most erotic for him. The sadistic cycle may be specific, following the narrative of an orgasmic-conditioned fantasy, or to varying degrees, may entail a level of improvisation and experimentation.

Dietz et al. (1990) report that 43% of the 30 sexual sadists in their study evidenced sexual dysfunction during their offenses, with Gratzer and Bradford's (1995) research supporting this finding. Specifically, 37% (11) of Dietz et al.'s total sample suffered from retarded ejaculation. MacCulloch et al. (1983) propose that for sexual sadists "by far the greatest amount of pleasure (normal or abnormal) is derived during the period of sexual pleasure prior to orgasm" (p. 20). If this is the case, it is logical for the offender to sustain the sadistic cycle, with either delayed ejaculation or no attempt to bring the act to an orgasmic conclusion. Gratzer and Bradford add that "sexual sadists appear not to be aroused by the sexual act itself. Rather the sexual act[s] seem to be used as vehicles for the degradation and control of the victims" (p. 452).

This paraphilia is strongly associated with psychopathy (see Chapter 9). On average, sexual sadism develops a few months after the age of 19 (Abel et al., 1988). Seventy-three percent of the sexual sadists in the study by Dietz et al. (1990) targeted only female victims, and 17% only males, which seems to indicate an overrepresentation of sexual sadism in the male homosexual community. This percentage might be inflated by the presence of one or more homosexual pedophiles in the study. Only 10% victimized both males and females. Regarding the victims' ages, 57% of the offenders preyed only on adults, 17% on children, while a staggering 43% of the total offenders victimized one or more children as well as adults. We hypothesize that this latter statistic is tied to the equal-opportunity victimization inherent in psychopathy (see Chapter 9).

The sexual sadists in the sample by Dietz et al. (1990) were often married at the time of the offense, had military experience[*] and some degree of postsecondary education, and presented as reputable citizens. For reasons already hypothesized, Gratzer and Bradford (1995) did not find this in their sample.

Roughly a third of sexual sadists seem to have a strong interest in the police (Dietz et al., 1990), with offenders such as Bianchi and Buono, John Wayne Gacy, and Ted Bundy actually posing as law enforcement in order to con some of their victims into getting into their cars. Similarly, Paul Bernardo owned handcuffs and retained a security guard outfit.

Frequently, sexual sadists will have abused drugs, and a look at their car's odometers will reveal that they are compulsive and often aimless drivers (Dietz et al., 1990).

Identifying and Investigating Sexually Sadistic Homicide Crime Scenes

Kingston and Yates (2008) have highlighted the troublesome fact that though certain crime scene behaviors have been associated with sexual sadism in academic publications, the offenders who committed these crimes are rarely if ever formally diagnosed with sexual sadism. Rather, sexual sadism is simply assumed to exist in such individuals because they have committed sexual homicides. Perhaps even more problematic is that excessive violence is also perpetrated by many nonsexually sadistic offenders.

One important exception is a recent study by Healey et al. (2013) in which crime scene behaviors were coded from 268 male offenders. Nineteen were identified as sexual sadists. They found that sexually sadistic offenders were more likely to premeditate their crimes, and to mutilate and humiliate their victims than nonsadists. In fact, the researchers discovered that some characteristics believed in previous studies to be particular to sexual sadists, such as kidnapping a victim or using excessive violence, were equally represented in nonsadists. Unfortunately, the authors do not define "excessive violence" or specify the nature of the mutilation (e.g., whether it took place before or after death, whether it was defensive or paraphilic).

Other crime scene behaviors listed here will be drawn from the study of 30 sexually sadistic offenders by Dietz et al. (1990), though we reiterate the important caveat that this research team only seem to include category 1 and 2 offenders in their studies. When this research is supported by Gratzer and Bradford (1995) and Healey et al. (2013), a footnote will be included indicating that this is the case.

According to Dietz et al. (1990), 66.6% of sexual sadists conceal their victims' corpses (Table 8.5). However, it should be noted that only 22 of the offenders in the study murdered their victims, so in actuality, 91% of sexually sadistic murderers conceal bodies. Taking this into consideration, a typical sexually sadistic homicide investigation will occur (1) when a body is anywhere from several days to years into the decomposition process, or (2) when a body remains undiscovered. Dietz et al. (1990) attribute this to the offender's obsessive planning in order to delay or prevent altogether the discovery of the body so as to avoid detection.

This first scenario applies to Paul Bernardo's known murder victims. Leslie Mahaffy's dismembered cement-encased remains were found 15 days after her disappearance, and 13 days after her murder, while Kristen French's body was located 14 days after her disappearance, and 11 days after her murder.

There are a number of telltale signs that a victim has been subjected to a sexually sadistic attack. *Signature* behaviors that a pathologist should be able to observe if the body is relatively intact include anal rape and forced fellatio, which occur in 73.3% and 70% of sexually sadistic offenses, respectively (Dietz et al., 1990). Nearly 67% of sexually sadistic offenders subject their victims to three or more of the following acts: sodomy, forced fellatio, vaginal rape, and foreign object insertion (Dietz et al., 1990). During a homicide investigation, if any victim's body shows evidence of anal rape or forced fellatio in conjunction with at least two other acts of sexual penetration, they should strongly be considered as the potential victim of a sexual sadist. Since 100% of the offenders in Dietz et al.'s (1990) sample tortured their victims, the coincidence of anal rape, forced fellatio, or *any* three or more acts of sexual penetration with evidence of torture should confirm the presence of a sexually sadistic perpetrator. Table 8.6 reveals the methods of physical torture Dietz et al. (1990) found among the 30 sexual sadists in their study. The table provides examples of the types of injuries that may be identified on the corpse of a sexual sadist's victim. For example, Paul Bernardo did not use specific "instruments of torture"; however, he had his accomplice violently insert a foreign object (a wine bottle) into his last victim's anus, beat and asphyxiated them, and occasionally cut them (Table 8.7).

---

[*] Given the vastly differing sizes of the American and Canadian militaries, it would be unreasonable to assume that the number of Canadian offenders with a military background would be anywhere near that of Americans.

Table 8.5 Characteristics of Offenses by Sexually Sadistic Offenders

Characteristics	n	%
A partner assisted in the offense	11	36.7
Careful planning of offense[a]	28	93.3
Impersonation of police in commission of offense	7	23.3
Victim taken to preselected[b] location	23	76.7
Victim kept in captivity for 24 hours or more[c]	18	60
Victim bound, blindfolded, or gagged[d]	26	86.7
Sexual bondage of victim (distinguished from bondage for the sole purpose of restraining the victim's movement)	23	76.7
Anal rape of victim	22	73.3
Forced victim to perform fellatio	21	70
Vaginal rape of victim	17	56.7
Foreign object penetration of victim	12	40
Variety of sexual acts with the victim (at least three of the following: vaginal rape, forced fellatio, anal rape, foreign object penetration)	20	66.7
Sexual dysfunction during offense	13	43.3
Unemotional, detached affect during offense	26	86.6
Told victim what to say during assault	7	23.3
Intentional torture	30	100
Murdered victim	22	73.3
Committed serial murders (three or more victims)	17	56.6
Concealed victim's corpse	20	66.6
Victim beaten (blunt force trauma)	18	60
Recorded the offense (includes recordings through writings, drawings, photographs, audio tapes, or video tapes)	16	53.3
Kept personal item belonging to victim	12	40

Source: Dietz, P., Hazelwood, R., and Warren, J. 1990. The sexually sadistic criminal and his offenses. *Journal of the American Academy of Psychiatry and the Law, 18*(2), 163–178.

[a] Supported by the research of Healey et al. (2013) who found that 89.5% (n = 17) of the sexual sadists in their sample premeditated their crimes, as opposed to 62% (n = 114) of nonsadists (Gratzer and Bradford, 1995).

[b] Supported by the research of Healey et al. (2013) who found that 89.5% (n = 17) of the sexual sadists in their sample premeditated their crimes, as opposed to 62% (n = 114) of nonsadists.

[c] 38.5% (n = 10) of the sadists in the study by Healey et al. (2013) kidnapped and confined their victims, as opposed to only 5.9% (n = 11) of nonsadists.

[d] Healey et al. (2013) found that 33.3% (n = 6) of sadists used physical restraints, more than triple that of nonsadists (n = 20) at 10.9%.

Case Study: David Parker Ray, Cindy Hendy, Roy Yancy, and Jesse Ray

Elephant Butte, New Mexico: A desert community of 1390 inhabitants. Late in the afternoon on March 22, 1999, the door to Darlene and Donald Breech's double-wide trailer burst open, and a young naked woman ran in screaming for help. Visibly injured, with a metal collar and broken chain fastened around her neck, she pleaded with Darlene not to let "them" get her. Darlene immediately realized the seriousness of the situation. Describing the young woman's physical state, she would later say, "Her wrists looked like hamburger meat. She had beautiful long brown hair and it was all matted with blood. She was dirty all over and it looked like she had pooped in her pants. Her poor little boobs were black and blue and there were bruises all over her arms and legs" (Fielder, 2003, p. 14). As Darlene did her best to comfort her, the woman began revealing more information: a couple named David and Cindy had abducted her, locked her in a trailer, then spent the past three days raping and torturing her. Today, David had put on a uniform and left for work, leaving Cindy to watch their chained captive. The young woman had managed to slip her locks, stab Cindy in the neck with an ice pick, and escape out of the window onto the desert road. Darlene called 911, and two Sierra County sheriff's deputies arrived to pick up the young woman, and took her immediately to the Sierra Vista County Hospital. She would eventually identify herself as Cynthia Vigil—a streetwalker from Albuquerque, a city approximately 150 miles north of Elephant Butte.

Table 8.6 Methods of Physical Torture Used by Sexually Sadistic Offenders

Method of Torture	n	%
Instruments of torture used[a]	8	26.7
Painful insertion of foreign objects	7	23.3
Beating[b]	6	20
Biting	5	16.7
Whipping	5	16.7
Painful bondage	5	16.7
Electrical shock	4	13.3
Twisting breasts until victim unconscious	4	13.3
Asphyxiation until victim unconscious	4	13.3
Burning	3	10
Amputation	2	6.7
Threatening with snakes	2	6.7
Cutting	1	3.3
Pulling out hair	1	3.3
Insertion of glass rod in male urethra	1	3.3
Injection	1	3.3
Submersion	1	3.3

Source: Dietz, P., Hazelwood, R., and Warren, J. 1990. The sexually sadistic criminal and his offenses. *Journal of the American Academy of Psychiatry and the Law, 18*(2), 163–178.

[a] This was the only behavior on this list that Gratzer and Bradford (1995) found to be present in their sample of sexual sadists.

[b] "Beating" was overwhelmingly the main method of torture in the Canadian sample (Gratzer and Bradford, 1995). Once again, this seems related to the impulsive seemingly *secondary psychopathic* nature of the sex sadists in this sample, as beatings can be improvisational.

The perpetrators, David Parker Ray, 59, and his 39-year-old girlfriend, Cindy Hendy, were found driving around the neighborhood looking for Vigil, and arrested.

Interviewed by Agent Wesley LeCuesta of the New Mexico State Police (NMSP), whom the case had been quickly turned over to, Cynthia Vigil explained that on the morning of Saturday, March 20, her pimp had introduced her to David Parker Ray and Cindy Hendy on Central Avenue in Albuquerque. She had gone to their RV expecting to exchange sexual favors for money, when suddenly, Ray produced a police badge and informed her that he was an undercover vice cop and was arresting her for solicitation. Cindy Hendy

Table 8.7 Cause of Death of 130 Murder Victims of Sexual Sadists

Cause of Death of 130 Murder Victims of Sexual Sadists	n	%
Ligature strangulation[a]	42 (one man responsible for 32)	32.3
Manual strangulation	34 (one man responsible for 25)	26.1
Gunshot wounds[b]	32 (one man responsible for 17)	24.6
Cutting and stabbing wounds	13	10
Blunt force trauma	4	3.1
Hanging	2	1.5
Suffocation	1	0.8
Torture	1	0.8
Exposure	1	0.8

Source: Dietz, P., Hazelwood, R., and Warren, J. 1990. The sexually sadistic criminal and his offenses. *Journal of the American Academy of Psychiatry and the Law, 18*(2), 163–178.

[a] This was the only means of murder that Gratzer and Bradford (1995) found was specifically associated with sexual sadism.

[b] As the Dietz et al. (1990) sample was American, and the sample by Gratzer and Bradford (1995) Canadian, there can be no meaningful interpretation of the number of murders committed by sexual sadists using firearms, given the different laws surrounding gun control in their respective nations.

had swiftly handcuffed her to the inside of the vehicle, and the two had stripped her clothes and threatened to electrocute her if she struggled. Transported to Ray's home, once inside, Vigil was played a lengthy tape recording of Ray describing how he planned to rape and torture her. Soon after, he penetrated her vaginally and anally with dildos while Hendy brandished a revolver. Ray attached cables to Vigil's breasts and genitalia and repeatedly shocked her with electricity. The following day she was chained to the ceiling where she was photographed and whipped, then raped with a large metal dildo.

Unlike the Bernardo case, where Toronto Metro Police had been aware of a sadistic rapist in their community and the Niagara Police had formed the GRT to investigate the murders of Leslie Mahaffy and Kristen French, until Cynthia Vigil's escape, nobody suspected that an abductor and serial torturer of women had been operating in Sierra County. Nevertheless, if Cynthia Vigil's account proved to be credible, investigators expected to find a trove of evidence at Ray's mobile home.

An initial search of the building by Deputy David Elston had revealed broken lamp on the floor of the bedroom, and blood-stained sheets. This seemed to corroborate Vigil's account of her escape in which she struggled with Cindy Hendy. Several elaborate instruments of sexual torture were also immediately observable: chains and hooks hanging from sliding steel rods on the ceiling and operated by a system of pulleys, a large dildo, and a box resembling a coffin pushed against the wall.

Arraigned separately on March 24, both Ray and Hendy requested public defenders. They were each charged on 25 felony counts, including kidnapping, criminal sexual penetration, aggravated assault, and criminal conspiracy.

A former friend of Hendy's, John Branaugh, soon appeared on KOB-TV, saying that on March 13, 1999, a drunken Hendy had told him and his wife, Jean, that her new boyfriend David Parker Ray was a serial killer responsible for hundreds of deaths. Ray preyed on prostitutes and drug addicts mainly, because of their place on the margins of society. Hendy had allegedly told Branaugh that she personally knew that the bodies of six or seven women were at the bottom of Elephant Butte Lake. Ray would eviscerate them, stuff the bodies with rocks, bind them back together with chicken wire, and then dump them in the water. Branaugh said that Hendy also complained about a drop of blood that she could not scrub off the floor. It had been there since David Parker Ray had shot a man in the head. Hendy had also allegedly said that she was looking forward to suffocating the next victim herself so that she could experience the rush of committing murder. At the time, the Branaughs had thought that Hendy was simply lying.

As the stories spread, another woman claiming to be a surviving victim of David Parker Ray came forward. On March 28, 27-year-old Angelique Montano entered the police station in Truth or Consequences where she spent the next 5 hours detailing how she had been repeatedly raped and tortured by Ray and Hendy from February 17 to 21, 1999. Unlike Cynthia Vigil who had escaped in time, Angie said that Ray had eventually taken her to a trailer on his property that he referred to as "The Toy Box." Montano soon sold the story of her capture to *Globe* reporter Joe Mullins, who published it on the front-page.

Following the arraignment, an obviously shaken Cindy Hendy offered to divulge new information to Wesley La Cuesta. She claimed that David Parker Ray had told her that he had murdered at least 14 people after subjecting them to prolonged sexual torture. Two of these supposed victims were identified from photographs already recovered from the "Toy Box." He said that he had buried or dumped his victims in the wilderness of New Mexico, and two other southwestern states. Hendy's confession was recorded on tape. Immediately after, the NMSP contacted the FBI's Behavioral Science Unit which was famous for dealing with cases of abnormal homicide. The two agencies decided to keep Hendy's revelation secret until they could ascertain the veracity of the murder claims. Interviewed a second time several days later, Hendy elaborated on her previous confession, adding that Ray claimed to have murdered his first victim as a teenager, binding a woman to a tree. She also mentioned an ex-boyfriend—Dennis Roy Yancy, whom she referred to as "Roy Boy"—who was a friend of Ray's, and had murdered a missing woman named Marie Parker in 1997.

Hendy then signed a "Plea of Disposition" in which she would plead guilty to the first-degree kidnappings and criminal penetrations of Cynthia Vigil and Angelica Montano, along with conspiracy to kidnap Vigil; assist with the investigation; and testify against David Parker Ray in return for a guarantee that she would serve between 12 and 54 years in prison and possibly pay as much as $60,000 in fines. The State would not file any further charges against Hendy; however, if more crimes were to surface, she could be susceptible to federal prosecution. Also, the agreement would be terminated in the event that Hendy ceased to cooperate with the investigators and prosecution.

The FBI took the lead on the investigation on March 29, with the NMSP providing crime-scene security. Along with searchers from the NMSP, they recovered a videotape which showed six minutes of footage in which a woman with a swan tattoo on her ankle was strapped to a bench and sexually assaulted by Ray.

Her eyes and mouth were covered with black duct tape as to significantly obscure her features. The victim, Kelli Van Cleave, was identified when her former mother-in-law saw coverage of the case on television, and telephoned the FBI. She told them that Kelli had gone missing for three days in July 1996 only to be brought back home by David Parker Ray who had told them that he had found her wandering on a nearby beach. Kelli was in a daze, messy and dirty, and missing her shoes and wedding ring. When asked, she had been unable to recall where she had been or what had happened to her. Convinced that Kelli had been cheating on him, the woman's son had told Kelli that he wanted a divorce and not to come in the house.

Hundreds of FBI agents had joined in the search of Ray's property by April. They located another video which showed a nude female, heavily drugged and on her back. Strips of duct tape covered her mouth and eyes. She was secured to a medical table by red nylon restraints in a spread eagle position. David Parker Ray stood over her in a black robe and a black leather mask freckled with gold. Beside him, Cindy Hendy pointed a handgun at the woman, threatening to kill her unless she cooperated. Laughing, Ray violently inserted a cattle prod into the woman's vagina. Her body visibly writhed in pain. Other acts of torture were to follow, physical and psychological—with Ray and Hendy ripping the duct tape off her mouth so that they could hear the woman scream and beg for her life. Eventually, blood suddenly began to pour out of the woman's mouth and ears, and her body fell limp and still. The investigators were convinced they had just witnessed a homemade snuff video showing a victim dying before their eyes.

Other evidence found behind the windowless trailer on blocks with the steel-reinforced double deadbolted door included:

- White sign with red letters saying "SATAN'S DEN"

- White sign with black underlined letters saying "THE BONDAGE ROOM"

- Replica skull with three white candles on top

- Bleached skull

- A motorized black leather gynecological chair with red plastic straps, metal stirrups, and electrodes on it. Elbow light fastened to end. Chair attached to six-foot tract so that it can slide backwards and forwards

- RCA Victor video camera on tripod pointed at chair

- RCA Victor television set placed so victims could observe what was being done to them

- Long black robe with red cape

- A clipboard with list of victims kidnapped between 1994 and 1997

- A cork bulletin board with photos and drawings pinned to it of adult females being tortured. Sign above it reads "THE LURE OF SATANISM"

- Instruments of torture, which included ammonia pills, branding iron, chains, chloroform (in bottles), clamps, clothespins, cotton, dildos (wooden, metal, latex, plastic), fishhooks, forceps, harnesses, handcuffs, K-Y jelly, latex gloves, lead sinkers, leather belts, needles, paddles, petroleum jelly, pins, pulleys, ropes, sandpaper, saw blades, screw clamps, soldering iron, suction cups, syringes, whips, wires

- Bathroom care products: baby oil, baby powder, body lotion, lipstick, mouthwash, nightgowns, perfume, shampoo

- A large generator with three switches "BUZZER," "LIGHT," and "PROBE," attached to fifteen-inch motorized dildo

- A miniature Barbie doll with chains hanging from neck, breasts, wrists, and ankles

- Aluminum drawer with six-foot-long cot as in a morgue

- Books on witchcraft and anatomy

There was also a note on the wall which read:

Remember		
A woman will do or say anything to get loose		
They will		
Kick	Scratch	Offer money
Bite	Yell	Beg
Scream	Run	Offer sex
Threaten	Lie	Wait for opportunity

Standard excuses and sob stories:

> Menstruating
> Pregnant
> V.D.
> Aids
> Sick
> Kids with babysitter
> Have to work
> A sick baby
> A sick parent
> Claustrophobia
> Missed by husband or friend
> Bad heart
> Can't miss school

> Don't let her get to you
> If she was worth taking-she is
> Worth keeping
> And
> She must be subjected to hypnosis before
> The woman can be safely released
> Never trust a chained captive

Underneath a drawing of a nude female with a hood over her head and clamps attached to her nipples:

1. Operate motor with the lever in the "up" position.

2. Attach clamps securely to each nipple.

3. Tighten cord until breasts are stretched to the maximum length.

4. Turn machine "on" and watch nipples for indication of tearing and check clamps for slippage. Continue to operate.

Note: This process is very painful and due to the constant motion, the body will not adjust to the pain. During the operation, the subject will remain in extremely painful distress.

Also recovered from the property was a five-minute-long audio tape, the content of which seemed to match the tape played in Cynthia Vigil's account of her abduction. Despite a thorough and ongoing search of the Ray property and Elephant Butte Lake by multiple police forces, no bodies were ever located.

That month, Kelli Van Cleave—now remarried and living in Craig, Colorado—was contacted by the FBI and met with agents from the bureau and NMSP. When shown the photograph of the swan tattoo, she tearfully confirmed that it was her and admitted that she had had amnesia and nightmares for years, but that gradually memories were returning to her. Kelli had been at the Blue Waters Saloon in Truth or Consequences on the night of July 25, 1996, and was the designated driver. At the end of the evening, Jesse Ray—David Parker Ray's lesbian daughter and a known dealer of marijuana, cocaine, and crystal meth—had offered to drive Kelli home on her motorcycle. Instead, she had taken her to David Parker Ray's house. There, Kelli was threatened to comply with a knife, and had duct tape placed over her eyes and mouth, was stripped nude, and had a dog collar fastened around her neck. She remembered being tortured for days as David Ray inserted large, sometimes spiked dildos into her vagina. Eventually, he had released her saying that he was part of a group of Satanists that had flagged her for a sex slave, but that he had subsequently decided she was too "tight between the legs for good sex." She had never told anybody in Truth or Consequences of her ordeal because she was certain that they would not believe her.

On April 9, after finishing his shift as a short-order cook at the Black Range Motel in Truth or Consequences, 27-year-old Roy Yancy, the man Cindy Hendy had implicated in Marie Parker's murder, was arrested by Wesley La Cuesta and Carlos Martinez and brought to an interview room in the state police office. Agent Norman Rhoades, who had dealt with the visibly apprehensive Yancy before, managed to get him to confess to the murder of Marie Parker within an hour.

Yancy said that at the end of the July 4 weekend, he and Jesse Ray had met Marie Parker, his former girlfriend, at the Blue Waters Saloon in Elephant Butte. Wanting to score some drugs, Marie had gone for a ride in David Parker Ray's white Dodge Charger with Jesse behind the wheel and Yancy in the back seat. Instead of taking Marie to find narcotics, Jesse and Roy Yancy had abducted her at gunpoint and brought her back to David Ray's double-wide trailer. Yancy then claimed that Jesse and David had taken Marie into the "Toy Box" while he watched TV. They had finally told him they were "done playing with her" on July 18, at which point Yancy said they made him strangle Marie to death in the Toy Box while Jesse threatened him with a gun. Yancy and the Rays had bundled Marie's corpse into a blanket, driven to Monticello Canyon, dumped it down the side of a ravine, and covered it with dirt. According to Yancy, the Rays had threatened him with death if he ever told anybody about the killing. He had spent the next year hiding out in Galveston, Texas with Jesse Ray until the fervor over Marie Parker's disappearance had dissipated, and in the summer of 1998, he had returned to Truth or Consequences.

By 10:30 p.m., Yancy had been charged with Parker's murder, kidnapping, tampering with evidence, and conspiracy to commit murder, and held without bond at Sierra County Detention Center. The following morning he escorted investigators to the place where he claimed they had buried Marie Parker's body, but they were unable to locate the remains. Yancy theorized that David Parker Ray had returned to remove them.

On April 12, Yancy pleaded not guilty to all of the charges at the Sierra Country Magistrates Court.

In mid-April, David Parker Ray attended a two-day preliminary hearing during which Angelica Montano and Cynthia Vigil both testified about the confinement, torture, and rape they had suffered at his hands. When shown the metal collar that she had been forced to wear, Vigil suffered a panic attack resulting in the judge having to temporarily clear the courtroom and ensure Vigil received medical attention to counteract her hyperventilating. Vigil also told of how Ray and Hendy had discussed kidnapping a 10-year-old girl in the near future to train as their sex slave, and that Hendy had claimed to be involved in other murders over the past year, but that she was a novice compared to Ray. The judge determined that Ray would stand trial on 37 counts.

The fourth and final suspect to be charged in the investigation, Jesse Ray, was arrested on April 26, and charged with twelve counts of kidnapping, conspiracy to kidnap, and criminal sexual penetration, and arraigned that afternoon. If convicted she could expect up to 150 years of incarceration. At her May 11 preliminary hearing, in which it was eventually determined that Jesse would stand trial, the judge allowed the audiotape found on David Parker Ray's property to be played for the first time:

"Hello there, bitch! Are you comfortable right now? I doubt it. Wrists and ankles chained, gagged, probably blindfolded. You are disoriented and scared, too, I would imagine.… Perfectly normal under the circumstances. For a little while at least, you need to get your shit together and listen to this tape. It is very relevant to your situation. I'm going to tell you in detail why you have been kidnapped, what's going to happen to you and how long you'll be here.

I don't know the details of your capture, because this tape is being created July 23, 1993, as a this-is-what's-going-to-happen-to-you tape for my captives. The information I'm going to give you is based on my experiences dealing with captives over a period of several years. If at a future date, there are any major changes in our procedures, the tape will be upgraded. Now, you are obviously here against your will. Totally helpless. Don't know where you're at. Don't know what's going to happen to you. You're scared or pissed off. I'm sure that you've already tried to get your wrists and ankles loose, and know you can't. Now you're waiting to see what's going to happen next. You probably think you're going to be raped, and you're fucking sure right about that.

Our primary interest is in what you've got between your legs. You'll be raped thoroughly and repeatedly in every hole you've got, because basically, you've been snatched and brought here for us to train and use as a sex slave. Sound kind of far-out? Well, I suppose it is for the uninitiated, but we do it all the time. It's gonna take a lot of adjustment on your part, and you're not going to like it a fucking bit, but I don't give a rat's ass about that. It's not like you're gonna have any choice about the matter. You've been taken by force, and you're going to be kept and used by force.

What all this amounts to is that you're going to be kept naked and chained up like an animal to be used and abused anytime we want to, any way that we want to. And you might as well start getting used to it, because you're going to be kept here and used, until such time as we get tired of fucking around with you, and we will eventually, in a month or two, or three.

It's no big deal; my lady friend and I have been keeping sex slaves for years. We both have kinky hang-ups involving rape, dungeon games et cetera. We found that it is extremely convenient to keep one or two female captives available constantly to satisfy our particular needs. We are very selective when we snatch a girl to use for these purposes. It goes without saying that you have a fine body, and you're probably young, maybe very young. Because for our purposes, we prefer to snatch girls in their early to midteens, sexually developed, but still small body, scared shitless, easy to handle and easy to train. And they usually have tight little pussies and assholes. They make perfect slaves.

Anytime we go on a hunting trip, if we can't find a little teenager, we usually start hitting the gay bars, looking for a well-built, big-titted lesbian. I thoroughly enjoy raping and screwing around with lesbians, and there's not as much danger of them carrying sexually transmitted disease, and I don't like using condoms. Also, even though they're a little older, unless they've been playing with dildos a lot, they still have tight holes between their legs, like the younger girls. If we can't find a lesbian that we want, we snatch anything that is young, clean and well built. We seldom come back empty-handed, because there's plenty of bitches out there to choose from. And with a little practice in deception, most of them is very easy to get with little risks.

At this point it makes little difference what category you fall into. You're here, and we're going to make the most of it. You're going to be kept in a hidden slave room. It is relatively sound-proof, escape-proof, and is completely stocked with devices and equipment to satisfy our particular fetishes and deviations. There may or may not be another girl in the room. Occasionally, for variety, we like to keep two slaves at the same time. In any case, as the new girl, you will definitely be getting the most attention for a while.

Now, as I said earlier, you're going to be kept like an animal. I guess I've been doing this too long. I've been raping bitches ever since I was old enough to jerk off and tie a little girl's hands behind her back. As far as I'm concerned, you are a pretty piece of meat to be used and exploited.

I don't give a flying fuck about your mind or how you feel about the situation.

You may be married, have a kid or two, boyfriend, girlfriend, a job, car payments—fuck it! I don't give a big rat's ass about any of that, and I don't want to hear about it. It's something you're going to have to deal with after you're turned loose. I make it a point to never like a slave, and I fucking sure don't have any respect for you. Here your status is no more than one of the dogs or one of the animals out in the barn. Your only value to us is the fact that you have an attractive, usable body. And like the rest of our animals, you will be fed and watered, kept in good physical condition, kept reasonably clean and allowed to use the toilet when necessary.

In return, you are going to be used hard. Especially during the first few days while you're new and fresh.

You're going to be kept chained in a variety of different positions, usually with your legs or knees forced wide apart. Your pussy and asshole is [sic] going to get a real workout, especially your asshole because I'm into anal sex. Also, both of those holes are going to be subjected to a lot of use, with some rather large dildos among other things. And it goes without saying that there's going to be a lot of oral sex. On numerous occasions you're going to be forced to suck cock and eat pussy until your jaws ache and your tongue is sore. You may not like it but you're fucking sure going to do it.

And that's the easy part. Our fetishises and hang-ups include stringent bondage, dungeon games, a little sadism, nothing serious, but uncomfortable and sometimes painful. Just a few little hang-ups that we like to use when we're getting off on a bitch [*laughs*]. If you're a young teenybopper, and ignorant about fetishes and deviations, you're about to get an enlightening crash course on sex ed. Who knows, you may like some of it. It happens occasionally.

Now, I've already told you that you're going to be here a month or two, maybe three, if you keep us turned on. If it's up to my lady, we'd keep you indefinitely. She says it's just as much fun and less risky. But personally, I like variety, a fresh pussy now and then to play with. We take four or five of the girls each year, depending on our urges and sometimes accidental encounters. Basically, I guess we are like predators; we're always looking. Occasionally some sweet little thing will be broke down on the side of the road, walking, bicycling, jogging. Anytime an opportunity like that presents itself, and if it's not too risky, we'll grab her.... Variety is definitely the spice of life. Now, I'm sure you're a great little piece of ass, and you're going to be a lot of fun to play with, but I will get tired of you eventually. If I killed every bitch that we kidnapped, there'd be bodies strung all over the country. And besides, I don't like killing a girl unless it's absolutely necessary, so I've devised a safe, alternate method of disposal.

I've had plenty of bitches to practice on over the years, so I pretty well got it down pat, and I enjoy doing it. I get off on mind games. After we get completely through with you, you're gonna be drugged up real heavy with a combination of sodium Pentothal and phenobarbital. They are both hypnotic drugs that will make you extremely susceptible to hypnosis, autohypnosis and hypnotic suggestions. You're gonna be kept drugged a couple of days while I play with your mind. By the time I get through brainwashing you, you're not gonna remember a fucking thing about this little adventure. You won't remember this place, us or what has happened to you. There won't be any DNA evidence because you'll be bathed, and both holes between your legs will be thoroughly flushed out. You'll be dressed, sedated and turned loose on some country road. Bruised, sore all over, but nothing that won't heal up in a week or two. The thought of being brainwashed may not be appealing to you, but we've been doing it a long time, and it works and it's the lesser of two evils. I'm sure you would prefer that in lieu of being strangled or having your throat cut..." (Fielder, 2003, pp. 104–109).

It is important to highlight that the negative psychological impact on those who heard this tape was readily observable to everyone in the courtroom.

At her arraignment in June 1999, Jesse Ray pleaded not guilty on all counts. In September, Judge Neil Mertz decided that David Parker Ray and Jesse Ray would be tried separately for their roles in the Van Cleave/Montano offenses.

Like Cindy Hendy, Roy Yancy had also signed a Plea of Disposition. He would plead guilty to second-degree murder and first-degree conspiracy to commit murder. In exchange, on December 2, 1999, Roy Yancy was sentenced to 20 years in prison followed by two years of parole. Yancy would be paroled early in 2010, only to return into custody upon violating the terms of his probation, where he will remain until 2021.

Meanwhile, David Parker Ray had used intermediaries to send letters to Cindy Hendy, managing to convince her not to testify against him. They had unsuccessfully filed a request to be married, which led many to conclude that they were attempting to exploit the law which prohibited compelling a spouse to testify against their partner. Though Hendy expressed her wish to change her plea to "not guilty," on November 10, Judge Mertz ruled that Hendy could not do so. Unfortunately, as Hendy's confessions had not been made under oath, and she would no longer be testifying against David Parker Ray, the prosecution's case against Ray was weakened considerably.

Ray's defense team was also successful in convincing Judge Mertz to have Ray tried separately—three trials in total—for the Montano, Vigil, and Van Cleave cases, largely on the premise that if Cynthia Vigil had another breakdown on the stand, it would bias the jury's judgment of the other two cases. Furthermore, in hopes of avoiding a mistrial, Judge Mertz ruled that Ray's first interviews with the NMSP and FBI were to be suppressed, that any information regarding Roy Yancy's confession and the murder of Marie Parker must be excluded from the trial, and that five expert witnesses for the prosecution could not testify because he did not receive information regarding their qualifications in time. Another unexpected blow to the prosecution came on May 7, 2000, when Angelica Montano suddenly passed away due to pneumonia.

That same month, Cindy Hendy was sentenced to 36 years imprisonment: 27 for the abduction and sexual assaults of Angelica Montano and 36 for that of Cynthia Vigil to be served concurrently.

David Parker Ray's trial for the 1996 kidnapping and sexual abuse of Kelli Van Cleave began on June 29, 2000. Crucially, Judge Mertz had ruled that photographs of torture apparatus, weapons found on the property, Ray's note regarding the treatment of his victims, and the audio tape which had shocked the courtroom during his preliminary trial were to be excluded from this trial. His basis for this decision was that the defense had argued that there was no proof that these items had been in Ray's possession in 1996. In summary, the defense's strategy was to (i) admit Ray's perversions, but to portray the sexual acts he had perpetrated on Van Cleave on the video footage as consensual BDSM, (ii) to reduce the credibility of Kelli Van Cleave by painting her as an impulsive party animal and adulterer, (iii) to dismiss her statements as unreliable due to her self-admitted memory loss, and (iv) to question the qualifications of Dave Spencer, Van Cleave's psychotherapist, who explained this loss of memory as resulting from posttraumatic stress disorder. It worked. Despite Van Cleave bravely taking the stand for 30 minutes to describe the horrors perpetrated on her, the testimony of NMSP Special Agent John Briscoe which described the shocking contents of the "Toy Box," and Spencer's divulgence, the jury was hung at ten-to-two, as two female jurors did not think there was significant evidence to convict Ray on the charges. Judge Mertz declared a mistrial.

Determined to have the retrial underway sooner rather than later, the prosecution had David Parker Ray back in court for his crimes against Kelli Van Cleave on April 9, 2001. Van Cleave, Briscoe, and Spencer took the stand once again, and for the most part, the defense's strategy was the same as in the first trial. This time, however, Judge Kevin Sweazea allowed the infamous audiotape to be played in court, eliciting a palpably mortified response from the jury. After five-and-a-half hours of deliberation, the jury found David Parker Ray guilty on twelve counts of kidnapping, sexual abuse, and conspiracy. He was sentenced to 130 years behind bars, and the Cynthia Vigil trial was still looming on the horizon.

The trial began on June 18, 2001, but after a week, Ray had his attorney contact the prosecution to negotiate a plea bargain. David Parker Ray pleaded guilty to the first- and second-degree kidnapping, criminal sexual penetration, and conspiracy to kidnap Cynthia Vigil. He waived his right to appeal the Vigil or Van Cleave cases, but would not be tried for Angelica Montano.

Jesse Ray was to be the fourth and final of the group to take a plea agreement on September 17, 2001. She was sentenced to nine years with six suspended, but having already spent two years in custody, was released on five-years probation.

At David Parker Ray's sentencing hearing, his attorney attempted to withdraw his plea bargain saying that Ray had been under the influence of heart medication which had affected his decision-making capacity. His motion was denied. He was sentenced to serve 223 years in jail—132 for the kidnap and torture of Kelli Van Cleave, and a further 36 years for Cynthia Vigil. He also agreed to the prosecution's request to increase each of the sentences by one-third for aggravation. The judge ordered the sentences to run consecutively. At the earliest, Ray would be eligible for parole in the year 2100. However, on May 28, 2002, he died of a heart attack in Lea County Correctional Facility.

Linkage Analysis

As we have seen, aside from homicides, Paul Bernardo and David Parker Ray also committed rapes in which the victim survived, before[*] and after their homicidal careers.

Every offender in MacCulloch et al.'s (1983) study who they deemed to be "sexually sadistic" engaged in "try-outs" before the commission of the crime for which they were incarcerated. These try-outs ranged from following a woman home at night to brutal assaults, and occurred with intervals whose durations differed from one offender to another. Nevertheless, there seems to be clear evidence that a sexually sadistic offender does not begin his violent career with murder, but builds up to it with a series of lesser crimes and/or preparatory activities. It may also be possible, then, to link sexually sadistic homicides to previous nonhomicidal crimes with sexually sadistic overtones. This does not mean that an otherwise good suspect should be disqualified because he lacks a criminal record, as the study by Dietz et al. (1990) reminds us.

The most obvious and easy crimes to link to sadistic homicides are sexual assaults. Paul Bernardo and David Parker Ray both committed rapes *before* and *after* their first known murders. These were *anger-excitation* rapes, in which the "rapist is sexually stimulated and/or gratified by the victim's response to the infliction of physical or emotional pain" (Hazelwood, 1995, p. 164). However, it is important to note that Bernardo began his career as a sexual criminal with voyeurism and progressed to attacking strangers by fondling them in the dark, before any sexually sadistic element became discernible in his attacks. This does not necessarily mean that the sexually sadistic murderer will have a history of criminal convictions that mirror his homicidal career. In their study, Dietz et al. (1990) found that before their arrest, 57% of the sexually sadistic murderers in their sample had no known criminal convictions, and that the remaining 43% had arrests or convictions for crimes that were not overtly sexual or sadistic in nature.

The rapes committed by sexual sadists are *high fantasy/high aggression* (Aggrawal, 2009), and as a result, have a number of signature elements which remain static. The nature and sequence of these acts should be obtained from the victim's testimony, forensic evidence, and any other reliable source (e.g., CCTV camera, witness) and documented, not only to link the crimes and determine the presence and specific expression of sexual sadism (consistently sadistic behaviors will be marked below with a #, but also to predict the likelihood and path of possible escalation). These behaviors include:

> *Information seeking*: Paul Bernardo would often ask the victims to tell him their name, their age, where they lived, if they had a boyfriend, what their boyfriend's name was, how old their boyfriend was, if they did these sex acts with their boyfriend, if they were a virgin, if the sexual assault felt good, etc. (Williams, 1996).
>
> *Scripting*: When an offender instructs his victims to repeat specific phrases which are usually integral to his sexual fantasy. Among the things Paul Bernardo instructed his victims to say in multiple incidents were:
>
> 1. That they hated their boyfriends
> 2. That they loved him (often he would make them repeat this over and over)
> 3. That the sexual assault felt good

He also routinely demanded that they refer to themselves as "bitch" and "slut"# (Williams, 1996; Mellor, 2012).

---

[*] Presumably before in the case of David Parker Ray, as the details of his first offenses remain conjecture.

In contrast, David Parker Ray would typically keep his victims gagged, and demand that they be quiet. Here we have conflicting behaviors which could help in separating one sexually sadistic offender from another in the unlikely event that there are two operating in the same location at the same time.

Humiliating or degrading acts[#]: Paul Bernardo rubbed dirt into some of his victims' hair, sodomized them before forcing them to perform fellatio on his soiled penis, and repeatedly called them derogatory names such as "bitch," "slut," and "cunt" (Williams, 1996). It should not be overlooked that these are the same slurs that he made the victims call themselves. Healey et al. (2013) found that humiliating victims was the most common behavior specifically shared by sexually sadistic rapists and murderers.

Physical torture[#]: This can range from Paul Bernardo's simple and brutish methods of inflicting pain (beating, strangling, painful object insertion) to the elaborate use of homemade torture devices such as David Parker Ray's electric breast stretcher, motorized dildo, and chain and pulley system to suspend his victims from the ceiling (Glatt, 2002).

Psychological torture: After her abduction, David Parker Ray played Cynthia Vigil a lengthy audio recording detailing what he was planning to do to her, terrifying her and reinforcing the helplessness of her situation (Glatt, 2002). He had set up a camera and monitor so that his victims were forced to watch themselves being tortured, and would lock them for long periods of time in coffins. Paul Bernardo took his victims' personal identification, threatening to attack them again if they called the police or left the scene before a specific period of time had elapsed. He also threatened to disfigure them or kill them and forced them to beg for their lives. Playing to the stigma surrounding rape, Bernardo would tell them that their friends would make fun of them and that their boyfriends would hate them when they found out about the rape (Williams, 1996; Mellor, 2012).

Sadomasochistic paraphernalia: Particularly in cases in which the rape victim is abducted and confined over a number of days, such as in the David Parker Ray case, they will encounter sadomasochistic paraphernalia such as Ray's costumes and masks, oversized dildos, customized restraints, chains, etc. Any surviving victim who reports being nonconsensually abused with these types of objects associated with BDSM culture has almost certainly encountered a sexually sadistic rapist.

In the absence of a confession or documentation, scripting and, with some rare exceptions, psychological torture and humiliating/degrading acts will not be evident in a sexually sadistic homicide as these signature elements are chiefly revealed through witness recall or video tapes of the attack. However, if there is reasonable certainty that a homicide victim was kept for a lengthy period of time before they were murdered, combined with a pathologist's determination that they were physically tortured, it is a sound assumption that they were the victim of a sexual sadist. Law enforcement can then look into rapes containing information seeking, physical and psychological torture, scripting, humiliating/degrading acts, and the use of sadomasochistic paraphernalia which had occurred prior to the murder to see if a link can be established. This is of paramount importance, as surviving victims are often able to provide descriptions of their attacker's voice and appearance. In the Paul Bernardo case, a police composite of "The Scarborough Rapist" was released to the public which resembled Bernardo exactly and led to his friend providing his name to law enforcement as a suspect. Taking into consideration Bernardo's startling likeness to the composite and that he resided in the geographical area FBI profilers had predicted in their profile, he should have been placed at the top of their priority list when he came to their attention a second time in 1990. Bernardo's DNA, which he provided willingly, should have then been analyzed years earlier, identifying him as "The Scarborough Rapist," and preventing the deaths of Tammy Homolka, Leslie Mahaffy, and Kristen French. Even still, the clear indications of physical torture on Kristen French's body should have immediately been compared to sexually sadistic rapes which had occurred before her murder, which would have allowed investigators to link her murder tentatively to the Scarborough attacks. At the time, the ViCLAS system was not in place in Canada, but the existence of the infamous and elusive Scarborough rapist was certainly known by the GRT.

Finally, it is also useful to acknowledge MacCulloch et al.'s (1983) finding that the content of a sexual sadist's fantasies typically changes in order to keep him stimulated. For this reason, the violence—though retaining sexual sadism as the primary paraphilia—may mutate in accordance with the offender's changing fantasy-life, and this typically gravitates toward an escalation in the amount of time spent with the victim and the intricacy or extremity of the acts. Mellor's Thematic-Derivative Model of Paraphilic Progression (detailed in Chapter 6) is a useful tool in charting this development. A few of the more common comorbidities with sexual sadism include:

Picquerism and mutilophilia: The fact that "cutting" was only evident in a single case in Dietz et al.'s (1990) study corroborates Mellor's (2016a) assertion that Geberth (2006) erred in incorporating sexual sadism into his definition of picquerism. For this reason, it is recommended that a determination of sexual sadism should not be made solely on the basis of fatal and nonfatal wounds inflicted with a cutting and/or stabbing weapon. That said, the longer time the offender spends with his victims and the greater variety of assaults that he commits on them increases the probability that superficial cutting and stabbing is linked to sexual sadism. There have been enough cases in which sexual sadism was comorbid with picquerism (e.g., Richard Cottingham, Robert Napper, Robert Boyd Rhoades) or mutilophilia (e.g., Cottingham and Napper—later in their careers, Dean Corll, Neville Heath, Gerard John Schaefer, Fred West) to merit noting that these activities can either derive from sexual sadism or vice versa. Healey et al. (2013) found that mutilation is one of the salient characteristics of sexual sadism, but unfortunately did not specify whether this mutilation was ante- or postmortem, or whether it was defensive, rage-based, or paraphilic. This leaves the possibility that they might actually have been conflating sexual sadism with necrophilia spectrum behavior.

Vincilagnia: As 86.7% of violent sexual sadists gagged, blindfolded, or bound their victims, evidence of any of these activities adds further credence to the presence of a sexually sadistic killer, particularly if the bondage was (i) tied in such a way as to be visibly painful to the victim and/or (ii) went beyond what was necessary to restrain the victim, as evidenced by a "variety of positions, excessive binding, symmetrical bindings, and neatness" (Dietz et al., 1990, p. 170).

One of the more common paraphilias that is comorbid with sexual sadism is vincilagnia: sexual gratification from binding or restraining a victim.

Asphyxiaphilia: Sexual sadists are often sexually aroused by the act of asphyxiating their victims, be it through strangulation or suffocation (Dietz et al., 1990; Healey et al., 2013), although this can also take the masochistic form of autoerotic asphyxiation (more details below).

Offender Profiling and Investigation Strategies

As the characteristics of a sexual sadist listed in Table 8.8 by Dietz et al. (1990) reveal, the only claims that we can make about such an offender is that he will almost always be a white[*] male. Contrary to the HNs we looked at in the previous chapter, it is not unlikely for the sexual sadist to be married with children.

In a small qualitative study of the wives and girlfriends of sexual sadists (n = 7), Hazelwood et al. (1993) proposed that all of the women in their sample reported being physically abused by their sexually sadistic partners. For this reason, the authors suggested that looking into domestic abuse complaints or reports might provide leads for investigators who are looking for a sexual sadist. If Paul Bernardo's DNA profile as "The Scarborough Rapist" had not emerged contemporaneously with the physical abuse charges filed against him by Karla Homolka, the latter might have flagged Bernardo as a potential suspect by members of the GRT. A simple check should have revealed that on March 31, 1992, a 27-year-old woman had reported that she and her sister had been followed by a man with a video camera in Port Dalhousie who drove a Gold Nissan SX with the license plate 660 HFH—a vehicle belonging to Paul Bernardo. The GRT could then have showed photographs of the car, Paul Bernardo, and Karla Homolka to the witnesses of the Kristen French abduction. Though one witness, who admitted to not being good with cars, had identified the abductor's vehicle as an ivory or cream-colored two-door Camaro or Firebird under the police's insistence that she make a judgment, it is possible that she might have identified the Nissan SX, Bernardo, or Homolka.

Hazelwood et al. (1993) further observed that many of the sexually sadistic acts that the sexual sadists had subjected their nonconsenting victims to were also inflicted upon their spouses or girlfriends. For this reason, interviewing the current or former sexual partners of a suspected HSS is advisable. Such individuals may be, to varying degrees, traumatized and/or terrified of the suspect, as well as embarrassed to speak about the peculiarities of their sex lives. This should be taken into consideration with regard to the who, how,

---

[*] It is not recommended that nonwhite offenders be eliminated as possible suspects due to this statistic, as the growth in interest and research pertaining to African American serial killers since this study has revealed a number of sexually sadistic black offenders (e.g., Samuel Dixon, Maury Travis, Anthony Sowell).

Table 8.8 Characteristics of Sexually Sadistic Offenders

Characteristics	n	%
Male	30	100
White	29	96.7
Parental infidelity or divorce	14	46.7
Physically abused in childhood[a]	7	23.3
Sexually abused in childhood	6	20
Married at time of offense	13	43.3
Incestuous involvement with own child (excluding childhood sex play)	9	30
Known homosexual experience	13	43.3
Known cross-dressing[a]	6	20
Known history of peeping, obscene telephone calls, or indecent exposure[a]	6	20
Shared sexual partners with other men	6	20
Education beyond high school	13	43.3
Military experience	10	33.3
Established reputation as solid citizen	9	30
Drug abuse (other than alcohol)	15	50
Suicide attempt	4	13.3
Excessive driving	12	40
Police "buff" (excessive interest in police activities and paraphernalia)	9	30

Source: Dietz, P., Hazelwood, R., and Warren, J. 1990. The sexually sadistic criminal and his offenses. *Journal of the American Academy of Psychiatry and the Law,* 18(2), 163–178.

[a] Though found in the sexual sadists in the study by Gratzer and Bradford (1995), the authors note that each of these antecedents is present in paraphilia in general, and are not specific to sexual sadism.

when, and where of the interview, and guarantees to protect the sexual partner's identity and person should be fully fleshed out and in place in order to provide them with emotional security. However, there is also room for investigative and prosecution errors in this approach (see "Assessing the Culpability and Agency of Accomplices" later in this chapter). Investigators should not be deterred from interviewing a suspect's sexual partner based upon the duration of their sexual relationship. The women in Hazelwood et al.'s (1993) study reported similar behavior even though the time they had been involved with their respective sexually sadistic partners ranged from 3 months to 13 years.

The degree to which the sexual partner of the HSS might be aware of his crimes may range from complete ignorance to having acted as an accomplice, so the primary investigatory goal here is to assess the sexual partner's knowledge of any criminal acts. Following that, the goal is to then determine whether the suspect is indeed a sexual sadist. The study by Hazelwood et al. (1993) indicates that women who have been in relationships with sexual sadists *should* report the following:

- His order of preference for sexual activities should be: anal, oral, vaginal, and foreign object insertion. All of these sexual activities will have occurred.

- Once anal intercourse has become part of their sexual relationship, he will no longer have had any interest in vaginal sex.

- He will be hypersexual, with sex always at the forefront of his mind.

- The women will have been approached by him during a time in which the woman lacked confidence and had low self-esteem. They will have been in a state of fear and/or depression throughout the relationship.

- The women will have been from middle-class backgrounds.

- The women will be passive, and ashamed that they had become involved with the man.

- The women will have been verbally and emotionally abused by him.

- The women will have been sexually naive when they met him, even though they may have had previous marriages, and they will have had no knowledge of sadomasochism.

- The women will have been secure in employment when they met him.

- Frequently, the women will have been whipped, hanged, burned in places on their bodies where the injuries are not visible when they are wearing clothes, kept captive, and coerced into committing criminal acts. That they will have been battered, painfully bitten, strangled during sex, and bound is almost certain, as is the fact they will have been *scripted*. Less commonly, they will have been penetrated anally with very large objects, urinated on, forced to participate in sex acts with other men or women (including being raped), made to sign a "slave contract," and to call themselves "evil."

- He will have strongly enjoyed ejaculating on her face.

- Often the man will have recorded their sexual behaviors through photography, diagrams, journals, etc.

- Often the man will have taken sexual photographs of the woman.

- The man will have socially isolated the woman from her friends and family.

Comorbid Paraphilias

According to a study by Abel et al. (1988), 46% of sexual sadists had also committed acts of rape, 33% of child molestation, 25% of voyeurism and frotteurism, and 18% were also masochistic. Therefore, a useful investigation strategy would be to look for local criminals with these behavioral antecedents.

HSSs who evidence sexual bondage (*vincilagnia*), and/or almost exclusively use ligature strangulation or hanging to kill, have an increased likelihood of practising autoerotic asphyxiation (AEA) (Blanchard and Hucker, 1991; Myers et al., 2008). AEA is the act of employing ligatures, plastic bags and other smothering instruments, and/or chest compression to decrease the flow of oxygen to one's own brain, reportedly enhancing sexual activity (*hypoxia*), whether this activity is mutual or masturbatory (Resnick, 1972). When this is an onanistic endeavor, the risk that accidental fatalities may occur is significantly elevated. The AEA deaths of pop singer Michael Hutchence and actor David Carradine have brought increased public attention to this sexual practice. Myers et al. (2008) noted five cases of serial murder in which sexual sadists who strangled or hung their victims are known to have also practiced autoerotic asphyxiation. The authors proposed that the link between sexual sadism and AEA can be attributed to (i) the association between sadism and masochism as posited by Krafft-Ebing, Havelock Ellis, and Freud, or (ii) the notion that the killer temporarily role plays a specific or hypothetical victim, often through cross-dressing. By experiencing an imperfect facsimile of the physical and psychological torment that his victim feels, the sexual sadist enhances his own sexual arousal. Knoll and Hazelwood (2009) have also proposed this as a theory. Mellor (2016b) couches Myers et al.'s second explanation in the social behaviorist concept of *play*, and notes that variations of this activity, which he dubs *autoerotic roleplay*, also occur in necrophilic offenders. Such activities may comprise the *play and surrogate enactment* phase of sexual progression in the Thematic-Derivative model.

Taking this into consideration, in sexual homicides where *vincilagnia* is evident, an investigatory strategy of appealing to the public to report any persons in the community known to engage in AEA is advisable. According to Douglas and Dodd (2008), the "BTK Killer" Dennis Rader was caught on two separate occasions by his wife participating in AEA. Paula Rader had seen television news reports featuring an audio recording of BTK telephoning the police and samples of his handwriting. She had remarked to her husband that the voice sounded like his, and that he spelled like "BTK." With her suspicions already aroused, the revelation that BTK may also have engaged in AEA might have been a key determinant factor in her passing her husband's name on to police. Regardless, the gleaning of alibis and collecting of voluntary DNA samples from autoerotic asphyxiation participants would, in the very least, eliminate a number of suspects and push those who refused to comply to the forefront of the investigation. To clarify, this is a dragnet strategy focusing on suspect prioritization. The *vincilagnic* sexually sadistic offender does not necessarily engage in AEA, so no suspect should be eliminated on these grounds alone.

Recommendations for Handling Cases of Sexual Sadists Who Kill

Arresting, Charging, and Prosecuting the Sexual Sadist

Above all other homicidal offenders, the sexual sadist meticulously documents his crimes and violent fantasies (Dietz et al., 1990), along with frequently modifying his home and/or vehicle to facilitate the restraint and torture of his victims. For this reason, it is advisable to keep the suspect unaware that he is on the police radar as much as possible before executing a search warrant on his property and vehicle. Among the standard forensic evidence such as fibers and DNA from the victim listed on the search warrant, it is recommended that the investigator add the following items:

1. *Restraints, including but not limited to handcuffs, rope, thumb cuffs, manacles, chains, zip ties, "torture" boards*

   If used in the commission of a crime, any restraints in the suspect's possession may contain traces of the victim's DNA, fingerprints, etc. It is also possible that the patterning and dimensions of ligature marks on the victim's body may be matched to restraints recovered from the suspect's possession. In the very least, the presence of elaborate restraints suggests that the suspect harbors sexually sadistic interests.

2. *Any sedatives or toxins that might have been found in the victim's system (e.g., Rohypnol and other date rape drugs, chloroform, ether, valium, halothane, Halcion)*

   Karla Homolka, Paul Bernardo, and David Parker Ray routinely drugged their victims. The presence of a particular substance found during medical testing of a victim's body which is also found in the possession of a suspected HSS constitutes a strong piece of circumstantial evidence.

3. *Homemade video recordings in a variety of different formats (VHS, film, DVD, on a digital device, etc.)*

   Among the most crucial evidence recovered in both the Bernardo and Ray cases was video footage showing the offenders sexually assaulting and torturing their victims. Dietz et al. (1990) found that 53.3% of sexual sadists recorded their offenses, whether through writings, drawings, photographs, audiotapes, or videotapes.

4. *Photographs*

   Same as above.

5. *Homemade audio recordings in a variety of different formats (cassette, CD, on a digital device, etc.)*

   Same as above.

6. *Computers and external hard drives*

   The Bernardo and Ray cases occurred before the ubiquitous presence of computers in our lives. However, if these HSSs were to have offended more recently, it is highly likely that they would have stored their photographs and videos on computers and/or external hard drives. For this reason, such materials should be seized as they are likely to contain evidence documenting the crimes.

7. *Souvenirs*

   Approximately 40–80% of sexually sadistic homicidal offenders collect personal items of little or no monetary value from their victims in order to recall their crimes (Dietz et al., 1990; Myers et al., 2006). Dietz et al. (1990) posit that the sexual sadist uses these to conjure up deviant fantasies, often for masturbatory purposes. Sadistic serial killer Gerard John Schaefer was found in possession of 200 items of jewellery which were linked to missing women not previously believed to have been his victims (Myers et al., 2006). This can directly link an offender to his victim.

8. *Pornography and detective magazines*

   Fifty-three percent of the sample by Dietz et al. (1990) collected pornography, with 23% collecting detective magazines, and a smaller 7% being avid readers of *Soldier of Fortune*. The contents of these publications might reveal inclinations toward or directly parallel the offender's crime scene behavior, and are therefore useful to collect. Investigators are however encouraged to seek the advice of experts on sexuality and pop culture regarding the prevalence and influence of each publication before forming any firm judgments about them. For instance, in the infamous case of the West Memphis 3, accused child killer Damien Echols's history of reading books about witchcraft and listening to heavy metal was taken as proof that he had ritualistically sacrificed the victims. Tens of millions of Americans read books about esoteric religions and listen to abrasive music, so unless the suspect's artistic property can be directly related to his crimes, this property is superfluous. It has since been learned that Echols played no part whatsoever in the murders.

9. *Diaries*

Perhaps one of the most important items a sexually sadistic offender harbors are diaries or journals. In both the Bernardo and Ray cases, these were invaluable, because they chronologically documented each man's history of violent offenses. This can not only lead to the discovery of additional victims, but will strengthen the prosecution's case significantly. They may also reveal details about the crimes or offender that will prompt interviewers to ask pertinent questions or follow lines of inquiry that otherwise would not have occurred to them.

10. *Drawings and sketches*

David Parker Ray, along with other HSSs such as Gerard Schaefer and Dennis Rader, plotted out their fantasies and illustrated past crimes in elaborate detail. These can be used to make a case for the existence of particular paraphilic interests in the suspect.

Interviewing

The sexual sadist, being typically either a psychopath or high in factor 1 psychopathic traits, is one of the most difficult offenders to interview due to their complete lack of a conscience, low trepidation, and the thrill they derive from playing "cat-and-mouse" with the police. An FBI agent once told this author of a sexually sadistic offender who had been arrested for the torture murder of a child because his truck got stuck in mud near the crime scene. When the interviewer entered the interrogation room, he immediately asked the offender why he had killed the child, to which the offender responded, "Where's my truck?" (Jeffrey Rinek, personal communication). For this reason, it is recommended that preparation and conduct for interviewing a sexually sadistic murderer should mirror that of interviewing the psychopath, as described in Chapter 9.

As cases of sexually sadistic homicide typically stir up strong emotions, even interviewers advised by experts not to appeal to the offender's conscience—as the interviewers in the Bernardo case had been on more than one occasion—may struggle with this professional requirement nevertheless. Frustrated when Paul Bernardo stonewalled their attempts to engage him in conversation with "no comments," one of the interviewers indignantly asked him whether knowing the pain Kristen's father was going through appealed "to some sense of decency and honesty inside you" (Williams, 1996, p. 421), and again, later raged "where's your decency, man? Where's your honesty?" (Williams, 1996, p. 422). Interestingly, the only technique that seemed to shake Bernardo during the questioning was showing him television news coverage of his arrest. Unfortunately, this breakthrough was not adequately capitalized on.

If an interviewer is fortunate enough to encounter a sexually sadistic murderer who works in tandem with one or more accomplices, then an oft-used and reliable (yet controversial) strategy is to offer a plea bargain or leniency to an accomplice in exchange for their testimony against a more dangerous, complicit, or obstinate offender. A caution: Before proceeding with this strategy, it is advisable to gather as much evidence as possible regarding the psychological state and complicity of the accomplice. For instance, in the case of David Parker Ray, there were multiple living witnesses who could attest to Cindy Hendy's enthusiastic participation in their rapes and torture. On the other hand, the infamous plea bargain with Paul Bernardo's wife and accomplice, Karla Homolka, would become one of the greatest blunders in the history of the Canadian criminal justice system, and continues to inspire anger and resentment across English-speaking Canada 20 years later. The error was in assuming that because Bernardo had physically abused Homolka, that her participation in the abductions and sexual assaults of Leslie Mahaffy and Kristen French was coerced. See "Assessing the Culpability and Agency of Accomplices" for more details.

The Bernardo and Ray cases have highlighted a number of issues that are likely to arise during the prosecution of a sexual sadist. These are briefly touched upon below:

> *Drugged witness*: Both surviving and murdered victims in the Bernardo and Ray cases had been drugged to ensure their submission. This is not uncommon in cases of sexually sadistic homicide. Richard Cottingham, Randy Kraft, and occasionally, Clifford Olson, and Dean Corll would also incorporate drugging into their MOs. In all six of these cases, there were surviving witnesses who had been drugged, and as demonstrated by the defense's treatment of Kelli Van Cleave, this can make their testimony particularly vulnerable during cross-examination. For this reason, prosecutors should act preemptively to counter the criticism of the witness's memory by the defense.
>
> *Collecting and processing evidence*: Though they were gifted a trove of evidence in the Bernardo and Ray cases, the GRT and FBI both managed, in different ways, to botch the location, collection, and/or processing of evidence. Despite the fact that Bernardo's house was searched over the course of two months, identification officers nevertheless failed to find the most crucial pieces of evidence—the 8-mm rape tapes—which had been hidden in a lighting fixture. This is worsened by the fact that one Constable Kershaw actually unscrewed the pot light, and noticed a 10″ × 10″ box in the attic above (Campbell, 1996). However, as it was out of his reach, he made no special effort to retrieve it.

In his review of the Bernardo investigation, Campbell (1996) concluded that as the GRT had not spoken in depth with Karla Homolka at the time, and because there was reason to believe that Bernardo's videocassettes either no longer existed or were hidden elsewhere, it is only in hindsight that it seems ridiculous that Kershaw did not go above and beyond to get the box. Campbell points out that because there was so little evidence against Bernardo in the Mahaffy/French homicides at the time of the search, Inspector Vince Bevan had to construct the warrant so that it minimized damage to the property, lest the identification officers violate the Charter of Rights principle of minimization, potentially rendering any evidence collected inadmissible. Essentially, the GRT had only been able to search the house based on similar fact evidence related to the Scarborough rapes. Campbell pointed out that, unlike narcotics officers, homicide identification officers are accustomed to preserving a scene rather than destroying it in the hopes of finding additional evidence, even if this evidence might turn out to be crucial. When combined with the strictness of the warrant, this made the identification officers extremely reluctant to damage the dwelling. Campbell concluded his report by recommending that after initial identification officers have finished searching such a crime scene that a secondary team be allowed to do so with a fresh set of eyes and ideas.

Instead of Justice Campbell's suggestions, we recommend here that homicide identification officers receive better training regarding what to expect when searching the homes of a person suspected or known to have paraphilic interests. In the study by Dietz et al. (1990), 53.3% of the sexual sadists recorded the offense through writings, drawings, photographs, audio tapes, or video tapes; while 40% took souvenirs from their victims. Regarding the first statistic, the advent of cell phone cameras and inexpensive recording technologies has likely led to an inflation in this statistic in modern HSSs.

Law enforcement also bungled in allowing Bernardo's defense team to enter 57 Bayview without close supervision, and granted them the right to remove remaining items, including the infamous rubber mallet, which the GRT would later have to ask Ken Murray to give back to them (Williams, 1996).

In another example, after discovering bags of cement—relevant to the Mahaffy body disposal—the officers neglected to log the bags of cement on the return for the first warrant because they were eager to discover something less obvious, and then ultimately forgot. Nor were the cement bags listed on the second warrant, leading to legal complications regarding whether or not they could be seized as evidence (Campbell, 1996).

The debacle in the Ray case concerned the FBI's failure to process the evidence collected in time to present it to the judge, resulting in him excluding important evidence from the first Van Cleave trial, as the judge had not had time to review it (Glatt, 2002).

> *Assessing the culpability and agency of accomplices*: In both the Bernardo and Ray cases, plea bargains with a female accomplice were botched because their antisocial tendencies were underestimated. With concern to Karla Homolka, it was simply assumed that she was the *compliant victim of a sexual sadist*, despite the many factors indicating otherwise that were not taken into consideration. Table 8.9 seems to indicate that Homolka did have many of the same experiences in her relationship with Bernardo as the "compliant victims of a sexual sadist" but with some important exceptions.

Though Bernardo was controlling and physically abusive, Karla was still living with her parents at the time of Tammy Homolka's death, and would only see Bernardo on weekends. This hardly reflected the level of

Table 8.9 Karla Homolka versus Compliant Victims of a Sexual Sadist

Features	Karla Homolka	7-Woman Sample	Match
Childhood			
Physically abused	No	2	N/A
Psychologically abused	No	6	No
Sexually abused	No	4	No
Background	Middle-class	All middle-class	Yes
Adult Life before Met Sex Sadist			
Sexually naive	Arguable	6	N/A
Low self-esteem	Yes	Yes	Yes
Professionally successful	Yes	6	Yes
In Relationship			
Partner is charming and thoughtful at first	Yes	7	Yes
Physically abused	On at least one occasion	7	N/A
Verbally abused	Yes	7	Yes
Strangled during sex	Yes	6	Yes
Bondage	Yes, but suggested it first	7	No
Forced oral sex	No, submitted willingly	7	No
Anal sex	Yes	6	Yes
Slave contract	No	3	N/A
Held captive	No	3	N/A
Sexually photographed	Yes	4	Yes
Scripted	Yes	6	Yes

Source: Mellor, L. 2012. *Cold North Killers: Canadian Serial Murder.* Toronto, Canada: Dundurn.
Note: N/A, Not applicable.

constant, oppressive control seen in the rest of the sample. Karla also remained close to her parents and had friends; in short, she could have easily maneuvered out of the relationship once Bernardo's violent sexual criminality and abusive nature became evident. She was also alone on multiple occasions when Leslie Mahaffy and Kristen French were confined at 57 Bayview, and could have easily freed the captives or telephoned the police.

This convenient designation as a compliant victim led the prosecution to sign a hasty plea bargain with Homolka, which would later result in a clear case of injustice, and nation-wide outrage that endures to this day. Before the hours of footage showing Homolka enthusiastically participating in the sexual assaults was revealed, she was considered a victim and key witness by members of the police force, prosecution, and Canadian mental health services. This seems to have skewed their assessment of her psychological makeup. Though the majority of the 16+ mental health professionals who examined her reached or supported the battered woman with PTSD diagnosis, there remains significant skepticism.

Dissenting voices such as Dr. Hubert Van Gijseghem who conducted a file review of Homolka drew attention to the fact that the origins of her supposed PTSD have never been adequately pin-pointed. Along with Dr. Robin Menzies, who examined Homolka in Saskatoon, he concluded that she suffered from antisocial personality disorder and was possibly psychopathic. It is our opinion that the most plausible diagnosis came from Dr. Graham Glancy who believes that Homolka has histrionic personality disorder combined with *hybristophilia*—sexual arousal from knowing that a lover or spouse has committed acts of violence.

When scrutinized, many of the mental health professionals who reached the PTSD/battered woman diagnosis become incredulous. Dr. Allan Long, for example, had committed an egregious error by recording Homolka's raw scores from the Minnesota Multiphasic Personality Inventory (MMPI) II onto first edition forms. This led him to characterize her as socially inadequate, alienated, untrusting, confused, and possibly schizophrenic. However, when her scores were processed properly, Homolka was shown to be histrionic with obsessive-compulsive and/or passive-aggressive features, a diagnosis which hinted at possible psychopathy. Long had validated his findings with TAT and Rorschach test interpretations, both of which are widely dismissed today as highly subjective.

Also using the MMPI, Dr. Peter Jaffe determined that Karla was paranoid, isolated, and anxious, alternately blaming herself and projecting anger outwardly. However, he attributed this to the trauma of her being abused and manipulated by Bernardo. He diagnosed Homolka as suffering from posttraumatic stress disorder. However, when scrutinized by one Dr. Pollack, it was revealed that Jaffe had based his conclusions on individual item content, an approach which Jaffe himself admitted should be approached with caution. Pollack believed that the results of Jaffe's MMPI-2 test of Homolka were accurate, but interpreted them not as a product of posttraumatic stress disorder, but rather as indicative of a serious personality disorder. This was more in keeping with Jaffe's second finding using the Rainwater computer program, which reported that Karla was prone to antisocial behavior.

On another occasion, a PCL-R assessment of Homolka had been conducted by Dr. Sharon Williams and reportedly scored somewhere in the vicinity of 5 (Mellor, 2012), which Hare proposes is the approximate score for an average member of the population. Yet Homolka evidences nearly all of the Factor 1 traits to some degree, along with meriting scores in the item promiscuous sexual behavior (Hare, 2003). A more accurate score would fall somewhere between 10 and 16, and could reflect primary psychopathy.

Unlike Karla Homolka, the failure of the Cindy Hendy plea bargain was the result of inadequate strategic measures to keep her isolated and out of communication with David Parker Ray. Though, generally, accomplices turn on the primary offender after they have been arrested, there are exceptions in which the partners of sexually sadistic offenders remain loyal, at least for a time, or who are capable of becoming loyal again after a momentary betrayal. As such, special precautions should be taken to ensure that a sexual sadist is completely unable to contact his accomplice before, during, and after trial, assuming that jurisdictional law permits this. Once again, it cannot be emphasized enough that the HSS is almost invariably highly psychopathic, which means that his ability to manipulate, deceive, and find ways to circumvent institutional rules and security should always be strongly considered. Nor should his accomplices be automatically placed into a different category of culpability or complicity, simply based on their gender. Rather, they should be subject to the same scrutiny as their male counterparts before any plea bargain is offered.

For instance, in the 2009 Canadian investigation into the sexual homicide of 8-year-old Tori Stafford which involved sadistic pedophile Michael Rafferty and his girlfriend Terri-Lynne McClintic, it was assumed that Rafferty, who had raped Tori, had also delivered the fatal blows. Eventually, McClintic admitted that she had been the one to bludgeon the 8-year-old to death with a hammer, a revelation that would never have come to light had McClintic not confessed (DiManno, 2012).

Treatment

As cognitive-behavioral therapy (CBT) is currently the most popular treatment for sexual offenders, unsurprisingly, it has also been recommended for sexual sadists (Marshall and Hucker, 2006a,b; Kingston and Yates, 2008). Naturally, there are factors that are specific to sexual sadism that need to be taken into consideration when treating homicidal offenders of this nature.

Generally, specialists in this field recommend that CBT is combined with pharmacological treatment in the form of antiandrogens (Marshall and Hucker, 2006a,b; Kingston and Yates, 2008). According to Kingston and Yates (2008), cyproterone acetate (CPA) and medroxyprogesterone acetate (MPA) have proven successful in the past; however, their significant side effects include diabetes, dyskinetic and feminization effects, increased blood pressure, and mellitus. A promising alternative is luteinizing hormone-releasing hormone (LHRH) which has inconsequential side effects. However, the downside to LHRH is that, as its usage is relatively new, its effectiveness as a form of treatment is not supported by the same amount of data as MPA or CPA.

Kingston and Yates (2008) list cognitive distortions, deviant sexual arousal and fantasy, emotion regulation, intimacy deficits, and offense-supportive attitudes as dynamic risk factors that should be targeted during CBT. Notably, they exclude "empathy deficits" because a significant number of academics believe that possessing empathy is intrinsic to the function of sexual sadism—if a sexual sadist is unable to perceive a victim's suffering, then they cannot be aroused by it. This gives rise to the frightening possibility that increasing a sexual sadist's empathy may actually allow him to develop enhanced methods of causing pain to future victims.

References

Abel, G. G., Becker, J. V., Cunningham-Rathner, J., Mittelman, M., and Rouleau, J. L. 1988. Multiple paraphilic diagnoses among sex offenders. *Journal of the American Academy of Psychiatry and the Law Online*, *16*, 153–168.

Aggrawal, A. 2009. *Forensic and Medico-Legal Aspects of Sexual Crimes and Unusual Sexual Practices*. Boca Raton, Florida: CRC.

American Psychiatric Association. 1987. *Diagnostic and Statistical Manual of Mental Disorders: DSM-III-Revised* (3rd ed.). Washington, DC: American Psychiatric Association.

American Psychiatric Association. 2013. *Diagnostic and Statistical Manual of Mental Disorders* (5th ed.). Washington, DC: American Psychiatric Association.

Blanchard, R. and Hucker, S. J. 1991. Age, transvestism, bondage, and concurrent paraphilic activities in 117 fatal cases of autoerotic asphyxia. *British Journal of Psychiatry, 159*, 371–377.

Brady, I. 2001. *The Gates of Janus: Serial Murder and Its Analysis.* Port Townsend, WA: Feral House.

Brittain, R. 1970. The sadistic murderer. *Medicine, Science and the Law, 10*, 198–207.

Campbell, A. G. 1996. *Bernardo Investigation Review: Report of Mr. Justice Archie Campbell.* Toronto: Solicitor General.

Crepault, E. and Couture, M. 1980. Men's erotic fantasies. *Archives of Sexual Behavior, 9*, 565–581.

Dietz, P. and Evans, B. 1982. Pornographic imagery and prevalence of paraphilia. *American Journal of Psychiatry, 139*, 1493–1495.

Dietz, P., Hazelwood, R., and Warren, J. 1990. The sexually sadistic criminal and his offenses. *Journal of the American Academy of Psychiatry and the Law, 18*(2), 163–178.

DiManno, R. 2012, March 14. Tori Stafford murder trial: Terri-Lynne McClintic describes killing little girl. *The Toronto Star.* Retrieved from http://on.thestar.com/1NR2Spa

Douglas, J. and Dodd, J. 2008. *Inside the Mind of BTK: The True Story behind the Thirty-Year Hunt for the Notorious Witchita Serial Killer.* San Francisco, CA: Jossey-Bass.

Egger, S. A. 1998. *The Killers among Us: An Examination of Serial Murder and Its Investigation.* New York, NY: Prentice Hall.

Englade, K. 1988. *Cellar of Horrors.* New York, NY: St. Martin's.

Fielder, J. 2003. *Slow Death.* New York, NY: Pinnacle.

Fox, J. and Levin, J. 2005. *Extreme Killing: Understanding Serial and Mass Murder.* Thousand Oaks, CA: Sage.

Fromm, E. 1973. *The Anatomy of Human Destructiveness.* New York, NY: Holt.

Gayford, J. J. 1978. Sex magazines. *Medicine, Science, and the Law, 18*(1), 44–51.

Geberth, V. J. 2006. *Practical Homicide Investigation: Tactics, Procedures, and Forensic Techniques.* Boca Raton, FL: CRC Press.

Giannangelo, S. J. 1996. *The Psychopathology of Serial Murder: A Theory of Violence.* Westport, CT: Praeger.

Glatt, J. 2002. *Cries in the Desert.* New York, NY: St Martin's. Kindle Edition.

Graber, B., Hartmann, K., Coffman, J., Huey, C. J., and Golde, C. J. 1982. Brain damage among mentally disordered sex offenders. *Journal of Forensic Science, 27*(1), 127–134.

Gratzer, T. and Bradford, J. M. W. 1995. Offender and offense characteristics of sexual sadists: A comparative study. *Journal of Forensic Sciences, 40*(3), 450–455.

Hare, R. D. 2003. *The Psychopathy Checklist-Revised* (2nd rev.). Toronto, Canada: Multi-Health Systems.

Hazelwood, R., Dietz, P., and Burgess, A. 1983. *Autoerotic Fatalities.* Lexington, MA: Health & Co.

Hazelwood, R., Warren, J., and Dietz, P. 1993. Compliant victims of the sexual sadist. *Australian Family Physician, 22*(4), 474–479.

Hazelwood, R. R. 1995. Analyzing the rape and profiling the offender. In: R. R. Hazelwood and A. Burgess (Eds.), *Practical Aspects of Rape Investigation: A Multidisciplinary Approach.* Boca Raton, FL: CRC Press, pp. 97–122.

Hazelwood, R. and Michaud, S. 2001. *Dark Dreams.* New York, NY: St. Martin's.

Healey, J., Lussier, P., and Beauregard, E. 2013. Sexual sadism in the context of rape and sexual homicide: An examination of crime scene indicators. *International Journal of Offender Therapy and Comparative Criminology, 57*(4), 402–424.

Holt, S. E., Meloy, J. R., and Strack, S. 1999. Sadism and psychopathy in violent and sexually violent offenders. *Journal of the American Academy of Psychiatry and the Law, 27*(1), 23–32.

Hucker, S. J., Langevin, R., Wortzman, G., Dickey, R., Bain, J., Handy, L., Chambers, J., and Wright, P. 1988. Cerebral damage and dysfunction in sexually aggressive men. *Annals of Sex Research, 1*, 33–47.

Hunt, M. 1974. *Sexual Behavior in the 1970's.* New York, NY: Playboy Press.

Jackman, T. and Cole, T. 1992. *Rites of Burial.* New York, NY: Pinnacle.

Karpman, B. 1954. *The Sexual Offender and His Offenses: Etiology, Pathology, Psychodynamics and Treatment.* New York, NY: Julian Press.

Kingston, D. A. and Yates, P. M. 2008. Sexual sadism: Assessment and treatment. In: D. R. Laws and W. T. O'Donohue (Eds.), *Sexual Deviance: Theory, Assessment, and Treatment* (2nd ed.). New York, NY: Guilford Press, pp. 231–249.

Kinsey, A., Pomeroy, W., Martin, C., and Gebhard, P. 1953. *Sexual Behavior in the Human Female.* Philadelphia, PA: Saunders.

Knoll, J. L. and Hazelwood, R. R. 2009. Becoming the victim: Beyond sadism in serial sexual murderers. *Aggression and Violent Behavior, 14,* 106–114. DOI: 10.1016/j.avb.2008.12.003.

Krafft-Ebing, R. 1886/2011. *Psychopathia Sexualis.* Philadelphia, PA: Bloat Books.

Krueger R. B. 2010. The DSM diagnostic criteria for sexual sadism. *Archives of Sexual Behavior, 39*(2), 325–345.

Langevin, R., Bain, J., Wortzman, G., Hucker, S., Dickey, R., and Wright, P. 1988. Sexual sadism: Brain, blood, and behavior. *Annals of the New York Academy of Sciences, 528,* 163–171. DOI: 10.1111/j.1749-6632.1988.tb50859.x.

Leith, R. 1983. *The Prostitute Murders: The People vs. Richard Cottingham.* Secaucus, NJ: Lyle Stuart.

Levin, J. and Fox, J. A. 1985. *Mass Murder: America's Growing Menace.* New York, NY: Plenum Press.

Lourie, R. 1993. *Hunting the Devil.* New York, NY: Grafton.

MacCulloch, M., Snowden, P., Wood, P., and Mills, H. 1983. Sadistic fantasy, sadistic behavior, and offending. *British Journal of Psychiatry, 143,* 20–29.

Marshall, W. L. and Hucker, S. J. 2006a. Issues in the diagnosis of sexual sadism. *Sexual Offender Treatment, 1*(2). Retrieved from http://www.sexual-offender-treatment.org/40.html

Marshall, W. L. and Hucker, S. J. 2006b. Severe sexual sadism. In: R. D. McAnulty and M. M. Burnette (Eds.), *Sex and Sexuality, Volume 3: Sexual Deviation and Sexual Offenses.* Westport, CT: Praeger, pp. 227–250.

Marshall, W. L., Kennedy, P., and Yates, P. 2002a. Issues concerning the reliability and validity of the diagnosis of sexual sadism applied in prison settings. *Sexual Abuse: A Journal of Research and Treatment, 14,* 310–311. DOI: 10.1023/A1019917519457.

Marshall, W. L., Kennedy, P., Yates, P., and Serran, G. A. 2002b. Diagnosing sexual sadism in sexual offenders: Reliability across diagnosticians. *International Journal of Offender Therapy and Comparative Criminology, 46,* 668–676. DOI: 10.1177/0306624X02238161.

McClellan, J. 2010. *Erotophonophilia.* New York, NY: Cambria Press.

McDougal, D. 1991. *Angel of Darkness.* New York, NY: Time Warner.

McGuire, C. and Norton, C. 1989. *The Perfect Victim: The True Story of the Girl in the Box by the D.A. That Prosecuted Her.* New York, NY: Dell.

Mellor, L. 2012. *Cold North Killers: Canadian Serial Murder.* Toronto, Canada: Dundurn.

Mellor, L. 2016a.[*] Mincing words: Refining the language of mutilation. In: L. Mellor, A. Aggrawal, and E. W. Hickey (Eds.), *Understanding Necrophilia: A Global Multidisciplinary Approach.* San Diego, CA: Cognella.

Mellor, L. 2016b.[*] Necrophilia and the thematic-derivative model of sexual progression. In: L. Mellor, A. Aggrawal, and E. W. Hickey (Eds.), *Understanding Necrophilia: A Global Multidisciplinary Approach.* San Diego, CA: Cognella.

Mellor, L. 2016c.[*] Whiter shades of pale: Expanding the necrophilic behavioral spectrum. In: L. Mellor, A. Aggrawal, and E. W. Hickey (Eds.), *Understanding Necrophilia: A Global Multidisciplinary Approach.* San Diego, CA: Cognella.

Mokros, A., Osterheider, M., Hucker, S. J., and Nitschke, J. 2011. Psychopathy and sexual sadism. *Law and Human Behavior, 35*(3), 188–199. DOI: 10.1007/s10979-010-9221-9.

Money, J. 1990. Forensic sexology: Paraphilic serial rape (biastrophilia) and lust murder (erotophonophilia). *American Journal of Psychotherapy, 44*(1), 26–36.

Myers, W. C., Bukhanovskiy, A., Justen, E., Morton, R. J., Tilley, J., Adams, K., and Hazelwood, R. R. 2008. The relationship between serial sexual murder and autoerotic asphyxiation. *Forensic Science International, 176,* 187–195.

Myers, W. C., Husted, D. S., Safarik, M. E., and O'Toole, M. E. 2006. The motivation behind serial sexual homicide: Is it sex, power and control, or anger? *Journal of Forensic Sciences, 51*(4), 900–907. DOI: 10.1111/j.1556-4029.2006.00168.x.

Newton, M. 2000. *The Encyclopedia of Serial Killers.* New York, NY: Checkmark Books.

Nitschke, J., Osterheider, M., and Mokros, A. 2009. A cumulative scale of severe sexual sadism. *Sex Abuse, 21,* 262–278. DOI: 10.1177/1079063209342074.

---

[*] These essays also available in Mellor, L. (in press). *Necrophilia: Theoretical Perspectives for the New Millennium.* Toronto, Canada: Grinning Man Press.

Porter, S. and Woodworth, M. 2006. Psychopathy and aggression. In: C. J. Patrick (Ed.), *Handbook of Psychopathy*. New York, NY: Guilford Press, pp. 481–494.

Power, D. J. 1976. Sexual deviation and crime. *Medicine, Science, and the Law, 16*, 111–128. DOI: 10.1177/002580247601600207.

Proulx, J., Aubut, J., McKibben, A., and Cote, M. 1994. Penile responses of rapists and nonrapists to rape stimuli involving physical violence or humiliation. *Archives of Sexual Behavior, 23*, 295–310.

Proulx, J., Blais, E., and Beauregard, E. 2006. Sadistic sexual offenders (Steven Sacks, Trans.). In: J. Proulx, E. Beauregard, M. Cusson, and A. Nicole (Eds.), *Sexual Murderers: A Comparative Analysis and New Perspectives*. Mississauga, Canada: John Wiley, pp. 107–122.

Resnick, H. L. P. 1972. Eroticized repetitive hangings—A form of self-destruction. *American Journal of Psychotherapy, 26*, 4–21.

Ressler, R., Burgess, A., and Douglas, J. 1992. *Sexual Homicide: Patterns and Motives*. New York, NY: The Free Press.

Robertson, C. A. and Knight, R. A. 2014. Relating sexual sadism and psychopathy to one another, non-sexual violence, and sexual crime behaviors. *Aggressive Behavior, 40*, 12–23. DOI: 10.1002/ab.21505.

Seto, M. C. and Kuban, M. 1996. Criterion-related validity of a phallometric test for paraphilic rape and sadism. *Behavior Research and Therapy, 34*, 175–183.

State of Kansas v. Dennis L. Rader. 2005a. *State's Summary of Evidence*. Retrieved from http://bit.ly/1mcpwSu

State of Kansas vs. Dennis L. Rader. 2005b. *Transcript of Pleas of Guilty*. Retrieved from http://bit.ly/1QPj94g

Williams, S. 1996. *Invisible Darkness*. Toronto, Canada: McArthur and Company.

Williams, S. 2004. *Karla: A Pact with the Devil*. Ontario, Canada: Seal Books.

Wilson, C. 1998. *The Corpse Garden: The Crimes of Fred and Rose West*. London, UK: True Crime Library.

III

Personality and Mentally-Disordered Homicide Offenders

9 Psychopathic Homicide Offenders

Lee Mellor, Katherine Ramsland, and Michel Funicelli

Contents

Introduction 165
Etiology 167
    Genetics 167
    Environmental Factors 168
Features and Assessment of Psychopathy 169
    Diagnosing Psychopathy 169
Typologies 171
Characteristics of Psychopathic Homicides and Their Perpetrators 173
Recommendations for Handling Cases of Psychopaths Who Kill 180
    Interviewing 180
    Treatment 181
References 182

Introduction

With 2500 peer-reviewed articles and numerous books on the topic of psychopathy, any attempt at an exhaustive review of the disorder here would be impossible. Rather, in this chapter, we provide a brief overview of the history of the term and construct, etiology, diagnostic instruments, typologies, characteristics, and treatment. Our objective is to equip law enforcement and mental health professionals with knowledge that is practically applicable during the investigation, interviewing, criminal justice, and treatment processes.

To begin, it is crucial to understand that the word "psychopathy"—frequently conflated with "sociopathy" or "antisocial personality disorder"—has been used to refer to many different mental disorders and constructs over the years. Conceptually, Western academics have been interested in unscrupulous persons since the works of the Greek philosopher Theophrastus in the third century BC (Millon et al., 1998). However, the first recorded use of the term "psychopathy" was in Germany in 1847, where it was referred to as *psychopatisch*. The label *psychopath* has been documented as being first used in 1885 in a court of law by one Dr. Balinsky to refer to a Russian woman who killed a little girl. Notably, Dr. Balinsky implored the jury to acquit the defendant precisely because she *was* a psychopath. This reflects an understanding of the term which is at odds with our contemporary understanding of psychopathy as typifying somebody who is "legally sane but morally insane." This is because, in its original usage, psychopathy simply referred to any mental disorder's (psycho) pathology (pathy).

Certainly, the concept of psychopathy, as we now understand it, preceded the actual word. In his 1801 work *A Treatise on Insanity*, Pinel described patients whose ability to reason was intact, but who were nevertheless dangerously impulsive and reckless, coining the term *manie sans délire*—"insanity without delirium"—to refer to them (1801/1962). The next 40 years saw the physicians Benjamin Rush of the United States and Carl Otto of Denmark along with the British alienist JC Prichard continue to explore Pinel's observations. Prichard is perhaps best known for his phrase "moral insanity"; though as Millon et al. (1998) observe, this was met with much criticism, as it introduced a moral component to Pinel's originally neutral concept. The debate as to whether morality should be associated with mental health diagnoses would rage on in Europe for the remainder of the nineteenth century with proponents and opponents on both sides, and still endures to varying extent to this day (Blackburn, 1988; Gunn, 1998). While the British continued to see and debate the psychopathic construct in moral terms, by the late nineteenth century German psychiatrists had adopted a more observational approach to understanding it. The first to formulate a psychological construct of psychopathy centered on the disorder's pathological need for dominance was Krafft-Ebing (1886/2011) in his landmark *Psychopathia Sexualis*, though he mainly emphasized psychopathy's high correlation with sexual sadism (see Chapter 8). Other influential German psychopathy researchers during this period included Koch, Meyer, and Kraeplin (Millon et al., 1998).

According to Hervé (2003), the term "sociopath" was coined by the German-American psychiatrist Karl Birnbaum in 1909, and was popularized by G.E. Partridge in the United States, around 1930. Hervé states that Partridge advocated this term for a number of reasons; first, Partridge believed that, given the extent to which the older term "psychopath" was being applied to patients with vastly different mental health problems, it had become a useless "waste-basket" category that needed to be replaced. Second, "sociopath" was also more suited to Partridge's notion that this personality disorder could result purely from environmental pressures, arising as a mode of social adaptation. Hervé points out that this was in opposition to the German concept of "psychopathy" which emphasized the role of genetics.

It is important to understand that both "psychopath" and "sociopath" arose to describe the same emerging psychological construct: *manie sans delire* or moral insanity (Hervé, 2003). However, the etiological pathways of the psychopath (genetic/nature) and sociopath (environmental/nurture) have been clearly demarcated since Partridge popularized the latter term.

Despite this distinction, there has been a problematic propensity for the general public, police, and academics alike to use the terms interchangeably. For example, in his "The Psychopathic or Sociopathic Personality," Begun (1976) switches casually between the two while referring to the same construct: a classic "jangle fallacy." Mohl (2013) does not distinguish between psychopaths, sociopaths, and individuals suffering from antisocial personality disorder, even though research has conclusively proven his standpoint to be false (Hare, 2003). Though preferring the term "sociopath," Mealey (1995) cites Hare's research on psychopathy to support her arguments. In fact, much of her essay concentrates on the genetic etiology of "sociopaths," as if unaware of the concept underlying the term altogether. Today, the term "sociopath" is rarely used in the mental health community, though Schlesinger (1980), Lykken (1998, 2000), and Perez (2012) have made convincing arguments for its reinstatement as a differentiating category.

The term psychopath started to reassert itself in the academic vernacular with the pioneering research of Hervey Cleckley, whose fifth edition of *The Mask of Sanity* (1976) was highly influential, and characterized psychopaths as individuals who are lacking any real structure to their personality, which leads them to destructive behavior, but who are able to outwardly mimic a functional member of society. Cleckley observed 16 traits in such individuals: superficial charm and good intelligence; absence of delusions and other signs of irrational thinking; absence of nervousness or psychoneurotic manifestations; unreliability; untruthfulness and insincerity; lack of remorse and shame; inadequately motivated antisocial behavior; poor judgment and failure to learn by experience; pathologic egocentricity and incapacity for love; general poverty in major affective reactions; specific loss of insight; unresponsiveness in general interpersonal relations; fantastic and uninviting behavior with drink and sometimes without; suicide threats rarely carried out; sex life impersonal, trivial, and poorly integrated; and failure to follow any life plan.

Inspired by Cleckley's work, the Canadian psychologist Robert Hare sought empirical data to substantiate Cleckley's construct, thereby refining it in the process. The result was the Psychopathy Checklist (and its Revised edition, the PCL-R), a clinical instrument for measuring psychopathy, and correspondingly, recidivism in incarcerated offenders. Widely and currently considered the "gold standard" in psychopathy assessment, the PCL-R will be discussed in further detail later in this chapter. Despite its popularity, the common tendency to conflate the PCL-R instrument with the construct of psychopathy has come under criticism by some academics (Skeem and Cooke, 2010).

Etiology

The genetic predisposition to psychopathy and the important contribution of nonshared environment are well established (Beaver et al., 2011a). "The genes load the gun and the environment pulls the trigger" (Fallon, 2006, p. 364). But neither perspective can explain alone the expression of psychopathy. Instead, both paradigms have to be viewed in how they relate with one another. This approach is favored in this chapter.

Genetics

To date, the psychopathic gene remains elusive (Gunter et al., 2010). Nevertheless, behavior genetics allow us to increase our genotypic and phenotypic knowledge base for this disorder. Studies of twins and adoptees reared together and apart are the bread and butter of behavior genetic research. Although this type of investigation may not be able to identify a specific gene, it does provide reliable data on the variance accounted for by genetic factors. For example, the more monozygotic (MZ) twins are alike in comparison to dizygotic (DZ) twins, the stronger the genetic effect; given that MZ twins share 100% of their DNA while the proportion of DNA shared by DZ twins is only 50%. Behavior genetics also concerns itself with environmental factors.

Evidence of genetic risk of psychopathy is not limited to adulthood. Indeed, it can be found in children, mid and older teens, and young adults. Viding et al. (2005) were the first to report on psychopathic tendencies in young children. They used data from the Twins Early Development Study (TEDS) to test the presence of two traits, callous/unemotional (CU) and antisocial behavior (AB), both known for their strong association with psychopathy. The TEDS is a birth record-based representative sample of twins born in the UK from 1994 to 1996. It includes teacher assessment, at school's year end, of CU and AB for 3487 pairs of twins at 7 years of age (Viding et al., 2005). Their findings of heritability factors of 0.67 (MZ vs DZ) for the extreme CU group, 0.81 for the extreme AB with CU, and 0.30 for the extreme AB without CU suggest that high level of callous/unemotional traits in 7-year olds is under strong genetic influence (Viding et al., 2005). More recently, Bezdjian et al. (2011) investigated two psychopathic personality traits, callous/disinhibited and manipulative/deceitful, and two types of aggressive behaviors, *reactive* and *instrumental*, as assessed by caregivers and child self-report using the Child Psychopathy Scale-Revised and the Reactive and Proactive Aggression Questionnaire. The participants were recruited from a large sample of twins from Los Angeles County aged 9 and 10 years old. Relative to child self-report, assessments from caregivers suggest that genetic effects explained a greater proportion of the variance, 53–57% compared to 33–38% (Bezdjian et al., 2011).

Studies involving teenagers and young adults arrived at similar conclusions. Larsson et al. (2006) examined a large sample (n = 2198) of MZ and DZ twins born in Sweden between 1985 and 1986. They measured psychopathy with the Youth Psychopathic Traits Inventory in 16–17-year-old twins and found comparable results. The genetic variance explained 0.51 of the grandiose/manipulative trait, 0.43 of the callous/unemotional feature, and 0.56 of the impulsive/irresponsible characteristic (Larsson et al., 2006). Interestingly, they found no significant sex differences in the genetic factors for psychopathy. Forsman et al. (2008) used the same sample to test two cohorts, one of 16-year-olds and another of 19 years of age. This study's findings suggest that higher-order psychopathic traits are stable across time and gender, and that stability for the callous/unemotional and impulsive/irresponsible dimensions is explained by unique genetic factors (Forsman et al., 2008). Finally, Beaver et al. (2011a) found that for males adoptees "having a criminal biological father increased the odds of scoring in the top 10% of the psychopathy scale by a factor greater than 8.5" (Beaver et al., 2011b, p. 430). Criminality in biological mothers was not associated with psychopathic personality traits in male or female adoptees (Beaver et al., 2011b). In spite of fairly solid evidence of genetic involvement in phenotypic psychopathy, much more research is needed.

A few genomic locations, however, appear promising for psychopathy and antisocial spectrum disorders. Two degradation enzymes, monoamine oxidase A (MAOA) and cathecol-*O*-methyltransferase (COMT), and the 5HTT gene are associated with antisocial behavior, and with functioning of the amygdala and prefrontal cortex (Fowler et al., 2009). These gene variants operate in brain regions implicated in psychopathy, and are related to genetic material involved in the regulation of emotional expression and antisocial behavior. Perhaps not surprisingly, Fowler et al. (2009) were first to report that MAOA, 5HTT, and COMT were significantly associated with emotional dysfunction scores, but only the first two were tied to total psychopathy scores. MAOA and COMT are enzymes that degrade amine neurotransmitters like dopamine, norepinephrine, and serotonin, while the 5HTT gene, located on chromosome 17, removes serotonin from the synaptic cleft back into the synaptic buttons (Gunter et al., 2010). As the logic goes, possession of a dysfunctional MAOA gene probably impairs the ability of serotonin transporters to function properly, and as a result reduces this neurotransmitter's inhibitory capacity on dopamine production. As mentioned earlier, once the dopamine/serotonin balance is destabilized, elevated expression of aggressive and impulsive behavior is a likely consequence. But these conclusions must be interpreted with caution. The study by Fowler's team contains a number of limitations such as small sample and effect sizes, the results are not generalizable beyond those with ADHD, and the fact that it was, to our knowledge, an inaugural experiment not since replicated.

Environmental Factors

As Fallon (2006) puts it, once the gun is loaded with genetic material, the environment pulls the phenotypic trigger. Research designs based on behavior genetics model enable investigators to disentangle genotypic, shared, and nonshared environment variance. The latter two components of variability relate, respectively, to experiences shared equally by all family members (e.g., socioeconomic status, same parents, home, community, schools, etc.), and environmental factors unique (unshared) to each sibling (e.g. birth order, accidents, traumas, illnesses, peer groups, etc.) (Plomin and Daniels, 1987).

With respect to psychopathy, the amount of variability explained by shared environment is hardly noticeable. Viding et al. (2005) found minimal influence (0.05) for shared environment in their sample of 7-year-old twins with extreme callous/unemotional scores. Findings from Larsson et al. (2006) in their study of 16- and 17-year-old twin teens reveal a variability of 0.00 from shared environment in callous/unemotional and impulsive/irresponsible traits, and only 0.03 with the grandiose/manipulative characteristic. Results from Forsman et al. (2008) and Bezdjian et al. (2011) appear to be in general agreement. This is not surprising for the study by Forsman et al. (2008). Even though they measured their data longitudinally at two time points, at ages 16 and 19, they used the same sample as in Larsson et al. (2006). In summary, there is little evidence that shared environment has any significant influence in the development of psychopathic traits (Da Silva et al., 2012). Consequently, one must look at unique events for potential answers.

The bulk of the environmental variance comes from nonshared experiences. Results range from 0.27 in 7-year-old twins scoring high on the callous/unemotional scale (Viding et al., 2005), to 0.37 in 16- and 17-year-old twins (Larsson et al., 2006), and 0.38 and 0.36, respectively, in 16- and 19-year-old twins (Forsman et al., 2008).

That environmental influence of the nonshared variety plays an important role in the development of psychopathy, at the expense of the shared type, is hardly earth shattering. Plomin and Daniels (1987) adroitly articulated how "non-shared environment is responsible for most environmental variation relevant to psychological development" (p. 4). In fact they conclude that unshared environmental impact preponderantly accounts for the variance in personality, psychopathology, and cognitive development (i.e., IQ) after childhood. If the development of healthy individuals is predominantly shaped by unshared environment and inheritable traits, each contributing roughly 40–60% of explained variability, why would the news of a similar breakdown in terms of psychopathy be any more remarkable? The distinctive input of nonshared environment is in the identification of unique life-altering events, without losing sight of two complicating factors, genotype–environment correlation (rGE) and genotype–environment interaction (G × E). Briefly, in regard to this last point, phenotypic variance in the development of children with latent psychopathic traits will be different according to how their genetic propensities correlate or interact with their environment.

Despite the dearth of scientific research in this domain, a few investigative leads are encouraging. In general, responsible and caring parents plant the seeds of empathy early on in the development of their children. Family offspring subsequently learn how to repress their destructive behavior, and incorporate their parent's attitudes, judgments, standards, and values (Torry and Billick, 2011). This upbringing shapes the development of a child's conscience, a central feature of psychopathy. Preliminary evidence suggests that parental incompetency and certain antisocial factors are associated with early onset of psychopathic traits (Salekin and Lochman, 2008; Gao et al., 2010; Da Silva et al., 2012). Lack of maternal care, characterized by low attachment and disengagement, predicted psychopathic variation in females, while only disengagement was associated in psychopathic personality traits in males (Beaver et al., 2012). Similarly, Gao et al. (2010) found support for poor parental bonding and its association with psychopathy, even after taking into account sex, social adversity, ethnicity, and abuse. The lesser the quality of the parental bond, as assessed retrospectively by participants at age 28, the higher the total psychopathic score. Harsh parental discipline was also associated with childhood psychopathy, especially in children who had extreme AB/CU scores and those with AB+ relative to those with CU+ scores and controls (Larsson et al., 2008). However, this relationship seems to be a child-driven effect. In other words, children with high AB or high AB/CU scores might evoke negative parental characteristics expressed by harsh disciplinary practices. Obviously, more research is necessary to determine directionality. Finally, having delinquent peers and being reared in a disadvantaged neighborhood was positively associated with psychopathy in both males and females (Beaver et al., 2012).

Another helpful direction is the interaction of the MAOA genotype with maltreatment and provocative environmental conditions. Genetic deficiencies in MAOA activity and child maltreatment have been associated with elevated aggression (Caspi et al., 2002; Weder et al., 2009). But not all children subjected to environmental insults develop antisocial behavior and problems with violent conduct. Caspi et al. (2002) first noted that the effect of male childhood maltreatment on antisocial behavior was significantly contingent on activity levels of MAOA. Male adults who had been severely mistreated as children and had low MAOA activity exhibited stronger antisocial behavior. Further analyses showed that those adults were more likely to develop conduct disorder, to be convicted of a violent crime as an adult, and to report (either self or informed) a disposition toward violence (Caspi et al., 2002). But in cases of children subjected to extreme levels of trauma (e.g., physical and sexual abuse, exposure to domestic and community violence, and multiple out-of-home placements), the effect of the MAOA genotype disappeared; ill-treated children were aggressive regardless of MAOA activity levels (Weder et al., 2009). It appears that MAOA activity explained aggressive behavior (expressed by fighting, rule breaking, and inattention) up to moderate levels of abuse. Last, in a laboratory experiment, adult males with a low activity form of the MAOA genotype, when placed in a highly provoking condition (the mistaken belief that 80% of their earnings had been taken by an adversary), reacted more aggressively (as measured by the amount of spicy sauce administered to their opponent) than their counterparts with the more active version of the gene (McDermott et al., 2009). Caution must be used with these recent developments. Much work remains to be done to replicate these studies. Results from studies examining G × E are preliminary, overshadowed by a number of limitations, and not generalizable beyond their sample population.

Features and Assessment of Psychopathy

Diagnosing Psychopathy

Dr. Robert Hare and his colleagues developed the Psychopathy Checklist (PCL) and its revision, the PCL-R, for the reliable and valid assessment of psychopathy (Hare, 1993; Forth et al., 2013). The PCL-R and its derivatives have also been hailed as among the most accurate instruments available for assessing the risk for violence and recidivism. (Dolan and Doyle, 2000; Hare, 2002). Influenced by prison psychiatrist Hervey Cleckley's list of 16 traits of psychopathy, Hare (1993) believes that among the condition's most devastating features are a callous disregard for the rights of others, a lack of remorse, and a propensity for predatory and violent behaviors.

Hare noticed throughout the early 1970s that other researchers were using different classification systems to address psychopathy, such as categories based on the Minnesota Multiphasic Personality Inventory and the California Psychological Inventory. The research was not unified. He set about creating a peer-validated checklist.

Hare's first published work on the 22-item research scale for the assessment of psychopathy (PCL) appeared in 1980. He later revised it to 20 items (PCL-R). It was scored on the basis of a semi-structured interview with the subjects along with information from files. Each trait and behavior was rated on a scale from 0 (the subject did not manifest it) to 2 (he or she definitely did manifest it). The total possible score was 40, and an individual was diagnosed as a psychopath if his or her score fell between 30 and 40. In 1991, Hare published a PCL-R manual, which has been updated over the years. Throughout the rest of the decade, more researchers affirmed the PCL-R's reliability and validity with male forensic populations (Kosson et al., 2002). The PCL-R generated a dramatic increase in basic research on the nature of psychopathy and on the implications of the disorder for the mental health and criminal justice systems.

Buzina (2012) points out that the condition of psychopathy is not interchangeable with antisocial personality disorder as measured with DSM-IV (now 5) criteria, or with the ICD-10 dissocial disorder. "Not all individuals with antisocial or dissocial personality disorder are considered psychopaths" (p. 134).

PCL-R items are grouped around two basic factors (Harris et al., 2001), *affective/interpersonal* features and *socially deviant lifestyle* (both of which have been divided further into two facets each for the two factors). Psychopathy is characterized by such traits as

- Factor 1 (affective/interpersonal)

  - Facet 1 (interpersonal): Glibness/superficial charm, conning/manipulative, grandiose sense of self worth, pathological lying

  - Facet 2 (affective): Lack of remorse or guilt, callous/lack of empathy, failure to accept responsibility for own actions, shallow affect

- Factor 2 (social deviance)

  - Facet 3 (lifestyle): Need for stimulation/proneness to boredom; parasitic lifestyle; lack of realistic, long-term goals; impulsivity; irresponsibility

  - Facet 4 (antisocial): Poor behavioral controls, early behavior problems, juvenile delinquency, revocation of conditional release, criminal versatility

  - Unaligned: Promiscuous sexual behavior, many short-term marital relationships (Hare, 2003)

During the early 1990s, the Research Network on Mental Health and the Law of the John D. and Catherine T. MacArthur Foundation examined the relationship between mental disorder and violent behavior directed against others. They listed 134 risk factors across four domains that had been associated with violence in prior research, and were believed to by clinicians to be linked to violence. Hare was asked to develop a tool, based on the PCL-R. He created the PCL:SV or Screening Version, which offered 12 items with the same factor structure as the PCL-R (Hart et al., 1995).

The items were submitted to a full-scale study involving nearly 1000 patients over 5 months after discharge from a psychiatric institute. Researchers measured the criterion variables by using official arrest and hospital records, regular self-reports, and collateral reports from knowledgeable informants. In this study, the PCL:SV proved to be the most reliable instrument for predicting the future risk of violence. Those with a score of 13 and higher were about three times more likely to have an episode of violence than were patients with lower scores (Hare, 2002).

A version of the PCL-R used for adolescents is the PCL:YV or Youth Version, developed with Dr. Adelle Forth and Dr. David Kosson (Kosson et al., 2002). For younger children, the antisocial process screening device (APSD), developed with Dr. Paul Frick, appears to be useful for distinguishing children who show risk factors for the development of psychopathy (Hare, 2002).

Hare was also asked by British probation officers to create a tool for them. "Four years ago," he explains (personal interview), "a senior probation officer in the UK organized a conference in Sheffield to convince me that probation and parole officers needed a tool to help them assess psychopathic features. They couldn't use the PCL-R or the 12-item PCL:SV, because these are controlled instruments that require professional qualifications."

Hare devised the Psychopathy-Scan (P-Scan), a nonclinical tool for developing general impressions into a hypothesis about whether a particular person might be a psychopath (Hare and Hervé, 1999). "It consists of 120 characteristics, 30 for impressions about interpersonal traits, like grandiosity and lying, 30 for impressions about affective traits, such as lack of remorse and shallow emotions, 30 for impressions about lifestyle features, such as impulsivity and stimulation-seeking, and 30 for impressions about antisocial behaviors. So, we have four components that match the new factor structure of the PCL-R. You don't have to be a clinician, you just have to have some experience with the individual" (personal interview).

Although the PCL-R is widely regarded as the gold standard for assessing psychopathy, other instruments have been designed as well. Concerns about access to files, the need for extensive clinical training, and the length of the assessment process for the PCL-R necessitated them (Fowler and Lilienfeld, 2013). "Some rely on self report, others on peer report, and still others on presumed implicit cognitive processes" (pp. 34–35).

Fowler and Lilienfeld summarize the primary alternative instruments to the PCL-R for assessing psychopathy. Among measures that have an inadequate research base are the Sociopathy Scale of the Minnesota Multiphasic Personality Inventory, the Psychopathic States Inventory, Levenson's Psychopathy Scale, the Social Psychopathy Scale, and the Antisocial Personality Questionnaire.

Among self-report measures are the following: the Levenson Primary and Secondary Psychopathy Scale (LPSP), Hare's Self-report Psychopathy Scale (SRP-III), and the Psychopathic Personality Inventory-Revised (PPI-R). The LPSP, with good internal consistency, contains 26 items in a Likert format. The primary psychopath is based on Cleckley's criteria and the secondary psychopath on "pseudo-psychopathy" measures. The SRP-III consists of 29 items that are highly correlated with the PCL-R, although there is currently less published research on it. The PPI-R offers 187 items in a Likert format and was intended to detect psychopathic traits in nonincarcerated populations. It has eight categorical subscales, including coldheartedness, egocentricity, and blame externalization. This assessment is considered to have good potential as a self-report measure.

Observer measures for psychopathy include the Interpersonal Measure of Psychopathy (IM-P), which has 21 observer-rated items, such as nonverbal behaviors and interactions with others. Some researchers suggest that the IM-P be used as an adjunct to the PCL-R, as it correlates well with Factor 1. The Psychopathy Q-sort (PQS) is derived from the 100-item California Q-set for personality assessment, but it seems to correlate toward DSM Cluster B personality disorders. Hare designed the P-Scan for nonclinical raters. The scales, with 30 items each, are interpersonal, affective, and behavioral. Its predictive validity is unknown, but internal consistency is high. The B-Scan, with four scales, was designed for use in a work environment (Babiak, 1995). Finally, the Minnesota Temperament Inventory is based on Cleckley's criteria. It can be used as a self-report inventory or be observer rated.

Widiger and Lynam (1998) have argued that psychopathy can be conceptualized on the five-factor model of personality (FFM) by high levels in the *antagonism* (the model's inverse of *agreeableness*) domain, low levels in the *conscientiousness* domain, as well as a low score in the *anxiousness* facet of the *neuroticism* domain.

Implicit measure devices include projective tests that use ambiguous stimuli (inkblots, images, drawings) and inductive reasoning tests. The Aggression Conditional Reasoning Test, for example, evaluates justifications for decisions and actions against six biases: hostile attribution, potency, retribution, retaliation, victimization, derogation, and social discounting. Test-takers are given 22 problems each of which has four possible solutions. Two are illogical, one is pro-social, and one reflects one of the biases.

The PCL-R appears to be most valuable for violence prediction. Rice and Harris (2013) have studied recidivism rates in psychopaths for decades. They say that those who score high on psychopathy assessment instruments are at high risk for repeat violence, especially associated with Factor 2 (social deviance) and Facet 4 (antisocial) of the PCL-R. Hare (2002) affirms this.

Typologies

The most widely accepted typology of psychopathy—*primary* (idiopathic or anethopathic) psychopathy and *secondary* (symptomatic) psychopathy—was identified by Karpman (1941), who believed that *secondary* psychopaths displayed the symptoms of psychopathy but that these symptoms were actually attributable to other mental diseases (Karpman, 1947, 1948a). Only 15% of those psychopaths remaining, Karpman claimed, were *primary* psychopaths.

Karpman (1948b) asserted that the presence or capacity for anxiety and impulsivity in *secondary* psychopaths is what chiefly differentiates them from *primary* psychopaths. In the 65 years since, this has been borne out by a plethora of research (Koenigs et al., 2010; Lee and Salekin, 2010; Vidal et al. 2010). Studies also seem to indicate that *primary* psychopaths have better interpersonal and manipulative skills than *secondary psychopaths* (Lee and Salekin, 2010) as well as thought facilitation and emotional management (Vidal et al., 2010) that they are more likely to commit acts of *instrumental violence*, and suffer from a malfunctioning amygdala (Chambers, 2010).

Adversely, *secondary* psychopaths have lower emotional intelligence, act impulsively (Vidal, Skeem, and Camp, 2010), and perpetrate acts of *reactionary violence*—likely resulting from deficits in their frontal prefrontal cortex. Unsurprisingly, Blagov et al. (2011) found that *primary* psychopaths scored high on Factor 1 (affective/interpersonal) of the PCL-R, and *secondary* psychopaths scored high on Factor 2 (social deviance). From a literature review on the interhemispheric dynamics of the brain, Hecht (2011) concluded that the right hemisphere of a *primary* psychopath's brain is hypoactive, while a *secondary* psychopath has a hypoactive left hemisphere.

Taking a much different approach, Millon and Davis (1998) have proposed that there are 10 subtypes of psychopaths: (1) unprincipled, (2) disingenuous, (3) risk-taking, (4) covetous, (5) spineless, (6) explosive, (7) abrasive, (8) malevolent, (9) tyrannical, and (10) malignant. Many of these subtypes do not seem to actually represent Hare psychopaths, but other conceptions of the disorder.

The *unprincipled* psychopath is a fearless risk-taker with strong narcissistic attributes, but is generally successful at avoiding police detection, the criminal justice system, and clinical treatment. He is frequently a confidence trickster and charlatan, and thrives on using and out-smarting people for his own personal gain.

Though the *disingenuous* psychopath shares many similarities, he tends to be more histrionic than narcissistic, and is motivated to seek attention, often employing seductive behavior to get it. He is habitually deceptive to others and himself, often believing that his motives—in actuality, to make people love him, believing that nobody will otherwise—are genuinely benevolent because he does not realize the extent of his own selfishness. Eventually, the desire for attention diminishes so that only interpersonal seductiveness and manipulation remains. Though he projects an air of sociability and geniality to strangers and acquaintances, he may express moodiness and resentment to people who he is closer to. Compared with other psychopaths he may be loyal, albeit inconsistently, and capable of reciprocating affection. Such psychopaths are characteristically impulsive and unreliable.

Combining antisocial and histrionic features, the eponymous *risk-taking* psychopath finds intrinsic worth in seeking out danger, as it gives him an adrenaline rush and allows him to experience the vitality of life. Values such a fame or material gain are of little worth to him. Naturally, he is impulsive in all areas of life, and has markedly reduced fear and anxiety. Personal autonomy and independence is his foremost priority, as he continues to seek out thrills in order to fill the persistent emptiness he feels inside. Unsurprisingly, such a hyperactive and volatile individual places absolutely no worth on self-discipline.

The *covetous* psychopath is basically a prototype of the individual with antisocial personality disorder as described in the DSM-5 or the ICD-10's dyssocial personality disorder. Believing that he has been given a raw deal where others have led comparatively pleasurable and easy lives, he seeks to even the odds by taking what he wants from others by way of physical force, manipulation, theft, and so on. For this reason, he has little to no remorse or guilt for any wrongdoings he has perpetrated, and is completely self-centered and without empathy. Ultimately, no matter how much he takes, it will never be enough to level the tables. Millon and Davis (1998) clarify that although the *covetous* psychopath seems to share many commonalities with the *unprincipled* psychopath, where the latter exudes a "benign, entitlement" (p. 165) the former comes across as "smug or justified" (p. 165).

A *spineless* psychopath sees others as powerful and hostile which makes him pathologically insecure. In order to scare would-be aggressors away he launches pre-emptive counterphobic strikes, demonstrating to the world that he is not to be messed with, even though he is not naturally cruel or violent. He takes no pleasure in his acts of aggression, but sees them as necessary, simultaneously trying to convince himself that he is not a coward or victim. Such psychopaths tend to inflict violence or domination through an institutional setting such as the government, military, church, or a political faction striking out against stigmatized groups who are perceived as dangerous.

In direct contrast is the *explosive* psychopath who, without warning, erupts into physically, verbally, or sexually violent rages in response to frustration or perceived threats. Such aggression is invariably *reactive* in nature, and is often the manifestation of many painful memories that he has suppressed. Specific people may trigger these emotional conflagrations because they symbolize his failures and inadequacies, and he seeks to destroy them as subjective symbols, not necessarily because of what they are in reality. The psychopath's anger is, therefore, best characterized as an emotional release.

The *abrasive* psychopath is essentially a constant critic and contrarian. Ever irritated, he antagonizes and quarrels with nearly everyone over the most pedantic points and frivolous issues. It is not unusual for him to claim that his devotion to his principles mandates him to hold his ground when he is in the right. However, for him it is not about finding the correct answer, but rather frustrating his opponents who he always considers to be unequivocally wrong. Although he berates and insults those who he disagrees with, he maintains that he is educating them for their own good. He has little or no guilt about his pugnacious behavior as he sees it not from stemming from his own personality, but rather it is justified by how unreasonable the other person is. There is comorbidity with paranoid personality disorder.

As "many murderers and serial killers fit this psychopathic pattern" (Millon and Davis, 1998, p. 168), the *malevolent* psychopath is of particular use to us here. He is fundamentally hostile and disdainful of social conventions, paranoid, selfish, cold-blooded, and ruthless. Like the *covetous* psychopath, he is driven by real or perceived injustices, but the *malevolent* psychopath can only be sated by revenge. He does not fear punishment; rather punishment simply adds further justification for his misanthropy. When he is unable to achieve his goals of dominance and fantastical success, he reacts with violent and vindictive retribution. Instead of experiencing guilt or remorse for his misdeeds, he is wickedly self-assured. Cognizant of the difference between right and wrong, but unable to emotionally experience this, he will push his victims to the brink as long as it does not compromise his own ends.

Similarly terrifying is the *tyrannical psychopath* who thrives on attacking—physically and/or verbally—those who oppose or show vulnerability to him. He takes pleasure in terrifying people into submission, and will actually exert tremendous effort to maximize the suffering he inflicts. His targets are not only his immediate victims, but any who would consider meddling with him in the future. Their aggression is not motivated by emotional factors but by actual sadistic pleasure. He is utterly without empathy or remorse.

Finally, the *malignant* psychopath has close ties to paranoid personality disorder. Believing himself to be threatened by society, he becomes lost in a world of fantasy where he builds up persecutory delusions in which he is certain that others are lying to sabotage him or break his will. Determined not to become a subordinate vassal of authority, he isolates himself and dreams of fighting back and exacting revenge, when in reality it is his own antisocial behavior that leads to people having bad impressions of him in the first place. The case of James Roszko, detailed below, provides us with a classic example of *malignant* psychopathy.

Case Study: James Roszko

On March 3, 2005, two bailiffs arrived at the chain-link fence-enclosed property of James Michael Roszko in Mayerthorpe, Alberta, Canada, with orders to repossess a 2005 Ford F-350 that Roszko had recently leased from a dealership in Edmonton. Roszko had a reputation as a dangerous man, and the two Rottweilers patrolling the grounds posed a clear threat. When the bailiffs shouted out to Roszko through the fence, he climbed into his truck and exited through a gate on the south side of his compound shouting obscenities at them as he drove off. The Royal Canadian Mounted Police soon arrived to assist the bailiffs, and having gained access to the Roszko property, they found a chop-shop, stolen property, and a marijuana grow-op. The RCMP soon obtained a search warrant, and began to methodically search the property.

At 8 a.m. the next morning, Constables Peter Schiemann, Brock Myrol, Anthony Gordon, and Leo Johnston decided to enter a Quonset hut on the premises. Little did they know that during the night, James Roszko had sneaked back into the compound with a Hechler and Koch .308 automatic assault rifle to prepare an ambush in the hut. Within seconds of entering, Roszko unloaded killing all four RCMP constables.

Likely believing that he had wiped out all of the policemen on the property, Roszko exited the Quonset hut only to come face-to-face with Constable Stephen Vigor who had overheard the gunshots. Roszko fired at Vigor and missed, and Vigor responded by shooting him twice, wounding him. Roszko fled back into the hut for cover, thus beginning a stand-off that would last for hours. Sometime before 2 p.m., Roszko committed suicide by shooting himself in the heart.

The Mayerthorpe massacre would go down as the single worst incident of police murder in Canadian history. In its wake, RCMP psychologist, Matt Logan, was assigned to interview those who knew Roszko as well as looking into his personal papers, police reports, and medical records to form a kind of psychological profile of the perpetrator. The aim was to determine whether anything could have been done beforehand to prevent the tragic murders of Schiemann, Myrol, Gordon, and Johnston. Logan learned that not only did Roszko have a pathological hatred of cops dating back to when he was a teenager, but that he had also been convicted on multiple counts of theft, break and enter, possession of stolen property, making harassing phone calls, breach of probation, uttering death threats, automobile offenses, and sexual assault. A photograph of a known cop-killer hung in his home, along with gun enthusiast magazines, and photographs of Roszko sexually assaulting two male adolescents. Roszko had also displayed marked behavioral problems from childhood, delving deep into drug and alcohol abuse and stealing a rifle from a local gun shop.

Ultimately, Logan concluded that James Roszko had been a classic psychopath and that he should have therefore been identified as such, considered a highly dangerous individual, and handled with much greater precaution. Mellor (2013) has also supported this diagnosis. As we shall see in the following section, Roszko's *instrumental* violence and indiscriminate sexual offenses are overrepresented in psychopaths.

Characteristics of Psychopathic Homicides and Their Perpetrators

O'Toole (2007) has proposed that the PCL-R items glibness/superficial charm, sensation-seeking (elsewhere referred to as "Proneness to boredom/Need for stimulation"), conning and manipulative, and impulsivity can be gleaned from careful analysis of one or more related crime scenes. In a later article, Smith et al. (2012) added lack of remorse or guilt, callous/lack of empathy, and grandiose sense of self-worth. This last item can only be reliably determined when a killer communicates with the police and/or media, targets a victim of social importance, or spends a significant amount of time with a witness. Promiscuous sexual behavior, poor behavioral controls, and criminal versatility are also sometimes discernable. Together, these ten items (Table 9.1) account for half of Hare's 20-item checklist, and find almost equal representation in each of the four facet (interpersonal, affective, lifestyle, and antisocial), with promiscuous sexual behavior remaining unaligned in the latest edition of the PCL-R (Hare, 2003).

Table 9.1 Ten PCL-R Items Discernible at a Crime Scene and Their Corresponding Factors and Facets

FACTOR 1 (Interpersonal/Affective)		FACTOR 2 (Social Deviance)		
Interpersonal	Affective	Lifestyle	Antisocial	Nonaligned
Glibness/superficial charm Conning and manipulative Grandiose sense of self-worth	Lack of remorse or guilt Callous/lack of empathy	Sensation seeking Impulsivity	Poor behavioral controls Criminal versatility	Promiscuous sexual behavior

According to the PCL-R, "Glibness/Superficial Charm" refers to "a glib, voluble, verbally facile individual who exudes an insincere and superficial sort of charm" (Hare, 2003, p. 21). Typically, these individuals seem very much at ease and employ a "gift of the gab" (Hare, 2003, p. 21) to spin endearing stories and portray themselves as more widely educated and intellectual than they actually are. This trait generally manifests in the approach phase preceding a murder, rather than during the actual attack itself. Thus, it is useful to consider crime scene elements such as the absence of forced entry into a victim's home. If the perpetrator is determined to be a stranger, a lack of defensive wounds may indicate that the assailant employed superficial charm to lower the victim's guard significantly before gaining control over them.

"Conning and Manipulative" refers to an individual who uses "deceit and deception to cheat, bilk, defraud, or manipulate others… motivated by a desire for personal gain (money, sex, status, power, etc.) and carried out with no concern for their effects on victims…in a cool, self-assured or brazen manner" (Hare, 2003, p. 29). This psychopathic trait yields a masterful con man, and though Hare speaks about it chiefly in terms of swindling for financial gain, such devious tricks may also be utilized for more nefarious purposes. The previously mentioned link between a lack of defensive injuries and glibness/superficial charm may also apply to the conning and manipulative individual.

Individuals with a "Grandiose Sense of Self-worth" are typically arrogant braggarts who believe that they should be afforded a great deal of respect despite having accomplished little of significance in their lives. They tend to look down on others and are often able to command the direction of an interview (Hare, 2003). This is most evident when a criminal communicates with the police, such as when the Zodiac Killer boasted of outwitting the police, although it could also be argued that posing a victim's body in a degrading position could reflect a sense of superiority.

"Sensation-seeking," also known as "Need for Stimulation/Proneness to Boredom," is a trait that leads the psychopath to quickly become disinterested and pursue thrills or novelty in order to overcome tedium. As a result, jobs and interpersonal relationships are fleeting, replaced by destructive or erratic behavior. Substance abuse is commonly associated with this item (Hare, 2003). Smith et al. (2012) refer to the Samuel Brown kidnapping, in which to the detriment of the abductor's plan, he kidnapped a high profile victim in broad daylight. They posit that this foolish decision was partially motivated by the excitement of executing such a risky criminal plot.

"Lack of Remorse or Guilt" is an affective item clustered with "Callous/Lack of Empathy," "Shallow Affect," and "Failure to Accept Responsibility for own Actions." Quite simply, it is the psychopath's inability to care about the consequences of his actions on the lives of others. This is demonstrated by him frequently placing his own needs first, and repeating criminal and/or immoral acts, despite claiming to regret them. He will tend to see himself as the victim even in problems of his own creation. Sometimes he openly admits that he does not feel guilty or remorseful for what he's done (Hare, 2003).

In some incidences, this "Lack of Remorse or Guilt" is flaunted, such as when Lawrence Bittaker and Roy Norris dumped the body of their last known victim, Leah Ledford, in a suburban neighborhood (*People v. Bittaker*, 1989). However, many killers do feel genuine remorse for their actions, which may occasionally be observable at their crime scenes. The most commonly observable behavior is "undoing"—in which the perpetrator makes *expressive/transformative* overtures to assuage his guilt regarding the crime. For instance, Chicago's "Lipstick Killer" scrawled the words "for heavens [sic] sake catch me before I kill more I cannot control myself" on the wall of his second victim's apartment.

One of the most crucial psychopathic items on the PCL-R, "Callous/Lack of Empathy" describes a self-centered individual who objectifies other people and can only understand their suffering in an abstract or intellectual sense (Hare, 2003).

Hare (2003, p. 40) describes "Poor Behavioral Controls" as an inability to "respond to frustration, failure, discipline, and criticism," including those of a trivial nature, without resorting to outbursts of violent anger. Interestingly, this explosion or rage is often fleeting, and within seconds, the offender may return to "normal" as if nothing untoward had occurred. Porter and Porter (2007) discuss a poignant example of poor behavioral controls in the case of a psychopath named "Glen":

I was asked to outline Glen's major risk factors for the court to which I responded that the major relevant characteristics included sadism, psychopathy, and a serious anger management problem… As I was giving the opinion that Glen's anger management problem was "the worst I had come across in all the offenders I have assessed," Glen attempted to bound out of the prisoner's dock screaming that he did not have a "f-ing anger management problem!" (p. 287)

Predictably, this type of spontaneous rage often manifests at the scene of a stranger homicide in the form of a sudden blitz attack of overwhelming ferocity with the attacker giving little consideration to his surroundings. Investigators should look for signs that something provoked the attacker, as in the case of the uncaught Scottish serial murderer Bible John, who seems to have killed upon discovering that his victims were menstruating (Wilson and Harrison, 2010).

Unlike some of the earlier more specific items, "Promiscuous Sexual Behavior" is a catch-all category for sexual acts and attitudes which Hare deems "impersonal, causal, or trivial" (Hare, 2003, p. 41). These include sexual assaults, a propensity to engage in one-night stands, multiple simultaneous sexual relationships, cheating on one's partner, prostitution (or using prostitutes), and openness to a range of sexual activities (Hare, 2003). Therefore, homicides involving a sexual or paraphilic element, where the perpetrator is an adulterer, or in which sex workers are victims could be considered to reflect the promiscuous sexual behavior item.

The term "Impulsivity" more or less speaks for itself but it is important to delineate this item from poor behavioral controls. Where the latter seems to hinge on reactive acts spurred by explosive anger, impulsivity refers more to doing things because the offender simply feels like it (Hare, 2003), rather than a lack of self-control. This may include sudden changes to lifestyle, or actions prompted by whim.

This item measures a criminal's willingness to perpetrate various types of crime. Smith et al. (2012) point out that the man who abducted Samuel Brown committed stalking, kidnapping, assault, extortion, and murder over a sustained period of time. The September 27, 1969 attacks in Napa believed to be perpetrated by the still uncaught Zodiac Killer—involving armed robbery, threatening, murder and attempted murder, and unlawful confinement (Graysmith, 2007)—reveal the offender's "Criminal Versatility" within a single incident.

Outside the realm of the PCL-R, research has also linked several other violent characteristics to psychopathy. Two studies in the late twentieth century found that offenders who committed at least one act of instrumental violence could be distinguished from nonviolent offenders and those who used only reactive violence based upon their PCL-R scores (Cornell et al., 1987, 1996). The researchers concluded that "although the Psychopathy Checklist includes no direct assessment of violent behavior, the construct of psychopathy appears to be associated with instrumental violence" (Cornell et al., 1996, p. 789). This theory was supported by Woodworth and Porter (2002), who examined the characteristics of murders committed by 125 Canadian offenders, 74 from Mountain and 51 from Springhill medium-security penitentiaries. They coded each of the homicides and found that 36% were purely instrumental, 23.2% were reactive-instrumental, 20% instrumental-reactive, and 12.8% purely reactive. Their research not only buttressed Cornell et al.'s, but in addition, they discovered that the higher a psychopath's PCL-R score, the greater the degree of instrumentality in his or her violence. The motives driving the crimes of instrumental violence included revenge (30.3%), monetary gain (22%), obtaining nonconsensual sex (19.3%), conflict over a female (11.1%), and obtaining drugs or alcohol (2.8%). The remainder (6.4%) consisted of various other motivations. Psychopaths did not seem to favor any one motive.

Porter and Woodworth (2007) have since reconfirmed these findings in a study of 21 homicidal offenders from Atlantic maximum-security institutions, along with 18 from the Springhill and 11 from the Dorchester medium-security institutions. 88.9% of psychopaths in the sample had primarily committed acts of instrumental violence, compared to 42.1% in the nonpsychopathic population.

More recently, Declercq et al. (2012) ran PCL-R tests on 82 incarcerated men in Flanders, Belgium who had committed a violent or sexually violent crime, or homicide. The researchers classified the subjects' crimes as predatory (instrumental), affective (reactive), or mixed. They learned that 75% of those offenders judged psychopathic (>30) had perpetrated an instrumental offence, and surprisingly, only 8% a reactive one. After conducting a thorough study on 158 offenders, Camp et al. (2013) determined that the most common goals which drive predators to instrumental violence are material gain and power/domination.

There is also a growing body of research showing that psychopathic offenders are more likely than nonpsychopaths to target victims of varying ages and genders. Porter et al. (2000) discovered that rather than being strictly rapists or child molesters, sexually criminal psychopaths tend to target a diverse group of victims. The researchers' sample was particularly large, representing 10% of incarcerated adult Canadian sex offenders at the medium-security Mountain Institution, of which 80% were assessed on the PCL-R. The only one of the five sex offender groups that Porter et al. (2000) identified as having more psychopaths than nonpsychopaths (64%) was the mixed rapist/molester. Among 95 psychopathic offenders, 16.8% had committed sex offenses against both children and adults compared to only 3.8% in the much larger nonpsychopathic population. Later studies by Porter et al. (2009) further substantiated this theory. Porter et al. (2009) proposed that "high-psychopathy offenders generally did not focus on a specific type of victim but, rather, were more prone to sexually assault victims opportunistically, or to change victim preferences over time in accordance with a thrill-seeking motivation (or simply getting 'bored')" (p. 110). As psychopathy does not seem to be overrepresented in sex crimes in general, Hare (2003, p. 138) speculates that "...the primary problem may not be that they are sex offenders but that they are *generalized offenders* whose sexual offenses are part of a *general propensity to violate the rights of others* [emphasis added]."

Considering this, might victim diversity also be true of nonsexual violence perpetrated by psychopaths? Canada's "Homicidal Drifter" Michael McGray—the epitome of a psychopath—is known to have killed two women, four adult males, and one female child. McGray is suspected of a further ten murders across Canada and the United States. Though he murdered a hitchhiker in Nova Scotia because she would not perform oral sex on him, none of the victims appear to have been sexually assaulted (Mellor, 2012). "Coast to Coast Killer" Tommy Lynn Sells was also a psychopath who reserved his sexual assaults for females, though like McGray, he is known to have killed men who were not in the company of women, as well as several children (Fanning, 2007). These are just two of numerous examples. Hare points out that while the majority of homicide victims are females who are known to the offender, statistics indicate that psychopaths actually tend to victimize male strangers most frequently (Hare, 2003). Given this information, it is hypothesized that nonsexual "equal opportunity" murder may also be characteristic of psychopathic homicide.

Over the past 20 years, there has been a great deal of interest in the link between psychopathy and acts of "gratuitous" or "excessive" violence (Meloy and Gacono, 1992; Hare et al., 1999), a term which in the context of homicide relates to physical torture, mutilation, "overkill" (driven by "pleasure" and not "rage"), and use of multiple crime scene weapons (Porter et al., 2003). Reviewing the literature on 279 murderers, Stone (1998) determined that in two-thirds of the cases in which a male psychopath committed homicide, he did so in a sadistic manner. Holt et al. (1999) assessed 41 violent or sexually violent inmates at a maximum-security penitentiary using the PCL-R, Scale 6 of the MCMI-II, and the PDE to determine the presence of sadistic personality disorder (SPD), as well as the DSM-IV for sexual sadism. They found far greater likelihood of sadism in psychopaths (>30) than nonpsychopaths (<24), though their sample was inconclusive regarding elevated rates of sexual sadism. The presence of SPD did not discern the violent from sexually violent.

A study of 38 incarcerated offenders who had committed sexual homicide—defined as a homicide with sexual activity before, during, or after the crime—by Porter et al. (2003) revealed that 84.7% of the offenders fell into the moderate–high range for psychopathy. 82.4% of the 18 psychopathic (≥30) offenders displayed sadistic behavior, which contrasted with 52.6% of the nonpsychopaths.

Case Study: Rodney Alcala

Tali Shapiro was just 8-years old when she went off to school alone on September 25, 1968. A man in a beige Mercury Comet picked her up, but an observant citizen called police, who chased him away before he could kill the girl. She had barely survived being sexually assaulted and strangled.

Despite items in the house that identified UCLA student Rodney Alcala (including hundreds of photos of girls), the investigation reached a dead end. An arrest warrant was issued, but Alcala had fled the state (Sands, 2011). Alcala went to New York City. Changing his name to John Berger, he enrolled in NYU's School of the Arts. "Berger" found a job as a security guard. People perceived him as charming. They did not know that the FBI had put him on its "Most Wanted" list. He was working in New Hampshire as a summer camp counsellor when the poster for his arrest went up in a nearby post office. Two girls from camp spotted it and told a counsellor, who turned him in.

The FBI returned Alcala to California to stand trial for kidnapping and child abuse. He pled guilty and served less than 3 years. He decided to stay in Los Angeles, possibly because he had killed Cornelia Crilley, 23, a flight attendant in New York. This case went cold and stayed that way for years until Alcala was caught in California (Weller, 2013).

Trolling for children, Alcala spotted "Julie J," who was saved by the timely intervention of a park ranger. Alcala went back for another short stint in prison. He managed to manipulate his parole officer into believing that a trip to New York during the summer of 1977 would be a positive thing (Sands, 2011).

It was around this time that heiress and socialite Ellen Jane Hover, 23, disappeared. This woman had rented an apartment at 686 Third Street in the bustling Midtown Manhattan. She had met "Berger," a photographer. Hover missed several appointments that day and did not answer her phone when her parents called. When police checked on her welfare, there was no sign of her. She had vanished (Hays, 2012). Berger transformed back into Alcala and returned to Los Angeles. He got a job with the *LA Times* as a typesetter. It wasn't long before he looked for another victim.

On November 10, 1977, a pair of patrol officers drove along a dirt road in response to a call in a secluded area of the Hollywood Hills near Mulholland Drive. They encountered an odd sight: a young woman had been beaten, murdered and posed in a strange position along the side of the road. It looked as if she'd been twisted into a ball. The top of the head, skull broken, touched the ground between the knees. The right arm was folded under the body, and the right hand was under the vaginal area, with the blood-drenched fingers curled upward (Sands, 2011). She was 18-year-old Jill Barcomb, from Syracuse, New York, where she had an arrest record for prostitution. She had come to California just the month before.

Alcala now had the credentials of a fine arts degree and employment with a prestigious newspaper, not to mention his photographic achievements in New York. He persuaded numerous young people to pose for him. He took photos of nude teenage boys, underage girls in sexual positions, and himself having sex with some of his subjects. He showed his collection to coworkers, assuring them that the parents of the photographed children had hired him. No one checked (Sands, 2011).

By this time, police in New York had learned that John Berger was Rodney Alcala, so they contacted the LAPD regarding his whereabouts (Secret, 2011). When questioned, Alcala said he had known Ellen Hover and had even been with her on the day she disappeared, but he had left her, after their lunch at her place, alive.

In December, a welfare check on a young woman named Georgia Wixted resulted in the discovery of her body. Wixted had been fatally beaten, strangled with pantyhose, and left naked on the floor, posed with her legs spread. Blood was spattered all over the walls, and a bloodstained claw hammer that matched her head wounds lay near the body. She had been raped vaginally and anally (Sands, 2011).

Despite knowing that he had been viewed as a viable suspect in several murders, Alcala seemed to think he was untouchable. By June 24, he had attacked his next victim. She was found in the laundry room of an apartment complex, naked and posed with her legs spread open. Her arms were bent under her back to prop and exaggerate her breasts, and she had been strangled with a shoelace. Having been beaten and bit, she had also been sexually violated. She was not a resident of that building, so it was difficult to identify her (Gardner, 2010).

Soon, the family of Charlotte Lamb reported her missing. Her description and the last time anyone had seen her matched the murdered Jane Doe. Investigators turned up information from Lamb's friends that she had gone on her own to a club. Somehow, she had crossed paths with her killer.

Close to the same time, a persistent police officer found the skeletal remains of Ellen Hover on the wooded Rockefeller estate in North Tarrytown, New York (Weller, 2013). It was where Alcala was known to go to watch sunsets. Despite his denials, he was now a firm suspect. Yet he remained free. Alcala was a contestant on The Dating Game on September 13. The young woman who picked him decided against going out with him.

On February 13th, Monique Hoyt was hitchhiking when a nice-looking man pulled over and asked for her help to win a photo contest. He took her to his house, where she spent the night. Then the man drove with her 80 miles east of Los Angeles, insisting that she accompany him deep into the woods. As she was posing for pictures, he bashed her head with a tree branch. She blacked out, reviving to the experience of rape. Hoyt passed out again. When she came to, she was bound. Later, her assailant removed the bindings and put her back in the car. When he stopped to use a restroom, she bolted and got someone to call the police. With her injuries, it was not hard to convince them that she had been assaulted. However, her attacker had already fled.

From a police line-up, Hoyt identified Alcala. He had no alibi when questioned, so he was placed under arrest. He admitted to rape and his mother posted his bail. The following month, he left his job at the *LA Times* (Pelisek, 2010).

On June 13, 1979, Alcala entered the second-floor Burbank apartment of Jill Parenteau by cutting a screen. After brutally beating, raping and strangling her, he placed a pillow under her to pose her, face-up, and before leaving, he spread her legs wide. He left a bite-mark on the right nipple.

At Huntington Beach that month, Alcala spent time taking pictures and hunting for prey. On June 20, Robin Samsoe and Bridget Wilvert, both just out of seventh grade, decided to go to the beach before

Robin's new job at a ballet studio (Sands, 2011). A photographer approached them to take pictures. Then Robin disappeared. Wilvert gave detectives a description of the photographer on the beach. It resembled Alcala's mugshot. One of the detectives happened to see a rerun of The Dating Game from 9 months earlier. This inspired the investigative team to hone in on him. They came across the case of Julie J, which had similarities. Six people who had been on the beach on the day that Robin Samsoe went missing identified Alcala as the photographer they'd seen (Sands, 2011). Then, her remains were found in the woods.

Alcala was arrested and booked. Police did not have much to use against him until they taped a conversation between Alcala and his sister about items in a storage locker in Seattle, WA that he asked her to remove. Detectives got there first. They found a large cache of photos that made them wonder how many victims they might be dealing with (Pelisek, 2010).

The case was largely circumstantial and depended on the jury believing the tale told by Dana Crappa, a forestry worker who had seen a man and a girl where Robin's remains were found. Items from Alcala's storage locker assisted the case: earrings in a small pouch had belonged to women. Robin Samsoe's mother identified a set of gold ball post earrings that she herself had modified, which made them unique. There were also plenty of provocative photos of young girls, including one that proved that Alcala was on or near the beach on the day in question. Alcala pled not guilty. He was convicted twice and given a death sentence, but both times the sentences were overturned (Sands, 2011).

By the time that Alcala's second conviction was overturned in 2001, DNA analysis had become a common procedure. The State of California forced Alcala to give a sample in 2002. This led to links between Alcala and the murders of Parenteau, Lamb, Wixted, and Barcomb (Pelisek, 2010).

In 2003, prosecutors from two jurisdictions joined to request that the five cases be joined in a single trial. In 2006, the judge granted it. In January 2010, Alcala came to court to act as his own attorney. His focus on minutiae was tedious. He completely ignored the DNA evidence and tried to twist interpretations of the circumstances. Nothing he did worked. For the third time, Alcala was convicted of Robin Samsoe's death, along with the other four murders (Gardner, 2010; Hays, 2012). During the penalty phase, psychiatrist Richard Rappaport claimed on Alcala's behalf that he suffered from borderline personality disorder with psychotic episodes that had erased some of his memory. This had occurred, said the psychiatrist, each time he had murdered one of the four women in Los Angeles. Because he had been shocked at what he had done, Alcala had developed a psychological defense mechanism that had blocked the incidents, allowing him to resume his life as if nothing had happened. Rappaport admitted that two psychologists who had also evaluated Alcala had disagreed with him, finding instead that Alcala had narcissistic personality disorder.

Mental health professionals had evaluated Alcala on a number of occasions. Although he'd grown up in a seemingly normal family, had a near-genius IQ, and seemed polished, skilled, and ambitious, while serving time in the military he had deteriorated. Two years after enlisting, he went AWOL several times. Eventually, he showed up at home, where he apparently exposed himself to his sister. His mother persuaded him to turn himself in, and those who examined him in the hospital ward where he was detained considered him unable to perform his duties in the foreseeable future. He was diagnosed at this time with antisocial personality disorder, "chronic, severe" (Sands, 2011).

He was admitted into a hospital in 1963 for observation. His initial diagnosis from the US Naval Hospital at Camp Pendleton was schizophrenic reaction, latent type. The psychiatrist at the receiving hospital disagreed. He believed that Alcala's irritability and aggression stemmed from an antisocial attitude. He was immature and impulsive, seemed to have no guilt over repeated acts of illegal behavior, and had an "absence of identity with or loyalty to a person, group or code." He was found to understand the difference between right and wrong but to have little concern about comporting himself according to the law.

The doctors found nothing in his background, aside from trauma over a deteriorating family structure, to explain his current issues. Alcala was born in San Antonio, Texas on August 23, 1943, and lived there until he was 9 years old. The Alcala family moved to Mexico, and at some point, his father, Raul, abandoned the family. They stayed in Mexico for 3 years and then moved to Los Angeles, California. Alcala was 12. He was raised Catholic and apparently had kept in touch with his father until Raul died in 1962.

Once discharged from the military in 1964, Alcala seemed to improve (Sands, 2011). He enrolled in college courses at Cal State before transferring to UCLA. He worked on a bachelor of fine arts degree in photography. But then he stumbled, kidnapping Tali Shapiro.

The next time Alcala was evaluated was almost 10 years later, in August 1972. This time his apparent drug use led to another diagnosis of "acute schizophrenic reaction," which was solely attributable to extensive ingestion of LSD. He was found to have a schizoid personality disorder with passive-aggressive tendencies. In addition, he had a psychosexual disorder that included homosexuality, incestuous tendencies, pedophilia, sadism, and exhibitionism (psychiatric report).

Other reports during Alcala's incarceration noted his "chameleon-like personality." He could be personable and charming when it served his objectives, but he used his skills and intelligence to lure victims into vulnerable situations. His IQ was listed as 135 from a 1972 evaluation (not 160, as some reports state).

He was considered to have "well-fixated erotic fantasies involving minor males and females." He liked them because they lacked body hair. Several witnesses supposedly heard Alcala say that he had raped and sexually assaulted many young boys and girls. He acted out when under stress. Without long-term intensive psychiatric care, he posed a danger to the community. Still, his psychosexual disorders, combined with his "hyper-intellectualization," would prevent psychotherapy from having much impact. He was considered to have a "sick" and "twisted" sexual pathology, and he presented "an absolute threat to any and all young boys and girls, and to any and all adult females" (psychiatrist's report).

At his third trial, Alcala had promised to explain a victim's DNA found on an earring in his possession, but he failed to provide it. After deliberations, on March 9, 2010, they handed him his third death sentence (Gardner, 2010).

Cops working the Crilley case had removed saliva from the bite mark on her body. DNA testing linked it to Alcala. So did the impression and a fingerprint on an envelope removed from under her body (Weller, 2013).

Then there was the Hover case. In 2011, a grand jury indicted Alcala for both murders. In June 2012, he was extradited to Manhattan. By June 2012, he had been extradited to Manhattan, and that December, Alcala pled guilty to both New York murders (Hays, 2012). New York added a 25-years-to-life sentence. New York added a 25-years-to-life sentence. It was the first time that Alcala had ever admitted to murder.

Investigators published many of the photos found in Alcala's storage unit, hoping to match some to cold cases of missing persons or Jane Doe murders. More than 900 could not be revealed, as they were too sexually explicit. Some women, still alive, came forward to identify themselves as the subjects in question. As of this writing, none of the photos have resulted in police closing a murder case.

It is notable that over the years, Alcala had been diagnosed with 75% of the DSM-5's current Cluster B personality disorders—antisocial, narcissistic, and borderline—along with schizoid personality disorder, which has been attributed to psychopathic sexually sadistic serial killers such as Ted Bundy (Moes, 1991) and Leonard Lake (Lasseter, 2000). Many of the ICD-10 diagnostic criteria for SPD overlap with those of psychopathy (Table 9.2).

As psychopathy has never been included in any of the editions of the DSM or ICD with a set of diagnostic criteria, and given that the PCL was not published until 1986, this instrument would not have been

Table 9.2 Comparing Schizoid Personality Disorder Criteria with Psychopathic Traits

Schizoid Criteria (ICD-10)	Psychopathic Traits
Emotional coldness, detachment, or reduced affect	Shallow affect (PCL-R item)
Limited capacity to express either positive or negative emotions toward others	Shallow affect (PCL-R item)
Consistent preference for solitary activities	Describing the PCL-R item callous/lack of empathy, Hare writes that a psychopath views others as objects, is selfish, and that his "contempt or lack of concern for others may lead him to describe himself as a loner by choice" (Hare, 2003, p. 35)
Very few, if any, close friends or relationships, and a lack of desire for such	Same as above
Indifference to either praise or criticism	There is no obvious corresponding psychopathic trait
Little interest in having sexual experiences with another person (taking age into account)	There is no corresponding psychopathic trait, however, this schizoid criterion does not describe the highly promiscuous and sex-offending Alcala whatsoever
Taking pleasure in few, if any, activities	Not enough evidence to comment on
Indifference to social norms and conventions	This basically characterizes psychopathy as a whole
Preoccupation with fantasy and introspection	Grandiose sense of self-worth (PCL-R item). Though not necessarily specific to psychopathy, this is certainly a characteristic of all paraphilic sex offenders, many of whom are not schizoid

available to the clinicians assessing Alcala in the sixties. With this in mind, it is likely that what now seems to be psychopathic traits in Alcala was misdiagnosed as schizoid personality disorder. Likewise, a majority of the traits of antisocial personality disorder, narcissistic personality disorder, and borderline personality disorder, for which he was also diagnosed, are also subsumed under psychopathy. Many researchers have found that borderline personality disorder is strongly related to secondary psychopathy (Blackburn, 1996; Edens et al., 2002; Sprague et al., 2012).

Alcala's "chameleon-like" charm, manipulativeness, grandiosity, lack of empathy or remorse, impulsivity, sexual promiscuity, and breach of bail conditions are all indicative of items found on the PCL-R. Furthermore, the fact that he committed instrumental sex crimes against both children and adults using excessive violence are all consistent with the features of psychopathic homicides discussed in the previous section. Though it is not known whether Alcala has been diagnosed as a psychopath, he has a multitude of psychopathic traits, and the culmination of this evidence certainly warrants such an assessment.

Recommendations for Handling Cases of Psychopaths Who Kill

Interviewing

Despite ample informal discussion in the police and psychological communities regarding the challenges of interviewing a psychopath, there is a surprising lack of academic literature on the subject (Quayle, 2008). Quayle (2008), who conducted a literature review on psychopathy and augmented it with his own experience in law enforcement, recommends a number of strategies.

Generally, Quayle favors a highly structured, fact-based, and sequential interview, in which the psychopath is presented with a growing, coherent mountain of evidence against him. In many cases, the psychopath will, at some juncture, rationally judge that he is going to be convicted, and may enthusiastically confess to the crimes, so that they can discuss how clever and difficult he was to catch.

Quayle urges that interviewers must, therefore, have complete familiarity with the case and the suspect they are investigating, as psychopaths are keen at spotting and capitalizing on deficits in an interviewer's understanding of the facts. This is important because Quayle emphasizes the need for the interviewer to never seem helpless or confused. Psychopaths look to exploit personal weaknesses, such as inexperience or uncertainty, in order to undermine an interrogation. Therefore, an interviewer must always come across as confident, seasoned, and professional, which includes wearing authoritative attire and addressing the suspect as "Mr," "Ms," or any other title they might hold. This operates on the principle that a psychopath's grandiosity demands that he be treated with respect, which also means that he must believe that he is interacting with top detectives or credentialed clinicians: people important enough to be worthy of him.

As psychopaths equate emotion with weakness, and have little to no conscience, displays of emotion or moral indignation will have no positive effect on the psychopath, and may diminish the interviewer's standing. The interviewer should never make the mistake of expecting a psychopath to have a conscience. An FBI agent once told of a case he worked in which a psychopathic sexual sadist had been apprehended after his truck became stuck near where he had just murdered a boy. When emotionally confronted by a detective with the question of whether he had killed the child, the psychopath responded, "Where's my truck?" (Jeffrey Rinek, personal communication).

This self-importance is arguably the psychopath's weakest spot in an interview, and thus displays of admiration and respect will engage them and sate their narcissistic desire for affirmation. O'Toole (personal communication) once advised that psychopaths are so self-aggrandizing that it is wise to give them a platform from which to pontificate. In this vein, Quayle advocates approaching the psychopath like the psychopath is an interesting person and that the interviewer wishes to learn something from them. Phrasing questions with "what do you think" is one way to go about this. Quayle specifies that interviewer and psychopath should have an inclusive rather than an adversarial rapport, which maintains a balance of power and respect on both sides. Attempts to deceive or trick the psychopath are not recommended, owing to their guile. Insulting a psychopath will also likely provoke him into refusing cooperation, either angrily, as a matter of policy, or amidst a veil of histrionics. When one must challenge the psychopath, Quayle recommends that it be done so cautiously, in a manner that is soft. The tone should be one of being puzzled, and asking the psychopath to help the interviewer understand.

Unlike many of the offenders discussed in this book, attempting to build rapport with a psychopath is discouraged. Quayle proposes that this is a waste of time as it is not possible to establish or expect trust with a psychopathic offender, due to their affective deficits. In fact, the psychopath may use this to gain knowledge and control of the conversation.

The ability to control a conversation using the interpersonal skills of glibness/superficial charm, conning and manipulation, and pathological lying is a powerful weapon in the psychopath's arsenal. A psychiatrist who interviewed Canadian serial killer Clifford Olson—who was scored as a 38/40 on the PCL-R by three separate mental health professionals (Semrau and Gale, 2002)—described him as almost being hypnotic. Quayle (2008) notes that he will attempt to control the interview by "talking at length about himself; asking the interviewers questions; provoking emotional responses or frustration in the interviewers; refusing to answer straightforward questions; requesting unnecessary breaks; attempting to intimidate the interviewers; and questioning the competence or authority of the interviewers" (p. 85). Other behaviors to expect include the use of police and legal terminology; insults, dismissals, or attempts at intimidation; direct eye contact; frequent and distracting hand gestures; attempts to read the interviewer's notes; and encroachment on the interviewer's personal space. Clifford Olson provided a chilling demonstration of this to Dr. Stanley Semrau when he managed to, without notice, seize and begin stroking Semrau's left hand and forearm while the doctor was making notes. Upon being noticed, Olson replied with, "Oh, am I making you uncomfortable?" (Semrau and Gale, 2002, p. 275).

Quayle (2008) proposes that the psychopathic traits of glibness/superficial charm, grandiose sense of self-worth, pathological lying, conning/manipulative, lack of remorse or guilt, shallow affect, callous/lack of empathy, failure to accept responsibility for own actions, need for stimulation/proneness to boredom, and poor behavioral controls could potentially become evident during the interview. Fortuitously, as previously discussed, seven of these ten traits may also emerge through crime scene behavior, making strategies to deal with them able to be prepared in advance.

Though Quayle does not comment on the Reid technique of interviewing which is in common use in the United States and Canada, he does point out that the British P.E.A.C.E. method of interrogation may be fundamentally counterproductive to successfully interviewing a psychopath.

Treatment

Hare believes that developing a good treatment plan is a new frontier of studying the psychopath. The received wisdom on the subject had been that psychopaths not only do not improve with treatment, but actually become more manipulative (Rice and Harris, 2013).

"We take the view," says Hare (personal interview), "that under the right circumstances, it's possible to modify the antisocial behaviors of anybody, although for psychopaths the task will be more difficult than for other offenders. Our philosophy, based on a lot of data, is that we are not going to target some of the core psychopathic features, such as lack of capacity for empathy, grandiosity, egocentricity, or shallow emotions. We think these features are fairly stable. But we're going to target features of psychopathy that may be modifiable. We have clues to what these might be."

"We look at the twenty items in the PCL-R and their scores as a function of the age at which offenders were assessed. And what we find, quite dramatically, is that across the age span from adolescence to 50 or 55, there are no appreciable changes in the interpersonal and affective characteristics of psychopathy, like egocentricity and lack of empathy. We also find that socially deviant behaviors, such as impulsivity, the need for stimulation, and irresponsibility, actually do decrease with age. So we have about seven or eight PCL-R features of psychopathy that are capable of changing. We can take features that change with age and use interventions to speed up the process. We know we're not going to instill in psychopaths a sense of empathy or a strengthened conscience, but we can probably work with characteristics related to their antisocial behavior, such as impulsivity, stimulation-seeking, and irresponsibility."

Whatever claims are made about any program's effectiveness for treatment must be evidence-based, use correct research models, and include regular evaluation intervals. With this in mind, we can evaluate the results of a program at the Mendota Juvenile Treatment Center (MJTC) in Madison, Wisconsin.

At the MJTC, psychologist Michael Caldwell and his mental health colleagues have developed an intensive treatment program for juvenile offenders, including those who are at risk for developing adult psychopathy. Caldwell et al. (2006) claim that the money spent upfront, which is considerable, more than pays itself back in social and judicial dividends and savings in the long run.

The MJTC is a hybrid correctional/mental health facility that serves the mental health needs of male adolescents transferred from institutions within the Division of Juvenile Corrections. It employs mental health experts rather than security guards or corrections officers. The ratio of therapist to resident is twice that of other programs. Within this clinical setting, residents undergo intensive individualized therapy designed to treat their emotional problems. The model relies on a variation of "decompression" treatment combined with Aggression Replacement Training (ART), a cognitive-behavioral treatment approach.

Program personnel attempt to erode aggressive adolescent offenders' antagonistic defiance, based on the notion that defiant behavior can become cyclical when the defiant response to a sanction is itself sanctioned. The MJTC program helps offenders accept responsibility for their behavior, learn better social skills, resolve mental health issues, deal with substance abuse or sexual disorders, and build solid relationships with their families.

A cornerstone of the intervention is the Today-Tomorrow Program, a highly sensitive point system that closely monitors each youth's behavior. Adolescents earn privileges following relatively short periods of positive behavior. Whenever youths in treatment act out or become unruly, they receive additional therapy as well as enhanced security.

Staff members Caldwell and Van Rybroek (2005) ran a study with colleagues to examine the cost benefits of this intensive treatment. A total of 101 boys who received the majority of their treatment services at MJTC were matched to a group of 101 juveniles who received treatment as usual (TAU) in a secured juvenile corrections setting. The sample was 52% African-American, 38% white, 9% Hispanic, and 2% Asian-American. To evaluate follow-up, the researchers used court and corrections department records to track each participant's pattern of reoffending. All participants were tracked for at least 2 years, with the average follow-up at four and a half years. Outcome data included the number and type of criminally charged offense. The MJTC group's 2-year recidivism rate was 52% versus 73% for the TAU group. While misdemeanor rates were not significantly affected, MJTC youths were only about half as likely to commit new violent and serious offenses. They also spent less time incarcerated and had a longer average "survival time" before reoffending. The authors attribute these results to the fact that the MJTC program had significantly increased their level of participation in rehabilitation services.

Caldwell et al. (2006) examined the treatment response of 141 juvenile offenders who had high scores on the PCL:YV, dividing them into two groups. One group of 56 participated in the MJTC program and the other group (85 participants) received treatment in conventional juvenile correctional institutions (JCI). During a 2-year follow-up study, offenders in the JCI group were more than twice as likely to violently recidivate in the community than those who had participated in the MJTC program. This treatment, then, is associated with relatively slower and lower rates of serious recidivism, even after controlling for the effects of nonrandom assignment to treatment groups and release status.

However, it is costly. Compared to the $150,000 per offender per year in JCI, the MJTC program costs twice as much. Yet in another study, over a 4-year period, researchers found that for every $10,000 invested in treatment, there was a $70,000 savings. Over the life of that offender, if the figures hold steady, this would be a potential savings of millions of dollars (Ramsland, 2011).

References

Babiak, P. 1995. When psychopaths go to work: A case study of an industrial psychopath. *Applied Psychology: An International Review, 44,* 171–178.

Beaver, K. M., Barnes, J. C., May, J. S., and Schwartz, J. A. 2011a. Psychopathic personality traits, genetic risk, and gene-environment correlations. *Criminal Justice and Behavior, 38*(9), 896–912. DOI: 10.1177/0093854811411153.

Beaver, K. M., Rowland, M. W., Schwartz, J. A., and Nedelec, J. L. 2011b. The genetic origins of psychopathic personality traits in adult males and females: Results from an adoption-based study. *Journal of Criminal Justice, 39*(5), 426–432. DOI: 10.1016/j.jcrimjus.2011.07.002.

Beaver, K. M., Vaughn, M. G., DeLisi, M., Barnes, J. C., and Boutwell, B. B. 2012. The neuropsychological underpinnings to psychopathic personality traits in a nationally representative and longitudinal sample. *Psychiatric Quarterly, 83*(2), 145–159. DOI: 10.1007/s11126–011–9190–2.

Begun, J. H. 1976. The sociopathic or psychopathic personality. *International Journal of Social Psychiatry, 22*(1), 25–46.

Bezdjian, S., Tuvblad, C., Raine, A., and Baker, L. A. 2011. The genetic and environmental covariation among psychopathic personality traits, and reactive and proactive aggression in childhood. *Child Development, 82*(4), 1267–1281. DOI: 10.1111/j.1467-8624.2011.01598.x.

Blackburn, R. 1988. On moral judgments and personality disorders: The myth of psychopathic personality revisited. *British Journal of Psychiatry, 153,* 505–512.

Blackburn, R. 1996. Psychopathy, delinquency and crime. In: A. Gale and J. A. Edwards (Eds.), *Physiological Correlates of Human Behavior: Vol 3. Individual Differences and Psychopathology.* Orlando, FL: Academic Press, pp. 187–205.

Blagov, P. S., Patrick, C. J., Lilienfeld, S. O., Powers, A. D., Phifer, J. E., Venables, N., and Cooper, G. 2011. Personality constellations in incarcerated psychopathic men. *Personality Disorders: Theory, Research, and Treatment, 2*(4), 293–315. DOI: 10.1037/a0023908.

Buzina, N. 2012. Psychopathy—Historical controversies and new diagnostic approach. *Psychiatria Danubina, 24*(2), 134–142.

Caldwell, M., Skeem, J., Salekin, R., and Van Rybroek, G. 2006. Treatment response of adolescent offenders with psychopathy features: A two-year follow-up. *Criminal Justice and Behavior, 33*(5), 571–596.

Camp, J. P., Skeem, J. L., Barchard, K., Lilienfeld, S. O., and Poythress, N. G. 2013. Psychopathic predators? Getting specific about the relation between psychopathy and violence. *Journal of Consulting and Clinical Psychology*. Advance online publication. DOI: 10.1037/a0031349.

Caspi, A., McClay, J., Moffitt, T., Mill, J., Martin, J., Craig, I. W., and Poulton, R. 2002. Role of genotype in the cycle of violence in maltreated children. *Science, 297*(5582), 851–854. DOI: 10.1126/science.1072290.

Chambers, J. C. 2010. An exploration of the mechanisms underlying the development of repeat and one-time violent offenders. *Aggression and Violent Behavior, 15*(4), 310–323. DOI: 10.1016/j.avb.2010.03.002.

Cleckley, H. 1976. *The Mask of Sanity: An Attempt to Clarify Some Issues about the So-Called Psychopathic Personality* (5th ed.). St Louis, MO: Mosby.

Cornell, D. G., Benedek, E. P., and Benedek, D. M. 1987. Juvenile homicide: Prior adjustment and a proposed topology. *American Journal of Orthopsychiatry, 51*, 383–393.

Cornell, D. G., Warren, J., Hawk, G., Stafford, E., Oram, G., and Pine, D. 1996. Psychopathy in instrumental and reactive violent offenders. *Journal of Consulting and Clinical Psychology, 64*(4), 783–790.

Da Silva, R. D., Rijo, D., and Salekin, R. T. 2012. Child and adolescent psychopathy: A state-of-the-art reflection on the construct and etiological theories. *Journal of Criminal Justice, 40*(4), 269–277. DOI: 10.1016/j.jcrimjus.2012.05.005.

Declercq, F., Willemsen, J., Audenaert, K., and Verhaeghe, P. 2012. Psychopathy and predatory violence in homicide, violent, and sexual offences: Factor and facet relations. *Legal and Criminological Psychology, 17*, 59–74.

Dolan, M. and Doyle, M. 2000. Violence risk prediction: Clinical and actuarial measures and the role of the Psychopathy Checklist. *British Journal of Psychiatry, 177*, 303–311.

Edens, J. F., Buffington-Vollum, J. K., Colwell, K. W., Johnson, D. W., and Johnson, J. K. 2002. Psychopathy and institutional misbehavior among incarcerated sex offenders: A comparison of the Psychopathy Checklist-Revised and the Personality Assessment Inventory. *The International Journal of Forensic Mental Health, 1*, 49–58.

Fallon, J. H. 2006. Neuroanatomical background to understanding the brain of the young psychopath. *Ohio State Journal of Criminal Law, 3*, 341–367.

Fanning, D. 2007. *Through the Window: The Terrifying True Story of Cross-Country Killer Tommy Lynn Sells*. New York, NY: St. Martin's.

Forsman, M., Lichtenstein, P., Andershed, H., and Larsson, H. 2008. Genetic effects explain the stability of psychopathic personality from mid- to late adolescence. *Journal of Abnormal Psychology, 117*(3), 606–617. DOI: 10.1037/0021-843X.117.3.606.

Forth, A., Bo, S., and Kongerslev. 2013. Assessment of psychopathy: The hare psychopathy checklist measures. In: K. Kiehl and W. Sinnott-Armstrong (Eds.), *Handbook on Psychopathy and Law*. New York, NY: Oxford University Press, pp. 5–33.

Fowler, K. and Lilienfeld, S. O. 2013. Alternatives to the psychopathy checklist-revised. In: K. Kiehl and W. Sinnott-Armstrong (Eds.), *Handbook on Psychopathy and Law*. New York, NY: Oxford University Press, pp. 34–60.

Fowler, T., Langley, K., Rice, F., van den Bree, M. B. M., Ross, K., Wilkinson, L. S., Owen, M. J., O'Donovan, M. C., and Thapar, A. 2009. Psychopathy trait scores in adolescents with childhood ADHD: The contribution of genotypes affecting MAOA, 5HTT and COMT activity. *Psychiatric Genetics, 19*(6), 312–319. DOI: 10.1097/YPG.0b013e3283328df4.

Gao, Y., Raine, A., Chan, F., Venables, P. H., and Mednick, S. A. 2010. Early maternal and paternal bonding, childhood physical abuse and adult psychopathic personality. *Psychological Medicine, 40*(6), 1007–1016. DOI: 10.1017/S0033291709991279.

Gardner, D. 2010, April 1. Rodney Alcala sentenced to death for murders of four women and girl, 12. *The Daily Mail*. Retrieved from http://dailym.ai/1YHCkvY.

Graysmith, R. 2007. *Zodiac*. New York, NY: Penguin.

Gunn, J. 1998. Psychopathy: An elusive concept with moral overtones. In: T. Millon, E. Simonsen, M. Birket-Smith, and R. D. Davis (Eds.), *The Psychopath: Antisocial, Criminal, and Violent Behavior.* New York, NY: Guilford Press, pp. 32–39.

Gunter, T. D., Vaughn, M. G., and Philibert, R. A. 2010. Behavioral genetics in antisocial spectrum disorders and psychopathy: A review of the recent literature. *Behavioral Sciences & the Law, 28*(2), 148–173. DOI: 10.1002/bsl.923.

Hare, R. D. 2003. *The Psychopathy Checklist-Revised* (2nd rev.). Toronto, Canada: Multi-Health Systems.

Hare, R. D. 1993. *Without Conscience: The Disturbing World of the Psychopaths among Us.* New York, NY: Simon & Schuster.

Hare, R. D. 2002. Psychopathy and risk for recidivism and violence. In: N. Gray, J. Laing, and L. Noaks (Eds.), *Criminal Justice, Mental Health, and the Politics of Risk.* London, UK: Cavendish, pp. 27–47.

Hare, R. D., Clark, D., Grann, M., and Thornton, D. 2000. Psychopathy and the predictive validity of the PCL-R: An international perspective. *Behavioral Sciences and the Law, 18,* 623–645.

Hare, R. D. and Hervé, H. 1999. *The Hare P-Scan: Research Version.* Toronto, Canada: Multi-Health Systems.

Hare, R. D., Cooke, D. J., and Hart, S. D. 1999. Psychopathy and sadistic personality disorder. In: T. Millon, P. H. Blanney, and R. D. Davies (Eds.), *Oxford Textbook of Psychopathology.* New York, NY: Oxford University, pp. 555–584.

Harris, G. T., Skilling, T. A., and Rice, M. E. 2001. The construct of psychopathy. In: M. Tonry and N. Morris (Eds.), *Crime and Justice: An Annual Review of Research.* Chicago, IL: University of Chicago Press, pp. 197–264.

Hart, S. D., Cox, D. N., and Hare, R. D. 1995. *Manual for the Psychopathy Checklist: Screening Version (PCL:SV).* Toronto, Canada: Multi-Health Systems.

Hays, T. 2012, December 14. Rodney Alcala, California killer sentenced to death, admits to killing two New York City women. *Huffington Post.* Retrieved from http://huff.to/1TkYq5P.

Hecht, D. 2011. An inter-hemispheric imbalance in the psychopath's brain. *Personality and Individual Differences, 51*(1), 3–10. DOI: 10.1016/j.paid.2011.02.032.

Hervé, H. 2003. *The masks of sanity and psychopathy: A cluster analytical investigation of subtypes of criminal psychopathy.* (Doctoral dissertation, University of British Columbia, British Columbia, Canada).

Holt, S. E., Meloy, J. R., and Strack, S. 1999. Sadism and psychopathy in violent and sexually violent offenders. *Journal of the American Academy of Psychiatry and the Law, 27,* 23–32.

Karpman, B. 1941. On the need of separating psychopathy into two distinct clinical types: The symptomatic and the idiopathic. *Journal of Criminal Psychopathology, 3,* 112–137.

Karpman, B. 1947. Moral agenesis. *Psychiatric Quarterly, 21,* 361–398. DOI: 10.1007/BF01562009.

Karpman, B. 1948a. Conscience in the psychopath: Another version. *American Journal of Orthopsychiatry, 18*(3), 455–491.

Karpman, B. 1948b. The myth of the psychopathic personality. *American Journal of Psychiatry, 104,* 523–534.

Koenigs, M., Kruepke, M., and Newman, J. P. 2010. Economic decision-making in psychopathy: A comparison with ventromedial prefrontal lesion patients. *Neuropsychologia, 48*(7), 2198–2204. DOI: 10.1016/j.neuropsychologia.2010.04.012.

Kosson, D. S., Cyterski, T. D., Steuerwald, B. L., Neumann, C. S., and Walker-Matthews, S. 2002. The reliability and validity of the Psychopathy Checklist: Youth Version (PCL:YV) in non-incarcerated adolescent males. *Psychological Assessment, 14,* 97–109.

Krafft-Ebing, R. 1886/2011. *Psychopathia Sexualis.* Philadelphia, PA: F.A. Davis Company.

Larsson, H., Andershed, H., and Lichtenstein, P. 2006. A genetic factor explains most of the variation in the psychopathic personality. *Journal of Abnormal Psychology, 115*(2), 221–230. DOI: 10.1037/0021-843X.115.2.221.

Larsson, H., Viding, E., and Plomin, R. 2008. Callous-unemotional traits and antisocial behavior: Genetic, environmental, and early parenting characteristics. *Criminal Justice and Behavior, 35*(2), 197–211. DOI: 10.1177/0093854807310225.

Lasseter, D. 2000. *Die For Me: The Terrifying True Story of the Charles Ng/Leonard Lake Torture Murders.* New York, NY: Pinnacle.

Lee, Z. and Salekin, R. T. 2010. Psychopathy in a non-institutional sample: Differences in primary and secondary subtypes. *Personality Disorders: Treatment Research and Theory, 1,* 153–169. DOI: 10.1037/a0019269.

Lykken, D. T. 1998. The case for parental licensure. In: T. Millon, E. Simonsen, M. Birket-Smith, and R. D. Davis (Eds.), *The Psychopath: Antisocial, Criminal, and Violent Behavior.* New York, NY: Guilford Press, pp. 122–143.

Lykken, D. T. 2000. The causes and costs of crime and a controversial cure. *Journal of Personality, 68*(3), 559–605.

McDermott, R., Tingley, D., Cowden, J., Frazzetto, G., and Johnson, D. D. P. 2009. Monoamine oxidase A gene (MAOA) predicts behavioral aggression following provocation. *PNAS Proceedings of the National Academy of Sciences of the United States of America, 106*(7), 2118–2123. DOI: 10.1073/pnas.0808376106.

Mealey, L. 1995. The sociobiology of sociopathy: An integrated evolutionary model. *Behavioral and Brain Sciences, 18*(3), 523–599.

Mellor, L. 2012. *Cold North Killers: Canadian Serial Murder.* Toronto, Canada: Dundurn.

Mellor, L. 2013. *Rampage: Canadian Mass Murder and Spree Killing.* Toronto, Canada: Dundurn.

Meloy, J. R. and Gacono, C. B. 1992. The aggression response and the Rorschach. *Journal of Clinical Psychology, 48(1)*, 104–114.

Mendota Juvenile Treatment Center Program. Retrieved from http://1.usa.gov/1YHEo72.

Millon, T., Simonsen, E., and Birket-Smith, M. 1998. Historical conceptions of psychopathy in the United States and Europe. In: T. Millon, E. Simonsen, M. Birket-Smith, and R. D. Davis (Eds.), *Psychopathy: Antisocial, Criminal, and Violent behavior.* New York, NY: Guilford Press, pp. 3–31.

Millon, T. and Davis, R. D. 1998. Ten subtypes of psychopathy. In: T. Millon, E. Simonsen, M. Birket-Smith, and R. D. Davis (Eds.), *Psychopathy: Antisocial, Criminal, and Violent Behavior.* New York, NY: Guilford Press, pp. 161–170.

Moes, E. 1991. Ted Bundy: A case of schizoid necrophilia. *Melanie Klein and Object Relations, 9*(1), 54–72.

Mohl, A. S. 2013. Sociopathic behavior and its relationship to psychohistory. *The Journal of Psychohistory, 41*(1), 2–13.

O'Toole, M. E. 2007. Psychopathy as a behavior classification system for violent and serial crime scenes. In: H. F. M. Hervé and J. C. Yuille (Eds.), *The Psychopath: Theory, Research, and Practice.* New York, NY: Routledge, pp. 301–325.

Pelisek, C. 2010, February 10. Rodney Alcala's final revenge. *LA Weekly.* Retrieved from http://bit.ly/1PopPmx.

People v. Bittaker. 1989. 48 Cal.3d 1046.

Perez, L. 2012. The etiology of psychopathy: A neuropsychological perspective. *Aggression and Violent Behavior, 17*(6), 519–522.

Pinel, P. 1962. *A Treatise on Insanity.* New York, NY: Hafner. (Original work published 1801).

Plomin, R. and Daniels, D. 1987. Why are children in the same family so different from one another? *Behavioral and Brain Sciences, 10*(1), 1–16. DOI: 10.1017/S0140525X00055941.

Porter, S., Fairweather, D., Drugge, J., Hervé, H., Birt, A., and Boer, D. P. 2000. Profiles of psychopathy in incarcerated sexual offenders. *Criminal Justice and Behavior, 27*, 216–233.

Porter, S., Woodworth, M., Earle, J., Drugge, J., and Boer, D. P. 2003. Characteristics of sexual homicide committed by psychopathic and nonpsychopathic offenders. *Law and Human Behavior, 27*, 459–470.

Porter, S. and Porter, S. 2007. Psychopathy and Violent Crime. In H. F. M. Hervé and J. C. Yuille (Eds.), *The Psychopath: Theory, Research, and Practice.* New York, NY: Routledge, pp. 287–300.

Porter, S. and Woodworth, M. 2007. 'I'm sorry I did it…but he started it': A comparison of the official and self-reported homicide descriptions of psychopaths and non-psychopaths. *Law and Human Behavior, 31*, 91–107.

Porter, S., Ten Brinke, L., and Wilson, K. 2009. Crime profiles and conditional release performance of psychopathic and non-psychopathic sexual offenders. *Legal and Criminal Psychology, 14*, 109–118.

Quayle, J. 2008. Interviewing a psychopathic suspect. *Journal of Investigative Psychology and Offender Profiling, 5*, 79–91.

Ramsland, K. 2011. Kent Kiehl: Peering inside the psychopath's mind. *The Forensic Examiner, 20*(3), 24–29.

Rice, M. and Harris, G. T. 2013. Psychopathy and violent recidivism. In: K. Kiehl and W. Sinnott-Armstrong (Eds.), *Handbook on Psychopathy and Law.* New York, NY: Oxford University Press, pp. 231–249.

Salekin, R. T. and Lochman, J. E. 2008. Child and adolescent psychopathy: The search for protective factors. *Criminal Justice and Behavior, 35*(2), 159-172. DOI: 10.1177/0093854807311330.

Sands, S. 2011. *The Dating Game Killer.* New York, NY: St. Martin's.

Schlesinger, L. B. 1980. Distinctions between psychopathic, sociopathic and anti-social personality disorders. *Psychological Reports, 47*(1), 15–21.

Secret, M. 2011, February 5. Forty years on, detective sees light shed on killing. *New York Times*. Retrieved from http://nyti.ms/1MA8yC8.

Semrau, S and Gale, J. 2002. *Murderous Minds on Trial: Cases from a Forensic Psychiatrist's Case Book*. Toronto, Canada: Dundurn.

Skeem, J. L. and Cooke, D. J. 2010. One measure does not a construct make: Directions toward reinvigorating psychopathy research—Reply to Hare and Neumann. *Psychological Assessment, 22*, 455–459.

Smith, S. S., O'Toole, M. E., and Hare, R. D. 2012. Predator: When the stalker is a psychopath. *FBI Law Enforcement Bulletin: Psychopathy, 81*(7), 9–13.

Sprague, J., Javdani, S., Sadeh, N., Newman, J. P., and Verona, E. 2012. Borderline personality disorder as a female phenotypic expression of psychopathy? *Personality Disorders: Theory, Research, and Treatment, 3*(2), 127–139.

Stone, M. H. 1998. Sadistic personality in murderers. In: T. Millon, E. Simonsen, M. Birket-Smith, and R. D. Davis (Eds.), *The Psychopath: Antisocial, Criminal, and Violent Behavior*. New York, NY: Guilford Press, pp. 346–355.

Torry, Z. D. and Billick, S. B. 2011. Implications of antisocial parents. *Psychiatric Quarterly, 82*(4), 275–285. DOI: 10.1007/s11126-011-9169-z.

Vidal, S., Skeem, J., and Camp, J. 2010. Emotional intelligence: Painting different paths for low-anxious and high-anxious psychopathic variants. *Law and Human Behavior, 34*(2), 150–163. DOI: 10.1007/s10979-009-9175-y.

Viding, E., Blair, R. J., Moffitt, T. E., and Plomin, R. 2005. Evidence for substantial genetic risk for psychopathy in 7-year-olds. *Journal of Child Psychology and Psychiatry, 46*(6), 592–597. DOI: 10.1111/j.1469-7610.2004.00393.x.

Weder, N., Yang, B. Z., Douglas-Palumberi, H., Massey, J., Krystal, J. H., Gelernter, J., and Kaufman, J. 2009. MAOA genotype, maltreatment, and aggressive behavior: The changing impact of genotype at varying levels of trauma. *Biological Psychiatry, 65*(5), 417–424. DOI: 10.1016/j.biopsych.2008.09.013.

Weller, S. 2013, January 13. A cold case of cold-blooded murder. *New York Times*. Retrieved from http://nyti.ms/1NPScr6.

Widiger, T. A. and Lynam, D. R. 1998. Psychopathy and the five-factor model of personality. In: T. Millon, E. Simonsen, M. Birket-Smith, and R. D. Davis (Eds.), *The Psychopath: Antisocial, Criminal, and Violent Behavior*. New York, NY: Guilford Press, pp. 171–187.

Wilson, D. and Harrison, P. 2010. *The Lost British Serial Killer: Closing the Case on Peter Tobin and Bible John*. London, UK: Sphere.

Woodworth, M. and Porter, S. 2002. In cold blood: Characteristics of criminal homicides as a function of psychopathy. *Journal of Abnormal Psychology, 111*, 436–445.

10 Psychotic Homicide Offenders

Michael H. Stone

Contents

Risk for Violence in Persons with Psychosis... 188
Psychosis and Homicide: A Neurological Risk Factor 190
Schizophrenia.. 190
Murder via Bizarre Acts as an Index to Schizophrenic Psychosis.......................... 194
Manic-Depressive Disorders with Psychosis 195
Autism-Spectrum Disorder 196
Head-Injury-Induced Psychosis.. 197
Drug-Induced Psychosis 198
Psychosis Not Otherwise Specified 199
Schizotypal Personality with Psychotic Episodes 199
Discussion 200
References 201

Psychotic homicidal offenders have in recent times received attention, at least in the United States, considerably in excess either of their number or of the number of victims they have killed. There are two main reasons for this disproportion. Some of the murders committed by psychotic persons, even where there are only one or two victims, are bizarre or else repugnant in nature—as if somehow the out-of-the ordinariness, the madness of the crime matches the madness of its perpetrator. This creates headline-grabbing news in the tabloids, contributing to the public's fearful assumptions that "crazy" people are especially dangerous, and worse than that—capable of inflicting suffering and horror beyond what a "normal" killer could inflict. Then there are the even rarer but still more dramatic incidents involving either serial sexual homicide or mass murder committed by persons who were described as mentally ill. From the standpoint of the public, such crimes have an even more electrifying impact, engendering widespread fear, and stirring up political conflict as to what should be done about the mentally ill—all of whom are suddenly lumped together in the public's mind as harbingers of unspeakable evil.

Before going further, it would be well to address the terminological confusion that surrounds the term "mentally ill." The phrase belongs to the domain of everyday speech by persons in everyday life. It is not a diagnosis in the official psychiatric nomenclature, although psychiatrists sometimes use the term. When psychiatrists do use the term, they are referring to persons who are *psychotic*. By this they mean: persons who exhibit a serious break from reality, often in the form of a delusion. Distortions that involve primarily thought ("cognitive" distortions) will be assigned a diagnosis of *schizophrenia*—as when someone insists that the government secretly places agents underneath his bed at night in order to record his thoughts.

This distinction is in keeping with the tripartite division regarding insanity outlined by Esquirol (1838); namely, "madness" of the intellect, of emotion (and morality), and of volition. Intellectual insanity, as characterized by Morrall (2000, p. 34), is usually in the form of delusions and command hallucinations. Distortions that involve primarily mood ("affective" distortions) are said to be *manic depressive*—as when someone insists he is Jesus or Napoleon (a grandiose delusion). Moral insanity (or "imbecility") involves that we now call psychopathy—which we no longer regard as a psychosis. Also included under the heading of mental illness are persons who function fairly well in most areas of everyday life, but who harbor a narrowly circumscribed delusion that, for example, unidentified flying objects [UFOs] are circling the earth, carrying creatures from another planet hoping to invade ours. There is also a grey zone of mental illness consisting of persons whose thoughts or moods are seriously derailed by abuse of mind-altering drugs. Still more subtle aberrations: persons with autistic spectrum disorders, such as Asperger's syndrome, where the derangement is not so much one of gross delusion as of a gross empathic deficit such that one cannot comprehend the feelings and the subtleties of language of ordinary people. Autistic persons are as baffled by us as we are of them, and often become social isolates. In severe cases, autistic persons may show paranoid peculiarities of thought, complaining that people are "against" them—but failing to understand that it is their own social incomprehension that alienates them from others. Autistic persons rarely commit violent crimes, but when they do, they are included among the "psychotic" offenders—not so much because of any frank delusions as because of their glaring incapacity to fit in socially. As we shall see, when they do commit violent crimes, they too are given the label of mental illness, the same as are the more widely recognized examples of persons with clear-cut schizophrenia and affective psychoses. There is yet another group of psychotic offenders: persons who—some with and some without preexisting vulnerability to mental illness—have made themselves psychotic through abuse of mind-altering drugs. The menu of such drugs has expanded greatly from what it was a generation ago: besides alcohol and abuse of marijuana in adolescence, we now contend with substances like methylenedioxymethamphetamine (ecstasy), methylenedioxypolyvalerone (bath salts), phencyclicine (angel dust), psilocybin (mushrooms), and others—any of which can provoke psychotic reactions and outbursts of violence—including homicidal violence (Teplin et al., 1993).

There is yet another category of homicide offenders who were regarded as psychotic at the time of their crime. These are men (the category seems one exclusively of men) who appeared fairly normal until they suffered a serious head injury—following which they experienced a dramatic change of personality, becoming psychotic in one or another manner (paranoid, grandiose, delusional, etc.) and in this altered state, committing one or a number of murders. With a few exceptions, these men did not appear to show antecedent risk factors, such as a family history of psychosis or incipient signs of mental illness in the premorbid/preinjury period of their lives (Hodgins et al., 2009).

Risk for Violence in Persons with Psychosis

Violence comprises both nonlethal and lethal acts. Because nonlethal acts, such as assaults and outbursts of rage, are much more common than murder, statistical data about the mentally ill mentioned in the forensic literature focus mainly on violence in general and only parenthetically on actual murder. The vast majorities of murders are committed by impulsive, antisocial, and psychopathic persons who are *not* mentally ill. In a large-scale multicenter epidemiological study of violence and mental disorder, funded by the National Institute of Mental Health [NIMH] in the United States, the focus was on violent acts such as using a weapon in a fight, hitting family members or others, or fighting while drinking. Murder was too rare an event to be captured even in a community sample of almost 18,000 persons. What emerged from the study was that the probability of violent behavior during a year of follow-up was low among those without mental disorder (1.38% in females, 2.45% in males), was substantially greater among those with affective disorder (5.7% in females, 8.4% in males), and greater still among those diagnosed "schizophrenic": (8.2% in females, 13.1 in males). Substance abuse (alcohol being the main contributor in this study) increased the risk, by itself, to 17% and 22% (female vs. male); the figures being just slightly higher in the *substance abuse and mental disorder* group (Swanson 1994). The presence of substance abuse doubled the likelihood of contact with the criminal justice system (from 13% to 27%). A history of psychiatric hospitalization elevated the violence risk still further. Those with either schizophrenia or major affective disorder showed a 1-year probability of 21% absent a history of arrest; this rose to 42% where there was mental illness, arrest, and psychiatric hospitalization. Adding substance abuse to the scenario nearly doubled the risk in the hospitalized (but not arrested) group to 40%; this rose to 64% when substance abuse was added to the mix (Swanson 1994, p. 129). These figures confirmed the generally held notion that psychiatric illness and substance abuse heighten the risk for violence, well above what is noted in the general population, although the mentally ill as a group do not pose a higher risk in absolute terms; that is, only about 7% of those with major mental illness (but without concomitant substance abuse) show assaultive behavior in a given year (ibid., p. 132). Needless to say, multivariate analysis of these data brings to the surface a host of other factors that either heighten or reduce the risk for violence, such as age, sex, marital history, socioeconomic status, education, and culture. We would be surprised, for example, to learn of violence, let alone murder, committed by an elderly highly educated wealthy woman of European background, as compared with a male of low educational and socioeconomic status during his "high testosterone" years (15–40) who came from a culture where violence is endemic. Elsewhere, Swanson et al. (1990) showed that persons with schizophrenia (diagnosed by DSM-III guidelines) were "…four to six times likely to report engaging in some form of violence than people without illness" (cf. Taylor et al. 1994, p. 119). The presence of delusions, as is particularly common in schizophrenia (their presence often triggers a subdiagnosis of "paranoid schizophrenia"), may add substantially to the risk of "criminal, mostly violent criminal, acts" (Taylor et al. 1994, p. 167). Persecutory delusions, in particular, may also be associated with hallucinations of a sort that appear to urge, or even compel, a psychotic person to assault or kill the person or group that is supposedly "threatening" his (or in rare instances, her) life. Symptoms of this sort are referred to as "control-override," the point being that the delusion or accompanying hallucination overrides the individual's capacity for internal (viz. frontal lobe) control of aggressive impulses (McNiel 1994). Examples of this sort are provided further on.

À propos psychotic symptoms, while the relationship between mental disorder and violent behavior appears "robust" (Monahan 1993), the main connection seems to be the *current* experience of psychotic symptoms (Link et al. 1992). Having been a *former* patient in a psychiatric hospital does not serve as a reliable indicator of future violence, according to Link, though there is a small number of repeat offenders among the psychotic patients who had earlier been in psychiatric facilities—including those who have gone on to murder someone. As Monahan argues (1993), "Compared to the magnitude of risk associated with the combination of male gender, young age, and lower socioeconomic status, the risk of violence presented by mental disorder is modest (p. 299), and even more modest when compared to risk posed by those who abuse alcohol or other substances." Monahan for these reasons decries the tendency of politicians (and journalists) of pandering to public fears. Pamela Taylor noted in her comment on the British prison/remand system vis-à-vis men ordered to prison on a murder charge that a comparison was often made between men with a psychotic illness versus men without—attention being paid more to the symptoms themselves than to the underlying diagnosis. A source for confusion here lay in the fact that psychotic symptoms (delusions, hallucinations, limited areas of paranoid beliefs, etc.) seldom point to one and only psychotic-level diagnosis. Within a sample of supposedly "schizophrenic" men (on cursory examination following arrest) who have committed murder, for example, there will be a proportion of unknown size who, upon more careful evaluation, might be diagnosed otherwise (bipolar manic, drug abuse with phencyclidine or methamphetamine, etc.)—leading to somewhat unreliable statistics concerning the risk of violence or murder of this or that diagnostic entity.

As a refinement to our understanding of the risk for *serious* violence (i.e., murder) among schizophrenics—as noted by Wallace et al. (2004)—Hodgins (2009), in reviewing a large-scale Danish epidemiological study, noted that persons with even one previous psychiatric hospitalization for schizophrenia showed about a 4.6 times elevation of violent crime rate among men, and a 23% elevation among women—compared with persons never psychiatrically hospitalized. As she mentions, "Although fewer women than men, both with and without schizophrenia, are convicted of crimes, schizophrenia confers greater risk of offending among women, than among men." Most of the violent acts are assaults; murders are rare. From cross-national studies, it appears that schizophrenic persons in countries with a high crime rate have a higher rate of committing violent crimes than their schizophrenic counterparts in countries with a lower crime rate. Persons from countries where attitudes of machismo prevail, or where the culture encourages the speedy avenging of romantic betrayals, are more prone to "take matters in their own hands," even to the point of committing murder (Erb et al. 2001). The violence risk among schizophrenics is greater than the risk among those without mental illness in whatever country is studied; even though the incidence of schizophrenia remains roughly the same (1%) worldwide, the proportion of those who commit violence, including murder, will be higher in the high crime countries than in the low-crime countries. A more difficult question: of all the murders committed in a certain country, what percent are committed by persons with schizophrenia? Estimates have ranged from 6% to 28% (Erb et al. 2001), but these figures do not address the differences among countries. A country with a large population where only 100 murders occur all year—where 28 are by schizophrenics—is a much safer place than a country with 20,000 murders a year—where only 1200 (6%) were committed by schizophrenic individuals.

Psychosis and Homicide: A Neurological Risk Factor

Though there is a variety of psychodiagnostic forms of psychosis, schizophrenia often serves as the *primus inter pares* of these forms: it is the psychosis that comes most readily to mind when referring to psychosis, and the one that receives the most attention. In the last generation, this has become all the more true, given that widespread abuse of psychotomimetic substances has added greatly to the number of persons considered to be psychotic—who get labeled schizophrenic, even though their primarily cognitive (hence schizophrenia-like) psychosis may have its origin not in a genetic predisposition to Kraepelinian (i.e., authentic) schizophrenia, but instead to the abuse of a drug. Mixed cases of course also occur—where a "genuine" genetic schizophrenia person self-medicates with one of these substances, ending up with a more intense form of schizophrenia, or one with an earlier than expected onset—say, at age 15 rather than at 20. As Adrian Raine (2013, p. 233) has pointed out, still other abnormalities may predispose to a schizophrenia-like psychosis, often involving some form of frontal lobe dysfunction. Fetal maldevelopment, perinatal complications, tumors in key regions of the frontal lobe, severe endocrine disturbances emanating from adrenal, thyroid, or pituitary abnormalities may all induce a psychosis that mimics the "real" schizophrenia, but to the clinician's eye during an initial examination, essentially "is" schizophrenia. This is particularly true in forensic work—where persons arrested for a violent crime, including murder, appear grossly psychotic when first apprehended—before there is any opportunity to discern whether the illness is of the uncomplicated genetic variety, or is instead a cognitive psychosis stemming from head injury, drug abuse, tumor, or some other factor not related to one's genome. In my study of 109 consecutive patients admitted to a forensic psychiatric hospital, for example, 80 were initially diagnosed as "schizophrenic" (59) or "schizoaffective" (21), but only 30 were considered examples of genetic schizophrenia upon reexamination months later. The remainder consisted of patients who abused marijuana and/or other drugs heavily during adolescence, or (in a few instances) who suffered traumatic brain injury, perinatal hypoxia, postsurgical dementia, or postpartum psychosis (one case, each). The rate for murder or attempted murder in the entire group was 44%: highest in those who never abused drugs (19 of 30, or 63%), lowest in the drug-induced group, where there was no known prior history of psychosis (9 of 29, or 31%), and intermediate in the drug-aggravated group (some history of mental illness; heavy drug abuse below age 18:20 of 39, or 51%)

Although the nature of symptoms and beliefs of certain schizophrenics make them seem more susceptible of violent behaviors: they are prone to paranoid ideation as though others are "against them," necessitating a "kill-or-be-killed" attitude toward the world—such an attitude is not the exclusive preserve of schizophrenia. Certain manic persons of the bipolar type 1 (extreme "highs" alternating with extreme depressions) have psychotic episodes in which they become either paranoid (and murder by way of a delusional "self-defense") or psychotically grandiose. This may move them to the point of believing, in their exalted state, that they possess God-like powers of life and death—in which state they feel justified to "eliminate" certain "unworthy" persons or groups. Persons with any of the "classic" psychoses (schizophrenia, bipolar disorder, delusional disorder) may feel prompted to "save the world" by killing all the blacks, Jews, Muslims, gays, prostitutes, conservatives, liberals, and so on, ending up committing what we denominate as murder, but which they experience as righteous acts deserving of admiration (cf. Raine, op cit, p. 235). Examples of this will be found below. Still, it does appear from the crime literature (and also from my forensic experience) that among psychotic persons committing murder, schizophrenics (both the genetic and the epigenetic) will outnumber those from the other diagnostic categories.

To illustrate the variety of psychotic conditions that have accompanied, and presumably contributed importantly, to mentally ill persons committing murder, I describe below a number of such murder cases, many of them "high profile" and well known, organized according to the type of mental illness involved. I derived these examples from a number of sources, including full-length "true-crime" biographies, clippings from newspapers and magazines, forensic hospital work, and my interviews for the Discovery Channel program, "Most Evil," where some of the offenders who had committed murder were also psychotic.

Schizophrenia

Peter Sutcliffe: Born in 1946, in Bingley, a town of some 20,000 in North West England, Sutcliffe came from a working-class Catholic family, was a loner at school, which he left at 15 to take a number of menial jobs, including that of grave digger. Sutcliffe was intimidated by his burly, extraverted father, and was much more at ease with his mother, a gentle and affectionate woman. Some have suggested that he may have been humiliated by his father—a man who embodied a violent macho culture that depreciated women (Burn 1985). When he was 23, he experienced what Adrian Raine (2013, p. 182) called the "pivotal moment of his life." He heard, or so he claimed, while he was digging a grave, a vague echoing voice that he felt emanated from the cross of a nearby Polish grave. This seemed to him something *fantastic*—in the sense of awesome, not fanciful—as though he had been singled out by God for some, at first unclear, purpose. In time, the "purpose" was revealed to him: he was singled out as the earthly agent to deal with God's wrath against sexual sin; specifically, against the sin of prostitutes. This "mission" may have derived some of its impetus from his father's conviction that his mother had been unfaithful (Newton 2006). Already, by 1967, Sutcliffe complained of having contracted a venereal disease from prostitutes in Leeds and Birmingham. Others suspected his antipathy toward prostitutes was fueled by his having been conned out of money in one such encounter in 1969, when an older prostitute tricked him out of 10£ (J Blanco; Wikipedia). Even so, 1967 on Valentine's Day was when he met Sonia Szurma, a woman of Czech-Ukrainian background—whom he married seven-and-a-half years later in 1974 (J Blanco). In what was perhaps his first act of violence against a prostitute, in the 1969 incident when tricked out of money, he followed the woman and struck her in the head with a stone that he had wrapped in a sock. The woman survived and did not press charges. Eleven months after his marriage, Sutcliffe bludgeoned a woman, Anna Rogulsky, who had been walking alone. He also slashed her abdomen with a knife. She survived. Sutcliffe was not suspected as the assailant. Six weeks later, in August 1975, he struck a 14-year-old girl as she was walking in a country lane; she too survived, but Sutcliffe was again not a suspect. He inaugurated his career as a serial killer, 2 months later in October 1975, when he killed Wilma McCann in Leeds, striking her with a ball-peen hammer and then stabbing her 15 times. Traces of semen were found in her underwear, but these were the days before DNA analysis, so the semen had no evidentiary value from a legal standpoint. Sutcliffe was not identified as the killer. Until his eventual arrest for murder in 1981, Sutcliffe killed a dozen more women, some prostitutes, some not. When he finally confessed, he acknowledged that he was indeed the man who had meantime earned the soubriquet as the Yorkshire Ripper. Shortly, thereafter, he claimed that God told him to murder the women, and went further in mounting his defense, adding that the voices he had heard (14 years earlier) came from the headstone of the dead Polish man, Bronisław Zapolski—and that the voices were those of God. This led to a back and forth between the defense and the prosecution, some asserting, on the strength of four psychiatrist reports, that Sutcliffe was a paranoid schizophrenic. Ten of the twelve jury members felt Sutcliffe was not insane, but was in fact and evil and sadistic murderer. The judge declared that he was sane, and had Sutcliffe sent to Parkhurst prison in 1981. But in 1984, he was transferred to Broadmoor, a forensic hospital, as though he was mentally ill, after all, to the point of manifesting "diminished responsibility." One can, of course, be psychotic but sane—the latter a legal term signifying merely that one knows the nature of one's act and whether it were right or wrong (after the M'Naghten Rule of 1843, defining "insanity"). Sutcliffe remains in Broadmoor to this day, having survived two assaults by other inmates—one in prison, the other at Broadmoor—rendering him blind in one eye. For me, the jury is still out vis-à-vis Sutcliffe's "schizophrenia." It is not common for truly and chronically schizophrenic men to marry, hold down a job, and to function adequately with prostitutes. He was not in psychiatric treatment before his arrest; he was not known either to psychiatry or to the authorities as a "crazy" person. There is a self-serving quality to a man, once arrested for a violent crime, to claim he "heard voices" urging to commit the crime for which he was now facing trial. Nor did his symptoms have the bizarre features that make a diagnosis of schizophrenia more compelling (as we shall see in some of the examples below). Prison being a less agreeable abode than a forensic hospital in the eyes of certain convicts, one must be wary of claims of madness lest they be invoked in the hopes of transfer to a pleasanter place in which to do one's time. Sutcliffe is a man of 70 as of this writing: he may have had some moments of psychosis during adolescence, but does not have the characteristics of chronic schizophrenia—which is often attenuated as one passes into the later years of life. Adrian Raine inclines toward the belief not only that Sutcliffe is psychotic, but that he was predisposed to this fate by virtue of having been born "premature," released from hospital after a "ten-day struggle for life" (p. 182), which Raine regards as an "early biological hit." But "premature birth" implies weighing *under* five pounds at birth. I can attest to this, having myself been regarded as "premature," though I too weighed five pounds at birth, and spent *fifteen* days in an incubator before release to home.

David Tarloff: In 2008, Tarloff, 39 at the time, had a two-decades-long history of paranoid schizophrenia, as manifest by delusions of communicating directly with God. He had been in and out of psychiatric hospitals in the intervening years, and bore a particular grudge against psychiatrist Dr. Kent Shinbach for having diagnosed him as severely mentally ill and in need of hospitalization some 20 years before. He had only been out of a psychiatric hospital a few weeks when, in February of 2008, he entered the east-side New York office of Dr. Shinbach, armed with hidden tools—intending to "get back" at the doctor, killing him, yet also with the alternative idea of robbing the doctor of $50,000 (as though he surely kept that kind of cash stowed in the drawer) by way of implementing the (truly) bizarre scheme of kidnapping his ailing mother from a hospital and then spiriting them both to Hawaii, where they could (so he planned) live happily ever after. Tarloff waited in the reception area and when psychologist Kathryn Faughey in the adjoining office was alone, he entered her office. Tarloff killed her with blows from his mallet, and with deep cuts from a meat cleaver. Dr. Shinbach, his original target, rushed in, trying to save Dr. Faughey, and ended up severely injured himself. Though arrested immediately, Tarloff was able to game the system, pleading insanity in hopes of dodging a prison sentence on the grounds of mental illness. Because the crime was premeditated, he was nevertheless declared competent to stand trial—but at trial several psychiatrists found him "mentally unfit." The jury was deadlocked, and a mistrial was declared—and then a second attempt ended in a mistrial. Finally, 6 years after the murder, Tarloff was found guilty of first degree murder and sentenced to life in prison without parole. This was a kind of mistrial in itself, insofar as Tarloff, unlike Sutcliffe, was unquestionably and profoundly schizophrenic day in and day out for at least the 20 years before the murder. Whereas, Sutcliffe was called "schizophrenic" because of his behavior (coshing and slashing a score of women), Tarloff had displayed bizarre paranoid ideation for decades, meaning that he had been diagnosed (correctly) as schizophrenic on the basis of his decades-long grossly disturbed cognition—which is the essence of schizophrenic psychosis. Because, at his trials, he realized his action (killing Dr. Faughey) was wrong, he failed to meet M'Naghten criteria for "insanity." Instead, he was psychotic but sane. Because the public in its understandable outrage, and mistrust of the mental health system is reluctant to trust that forensic hospitals will keep such persons safely incarcerated—forever, if need be—prison is chosen as the correct venue, rather than hospital. This is a recurring problem in the arena of forensic psychiatry, and will be addressed in greater detail below.

Diana Gallow, née Skidmore, also known as "Dial": Unlike David Taroff, who exemplifies classic genetic-based schizophrenia (with both the "positive signs" of delusions and hallucinations, but also the important accompaniment of a formal thought disorder, and blunting of affect), Diana Dial (as she came to call herself) had functioned well—college graduate, tennis buff, mother of two—until a third pregnancy, which ended in miscarriage but also in a profound and irremediable cognitive psychosis, culminating in the murder of a man whose house she shared after her husband had divorced her. She had become fearful and irrational, convinced that Nazis were endangering both herself and her two sons (whom she forced to wear special amulets to ward off the Nazis). After the divorce, she traveled from one state to another, trying to escape from the clutches of her supposed Nazi pursuers. Eventually, she settled in a rooming house in Texas owned by Jack Ferris. She complained to the police multiple times a day to complain about her predicament with the "Nazis"—and refused therapy or medications since she was convinced that her delusions were reality. Her bizarre beliefs and actions escalated to the point where she imagined someone in the library where she had secured (and quickly lost) a job—was accosting her and poking at her ear with an ice pick. She became convinced that Mr. Ferris was in league with the Nazis and was trying to put poison in her tea or coffee, such that she was slowly dying. Her bizarre beliefs assumed new heights, as she felt she was being stalked by President Clinton, though she was also the heiress of Howard Hughes. She changed her name to "Dial" as though she were the heiress to the Dial Soap fortune, somehow overlooking the fact that *Dial* was a trade name (like the *Ivory* of Ivory Soap), not a family name. As her paranoia heightened to where she felt Mr. Ferris was going to harm her children as well, she shot him to death—and then reported the incident to the police, out of her conviction she was doing the right thing. Unlike Tarloff, she has never to this day acknowledged what she had done was wrong and that she had been driven to do so out of mental illness. When I interviewed her in prison in 2007, she expanded her delusion to encompass the Kennedys along with the Nazis in a grand scheme to "take over our country," and was baffled by my incomprehension as to why the Kennedys of all people would team up with the Nazis. But *on any other topic*, Diana was perfectly lucid: she could talk about her prowess on the tennis court, about her wide knowledge of Egyptian history, and a host of other subjects. There were, in other words, islands of normalcy in her thinking, unlike Tarloff, who could not talk intelligibly even on areas distinct from the murder. I asked the warden whether she could have Diana evaluated by modern brain imaging techniques, but the prison budget did not allow for this. Hers may not have been a classic genetic schizophrenia like Tarloff's, but may have come about from some neurochemical derangement following the last pregnancy—that led to a cognitive psychosis just as perduring as Tarloff's (Taylor et al., 1993; Hodgins, 2009).

Patient A (at forensic hospital): A man from a well-to-do New England family had complied an excellent record at university and was then accepted at a prestigious law school. During the middle of his studies there, he experienced a psychotic episode, diagnosed paranoid schizophrenia, for which he was hospitalized and treated with neuroleptic medications. He was then able to resume his studies and to graduate on schedule. His mental health seemingly restored; he was then able to secure a position at a law firm. He now formed a romantic relationship with a woman 2 years his junior. This progressed to where they became formally engaged. His fiancée became pregnant. This unexpected turn of events involving not only the necessity of becoming a husband but also a father in this abrupt fashion proved overwhelming for him. When his fiancée was in her fourth month, he went to her apartment and stabbed her to death. He was laboring under the delusional conviction that she was somehow an alien person whom powerful but unidentified forces within the Communist government—to whom he had now become subservient—had compelled him to "eliminate." This event heralded the resurgence of his schizophrenic breakdown. He was quickly arrested, but because of his evident psychotic state, he was transferred to a forensic hospital. Neuroleptic medications (which he had for a time omitted to take) were reinstituted. This regimen restored a measure of calm, but had no impact on his delusion. He could, for example, discuss the political events of the day, or expatiate upon his favorite topic of medieval French poetry with great clarity. But when questioned about the death of his fiancée, he immediately reverted to the delusory ideas of being controlled by the nameless authorities in a faraway Communist government. I worked with this man for 2 years in twice-weekly therapy of a mixed supportive and analytically oriented type. Toward the end of that time, I posed the question: "Don't you think it's at least possible that in the urgency of the moment you were feeling extremely fearful of embarking, and all so suddenly, on a life of husband and father—at a time when you were feeling unselfconfident about being able to support a family and to relate to a child? Worries, that is, that would be terribly embarrassing to acknowledge—so that your mind, by way of helping you to save face, urged you to do away with your fiancée, but conjuring up a story that it was not you who were behaving as you did, of your own will—but rather that you were instead the helpless agent of some malevolent foreign power?" "Ah," he said, "I can see your reasoning…but never having been under the power of a tyrannical government, you cannot really imagine what it must be like, and what a man may be driven to do!" He remains, in other words, to this day (12 years after the murder) in the same state of paranoid delusory ideation as had prevailed at the onset of the psychotic breakdown. He does, however, experience intense remorse. Whenever the hospital feels he may be ready for transfer to a conventional psychiatric facility, he begins to behave in inappropriate ways, forestalling any plans for such a move.

Robert Napper: In contrast to Peter Sutcliffe, whose record as a serial killer is beyond question, but whose diagnosis of schizophrenia is debatable, Napper's schizophrenic psychosis is as firmly established as his conviction for serial sexual homicide. It was his genuine psychosis that led to his remand to Broadmoor Hospital for the criminally insane (Alison and Eyre 2009). In Napper, a genetic tendency to a schizophrenic psychosis was complicated by an abysmal childhood. His father, Brian, was violent toward his mother, Pauline—who in turn was violent toward Robert, the eldest of four children. After the parents divorced (when Robert was 4), the children were all placed in fosterage. When he was sodomized at age 12 by a gay family friend, he became embittered, introverted, and reclusive. Already at 13, he was hospitalized after raping a woman and taking an overdose. He raped a woman when he was 23 (but was not arrested). His first murder came 2 years later, when he was 25, stabbing a woman to death. Thereafter, a pattern emerged: he would rape, murder, and sometimes disembowel or otherwise mutilate a mother in front of her small child. He earned the soubriquet: the Green Chain rapist because of his savage attacks of some 70 women in South East London during the years 1991–1994. At times, he would sexually assault and kill the daughters of the women he accosted. Some psychologists who evaluated him felt that the schizoid and friendless person he had become, represented an "acting out" of the violence done to him. Others read his being a loner and his having an "*encompassing preoccupation with one stereotyped and restricted pattern of interest that is abnormal in intensity*" as a manifestation of an Asperger-type autistic disorder (as defined in DSM-IV). When finally arrested at age 27, however, he was found to have a profound and "formal" thought disorder that was indicative of paranoid schizophrenia. Napper, for example, considered himself "untouchable" and believed he could transmit his thoughts via telepathy. He thought strange changes had been made in the calendar that then affecting his thinking. In a mixture of grandiose and bizarre delusions, he also insisted that he had won the Nobel Peace Prize, had earned a master's degree in math, had won medals for fighting in Africa, and that he had millions of pounds stored in a bank. More astonishing still: he spoke of how his fingers had been blown off by an IRA bomb but had then miraculously grown back. The grotesque nature of Napper's murders, in and of itself, pointed to mental illness.

An illustrative case was that of his 1992 murder of Rachel Nickell—a 23-year-old model and mother of a young son, Alex. After stalking her as she and the boy walked through London's Wimbeldon Common, Napper slit her throat and stabbed her 49 times—most of the blows coming postmortem. She had been sexually assaulted and left half naked, her boy then clutching her body, crying "Get up, Mummy." Napper's actions establish him also as a "sexual sadist," in the sense of feeling arousal during the act of murder. Many serial killers are sexual sadists; few are in addition psychotic. In Napper, all these facets were combined.

Patient B: In forensic psychiatric settings, there are many patients whose murders were in and of themselves were unspectacular, but had been set in motion by thoughts of a bizarre nature. A policeman in his early 30s had never dated or formed any close attachments. He lived with his widowed mother—for which he was sometimes taunted by the other men in his precinct as being a "mama's boy." In this context, his mind began to unravel to the point where he began to believe that his mother was the "Queen of the Mafia," even though she had come from a Polish background. Further, he developed the delusion that he himself had been born to Hitler and Mussolini. Convinced that the world would be a better place with the Mafia-Queen no longer in the picture, he shot his mother to death. Quickly apprehended, he spouted his bizarre rationale for the murder—for which he was then sent to a forensic hospital. Seemingly without animosity except for his mother, he has been calm and quiet on the ward for the past 25 years—thanks in part to his neuroleptic medications, which have not, however, succeeded in dampening his bizarre beliefs.

Murder via Bizarre Acts as an Index to Schizophrenic Psychosis

Whereas, bizarre thoughts were the defining features of Napper's schizophrenia, in some instances it is the bizarre nature of the murderous *act* that suggests the presence of a schizophrenic psychosis—usually corroborated afterwards when we learn of the bizarre thoughts that precipitated the act.

Patient C: A woman of 35 was remanded to a forensic hospital in the aftermath of a violent confrontation with her mother, a woman of 71. The patient lived with her mother in a tempestuous relationship going back nearly 20 years. She experienced her mother as highly critical and punitive, while at the same time had grown totally dependent upon her. It was her mother who looked after her when she would return from her many hospitalizations for schizophrenia—not well controlled with medications, owing to the patient's poor compliance with their use. Her mother often rebuked her for neglecting to take her medication. The offense that necessitated forensic hospitalization consisted of the woman having pushed her mother to the floor, following such a rebuke—at which point the woman shoved a long knife through her mother's vagina, killing her. In the patient's mind, she had a "rationale" for this act; namely, to facilitate the escape of the "good mother" who lay buried within the mother's exterior—or "bad"—body. To the surprise of no one except the patient, both the "good" and the "bad" mother succumbed to the knife wound. But as should be obvious from the story, the act itself was unmistakably the behavioral expression of a grossly psychotic and bizarre delusion.

Richard Chase: Bizarre acts helped confirm the schizophrenic nature of Chase's psychosis, though early abuse of psychotomimetic and psychostimulant drugs created a confusing picture: would he have suffered a schizophrenic breakdown even if he refrained from such drugs? Did the drugs produce a schizophrenia-like syndrome *de novo*, in someone who may otherwise have avoided a psychotic breakdown? He did, already in early adolescence, exhibit strange behaviors—such as killing and burying cats in his backyard. Born in Sacramento, California, in 1950, his earliest years seemed unremarkable. There was no history of parental neglect or abuse. His parents, both of whom appeared to have paranoid tendencies, divorced when Richard was already 23. He had friends of both sexes in high school, and enjoyed a measure of popularity. But finding himself impotent with three different girls, he underwent a change of personality. He was disorganized in his habits, defiant of authority, became egocentric, and started to abuse a variety of drugs: marijuana, amphetamines, alcohol, and LSD. His hygiene deteriorated; he withdrew from people, and behaved in strange ways—such as walking out of his room naked and speaking unintelligibly. For this, he was hospitalized briefly at 23—where he was diagnosed as paranoid schizophrenia. Shortly afterwards, he began to steal rabbits, taking them back home and eviscerating them. He would drink their blood, hoping thereby to cure his impotence by having the extraneous blood somehow settle in his penis. He added the blood of other animals to the mix, capturing and killing cats and dogs; even a cow. He once walked into a hospital emergency room and complained to the nurse that someone had stolen his pulmonary artery. He felt also that bones were coming out of the back of his head, that his heart would stop beating, and that his stomach was "backwards." He was again diagnosed as a paranoid schizophrenic, though the doctors suspected that drug abuse may have exaggerated his symptomatology. Unable to fend for himself, he now lived with his mother—who decided he did not need his medications, so she weaned him from them. He once came home holding a dead cat, which he tore apart in front of her, smearing its blood over his face. His mother did nothing and did not alert anyone about this unsettling behavior. It was at this point, when he was 26 that he began to kill humans and to drink their blood—ending up killing and eviscerating three adults and three children. One of his last victims was a pregnant woman of 22, whom he shot to death, and then raped and bit off her nipple, drinking blood from her disemboweled body. He had also stuffed animal feces in her mouth. Finally caught and arrested when he was 28, he was convicted and sentenced to death in 1978. Two years after his incarceration, Chase committed suicide via an overdose of antidepressants (Biondi and Hecox, 1992).

Manic-Depressive Disorders with Psychosis

Laurie Wasserman Dann: Born in 1958 into a prosperous Jewish family in a Chicago suburb, Laurie was shy and withdrawn as a child, and did poorly at school. She attended college thinking to become a teacher, but dropped out and never graduated. At 22, she married a Russell Dann, a successful insurance executive, but the marriage soon failed, owing to her obsessive-compulsive disorder and strange behavior—leaving trash all over the house. She saw a psychiatrist briefly but then quit. During the divorce proceedings, she harassed her husband with repetitive phone calls, accused him of burglarizing her parents' home, and then bought a gun (and later, a second) as if for "self-defense." Now living separately, she once sneaked into Russell's house and stabbed him (nonfatally) with an ice pick. Her behavior deteriorated further to the point where she prepared cookies and fruit juice boxes with arsenic she had managed to steal, and then delivered them to various people, including a psychiatrist (who had the wisdom not to trust a "gift" from her). He had made a diagnosis of obsessive-compulsive disorder and bipolar disorder, with mainly depressed features. She made death threats by phone, shoplifted wigs and clothes with which to disguise herself, accused an ex-boyfriend of rape, and was found by the janitor of her building one day scrunched up in a garbage bag in the cellar. She was noted to ride up and down elevators for hours at a time, to wear rubber gloves to avoid touching metal, and to leave rotting meat in sofa cushions. As her depression and desperation intensified, she drove to a nearby elementary school, where she entered a second-grade classroom, and commenced firing one of her two pistols, shooting six children—killing an 8-year-old boy and wounding the other five. Then fleeing by car to a house in the vicinity, she begged entry on the grounds she had been "raped." The family noted she had two guns, and tried to persuade her to give them up. They managed to call the police. The scene ended when the police entered the house—only to discover that Laurie had shot herself to death, thus ending a life of failure, depression, strange compulsions, rage—and suicide (Kaplan et al. 1990).

Patient E: Raised in an upper-middle-class family of Irish-American background, this woman—before her placement in a forensic hospital—had been a bright high school student who married shortly after high school to a man from a traditional Italian-American family. His parents were born in Palermo and espoused old-fashioned views about the proper virtues of women; namely, that a woman's role was to devote herself to the three spheres of womanly life—as captured in the German phrase: *Kinder, Kirche, Küche*. The Italian equivalent would be something like *Bambini, Chiesa, Cucina*. She had two sons during the first few years of their marriage. When the boys, now six and eight, were in school, she yearned to go to college and fulfill her dream of becoming a teacher. This idea was abhorrent to both her husband and his parents—a violation of God's prescription for the roles of married partners. The more she spoke openly about her ambition, the more her husband and her in-laws heaped scorn on her. During this time of intense conflict, she began to experience sharp alterations of mood, swinging between episodes of manic energy, sleeplessness, and overactivity—to bouts of profound depression and avoidance of household obligations. At one point, she did summon the energy—and the daring—to make a formal application to a college that allowed a half-time curriculum that could take place while the boys were in school. This led to a terrible scene in which her husband and his parents forbade her to submit her application. That night, while in the grips of a towering rage, she stabbed to death first her two sons and then her husband. Apprehended immediately, she was diagnosed as suffering from a bipolar psychosis and sent to a forensic hospital. While there, medicated with lithium and (briefly) with an antipsychotic medication, she gradually recovered, albeit struggling with intense remorse. After 3 years at hospital, she was considered sufficiently restored to warrant transfer to a conventional psychiatric hospital. Two years later, she was released back into the community. Several years further on, she had remarried to a more liberal-minded husband, with whom she had a child. Now in her mid-thirties, she has remained well on mood-stabilizing medication, but has not as yet been able to fulfill her educational ambitions.

Patient F: A young man of 19 had emigrated with his sister and their father to the United States from Pakistan. The father had divorced the mother some 10 years earlier, just before leaving his native country. A harsh, controlling, and abusive man, the father would not allow either child to leave the apartment once they returned from school and forbade them either to have friends visit or to go to their friends' homes. Also forbidden was any contact with their mother, whether by phone or by mail. The father beat both children severely even for the most trivial offenses. Prisoners in their own home, the young man and his sister had only each other to talk with, though that too was discouraged. The young man's bitterness and resentment were intense but remained just below the boiling point, until he learned from his sister that their father had begun to molest her sexually. At that point, he suffered what was understood in retrospect as an acute manic episode. On his way back from school, he bought a large knife—a machete—and when he got home, he bludgeoned his father's head with the flat of the machete, rendering him unconscious. He then severed his father's head and, gripped in his psychotic state with the fear his father's head might re-attach itself, becoming his fearful, tyrannical self all over again, he tossed the head out the window onto the street below. This became a sensational news item, and he was arrested shortly thereafter and consigned to a forensic facility. He was treated with lithium, and made a swift recovery, experiencing remorse for the murder, though also relief at no longer having to endure his father's oppressive behavior. After 2 years at hospital, he was adjudged a recovered manic and permitted to apply for college, with the proviso that he be monitored as to his lithium level.

Andrea Kennedy Yates: Born in 1964 to a Catholic family in Houston, Texas, Andrea Kennedy was valedictorian of her high school and captain of its swimming team. She then completed nursing school and worked at a University of Texas hospital. At 29, she married Russell Yates, both agreeing to have as many children as Nature allowed. After the birth of their fourth son, she experienced a postpartum depression. Russell and she then came under the influence of a charlatan cult-preacher, Michael Woroniecki, who counseled total avoidance of the "corrupt" outer world. He sold the couple a used Greyhound bus—which was to be their new "home": 350 square feet in all for the couple and their four (and soon to be five) children. Russell could leave the bus for his engineering job but Andrea had to remain inside—to care for the children, homeschool, and homechurch them. She had several depressive episodes for which she received various antidepressants and spent a few days in a psychiatric hospital. Russell refused to lighten her burden by hiring babysitters, since they were "too secular." Feeling depressed and overwhelmed, Andrea began to hallucinate voices urging her to get a knife. Rehospitalized briefly for suicidal feelings, and now pregnant with her fifth child, she refused medication. She had fears she would kill the children, and now thought of suicide as a way of sparing them. Her mother managed to persuade Russell to move from the bus to a house. Six months after delivering her fifth child, Andrea's father died. Two months later she had become mute, depressed, and suicidal, but when briefly hospitalized again was given a few pills and sent home. There at home she filled up a bathtub with water and drowned her five children, then calling the police to tell them what she had done. Because of the high-profile nature of the crime, Andrea was at first sent to prison. Errors had been made at that trial, and a second trial was scheduled—at which the more merciful (and correct) decision was made, because of her depressive psychosis, to have her remanded to a forensic hospital where she remains to this day.

Autism-Spectrum Disorder

Autistic-spectrum disorders are becoming more recognized currently, and perhaps also more frequently in their occurrence—but are still not as common within the general population as are schizophrenic and manic-depressive disorders, and are seldom associated with violent crimes. One formerly referred to autistic persons with fairly good function and good language skills as manifesting the Asperger Syndrome, features of which include inability to make friends, poor eye contact in social encounters, low empathic capacity, and obsessive preoccupations with one or a few activities—often odd ones like memorizing train schedules or playing make-believe sports events via the Internet. There have been several mass murders in the United States in the past 10 years carried out by autistic young men; the publicity about them electrified the public about the supposed dangers of Asperger's Syndrome. The first such case was that of Seung-Hui Cho, an immigrant to the United States from Korea and a student at Virginia Technical College. Unable to socialize in any way, and reluctant to respond verbally to anyone, he was mocked in school for his oddities—which grew more marked when he entered college. He behaved menacingly to teachers and classmates, could not relate to girls, and felt resentful when his advances were rebuffed. This contributed to his determination to "get even," and prompted his purchasing two semiautomatic pistols in March of 2007—in preparation for the mass murder he was to carry out a month later. He killed 32 in all, including several teachers—before committing suicide.

Adam Lanza: In December 2012 a 20-year-old man from Newtown, Connecticut entered a nearby school, carrying several semiautomatic rifles, and proceeded to kill 6 teachers, 20 pupils (ages from 5 to 10) and then himself. He had first, before leaving home, killed his mother with several shots to the head. Recognized as autistic as a toddler, Lanza could make no eye contact with others, and was electively mute much of the time. Bullied because of his peculiar behavior, he was eventually cared for at home by his mother, a divorcée, who also had another son, psychologically normal, who was 4 years older and lived in another town. The mother was a paranoid woman—an avowed Doomsday Prepper (a club for people who hoard dry food and essentials in preparation for the cataclysmic invasion of the country they anticipate). Fearing to live alone, she denied him psychiatric treatment or hospitalization. She took him to shooting galleries regularly where the two practiced at rifle ranges. The mother owned at least five semiautomatic rifles and several pistols. She gave Adam yet another for Christmas. Toward the end, Adam became increasingly bizarre, isolating himself in his room, blackening the windows, and communicating with his mother in their large home—only via computer. As best we can ascertain (from neighbor's accounts and the media), she was finally aware that he needed institutional care. This seemed to be the triggering event, since Adam would now be cut off from his only human contact (his father and brother having long since declined any involvement with him). It is thought that he chose to kill the elementary school children, because his mother once had a volunteer position at the school—leading him to suppose she loved those children more than she did him. The true dynamics can never be known for certain, since all the main persons are dead.

Eliot Rodger: Twenty-two at the time, he committed a mass murder in Isla Vista, California, near one of the University of California campuses, Eliot came from a prominent family: his father, a British filmmaker; his mother, a Malaysian research assistant for a film company. Though he got on well with his mother and his female teachers when he was quite young, he was notably disturbed emotionally by the time he was around eight—bullied by other students because of his social awkwardness and inability to relate to girls—though he craved their attention. He was diagnosed with Asperger's Syndrome, and for a time treated with medications usually prescribed for schizophrenia or manic depression. Gradually, because of his marked social handicaps and lack of empathy, he became progressively more furious at the girls who (understandably) rejected his advances; he became extremely misogynistic, isolate, and filled with murderous fantasies directed toward all women (setting aside some hatred, also, for normal men who were successful in their romantic ventures). On several occasions, when he was twenty, his jealousy led him to toss fluids at girls in cafes or parks. He developed great contempt for his "inferiors"—especially if they were adept in the dating scene. In his book-length Manifesto written shortly before the massacre, he wrote, for example: "How could an inferior, ugly Black boy be able to get a white girl and not me? I am beautiful, and I am half white myself. I am descended from British aristocracy. He is descended from slaves" (Manifesto, p. 84). Rodger was able to purchase a Glock-34 handgun in 2012 and two SIG-Sauer pistols in 2013. On the day of the massacre in May of 2014, he killed three students with a knife, and three others with the handguns: four male and two female victims—and then shot himself to death. Rodgers shares with Seung-Hui Cho and a number of other men with Asperger's—who have committed mass murder, spurred in part at least by their extreme social handicap and inability to make any connection with women. Rather than recognizing their disability, they blamed the women as being "hateful," deserving of being killed one and all.

Head-Injury-Induced Psychosis

Phil Garrido: Born in 1951 in Pittsburgh, California—a small town in the San Francisco Bay area, Phil was known as a "sweet, gentle, well-behaved child who loved making people laugh…bright, intelligent and polite" (Glatt 2010, p. 8). When he was 14, he borrowed his older brother's motorcycle without permission and took it for a spin. The motorcycle crashed minutes later and Phil was thrown to the ground, unconscious, sustaining a serious head injury that necessitated surgical removal of a subdural hematoma. Thereafter, his personality underwent a transformation—for the worse. He neglected his studies, seldom attended classes, let his hair grow long, and began to abuse marijuana and LSD—and to sell illegal drugs in order to pay for his illegal drugs. He got into a bad crowd, became preoccupied with pornography—and with fantasies of raping women. He also formed grandiose schemes, hoping to make millions of dollars, and told his father he could now speak with God. Phil would also lure young girls to a motel, dope them with barbiturates till they were unconscious, and then rape them. After several arrests for marijuana and LD, he raped a woman in Nevada for which he was arrested and sentenced to 50 years in prison. But the authorities there released him on parole after only 11 years. He then kidnapped 11-year-old Jaycee Dugard, sequestering her in a walled-off area that he constructed in his backyard. Phil, now married but without children by his wife, kept Jaycee imprisoned there for 18 years, siring two daughters by her: Angel and Starlit. During those years, which did not end until Jaycee and her daughters escaped in 2009, Phil was now a grossly psychotic man, often hallucinating the voices of angels, who fancied himself the leader of a new religion—and founder of his self-styled Church of God's Desire. Two years after Phil's arrest, he was sentenced to 431 years in prison for the kidnap, repeated rape, and unlawful confinement of Jaycee.

The number of violent crimes, including murder and serial sexual homicide, committed by men who had undergone a radical change of personality following a serious head injury, is quite large. Within the ranks of serial killers, for example, there are the dramatic cases of Fred and Rose West in the English Midlands (Sounes 1995) and Richard Starrett in the United States (Naifeh and Smith 1995). Fred West suffered two serious head injuries: the first when he fell from a motorcycle at age 16; the other, when at 19 he was pushed to the ground by a woman he was trying to molest sexually. He had become aggressive after the first injury, and also hypersexual and preoccupied with various unconventional approaches. Richard Starrett fell off a playground jungle gym twice around the ages of 7 and 10, becoming hypersexual afterwards and obsessed with rape fantasies (he also suffered headaches and bouts of dizziness as neurological sequelae of the brain damage).

Drug-Induced Psychosis

Jared Loughner: The only child of a working-class couple in Arizona, Loughner's life seemed unremarkable in his early years. He was described as "sweet and caring" by a former girlfriend in his mid-adolescence. But following the rejection by a girl he dated when he was 14 or 15, he began to abuse a whole menu of street drugs (in addition to alcohol), including marijuana, LSD, salvia divinorum, and psilocybin ("shrooms"—from a hallucinogenic mushroom). As a result, he underwent a transformation of personality. He became rude, paranoid, and spoke in riddles, uttered senseless comments, and developed sharp anti-government views. He was kicked out of classes at school, fired from jobs, shunned by former friends. He was particularly hostile toward US congressman, Gabrielle Giffords, all the more so when she gave no response to a senseless question he once posed to her at a meeting: "what is government if words have no meaning?" He began to conjure up assassination plots, and to load up on weapons, in preparation for his attack on the congressman. When she held a meeting for her constituents on January 8, 2011, Loughner approached and began firing. Before he was finally subdued by others who had come to listen, six people lay dead, 13 were wounded, and Gabrielle Giffords was shot in the head, critically wounded. Examined psychiatrically after his capture, he was considered a "paranoid schizophrenic," and declared not competent to stand trial (Conant and Martin 2011). After treatment with antipsychotic medications, competency was restored a year and a half later, at which time he was sentenced to life without parole. In retrospect, the schizophrenia in Loughner's case was not of the hereditary type (which was formerly true of most persons given that diagnosis), but rather of a secondary type in which abuse of psychotomimetic drugs can induce a schizophrenia-like clinical picture. The latter usually consists of the "positive" signs of the psychosis: delusions and hallucinations, but not the "negative" signs of emotional blunting and loss of volition. Cases such as Loughner's are often (and more correctly) labeled "schizophreniform"—indicating its resemblance to the hereditary condition (Stone, 2015a).

Herbert Mullin: Born in 1946 in the San Francisco Bay area, Mullin was raised in a middle class, nonabusive home. He was outgoing, friendly, and a good student. Shortly after his high school graduation, however, his best friend died in a car accident. He then began to abuse marijuana and LSD heavily. His behavior deteriorated and he became overtly psychotic. He was arrested on "drunk and disorderly" charges; also, for drug possession, dropped out of college, developed a violent temper, and was rejected by his girlfriend. In 1972, Mullin went on a killing spree, murdering 13 people over a 2-month span. What inspired the spree was a delusion in which he believed that a *big* disaster (he was thinking about an earthquake that might destroy Los Angeles) could be averted via a *minor* disaster—such as his murder spree. As he told the psychiatrist who interviewed him (and who wrote a book about the case: Dr. DT Lunde 1980), "We human beings throughout history have protected our continents from cataclysmic earthquakes by murder…In other words, a minor natural disaster avoids a major natural disaster." As for the number 13 of his murders, he alluded to the 12 gospels plus Jesus = 13. He also argued that Einstein had died on Mullin's birthday—which gave him a "dominant position in the reincarnation." Mullin's psychosis was attributed to his abuse of LSD, which led to a courtroom dispute after his capture: the defense arguing that he was legally insane; the prosecution, contending that he was psychotic but legally sane. The latter opinion prevailed, and Mullin was sentenced to life imprisonment.

Psychosis Not Otherwise Specified

Hadden Clark: Born in 1951, Clark came from an upper-class New England family, dating back to the Mayflower on his father's side, but now in a state of social decline (Havil 2001). Both his parents were alcoholics. They fought in front of the children, and the father had sex with a babysitter in front of Hadden when he was in his teens. The parents had wanted a girl, to which end they dressed him in girl's clothing and called him Kristen. Hadden showed cruelty early, killing and eviscerating cats and dogs. He was emerging as an effeminate homosexual, which his father, albeit having wanted a daughter, tried to "cure" him via beatings. For a time, Hadden worked as a cook, but was fired for his antisocial and weird behavior. He joined the Navy but was soon discharged as mentally unfit (Biondi and Hecox, 1992). He was given a diagnosis of paranoid schizophrenia eventually, but was first called "psychotic" and had been mocked because of his effeminacy and homosexuality. Clark then lived with his brother FGeoff, but was arrested for stealing women's underwear. Meantime, his elder brother Brad had been arrested for murdering a woman after biting off her breast and eating it. Hadden continued to pose as a woman, leading some, during his multiple psychiatric hospitalizations, to consider him a "multiple personality" with two "alters": Hadden and Kristin. He killed at least two women, and like his brother, also cannibalized their bodies. Arrested in 1992, he claimed to have killed as many as 13 or more. At trial he was adjudged mentally ill, psychopathic and "evil," and sentenced to 70 years in prison. In personality, he shows a mixture of schizoid (loner, no friends), sadistic, narcissistic, antisocial/psychopathic traits. The nature of the psychosis is not clear. He seemed not to have a formal thought disorder—which would have bolstered a diagnosis of schizophrenia. His father was manic depressive for whom lithium was prescribed, so it is possible that Hadden (and his elder brother) may have inherited "risk genes" for bipolar disorder. This in turn, complicated by his exposure to an extremely chaotic and violent family life, may have contributed to a psychosis that does not fit neatly into our standard nomenclature. He did not appear to have abused alcohol (as did the rest of his family) or drugs. One psychiatrist had said that Hadden's mental state is psychosis with questionable etiology, mentioning that Hadden told him that birds and squirrels talk to him and keep him company. This is suggestive of psychosis, but not one of a specific type. His homicidal propensities stemmed more, it would seem, from his early exposure to, and victimization from a violent family. His psychosis, whatever its nature, appears merely to have reduced his capacity to inhibit morally repugnant (including murderous) impulses.

Schizotypal Personality with Psychotic Episodes

James Holmes: The perpetrator of the mass murder at the Aurora, Colorado movie theater on July 20, 2012 was 24 at the time and had shortly before dropped out of university after failing a key examination. He had been born into an upper-middle-class California family: his father, a mathematician and scientist; his mother, a nurse. At age twelve, he began to decline socially, and had attempted suicide the year before. Even as a child, however, Holmes saw disturbing "visions," including flickers at the corners of his eye—which he imagined were fighting one another with weapons. He became obsessed with killing people from this time forward. Socially ill at ease, he alienated a girlfriend via his talk about wanting to kill people. One such girl recommended he get psychiatric help in January 2012, half a year before the massacre—but he declined. Earlier, while in high school, he was described as stubborn, uncommunicative, and socially inept. Yet he was academically brilliant, though odd in some of this ideas. He lectured to a class, for example, that he had developed a method for "changing the past." That would be a sure sign of thought disorder, but no one paid attention to it at the time. In college as well, he did brilliantly graduating ΦBK. He won a large scholarship to graduate school, where he studied neuroscience. But in 2012, his academic performance declined. He saw a psychologist briefly, to whom he spoke of his homicidal ideas. He wavered between thoughts of suicide and thoughts of murder, shifting to the latter after being rejected by a girl he had been dating. In the weeks before the massacre, he bought a pistol and a rifle—with no difficulty, since he had no record of previous arrests or psychiatric hospitalizations. Besides booby-trapping his apartment (in order to kill any policemen who chose to enter), he then picked the late performance at the movie theater for the massacre—so as to minimize killing children. While there, dressed as his comic book hero Batman, and dyeing his hair orange, he shot to death 12 people and wounded 70. During the psychiatric evaluation that followed his arrest, Dr. William Reid testified that Holmes was legally sane and met diagnostic criteria for schizotypal personality disorder. I had made the same assessment about Holmes during my lecture in Oslo to the Norwegian Psychiatric Association at the time of the sentencing of the Norwegian mass murderer, Anton Breivik (Stone 2012). Holmes met at least five criteria, sufficient to establish the diagnosis of schizotypal personality disorder: odd thought (his conviction he could direct his brain to change the past), odd speech, odd behavior (painting himself orange at the time of the murders), odd affect (piercing eyes, insincere smile, rigid faces), and absence of friends or confidantes. To avoid the death penalty, Holmes pled guilty and was sentenced to prison for life without parole. This personality disorder is considered as a condition within the schizophrenia "spectrum"; those who manifest it are prone, when under great stress, to suffer a temporary psychotic episode that would correctly be diagnosed at the time as schizophrenic. Drug abuse was not a factor in Holmes' breakdown. Many persons with this personality configuration have close relatives with frank schizophrenia, but no one in Holmes' immediate family appears to have suffered from any form of schizophrenia (Eliot, 2015).

Discussion

As the examples above indicate, psychotic homicidal offenders come in many forms and exhibit a wide variety of underlying motives and psychological conflicts. It is consistent with crime statistics in general that among psychotic persons who commit murder, men considerably outnumber women, as is the case with the larger nonpsychotic population. Women are not only less likely to murder, but when they do, their victims are more likely to be family members; only rarely, strangers. Men commit their acts of violence in both spheres: family, and the outside world. Mass murder is almost exclusively a male preserve (Stone 2015b). The typical mass murderer is a disgruntled male with paranoid personality traits—recently fired from a job or rejected by a lover or spouse (Fox and Levin, 2012). Only about 22% are in addition psychotic (as in the example of James Holmes above). Serial sexual homicide is a male-only phenomenon—apart from the only two women I am aware of who experienced orgasm while killing their numerous victims: the sixteenth century Hungarian Countess Erzsebet Báthory (Penrose 2006) and the Boston nurse, Jane Toppan (Schechter 2003) from the late nineteenth century. In my series of 168 serial killers about whom a full-length biography was written, only 12 (7%) could be considered psychotic (such as Robert Napper from the vignette above).

Many instances of infanticide, in contrast, are committed by women, a large proportion of whom are mentally ill. This is especially true in forensic hospital settings, where most of the women who had killed one or more children were either schizophrenic or manic depressive (Stone et al. 2005). The exception is neonaticide: many mothers who kill an infant immediately after birth are unwed but not psychotic and do so for reasons of poverty or to avoid embarrassment.

In forensic settings, schizophrenic men and women who have committed murder have usually killed one or two persons, often family members—such as the woman who hoped to "release" the good mother inside the external "bad" mother in the example above. Another such woman stabbed her grandmother 600 times—in the kind of "overkill" that is often a reflection of madness and ungovernable rage. A schizophrenic mother in California, LaShuan Harris, was answering the hallucinatory voice of God commanding her to toss her three children into the San Francisco Bay. Yet another, Otty Sanchez, decapitated her baby and ate its brain tissue—an act whose bizarre nature points to the likelihood of an underlying psychosis.

When homicides are committed by persons suffering from manic depression (particularly bipolar type 1) they have often been in a state of rage, though with less of the bizarre qualities seen in schizophrenic offenders. The mother, cited above, who stabbed her husband and two sons to death was simply in a state of rage; there was no element of "command hallucinations" urging her to act as she did. The same is true of another forensic patient: a mother who, in a state of depression and anger, stabbed to death her 6-year-old daughter to avenge her husband, who threatened to take the girl back to his country in the Middle East.

Regarding the impact of head injury in certain cases of adolescent or adult males who afterwards experience marked personality changes of a sort that heighten the risk of violent sexual crimes, there have been several recent studies of brain imaging that may shed some light on this otherwise puzzling phenomenon. As Adrian Raine has summarized, damage to key areas in the frontal lobes may have dramatic effects on social behavior. The medial prefrontal cortex, for example, subserves behavioral control and moral decision-making, empathy, and social judgment. The ventral prefrontal cortex, including the orbitofrontal cortex, mediates emotional regulation and impulse control (Raine p. 310). Persons like Phil Garrido and Fred West, cited above, probably suffered damage in these areas (their captures antedated the availability of such imaging studies); their sudden preoccupation with rape, and their diminished capacity to inhibit their newly emerging violent tendencies may have stemmed from frontal lobe damage sustained after their injuries. Other imaging studies focusing on pedophilia point to other brain regions that mediate sexual object choice (hetero- vs. homosexual; adults vs. children), such as certain limbic and other structures: the substantia nigra, caudate nucleus, anterior cingulate gyrus, the amygdala, the thalamic nuclei, and globus pallidus (Schiffer, Paul et al. 2008; Schiffer, Krueger et al. 2008). Damage to some of these structures may have significant explanatory value concerning the radical changes in sexual predilection and impulse control in the aftermath of severe frontal lobe and limbic area injury.

Although men with Asperger's type of autistic spectrum disorder rarely commit violent acts, let alone murder, the recent mass murders by such men have created unnecessary, though understandable, worries in the public. Usually the condition is a kind of *social* psychosis rather than the traditional *cognitive* psychosis of which schizophrenia is the standard-bearer. The ones who commit murder have been in the grips of paranoid beliefs—to the effect that others are "against" them, whether other boys or men who mock them because of their social awkwardness or girls who reject them (for the same reason). In trying to understand the rage that sometimes follows from these taunts and rejections, it is important to recognize how extraordinarily embarrassing it must be for a Asperger patient to *acknowledge* and then to *accept* that, in all likelihood, he will never be able to form or sustain a conventional intimate relationship or even to form and retain ordinary friendships with others. From my perspective as a psychoanalyst, it is understandable that in some instances, the "blame" would instead be deflected *away* from oneself and one's serious social deficiencies, and *onto those doing the rejection*: in the case of Eliot Rodgers or Seung-Hui Cho—"blameworthy" persons were the girls in their classrooms who were spooked by weirdness of those men. For most such autistic men, the answer is rather a retreat from social interaction and a quiet giving up of any hope for fulfillment in the social arena. But for the tiny minority—the answer is murder.

To summarize, the importance of psychotic homicidal offenders lay not so much in their frequency as in their impact. While it is not clear what precise percentage of all the murders in a given year—in the United States, for example—can be attributed to persons suffering from a psychosis, the number is small. As to mass murder, about 1% of the 16,000 murders per year (in recent years) stem from mass murder, but only about a fourth of that number result from the actions of psychotic persons; that is, about 40 deaths. The number lost to serial killers would be in the same range. In most European countries where gun ownership by citizens is infinitesimal compared with United States figures, these number would be smaller still. Mothers who kill a child beyond the first few days of life will often be found to suffer from mental illness: schizophrenia more often than manic depression, but again the total number is small (Resnick 1970; Friedman et al. 2005; Daly and Wilson 1988).

Similarly, small fractions pertain to the percentage of murders of other types committed by the mentally ill, the majority of who kill just one or two victims, as in the case of David Tarloff cited above. Vitali Davydov, a schizophrenic man of 20, for example, killed his psychiatrist Wayne Fenton in 2006. Another paranoid schizophrenic man, Bart Ross, killed the husband and mother of the female judge involved in his trial.

Among the 310 mass murderers (the majority of whom are from the United States) that I have studied, 33 had committed familicide (the murder of all their family members). Of these, eight were clearly mentally ill—with schizophrenia or delusional disorder (5) or psychotic depression (3).

But the *impact* of these murders outweighs their frequency. I believe, this is owing in great measure to the unpredictability and hence shock value in the community. Dr. Fenton, for example, could not have guessed that his young patient would suddenly rise out of his chair and pummel the doctor to death in his own office. In some instances of murder by mentally ill persons, it is the weirdness or unconventionality of the act that proves particularly frightening to the public—as in the case of Otty Sanchez, cited earlier, who decapitated her baby and cannibalized its brain tissue. This weirdness then leads to exaggerated fears within the community about the threat to public safety that the mentally ill people actually pose. As a result, some have advocated stern measures such as making the names of persons seeking psychiatric help more available to the authorities, curbing some of their civil rights, and so on. Such measures are statistically unwarranted and ineffective, as well as prejudicial to the rights of the mentally ill.

References

Alison, L. and Eyre, M. 2009. *Killer in the Shadows: The Monstrous Crimes of Robert Napper.* London: Penguin.

Biondi, R. and Hecox, W. 1992. *The Dracula Killer: The True Story of California's Vampire Killer.* New York: Pocket Books.

Blanco, J. I. (Ed.), *Murderpedia [an Internet encyclopedia of murderers].*

Burn, G. 1985. *Somebody's Husband, Somebody's Son. The Story of the Yorkshire Ripper.* New York: Viking.

Conant, E. and Martin, C. 2011. *Jared Loughner's Mental State.* Newsweek, Jan. 10.

Daly, M. and Wilson, K. 1988. Killing children. In: M. Daly and K. Wilson (Eds.), *Homicide.* New York: Aldine de Gruyter, pp. 61–93.

DSM-III. 1980. *Diagnostic and Statistical Manual of Psychiatric Disorders* (3rd ed.). Washington, DC: American Psychiatric Press.

Elliot, D. 2015. *Psychiatrist: Colorado Shooter Knew What He Was Doing*. Chicago, IL: Associated Press, May 29.

Erb, M., Hodgins, S., Freese, R., Müller-Isberner, R., and Jöckel, D. 2001. Homicide and schizophrenia: Maybe treatment does have a preventive effect. *Crim Behav Ment Health 11*, 6–26.

Esquirol. J.-E. 1838. *Des Maladies Mentales*. Paris: J-B Baillière.

Fox, J. A. and Levin, J. 2012. *Extreme Killing: Understanding Serial and Mass Murder*. London: Sage Publications.

Friedman, S. H., Horwitz, S. M., and Resnick, P. J. 2005. Child murder by mothers. *Amer J Psychiatry 162*, 1578–1587.

Glatt, J. 2010. *Lost and Found: The True Story of Jaycee Lee Dugard and the Abduction That Shocked the World*. New York: St. Martin's Paperbacks.

Havil, A. 2001. *Born Evil*. New York: St Martin's paperbacks.

Hodgins, S. 1993. The criminality of mentally-disordered persons. In: S. Hodgins (Ed.), *Mental Disorder and Crime*. London: Sage Publications, pp. 3–21.

Hodgins, S. 2009. Violent behavior among people with schizophrenia: A framework for investigations of causes, effective treatment, and prevention. In: S. Hodgins, E. Vidding, and A. Plodowski (Eds.). *The Neurobiological Basis of Violence: Science and Rehabilitation*. New York: Oxford University Press, pp. 43–64.

Hodgins, S., Viding, E., and Plodowski, A. 2009. *The Neurobiological Basis of Violence: Science and Rehabilitation*. New York: Oxford University Press.

Kaplan, J., Papajphn, G., and Zorn, E. 1990. *Murder of Innocence: The Tragic Life and Final Rampage of Laurie Dann*. New York: Warner Books.

Link, B., Andrews, H., and Cullen, F. 1992. The violent and illegal behavior of mental patients reconsidered. *Amer Sociol Rev 57*, 275–292.

Lunde, D. T. and Morgan, J. 1980. *The Die Song: A Journey into the Mind of a Mass Murderer*. New York: WW Norton.

McNiel, D. 1994. Hallucinations and violence. In: J. Monahan and H. J. Steadman (Eds.), *Violence and Mental Disorder: Developments and Risk Assessment*. Chicago: University of Chicago Press, pp. 183–202.

Monahan, J. 1993. Mental disorder and violence. In: S. Hodgins (Ed.). *Mental Disorder and Crime*. London: Sage Publications, pp. 287–302.

Morrall, P. 2000. *Madness and Murder*. London: Whurr Publishers.

Naifeh, S. and Smith, G. W. 1995. *A Stranger in the Family: A True Story of Murder, Madness, and Unconditional Love*. New York: Dutton.

Newton, M. 2006. *The Encyclopedia of Serial Killers* (2nd ed.). New York: Checkmark Books.

Penrose, V. 2006. *The Bloody Countess*. (tr. Of La Condeza Sangrienta by Alejandra Pizarnik) Solar Books.

Raine, A. 2013. *The Anatomy of Violence: The Biological Roots of Crime*. New York: Pantheon Books.

Resnick, P. J. 1970. Murder of newborns: A psychiatric review. *Amer J Psychiatry 126*, 58–64.

Rodger, E. undated. *My Twisted World: The Story of Eliot Rodger*. (downloaded from the Cloud of digitized information).

Schechter, H. 2003. *Fatal: The Poisonous Life of a Female Serial Killer*. New York: Pockeet Star Books.

Schiffer, B., Krueger, T., Paul, T., de Greiff, A., Forsting, M., Leygraf, N., Schedlowski, M., and Gizewski, E. 2008. Brain response to visual sexual stimuli in homosexual pedophiles. *J Psychiatry Neurosci 33*, 23–33.

Schiffer, B., Paul, T., Gizewski, E., Forsting, M., Leygfraf, N., Schedlowski, M., and Krueger, T. 2008. Functional brain correlates of heterosexual pedophilia. *Neuroimage 41*, 80–91.

Sounes, H. 1995. *Fred & Rose: The Full Story of Fred and Rose West and the Gloucester House of Horrors*. London: Warner Books.

Stone, M. H. 2012. Lecture and Power Point presentation: "Mad versus Bad" at the Norwegian Psychiatric Association, August 23rd.

Stone, M. H. 2015a. Marijuana and psychosis: The effects of adolescent abuse of marijuana and other drugs on a group of forensic psychiatric patients. *J Child Adol Behav* DOI: 10.4172/2375-4494.1000188.

Stone, M. H. 2015b. Mass murder, mental illness, and men. *Violence Gender 2*, 51–86.

Stone, M. H., Krischer, M., Dreher, J., and Steinmeyer, A. 2005. Infanticide in forensic mothers: An evolutionary perspective. *J Practical Psychiatry 11*, 35–45.

Swanson, J. W. 1994. Mental disorder, substance abuse, and community violence: An epidemiological approach. In: J. Monahan and H. J. Steadman (Eds.), *Violence and Mental Disorder: Developments and Risk Assessment*. Chicago: University of Chicago Press, pp. 101–136.

Swanson, J. W., Holzer, C. E., Ganju, V. K., and Jono, R. T. 1990. Violence and psychiatric disorder in the community: Evidence from the Epidemiological Catchment Area surveys. *Hosp Commun Psychiatry 41*, 761–770.

Taylor, P. J. 1993. Schizophrenia and crime: Distinctive patterns in association. In: S. Hodgins (Ed.), *Mental Disorder and Crime*. London: Sage Publications, pp. 63–85.

Taylor, P. J., Garety, P., Buchanan, A., Reed, A., Wessely, S., Ray, K., Dunn, G., and Grubin, D. 1994. Delusion and violence. In: J. Monahan and H. J. Steadman (Eds.), *Violence and Mental Disorder: Developments and Risk Assessment*. Chicago: University of Chicago Press, pp. 161–182.

Teplin, L. A., McClelland, G. M., and Abram, K. M. 1993. The role of mental disorder and substance abuse in predicting violent crime among released offenders. In: S. Hodgins (Ed.), *Mental Disorder and Crime*. London: Sage Publications, pp. 86–103.

Wallace, C., Mullen, P. E., and Burfgess, P. 2004. Criminal offending in schizophrenia over a 25 year period marked by deinstitutionalization and increasing prevalence of comorbid substance use disorders. *Amer J Psychiatry 161*, 716–727.

Wikipedia: https://en.wikipedia.org/wiki/Peter_Sutcliffe.

IV

Homicide Offenders in Special Populations

11 Battered Women Homicide Offenders

Joan Swart and Lenore E. A. Walker

Contents

Introduction 207
    Characteristics of Battered Women Homicide Offenders and Their Crimes 208
Cycles of Abuse and Psychological Trauma 209
    Stages of Battered Woman's Syndrome 209
    Cycle Theory of Violence 210
    Learned Helplessness 212
Features and Assessment of BWS 213
    Symptoms of BWS and Beliefs of the Victim 213
    Batterer Typology 214
    Assessment Protocols 216
Criminal Defenses Utilizing the BWS 221
    Admissibility of Evidence 222
    Case-Specific v. General Expert Testimony 223
    Justification v. Excuse Defenses 223
    The Issue of Imminence in Self-Defense 224
    The Problem of Syndrome Defenses 225
Recommendations for Handling Cases of Battered Women Who Kill 228
    Criminal Investigation and Interviewing 228
    Forensic Psychological Assessment 229
    Expert Testimony 229
    Clinical Treatment 230
References 230

Introduction

Battered woman syndrome (BWS) is a typical pattern, or patterns, of signs and symptoms of psychological and behavioral reactions after sustained abuse. From the outset it has to be emphasized that BWS is not an officially recognized distinct psychological disorder in the *American Psychiatric Association's Diagnostic and Statistical Manual of Mental Disorders* (DSM), but it is recognized in the World Health Organization's International Classification of Diseases (ICD). However, both of these diagnostic systems are used to assess signs and symptoms often associated with BWS and neither is it a legal defense per se. The presence of certain groups of signs and symptoms are explored to determine the likelihood that such abuse took place and the severity thereof for the purpose of establishing an underlying basis for intervention, treatment, and/or legal reasons. Although BWS itself is not a legal defense, per se, it may be used to demonstrate why someone needed to use self-defense or exculpation in criminal defense. Yet the term continues to be misunderstood and incorrectly applied as it is often interchangeably referred to as a psychological disorder and a legal defense.

"Colloquially known as 'battered woman syndrome', this psychological disorder (*sic*) is said to establish a causal relationship between the pattern of abuse suffered by the defendant, her psychological reactions to it, and her perception of her subsequent conduct" (McEwan, 2014, p. 152). BWS results from repeated exposure to forceful physical or psychological abuse from a partner (Walker, 2009), resulting in physical and mental harm that influences the victim's state of mind and decision making (Biggers, 2003). After enduring years of abuse, victims might feel fearful for their lives, leading them to engage in actions that may kill their partner. Such situations are the foundations of BWS as an element of defense. In many states, the legislative and case laws actually mention BWS as part of self-defense or other statutes. However, in most of those laws, BWS is defined as including the dynamics of a domestic violence relationship in addition to the resulting psychological signs and symptoms. This section discusses the characteristics and development of BWS in the context of female homicide offenders and the use of BWS as a legal defense at the hand of two case examples and the development of guiding case law.

According to the U.S. National Violent Death Reporting system, or NVDRS, about 80% of intimate partner-related homicides were perpetrated by a male offender against his female partner or ex-partner. Nearly 40% of these were homicide-suicides. It is estimated that one-in-three female homicide victims in the United States are murdered by a current or former partner each year. In addition, a significant number of the 6000 or so women who commit suicide in each year likely do so because of being abused by an intimate male partner—indications are that almost 30% were battered and more than 22% had at least one documented incident of domestic abuse in their records (Websdale, 2003). On the contrary, very few abused women end up committing acts that result in the death of their abusive partners.

Characteristics of Battered Women Homicide Offenders and Their Crimes

Although women commit only about 10% of overall homicides, the large majority of those involve women affected by domestic violence and abuse. Consequently, homicides committed by women are more consistent in characteristics and circumstances than those by male offenders. The killings most frequently take place in the home and involve little planning, follow sudden aggression or provocation by the victim, and there are no co-conspirators (Ogle and Jacobs, 2002). Female killers also tend to be more socially conforming in terms of gender roles and lifestyle expectations, and report enduring "insurmountable life pressures, depression, despair, and desperation" at the time of the offense (Ogle and Jacobs, 2002, p. 44).

The emotional and psychological injuries sustained by women who are victims of intimate partner violence have been recognized in the mental health field for almost 40 years. Although men also become victims, it is usually women who are most likely to be hurt through physical, sexual, and psychological abuse in domestic environments. Lenore Walker describes a "battered woman" as any woman "18 years of age or older, who is or has been in an intimate relationship with a man who repeatedly subjects or subjected her to forceful physical, sexual, and/or psychological abuse" (Beecher-Monas, 2007, p. 221). Although women are affected differently—some are inherently more resilient and there is a gamut of contextual permutations that impact on the interpersonal dynamics—there is a typical constellation of symptoms that often develop, which makes it difficult for victims to regain control of their lives. According to Walker et al. (2008), BWS can best be conceptualized as …

> A combination of posttraumatic stress symptomatology, including re-experiencing a traumatic event (i.e., battering episode), numbing of responsiveness, and hyperarousal, in addition to a variable combination of several other factors. These additional factors include, but are not limited to, disrupted interpersonal relationships, difficulties with body image, somatic concerns, as well as sexual and intimacy problems. (Walker et al., 2008, p. 42)

Female domestic killers are from a wide range of socioeconomic classes, and different races and cultures, although the situations of lower-class women and those from minority and other vulnerable groups are thought to favor the inherent oppression that most of these offenses are associated with. Therefore, social, cultural, structural, and situational variables all have significance in battered women who kill. According to Stack (1997), women in battered relationships are more likely to kill to survive, while men are more likely to kill their partners in a rage and then commit suicide. Younger people are more likely to be perpetrators and victims of domestic homicides, with the prevalence increasing as the age differential between partners increases (Websdale, 1999). Female intimate homicides are often preceded by an injury in the year before the incident, and support the notion that such acts are linked to defensive reactions resulting from prior abuse (Swatt and He, 2006). Compared to male intimate homicides, offenses committed by battered women are slightly less likely to involve substance use, and nearly three times more likely to use a knife than their male counterparts (Swatt and He, 2006). However, in instances ranging from 55% (Mann, 1996; Fox and Zawitz, 2006) to 80% (Walker, 1990), females used a firearm to commit intimate homicides, compared to 37% of males. This level depended mostly on the availability of a gun in the home, in which case it is usually the weapon of choice due to limited upper body strength of most women and close combat skills required to use a knife effectively.

Cycles of Abuse and Psychological Trauma

After experience of a traumatic event, there is a psychological and neurobiological cascade that are primarily designed to facilitate short-term coping and survival. Biologically, extraordinary stress hormone levels cause changes to the functioning of the pre-frontal cortex, hippocampus, and amygdala areas of the brain, also referred to as the H–P–A system. As a result, syndromal symptoms start to appear. After most instances of trauma, the disturbances naturally dissipate, some form of resolution is achieved, and psychological conditions return to the pre-event baseline.

However, when trauma is severe and/or repetitive, the victim is vulnerable, and lacks—or is prevented from accessing—supportive resources, traumatic symptoms worsen and become continuous. Soon functioning also deteriorates, and maladaptive coping emerges. The appearance of co-occurring disorders is typical, such as depression, anxiety, substance abuse, and bipolar and obsessive–compulsive disorders. After a period when no positive changes are made, the condition becomes chronic and effective intervention more challenging. In the case of sustained domestic abuse, four typical stages in the psychology of the victim are found in the development of BWS, namely (1) denial, (2) guilt, (3) enlightenment, and (4) responsibility (Skaine, 2015).

Stages of Battered Woman's Syndrome

In the denial phase the victim refuses to admit to herself, or anyone else, that she has been abused or that there is a problem in her relationship. In some cases of subtle emotional or psychological abuse she may not even be aware that there are intentional and systematic malevolent actions against her. She tends to justify and minimize the actions, seeks excuses for the abuser's behavior, and firmly believes that it will never happen again. After a while, in the second phase, guilt sets in. She now acknowledges that there is a problem, but blames herself for being responsible, and therefore accepts that she deserves the punishment because of personal defects or being unable to meet expectations. It is vital to recognize that, for many reasons including obligations, dependency, and shame, many women find it difficult to move on from this stage, thereby remaining stuck in an abusive cycle that becomes ever more intense. The nature of the cycle of abuse is such that it forms and sustains an emotional bondage between abuser and victim. In the process, the victim reconciles her pain and disharmony by adopting beliefs and attitudes that are in harmony with her situation, changing perceptions about her partner's abusive behaviors, and changing her own behavior to match her beliefs and attitudes and minimize the disruption. However, their coping strategies are doomed to fail and take a high toll as it is not sustainable.

At some time, for most women, a sense of awareness sets in. The cognitive dissonance becomes unbearable and she starts to realize that her continued feelings and experiences of discomfort and disharmony are incompatible with her acceptance and justification of her partner's behavior, and her loyalty and hope that there will be positive change. It becomes increasingly difficult to adapt her beliefs and behaviors to accommodate her subconscious fears. She becomes unable to reconcile their thoughts and actions any longer and starts to appreciate the fact that no one deserves to be abused and battered. She realizes that such behavior is not justified and that her partner has a serious problem. However, for various reasons, she is not yet ready to abandon hope and continues to try to keep the relationship intact. It may be for the sake of her marriage, her children, cultural expectations, financial restraints, uncertainty, fear, or psychological dependency. She still has an inkling of hope for future change, but starts to realize the improbability of it and the risk that she faces.

In stage four, she knows that her partner has a serious problem that will not go away and that only he can fix. She understands that nothing she does or says will help her abuser or change his behavior. She is ready to choose to take the necessary steps to leave her abusive partner. At this time, the risk of lethal violence typically heightens. The woman prepares to leave the relationship or take other protective measures such as an order of protection or reporting the abuse to authorities. In the presence of certain circumstances or factors this can cause a sudden escalation of violence that can become deadly, especially in the presence of weapons, excessive use of substances, and antisocial behaviors. For the battered woman it may generate a fight-or-flight response. Recognizing the increasing danger to her life, when she is prevented from leaving, her state of mind may induce measures of self-defense. This may include the resolve to act when attacked again, or even to strike preemptively or preventatively, as she is at a physical disadvantage in an attack situation.

It is important to note that these stages should only be used as a guideline to help understand the dynamics and psychological and emotional progress of many abusive relationships. As such, it is a broad generalization that has not been qualified by scientific evidence. The stages should not be used in the legal sense to confirm guilt by pointing at atypical behavior. For example, many women do not feel guilt that it is their fault—rather, they wish they could have done something to help the batterer stop his violence but are clear that it is his problem—not theirs.

Cycle Theory of Violence

The typical cycle of violence within an individual person's pattern of abuse encompasses the time between the batterer's threat to kill or cause bodily harm to a victim and her behavioral and psychological responses. According to Walker (2009), there are three stages that tend to progress and repeat to form an increasingly destructive spiral, namely "(1) tension-building accompanied with rising sense of danger, (2) the acute battering incident, and (3) loving-contrition" (Walker, 2009, p. 91). The third stage, also sometimes referred to as the honeymoon phase, is sometimes further divided into two phases: reconciliation and calm (or "pretend normal") (Haley and Braun-Haley, 2003; Skaine, 2015).

Each completed sequelae is often more disruptive and harmful than the one before. Although the cycle is not confined to heterosexual relationships, marriage, and dating, and does not always lead to physical abuse, the concept is widely used in domestic violence programs. The cycle usually progresses in the following order and will continue until it is stopped, mostly by the survivor completely abandoning the relationship, by some form of intervention, or, in a few but too many cases, by lethal action. According to the FBI crime reports, in total about 1300 spouses, girlfriends, and boyfriends are murdered by their intimate partners in the United States each year. This underscores the importance of understanding and being able to raise awareness and identify at-risk persons in time to prevent such outcomes.

1. *Tension-building phase.* There is a buildup of minor abusive incidents, such as name-calling, emotional threats, and verbal outbursts in which the victim becomes hyper-vigilant to her abuser's cues and attempts to change her behavior accordingly. The tension builds and there is a breakdown of communication. The batterer expresses his dissatisfaction and hostility, but remains controlled. The victim becomes confused and fearful and tries to placate the abuser and to meet his perceived expectations. She does what she thinks might please him and tries to calm him down so as not to upset him further. There may be small incidents of violence that are quickly terminated (McMahon, 1999), and to which the victim tries not to respond. During this stage, the victim often rationalizes that they might have brought the abuse on themselves (Biggers, 2003). She might manage to hold him back from escalation for varying amounts of time, which contributes to the unpredictable response-outcome pattern that is instrumental in creating learned helplessness. Unrealistic beliefs that she has some control may be reinforced (Walker, 2009). This is a critical phase as it establishes anticipatory anxiety that erodes the victim's sense of self-value, control, and emotional balance. Such psychological effects of an abusive relationship are often more devastating and debilitating over the longer term than physical injuries sustained as it gradually shifts to a chronic condition.

2. *Acute battering incident.* The second stage is where the severe or potentially lethal violent battering incident occurs, generally accompanied by psychological abuse (Walker, 2009). When the tension continues to escalate in the first phase, the victim is eventually unable to maintain the illusion of control. She is exhausted from the continued stress and becomes more fearful. Noticing her frightened withdrawal, the abuser becomes more oppressive and bold. By an uncontrollable discharge of tensions that have been building up, the batterer may only need a small tipping point to enter a blind rage and physically attack the victim (Cipparone, 1987; Walker, 2009). Usually an external event

or internal state of the abuser triggers the incident. It may be a response to loss of control (real or perceived), unmet dependency needs, fears, anxiety, frustrations, and threats to self-esteem—both inside and outside the home. The tensions that have built up in the first phase are not sustainable and release is sought by confirming physical control and subjection of the victim—who is the subject of the abuser's rage or a vulnerable substitute. As a result he experiences the psychological satisfaction of power, superiority, dominance, and entitlement. The physical aggression is typically accompanied by a barrage of verbal insults and threats. Most injuries occur during the second phase, including defensive injuries, and it is also the time that law enforcement becomes involved and visits are made to the emergency room shortly afterward. The phase is concluded when the battering stops, and there is a sharp reduction in tension, which, together with the satisfaction that the batterer experiences, and the victim's relief that the attack is over, produces a natural reinforcing effect with the infusion of stress hormones. For the batterer, the violence is both satisfying and useful. The victim is reminded that there is no out, and that the only alternative is to hope that the cycle does not get to that stage again. It is also during or closely before an acute battering incident that most homicides committed by the abuse victim take place, either in direct self-defense, or in anticipation of another serious, and possibly lethal attack.

3. *Loving-contrition*. In the third stage, the batterer is remorseful, promises never to harm the woman again, and uses his charm to make his promises believable (Walker, 2009). He displays kindness, shower her with gifts and special treats, and may genuinely believe that he will not go to those lengths again. Needing to believe her partner's remorse and resolve, the woman's hope is renewed that it will not happen again and that he has come to his senses and will change. The love that there is, is rekindled and she is reminded of the good times during their courtship and before the abuse started. According to Walker (2009), "loving-contrition behavior" (p. 95) is sometimes not present, but as the tension and violence is absent, the victim experiences a respite. If there is not a return to such a loving-contrition baseline and the perception of tension and danger remains high, it is a sign that the cycle is in an advanced state of repeated escalation and the risk of a lethal incident is even higher.

4. *Calm phase*. Although not part of Walker's cycle of violence, and therefore not easily distinctively separated from the loving-contrition behavior of the third phase, the calm phase can be seen as an extension of the loving-contrition phase. Whether there are signs of loving-contrition or only a relief from serious incidents of abuse, the situation has stabilized and some sense of calm has been restored. Both may be at their best behavior, but expectations are often too high and unrealistic. When expectations are not met, the cracks start to show again. The abuser feels the need to reassert his dominance, possibly sparked by feelings of insecurity that are resurfacing. Soon, the victim may begin to feel uncomfortable again. Rewards and appeasing behavior dwindle, while threats and coercion increase. Having been able to restrain himself to this stage, possibly meeting some promises made after the previous battering incident, the abuser abandons his peaceful and kind approach. He blames his partner for his dissatisfaction. Conflicts arise, which lead again into another tension building phase (Figure 11.1).

The cycle of abuse repeats over time and becomes an integral part of the dynamic of the BWS. The duration of the cycle and its stages are not the same for all abusive relationships; nor are the behaviors and patterns that take place in each. Yet, the cycle is reinforcing and self-sustaining by the rewards and dependency that are intrinsic in abusive relationships. Walker (1988) argues: "These patterns lead to an intensity in the relationship, with participants always expecting to be overwhelmed by the rapidity of the abusive acts, yet also reinforced by the rewards in the third phase of the cycle" (p. 141). However, as the potential for lethality increases, the cycle becomes unsustainable and it becomes progressively an issue of survival for the victim. In the context of battered women who end up killing their partners, it is important to explore the progression and nature of their individual cycle of abuse, thereby understanding unique demands placed on the victim and her perception of the level and imminence of the danger that she faced. In a study based on 1000 battered wives, Bowker (1998) found that victims utilize one or more of several coping strategies to manage the threat against them: talking, extracting promises, nonviolent threatening, hiding, passive defense, avoidance, counter-violence, and seeking formal and informal help and support. Due to the unique circumstances of each individual case, not all may be available or possible to pursue. It is when other options largely run out

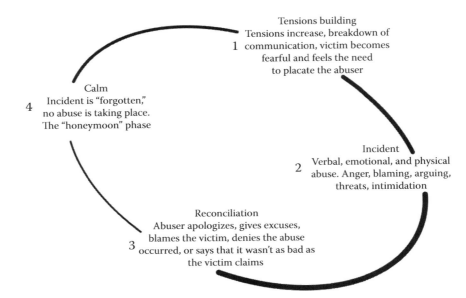

Figure 11.1 Cycle of abuse.

that counter-violence becomes a viable measure. Bowker also conceptualized four common patterns that diverge from the typical cycle of violence:

1. In some cases battering remains stable over a longer term. There is some form of restraint and stability present that prevents the need for escalation and incidents are likely less severe and less frequent.

2. In other cases, acute battering is less severe, and the contrition state is diminished or absent. It is likely that the woman is completely controlled, obedient, and isolated. The abuser does not perceive the need to execute a serious physical attack, or is able to exert some self-control.

3. Potential lethal levels of acute battering followed by contrition occur, but are not sustainable over repeated cycles. Contrition disappears as time passes and the tension becomes chronic and unbearable for the victim as she abandons hope of change.

4. Once an acute battering stage is reached, it remains at lethal levels. It is also not sustainable and various outcomes are likely in the shorter and medium term, including death and/or suicide, separation, or criminal justice intervention.

Another psychological phenomenon that influences the victim's decision making in the cycle of abuse is learned helplessness. In many cases, her motivation to escape the abuse is countered by a perception that it is not possible to do so.

Learned Helplessness

The theory of learned helplessness was first developed by Martin Seligman and his team who conducted experiments in 1967 where dogs were trapped in cages and given inescapable random shocks. After a while, the dogs stopped attempting to leave the cage even at times when escape routes were made available, leading researchers to argue that they have lost motivation to change their situation.

Walker (2009) analogized this condition to those that battered women find themselves in as their motivation to respond to acts of abuse diminishes over time. As such, learned helplessness became another psychological theory associated with BWS and the cycle of abuse that they are subjected to (McMahon, 1999). Learned helplessness occurs when a woman realizes that she is unable to prevent being battered after repeated cycles and escalations of violence left her feeling helpless and without hope and will to change her situation and fate (Walker, 2009). Perceiving no viable alternatives, she feels forced to endure the abuse, rather than avoiding subsequent incidents, even if they are escapable. In an important sense, she attempts to trade escape skills for skills to lower the level and intensity of the violence. As such, she is often taking action to protect herself but she rightfully recognizes that escape will be more dangerous than staying and coping with the abuse.

This is one explanation offered to the inevitable question when dealing with a victim of abuse—why does the victim often stay or keep going back to the abuser? When the victim perceives that their behavior has no effect on the abusive environment, they also invariably tend to become apathetic, depressed, and unwilling to try previous or new behavior (Engel, 2007). As part of his threats and controlling behavior, an abuser will often tell a victim that there is nothing that she can do to resist or escape, and it becomes a powerful perception and demotivation where future violence is accepted as inescapable. Breaking free and recovering from learned helplessness can be an arduous process but once the woman is able to identify her reinforcers, those behaviors in the loving-contrition phase that keeps her believing he really will change and sees her partner's manipulative behavior for what it really is, she is able to break free from learned helplessness. In this sense, the term learned helplessness is not an ultimate state, and even Seligman has focused instead on learned optimism or positive psychology as the way to break the cycle. Nevertheless, without solid resolve and courage, the possibility of freedom, together with the onslaught of decisions that have to be made, can overwhelm and condition victims to stay at their abuser's side—literally and figuratively.

Nonetheless, in legal contexts, the concept of learned helplessness and its effect on an abuse victim is often viewed as a psychological pabulum created to excuse women who kill their partners, especially without an immediate lethal threat present. Criticists have pointed out that the passivity observed among victims of abuse may be instrumental behaviors that are utilized to minimize the risk of violence, instead of being truly helpless (Dutton, 2009). By intentionally using passive behavior, battered women hope to stay safe. As the violence increases it is possible that both passive (placating) and active (resisting) may increase. Although seemingly passive or not taking any action, they may still actively expend effort to reduce the risk of violence and abuse to themselves and their children. These strategies can only be understood in the context of the individual woman, her partner, their relationship, and their environmental parameters.

This leads to another criticism of the theory of learned helplessness and BWS: the concept of a "syndrome," the inconsistency of effects across individual battered women, and the danger of stereotyping and excluding those who do not fit the perceived type. These issues are discussed further in the paragraph about the perils of syndrome evidence in legal application. Nevertheless, despite the concerns, learned helplessness manages to explain in general terms why many battered women see no viable option other than to stay with their abusive partners, and should highlight the fact that there are indeed for many too little support, and too much ignorance, apathy, and doubt from outside to provide safe alternatives.

Features and Assessment of BWS

The definition of a syndrome is a set of medical and psychiatric signs and symptoms that are correlated with each other, and with a specific disease or pathology. It is assumed that the collection of signs and symptoms is distinct in the context of their combination and underlying cause than by chance or any other circumstance. In the case of battered women it is the physical and psychological condition of a person who has suffered emotional, physical, and sexual abuse from another person, most likely a romantic partner.

Symptoms of BWS and Beliefs of the Victim

As battered women suffer from chronic stress and trauma, the syndrome has features similar to posttraumatic stress disorder (PTSD), but the intimacy and longevity of the abuse also present in other ways. According to Walker (2006), BWS consists of the following symptoms:

1. Re-experiencing the battering as if it were recurring even when it is not

2. Attempts to avoid the psychological impact of battering by avoiding activities, people, and emotions

3. Hyperarousal or hypervigilance

4. Disrupted interpersonal relationships

5. Body image distortion or other somatic concerns

6. Sexuality and intimacy issues

7. Cognitive confusion, attention deficits, and lack of concentration

Additionally, the repeated cycles of abuse shape and strengthen the following dysfunctional beliefs of the victim (Walker, 2009):

1. The woman believes that the violence was or is her fault.

2. The woman has an inability to place responsibility for the violence elsewhere.

3. The woman fears for her life and/or her children's lives.

4. The woman has an irrational belief that the abuser is omnipresent and omniscient.

When these symptoms and cognitive beliefs are present in the presence of escalating violence that may seem to approach lethal levels, the victim's perception of the lack of options and support is amplified. She sees no reasonable chance of escape as her dependency and his threats and behavior lock her into a life-threatening situation. Accordingly, Browne (1989) noted seven factors that are prevalent with women who have killed their abusers compared to those who had not killed (Ogle and Jacobs, 2002, p. 48):

1. An increased frequency of abuse

2. Frequent intoxication and drug abuse

3. High level of seriousness to injuries

4. Increased seriousness of sexual abuse

5. High levels of isolation of the victim

6. The existence of threats to kill

7. Failed attempts by the victim to leave or utilize outside assistance that caused feelings of hopelessness

This is an important distinction as it provides the basis to understand the cognitive perception of a battered woman who is unable to see another outcome apart from death—her own or her partner's. By exploring and assessing these factors in an abusive relationship, the risk of lethal violence from the victim's perspective can be determined both retrospectively and prospectively.

Batterer Typology

Examining the characteristics of the batterer is also useful to determine the risk that was likely presented to the victim. Although samples of men who are violent and abusive in relationships are heterogeneous, subtypes of batterers have been identified to assist with intervention, risk assessment, and forensic decision making. Batterer subtypes are classified among three descriptive dimensions: (1) the severity and frequency of the domestic battering incidents, (2) the generality of the man's violence, and (3) the batterer's psychopathology and personality disorder characteristics (Holtzworth-Munroe, 2008). Using these three dimensions, three subtypes of batterers have been identified, namely family-only batterers, dysphoric/borderline batterers, and generally violent/antisocial batterers.

1. *Family-only batterers.* This group is predicted to be the least violent of the domestic batterers. They are believed to engage in the least amount of violence in- and outside the home, as well as the lowest levels of psychological and sexual abuse against their partners. They have little or no psychopathology and incidents are infrequent and contextual. Abusive events are related to a combination of stress (personal and/or relationship, financial, work, and other responsibilities), and lower level risk factors (lack of social and relationship skills, occasional substance use, and domestic violence in

the childhood home) (Holtzworth-Munroe, 2000). For these men, abusive behavior is triggered by occasional high-stress situations and they feel guilt and remorse afterwards. They tend to have more liberal sex role attitudes and they generally do not justify violence.

2. *Dysphoric/borderline batterers.* This group of men typically has attachment issues that stem from a childhood of parental neglect and rejection. As a result they have difficulty forming a secure and trusting adult attachment with a romantic partner. They can be very jealous and engage in obsessive behavior because of their dependence and fear of losing their partners. Their possible borderline personality traits cause impulsive and unstable behavior, which may result in violence when angry and frustrated. They tend to have high levels of depression, especially when feeling uncertain and stressed, which may lead to substance use, and violent and suicidal behavior. They have relatively conservative attitudes toward the roles of women and can become extremely jealous and reactive aggressive when their expectations are not met or when they perceive that their relationship is threatened. In some cases this may result in lethal violence, sometimes with psychotic aspects, and is often followed by suicide.

3. *Generally violent/antisocial batterers.* This group perpetrates the highest level and frequency of domestic violence. Their antisocial or psychopathic tendencies include impulsive and high-risk behavior, a lack of empathy and remorse, a pathological need for power and control, and a rigid expectation of women's sex roles. Their personality style is likely rooted in a history of violence and delinquency from their parental homes, and they associate with deviant peers and criminal activities outside the home. They have hostile attitudes toward women and other vulnerable groups and justify violence as acceptable to achieve their own goals. Relationship violence is a part of their antisocial lifestyle and general aggressive tendencies. Of the three batterer types, their domestic abuse leads to the highest level of victim injuries, which is most often preceded and exacerbated by substance use and problems with the law.

A summary of the typical characteristics of batterers from the three subgroups is presented in Table 11.1, as adapted from Holtzworth-Munroe and Stuart (1994). The distinction between the three groups highlights the fact that batterers from the GVA group are more likely to commit sustained serious and lethal violence against a partner, is less likely to commit to treatment or accept an intervention (or resistance), and will probably not cease the abusive behavior unless the women is supported to safely leave the relationship. Another analogy made by Gottman and Jacobson (2007) is the characterization of male batterers as pit bulls and cobras. The cobra is quiet and focused before striking unexpectedly, while the pit bull's fury smolders and burns before attacking ferociously, losing control in the process. "Pit bulls confine their monstrous behavior to the women they love, acting out of emotional dependence and a fear of abandonment. Pit bulls are the stalkers, the jealous

Table 11.1 Male Batterer Typologies and Their Characteristics

Characteristic	Family-Only	Dysphoric/Borderline	Generally Violent/Antisocial
Severity of partnership violence	Low	Moderate-high	Moderate-high
Emotional and sexual abuse	Low	Moderate-high	Moderate-high
Extra-familial violence	Low	Low-moderate	High
Criminal behavior, legal involvement	Low	Low-moderate	High
Personality disorder	None or passive/dependent	Borderline or schizotypal	Antisocial or psychopathy
Substance abuse	Low-moderate	Moderate	High
Depression	Low-moderate	High	Low
Anger	Moderate	High	Moderate
Parental violence	Less likely	Mixed	More likely
Parental style	Discipline or rejection	Insecure or absent	Physically abusive
Juvenile delinquency	Less likely	Internalized	More likely
Attachment	More stable and committed	Insecure and dependent	Unstable and uncommitted
Remorse and empathy	Moderate	Low-moderate	Low
Anger proneness	Mixed	Tendency to overreact	Low
Problem-solving	Negotiation	Obsessive tendencies	Violence and intimidation
Attitudes toward women	Most liberal sex role attitudes	Relatively conservative sex role attitudes	Most rigid and conservative sex role attitudes
Attitudes toward violence	Not justified	Sometimes justified	Permissible and justified

husbands and boyfriends who are charming to everyone except their wives and girlfriends" (Newberger, 2000, p. 161). They monitor the woman's every move and see betrayal in everything she does, which infuriates them as they feel they are the victims. The cobra type does not have the same level of emotional dependence but they crave dominance and expect submission from their partners. They have antisocial tendencies and are likely to be aggressive toward others as well. For them, violent behavior is triggered when they believe their dominance is being challenged. They use violence as a tool to establish and maintain complete control. They are similar to the GVA type in the Holtzworth-Munroe and Stuart classification, while the pit bull type shares similarities, especially the unstable dependence factor, and obsessive and paranoid tendencies with the dysphoric/borderline type. Assessing the personality type of the batterer and his behavior is useful to determine the risk of serious and lethal violence, both in retrospect or future likelihood.

Appreciating that BWS is a group of signs and symptoms most associated with domestic abuse and violence that contain some heterogeneity among victims, it is advisable to explore psychological and behavioral characteristics of both abuser and victim, as well as their relationship, to ascertain the likely course and risk of lethal violence. As the most common evidence used for BWS involves the principles of "cycle of violence" and "learned helplessness," the presence and status of these processes are examined in each case to determine the woman's most likely state of mind, including perceptions and beliefs, before or after lethal violence occurred (Walker, 2009). This is best achieved by following a systematic and comprehensive protocol that includes clinical inquiry and psychological testing.

Assessment Protocols

As BWS is not a singular or homogeneous condition, assessment protocols have to be sufficiently broad and robust to cover a broad but individualized overview of the woman's functioning, history, and battering relationship. Therefore, a battery of tests is used in order to assess the myriad of areas that establish such a relationship, focusing on cross-cultural similarities in body distortion, PTSD symptoms, and power, control, and sexuality issues. The protocol favored by Lenore Walker, leading domestic violence expert, includes the following assessment procedures, in order of administration: (1) Battered Woman Syndrome Questionnaire-3, BWSQ-3, (2) Revised Adult Attachment Scale, (3) Derogatis Interview for Sexual Functioning, (4) Objectified Body Consciousness Scale, (5) Detailed Assessment of Posttraumatic Stress, and (6) Trauma Symptom Inventory. These assessment procedures combined, on average, take approximately three hours to accurately complete. In addition to these instruments, the Personality Assessment Inventory (PAI) is often used to explore nuances of trauma-based psychopathology. In the self-report 344-item questionnaire statements are rated by the respondent with a 4-point scale (1—"Not true at all," 2—"Slightly true," 3—"Mainly true," and 4—"Very true"). It shows good convergence with other personality tests including the Minnesota Multiphasic Personality Inventory (MMPI-2), but is considered more cost-effective and relevant to explore the nuanced effects of trauma exposure.

In some cases, the Wechsler Adult Intelligence Scale (WAIS) is used to evaluate how the woman's emotional status impacts on her cognitive abilities and judgment. A lethality assessment is also done by identifying dynamic and static risk factors present and the nature of the battering incidents in order to determine the protection required for the victim or her perceived need for self-protection at any time.

> *BWSQ-3.* The BWSQ-3 is a semi-structured interview with both quantitative and qualitative contents, in which participants are asked questions regarding their history of abuse in childhood and adulthood, current functioning, trauma symptoms, and body image. Included in the qualitative analysis are the women's narrative experiences of battering in general and descriptions of four specific incidents (i.e., first, worst, most recent, and typical). The narratives are examined for themes of power and control, cycle of violence, and learned helplessness (Walker et al., 2008).
>
> *Revised Adult Attachment Scale.* The RAAS is a self-report that consists of 18 items scored on a 5-point Likert scale ranging from "not at all characteristic of me" to "very characteristic of me." Three adult attachment styles are measured, namely Secure (high scores on Close and Depend subscales, low score on Anxiety subscale), Anxious (high score on Anxiety subscale, moderate scores on Close and Depend subscales), and Avoidant (low scores on Close, Depend, and Anxiety subscales). According to research by Walker (2009), battered women predominantly exhibited an avoidant attachment style, with a secure attachment style the least likely.
>
> *Derogatis Interview for Sexual Functioning.* The DISF is a brief semi-structured interview designed to measure the quality of a person's sexual functioning. The 26 interview items are arranged into five

domains of sexual functioning, namely Sexual Cognition/Fantasy, Sexual Arousal, Sexual Behavior/Experience, Orgasm, and Sexual Drive/Relationship. The total score summarizes the quality of sexual functioning across all domains. There is also a self-report version, the DISF-SR, which matches the DISF interview on an item-for-item basis (Derogatis, 1997).

Objectified Body Consciousness Scale. The OBCS has 24 items that are scored on a 7-point Likert scale ranging from "strongly disagree" to "strongly agree." Three scales are scored, namely (1) surveillance (viewing the body as an outside observer), (2) body shame (feeling shame when the body does not conform), and (3) appearance control beliefs (McKinley and Hyde, 1996). Among battered women body image problems are linked to their low self-esteem and have a powerful influence of their thoughts, feelings, and behaviors (Russo and Pirlott, 2006). According to Walker (2009), most battered women reported being never/rarely satisfied with their unclothed physical appearance (61%), never/rarely having knowledge that their weight is appropriate (63%), and often/always think their stomach is too big (68%). Almost half (43%) of battered women occasionally, often, or always restrict their food intake. Results also reveal that physical, sexual, and emotional abuse produce similar distortions in body image.

PTSD Assessment. A comprehensive PTSD assessment is conducted according to the diagnostic criteria stipulated by the *Diagnostic and Statistical Manual of Mental Disorders*, Fifth Edition (DSM-5; American Psychiatric Association, 2013), or the *World Health Organization's International Classification of Diseases*, 10th Revision (ICD-10). Criteria include the presence of a stressor, functional impairment, and symptoms such as re-experiencing, avoidance, amnesia, numbing, and arousal from three symptom clusters, namely intrusive recollections, avoidant symptoms, and hyperarousal symptoms. In addition to the Structured Clinical Interview for DSM-5 (SCID-5), the PTSD Checklist (PCL) and Trauma Symptom Inventory (TSI) are the two most widely used self-report instruments to assess posttraumatic effects (Elhai et al., 2005).

Trauma Symptom Inventory. Walker's research has found that three clinical criteria for PTSD (re-experiencing the trauma, high arousal, and emotional numbing and avoidance) are linked to BWS (Walker, 2009). The TSI-2 has 136 questions that takes 20 minutes to complete and is used in the evaluation of acute and chronic posttraumatic symptomatology related to various types of traumatic events and experiences. It utilizes three validity scales, mainly to identify malingering—response level, atypical response, and inconsistent response—as well as 10 clinical scales—anxious arousal, depression, anger/irritability, intrusive experiences, defensive avoidance, dissociation, sexual concerns, dysfunctional sexual behavior, impaired self-reference, and tension reduction behavior, which inform the specific presentation of trauma symptoms. Women from domestic violence populations typically have elevated scores (above 60) on the dysfunctional sexual behavior, tension reduction behavior, intrusive experience, and defensive avoidance scales, while scoring lowest on the sexual concerns, anger/irritability, and anxious arousal scales (Walker, 2009). Saunders (1994) also found that nightmares, intrusive memories of the abuse, avoiding reminders of the abuse, and hyperarousal were the most common PTSD symptoms among battered women.

Detailed Assessment of Posttraumatic Stress. The DAPS is a self-report instrument consisting of 104 items that assesses peri- and posttraumatic symptoms and associated features related to a specific traumatic event. According to the developers, it provides a tentative diagnosis of PTSD or acute stress disorder that can be confirmed by a clinical interview (Briere, 2001). The DAPS includes three PTSD symptom clusters (Reexperiencing, Avoidance, and Hyperarousal) and three associated features of posttraumatic stress (Trauma-Specific Dissociation, Suicidality, and Substance Abuse). This measure has good sensitivity (0.88) and specificity (0.86) with respect to a clinician-administered PTSD assessment (Briere and Scott, 2015).

Minnesota Multiphasic Personality Inventory. Despite the fact that many experts consider the MMPI-2 inadequate to reliably assess PTSD without supporting evidence, it is frequently used in court for this purpose, of which the following case study is one example (Butcher et al., 2008). As such, a potential for bias in PTSD assessments is introduced, which raises questions about its reliability and admissibility in court. Keeping these issues in mind, research has shown that although many women do not show psychopathology on the MMPI-2 test, elevation on scales 4, 6, and 8 is often found, which represents a high level of family discord, fear, feeling threatened, and disruptions in their boundaries or reality testing (Kaser-Boyd, 2004). This is similar to profiles found in paranoid schizophrenia, PTSD, and other forms of trauma-related conditions. Conversely, battered women tend to have lower scores on ego strength and dominance (Barnett et al., 2011). Overall, battered women who kill their abusers have higher elevations. Furthermore, the MMPI-2 is particularly useful in detecting underlying anxiety and depression in women whose behavioral coping style may mask such problems, which is a common issue with battered women (Roberts, 1996). The Harris-Lingoes subscales are used to interpret clinical scale elevations more accurately—in particular, elevation is often found on the Family Discord subscale (Kaser-Boyd, 2004). Interpreters must also consider that profiles of battered women may vary by reflecting differences in premorbid adjustment.

Wilson and Walker (1990) reported that Scale 2 may capture the PTSD symptom of emotional numbing; Scale 4 may capture the emotional detachment, alienation, or anger seen in cases of interpersonal violence; Scale 6 measures the hypervigilance to danger; and Scale 8 may reflect intrusive reminders of the trauma, or profound vulnerability and fragmentation. Kahn et al. (1993) found that the supplementary scales MAC-R, Mt, PK, and PS were also often elevated in MMPI-2 profiles of battered women, while scales 2 and 7, which are often associated with depression, anxiety, and other forms of subjective distress, were not consistently elevated. Battered women, based on MMPI-2 results, may also appear to be suffering from a variety of psychopathologies, including but not limited to borderline personality disorder, paranoia, histrionic personality disorder, and even schizophrenia (Erickson, 2005). Therefore, an experienced analyst will investigate battering as an alternative conceptualization for the client's psychopathological presentation.

Finally, a question that routinely comes up in expert testimony is whether BWS or the effects of battering can be faked. In addition to a thorough clinical judgment that includes a battery of tests and supportive evidence, the MMPI-2 is very difficult to fake. It has a standard set of validity scales (L, F, and K, plus TRIN, and VRIN) to evaluate test-taking stance. Khan et al. (1993) highlighted typical battered women's elevations on scale F, which they associated with ordinary distress when accompanied by low L and K scale scores.

Lethality Assessment. Although there is no single formula for predicting lethal violence, there are common factors that indicate an increased risk of lethal violence that a batterer poses to his victim, which include:

1. Threats to kill the victim

2. Talk of suicide by the batterer

3. Fantasies of homicide or suicide

4. Availability of weapons

5. Use of weapon in prior abusive incidents

6. Threats with weapons

7. Serious injury in prior abusive incidents

8. Extreme controlling, jealous, or obsessive behavior

9. Frequent use of drugs and alcohol by the batterer

10. Depression of the batterer

11. Isolation of or dependency on the victim

12. Escalation of violence and/or risk-taking

13. Acts of abuse in public
14. Leaving or trying to end the relationship
15. Use of choking or strangling
16. Forced sex of female partner
17. Stalking, abduction, or hostage-taking behavior
18. History or threats of arson
19. Familiarity with the use of violence
20. Police contact (e.g., complaints, restraining orders, questioning)
21. History of antisocial behavior (e.g., public fighting, gang-related violence, vandalism, and job-related violence)
22. Violence in his family of origin or during childhood
23. Cruelty to animals
24. Violation of protective orders
25. History of mental health problems

Although many of these factors are present in a significant number of domestic abuse situations, the intensity of indicators is linked to a higher likelihood of a life-threatening or lethal attack, which has bearing on the effect of the BWS and state of mind that pertains to the victim's assumed need for measures that may include lethal self-defense, even if preemptive or anticipatory.

Therefore, the assessment of BWS and its particular case-by-case psychological presentation and effect on the victim's state of mind is best done by an experienced clinician using a systematic inquiry with the aid of a battery of psychological tests. No single area of inquiry can be expected to yield a reliable and valid answer, but by piecing together representations and accounts of the victim's history, behavior, psychological and social functioning, relationship dynamics, battering incidents, and her partner's behavior, a case-specific profile can be retrospectively constructed to reflect her state of mind and perceptions of the options available to her with high accuracy. Such a representation has to remain individualized and culture-sensitive, taking care not to stereotype the victim as a mild and meek partner without blemishes. Otherwise, consideration of the BWS in legal decision making has the unintended potential to reject valid self-defense and duress claims of women that purportedly do not fit this stereotype on the one hand, and increase the likelihood of false claims on the other hand. Opportunistic attempts to claim BWS in murder defenses unfortunately tend to negate claims that are valid, produce bias against objective examinations of abuse, and discourage the criminal justice system from considering such factors in decision making and intervention.

Case Study: Jodi Arias

Despite the increased acceptance and broad interpretations of conduct of the BWS as a criminal defense, it is still often criticized for lacking in empirical support and definitive measurement, which opens the doors to false and exaggerated claims. In many instances, the court has to pick carefully through clues in historical accounts and psychological interpretations to find the most reasonable approximation of proof. Although lawyers and judges are becoming better consumers of science, it is still a task fraught with subjective views and time-consuming investigations. The Jodi Arias case is an unfortunate example of largely unsubstantiated claims of abuse offered in an attempt to escape a murder conviction.

On June 4, 2008, Jodi Arias killed Travis Alexander by stabbing him 27 to 29 times, slitting his throat, and shooting him in the head. Arias started dating Alexander in February 2007, but trouble started soon after when Arias found text messages from another girl on Alexander's phone in June 2007. They split up, but continued to have sex and in July 2007 Arias moved from California to Mesa, Arizona to be closer to him. When Alexander began dating someone else, Arias reportedly started following them, sent the other woman threatening emails, and slashed his tires. Arias moved back to California in March 2008. On June 2, Arias rented a car in Redding, California, which she returned on June 7, after driving 2,800 miles. Timestamped photographs of her and Alexander, many sexually suggestive, including one of his apparent dead body, and her DNA in a bloody palm print was found at his apartment after his body was discovered in the shower of the master bathroom.

Arias initially claimed that she was not in Mesa at the time before blaming the murder on two masked home intruders. Two years after her arrest, Arias told police that she killed Alexander in self-defense, claiming that she had been a victim of domestic violence. During her trial, Arias testified that she had been violently abused by her parents beginning when she was approximately 7-years-old, and that her relationship with Alexander became increasingly physically and emotionally abusive. According to her, she killed him after he became enraged when she dropped his camera and she feared for her life. Three psychologists, Richard Samuels, Alyce LaViolette, and Robert Geffner, testified for the defense that Arias likely suffered from acute stress, anxiety disorder, and PTSD stemming from domestic violence-related trauma.

The prosecution's expert witness, Janeen DeMarte, disagreed and offered a different view—that there were no signs that Arias suffered from PTSD or amnesia, nor that she was a victim of abuse. Instead, DeMarte said Arias suffered from borderline personality disorder, showing signs of immaturity and an "unstable sense of identity." DeMarte also told jurors that people who suffer from such a disorder tend to "have a terrified feeling of being abandoned by others." No evidence could be found suggesting that Alexander had ever physically abused Arias, although there were many indications of power and control issues, psychological cruelty, and other abuse issues commonly found in domestic violence situations. The presence of the pictures and testimony about Alexander sexually using her could also be indicative of an abusive relationship. However, it does not seem that Arias was ever properly questioned about sexual abuse. After a hung jury and a sentencing retrial Arias was sentenced to life imprisonment without the possibility of parole on April 13, 2015.

As her whole defense rested upon claims of abuse in order to establish ground for self-defense, the Arias case is a good example of the process to investigate and prove or disprove such notions. As BWS is neither a recognized mental illness nor standalone legal defense, but rather a contextual grouping of characteristics, both personal (psychological and behavioral) and situational, a holistic picture has to be painted to support state of mind and intent. In most jurisdictions, the basis of self-defense rests on establishing that the accused must have had a reasonable apprehension of imminent death or grievous bodily harm and had a reasonable belief that force was necessary to preserve herself from such death or grievous bodily harm.

The defense did not present evidence that Arias was in fear of her life when she killed Alexander, only making an argument of BWS, which is not sufficient justification to establish self-defense. Instead, evidence of BWS is used to bridge the gap between self-defense and a reasonable fear of serious bodily harm or death based on a pattern of past battering incidents. The differences between male and female perceptions of lethal danger were highlighted by the *Washington Supreme Court in State v. Wanrow* (1977):

> The respondent was entitled to have the jury consider her actions in the light of her own perceptions of the situation, including those perceptions which were the product of our nation's long and unfortunate history of sex discrimination...Until such time as the effects of that history are eradicated, care must be taken to assure that our self-defense instructions afford women the right to have their conduct judged in the light of the individual physical handicaps which are the product of sex discrimination (Stark, 2007, p. 150).

The most common standard now to determine the most likely perception of any reasonable woman in the same situation, which is a combination of objective and subjective perception of imminent harm—objective being anyone would agree what is reasonable while subjective is what any battered woman would perceive.

Finally, in some jurisdictions, there used to be a requirement that the accused must not have been able to retreat from the situation, especially if not in her own home but has been reversed in *Weiand v. State* (1999). Receding the view it has held since *State v. Bobbitt* (1982), the Supreme Court held that a person does not have a duty to retreat from the residence before using deadly force in self-defense against a co-occupant. In the majority ruling, Justice Pariente wrote: "(W)e hold that there is no duty to retreat from the residence before resorting to deadly force against a co-occupant or invitee if necessary to prevent death or great bodily harm, although there is a limited duty to retreat within the residence to the extent reasonably possible."

As was done in Arias' case, such an effort entails behavioral history obtained through witness and other accounts, past psychiatric, medical, and arrest reports, and psychological evaluation. In order to substantiate claims of abuse that could have led to BWS, this information has to establish a pattern consistent with chronic abuse. In the Arias trial, although Alexander's friends testified to his behavior as crude, rude, and disrespectful—maybe even psychological abusive to women—such consistency did not exist, or did not rise to sufficient levels of danger. In this regard, Arias' claims fell short of establishing either imminent physical violence or consistent, chronic abuse that could satisfy self-defense.

In most jurisdictions, the force or threat by the abuser must be perceived as imminent by the victim. In an appropriate case, the testimony of the battered woman about the abuse over a period of time, her belief that she could not escape her abuser in any real way, together with the expert testimony about the reality of these beliefs provides a context that fits a test of imminence, grounded in her experience even if the man's back was turned or she was responding to an unarmed assault. It is the objective of the psychiatric experts to establish whether such a perception of imminent serious threat existed and why.

Arias claimed that the assault on her was imminent and potentially lethal, and that it was part of a pattern of emotional and physical abuse that she has already endured. But not only were there no corroborating evidence of any kind—no complaints or reports of previous abuse. She did not give a coherent explanation of why she felt that there was a reasonable belief that she was about to be seriously bodily harmed or killed. She did not attempt to avoid him but exhibited stalking behavior, which battered women sometimes do in a watchful attempt to gain some form of control. No evidence was presented that she ever acted in a hyper-vigilant, hyper-aroused, or anxious way that is typical of abuse victims. Neither did she have a negative body image, but instead seems to be high on the narcissistic continuum, possibly using her sexuality to lure men into her personal space. The limited psychological evaluation evidence available suggests the possibility of serious mental disorder that may have obscured symptoms of BWS if present. With no 911 calls, no injuries, no emergency room visits, hospital reports, bruises, broken bones or injuries noted by family or friends, Arias' claims of self-defense in the context of BWS were dismissed by the jury. In addition, Arias had no defensive wounds (Alexander had several) and some experts claim that the level of overkill evident in her attack is indicative of extreme personal anger or retaliation (Keppel and Birnes, 2003). The FBI Behavioral Sciences Unit's John Douglas characterized such an event as an anger-retaliation murder by overkill, typically involving the use of more than one weapon (Flowers, 2013). According to Campbell (1992), sadism and excessive violence were found in 61% of intimate partner homicides. However, acts resembling excessive self-defense—uses of force and violence beyond that required by the occasion to eliminate the threat—have also been linked to fear in domestic violence contexts, desperate to prevent retaliation, even after the abuser is dead (*People v. Day*, 1992).

Although the MMPI-2 was administered and discussed at great length in expert witness testimony, there did not seem to be much supportive information in terms of possible malingering and cognitive abilities, especially as Arias had changed her story several times (Eisner, 2014). Although some of her MMPI-2 results were suggestive of someone who had been traumatized or had been in an abusive relationship, scores should be analyzed in the context of the individual being tested, and administered as a part of a battery of psychological tests, which, together with collaborative sources, can either confirm or deny the hypotheses the MMPI-2 might suggest in the context of overall psychopathology.

Although a 468 code type is sometimes associated with possible BWS, and Arias had much higher scores than research benchmarks for abused women (Erickson, 2005), the MMPI-2 remains an inadequate test to establish evidence of BWS in isolation. Overall, there was insufficient evidence that (1) there was a sufficiently abusive relationship to cause her to have reasonable fear of imminent harm, (2) the psychological evaluation did not look carefully for evidence of other explanations such as a coexisting disorder even if BWS was found, and (3) there was no evidence at trial that she was in fear for her life at the time she killed Alexander. The Jodi Arias demonstrates the importance that claims of abuse and battering in relation to homicide committed by the defendant are thoroughly investigated by appropriate means. These have to include a battery of tests, behavioral analysis of crime scene evidence, and collateral sources attesting to the veracity of the claims in terms of psychological and behavioral history of the claimant, victim, and their relationship.

Criminal Defenses Utilizing the BWS

From the beginning of time women were seen as inferior to men who were allowed to treat their wives as property, authorized to use reasonable violence to chastise and control them. For instance, in Roman law blackening a woman's eyes or breaking her nose was permitted, and under English laws marital rape was inconceivable as it was the husband's right to command his wife to meet her conjugal obligations. In many parts of Europe a man was not punished for murdering his wife, while a woman who killed was severely penalized. Even by 1910, only 35 out of 46 U.S. states classified wife beating as assault. It is only in the past 20 years that most states have criminalized marital rape. Currently, in the United Nations, of the 193 member states, only 125 nations outlaw domestic violence, and marital rape may be prosecuted in 104 states, but is a specific criminal offense in only 32 (United Nations, 2006).

Even in jurisdictions where legislation is in place to penalize perpetrators of domestic violence, the past patriarchal societal state of mind is not easily changed. The real test of the application of these laws and practices lies in our perceptions of the duties, obligations, and image of a "good" woman in the home. Add the fact that family matters were always considered to be a private matter, and the odds are stacked against women being protected from harm in the home. It seems the same attitudes that have accepted wife beating had little tolerance for women who dared to fight back, perhaps because they did not fit the expected mold, or dared to bring private problems into the open. Neither did it fit the usual defense requirements. On the rare occasion that a battered woman was successful at trial their defense was premised on the concept of insanity (Dowd, 2008). One such a case, widely known as "The Burning Bed," was seen as a landmark in recognition of the daily difficulties that battered women face when Francine Hughes was acquitted of murdering her abusive husband by setting fire to the bed in which he was sleeping on grounds of temporary insanity. Although many criticized such an apparent expansion of the self-defense argument to non-confrontational murder cases, her experiences helped people understand the complexity of battered women's lives and the impact that the abuse has on their psychology, perceptions, and choices (Hinton-Johnson, 2013). Another case, the appeal of Yvonne Wanrow, decided by the Supreme Court in the State of Washington in 1977, set the stage for abused women to argue self-defense in the context of gender-based standards when determining whether their conduct and use of force was justified under the circumstances of domestic abuse. Only, until today it still remains uncertain which standard (i.e., male standard, battered woman standard, reasonable woman standard, or sex-neutral) is the most appropriate to serve justice and prevent gender stereotyping.

Partly as a result, the BWS was defined to help set a standard in understanding the battered woman's experiences and perceptions. BWS was first introduced as an element in a legal defense in *Ibn-Tamas v. U.S.* (1979) (Meyer, 2012). In *Ibn-Tamas*, the defendant challenged her second-degree murder conviction for killing her husband. The appellate court found that the jury could not adequately evaluate from the evidence itself, without the explanation of an expert, the defendant's relationship with her husband. Therefore, it has been established that providing a description of the BWS, explanations of the effect that severe abuse has on women and how they are influenced to stay in those situations, and characteristics of the battering male and abusive relationship, has probative value (Brown, 1980).

Admissibility of Evidence

In the U.S. federal courts, the admissibility of expert evidence in criminal trials is determined by the Federal Rules of Evidence (FRE), which was drafted between 1969 and 1972 and was signed into federal law in 1975. In addition, many states in the United States have either adopted FRE, with or without local variations, or have revised their own evidence codes based in part on the federal rules. The evidence admissibility laws of many other developed countries are also influenced by American law or similar principles (Glancy and Bradford, 2007). Based on the FRE, in order to determine whether expert testimony in criminal trials is admissible, including defenses presenting case-specific or general expert testimony related to BWS, the following process is required:

1. *Relevance.* Does the evidence have any tendency to make the existence of any fact that is of consequence to the determination of the action more probable or less probable than it would be without the evidence? [FRE 401].

2. *Probative Value.* Does the probative value substantially outweigh the danger of unfair prejudice, confusion of the issues, or misleading of the jury, or by considerations of unfair delay, waste of time, or needless presentation of cumulative evidence? [FRE 403].

3. *Expert Opinion.* Is the testimony in the form of an opinion, that is, is the opinion one that is rationally based on the perception of the witness and would be helpful to a clear understanding of the witness' testimony or determination of a fact in issue? [FRE 701].

4. *Expert Qualification.* Is the witness qualified by knowledge, skill, experience, training, or education to testify as an expert witness on an issue that is properly the subject matter of expert testimony? [FRE 702].

5. *Acceptance.* Is the opinion based on facts or data of a type reasonably relied upon by experts in the particular field as based on reliable principles and methods? [FRE 703].

6. *Ultimate Issue.* If all other previous conditions are satisfied and the opinion is not on an ultimate issue, or the expert witness is testifying with respect to the mental state or condition of the defendant as to whether the defendant did or did not have the mental state or condition constituting an element of the crime charged or of a defense thereto, the testimony is admissible. [FRE 704].

Case-specific evidence related to BWS may include an assessment of the defendant's mental state, habit, character, or a character trait, if it is an essential element of the charge, claim, or defense and can be proven by valid and reliable test methods or specific instances of the person's conduct [FRE 405]. The defendant's evidence of self-defense does not automatically put character at issue. Similar guidelines apply to presenting character evidence in instances where the victim has been battering or abusing the defendant in which case reputation or opinion "bad character" evidence is presented by the defendant. It is especially the violent predisposition of the "victim" that is relevant in self-defense cases to establish whether the defendant's fear was reasonable and/or the victim was the aggressor [FRE 404].

Case-Specific v. General Expert Testimony

The admissibility of expert evidence in battered woman cases is often appealed, including whether such evidence can include case-specific aspects or must remain general in terms of the effect of battering on a woman's state of mind, beliefs, perceptions, and behavior. General testimony of BWS has the objective to establish a social framework whereby abused women typically act in a certain way (e.g., fail to leave), have similar beliefs and perceptions (i.e., being lethally threatened and having no escape/support available), and exhibit a common state of mind (e.g., learned helplessness) that affect their decision making and actions. It is also used to dispel myths of BWS that are commonly held by the public, such as that a battered woman can leave the batterer at any time, has in some way provoked or can be blamed for the abuse, or is simply seen as an excuse to get away with murder, especially in cases where they kill in circumstances that do not include a traditionally defined imminent threat or serious bodily harm (Russell, 2010). Another danger is that battered women are stereotyped as mentally ill, and expected to be meek, subservient, passive, and "flawless" in character and behavior. When a defendant does not fit this mold, her perceptions and motivations are not easily believed unless countered by expert testimony (Russell and Melillo, 2006).

Therefore, presenting evidence of BWS as social framework testimony is employing social science research "to provide a social and psychological context in which the trier can understand and evaluate claims about the ultimate fact" (Vidmar and Schuller, 1989, p. 135). However, although general expert testimony is generally accepted in battered woman cases, case-specific evidence is often disallowed because the courts feel that expert testimony does not offer sufficient probative value compared to the danger of prejudice, and that it is within the purview of the jury to reach a decision based on other evidence. In their amici brief, Dorchen A. Leidholdt Sanctuary for Families et al. (2013) disagreed, claiming that both general and case-specific evidence is crucial in explaining the peculiarities of the defendant's situation and the reasonableness of her fear at the time of the charged offense. Case-specific evidence can assist the jury to appreciate the facts specific to the particular case, including discussing the Danger Assessment tool and the defendant's ability to appraise the likelihood of being killed by her partner. These are highly probative facts to support the defendant's belief that she was in imminent danger, thereby better formulating the individual defendant's state of mind at the time of the offense. Therefore, both case-specific and general expert evidence testimonies are important to present a complete defense.

Justification v. Excuse Defenses

According to the Model Penal Code of the United States, a person is criminally responsible for the harm that he causes "when the state proves beyond a reasonable doubt that he acted voluntarily, with a wrongful state of mind, and in the absence of any excusing conditions" (Appelbe, 2005, p. 1). In the case of justification the assumption is that despite the act's harmful effect, there is an overall benefit to society that outweighs the harm; as such, the act is considered justified and the actor not punished. Excuse covers the situation where there is both a harm and a wrong, but individual and subjective grounds exist for not attributing harm to the actor.

Although BWS is not accepted as a legal defense *per se*, the courts in the United States, United Kingdom, Australia, Canada, and New Zealand have recognized that such evidence may support a variety of defenses to a charge of murder, including mitigating the sentence. As such, evidence of BWS may legally constitute elements of justification and/or excuse:

The justification defense. As more than two-thirds of battered women who kill their partners act during a confrontation, a justification defense is mostly appropriate to employ. However, self-defense is rarely without challenges. Although using a reasonable and proportionate degree of violence in response to the abuse might appear to be the most appropriate defense, it rarely succeeds. Although some women are acquitted, many continue to be convicted of murder or manslaughter. A study by Charles Patrick Ewing of 100 homicide cases between 1978 and 1986 where BWS was argued,

> Nine pleaded guilty, three were acquitted on grounds of insanity, and three had the charges dropped. Of the remaining 85 who went to trial claiming self-defense, 22 were acquitted whilst 63 were found guilty of some type of homicide; 12 of the latter received life imprisonment sentences. Fifty-five of the 63 appealed; 22 convictions were affirmed, 22 got new trials, and four had their cases dismissed. (Easteal, 1991, p. 38)

For BWS to be successful as self-defense, four elements must be met. First, the defendant must believe that she was in immediate danger of death at the time of the act. Second, the defendant responding to the threat must have used a reasonable amount of force. Third, the defendant cannot have been the aggressor. Fourth, harming the perpetrator must have been the only opportunity to reach safety (Biggers, 2003). Therefore, the questions of whether the defendant met the threat with excessive force and whether she had a duty and opportunity to retreat are also valid, although the latter is sometimes not required in her own residence.

In battered women defenses the issues that often attract debate are the generally accepted self-defense requirement of imminence of a lethal threat, the duty to retreat, and what standard should be applied to determine a reasonable and proportionate degree of violence. General expert testimony about BWS can educate the jury on these three matters in typical situations, while case-specific expert testimony can evaluate it in terms of the specific pattern and level of violence and the defendant's state of mind.

Excuse defenses. Before 1980, battered women who killed their partners most often used an excuse theory of defense, either insanity (usually within the meaning of the M'Naghten rules) or provocation, both diminished responsibility elements. In claims of both provocation and insanity psychiatric evidence is relevant to illustrate the abuse and its effects on the defendant, either temporary in cases where there are provocative words and/or behavior and a lethal reaction is provoked in the moment, or where aspects of psychopathology related to the abuse interfere with mental capacity. The characteristics of the batterer are also elucidated, and, with contextual factors such as substance abuse, associated with the dynamics of the abusive relationship as it culminated into homicide.

The Issue of Imminence in Self-Defense

As such, Graff (1988) explained that two fact patterns exist in battered women's cases that pose separate legal issues. In the first scenario, women kill their abusive partners in response to an imminent or actual attack. In American law, the killing can be justified if the defense was both necessary (no lesser means available), and proportional (the harm caused by stopping the attacker is not disproportional to the potential harm to be suffered by the defender).

In the second and more difficult fact pattern, women kill their abusive partners when there is no present attack. Utilizing such opportunities are attributed to the physical disparity between women and men, which leads women to kill when their mates are asleep, drunk, ill or otherwise unable to resist. There has been controversy as to whether either justification defenses (e.g., self-defense, preventative defense, self-defense analogous situations) or exculpation (or excuse) defenses (e.g., necessity, duress, provocation) offer an appropriate means of disposition of battered woman homicide trials, especially the "burning beds" cases. With the support of psychological research, law practitioners and reformers recognized that the usual standards for self-defense are gender biased. As a result of placing more emphasis on the context of a woman defendant's actions, "The sex symmetrical survival construction of battered women led to statutory and case law reforms that expanded self-defense options for battered women" (Dixon, 2014, p. 1615). With such an expansion of justification defenses a wider range of abuse cases are included, including the battered woman defense, which is then viewed as a specialized version of self-defense. Nevertheless, the immediacy aspect of the lethal threat often remains a contentious issue, especially when reasonable person standards remain male-dominated. But, Maguigan (1991) pointed out that the problems do not lie as much with the laws as with the ways that they are applied:

> Fair trials should be defined as those in which a defendant is able to put her case fully before the finder of fact, to "get to the jury" both the evidence of the social context of her action and legal instructions on the relevance of that context to her claim of entitlement to act in self-defense. (Maguigan, 1991, p. 383)

By taking into account the mental and physical status and capacity of the woman in the context of her relationship, abuse, and partner, the jury is able to apply appropriate and objective standards to the woman's actions, especially when clarified by expert testimony. In opposition, Dressler (2006) asserts that "[t]he proposition that a battered woman is justified in killing her sleeping abuser, although well-meaning, is wrong, and ... any serious effort to expand self-defense law ... to permit such killings [risks] ... the coarsening of our moral values about human life and, perhaps, even the condonation of homicidal vengeance" (p. 458). In place of self-defense, Dressler proposes an expanded use of the duress doctrine to excuse rather than justify the battered woman's actions, permitting society to condemn the killing while simultaneously acknowledging that the defendant lacked a "fair opportunity to conform her conduct to the dictates of the law" (p. 469). However, in response, Krause (2007) pointed out that the definition of imminent as it relates to self-defense is both imprecise and subjective. Although most battered women who kill are under confrontational circumstances at the time, even those who are not confronted at the time may be compelled to act with deadly violence, may believe that it is a matter of survival. If a jury finds such a belief "both subjectively reasonable, in that the actor herself truly believes it, and objectively reasonable, in that a reasonable person would similarly so believe" (p. 557), the requirements of self-defense is arguably met. In such cases, a thorough assessment of the nature and level of abuse and victim's state of mind, as well as general characteristics of BWS, should be used to inform the jury in order to define the standards of reasonableness that apply.

The Problem of Syndrome Defenses

There are three levels of inquiry needed to establish the legal standard of BWS evidence. Before expert testimony becomes relevant, the party seeking to use it must establish that the victim is a battered woman and that the legal decision making would be aided by such evidence to explain her behavior. Once determined to be relevant, the testimony must pass an admissibility test and the probative value must outweigh its prejudicial impact.

To pass the admissibility hurdle, the BWS testimony must also pass a three-prong test formulated by *Dyas v. United States*:

1. The testimony's subject matter "must be so distinctly related to some science, profession, business or occupation as to be beyond the ken of the average layman."

2. Second, "the witness [must] have sufficient skill, knowledge, or experience in that field or calling as to make it appear that his opinion or inference will probably aid the trier in his search for truth."

3. Finally, expert testimony is inadmissible if "the state of the pertinent art or scientific knowledge does not permit a reasonable opinion to be asserted even by an expert."

Then, having proved both relevant and admissible, the probative value of the BWS testimony must also outweigh its prejudicial impact by being directly related to the defendant's perceptions and actions at the time of the crime. In *State v. Yusuf* (2002), the court also allowed expert testimony that was useful to help the jury understand why the victim did not end her relationship with the defendant, why she did not report prior assaults to the police, why she did not leave the scene after the assaults, and why she complied with the abuser's demands.

By definition, a psychological syndrome is defined as a distinct group of signs, symptoms, or patterns of behavior, or "evidence elicited from an expert that a person is a member of a class of persons who share a common physical, emotional, or mental condition" (Gupta, 2013, p. 414). BWS was introduced in the 1970s and is based on two core principles that are argued to delineate the effects of domestic abuse on a typical victim: the cycle of violence and learned helplessness. Although these concepts are helpful to explore and understand the effects that battering can have on the beliefs and perceptions of victims, it is by no means definitive. There are innumerable individual characteristics and relationship/contextual parameters, both baseline and abuse-related, that play a role to determine each situation. None are exactly alike and it is even difficult to approximate a common profile or expected/reasonable behavior of a battered woman. As such, the BWS in a criminal defense is particularly problematic for women who do not fit stereotypical expectations of how battered women should behave. The syndrome also often do not adequately address the experiences of racially and economically marginalized women, immigrants, lesbians, and transgendered persons who do not have access to the same sources and levels of support than other women (Zatz and Gough, 2014). The many counterintuitive behaviors can easily confuse or misguide a jury. The causation between lethal violence and being abused is not always straightforward. Therefore, especially after the introduction of more stringent standards of admissibility of expert evidence, there has been a continued controversy about such testimony.

One problem is that courts vary to great extremes in their approaches to the admissibility and interpretation of such syndrome evidence (Gupta, 2013). Courts also routinely disagree whether it relates to claims of justification or excuse. Furthermore, both legal practitioners and mental health professionals struggle to conceive how the psychological construct of BWS fits within legal theories and concepts (Follingstad, 2003). However, despite the issues, BWS expert testimony is allowed in almost all U.S. states and other developed countries, including Canada, the United Kingdom, Australia, and New Zealand. This is mostly in recognition of the serious social problem of domestic violence and the need to manage and represent victims appropriately.

Therefore, there is usually agreement that full knowledge of a case and its circumstances is required to make informed decisions about personal responsibility and accountability. As BWS testimony is meant to educate the jury about the realities of domestic violence, it is currently the best construct by which to explore cases of battered women who killed their partners. By providing a structured theory and assessment protocol, objectivity and a scientific basis is preserved in the best way possible to ensure that a battered woman's situation is considered in order to reach an appropriate judicial outcome. Despite concerns, there are no indications that such evidence is resulting in negative consequences such as the growth of the use of lethal violence by battered women and that such perpetrators are unjustly exonerated. On the contrary, the introduction of BWS into expert evidence and public parlance has led to an increased understanding of the prevalence and experiences of battered women, which has arguably resulted in increased societal efforts to ensure their proper treatment. The recent case of Barbara Sheehan is an example of the use of expert testimony in court related to BWS to inform the jury of the unique circumstances of domestic abuse and how the victim's perceptions and alternatives are altered during the course of an abusive relationship.

Case Study: Barbara Sheehan, Wife of an NYPD Sergeant

Fifty-year-old school secretary Barbara Sheehan had been married to retired NYPD sergeant Raymond Sheehan for 24 years when they had another fierce argument, this time over a vacation in Florida that she did not want to accompany him on. This was just another of many over the years. On that evening of February 17, 2008, while heading home from watching their son play football as a freshman at a college in Connecticut—their usual weekend ritual that included dinner and delivering clean laundry—Raymond punched Barbara in the face and broke her nose. This was part of Raymond's habit of serial rages and battery, which could (and did) often erupt unexpectedly. He always carried a firearm strapped to his ankle and another around his waist, even when eating breakfast or watching television. According to *New York Times* court reporter, Jim Dwyer (2011), he also patronized transvestite hookers, wearing diapers and sucking pacifiers, before returning home to beat his wife.

The morning after, when she tried to leave their Queens house, carrying one of her husband's guns for protection, he picked up his gun from the bathroom vanity and pointed it at her, as he had apparently done many times before, and worse. When he went into the bathroom to shave, Barbara shot him five times with his .38-caliber revolver, which he had left in the bedroom. When it was empty, she picked up his Glock and shot him six more times. The police arrived to find him dead on the bathroom floor. She was charged with second-degree murder. This is an example of fear-based overkill that was mentioned earlier.

Initially her defense team had been barred from presenting testimony by psychiatric experts about her long-term abuse, but after an appeal overturned the decision. However, only generic testimony on the cycle of violence and the concept of "learned helplessness" was allowed. Case-specific testimony such as the fact that of the 20 or so indicators of lethality in a battering relationship, nearly all were present in Barbara's situation in the year preceding the shooting (e.g., escalating level of violence, threats to kill, presence of firearms, his talks of suicide, his use of choking, and complete control of her daily activities) was not admissible.

Few important facts appeared to be in dispute. She admitted that she had shot him, and their children, extended family, friends, domestic violence counselors, and medical records all confirmed her accounts of the abuse. The most important question to be resolved by a trial was Barbara's state of mind at the time she killed her husband. This was informed by the typical dynamics of BWS as victims become so emotionally paralyzed that they are unable to leave the relationship, but simultaneously fear for their lives. Furthermore, they could find it difficult to conceptualize or explain their experience of the escalation of fear when the autonomic nervous system response of paralysis may be accelerating from the re-experiencing fragments of the prior abuse incidents at that time.

By Barbara and her children's accounts, their household was dominated by Raymond's rages. One day, unhappy with dinner, he flung a pot of boiling sauce over her. Their daughter, Jennifer, a chemotherapy nurse, also testified that on another occasion he pinned her mother to the floor while punching her. Several other times he knocked her bedroom door down, or threw her down. Another time her face was injured during a family vacation to Jamaica. Raymond told their son and friends that she tripped in the tub and hit her head, while he had smashed her head against a cinder-block wall. He would also remind her that he had worked in a crime scene unit and could dispose of her body without leaving evidence if she dared call the police. During that last evening, when she visited the emergency room to have her broken nose treated, he repeated those threats. The next morning he was still furious that she did not want to go on a Florida vacation with him. She said that he pointed his Glock at her as he shaved, threatening to kill her, but she had already picked up his revolver. Then she fired at him.

Although the prosecution tried to discredit and minimize her claims of abuse and injuries, her children, friends and coworkers, a banker, a sanitation worker, a school security guard, and a secretary all told a consistent story of long-term and severe battering. Their son, Raymond Jr. described his father as a monster. Reaching a consensus in their third day of deliberations, the 12-person jury acquitted Barbara of the second-degree murder charge in the case that proved to be a strenuous test of the BWS in support of self-defense. The critical question at trial was whether Barbara was in imminent danger when she killed her husband as required by New York's self-defense law. However, in what many view as a "split the baby in half" legal compromise, they found her guilty of the second gun possession charge for which she received a 5-year sentence. Afterward a jury member said that they had believed that Barbara reasonably feared she faced an imminent threat of bodily harm when she shot her husband the first time. The guilty verdict was because she continued to shoot her husband even after he no longer posed a danger.

"The case is a good marker of the willingness of jurors to realize that a history of abuse can inform a woman's sense of the need to act in self-defense," said Holly Maguigan, a law professor at New York University. "There is no joy today," her defense counsel, Michael G. Dowd said. "The only thing that can bring joy to this family would be to bring them back 17 years before the first blow was struck."

Although the Barbara Sheehan case did not constitute a "burning bed" defense, where imminence of a potentially lethal threat was claimed, BWS testimony could be used to inform the objective analysis required in self-defense law, namely to show that any reasonable battered woman would believe that the abuser represents an immediate threat to her life even in non-confrontational circumstances. Currently, New York is one of the few states where the law is based more on an objective standard for reasonable belief of imminent danger. *People v. Goetz*, 68 N.Y.2d 96, 497 N.E.2d 41, 506 N.Y.S.2d 18, 1986 N.Y. 19388, modified the standard to a quasi-objective–subjective standard, finding that lethal force is only permissible if a reasonable person would believe that he is in imminent fear of serious physical injury or death under similar circumstances and with the background and other relevant characteristics of the perpetrator (DuCharme, 2002). Many other states do not have such a strict standard, rather allowing testimony of what the particular woman believed based on everything she knew and experienced—understanding and considering the effects of enduring stress on her perceptions and behavior.

The introduction of syndrome evidence in such an approach to self-defense has been very controversial, and is said to be an argument of excuse rather than justification that tends to pathologize a battered woman defendant. But, the battered woman defense "defines the woman as a collection of mental symptoms, motivational deficits, and behavioral abnormalities; indeed, the fundamental premise of the defense is that women lack the psychological capacity to choose lawful means to extricate themselves from abusive mates" (Coughlin, 1994, p. 7). Such argument, by implication, questions the reasonableness of her state of mind, and renders such a defense closer to a mental incapacity defense (Dressler, 2006). However, many jurisdictions increasingly apply a hybrid subjective–objective standard of self-defense. This affords a jury more leeway—with the input of an expert witness—to consider the impact of sustained abuse on a battered woman's perceptions and beliefs that likely contributed to her killing her partner.

Recommendations for Handling Cases of Battered Women Who Kill

As a forensic psychologist or legal counsel with a battered woman who has killed her partner as client, there are a few important considerations to apply in order to maintain a standard of best practice. In these roles you will likely be involved in investigating, prosecuting, defending, or testifying in the defendant's case, but may also be in a position to advise on clinical services in- and outside a custodial setting. The following strategies and protocols are proposed.

Criminal Investigation and Interviewing

Besides the standard crime scene investigation, forensic analyses, autopsy, canvassing, and witness interviewing, in investigating a death where domestic violence may have been a factor there are factors that are of additional importance. To be effective, the interviewer must learn as much as possible about the individual actors and incidents in question, including exactly what had happened, what each person did, if there is any other evidence available, and what events preceded the incident. In addition, particulars of previous battering are very important to help determine the context of the last incident. In an interview with an abused woman offender a police officer or attorney should:

1. Establish the pattern of battering behavior in terms of last, worst, and first; escalation of violence; involvement of a weapon; injuries; and threat to children.

2. Utilize reflective listening techniques to clarify all statements accurately and objectively.

3. Accept that ambivalence is normal and do not express judgment or disbelief.

4. Be aware of factors that may be affecting the interviewee's ability or willingness to cooperate, such as fear, embarrassment, or confusion. Rather than indicating unreliable information, these psychological vulnerabilities can interfere with fairness and justice.

5. Ascertain if the interviewee has made any attempts to leave the relationship, and what prevented her from doing so. Factors may be fear of retaliation, financial hardship/uncertainty, isolation, and lack of support.

6. Ascertain if the interviewee has sustained injuries that caused medical attention or a visit to the emergency room.

7. Ask the interviewee if she had made use of other options, including reporting the abuse to authorities, calling the police, getting a protective or restraining order.

8. Enquire if there were ever any witnesses to the abuse.

9. Be mindful of legal requirements, including Miranda warnings and videotaping statements.

10. Manage the interview duration according to the interviewee's emotional status, attentional focus, energy, and cooperativeness. Do not use any coercive techniques or deception. Some women only open up to talk about the abuse hours into the interview.

Many of the same guidelines will also apply to an interview conducted by a public defender or private attorney. In addition to a clinical interview by a psychologist/expert witness, also have a psychologist present at other interviews. The locale should be as private, safe, quiet, and neutral as possible; preferably not the jail, where possible. Furthermore, an interviewer should always explain their role and exceptions to confidentiality. As with most other forensic and custodial interviews, ask open-ended questions and listen to the narrative as it is the most effective way to highlight the emotional impact, patterns, and inconsistencies, both important aspects in cases involving battered woman offenders. Be cognizant that trauma can distort memories and perception of time. Always remember that the truth is in the details. Only ask clarifying questions that are essential to your understanding of her story. Also listen to what has not been said and follow up with specific questions to fill in any gaps. Strive to reconstruct an incident and all underlying aspects such as perceptions and emotions in frame-by-frame detail. Look at the broader perspective and consider preceding and subsequent events. Be aware of context and anticipate issues that the other side are likely to raise. In cases involving domestic abuse, it is even more important to resolve inconsistencies and explore past abuse, including sexual violence. Conclude the interview by inviting final comments and explain the options and process going forward.

Forensic Psychological Assessment

In addition to the forensic assessment protocol that was discussed before, there are certain general guidelines and aspects specific to domestic violence that have to be followed. Typically, a psychological assessment in a forensic setting has the objective to inform a legal question, such as whether the defendant was legally sane at the time of the event, was her actions and state of mind pursuant to self-defense, and does she have the capacity to stand trial. In cases raising BWS as an element in the defense, the state of mind of the defendant and how it was influenced by a history of abuse is vital evidence.

Clinical interviews and a battery of test instruments are used to obtain such a picture and place it in the context of the accepted signs and symptoms of BWS. Concepts such as cycle of violence and learned helplessness are utilized to explain the woman's actions based on the perception of options that she had at the time. If allowed in a particular trial, the assessment forms part of case-specific expert testimony to prove or disprove that the defendant's behavior was consistent with being a victim of abuse and how it was likely influenced by such abuse, thereby creating a context of self-defense or reduced culpability.

Expert Testimony

Although the admissibility of expert testimony in court differs between jurisdictions, with few exceptions general expert testimony about BWS is allowed. Case-specific testimony is allowed in fewer instances, and is determined by the court's view of its probative value compared to the prejudicial effect that it is expected to introduce. In *State v. Goff* (2010), the court ruled that the prosecution has the right to appoint their own expert and compel psychiatric examinations when the defense counsel raises BWS as an element of defense. On appeal the Ohio Supreme Court argued that expert testimony on BWS addresses the second element of the affirmative defense of self-defense, specifically the "bona fide belief that she was in imminent danger of death or grave bodily harm and that her only means of escape was the use of force" (*State v. Thomas*, 1997). This is especially important in jurisdictions that apply a subjective test for self-defense (Kimmel and Friedman, 2011). Typically, such evidence is limited to "testimony about the syndrome in general, testimony regarding whether the defendant experienced the syndrome, and testimony concerning whether the syndrome accounts for the requisite belief of imminent danger of death or great bodily harm to justify the use of the force in question" (*State v. Goff*, 2010, p. 1087).

It appears that only four jurisdictions in the United States adopt a purely subjective test of self-defense: Ohio, Georgia, North Dakota, and Washington. Others apply an objective test based on a reasonable person standard consisting of the presence of an imminent lethal threat, and a proportionate response. A subjective test would consist of whether the defendant believes that she faced a lethal threat from which she could not escape by other means. Even then, their distinction is not definitive, but fall somewhere on a continuum (Ogle and Jacobs, 2002), and, increasingly, states' legislation codes hybrid tests that incorporate both objective and subjective standards, and include the following.

1. The qualifications of an expert witness is first established by presenting experience and achievements, including present and past employment positions, education, membership of professional associations, training programs attended or participated in, special awards or honors, case studies or reports in which the expert participated, the number of times the witness has been qualified as an expert in court, the number of victims contacted/assisted, and research conducted, and publications issued.

2. The technology in question, in this case BWS, is qualified as scientific, including titles and authors and whether these articles' conclusions are generally accepted in the relevant scientific community.

3. As a general expert witness on BWS, testimony is provided to address the myths generally held about battered women and their behavior (e.g., that they choose to stay in an abusive behavior, that they are mentally ill, and are either passive or partly to blame), explain typical patterns of abuse, the cycle of violence, and learned helplessness, and the psychological effects that it has on a battered woman's state of mind.

4. The expert witness who testifies regarding case-specific aspects addresses any counterintuitive behavior that a defendant may have exhibited (e.g., minimization of violence, delayed or not reporting abuse, recantation or reluctance to testify, continued contact with the batterer, or flat affect), as well as other signs and symptoms that are indicative of a battering relationship, and explain it in the context of BWS.

5. The expert witness and retaining counsel should verify limits of admissibility.

6. Preparation to provide expert testimony (including cross-examination) is vital: Ensure that all reports, data, copies of professional ethical codes, and any other sources are at hand.

7. Bolster credibility with professional appearance and demeanor.

The quintessential role of the expert witness is to educate the attorneys, the judge, and the jury about the dynamics of violent relationships and the effects of continued physical abuse on the victim, in general or specific terms. As there are many public misconceptions about battered women and their behavior, effective expert testimony in this regard can have a very powerful effect on jury's perceptions and decision-making as they are able to put the woman's actions in better context with her state of mind and experiences.

Clinical Treatment

In conclusion of the topic on battered women who kill their partners, their assessment and trial considerations, it is fitting to discuss treatment options in very brief terms. As it is outside the scope of the current discussion, only the most salient principles are mentioned. The foremost two elements are safety and validation. A clinician should take all reasonable steps to identify and manage risk factors that a woman may continue to face after an abusive relationship. These may include suicidal ideation, emotional instability, feelings of hopelessness, low self-esteem, anger issues, and propensity to engage in a similar relationship. In a top-down approach, the most pressing issues are dealt with first, usually in individual therapy supplemented with group sessions and/or medication as required. By using a validation-based psychotherapy approach such as a Mindfulness-Based Cognitive Behavioral Therapy (MCBT), Acceptance and Commitment Therapy (ACT), or Dialectical Behavior Therapy (DBT), the therapeutic relationship is strengthened, which supports empowerment of the abuse survivor.

A treatment plan has to be based on a thorough and systematic evaluation process, including dysfunctional beliefs and personality disordered traits that may be a result of sustained abuse, but also make it difficult for a woman to break free from her lifestyle. However, it is not only about treating the trauma-related symptoms; improving the client's social and coping skills have also proven to be effective in changing the parameters of a person's relationships and environment by working from the inside out to boost self-confidence and empowerment. Such a treatment plan is based on a cognitive problem-solving model that has the objective to change a victim's thinking pattern to become a survivor who has the ability and power to change the course of her own life.

References

American Psychiatric Association. 2013. *Diagnostic and Statistical Manual of Mental Disorders* (5th ed.). Washington, DC: Author.

Appelbe, D. 2005. The theory of justification and excuse and its implications for the battered woman. *Cork Online Law Review*, 2, 1–15.

Barnett, O. W., Miller-Perrin, C. L., and Perrin, R. D. 2011. *Family Violence across the Lifespan* (3rd ed.). Thousand Oaks, CA: Sage.

Beecher-Monas, E. 2007. *Evaluating Scientific Evidence: An Interdisciplinary Framework for Intellectual Due Process*. New York, NY: Cambridge University Press.

Biggers, J. R. 2003. A dynamic assessment of the battered woman syndrome and its legal relevance. *Journal of Forensic Psychology Practice*, 3(3), 1–22. DOI: 10.1300/J158v03n03_01.

Brief for Dorchen A. Leidholdt Sanctuary for Families et al. as Amici Curiae supporting defendant-appellant, *People v. Sheehan*, 2013 NY Slip Op 03859 [106 AD3d 1112].

Bowker, L. H. 1998. *Ending the Violence: A Guidebook Based on the Experience of 1,000 Battered Wives*. Baltimore, MD: Human Services Library.

Briere, J. 2001. *Detailed Assessment of Posttraumatic Stress* (DAPS). Odessa, FL: Psychological Assessment Resources.

Briere, J. and Scott, C. 2015. Assessing trauma and posttraumatic outcomes. In: *Principles of Trauma Therapy: A Guide to Symptoms, Evaluation, and Treatment.* Thousand Oaks, CA: Sage, pp. 63–94.

Brown, L. R. I. 1980. Admissibility of expert testimony on the subject of battered women. *Criminal Justice Journal*, 4(1), 161–179.

Browne, A. 1989. *When Battered Women Kill.* New York, NY: The Free Press.

Butcher, J. N., Gass, C. S., Cumella, E., Kally, Z., and Williams, C. L. 2008. Potential for bias in MMPI-2 assessments using the Fake Bad Scale (FBS). *Psychological Injury and Law*, 68(1), 203–210. DOI: 10.1007/s12207-007-9002-z.

Campbell, J. 1992. "If I can't have you, no one can": Power and control in homicide of female partners. In: J. Radford and D. E. H. Russell (Eds.), *Femicide: The Politics of Woman Killing.* New York, NY: Twayne, pp. 99–113.

Cipparone, R. C. 1987. The defense of battered women who kill. *University of Pennsylvania Law Review*, 135, 427–452.

Coughlin, A. M. 1994. Excusing women. *California Law Review*, 82(1), 1–93. DOI: 10.15779/Z38QH9P.

Derogatis, L. R. 1997. The Derogatis interview for sexual functioning (DISF/DISF-SR): An introductory report. *Journal of Sex & Marital Therapy*, 23(4), 291–304. DOI: 10.1080/00926239708403933.

Dixon, J. 2014. Feminist theory and domestic violence. In: G. Bruinsma and D. Weisburd (Eds.), *Encyclopedia of Criminology and Criminal Justice.* New York, NY: Springer, pp. 1612–1617.

Dowd, M. 2008. The "battered woman's defense": Its history and future. *FindLaw.* Retrieved from http://tinyurl.com/dowd2008.

Dressler, J. 2006. Battered women and sleeping abusers: Some reflections. *Ohio State Journal of Criminal Law*, 3, 457–471.

DuCharme, S. D. 2002. The search for reasonableness in use-of-force cases: Understanding the effects of stress on perception and performance. *Fordham Law Review*, 70(6), 2515–2560.

Dutton, M. A. 2009. *Update of the "Battered Woman Syndrome" Critique.* Harrisburg, PA: VAWnet. Retrieved from http://goo.gl/iZ0tph.

Dwyer, J. 2011, April 26. A court battle over a husband's rage and a wife who'd had enough. *The New York Times*, p. A21.

Dyas v. United States, 376 A.2d 827 (D.C. 1977).

Easteal, P. W. 1991, September 24. Battered women who kill: A plea of self-defense. *Women and the Law.* Paper presented at the *Australian Institute of Criminology (AIC) Conference*, Canberra, Australia.

Eisner, D. A. 2014, March 29. How not to be an expert witness: Lessons from the Jodi Arias trial. Paper presented at the *30th Annual Symposium of the American College of Forensic Psychology*, the Westgate Hotel, San Diego, CA.

Elhai, J. D., Gray, M. J., Kashdan, T. B., and Franklin, C. L. 2005. Which instruments are most commonly used to assess traumatic event exposure and posttraumatic effects? A survey of traumatic stress professionals. *Journal of Traumatic Stress*, 18(5), 541–545. DOI: 10.1002/jts.20062.

Engel, B. 2007. *Breaking the Cycle of Abuse: How to Move Beyond Your Past to Create an Abuse-Free Future.* New York, NY: John Wiley & Sons.

Erickson, N. S. 2005. Use of the MMPI-2 in child custody evaluations involving battered women: What does the psychological research tells us? *Family Law Quarterly*, 39(1), 87–108.

Flowers, R. B. 2013. *The Dynamics of Murder: Kill or Be Killed.* New York, NY: CRC Press.

Follingstad, D. R. 2003. Battered woman syndrome in the courts. In: A. M. Goldstein and I. B. Weiner (Eds.), *Handbook of Psychology: Volume 11, Forensic Psychology.* Hoboken, NJ: John Wiley & Sons, pp. 485–507.

Fox, J. A. and Zawitz, M. W. 2006. *Homicide Trends in the United States.* Washington, DC: Bureau of Justice Statistics.

Gottman, J. and Jacobson, N. 2007. *When Men Batter Women: New Insights into Ending Abusive Relationships.* New York, NY: Simon & Schuster.

Graff, S. 1988. Battered women, dead husbands: A comparative study of justification and excuse in American and West German law. *Loyola of Los Angeles International and Comparative Law Journal*, 10(1), 1–55.

Gupta, N. 2013. Disillusioning the prosecution: The unfulfilled promise of syndrome evidence. *Law and Contemporary Problems*, 76, 413–431.

Haley, S. D. and Braun-Haley, E. 2003. *War on the Home Front: An Examination of Wife Abuse*. New York, NY: Berghahn Books.

Hinton-Johnson, K. 2013. Francine Hughes. In: L. L. Finley (Ed.), *Encyclopedia of Domestic Violence and Abuse*. Santa Barbara, CA: ABC-CLIO, pp. 228–231.

Holtzworth-Munroe, A. 2000. A typology of men who are violent toward their female partners: Making sense of heterogeneity in husband violence. *Current Directions in Psychological Science*, 9(4), 140–143.

Holtzworth-Munroe, A. 2008. Batterer typology. In: N. A. Jackson (Ed.), *Encyclopedia of Domestic Violence*. New York, NY: Routledge, pp. 98–103.

Holtzworth-Munroe, A. and Stuart, G. L. 1994. Typologies of male batterers: Three subtypes and the differences among them. *Psychological Bulletin*, 116(3), 476–497.

Ibn-Tamas v. United States, 407 A. 2d 626, 1979.

Kahn, I., Welch, T. L., and Zillmer, E. A. 1993. MMPI-2 profiles of battered women in transition. *Journal of Personality Assessment*, 60(1), 100–111. DOI: 10.1207/s15327752jpa6001_7.

Kaser-Boyd, N. 2004. Battered woman syndrome: Clinical features, evaluation, and expert testimony. In: B. J. Cling (Ed.), *Sexualized Violence Against Women and Children: A Psychology and Law Perspective*. New York, NY: Guilford Press, pp. 41–70.

Keppel, R. D. and Birnes, W. J. 2003. *The Psychology of Serial Killer Investigations: The Grisly Business Unit*. San Diego, CA: Elsevier.

Kimmel, S. and Friedman, S. H. 2011. Limitations of expert testimony on battered woman syndrome. *The Journal of the American Academy of Psychiatry and the Law*, 39(4), 585–587.

Krause, J. H. 2007. Distorted reflections of battered women who kill: A response to Professor Dressler. *Ohio State Journal of Criminal Law*, 4, 555–572.

Maguigan, H. 1991. Battered women and self-defense: Myths and misconceptions in current reform proposals. *University of Pennsylvania Law Review*, 140(2), 379–486.

Mann, C. R. 1996. *When Women Kill*. Albany, NY: State University of New York Press.

McEwan, J. 2014. Behavioral science evidence in criminal trials. In: G. Bruinsma and D. Weisburd (Eds.), *Encyclopedia of Criminology and Criminal Justice*. New York, NY: Springer, pp. 145–154.

McKinley, N. M. and Hyde, J. S. 1996. The objectified body consciousness scale: Development and validation. *Psychology of Women Quarterly*, 20(2), 181–215. DOI: 10.1111/j.1471-6402.1996.tb00467.x.

McMahon, M. 1999. Battered women and bad science: The limited validity and utility of battered woman syndrome. *Psychiatry, Psychology and Law*, 6(1), 23–49. DOI: 10.1080/13218719909524946.

Meyer, C. 2012. *Young, Educated Voters' Opinions of Battered Person Syndrome as a Legal Excuse in Self-Defense Cases*. Los Angeles, CA: Alliant International University.

Newberger, E. 2000. *The Men They Will Become: The Nature and Nurture of Male Character*. Cambridge, MA: De Capo Press.

Ogle, R. S. and Jacobs, S. 2002. *Self-Defense and Battered Women Who Kill: A New Framework*. Westport, CT: Praeger.

People v. Day 1992. 2 Cal. App. 4th 405, 2 Cal. Rptr. 2d 916.

People v. Goetz, 68 N.Y.2d 96, 497 N.E.2d 41, 506 N.Y.S.2d 18, 1986 N.Y. 19388.

Roberts, A. R. 1996. *Helping Battered Women: New Perspectives and Remedies*. New York, NY: Oxford University Press.

Russo, N. F. and Pirlott, A. 2006. Gender-based violence: Concepts, methods, and findings. *Annals of the New York Academy of Sciences*, 1087, 178–205. DOI: 10.1196/annals.1385.024.

Russell, B. L. 2010. *Battered Woman Syndrome as a Legal Defense*. Jefferson, NC: McFarland.

Russell, B. L. and Melillo, L. S. 2006. Attitudes toward battered women who kill: Defendant typicality and judgments of culpability. *Criminal Justice and Behavior*, 33(2), 219–24. DOI: 10.1177/0093854805284412.

Saunders, D. G. 1994. Posttraumatic stress symptom profiles of battered women: A comparison of survivors in two settings. *Violence and Victims*, 9(1), 31–44.

Skaine, R. 2015. *Abuse: An Encyclopedia of Causes, Consequences, and Treatments*. Santa Barbara, CA: Greenwood.

Stack, S. 1997. Homicide followed by suicide: An analysis of Chicago data. *Criminology*, 35(3), 435–453. DOI: 10.1111/j.1745-9125.1997.tb01224.x.

Stark, E. 2007. Representing battered women. In: *Coercive Control: The Entrapment of Women in Personal Life*. New York, NY: Oxford University Press, pp. 133–170.

State v. Bobbitt, 415 So.2d 724 (Fla.), 1982.

State v. Goff, 942 N.E.2d 1075 (Ohio), 2010.

State v. Thomas, 673 N.E.2d 1339, 1342 (Ohio), 1997.
State v. Wanrow, Wash. Sup. Crt. 88 Wash. 2d 221, 559 P.2d 548, 1977.
State v. Yusuf, 800 A.2d 590 (Conn. App. Ct.), 2002.
Swatt, M. L. and He, N. 2006. Exploring the difference between male and female intimate partner homicides: Revisiting the concept of situated transactions. *Homicide Studies*, *10*(4), 279–292. DOI: 10.1177/1088767906290965.
United Nations. 2006. *Ending Violence Against Women: From Words to Action*. New York, NY: Author.
Vidmar, N. J. and Schuller, R. A. 1989. Juries and expert evidence: Social framework testimony. *Law and Contemporary Problems*, *52*(4), 133–176.
Walker, L. E. 1990. *Terrifying Love: Why Battered Women Kill and How Society Responds*. New York, NY: HarperCollins.
Walker, L. E. 1988. The battered woman syndrome. In: G. Hotaling, D. Finkelhor, J. Kilpatrick, and M. A. Strauss (Eds.), *Family Abuse and Its Consequences: New Directions in Research*. Newbury Park, CA: Sage, pp. 139–147.
Walker, L. E. 2006. Battered woman syndrome: Empirical findings. *Annals of the New York Academy of Sciences*, *1087*, 142–157. DOI: 10.1196/annals.1385.023.
Walker, L. E. 2009. *The Battered Woman Syndrome* (3rd ed.). New York, NY: Springer.
Walker, L. E., Duros, R., and Tome, A. 2008. Battered woman syndrome. In: B. Cutler (Ed.), *Encyclopedia of Psychology and Law*. Thousand Oaks, CA: Sage, pp. 40–44. DOI: 10.4135/9781412959537.n17.
Websdale, N. 1999. *Understanding Domestic Homicide*. Lebanon, NH: Northeastern University Press.
Websdale, N. 2003. Reviewing domestic violence deaths. *Journal of the National Institute of Justice*, *250*, 26–31.
Weiand vs. State, WL 125522 (Fla. 3/11/99).
Wilson, J. P. and Walker, A. J. 1990. Toward an MMPI trauma profile. *Journal of Traumatic Stress*, *3*(1), 151–168. DOI: 10.1002/jts.2490030111.
Zatz, M. S. and Gough, H. R. 2014. Gendered theory and gendered practice. In: G. Bruinsma and D. Weisburd (Eds.), *Encyclopedia of Criminology and Criminal Justice*. New York, NY: Springer, pp. 1876–1883.

12 Child and Adolescent Homicide Offenders

Joan Swart

Contents

Introduction 236
The Psychology of Youth Violence and Homicide 236
    Youth Violence and Homicide by the Numbers 236
    Neuropsychology and Youth Violence 238
    Reactive Aggression 239
    Emerging Psychopathy 239
    Developmental Disorders 240
    Other Risk Factors 241
    Typology of Homicidal Youth 242
        Anger 242
        Resentment 242
        Fear 242
        Depression 243
        Belonging 243
        Entitled/Egoistic 243
        Conviction of Beliefs 243
        Reactive Aggressive Killer 243
        Revenge Killer 243
        Thrill Killer 243
        Domestic Killer 243
        School Shooter 244
    Media and Youth Violence 245
The Criminal Justice System and Youth Homicide 246
    Investigating and Interviewing Youth 246
    Sentencing Youth 247
    Treatment and Prevention of Youth Homicide 249
    Reintegration into Society 250
References 253

Introduction

According to Federal Bureau of Investigation (FBI) statistics, homicide is the second leading cause of death in the age group under 18-years, with 1085 victims in 2014 in the United States. In the same year, 653 youths aged under 18 years were arrested for murder. The majority of adolescents with violent and homicidal behavior have multiple personality disorders (e.g., antisocial, borderline, and narcissistic features) and other coexisting conditions such as developmental disorders, post-traumatic stress disorder (PTSD), mood disorders, and substance abuse issues. Violence among youth is also associated with other criminal activities and conduct problems. This seems to be rooted in early childhood maltreatment in the context of other proximal factors such as violence, substance abuse, and psychiatric problems in the family, poor/absent parenting, antisocial peer associations, and poor school/vocational performance.

Distal risk factors also play a role, including impulsive, aggressive, and intense temperament, socioeconomic issues, and poor and unstable living conditions. As such, their behavior is linked to dysfunctional attitudes, values, and beliefs that have been found to be changeable by cognitive behavioral therapeutic interventions. In addition to these developmental considerations, the investigator and the legal professional will have to take their cognitive and emotional maturity into account when communicating and assessing the behavior and culpability of a youth offender. At this age, an adolescent's trajectory is not set, and there is room for correctional efforts. A youth's homicide offending is likely to be reactive aggressive (e.g., related to a perceived provocation or threat). As such, it is usually situational driven, or, in some cases functional (e.g., with an objective of material gain), or expressive (e.g., driven by feelings of jealousy or revenge).

The Psychology of Youth Violence and Homicide

Although the types, methods, and motivations of youth homicide are varied, the personal characteristics and circumstances are relatively consistent. Even though incidences have steadily declined in most developed countries over the past years, it remains a serious and costly issue that requires better understanding to develop more effective interventions. Most youth homicides are associated with difficult personal circumstances, including dysfunctional families, abuse, and mental health issues, substance abuse, and negative peer influences. The following section analyzes the statistics of youth violence in the United States, thereafter characteristics linked to youth homicide offenders are explored. These include neuropsychology, reactive aggression, emerging psychopathy, and developmental disorders, before highlighting different offender typologies. These aspects are illustrated with the discussion of the first of two case studies.

Youth Violence and Homicide by the Numbers

According to the United States Federal Bureau of Investigation (FBI) homicide offender statistics of 2014, only 4.7% of all homicide offenders were under 18 years and only 7.7% of this group were females. The 10-year trend is illustrated in Figure 12.1. It indicates an overall drop in under-18 offenders as a percentage of all offenders in the 7 years since 2006. However, the trend has reversed in 2014, primarily caused by a 39% increase of female homicide offenders between ages 16 and 18. There has also been a decrease in the ratio of female and male homicide offenders in the same age group. Of the child and adolescent murderers in the United States in 2014, two-thirds killed victims aged 18 and over, while only one-third offended against victims the same age or younger. Forty percent of under-18 murderers were white, and 59% African-American.

Where information is available, their weapons of choice were firearms (56%), personal weapons (e.g., fists and feet) (23%), sharp instruments (9%), and blunt objects (5%). Asphyxiation (4%), strangulation (1%), narcotics (1%), and fire (1%) were less often applied. Compared with over 18-year-old murderers, youths used fewer firearms (56% vs. 75%) and knives (9% vs. 15%), while favoring hitting and kicking (23% vs. 4%) and asphyxiation (4% vs. 0.6%). One can argue that these differences are primary because of smaller availability of weapons in the younger age group, and more spur-of-the-moment incidents that involve personal physical violence.

In 2010, 85% of the victims of juvenile murderers were male (Sickmund and Puzzanchera, 2014), while 77% of the victims of all homicides were male in the same period (Federal Bureau of Investigation [FBI], 2014). There are interesting differences among the victims of fatal violence perpetrated by male and female youth, as illustrated in Figure 12.2. Aside from the preponderance of acquaintance victims, males and females tend to kill different types of victims. Females were more likely than males to kill family members, whereas males were more likely than females to kill strangers. Finkelhor and Omrod (2001) pointed out that

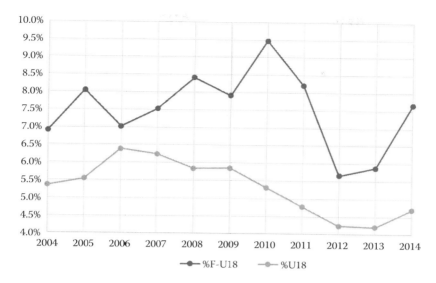

Figure 12.1 Percentage of youth homicide offenders in the United States between 2004 and 2014.

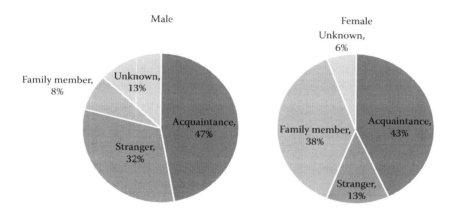

Figure 12.2 Youth murderers relationship with their victims. (Adapted from Snyder, H. N., Sickmund, M., and Poe-Yamagata, E. 1996. *Juvenile Offenders and Victims: 1996 Update on Violence*. Washington, DC: Office of Juvenile Justice and Delinquency Prevention. With permission.)

a murder of a stranger by an adolescent is most likely, 92% of the time, committed using a firearm, whereas a firearm is used in less than half (44%) of the murders of nonstrangers. These homicides are two times more likely to involve a knife or blunt object, and 18 times more likely to involve punching, kicking, or asphyxiating a nonstranger to death than a stranger. Gang killing and robberies account for more than half of stranger deaths committed by youth.

A more recent analysis by Sickmund and Puzzanchera (2014) indicated that almost two-fifths (38%) of murders involving a juvenile offender also involved an adult offender. This ratio increased steadily over the past 3 decades. Regarding incarceration, on a typical day in 2010, there was about 7600 persons younger than 18 in adult jails, mostly males (87%), minorities (58%), and person offenders. Of the new admissions, 71% were for violent offenses, including 7% for homicide (Sickmund and Puzzanchera, 2014). Although most states report recidivism rates, their methodology of calculation varies significantly, which makes comparisons challenging. Nevertheless, a meta-analytic study has shown that violent juvenile offenders who have been transferred to adult court are typically rearrested before those who were processed as juveniles (Cottle et al., 2001). Furthermore, as a child and adolescent brain and personality continue to develop, many young offenders naturally desist from crime into adulthood. A Pittsburgh Youth Study found that only just more than half of juvenile offenders continue to offend up to age 25 (Loeber et al., 2012). In the past 5 years, this number dropped by two-thirds. However, a large number of individual differences, both personal and contextual, determine the outcome, in particular how the young person's brain matures in terms of emotion regulation and judgment.

Neuropsychology and Youth Violence

Victor Streib, a retired professor of law and ex-dean of the Ohio Northern University College of Law, argued that many juvenile homicides do not compare with adult variants. "Premeditation assumes an adult mind of intending, planning and premeditating. You'll read the casual comment that even a small child knows this is wrong…Most kids I've worked with have a Nintendo view of this stuff: They're surprised the person is still dead." (Jones, 2014, p. 39).

In their preteen and teenage years, youths develop intense social relationships, and peer pressure can lead to risky choices and behavior. The adolescent brain is not yet fully able to set limits and see the world from someone else's point of view. The prefrontal cortex, the part of the brain that controls critical thinking, judgment, and deliberation, only matures when a person is in his mid-20s. Because it has not yet fully developed, a young person's behavior is more impulsive, influenceable, and ignorant of consequences. Extreme trauma and abuse in childhood stunts or delays this maturation process, and can also produce permanent neurological changes and deficits. Similarly, traumatic brain injuries in children are also linked to an increased risk of violent and aggressive behavior.

Therefore, in the context of child and adolescent homicide offenders and their neuropsychological development, there are two considerations. The first is the fact that their immature brains do not yet equip them to exercise fully developed control and judgment. The second is the link between traumatization and brain development.

Reduced legal accountability for their actions has made an important part of the arguments against the capital punishment for adolescents in the landmark case of *Roper v. Simmons*, 543 U.S. 551 (2005). In their briefs, proponents of its abolishment argued adolescents are not as morally culpable as adults, in particular, as the brain's frontal lobe that enables restraint over impulsive behavior only begins to mature at age 17. Normal brain maturation only peaks after the age of 21. The adolescent brain also lacks an integration of information from other regions and functioning is more localized. Areas that govern impulses and instincts are therefore far more isolated and unmoderated. Furthermore, the amygdala, a brain region that processes emotion, is not yet fully able to accurately distinguish emotional cues and expressions in adolescence. The other two functions of the adolescent brain that still lack mature functioning are the ability to perceive consequences and sensitivity to negative external influences such as peer pressure. Moreover, as a young person is still in the process of forming a coherent personality, their behavior reflects the transient qualities of a person in the process of maturing. Experts, therefore, argue that criminal tendencies of an adolescent will not necessarily continue into adulthood, and they are amenable to positive change (*Roper v. Simmons*, 2005).

The second neuropsychological consideration that applies to many youth murderers is the effect that childhood trauma has had on their psychosocial functioning and brain development. According to Tsavoussis et al. (2014), poor childhood conditions cause biological and structural alterations in the brain. These typically affect the midbrain, cerebral cortex, limbic system, corpus callosum, cerebellum, hypothalamus, pituitary, and adrenal glands. PTSD is common among children who have been subjects of trauma. Resulting neurological changes predict cognitive difficulties. These include poor academic performance, impaired language skills, memory deficiencies, lack of inhibition, and attention issues (Tsavoussis et al., 2014). Therefore, child maltreatment compromises both brain anatomy and function by affecting the structure, physiology, and signaling pathways. These outcomes include "relatively decreased activation of the middle frontal cortex and increased activation in the left medial frontal gyrus and the anterior cingulate gyrus" (p. 3). Typically, affected children have difficulty sustaining attention and easily become distracted.

Also, changes to the limbic system involve more intense experiences of fear, anger, and pleasure, but there is an added lack of ability to regulate these emotions. Delayed maturation or underdevelopment of the prefrontal cortex is another possible outcome of childhood trauma with a negative effect on morality, empathy, and decision-making. The corpus callosum is a broad bundle of neural fibers that connects the right and left cerebral hemispheres and facilitates the transfer of signals. Trauma can also cause decreased functioning of the corpus callosum, of which the risk of psychological symptoms such as depersonalization, derealization, and delusions increases. Finally, the hypothalamic-pituitary-adrenal (HPA) axis that activates during stress responses develops into chronic hypervigilance and hyperarousal. The resulting elevated cortisol levels in the brain further slows immunity, metabolism, cognition, and brain development (Tsavoussis et al., 2014). It also exacerbates problems with aggression, anxiety, depression, and irritability. Thus, the immature human brain is subject to heightened responsiveness to incentives and socio-emotional contexts with insufficient impulse control and emotional regulation to counter it (Casey et al., 2008). Experiences of chronic and severe trauma worsen these effects.

Reactive Aggression

Another chapter covers the presentation of reactive aggression in the adult context in greater detail. Here, the focus is on its role in youth violence, specifically homicides. We have already ascertained that arguments and disagreements that lead to physical altercations precede most murders committed by juveniles. Angry, retaliatory responses to a perceived provocation or threat characterize reactive aggression. It is more common in violent juvenile behavior than proactive aggression, which refers to premeditated and goal-directed predatory attacks aimed at achieving a material or psychological reward. The incidence of reactive aggression in children and adolescents is higher than that of proactive aggression, by a factor of about 2.3:1 (Swart et al., 2015). However, these two types of aggressions are not mutually exclusive. Although distinct in its motivation and presentation at any time, it can co-occur in the same individual. Antisocial behavior, which tends to be more severe and intractable, the earlier the onset, is typically associated with a combination of aggression types (Rappaport and Thomas, 2004). Whereas proactive aggression is a predictor of antisocial behavior, it is not associated with negative affect. In contrast, reactive aggression is linked to negative affect and does not imply antisocial or psychopathic traits (Fite et al., 2009).

As such, instinctive hostile reactions are marked by impulse and emotion regulation deficiencies. Early precursors of such difficulties include conflict and violence in the family home, poor parental skills and attitudes, in particular, a lack of supervision or harsh discipline, low socioeconomic status, and family dysfunction. The frustration-aggression hypothesis best explains reactive aggression by suggesting that aggression is an angry and hostile reaction when circumstances prevent a person from achieving their goals (Fite et al., 2015). It is an attempt to justify anger and violence as having an uncontrollable and external cause. Reactive aggression is consistent with having poor attachments and a hypervigilance toward and tendency to misinterpret social cues. Also, states of frustration and anger interfere with helpful social information processing. According to Fite et al. (2015), anger skews a person's attribution of intent and reinforces aggressive scripts and schemes. Anger coping is another useful distinction between reactive and proactive aggression types. A young person's ability to regulate their emotions and cope with anger correlates with reactive, but not proactive, aggression.

Emerging Psychopathy

A proactive aggression style is a hallmark of psychopathic traits. Where ineffective emotional and social responses characterize reactive aggression, the inability to form associations between stress cues and conditioned stimuli that inhibit violent behavior presents in the emerging psychopath. Those children and adolescents with callous/unemotional traits represent a distinct subgroup with elevated proactive aggressive tendencies. They are genetically more vulnerable to violence and antisocial behavior compared to reactive aggressive children who have primarily environmental etiology (Viding et al., 2012). They also appear emotionally underreactive, especially about others' distress. The presence of a genetic component implies that early onset of callous/unemotional traits is relatively stable over time, and the prognosis is thought to be poor (Swart et al., 2015).

Experts disagree about the moral implications and usefulness of diagnosing children with personality disorders, although it is clear that personality development starts in early childhood (Vizard, 2008). Such fears are in part linked to potential negative consequences of labeling a child as antisocial or psychopathic, as well as the notion that many problems naturally remit into adulthood. However, as antisocial personality disorder and psychopathy is overrepresented among adolescent and adult homicide and violent offenders, early identification is clearly important. According to Vizard (2008), about 40% of children diagnosed with conduct disorder continue to have serious psychosocial disturbances in adulthood.

Kimonis and her colleagues distinguish between two variants of juvenile psychopathy. Low anxiety characterizes the primary type while high anxiety is an element of the secondary type (Kimonis et al., 2012). Juveniles in the secondary group are more likely to have suffered a history of abuse and present with emotional and attentional problems than those in the primary group. The main qualities of the primary variant are low arousal of fear and poor ability to sympathize with distress in others. Secondary variants are better at recognizing emotional tone and content. Although both groups have similar callous/unemotional trait levels, the primary group is closer to the prototypical adult psychopath because of their fearless temperament and lack of conscience. Essentially, it may, therefore, be that the callous/unemotional traits of the secondary variant of juvenile psychopathy are mechanisms to cope with being overwhelmed in negatively charged situations. Whereas, in the primary variant, the same traits are present because of their innate inability to connect emotionally.

Lindberg and her colleagues found that one in five homicidal male adolescents in their sample met their criteria for psychopathic personality by scoring 26 and above on the Psychopathy Checklist-Revised (PCL-R) test. Compared to those who scored lower, the following differences became apparent (Lindberg et al., 2009):

- They had a criminal history more often.

- They used excessive violence more frequently.

- They more rarely lived with both parents until age 16.

- They had more institutional or foster home placements.

- They had more school difficulties, including receiving special education.

- They more often had contact with mental health services.

- Their parents and relatives more often had criminal histories, including homicide.

- Their crimes were more often associated with another crime (e.g., property, drug crime).

- Their homicides were twice as likely to involve multiple offenders.

Despite the fact that many view psychopathy as untreatable, juveniles in a test group who were treated with an intensive program utilizing the decompression model were more than twice less likely to reoffend than others. The decompression treatment model is based on the theories of defiance and social control. Youth offenders with psychopathic features have the tendency to react to punishment with increasingly frequent and serious violent and criminal behavior. The cycle deteriorates with the youth further removed from acceptable goals and values. Therefore, they become compressed or trapped in defiant behavior patterns. This also contributes to strained social bonds, which is another risk factor for continued antisocial behavior. The Mendota Juvenile Treatment Center, a correctional facility in Madison, Wisconsin, applies the decompression treatment model, in which they use cognitive-behavioral techniques, primarily aimed at anger replacement (Caldwell et al., 2006). The development of prosocial skills, positive family relationships, and acceptance of responsibility forms part of the approach. The average length of treatment ranges from 45 to 83 weeks.

Developmental Disorders

Developmental disorders represent a group of psychiatric conditions that originate in childhood. These present with impeded functioning in a variety of areas, including speech, learning, movement, coordination, and social and communication difficulties. Autism and Asperger syndrome—now combined as autism spectrum disorder (ASD) in the DSM-5—are the two developmental disorders most associated in the literature with violent behavior. Although a link between ASD and violence appears to be tenuous and confounded, experts have argued that risk factors associated with the condition may result in violent and criminal behavior (Haskins and Silva, 2006). These include deficient social awareness, inappropriate interpersonal behavior, inflexible preoccupations, and poor empathy and emotional reciprocity. Comorbid psychotic and substance use disorders also increase the likelihood of violent offending. Personality disorders with antisocial and psychopathic features heighten the risk even further. In fact, it appears that the presence of comorbid conditions correlates much more with the potential for violent behavior than the coexisting ASD (Långström et al., 2008).

A long-term follow-up study of a group of former atypical autistic child, psychiatric inpatients at a hospital in Denmark, showed that a smaller percentage compared to a general population control group had criminal records. However, those with autism were more likely to have been convicted of violent crimes (+43%), robbery (+575%), weapons possession (+288%), and arson (+575%) than their peers from the general population (Mouridsen et al., 2008). Comparing those with Asperger syndrome had different results, leaning more toward sexual offending (+389%), and less to violent crimes (−78%) than the control group. The potential influence of comorbid conditions in the experimental group is not known and, unfortunately, limits the meaningfulness of the comparisons.

Schwartz-Watts (2005) pointed out that the prevalence of autism spectrum disorders in forensic settings is "startling" (p. 390). There appears to be a lack of data regarding the presentation of ASD in correctional facilities, which indicates a broader inability to recognize and deal with the repercussions of the condition in the criminal justice system (Freckelton, 2011). Violence and sexual assault perpetrated by those with autism are linked to sudden invasion of personal space and the inability to interpret emotional responses of the people whom they interact with. The intention is not violence, but rather a primitive response based on inaccurate interpretation of cues. Arson is an interesting criminal endeavor of many autistic offenders. Some have an obsessive preoccupation with flames, cinders, colors, and heat. The fascination drives their behavior rather than the intention to damage property or put lives at risk.

Several court cases addressed the aspect of ASD and criminal accountability. In *McKinnon v. Secretary of State for the Home Department* (2009), a psychiatric expert testified that the defendant, who was diagnosed with Asperger syndrome, "does not appreciate the relative priorities of societal rules and so has difficulty in judging what is serious offence and what is minor and balancing this against the perceived rightness of his cause." The testimony also highlighted difficulties that an autistic person often has in prison. They are more vulnerable to victimization, find the environment threatening, and are prone to depression, anxiety, and suicide. They do not have the social skills required to cope in prison, and typically find sharing a cell, groups of people, and loud noises aversive and traumatic. In an Australian criminal case against a defendant accused of raping his 11-year-old daughter, the defense pointed out that autism can be associated with deficient empathy, interpersonal naivety, and sexual frustration and preoccupations (*DPP v. HPW*, 2011). This is a combination often found in sexual assaults. The ruling in this case established that "the fact alone that a person has an Autism Spectrum Disorder does not necessarily exculpate or even mitigate an accused person's conduct" (Freckelton, 2011, p. 265).

Expert testimony in a Canadian criminal trial involving a defendant with Asperger syndrome who was charged with aggravated assault stated that people with this condition often have difficulty developing peer relationships (*R v. Kagan*, 2007). They tend to be blunt in their interactions, have mild paranoia, and a low tolerance for change. This can lead to frustration and anxiety leading them to misconstrue others' behavior as aggressive or threatening. These and other similar criminal trials demonstrated that ASD should be considered in legal decision-making (e.g., sentencing, intervention, and rehabilitation efforts). Interviewers should also consider features of the condition that may influence the effectiveness of questioning. This is because they are often more compliant and deferential and tend to be fearful of figures in authority, therefore, feeling more pressurized and anxious than others. Courts usually find defendants with ASD are able to appreciate the wrongfulness of their conduct and are fit to stand trial.

Other Risk Factors

As previously mentioned, there is a wide variety of factors that contribute in combination to initiate and sustain developmental trajectories of violence. These can be divided into three types, namely (1) extent of meeting a child's developmental needs, (2) parenting capacity, and (3) other family and environmental factors. If these elements are positive and balanced, the child is receiving the best safeguards to promote the welfare and desistance from violence and criminality. The following diagram is adapted from work by Vizard (2008, p. 393) that looks at treatment and intervention in the context of child personality development and the link with conduct disorders.

The importance of stability and function in the familial environment to promote psychological health and prevent violent and criminal behavior is clear. High levels of physical violence in children are linked to high trajectories of vandalism, theft, and alcohol use between ages 10 and 14 (Van Lier et al., 2009). At these ages, key aspects that mediate the presence of early risk factors on the trajectory of violence and aggression emerge. These include failure to perform well in school and contact with deviant peers (Aber et al., 2003). There are two basic trajectories that are problematic regarding youth violence, namely a steady increase and late acceleration. Although it is not easy to delineate, one can argue that the family context will have a crucial early impact, followed later by neighborhood, school, and peers. A study by Nash and Kim (2006) found that adolescent onset of violence (12% of their sample) is more than twice as prevalent as childhood onset that became chronic (5%). They concluded that three factors best predicted this late-onset trajectory: presence of a high strength of beliefs legitimizing aggression, bonding with delinquent peers, and lack of involvement in conventional activities.

Typology of Homicidal Youth

Cornell et al. (1987) proposed a typology of juvenile homicide offenders that consists of three categories based on the circumstance of the offense. The first is a psychotic type, which refers to youths who had symptoms of severe mental illness that included hallucinations or delusions. The second is a conflict type, where youths were engaged in an argument or dispute when the murder occurred. The third is a crime type, involving youths who killed during the commission of another felony such as rape or robbery. The consistency of the typology was tested using eight composite categories, namely family dysfunction, school adjustment, childhood problems, violence history, delinquent behavior, substance use, psychiatric problems, and stressful life events before the offense. Based on the information of 72 participants, 7% of the juvenile homicide offenders were assigned to the psychotic subgroup, 42% to the conflict subgroup, and 51% to the crime subgroup (Heide, 2013).

Further analysis revealed distinctions between the three types based on the eight life facets. Psychotic offenders typically have a history of mental health issues, including diagnoses and institutionalizations. They tend to have less prior criminal involvement. Compared to the conflict subgroup, the crime subgroup presents more school adjustment problems, substance abuse, and criminal activity. They also scored lower in the stressful life events category and had higher levels of psychopathology on the Minnesota Multiphasic Personality Inventory (MMPI-2) test. Furthermore, these young crime-type offenders are more likely to offend with others and be under the influence of drugs and alcohol at the time of the murder. Offenders in the crime subgroup also tend to dehumanize victims to a higher degree and to have more severe developmental deficits than offenders in the conflict subgroup (Heide, 2013).

Within the conflict subgroup, there are differences depending on whether the victim is a family member or not. Juvenile parricide offenders typically have a history of family dysfunction, but less school adjustment problems and delinquency than others in the conflict subgroup.

This information can be used to distinguish types of youth offenders from one another, which is useful in prevention and rehabilitation efforts. These distinctions link up with the crime classifications formulated by the FBI. At the highest level, The Crime Classification Manual divides homicide into four basic types. These are criminal enterprise, personal cause, sexual cause, and group cause (Douglas et al., 2006). A study by Myers and his colleagues with 25 juvenile homicide offender participants explored distinctions between two of these categories, namely criminal enterprise and personal cause (Myers et al., 1995). Ten profile characteristics were identified that applied to most of the sample. These consisted of familial factors such as family dysfunction, emotional abuse by a family member, and family violence. Personal and behavioral characteristics that are common in youth murderers are a history of violent acts, conduct disorders, learning disabilities, failing at least one grade, prior arrests, and psychotic symptoms. The availability of a weapon is the tenth factor. The research established significant differences between the criminal enterprise and personal cause youth homicide offenders on victim age, victim relationship, and physical abuse. Those with instrumental motives are more likely to have been abused and to have killed an adult whom they did not know (Heide, 2013). They tend to have more prominent personality disorders as well. Personal cause offenders typically have psychotic and/or mood disorders and choose a younger victim whom they know.

Therefore, juvenile homicides can be classified based on the primary motivation and attitude of the offender prior and during the offense. Any homicide likely contains a combination of these aspects leading up to the criminal act, but a deeper look could enable improved risk prediction. In general, youth offenders are callous and pursue their interest without regard for others, or they are emotionally and psychologically unstable.

Anger

Many tend to be angry at the world for standing in their way or not giving them what they deserve. They internalize their aggression, which presents as depressed and anxious feelings, or they externalize their aggressive tendencies as maladaptive behavior.

Resentment

Many youth homicide offenders, especially those in the personal cause subgroup, harbor a deep resentment toward peers and authority figures. They believe that the authority figures and peers unnecessarily disrespect, criticize, and deprive them of needs. With time, their hatred grows and becomes uncontrollable.

Fear

Fear and anticipatory anxiety are typical result of experiencing or witnessing abuse. Experts associate common coping mechanisms with paranoia and delusional beliefs. These can include paranoid delusions and the genuine belief that the violent behavior is necessary for protection and survival.

Depression

Feeling hopeless, unloved, and rejected often preempts the need to annihilate oneself and others. It is a form of a last desperate stance against injustices of the world and the inability to cope and achieve one's goals. We often see this typology in murder-suicide offenders or mass murderers who do not have an escape strategy.

Belonging

The most profound need of human beings is to belong and be accepted. Belongingness has multiple and strong emotional patterns and cognitive processes (Baumeister and Leary, 1995). Lack of positive attachments has an ill effect on health and psychological well-being, including resilience and adjustment. The need to belong can also make a young person suggestible to delinquent and criminal influences.

Entitled/Egoistic

Narcissistic and/or psychopathic personality traits present as beliefs of entitlement and pursuing egoistic interests. The notion that a person is somehow more important than the other underlies many criminal activities that involve instrumental motivations. There is a selfish, callous, and unsympathetic disregard for others. A parasitic, risk-seeking, and impulsive lifestyle is common in this type of offender.

Conviction of Beliefs

This type of juvenile homicide offender can present with psychotic delusions or hallucinations, and extreme ideologies or ideas influenced by others. They often have an inner conviction that others present a threat or believe that members of other groups are undeserving. Their beliefs can be influenced and radicalized by those with whom they associate.

At an early onset, these motivations are most often underlain by psychopathology due to traumatization by forms of abuse, neglect, or the deprivation of basic needs. An external influence that strengthens preexisting personal conditions and needs can also play an important role to predispose a juvenile to violence. Different types of youth homicide events associate with various situational contexts.

Reactive Aggressive Killer

This type of juvenile killer has poor impulse and emotional regulation skills and is sensitive to perceived criticism or disrespect. An argument or disagreement typically precedes a murder that was not premeditated, to which he reacts violently and instinctively. The risk of fatal violence increases if a weapon is present.

Revenge Killer

The juvenile revenge killer acts out of anger toward nonstrangers (or anyone who represents them) with the belief that they have somehow wronged him. These murders usually involve detailed preplanning, and the offender typically has delusions or psychopathic traits (Hickey, 2016). They seek to get even, most often against teachers, classmates, and family members.

Thrill Killer

The excitement of the act is the primary motivation for this type of juvenile homicide offender. They often have a need to feel powerful, which may involve taunting or torturing a victim. The suffering of their victims makes them feel more meaningful and in control. They are hedonists who target strangers and derive satisfaction from acts leading up to the murder, rather than the killing itself. They stalk and hunt their prey to increase the thrill.

Domestic Killer

Many juvenile homicide offenders who murder family members do so for revenge or instrumental gain. Violence by parents often precipitates child-to-parent violence, including violence between parents, corporal punishment of children, or physical abuse (Siegel, 2010). In addition to abused children, there are also cases where severely mentally ill children and juveniles and violent-prone antisocial children and juveniles have targeted their parents and family members (Hart and Helms, 2003). Research by Amorado et al. (2008) found that the majority of parricides by juveniles involve a measure of overkill. They also established that young domestic murderers less often move the bodies than older parricide offenders, suggesting less planning may be involved.

School Shooter

Of the school shooters who were minors, almost two-thirds obtained weapons from their home. In a sizeable portion of cases, about one-third, an argument preceded the shooting. Similar to juvenile domestic murderers, three types describe rampage school shooters. These are psychopathic, psychotic, and traumatized types (Langman, 2012). Psychopathic offenders oppose authority and order. Violence and the notoriety associated with it produces thrill. They put their goals and satisfaction first. They are often not from abusive homes, but their caretakers may have overindulged them. Psychotic killers are also often from stable family situations but have symptoms of schizophrenia and schizotypal personality disorders. As a result, hallucinations, delusions, and severe social and emotional impairment are present. Traumatized school shooters have histories of physical, emotional, and sometimes sexual abuse in their family homes. Their parents often abuse substances and engage in criminal activities (Langman, 2009).

However, as the following case study demonstrates, some murders or attempted murders are not that easy to fit neatly into a standard category. Children's minds have not yet developed abstract thinking and reality testing skills that are required to separate fantasy from real life, and they are highly suggestible too. The behavior and beliefs of role models and peers can have a profound impact on their judgment and understanding of consequences.

Case Study: Slender Man Stabbing

On Saturday, May 31, 2014, two 12-year-old girls lured another girl of the same age into woods in Waukesha, Wisconsin and stabbed her 19 times. They have apparently planned the attack since December 2013 to kill Payton Leutner, a classmate, allegedly believing Slender Man, a fictional Internet character, was going to harm their families if they did not please him. The day before, they convinced Leutner to join them for a sleep over to celebrate one girl's 12th birthday. The next morning they lured her into the forest in the Milwaukee suburb for a game of hide-and-seek. They pushed her down, and when Anissa Weier could not stab her, she gave the knife back to Morgan Geyser and told her to do it. After stabbing her 19 times, piercing her liver, pancreas, and stomach, they told her to lay still and be quiet. They fled, hoping that her death would appease Slender Man. After the attack, the victim crawled to a road and was found on the sidewalk by a passing cyclist. She was critically injured but survived. She was able to tell police who attacked her.

Police found the girls near Interstate 94 more than 4 h later and arrested them in as they were walking toward what they believed was Slender Man's mansion in Nicolet National Forest, a Wisconsin state park. One of them had a 5-inch bladed knife in her backpack. They expressed regret mixed with cold-blooded intent. The two girls were charged with attempted first-degree and attempted second-degree murder and on March 13, 2015, Judge Michael Bohren decided to keep their prosecution in adult court. They argued for transfer to juvenile court at another hearing in August, but the earlier decision was upheld. The judge cited the need to protect the public and concern that the girls would stop receiving mental health treatment and be released with no supervision when they exited the juvenile system at 18 (Joshi, 2015).

During interrogation, the girls revealed that they wanted to prove Slender Man exists, become his proxies, and live in his Northwood mansion, which was considered nonfear motives by the court. Premeditation to commit murder requires that a first-degree charge must start in adult court according to Wisconsin law, even for defendants as young as 10. To get the cases sent to juvenile court, the defense had to convince the court of three things: (1) that the girls could not receive adequate treatment in the criminal justice system, (2) that the move would not "depreciate the seriousness of the offense" and (3) that keeping the case in adult court is not necessary to deter other juveniles from similar offenses (Vielmetti, 2015).

Both girls have been assessed to determine competency to stand trial. Weier was deemed competent, and while Geyser was initially ruled incompetent, she was found to have regained competency. She had also been diagnosed with schizophrenia. According to court testimony of adolescent psychiatrist Dr. Kenneth Casimir, when asked what she would do if Slender Man asked her to kill again, Geyser replied: "Well if he told me, meaning Slender Man, if he told me to hurt more people, I'd have to do it. If he told me to break into someone's house and stab them, I would have to do it" (Sassoon, 2015, para. 3). She also reportedly said that it was weird that she did not feel remorse.

Doctors claimed that Geyser masterminded the plot and continued to believe that Slender Man is real and that she has ongoing relationships with several characters from the Harry Potter books who she feeds and sometimes sleep over. Disturbing scrawling and drawings were also found in a notebook belonging to Geyser that professes "I love killing people" and "I want to die," and depict supernatural characters. Also, more than

60 sketches of Slender Man—many included notes such as "not safe even in your own house" and "he is here always"—and Barbie dolls disfigured with cult symbols were found in her bedroom. Both girls believed Slender Man, who evolved from two black-and-white supernatural photos entered into a Photoshop contest through fan fiction into a kind of modern-day, tech-fueled folklore, is real. Geyser described him as a tall, faceless man with tendrils that are very sharp who preys on children. She told Weier that she had made a deal with Slender Man that if they killed Leutner, he would not kill their families and everything that they love.

In an interview with Newsweek, juvenile homicide expert and professor of criminology at the University of Southern Florida, Kathleen Heide, said that although highly publicized cases such as these create the impression that girls are becoming more violent, there is no evidence to support such a notion (Jones, 2014). Other noteworthy cases involving homicides committed by young girls exemplify how newsworthy these stories can be, creating a burstiness effect or frequency illusion. Examples that come to mind are:

- *Mary Bell*, a British girl who was convicted of manslaughter in 1968 after strangling two boys aged 4 and 3, respectively, to death when she was 11 years old. Based on psychiatric testimony that she was displaying classic signs of psychopathy and posed a very grave risk to other children, she was given an indefinite sentence of incarceration (Paul, 2011). She was released from prison in 1980 at the age of 23 and with a permanently protected identity, reportedly integrated successfully into the community.
- In 1986, *Paula Cooper* was the youngest person on death row in the United States. As a 16-year-old, she was found guilty of murdering a 78-year-old Bible teacher in Indiana whom she stabbed 33 times during a robbery attempt a year before. She was released from prison in 2013 and committed suicide 2 years later.
- In July 2012, 16-year-old *Shelia Eddy and Rachel Shoaf* lured their best friend into the woods of West Virginia and stabbed her to death stating as a reason that they did not like her. They were tried as adults. Eddy was sentenced to life and Shoaf to 30 years in prison. Eddy is eligible for parole in 2029 and Shoaf in 2025.

In reality, it is extraordinarily rare for girls to commit murder. In the last 30 years between 1976 and 2007, girls under 13 represented 4% of all female juveniles arrested for murder and nonnegligent homicide in the United States. With little exception, group dynamics play an important role in developing the fantasy and evolving it into reality. There is a motion pending, challenging the Wisconsin law that allows a child so young to be charged as an adult based on the argument that it is cruel and unusual punishment. Nevertheless, the Wisconsin judge ruled that the two girls who are now 13 years old will stay in adult court. If convicted as adults, they could face up to 65 years in a state prison where the system is not geared toward rehabilitation as is the juvenile system.

Media and Youth Violence

Exposure of young people to the violence depicted in various forms of media is often blamed for their violent behavior. Several studies have claimed that the introduction of television into countries was directly responsible for an increase in youth violence (Williams, 1986; Centerwall, 1989, 1992). However, these claims generally do not consider the concurrent effect of other demographic and environmental factors. Most evidence, however, establishes that exposure to violence in television, movies, and video games increases the likelihood of immediate violent behavior while the effect over the longer term remains unknown. Studies in the United States showed that an average youth between ages 8 and 18 watches about 10,000 violent acts each year on television (Krug et al., 2002). Several meta-analyses concluded that media exposure generally leads to increased aggression regardless of age. Even brief exposure to violence on television or film produced a short-term effect. It is especially those children who already have aggressive tendencies or are easily provoked or aroused that are affected. Media violence also increases attitudes and beliefs that legitimize anger and aggressive behavior, which is an important factor in youth violence as highlighted earlier.

The increase in electronic communication and online activities has also changed behaviors. Young people do not engage so much in face-to-face communications anymore. As a result, their social skills, including being able to distinguish between appropriate and inappropriate interpersonal conduct and interpret social cues correctly, lack development. They become more depersonalized and the consequences of their online behavior are not clearly apparent. This can lead to bullying, threatening, harassing, and victimizing behavior online. Perpetrators of electronic aggression typically extend their attitudes into the real world as well, failing to see potential consequences of their actions. Research has estimated that between 4% and 9% of the youths have committed electronic aggression in previous months (Williams and Guerra, 2007; Ybarra et al., 2007). These youths are also more likely to believe that physically bullying peers and face-to-face aggression are acceptable behaviors.

The Criminal Justice System and Youth Homicide

Appropriate evaluation and management of child and adolescent homicide offenders are important across all stages of the criminal justice process, from investigation and sentencing to rehabilitation and reintegration. For various reasons, proper responses are often not made. In cases of serious offenses, such as homicide, the need to close a case and punish the offender sometimes takes precedence over rehabilitative approaches. Most young homicide offenders have serious mental health issues, in the clinical, if not legal sense. Their circumstances and fate are still largely determined by others, which may cause distress and frustration. Their brains are still developing and they have a better chance of changing and recovering than their adult counterparts. Any condition except antisocial and psychopathic features is usually highly treatable in this population. Therefore, the forensic considerations in the management of a child or adolescent offender in the criminal justice system are important to ensure an effective yet fair system, which begin in the pretrial phases.

Investigating and Interviewing Youth

The best practices of the investigative interviewing of a child and an adolescent offender is a topic that could fill an encyclopedia. As the scope is limited here, such a discussion is condensed to a few brief guidelines. The most important principle is to evaluate the young person's abilities and attitude as accurately as possible. What is his cognitive level of understanding? Does he have mental health conditions that may interfere with or influence questioning? What is his general attitude and personality? An open and objective assessment of these factors at the start of the session forms a solid basis. Next, use a structured investigative interview protocol. Although it can deviate as the circumstances and information change, there are usually five stages. First, an introduction is made and the roles, process, and objectives explained. As much as possible, a relationship is established between the interviewer and suspect. Second, the suspect is given the opportunity to provide a narrative of the events involved in the offense. It is as uninterrupted and open-ended as the suspect offers, but momentum is maintained with well-paced prompts. Based on the contents of the narrative, the interviewer elicits additional information by guiding the suspect through information-rich narratives, ensuring that all detail is covered to construct a vivid picture. The information is reviewed with the suspect. Finally, the session is closed in a manner that can facilitate follow-up. The following are general guidelines for young suspects who are cognitive and emotionally immature, or present with developmental difficulties:

- Always have a parent, guardian, or legal representative present, videotape the interview, and conduct an informed consent process in very simple terms.

- This includes assessing whether they understand the process, the reason that they are interviewed, and their rights.

- With the help of others who know the suspect, determine his or her cognitive and communication strengths or deficits.

- Review all records of assessment that are available, including medical and psychiatric reports.

- Plan and conduct questioning based on the youth's cognitive and communication abilities.

- Address him or her personally, and always with a nonthreatening attitude and demeanor.

- Demonstrate respect and objectivity.

- Use simple and direct language, deal with one issue at a time, and do not use abstract concepts, hypotheses, or metaphors that can be confusing.

- Each question should be direct, clear, and concise.

- Give the youth an opportunity to recreate events in their own words—interrupt only to keep up the momentum.

- Use active listening techniques to ensure that your understanding of everything that is said is exactly the same as that of the youth.

- Be patient, calm, and nonjudgmental; avoid any statement or gesture that can be construed as confrontational, coercive, or deceptive.

- Ascertain whether the person understands the concept of truth and can distinguish between right and wrong.

- Take frequent breaks as younger people, especially those with developmental disorders, tend to have shorter attention spans.

- Be alert to nonverbal clues, but clarify them instead of making assumptions. Many gestures and signs that are commonly associated with deceit or guilt are prevalent in children who find themselves in overwhelming situations.

- If the youth appears belligerent, evasive, argumentative, or stubborn, rephrase the question, or take a break.

- As young and mentally ill offenders are very conducive to false confessions, 69% of 12–15-year-old exonerees in the United States from 1989 to 2004 involved false confessions (Owen-Kostelnik et al., 2006), be careful to avoid suggestions and emotional pressure.

- Remember that young people are more likely to favor perceived short-term gains over long-term consequences.

- Appreciate the fact that young people have different memory processing that may cause them to regurgitate their perception of experiences in vivid detail without proper comprehension of what it means.

- Depending on the circumstances and personality of the child, they may naturally trust or distrust authority figures; guide them away from either extreme by being factual and objective but friendly (do not use the friendly–unfriendly interrogation technique).

- Use open-ended questions that rely on narrative responses instead of leading questions.

- Seek the advice of a legal professional or psychologist who is familiar with interviewing young people and/or their specific mental health status.

These 22 guidelines should ensure that your interview with a young suspect goes smoothly and is effective unless they have severe deficits, resistance, or instability. If there are indications that the interviewee has psychopathic tendencies, be even more professional, thorough, and prepared. Know everything possible about the suspect. Do not criticize. More than others, young people like compliments and recognition. A custodial interview that is done thoroughly and effectively forms an important basis when the trial goes to court.

Sentencing Youth

Many countries in the world, including the United States and the United Kingdom, move juvenile cases of serious offenses such as homicide to adult courts. In exceptional cases, children as young as 10-year-old have been tried as adults for murder and attempted murder. The two case study presentations are examples of such decisions. In the first, two girls who were 11-year-old at the time of an attempted murder are being tried in an adult court in Wisconsin, the United States. The second case elaborates a murder committed in England after which two 10-year-old boys were also tried in an adult court. There has been a long-standing question of criminal responsibility and culpability that children should have for their crimes. The appropriate punishment has also been fiercely debated. While the United Nations and human rights groups work tirelessly to get countries to increase the age of criminal responsibility to 14, case law has led the way in sentencing options. Three landmark court rulings had particular importance: *Roper v. Simmons*, 543 U.S. 551 (2005), *Graham v. Florida*, 130 S. CT. 2011 (2010), and *Miller v. Alabama and Jackson V. Hobbs*, 132 S. CT. 2455 (2012).

The Supreme Court ruled in *Roper v. Simmons* that juveniles cannot be sentenced to death. They argued it is a disproportionate sentence for young people whose immaturity and susceptibility to outside pressures and influences diminish their culpability. The court also held that such a sentence is cruel and unusual in the context of the nation's evolving standards of decency. In the 30 years before the *Roper* decision, 22 prisoners were executed for crimes they committed as juveniles. Because of *Roper*, 72 juveniles were removed from death row in 12 states. As a result of the court decision, the harshest sentence available for offenses committed by those under 18 was life without the possibility of parole (LWOP).

In *Graham v. Florida*, the court abolished the use of LWOP for all crimes except homicide as it was also deemed disproportionate and cruel and unusual. The *Graham* ruling affected at least 123 prisoners, of which 77 had been sentenced in Florida. Therefore, after *Graham*, juveniles could only be sentenced to LWOP for crimes involving homicide. Although the new sentences did not necessarily guarantee release, it guaranteed a "meaningful opportunity" for eventual parole.

Following *Graham*, about 2500 offenders who were juveniles at the time of their crimes were serving sentences of LWOP for homicides. In 2012, the Supreme Court decided the cases of *Miller* and *Jackson* jointly, ruling that mandatory LWOP sentences for juveniles violate the Eighth Amendment. The majority argument called for consideration of the characteristics of a juvenile defendant to ensure a fair and individualized sentence. Young people are prone to "transient rashness, proclivity for risk, and inability to assess consequences," factors that should be taken into account on a case-by-case basis. Although the ruling in *Miller v. Alabama* did not explicitly forbid life terms for young murderers, the court found, with a 5–4 majority, that an LWOP sentence for a 14-year-old child did not necessarily violate the Eighth and Fourteenth Amendments' prohibition against cruel and unusual punishment. However, case-by-case consideration is required as LWOP constituted an unconstitutionally disproportionate sentence in some cases. Concurring opinions argued that the court has to determine whether the offender actually killed (e.g., not an accomplice felony murder situation) or intended to kill the victim to justify such a harsh sentence. Of the 46 U.S. states that have some form of felony murder rule on their statute books, 11 unambiguously allow for individuals who commit a felony that ends in a death to be charged with murder. This applies even when they are the victims, rather than the agents, of the killing (Pilkington, 2015).

A recent poll conducted in Massachusetts indicated that the majority of the general public in the United States supports a punishment that offers a juvenile convicted of a homicide the opportunity of parole (see Figure 12.3) (J. Trounstine, personal communication, October 14, 2015). Only 21% of the respondents favored a sentence of life without the possibility of parole for an offender under 18. Sixty percent of respondents also indicated that they do not believe adult prison is an appropriate placement for a juvenile. More than half (53%) were of the opinion that a person who committed a homicide while under the age of 18 should be released when they are a maximum of 33-years-old (Figures 12.4).

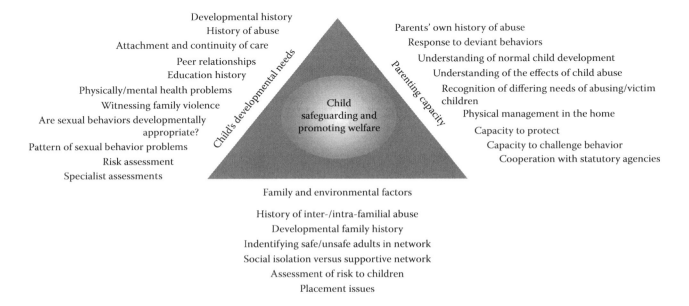

Figure 12.3 Factors that influence child welfare.

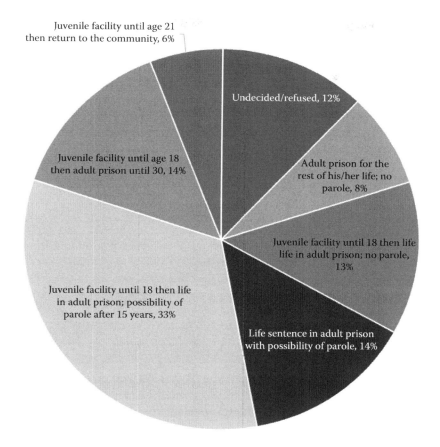

Figure 12.4 Juvenile homicide offenders punishment poll.

After the court decision in *Miller v. Alabama*, the debate continued about the appropriateness of LWOP sentences for juvenile homicide offenders. Courts and state legislatures also continue to review and test the arguments on specific cases. The Louisiana Legislature enacted a law in 2013 making juvenile homicide offenders eligible for parole after serving 35 years of their life sentences but did not apply it retroactively. A petition to do so was filed in the Supreme Court of Louisiana. In *State v. Darryl Tate* (2013), the court ruled that the Miller decision was not retroactive. The ruling was based on the argument that Miller "merely sets forth a new rule of constitutional criminal procedure, which is neither substantive nor implicative of the fundamental fairness and accuracy of criminal proceedings." Currently, there are about 2000 inmates in the United States who have been convicted as juveniles (Mills et al., 2015).

Treatment and Prevention of Youth Homicide

As has been highlighted previously, there are individual-, family-, and community-level risk factors involved in the occurrence of youth violence, which can be addressed by national and local initiatives. The most common intervention strategy is to identify at-risk individuals and conduct programs at school or elsewhere to improve their individual skills, attitudes, and beliefs. Social development programs improve competency and social skills and promote behavior that is prosocial by focusing on anger management, social perspectives, conflict resolution, and moral development. According to Krug et al. (2002), such programs have been offered in Norway, England, Germany, and the United States and, as a result, bullying was reduced by half within 2 years. Planned Parenthood programs, parental training, after-school programs and extracurricular activities, mentoring, and home-school partnership programs have also proven effective in reducing the risk factors for youth violence. Heide and Solomon (2003) proposed 12 components of effective treatment for juvenile homicide offenders. These are (pp. 13–19):

1. *Effective and extensive assessment.* A thorough medical, psychiatric, and risk assessment based on multiple sources forms the foundation of an effective treatment and intervention plan. This includes

exploring the youth's history of victimization and abuse, and dysfunctional behaviors such as self-harm, suicide attempts, substance abuse, risk-seeking activities, and anger outbursts.

2. *Comprehensive cognitive behavioral restructuring.* Legitimizing beliefs about violence and dysfunctional behavior are strongly linked to homicide. Cognitive behavioral-based treatment has proved effective to improve these issues.

3. *Prosocial skills training.* Antisocial behavior is characterized by poor impulse control and judgment. Learning prosocial skills improves conflict resolution, emotion regulation, anger management, and self-control.

4. *Positive peer communities.* Contact with delinquent peers is another important risk factor in youth violence. By structuring a positive peer culture in schools, churches, sports clubs, and other places, healthy role models are fostered. As a result, moral leadership, tolerance, and respect are improved.

5. *Anger management.* By teaching youth to recognize the triggers of anger and frustration, they can develop adaptive alternatives to manage it. They are also guided to recognize, acknowledge, accept, and validate their feelings.

6. *Empathy training.* Empathy enables a person to put himself in the shoes of another person, understand what they are feeling, and why. It is a quality that is often lacking in juvenile offenders. Empathy involves perceiving and communicating—verbal and nonverbal—skills. Emphatic techniques, such as reflective listening and body language, can be taught.

7. *Clear, firm, and consistent discipline.* Most juvenile homicide offenders lack self-control and self-discipline due to the absence of a male role model, or limits and boundaries. Setting and enforcing structure, boundaries, and norms is important to promote socialization.

8. *Drug and alcohol education and counseling.* Substance abuse is common among juvenile homicide offenders. Therefore, assessment and intervention are critical.

9. *Transition services.* Based on the needs of the juvenile, services and resources have to be identified and provided to assist with the reintegration process after release. If possible, family counseling is advisable. Assistance in basic life skills is often required.

10. *Aftercare.* Continued supervision is another important element in the prevention of recidivism, especially as juvenile homicide offenders usually have long-standing, multifaceted issues. Intensive aftercare programs should be conducted and inpatient treatment provided, where required.

11. *Psychopharmacological management.* Juveniles with disorders such as attention deficit hyperactivity disorder (ADHD), psychotic disorders, depression, or bipolar disorder need medication. Noncompliance is often a problem and juveniles have to be monitored.

12. *Educational and vocational programs.* Stable employment is the most important protective factor to prevent reoffending. Academic improvement and job skills will provide an alternative to crime and improve their self-esteem.

Family therapy programs are relatively costly, but can be effective to improve family functioning and reduce behavioral problems in children. Initiatives to address gang activities, substance abuse, and firearm availability also had some success for adolescents. The overall objective is to identify at-risk youth as early as possible, understand the problem and causes of youth violence, utilize multifaceted strategies, and identify interventions that are successful. Ultimately, the approach to achieve and sustain reduced violence among youth is to promote economic opportunities and growth, which will help make communities more stable and viable, what Douglas and Bell (2011) referred to as "Rebuilding the Village."

Reintegration into Society

There are several programs targeting successful reintegration of juvenile offenders into their communities after release. The focus is twofold. Programs that are conducted in the years before release focus on fostering empathy, responsibility, and verbal expression, while decreasing feelings of hostility and aggression (Heide, 2013). The Capital Offender Program (COP) offered at the Giddings State Home and School in Lee County, Texas is one example. Evaluations of the outcome of the program showed that "youths became significantly less hostile and aggressive, assumed more responsibility, and had more empathy for their victims" (p. 238) as a result of the COP. Furthermore, the likelihood of capital offenders being rearrested for a violent crime within a year after release dropped by 53%, an improvement which was relatively maintained at the 3-year interval (43%).

A program that is offered after release to improve reintegration into the community is Project CRAFT, or the Community Restitution and Apprenticeship-Focused Training program, which is designed to promote employment of previously incarcerated youth by providing home building skills. CRAFT was implemented at multiple sites in six U.S. states, namely Maryland, Nevada, Tennessee, Colorado, Florida, and Ohio. The CRAFT model emphasizes cooperation between the juvenile justice system, parole, probation, and community-based service providers. The model consists of 10 components: (1) outreach and recruitment; (2) assessment and screening; (3) individualized development plans; (4) case management services; (5) industry-validated, trades-related training; (6) building industry-related academics; (7) community service; (8) academic preparation and substance abuse treatment; (9) employability and life skills training; and (10) community transition and long-term follow-up (Hamilton and McKinney, 1999). Participants receive 840 h of practical training and classroom instruction in trades-related skills before graduating. Outcome studies have shown that the program has a high rate of job placement after reintegration, with a recidivism rate that is substantially below the national average, which is estimated at 50% for serious juvenile offenders (Lipsey, 1999). This program demonstrates how important stable employment with improved social skills and lifestyle is in the successful reintegration of youth offenders. The second case study follows the lives of two child murderers who have seemed to take very different directions, probably due to different attitudinal risk factors.

Case Study: The Jamie Bulger Murder

Two-year-old Jamie Bulger disappeared from the New Strand Shopping Center in Bootle, a town in North West England, on February 12, 1993, while accompanying his mother. His body was found two days later on a railway line two-and-a-half miles away in Walton. CCTV footage from the shopping center showed two local 10-year-old boys, Jon Venables and Robert Thompson, abducting Bulger. They often played truant from school, as they had done that day at the mall. The footage showed that they had been stealing various items and casually observing children all day. Around 4:30 p.m., they took the child outside and on a walk across Liverpool to the Leeds and Liverpool Canal. Here, they dropped him onto his head, and he suffered injuries to his face. Then, they walked to the railway line near the disused Walton and Anfield railway station, close to Anfield Cemetery. They put paint into his left eye, kicked and stomped on him, and threw bricks and stones at him. They also dropped a 22-pound iron bar on him and stuffed batteries into his mouth. He sustained a total of 42 injuries, many of which could have been the cause of his death, according to the coroner's testimony. Venables and Thompson also removed the boy's socks, trousers, and underpants. They left him on the rail tracks in the hope that a train hitting him would cover their tracks.

After a witness had identified Venables from the CCTV footage, he was arrested along with Thompson. Forensic evidence linked them to the crime, and prosecutors tried them in 1993 in public as adults. At trial, the principle of *doli incapax*, which presumes that young children cannot be held legally responsible for their actions, was rejected. The court ruled that they knew the difference between right and wrong. Thompson was considered to have taken the leading role in the abduction. Venables described how Bulger held his hand and allowed him to pick him up during their walk. The Lord Chief Justice ordered them to serve a minimum of 10 years in prison.

Venables' parents and Thompson's mother visited them every few days at their respective custodial facilities. Both boys received education and rehabilitation and made good progress, suffering from PTSD. After appeals to the European Court of Human Rights, their sentences were reduced to 8 years, and British authorities released them in 2001. They assumed new identities and locations, which the court prohibited the media from publishing. Reports revealed that psychiatric experts suggested that Thompson was a psychopath, which the parole panel dismissed (Harris and Bright, 2001). Another psychiatric report of Venables concluded that rehabilitation efforts had been successful; he was unlikely to reoffend.

As a result of the controversy that followed the murder, the Criminal Justice and Public Order Act 1994 clarified the rules on the availability of certain types of video material to children. The change was after the media had claimed that the murder reminded of scenes in "*Child's Play 3*" (1991), a movie that the Venables' had rented before the killing. In March 2010, the Children's Commissioner also called on the U.K. Government to raise the age of criminal responsibility from 10 to 12 (Lipscombe, 2012). In the United States, 33 states have set no minimum age of criminal responsibility but apply a capacity related test. The lowest set threshold among the U.S. states is North Carolina at 7 years, and the highest is Wisconsin at 10 years. In most of Europe, no child can be subject to criminal penalties under the age of 14, including Germany, Italy, and Austria, which is also the minimum age proposed by the Council of Europe. The U.N. Convention on the Rights of the Child does not consider a minimum age of criminal responsibility below the age of 12 years to be internationally unacceptable, and also proposes 14 as the appropriate age. The Ministry of Justice rejected the appeal of the Children's Commissioner, stating that children over the age of 10 know the difference between bad behavior and serious wrongdoing. On June 2, 2015, Lord Dholakia presented a bill to the U.K. Parliament that would raise the minimum age of criminal responsibility if voted in, probably to 14 in line with international guidelines (UK Parliament, 2015).

In March 2010, Venables was arrested and charged with the possession and distribution of child pornography and sentenced to 2 years in prison. In September 2013, the parole board approved his release. According to media reports, Venables, who is drinking heavily and using drugs, recently told a stranger in a pub that he blamed Bulger's mother for his death as she left him unattended. Robert Thompson appears to have lived a more quiet and uneventful life after his release.

After the Bulger murder, their upbringing was scrutinized for signs of lack of love, care, and parental control that could explain their behavior. Both had parents who were separated, and each had difficulties with attendance, learning, and behavior at school. They played truant, shoplifted, and were violent. The Thompson family was terribly dysfunctional (Gillan, 2000). Gillan went on to report that Ann Thompson's husband abandoned her and her seven children 5 years before the Bulger killing. She started to drink heavily. There were many violent incidences between the boys. The mother and two boys attempted suicide on different occasions.

The Venables household was also dysfunctional but in a different way (Gillan, 2000). Jon's parents divorced when he was 3 years old. They lived in separate houses a mile apart, where the children spent equal time. Jon's brother and sister both had learning difficulties and attended special schools. Jon was hyperactive and always acting out. He threw tantrums at home and school whenever he was not the center of attention. He already had a record of violence for attempting to choke another boy at school. His mother was severely depressive, which attributed to Jon's suicidal ideation. In 1987, neighbors called the police because the children (then aged 3, 5, and 7) were left alone for 3 h. His mother apparently had a harsh parenting style, including regular beatings that made Jon afraid of her. Despite these reports and appearances, there are many families and children in similar conditions that do not resort to violence. It does not automatically condemn the parents for their children's wrongdoing, although it is widely accepted to play a large part in a child predisposed to violent behavior (Figure 12.5).

Figure 12.5 Drawing by Venables weeks before the murder.

Investigators found a drawing at his father's home that revealed Jon's deeply disturbed mind, which was helped along by his fondness for horror movies. Regarding the boys' personalities, Thompson was the instigator with a harder and colder demeanor, showing signs of psychopathy, while Venables was an attention-seeker (Wright et al., 2010). His personality style could explain why Venables have had an extremely difficult time coping with a secret identity. People in his position have to blend in with ordinary people and live humdrum lives under immense psychological pressure to prevent exposure.

The Bulger case is another reminder of how important secure attachments in childhood are. Although the boys did not experience extreme abuse, early neglect had apparently taken its toll. Their identities are still protected, but neither has been known to have committed a violent offense since the 1993 murder. According to a report by Sir David Omand issued after the 2010 arrest of Venables, he had difficulty keeping a job, was addicted to alcohol and drugs, and had problems with depression. He conceded that, upon obtaining this knowledge, they should have imposed a curfew, random drug testing, and substance abuse treatment (Omand, 2010). According to media speculation, Thompson is involved in a long-term relationship with another man and it is believed that he has settled into the community without problems (Jeeves, 2010). As the Bulger case illustrates, the outcomes of released juvenile homicide offenders vary greatly, and it is extremely difficult to predict.

There are only a handful of studies that measure recidivism rates of juvenile homicide offenders. Three studies with a reasonable sample size are worth mentioning. In the first, Howell (1995) reported on 128 subjects who were divided into a treated and untreated group. He found that the conviction rate of any crime post release from prison was 22% of the treated offenders and 40% of the untreated offenders after the first year. However, this difference almost disappeared after 3 years. Heide, Spencer, Thomson, and Solomon (2001) found a recidivism rate in a sample of 59 juvenile homicide offenders at 60% after 15 years. A more recent study by Vries and Liem (2011) reported a general recidivism of 59% 5 years after release among 137 juvenile homicide offenders which increased to 71% at 10 years. A total of 16 offenders (3%) were convicted of another murder, and 20% for a violent crime.

The profile of the offenders was very similar. More than half of the juveniles had at least one psychological disorder while about 20% had two or more. Nearly 50% had poor impulse control, 60% were from a problematic family background, and 20% had a history of physical abuse by a parent. Almost half of the study population had criminal offenses before the homicide event, of which half were property offenses and one-quarter violent offenses. On average, they have committed their first offense 2 years before the homicide, at the age of 15. Furthermore, nearly half of the juveniles had contact with delinquent or convicted friends and two-thirds frequently used alcohol or drugs (Vries and Liem, 2011).

These findings underscore a couple of very important points in the prevention of juvenile homicide offending. The first is the need for early identification and treatment of mental health disorders, including drug and alcohol abuse. Second, treatment and monitoring should begin when a youth first offends and continued after release from prison or other secure placement. Third, social programs should be available to target establishing and strengthening of healthy relationships while discouraging delinquent peer contact.

References

Aber, J. L., Brown, J. L., and Jones, S. M. 2003. Developmental trajectories toward violence in middle childhood: Course, demographic differences, and response to school-based intervention. *Developmental Psychology, 39*(2), 324–348. DOI: 10.1037/0012-1649.39.2.324.

Amorado, R. M., Lin, C., and Hsu, H. 2008. Parricide: An analysis of offender characteristics and crime scene behaviors of adult and juvenile offenders. *Asian Journal of Domestic Violence and Sexual Offense, 4*(1), 1–32.

Baumeister, R. F. and Leary, M. R. 1995. The need to belong: Desire for interpersonal attachments as a fundamental human motivation. *Psychological Bulletin, 117*(3), 497–529.

Caldwell, M., Skeem, J., Salekin, R., and Van Rybroek, G. 2006. Treatment response of adolescent offenders with psychopathy features: A 2-year follow-up. *Criminal Justice and Behavior, 33*(5), 571–596. DOI: 10.1177/0093854806288176.

Casey, B. J., Jones, R. M., and Hare, T. A. 2008. The adolescent brain. *Annals of the New York Academy of Sciences, 1124*, 111–126. DOI: 10.1196/annals.1440.010.

Centerwall, B. S. 1989. Exposure to television as a cause of violence. *Public Communication and Behavior, 2*, 1–58.

Centerwall, B. S. 1992. Television and violence: The scale of the problem and where to go from here. *Journal of the American Medical Association, 267,* 3059–3063.

Cornell, D. G., Benedek, E. P., and Benedek, D. M. 1987. Juvenile homicide: Prior adjustment and a proposed typology. *American Journal of Orthopsychiatry, 57*(3), 383–393. DOI: 10.1111/j.1939–0025.1987.tb03547.x.

Cottle, C. C., Lee, R. J., and Heilbrun, K. 2001. The prediction of criminal recidivism in juveniles: A meta-analysis. *Criminal Justice and Behavior, 28*(3), 367–394. DOI: 10.1177/0093854801028003005.

Douglas, K. and Bell, C. C. 2011. Youth homicide prevention. *The Psychiatric Clinics of North America, 34*(1), 205–216. DOI: 10.1016/j.psc.2010.11.013.

Douglas, J. E., Burgess, A. W., Burgess, A. G., and Ressler, R. K. 2006. *Crime Classification Manual: A Standard System for Investigating and Classifying Violent Crimes* (2nd ed.). San Francisco, CA: Jossey-Bass.

DPP v. HPW. 2011. VSCA 88.

Federal Bureau of Investigation. 2014. Uniform crime reports: 2014 Crime in the United States. *FBI.* Retrieved from http://1.usa.gov/1MNFzhq.

Finkelhor, D. and Omrod, R. 2001. Homicides of children and youth. *OJJDP Juvenile Justice Bulletin,* NCJ 187239, 1–12. Retrieved from https://www.ncjrs.gov/pdffiles1/ojjdp/187239.pdf.

Fite, P. J., Poquiz, J., Cooley, J. L., Stoppelbein, L., Becker, S. P., Luebbe, A. M., and Greening, L. 2015. Risk factors associated with proactive and reactive aggression in a child psychiatric inpatient sample. *Journal of Psychopathology and Behavioral Assessment, 36,* 338–347. DOI: 10.1007/s10862-015-9503-0.

Fite, P. J., Stoppelbein, L., and Greening, L. 2009. Proactive and reactive aggression in a child psychiatric inpatient population. *Journal of Clinical Child & Adolescent Psychology, 38*(2), 199–205. DOI: 10.1080/15374410802698461.

Freckelton, I. 2011. Autism spectrum disorders and the criminal law. In: M. Mohammadi (Ed.), *A Comprehensive Book on Autism Spectrum Disorders.* Rijeka, Croatia: InTech, pp. 249–272.

Gillan, A. 2000, November 1. Did bad parenting really turn these boys into killers? *The Guardian.* Retrieved from http://bit.ly/1jfLwcP.

Graham v. Florida. 2010. 130 S. CT. 2011.

Hamilton, R. and McKinney, K. 1999. *Job Training for Juveniles: Project CRAFT.* Washington, DC: Office of Juvenile Justice and Delinquency Prevention, U.S. Department of Justice.

Harris, P. and Bright, M. 2001. The secret meetings that set James's killers free. *The Guardian.* Retrieved from http://bit.ly/21citcg.

Hart, J. L. and Helms, J. L. 2003. Factors of parricide: Allowance of the use of battered child syndrome as a defense. *Aggression and Violent Behavior, 8*(6), 671–683. DOI: 10.1016/S1359-1789(02)00103-9.

Haskins, B. G. and Silva, J. A. 2006. Asperger's disorder and criminal behavior: Forensic-psychiatric considerations. *Journal of the American Academy of Psychiatry and the Law, 34*(3), 374–384.

Heide, K. M. 2013. *Young Killers: The Challenge of Juvenile Homicide.* Thousand Oaks, CA: Sage.

Heide, K. M. and Solomon, E. P. 2003. Treating today's juvenile homicide offenders. *Youth Violence and Juvenile Justice, 1*(1), 5–31. DOI: 10.1177/1541204002238361.

Heide, K. M., Spencer, E., Thomson, A., and Solomon, E. P. 2001. Who's in, who's out, and who's back: Follow-up data on 59 juveniles incarcerated in adult prison for murder or attempted murder in the early 1980s. *Behavioral Sciences and the Law, 19*(1), 97–108. DOI: 10.1002/bsl.423.

Hickey, E. W. 2016. *Serial Murderers and Their Victims* (7th ed.). Boston, MA: Cengage.

Howell, J. C. 1995. *Guide for Implementing the Comprehensive Strategy for Serious, Violent, and Chronic Juvenile Offenders.* Washington, DC: U.S. Department of Justice, Office of Justice Programs, Office of Juvenile Justice and Delinquency Prevention.

Jeeves, P. 2010, March 6. Now James' other killer wants 24-hour protection. *Daily Express.* Retrieved from http://bit.ly/1PJKsMq.

Jones, A. 2014, August 13. The girls who tried to kill for Slender Man. *Newsweek.* Retrieved from http://bit.ly/1pNHjMu.

Joshi, P. 2015, August 21. Slender Man obsessed teens Morgan Geyser, Anissa Weier plead not guilty to stabbing. *International Business Times.* Retrieved from http://bit.ly/1NKT9QH.

Kimonis, E. R., Frick, P. J., Cauffman, E., Goldweber, A., and Skeem, J. 2012. Primary and secondary variants of juvenile psychopathy differ in emotional processing. *Development and Psychopathology, 24*(3), 1091–1103. DOI: 10.1017/S0954579412000557.

Krug, E. G., Dahlberg, L. L., Mercy, J. A., Zwi, A. B., and Lozano, R. 2002. *World Report on Violence and Health*. Geneva, Switzerland: World Health Organization.

Langman, P. 2009. School shooters: A typology. *Aggression and Violent Behavior*, *14*(1), 79–86. DOI: 10.1016/j.avb.2008.10.003.

Langman, P. 2012. Thirty-five rampage school shooters: Trends, patterns, and typology. In: N. Böckler, T. Seeger, P. Sitzer and W. Heitmeyer (Eds.), *School Shootings: International Research, Case Studies, and Concepts for Prevention*. New York, NY: Springer, pp. 131–156.

Långström, L., Grann, M., Ruchkin, V., Sjöstedt, G., and Fazel, S. 2008. Risk factors for violent offending in autism spectrum disorder: A national study of hospitalized individuals. *Journal of Interpersonal Violence*, *24*(8), 1358–1370. DOI: 10.1177/0886260508322195.

Lindberg, N., Laajasalo, T., Holi, M., Putkonen, H., Weizmann-Henelius, G., and Häkkänen-Nyholm, H. 2009. Psychopathic traits and offender characteristics: A nationwide consecutive sample of homicidal male adolescents. *BMC Psychiatry*, *9*(18), 1–11. DOI: 10.1186/1471-244X-9-18.

Lipscombe, S. 2012. *The Age of Criminal Responsibility in England and Wales*. Briefing Paper Ref. No. SN/HA/3001. London, England: U.K. Parliament. Retrieved from http://researchbriefings.parliament.uk.

Lipsey, M. W. 1999. Can intervention rehabilitate serious delinquents? *The Annals of the American Academy of Political and Social Science*, *564*(1), 142–166. DOI: 10.1177/000271629956400109.

Loeber, R., Menting, B., Lynam, D. R., Moffitt, T. E., Stouthamer-Loeber, M., Stallings, R., and Pardini, D. 2012. Finding from the Pittsburgh Youth Study: Cognitive impulsivity and intelligence as predictors of the age-crime curve. *Child & Adolescent Psychiatry*, *51*(11), 1136–1149. DOI: 10.1016/j.jaac.2012.08.019.

McKinnon v. Secretary of State for the Home Department. 2009. EWHC 170.

Miller v. Alabama. 2012. 132 S. Ct. 2455, 567 U.S., 183 L. Ed. 2d 407.

Mills, J. R., Dorn, A., and Hritz, A. C. 2015. Juvenile life without parole in law and practice: The end of super predator era sentencing. *American University Law Review*. Advance online publication. Retrieved from http://bit.ly/1VRvTu7.

Mouridsen, S. E., Rich, B., Isager, T., and Nedergaard, N. J. 2008. Pervasive developmental disorders and criminal behavior: A case control study. *International Journal of Offender Therapy and Comparative Criminology*, *52*(2), 196–205. DOI: 10.1177/0306624X07302056.

Myers, W., Burgess, S., and Burgess, A. 1995. Psychopathology, biopsychosocial factors, crime characteristics, and classification of 25 homicidal youths. *Journal of the American Academy of Child and Adolescent Psychiatry*, *34*(11), 1483–1489. DOI: 10.1097/00004583-199511000-00015.

Nash, J. and Kim, J. S. 2006. *Trajectories of Violent Offending and Risk Status in Adolescence and Early Adulthood*. Washington, DC: U.S. Department of Justice National Criminal Justice Reference Service.

Omand, D. 2010. *Omand review: Independent serious further offense review*. Retrieved from http://bit.ly/1hDVpQL.

Owen-Kostelnik, J., Reppucci, N. D., and Meyer, J. R. 2006. Testimony and interrogation of minors: Assumptions about maturity and morality. *American Psychologist*, *61*(4), 286–304. DOI: 10.1037/0003-066X.61.4.286.

Paul, J. 2011. *When Kids Kill*. London, England: Virgin Books.

Pilkington, E. 2015, February 26. Felony murder: Why a teenager who didn't kill anyone faces 55 years in jail. *The Guardian*. Retrieved from http://bit.ly/1AaAE0N.

Rappaport, N. and Thomas, C. 2004. Recent research findings on aggressive and violent behavior in youth: Implications for clinical assessment and intervention. *Journal of Adolescent Health*, *35*(4), 260–277. DOI: 10.1016/j.jadohealth.2003.10.009.

R v. Kagan. 2007. 261 NSR (2d) 285; 2008 261 NSR (2d) 168.

Roper v. Simmons. 2005. 543 U.S. 551.

Sassoon, L. 2015, June 20. Slender Man stabbing girl "could try to kill" again it let out of jail. *Mirror Online*. Retrieved from http://tinyurl.com/n9q3lzq.

Schwartz-Watts, D. M. 2005. Asperger's disorder and murder. *Journal of the American Academy of Psychiatry and the Law*, *33*, 390–393.

Sickmund, M. and Puzzanchera, C. 2014. Juvenile offenders and victims: 2014 National report. Washington, DC: National Center for Juvenile Justice. Retrieved from http://www.ojjdp.gov/ojstatbb/nr2014/downloads/NR2014.pdf.

Siegel, L. J. 2010. *Criminology: Theories, Patterns, and Typologies* (10th ed.). Belmont, CA: Wadsworth.

Snyder, H. N., Sickmund, M., and Poe-Yamagata, E. 1996. *Juvenile Offenders and Victims: 1996 Update on Violence*. Washington, DC: Office of Juvenile Justice and Delinquency Prevention.

State v. Darryl Tate. 2013. 12–2763 (La. 4/19/13), 111 So.3d 1023.

Swart, J., Bass, C. K., and Apsche, J. A. 2015. *Treating Adolescents with Family-Based Mindfulness.* New York, NY: Springer.

Tsavoussis, A., Stanislaw, S. P. A., Stoicea, N., and Papadimos, T. J. 2014. Child-witnessed domestic homicide and its adverse effects on brain development: A call for societal self-examination and awareness. *Frontiers in Public Health, 2*(178), 1–5. DOI: 10.3389/fpubh.2014.00178.

UK Parliament. 2015. *Age of Criminal Responsibility Bill* [HL] 2015-16. Retrieved from http://bit.ly/1jfL26u.

Van Lier, P. A. C., Vitaro, F., Barker, E. D., Koot, H. M., and Tremblay, R. E. 2009. Developmental links between trajectories of physical violence, vandalism, theft, and alcohol-drug use from childhood to adolescence. *Journal of Abnormal Child Psychology, 37*(4), 481–492. DOI: 10.1007/s10802-008-9289-6.

Viding, E., Fontaine, N. M. G., and McCrory, E. J. 2012. Antisocial behavior in children with and without callous-unemotional traits. *Journal of the Royal Society of Medicine, 105*(5), 195–200. DOI: 10.1258/jrsm.2011.110223.

Vielmetti, B. 2015, March 13. Judge keeps two girls in Slender Man stabbing in adult court. *Milwaukee Journal Sentinel.* Retrieved from http://tinyurl.com/ofnbj6s.

Vizard, E. 2008. Emerging severe personality disorder in childhood. *Psychiatry, 7*(9), 389–394. DOI: 10.1016/j.mppsy.2008.07.009.

Vries, A. M. and Liem, M. 2011. Recidivism of juvenile homicide offenders. *Behavioral Sciences and the Law, 29*(4), 483–498. DOI: 10.1002/bsl.984.

Williams, K. R. and Guerra, N. G. 2007. Prevalence and predictors of internet bullying. *Journal of Adolescent Health, 41*(Suppl.), 14–21.

Williams, T. M. 1986. *The Impact of Television: A Natural Experiment in Three Communities.* New York, NY: Academic Press.

Wright, S., Sims, P., and Freeman, S. 2010, March 9. Revealed: The horror image drawn by Jon Venables just weeks before he killed James Bulger. *Mail Online.* Retrieved from http://dailym.ai/1ldGzCw.

Ybarra, M., West, M. D., and Leaf, P. 2007. Examining the overlap in internet harassment and school bullying: Implications for school intervention. *Journal of Adolescent Health, 41*(Suppl.), 42–50.

13 Intellectually Disabled Offenders

Joan Swart

Contents

Introduction 257
  Factors Contributing to Mental Health Problems in People with Intellectual Disability 258
  Clinical Definition and Criteria of ID 259
Effect of Susceptibility and External Influence on an Intellectually Disabled Person 260
  ID, Comorbidity, and Criminal Behavior 260
Interviewing Intellectually Disabled Suspects and Witnesses 261
  Assessing Fitness to Attend a Police Interview 262
  Guidelines for Interviewing an Intellectually Disabled Person 263
ID and the Death Penalty 264
  Atkins v. Virginia 264
  Death Penalty and ID after Atkins 265
  Hall v. Florida 266
  Determination of IQ 267
  Determination of Functional Impairment 267
Risk Assessment, Restoration of Competence, and Rehabilitation of Intellectually Disabled
Offenders 268
  Risk Assessment of Intellectually Disabled Offenders 268
  Restoration of Competence 270
    Measuring Adjudicative Competence 270
    Restoring Adjudicative Competence 271
  Rehabilitation of Intellectually Disabled Offenders 272
References 272

Introduction

The definition and criteria of intellectual disability (ID) have changed in the past 10 years with less emphasis on a numerical overall intelligence quotient (IQ) score to reflect the significance of adaptive functioning, both behaviorally and intellectually. In addition to definitions by the American Association on Intellectual and Developmental Disabilities (AAIDD) and diagnostic criteria of the *Diagnostic and Statistical Manual of Mental Disorders, Fifth Revision* (DSM-5; American Psychiatric Association, 2013), case law has followed to reflect these parameters. The *Atkins* ruling set out to protect intellectually disabled offenders; it largely failed to set guidelines for the legal determination of ID, or mental retardation as it was previously referred to, but most U.S. death penalty states used an IQ cutoff of 70 to guide their *Atkins* decisions, which ruled the death penalty unconstitutional for intellectually disabled offenders. In *Hall*, the Supreme Court ruled that such a bright line cannot be used to determine exclusion from the death penalty based on ID.

There is little evidence that ID is linked to violent and criminal behavior. There are, however, certain factors that may predispose an intellectually disabled person to violent and homicidal behavior. These include factors and characteristics that are typical in this population, including a high level of comorbidity (i.e., coexisting mental health disorders), substance abuse, limited independence, susceptibility, and a history of abuse, victimization, and exploitation. But it is especially adverse childhood conditions and psychopathic or antisocial personality traits that put intellectually disabled individuals at risk of violent behavior. Having been sexually abused and a possessing lower level of social integration increases the risk of sex offending, which can cause distorted cognitions, more so when associated with poor impulse control; lack of emotion regulation, guilt, and remorse; callousness; and unmet needs.

Factors Contributing to Mental Health Problems in People with Intellectual Disability

ID per se does not predispose a person to violent behavior, but various biological, social, and psychological factors contribute to a higher risk when present with low intellectual functioning (see Figure 13.1). As a result, the intellectually disabled person may lack social integration and skills, experience a lack of support, have difficulty managing adverse life events, and engage in maladaptive behavior.

According to Gates and Barr (2009, p. 229), the following factors in an intellectually disabled person's life and upbringing contribute to a higher risk of delinquency and violence:

1. High levels of social deprivation or poverty

2. Family composition (i.e., raised in a single-parent home)

3. Family or primary caregiver history of mental health

4. Presence of family disharmony and negative role models

5. Negative life events (i.e., abuse, accidents, domestic violence, and bereavement)

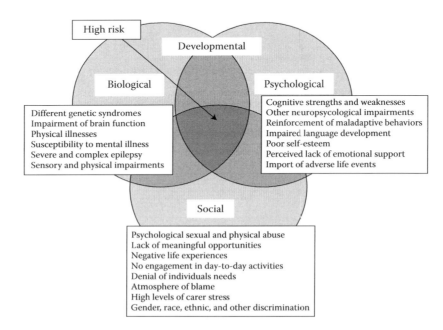

Figure 13.1 Contributing factors to mental health problems coexisting with intellectual disability.

6. Lower opportunities for employment, education, and recreation
7. Excessive amounts of free time
8. Limited relationships and friends—social exclusion
9. Lack of meaning in life

In the following sections, different aspects of intellectually disabled homicide offenders are discussed, focusing on their contact with the criminal justice system and typical behavior in the context of crime and law, namely, how their typical characteristics may influence them to become involved in homicide, the problem of false confessions, assessment of ID in death penalty cases, and risk prediction in legal decision-making.

Clinical Definition and Criteria of ID

The *DSM, Fourth Edition, Text Revision* (DSM-IV-TR; American Psychiatric Association, 2000) estimated that 2–3% of people meet the criteria for ID, for which the diagnostic criterion required an IQ score of approximately 70 and below. The DSM-5 has moved away from specific IQ scores and instead relies on adaptive functional abilities to diagnose ID, and an estimate based on the changed criteria is that about 1% of the general population qualifies as intellectually disabled. The DSM-5 definition and criteria for ID are (American Psychiatric Association, 2013, p. 33):

Intellectual disability (intellectual developmental disorder) is a disorder with onset during the developmental period that includes both intellectual and adaptive functioning deficits in conceptual, social, and practical domains. The following three criteria must be met:

1. Deficits in intellectual functions, such as reasoning, problem solving, planning, abstract thinking, judgment, academic learning, and learning from experience, confirmed by both clinical assessment and individualized, standardized intelligence testing.
2. Deficits in adaptive functioning that result in failure to meet developmental and sociocultural standards for personal independence and social responsibility. Without ongoing support, the adaptive deficits limit functioning in one or more activities of daily life, such as communication, social participation, and independent living, across multiple environments, such as home, school, work, and community.
3. Onset of intellectual and adaptive deficits during the developmental period.

A specifier is assigned to indicate the current severity: mild, moderate, severe, and profound. Unlike previous DSM versions, no full-scale IQ score ranges are attached to each level of disability. Instead, qualitative descriptions are assigned to each in three domains: conceptual, social, and practical, reflecting the increased focus on the adaptive functional components of intellectual ability. This interpretation is also reflected in the *Hall* ruling, which is discussed in a later paragraph. In the DSM-IV-TR (American Psychiatric Association, 2000), classifications were made according to IQ ranges, as follows:

Clinical Term	IQ
Borderline intellectual functioning	71 up to 84
Mild	50–55 up to around 70
Moderate	35–45 up to around 50–55
Severe	20–25 up to around 35–40
Profound	Below 20–25

Of persons suffering from ID in the "mild" and lower categories, 85% of those fall in the "mild intellectual functioning" category (Fabian et al., 2011). Most criminal defendants who have ID will function in the upper end of these four categories and will also qualify for a mild specifier. However, as *Hall v. Florida* (2014) has ruled: the interpretation of ID for forensic purposes such as qualification for the death penalty under *Atkins* cannot rely on a finite numeric cutoff IQ value, but has to account more strongly for adaptive functioning. Therefore, using the more recent diagnostic criteria, ID is reflected more in the adaptive functioning and behavior of a person than intellect alone. If such a person is poorly adapted to daily life, including dysfunctional relationships and distorted needs, the risk of involvement in criminal and violent behavior increases.

Effect of Susceptibility and External Influence on an Intellectually Disabled Person

It is widely recognized that most intellectually disabled persons are very susceptible to external influences and ideas, especially from those whom they consider authority figures or role models, or are dependent upon. As a population, intellectually disabled persons are neither more violent than the general population nor more prone to engage in homicidal activity. For those who engage in criminal activities, their preference seems to be vandalism of property, arson, and drug dealing. Instances where homicide is involved are often accompanied by one of a few factors: an unintended accident, momentary reactive anger, or manipulation by a partner or acquaintance.

ID, Comorbidity, and Criminal Behavior

Research has found that the level of offending behavior among the moderate-to-severe intellectually disabled population is "strikingly low" (Holland et al., 2002, p. 6). It is estimated that 4% of the total U.S. prison population is borderline and lower intellectually disabled, compared to 7% with psychotic disorders, and 12% with other psychological disorders (Petersilia, 2000). The crimes most associated with ID are property crimes (e.g., vandalism and arson), petty theft, and drug crimes. Similar characteristics and risk factors apply to intellectually disabled persons and the general population alike that lead to offending behavior, including psychosocial disadvantage, familial offending, a history of behavioral problems, unemployment, and comorbid mental health needs (Jones, 2007). They are, however, at increased risk due to the demands of community living, poor coping strategies, limited independence, and vulnerability to victimization and exploitation.

However, physical violence and injury are uncommon among offenses committed by intellectually disabled offenders, and only a minority is involved in homicide. Many of these cases involve influence of a more intelligent and dominant partner who exploits the intellectually disabled person's compliant and dependent nature.

About 60% of intellectually disabled adult offenders also suffer from one or more additional psychiatric disorders (Su et al., 2000). These coexisting conditions are typically substance abuse (68%) and antisocial personality disorder (25%); psychotic disorder (5%), obsessive-compulsive disorder (5%), and depressive disorder (2%) presented at much lower rates (Salekin et al., 2010). Such diagnoses are often challenging as ID masks some of the comorbid symptoms and present difficulty in communication, expression, and language use. The presence and degree of ID also modifies manifestation of these coexisting conditions. In addition, response to treatment may not be favorable compared to nonintellectually disabled patients with similar conditions (Girimaji, 2000).

Intellectually disabled offenders who exhibit violent behavior that may result in physical assault and homicide are associated with antisocial and psychopathic personality traits (Hogue et al., 2006). They require referral to higher security placement, present higher risk of reoffending, and are linked to poor treatment outcomes (Morrissey and Hollin, 2011). It is now recognized that there is no association between global IQ and antisocial or psychopathic personality traits, although some symptoms may overlap, such as affective lability, self-harm, impulsivity, and aggressive behavior (Forth et al., 1990). Furthermore, young people with ID are at increased risk of victimization and sexual abuse. Firth et al. (2001) found that intellectually disabled persons who sexually abuse younger victims were likely victims of earlier multiple forms of abuse themselves. Physical and sexual abuse during childhood tend to perpetuate a cycle of violence where the victim eventually becomes the abuser due to dynamics where coping mechanisms and strategies become habitual and fixed. Together with ID and other mental health disorders, poor living conditions and instability, substance abuse, and domestic violence in the family, the risk of violent behavior in adolescence and adulthood increases. Negative labeling in the community and their limited independence also increases susceptibility to negative role models, especially in contexts of disharmony or unmet needs.

Case Study: Teresa Wilson

Teresa Wilson was born in 1969 and grew up in poverty in Danville, Virginia. She dropped out of school at age 16 to marry, and gave birth to a daughter. The marriage soon ended and Teresa started to use alcohol and painkillers. After several low-paying jobs, Teresa found employment at the Dan River textile mill and married her supervisor within months. Her second husband, Julian Lewis, had two sons and a daughter and when the eldest died in a car accident, he used the life insurance money to buy a manufactured home on 5 acres of land in Pittsylvania County, Virginia. In August 2002, Julian's younger son, Charles J. Lewis, obtained a $250,000 insurance policy in preparation for his impending deployment to

Iraq as part of the U.S. Army Reserve. Charles designated his father as the primary, and Teresa Lewis as the secondary beneficiaries.

Soon after Teresa met 21-year-old Matthew Jessee Shallenberger and 19-year-old Rodney Lamont Fuller, she started a sexual relationship with both. In October 2002, Charles came home for a visit from army training in Maryland. Shallenberger and Lewis discussed killing Charles and his father Julian with Fuller's help to get access to the insurance. She gave them $1200 to buy firearms and ammunition. On the night of October 30, 2002, they put their plan in motion. Shallenberger and Fuller entered the Lewis mobile home through the back door that Lewis had left unlocked. While she waited in the bathroom, Shallenberger shot the sleeping Julian several times, while Fuller shot Charles three times in his bedroom with a shotgun. Teresa waited 45 min before calling the police at 3:55 a.m., taking $300 from her husband's wallet, which she gave to Shallenberger and Fuller before they left. When the deputies arrived, Julian was still alive and managed to indicate that his wife knew the assailants before passing away. Teresa maintained that it was a home invasion by two unidentified men.

Shortly afterward, when Teresa tried to withdraw $50,000 from her husband's Prudential Securities account with a forged check, she was arrested and confessed to police that she had offered money to Shallenberger to have her husband killed. At trial, a court-appointed psychiatrist testified that Teresa had a full-scale IQ of 72. Appeals for leniency were unsuccessful and she was sentenced to death. Shallenberger and Fuller were sentenced to life imprisonment in separate trials. Two years later, in 2004, Shallenberger wrote in a partially transcribed affidavit that Teresa was in love with him, was eager to please him, and was not very smart (Hammack, 2010). Shallenberger also wrote to a friend that the only reason he ever had sex with Lewis was to get her to fall in love with him so she would give him the insurance money, which he needed as seed money to establish a drug trade operation and become a hitman after making a name for himself. He committed suicide in prison 2 years later. Fuller confirmed the theory that Lewis was not the mastermind, writing in a sworn affidavit dated August 12, 2010 that Shallenberg came up with the plan to kill Teresa's husband and that he was the dominant one in the relationship. Shallenberg, with an IQ of 113, was known to be intelligent and manipulative. Her defense also pointed out that her addiction to painkillers clouded her judgment and her diagnosis of dependent personality disorder put her further at risk of exploitation. After all appeals failed, Lewis was executed on September 23, 2010.

Teresa Lewis is a good example of the risks that an intellectually disabled person faces of being manipulated by a dominant partner, especially with comorbid substance abuse and personality disorders that further increased her dependence and affected her judgment. The judge's rationale in giving Lewis a death sentence was that she was more culpable than the men, but evidence suggests that she was compliant and dependent, and lacked the skills required to organize and lead a conspiracy.

Interviewing Intellectually Disabled Suspects and Witnesses

Inappropriate interviewing of intellectually disabled suspects and witnesses has a high probability to produce inaccurate or false information. Besides the possibility to derail or delay a criminal investigation, false confessions also result in wrongful convictions and often the actual offender remains undiscovered. According to the Innocence Project, more than one in four people wrongfully convicted but later exonerated by deoxyribonucleic acid (DNA) evidence made a false confession or incriminating statement. Although the reasons that people falsely confess are complex and varied, intellectual impairment is often a factor. People with IDs are typically susceptible and tend to agree with authority figures. As a result, they have a natural tendency to acquiescence response bias, and will answer "yes" to a wide range of questions, even when it is incorrect, inappropriate, or absurd.

Many law enforcement interviewers also do not have adequate training to deal with mental illness. Additionally, there is often pressure and zeal to obtain a confession or information that would facilitate a conviction. In some cases, threats, coercion, or some form of torture are applied to expedite the process. It may also involve more subtle methods, including withholding sleep and food, irregular and extended hours, deceit (e.g., making promises, misrepresenting evidence, and lying about polygraph results), and circumventing the Miranda warning. Such approaches are incredibly misguided and irresponsible. Not only does it not guarantee accurate information but it is also a blatant disregard of the rights of the interviewee, and increases the probability of a wrongful conviction. In the Drizin and Leo (2004) sample of false confessors, about 22% were diagnosed with ID. The case of Earl Washington Jr. is a good example of a wrong and irresponsible approach to interview an intellectually disabled suspect, which created a travesty of justice while many measures and safeguards exist to prevent such an injustice.

Case Study: Earl Washington Jr.

In June 1982, Rebecca Lynn Williams, a 19-year-old mother of three, was raped and stabbed 38 times in her Culpeper, Virginia apartment. Almost a year later, Earl Washington Jr. was arrested in neighboring Fauquier County for an alleged burglary and malicious wounding. After 2 days of questioning, police claimed that he had confessed to five different crimes, including the murder of Rebecca Williams. The first four confessions were rejected on the basis of inconsistencies and inability of witnesses to identify Washington. Despite the fact that Washington did not know the race of the victim, that she was raped, or the address of the apartment, described her incorrectly as "short," claimed to have stabbed her only two or three times, and that there were no one else in the apartment at the time (her two young children were there when she was murdered), the confession was accepted after multiple rehearsals.

Washington picked out the scene of the crime after being taken there three times in one afternoon by police. The confession was the only "evidence" that linked him to the crime. Psychological analysis reported that he had a full-scale IQ of 69, the intellectual functioning of a 10-year-old child, and that he was compliant with authority figures, seeking their approval. When a rare plasma protein was identified on a shirt found at the crime scene and did not match Washington, the test was ruled inconclusive. In 1984, a jury sentenced Washington to death for the murder of Rebecca Williams. A direct appeal failed, but a habeas corpus petition secured a stay of execution in 1985, 9 days before it was scheduled to take place. In 1993, parties involved in the case agreed to conduct DNA testing on the biological evidence. The test results revealed that Washington was excluded as a contributor of the seminal stain, and Washington's sentence was commuted to life imprisonment. Only in 2000 did the newly elected Governor of Virginia agree to additional DNA testing, and Washington was granted an absolute pardon for the capital murder conviction. In 2007, the State agreed to settle a lawsuit brought on behalf of Washington for $1.9 million.

Although at the time intellectually disabled offenders were not yet excluded from the death penalty on the basis of their impaired functioning, the police conduct in Washington's case were inexcusable. Leading questions and deceit were used to coax a confession; Washington was relentlessly interrogated for 2 days, asked leading questions, provided with information and scenarios about the crime, and coached to provide the desired confession. All of these techniques are especially inappropriate for an intellectually disabled suspect. If there was no DNA evidence that could eventually be tested to exclude him, he would have been executed in 1985.

Assessing Fitness to Attend a Police Interview

If the suspect is in a custodial situation where Miranda rights are required, the investigator (or a medical or mental health professional) must be able to determine whether the person has the mental capacity and understanding of his constitutional rights in order to waive it in an intelligent and thoughtful manner. He should be asked to explain his rights back in his own words. This technique is referred to as reflective interviewing and it is very useful when dealing with a wide variety of personalities and abilities. Confession plays a significant role in solving a crime—an American study indicated that interrogation was necessary to obtain a conviction in 17% of cases (Wald et al., 1967), and a similar study in England and Wales indicated 30% (Baldwin and McConwell, 1980). Therefore, safeguards are required to ensure a fair process. This includes assessing the fitness of an interviewee to be interviewed as a first step.

In England and Wales, a code of practice was implemented in 1984 to regulate protocols with respect to a number of matters, including the detention, treatment, and questioning of persons by police officers (Ventress et al., 2008; Norfolk and Stark, 2011). The Police and Criminal Evidence Act (PACE) set standards, which, if breached, will render confessions inadmissible. PACE specifically states that "a detainee may be at risk in an interview if it is considered that:

1. Conducting the interview could significantly harm the detainee's physical or mental state.

2. Anything the detainees say in the interview about their involvement or suspected involvement in the offense about which they are being interviewed might be considered unreliable in subsequent court proceedings because of their physical or mental state." (Norfolk and Stark, 2011, p. 346).

Such examination is conducted by a medical or mental health professional and includes observations on the general appearance, physical examination when appropriate, mental state examination, and functional assessment. The latter covers whether the interviewee is aware of and understands the reason of arrest, purpose of the interview, and his/her legal rights. A determination is also made whether the interviewee has the capacity to make rational and informed decisions and is able to carry out that decision. This procedure is particularly valuable to prevent mistreatment of mentally vulnerable individuals that could lead to miscarriages of justice. After being found fit to be interviewed, there are various further measures that can be taken to ensure that good information is obtained during an interview with an intellectually disabled individual.

Guidelines for Interviewing an Intellectually Disabled Person

By using a sensible and knowledgeable approach to interviewing an intellectually disabled suspect or witness, the interviewer is in the best possible position to extract accurate and reliable information, thereby solving a case and obtaining a just conviction.

1. Limit the duration of an interview session to less than 6 h. A study by Drizin and Leo (2004) found that 84% of false confessions occurred after 6 h of interviewing. The average duration in their sample was more than 16 h of uninterrupted interviewing.

2. Polygraphs and voice stress analyzers are not reliable lie-detection technology and are problematic with intellectually disabled persons who are susceptible and vulnerable to deceit, often believing that such tests are infallible.

3. Lying, deceit, and misrepresenting evidence by interviewers should not be allowed when interviewing an intellectually disabled suspect, as it plays a significant role in many false confessions.

4. Implicit promises of leniency should not be used. Pragmatic implication, such as suggesting alternative scenarios for crimes and outcome, unduly promotes false confessions.

5. Any voluntary confession, especially by an intellectually disabled person, should be examined for reliability and supported by substantial corroboration.

6. Use simple language and have the person explain important points in their own words; also consider the interviewee's development when assessing his answers and judgments.

7. Consider the cognitive and emotional development and any other mental health conditions that may be presented.

8. Interviewing is a learning process and has an impact on the interviewee's memory and recall; take care not to lead these individuals or inadvertently taint their statements.

9. Accept that there are no behavioral manifestations that can be specifically and reliably linked to criminal behavior or adverse experiences; it should only provide cues to be corroborated by other means.

10. The NICHD protocol that was developed by the National Institute of Child Health and Human Development in Bethesda, Maryland has proven effective to develop reliable information from an intellectually disabled interviewee (Fleisher and Gordon, 2006, p. 213):

    a. The interviewer should properly introduce himself or herself.

    b. Develop rapport with the interviewee.

    c. Establish the purpose of the interview.

    d. Establish that the interviewee is willing to talk to the interviewer.

    e. Establish that the interviewee understands that they do not have to know the answer to every question.

    f. Establish that the interviewee knows the difference between telling the truth and lying.

    g. Establish that the interviewee understands that they can correct the interviewer if they feel something is said that is not true.

h. Utilize investigative questions that do not influence the quality and accuracy of the information obtained.

11. Entire interviews (not only the confession) with intellectually disabled suspects should be videotaped from a vantage point that shows the interviewer and interviewee equally.

Investigating and interviewing a person with intellectual abilities is a sensitive process that can be expected to take more time than usual. Specialized expertise and knowledge is required, including the management of typical traits and abilities, and common co-occurring mental health conditions that may be present. The ability and development of the intellectually disabled person always has to be taken into account in the planning and management of a case and its evidence. A transparent, sensitive, and thoughtful approach is much more effective in generating reliable and accurate information than threats, coercion, or deceit. Such considerations will significantly reduce false confessions and wrongful convictions of intellectually disabled persons.

ID and the Death Penalty

Although the objectives of modern criminal justice systems are to punish the offender, appease society, and keep it safe, the central philosophy has been that the offender should have been culpable to justify punishment. He or she must have known that the criminal act was wrong and understood the quality and nature of the act. Even if there is a lesser or greater degree of culpability, offenders should be able to understand the basic legal processes and its potential consequences. The same applies to the death penalty. By its nature, the presence of ID places a question over the ability of an offender to understand and appreciate his or her behavior and its impact, and the reason and meaning of execution.

Atkins v. Virginia

In *Atkins v. Virginia*, 536 U.S. 304 (2002), the Supreme Court of the United States ruled 6–3 that execution of an intellectually disabled person constituted cruel and unusual punishment, and thus violates the Eighth Amendment. However, they left the definition and determination of intellectual ability to the discretion of individual states. Daryl Atkins was charged for abducting a person from an ATM, robbing and shooting him. During the penalty phase of the trial, a forensic psychiatrist testified that Atkins was mildly mentally retarded, with an IQ of 59. He corroborated his conclusion with interviews he had with Atkins and with others who knew him, review of school reports, and court records of other crimes. In the first and second sentencing, the jury sentenced Atkins to death.

The Supreme Court overruled the sentence, concluding that the death penalty is not a suitable punishment for a mentally retarded offender, as there is a concern that the justification underpinning the rationale for the death penalty—retribution and deterrence of capital crimes—does not apply due to the reduced culpability of such offenders. The majority opined that the "evolving standards of decency" in American law prohibits excessive punishment such as the execution of mentally retarded offenders. In their amicus brief, the American Psychological Association (APA) joined others such as the AAIDD, arguing that imposition of the death penalty on mentally retarded persons offends the shared moral values of the American people, that mentally retarded offenders are not responsible for their condition, but that it reduces their culpability and increases the likelihood of the conviction and execution of a factually innocent individual beyond what is tolerable. In his dissent, Justice Scalia warned against feigning of symptoms of mental retardation in future cases, a valid argument, but one that must be contended with in other ways (e.g., comprehensive and valid assessments).

However, although the court ruled executing a mentally retarded offender unconstitutional, it failed to endorse clinical definitions of and/or guidelines for the determination of mental retardation (Blume et al., 2009). Their contention that states must "generally conform" to their understanding has proven sufficiently ambiguous to permit states to set their own, greatly varying, eligibility criteria for mental retardation that are often subjectively motivated. The case of Marvin Lee Wilson is a good example of irregularities in state-applied definitions and criteria.

Case Study: Marvin Lee Wilson

Marvin Lee Wilson was born in Southeast Texas on August 5, 1958. He was the second eldest child of six children, had little contact with his father and went to special education classes throughout his 11 years of formal education. According to his psychological assessment, his reading, writing, and math skills never progressed beyond early elementary level. He dropped out of high school to work in a construction company in order to help his sick mother take care of the household. Soon after he fathered a son, he looked for a "decent" job for more than a year in order to rent a home and marry his son's mother. Eventually he turned to the streets where he did make money. However, he was soon arrested for robbery and served 4.5 years in prison. After his release, he again looked for a job for a short while before returning to crime for an income. His second arrest got him another 6 years in prison. When he got out again, he worked in his cousin's construction company and returned to live with his son and his mother again, but with the rainy season he ran out of money, turning to the streets again, this time selling drugs. It was only 4 months after his release. He made money "easy and quick," but 16 months later he was arrested one last time, for murder.

On November 4, 1992, police officers entered Wilson's apartment pursuant to a search warrant. Police informant, 21-year-old Jerry Williams, entered and left the building shortly before. Wilson, Vincent Webb, and a juvenile female were present in the apartment where over 24 g of cocaine was found. The men were arrested for possession of a controlled substance. Wilson was released on bond. Wilson told Terry Lewis that someone snitched on him and he "was going to get him." On November 9, 1992, witnesses observed Wilson in the parking lot of a grocery store, beating Williams, who ran away across the street into a field. Wilson chased and caught up with him. Andrew Lewis, Terry's husband followed them by car and together they forced Williams into the vehicle. His nude body was discovered next to a road the next morning. The autopsy showed that he died from close range gunshots to the head and neck. No forensic evidence or eyewitness testimony could determine the identity of the shooter. Lewis' wife testified that Wilson confessed to pulling the trigger and as a result, Lewis was sentenced to life in prison without the possibility of parole. Wilson was sentenced to death.

Wilson's final appeals focused upon his alleged mental retardation. IQ tests were administered throughout his life. In the first test, given at school, when he was 13, he scored 73. The next test was given by Texas Department of Criminal Justice when Wilson was 29, when he scored 75. Wilson took three more IQ tests as part of the evidentiary hearing. His scores in those were 61, 75, and 79. Despite the controversy, wide-spread condemnation, and last-minute appeals, Marvin Wilson was executed by lethal injection on August 7, 2012. Wilson's execution was largely criticized as arbitrary, unconstitutional, and a blatant disregard of the *Atkins* ruling (NAACP Brief, 2009; AAIDD Brief, 2011).

Death Penalty and ID after Atkins

There continue to be various interpretations of and standards for considering ID in death penalty determinations after the *Atkins* ruling among the 31 states with the death penalty. Many argue it is due to the fact that *Atkins* came short of setting appropriate definitions, standards, and guidelines for the assessment of ID. Although the total national number of annual executions has been declining in the United States since 1999, three states in particular show no indication of decline and contributed more than two-thirds of U.S. executions in 2013 and 2014—Texas, Florida, and Oklahoma. Although Georgia, for example, is the only state in the nation that still requires the condemned to bear the burden of proving his or her retardation beyond a reasonable doubt—the highest legal standard—it is mostly the decisions of Texas and Florida that continue to come under fire. It is especially in the South where the legal rules of ID seem to have been manipulated by local officials and judges in a way that undermines the *Atkins* decision.

Despite the fact that Marvin Wilson was subjected to a battery of internationally recognized clinical procedures and tests, including extended interviews and analysis of his school records that showed he had a reading and writing level of a 7-year-old, having been bullied and widely regarded as "stupid" and "retarded," and unable of normal everyday functioning such as managing money, dressing without assistance, and self-direction, he was deemed fit to be executed under state-developed guidelines. Texas accepts the definition of mental retardation set forth by the AAIDD (formerly, the American Association of Mental Retardation, AAMR) as: Under the AAIDD definition, mental retardation is a disability characterized by three prongs: (1) "significantly subaverage" general intellectual functioning, (2) accompanied by "related" limitations in adaptive functioning, and (3) the onset of which occurs prior to the age of 18. However, Texas has developed a novel set of guidelines to determine such functioning, referred to as the Briseño factors, which is considered by most mental health professionals as completely misguided and arbitrary. The following are weighed as evidence indicative of such ID (In re Briseno, 2004):

1. Did those who knew the person best during the developmental stage—his family, friends, teachers, employers, authorities—think he was mentally retarded at that time, and, if so, act in accordance with that determination?

2. Has the person formulated plans and carried them through or is his conduct impulsive?

3. Does his conduct show leadership or does it show that he is led around by others?

4. Is his conduct in response to external stimuli rational and appropriate, regardless of whether it is socially acceptable?

5. Does he respond coherently, rationally, and on point to oral or written questions, or do his responses wander from subject to subject?

6. Can the person hide facts or lie effectively in his own or others' interests?

7. Putting aside any heinousness or gruesomeness surrounding the capital offense, did the commission of that offense require forethought, planning, and complex execution of purpose?

If one or more of these factors are deemed present or true, even by subjective standards, appeals on the grounds of ID are rejected, as have happened with Marvin Wilson. There is neither scientific or theoretical basis that ties these factors to sufficient grounds to reject the intent of *Atkins*, nor can it be measured objectively and reliably. It is an example of an arbitrary system, similar to approaches in other states, that has effectively circumvented the intention of *Atkins* to safeguard intellectually disabled offenders from cruel and unusual punishment as promised by the Eighth Amendment.

Hall v. Florida

After *Atkins*, a few states instituted legislation that drew a hard line on IQ scores without any consideration of adaptive behavior: Alabama, Kentucky, Virginia, Idaho, and Florida all required defendants to scores below 70 on an IQ test to be deemed intellectually disabled. Many other death penalty states also use such a finite cutoff, which is either 65 (Arkansas) or 70 (Maryland, New Mexico, Nebraska, North Carolina, South Dakota, Tennessee, and Washington). Most of these states apply the three-pronged definition of ID, but does not define or specify an appropriate measurement of "deficits in adaptive behavior." The lack of a legal definition of ID as applied to *Atkins*, including the hard line distinction based on IQ scores, resulted in an inconsistent, arbitrary, and objective interpretation and application of intellectually disabled persons' rights under the Eighth Amendment. After many highly publicized executions of intellectually disabled prisoners, it was time to change.

Twelve years after *Atkins* and many controversies and appeals, in *Hall v. Florida* (2014), the U.S. Supreme Court narrowed the discretion by a narrow (5–4) majority under which U.S. states can designate a defendant as too intellectually disabled to be executed. The ruling has started to clarify the rules that state officials have to follow in order to determine whether or not intellectually disabled defendants qualify to be precluded from execution under the Eighth Amendment. Despite the fact that Florida Courts agreed that Freddie Lee Hall has been retarded his whole life and has been repeatedly tested as such, state judges ordered him executed because *Atkins* failed to set uniform standards in the determination of ID, leaving this discretion up to individual states. Relying only on their qualifying standard of an IQ score of 70—Hall had scored 73 and 80 on the Wechsler Adult Intelligence Scale-Revised (WAIS-R) and 71 on the Wechsler Adult Intelligence Scale-III (WAIS-III)—Florida Courts maintained that he did not establish the first element of a mental retardation claim and rejected his appeals.

However, according to the *Hall* ruling, the Florida courts have interpreted the statute too narrowly by relying only on an IQ test score—which itself is not infallible as it has a standard error of measurement—instead of allowing for the consideration of other evidence regarding the defendant's ID. The mandatory cutoff at an IQ of 70 is therefore unconstitutional. In dissent, Justice Alito argued that there was no evidence that the new method the majority opinion favored was any more accurate than the IQ test. In their amicus brief, the APA (2014) argued that there is "unanimous professional consensus that the diagnosis of intellectual disability requires comprehensive assessment and the application of clinical judgment" (p. 8) and that such a comprehensive assessment requires "concurrent analysis of intellectual and adaptive functioning" (p. 10). Furthermore, the interpretations of IQ scores are subject to a standard error of measurement and must take the test's reliability into account. The majority rule concurred. If a person is unable to make calculated judgments, the death penalty does not serve a legitimate purpose. Although *Hall v. Florida* still does not propose a uniform standard for the determination of ID in death penalty cases, the ruling was another step in the process to ensure responsible and consistent treatment of intellectually disabled defendants who face execution.

Determination of IQ

As noted by now, there are several issues with the determination of an accurate IQ. An IQ is a score derived from one of several standardized tests designed to measure human intelligence. The WAIS is the most widely used instrument to measure IQ. Wechsler defined the concept of intelligence as "the capacity of the individual to act purposefully, to think rationally, and to deal effectively with his environment." The current version, WAIS-IV, measures four index scores representing major components of intelligence: Verbal Comprehension Index (VCI), Perceptual Reasoning Index (PRI), Working Memory Index (WMI), and Processing Speed Index (PSI). Each scale consists of different subtests.

Before WAIS, the Binet scale was considered the supreme authority in intelligence testing, but Wechsler believed that nonintellective factors played a role, which the Binet scale did not adequately incorporate; he opposed the idea of a single score; the Binet scale was not valid for adults, and it did not cater correctly for older adults. It is especially the continued significance that is given to a single score to measure intelligence that remained a concern for Wechsler and others.

Furthermore, factors such as anxiety and stress are correlated with worse performance, which raises concerns about the accuracy and reliability of test outcomes (Chaudry and Ready, 2012). Age has an influence too, as do point conditions, including mental health (other than ID), medication and other substances, and executive skills such as motivation, goal awareness, flexibility, impulsivity, and planning ability. According to Whitaker (2012), there are other concerns regarding the validity and reliability of the WAIS-IV too, especially regarding its use for individuals with low intellectual abilities. The stability of the test in the low range is questioned. The degree to which full-scale IQ and index scores are artificially increased by a floor effect is uncertain. The percentiles cited in the manual below 1% would appear to be incorrect. It is possible that the full-scale IQ and index scores are systematically higher than their equivalents on the similar instrument for children (Wechsler Intelligence Scale for Children, WISC-IV). These are added problems in the use of adult intelligence instruments for use with the intellectually disabled, and should be considered as part of a more holistic approach to the determination of such disability.

After all, as illustrated in the *Hall* ruling, an IQ score in isolation is not an adequate representation of a defendant's intellectual functioning and qualification under *Atkins*. Although a low IQ score (representing general intellectual functioning) is one element of four in the determination of ID in legal contexts, it has to be considered with the three other elements: adaptive functioning deficits, adaptive behavioral deficits, and onset before age 18 to satisfy a claim of mental retardation for setting aside the death penalty. In addition, psychologists retained by the defense or prosecution have to adhere to the laws of their jurisdiction and the ethics code of their profession (Duvall and Morris, 2006). This includes informed consent, boundaries of competence, selecting appropriate test instruments, acknowledging the limitations of such instruments, multicultural competence, multiple roles (e.g., not providing forensic and clinical services to the same client), and avoiding any form of bias and discrimination. When there is any personal conflict between personal values or professional ethics, professionals are advised not to participate in death penalty proceedings, as it may compromise themselves and the client. In closing, intelligence testing is not the all-important factor in the legal determination of ID, as per the *Hall* ruling. Assessment of adaptive functioning—intellectually and behaviorally—completes the picture.

Determination of Functional Impairment

The concept "deficits in adaptive behavior," which is one of the AAIDD's three prongs of mental retardation, has proven difficult to define and assess consistently and reliably. Adaptive functioning is determined by three basic skill sets:

1. *Conceptual skills*: Reading, numbers, money, time, communication, etc.

2. *Social skills*: Understanding and following social rules and customs, obeying laws, and interpreting motivations and intentions of others to avoid victimization, deception, exploitation, etc.

3. *Practical life skills*: Feeding, dressing, bathing, navigation, occupational skills, etc.

In legal settings, it is imperative that forensic mental health professionals choose standard methods of adaptive functioning that have well-established psychometric properties (DeMatteo et al., 2011). In 2002, the AAIDD (then the American Association on Mental Retardation; AAMR) mentioned several instruments that can be used for this purpose, including the Vineland Adaptive Behavior Scales, the AAIDD Adaptive Behavior Scales, the Woodcock–Johnson Scales of Independent Behavior, and the Adaptive Behavior Assessment System. The measure that a professional selects will be based on his or her familiarity and experience with it, whichever instruments are mandated for use in the particular jurisdiction, the profile of the test subject, and resources available, including access to third parties with sufficient knowledge of the defendant. The defendant's adaptive functioning can also be assessed through other means, such as self-report, behavioral observation, and information from third parties and collateral sources such as school, work, and previous mental health reports (DeMatteo et al., 2011). If done in a systematic and structured way, these sources can provide valuable support to psychological test interpretations, which should be collated to present a comprehensive and coherent picture of the defendant's adaptive functioning by covering multiple domains.

Assessors are also advised to obtain additional expert opinions where appropriate and present a balanced interpretation of their results by acknowledging potential limitations of the test instruments used and their entire approach. One example is the possibility of malingering, or "faking bad," which is a real possibility when a defendant faces the death penalty (Tassé, 2009). It is another reason why an assessor should not solely rely on a defendant's self-report in the determination of adaptive functioning deficits. Intellectually disabled individuals have a greater natural tendency to "fake good," which can also have an undue negative effect on their assessment under *Atkins*. Furthermore, the assessor should be cognizant of any changes of functioning that could have occurred due to medication changes, rehabilitation efforts, detainment conditions, memory degradation, etc. Sometimes, a retrospective evaluation is a good option, keeping in mind that it is challenging and untested.

Risk Assessment, Restoration of Competence, and Rehabilitation of Intellectually Disabled Offenders

Although ID is not specifically correlated with sexual and violent offending and recidivism, there are indications that certain factors that co-occur with ID increases the risk of offending. Some typical traits of an intellectually disabled person such as limited independence, poor decision-making and judgment, naivety, susceptibility, and awkward social interactions may put the person at risk of being physically or sexually abused or exploited. Such negative interactions tend to perpetuate a cycle of sexual and physical violence with the victim later becoming the perpetrator. If accompanied by antisocial or psychopathic personality characteristics and substance abuse, the risk is further increased. If a person with ID and dysfunctional or offending behavior is timely identified, assessed, and treated, such risks can be successfully minimized to reduce reoffending and escalation of criminal behavior.

Risk Assessment of Intellectually Disabled Offenders

The prediction of future risk is in many aspects an imprecise art with a significant probability to produce false negatives and positives. A meta-analytic study by Fazel et al. (2012) found that risk assessment tools produced low-to-moderate positive predictive values—achieving a median accuracy 41% of the time—and at 91%, higher negative predictive values. However, with a multifaceted systematic approach, accuracy can be optimized to acceptable levels. Several demographic variables and substance abuse have been linked to an increased risk of violence and recidivism. Although mental illness in general is not strongly associated with violent and criminal behavior, some types, including ID, represent a modest risk factor under certain circumstances (Norko and Baranoski, 2007).

The strongest predictor of future behavior is past behavior. The nature and frequency of past violent behavior in the specific context that it occurred is the best indicator of what to expect of a person, particularly if the motivator or mechanism is psychological, for instance, the achievement of sexual gratification or power, lack of remorse or guilt, callousness, or poor impulse control and emotional regulation. Although ID per se does not significantly elevate the potential for violent behavior, several aspects thereof can influence such propensity. These include substance abuse, risk of being victimized and abused themselves, dependence on others, and susceptibility to outside influence. Risk assessment is best approached by a combination of various means, including clinical interviews, collateral sources such as witnesses, medical, school, work, and arrest records, and actuarial and clinical assessment instruments.

A study by Lindsay and his colleagues (2008) found that the Violence Risk Appraisal Guide (VRAG), Historic Clinical Risk Management-20 (HCR-20), Short Dynamic Risk Scale (SDRS), and Emotional

Problems Scales (EPS) instruments successfully distinguished between prisoners with IDs who needed high-, medium-, and low-security settings. The two latter instruments are dynamic measures, while the VRAG is a static measure of risk. Gray and her colleagues (2007) also tested the VRAG and HCR-20 to predict future reconviction of offenders with IDs and confirmed that these instruments are significant predictors of violent reconviction in their sample, even at greater rates than a control sample without ID. In addition, they concluded that the Psychopathy Checklist: Screening Version (PCL:SV) is equally useful for this purpose. Comorbidity was high in their subject sample with 48% diagnosed with delusional disorders and almost 20% with personality disorders, which is not surprising as participants were solicited from a group of prisoners who were referred to psychiatric hospitals. All three instruments were able to predict violent recidivism over a 5-year period with large effect sizes. Another static measure of risk, the Sex Offender Risk Appraisal Guide (SORAG), was found to be as accurate with offenders who had intellectual limitations as with offenders who did not (Quinsey et al., 1998). Camilleri and Quinsey (2011) also agreed, but urged a better understanding of the link between ID while avoiding assessments that require clinical judgment. Lofthouse et al. (2014) recommended that static and dynamic assessments are used in conjunction as dynamic risk factors appear to act as "proxy risk factors" for static risk, while both capture elements of an underlying risk of violent behavior.

Case Study: Duane Taylor

Duane Taylor admitted that he molested young girls and boys at parks and playgrounds since he was 8 years old. He was raised by his biological parents until that time when he was sent to training school. He recalled his father always being drunk and that he abused his mother. At training school, he saw his parents once a year. School records indicated that he was found sexually fondling both male and female children on several occasions.

In 1978, Taylor was sent to prison for 4 years, after he tried to rape a 4-year-old girl in Cobourg. He was 17 when he arrived at Kingston Penitentiary. Having served two-thirds of his sentence, he was freed on mandatory supervision after less than 3 years, although the 20-year-old was clearly deeply troubled and borderline intellectually disabled.

On August 10, 1981, he went to a halfway house in Ottawa, and officials decided within days that Taylor needed to be institutionalized, but a bed was not immediately available at Whitby Psychiatric Hospital. Taylor returned to Kingston on August 12 where he was provided temporary accommodation at the Sally Ann's Harbor Light Centre. According to witnesses, he was at a rooming house at 179 Montreal Street on August 18, where his window overlooked a park across the street.

Three doors away from Taylor, lived 2-year-old April Marie Morrisson with her single mother and two older brothers. She frequented the park across the street. On August 21, she was walking along the street when Taylor randomly approached her. When she did not return home by 8:30 p.m., police was called. Having received a tip, they went to Taylor's room where Officer Harpell found April's body under the bed. She had been dead for 2 h. As recorded during a parole hearing conducted by Sharon Gail Perrault and Craig Allan in 2010, Taylor confessed, stating:

> I asked her if she would like to go for a walk. She said yes, so I took her to my house. I took her upstairs to my bed. I had intercourse with her. I put it into her rectum. I put it into her vagina. She started to bleed from her rectum, then her vagina. I tried to kill her by punching her in the throat. I was sitting on top of her, face down on the chair. After that I got off and she stayed there. She woke up after about 10 minutes and started crying. I sat back down on her head. I stayed on her for about 20 minutes, when I got up she was dead. That's it. (p. 3)

He pleaded guilty to first-degree murder, abduction, and sexual assault of the 2-year-old girl and was sentenced to life in prison with no chance of parole for 25 years. He had been charged six different times with institutional offenses by 2010, including two acts of violence with other inmates. His other offenses involved being abusive toward staff members. Although he underwent sex offender programs and counseling, he continued to lack insight into his offending behavior and the consequences thereof. He also never expressed any regret or remorse. Taylor was murdered by a fellow inmate in a Manitoba prison on August 17, 2014.

The case of Duane Taylor is a good example of risk assessment that was not done or failed. There are clear indications of psychopathic traits together with borderline intellectual functioning and pedophilia. He failed to comply with community supervision, breached parole, and had a history of institutional violence. There is no record of Taylor receiving psychological assessments or being assigned to a sex offender program during his first incarceration, despite his obvious risk of sexual and violent recidivism. Furthermore, since a young age, there was a degree of planning evident in his offending pattern. Taylor also objectified his victims by not seeing them as persons and not acknowledging the impact of his behavior on them and their families. He had a temper, but never took responsibility for his own anger, but blamed others and his situation. These tendencies were all evident at the time of his first arrest and should have raised the requirement for a thorough risk assessment, supervision, counseling, and institutionalization at the time. Just considering the PCL:SV and SORAG risk assessment instruments, Taylor would have scored well into the high-violent recidivism category. Using conditions after his first arrest retrospectively, total scores of 18 on the PCL:SV and 24 on the SORAG would have put him in upper quadrants, especially the Part 2 score of the PCL:SV would have put him at a percentile rank of 95.8% relative to others in the forensic/psychiatric comparison group. As a result, he should have been closely supervised and participated in a sex offender program after his first arrest.

Restoration of Competence

Most modern criminal justice systems that are based on the adversarial system require defendants to be competent to stand trial before the court proceedings begin. Due to their intellectual and cognitive impairment, this is an issue that has to be addressed with intellectually disabled offenders. The modern standard in the U.S. law was established in *Dusky v. United States* (1960), of which all states use slightly different wording to define the requirements of adjudicative competency (Roesch et al., 1999). In Dusky, the Supreme Court held that:

> It is not enough for the district judge to find that "the defendant is oriented to time and place and has some recollection of events", but that the test must be whether he has sufficient present ability to consult with his lawyer with a reasonable degree of rational understanding—and whether he has a rational as well as factual understanding of the proceedings against him. (Favole, 1983, p. 402)

Although the Dusky standard has been applied for many decades, its definition has never been explicit. Therefore, a typical forensic evaluation of adjudicative competency remains relatively unguided, although proposed protocols and instruments have emerged in the past 15 years or so. Using evaluees from a federal evaluation center, Cochrane et al. (2001) reported that 30% of defendants who have been diagnosed with ID were assessed as incompetent by forensic evaluators. A study by Petrella (1992) confirms this order of magnitude, finding that about 35% of defendants with ID referred for evaluation, are not competent to stand trial.

Adjudicative competence has two basic components, namely, foundational and decisional competence. Foundational competence refers to the defendant's ability to

1. Understand the basic elements of the adversary system (e.g., prosecutor, judge, and jury)

2. Inform their counsel of information relevant to the case

3. Understand their situation as a criminal defendant

Decisional competence refers to the defendant's ability to

1. Understand information relevant to the decisions they must make (e.g., pleading, waiving a jury trial)

2. Think rationally about alternatives involved in the decisions

3. Appreciate decisions that need to be made in their best interest

4. Make a choice among the available defense strategies

These are the basic abilities that a defendant has to possess in order to participate and add value to his or her defense. A variety of screening and test measurements have been developed to determine whether a defendant has these abilities in order to ensure a fair trial.

Measuring Adjudicative Competence

Competency to stand trial with intellectually disabled offenders is usually determined with the Competence Assessment for Standing Trial for Defendants with Mental Retardation (CAST-MR; Everington and Luckasson, 1992), but as thorough screening can be time consuming and costly, a screening test is used to identify clearly competent defendants and eliminate them from the process. A variety of tests are available, of which the *Competency Screening Test* (CST: Lipsitt et al., 1971) is widely used. The CST is a 22-item sentence completion task that addresses the defendant's perceptions of counsel and aspects of the trial that might induce emotional reactions (Grisso, 1986). Responses are scored on a three-point Likert scale, with total scores of 20 and higher considered indicative of competency. Administration time is 25 min or less. As the false-negative rate is relatively low, the CST is deemed an effective screening measure. Sample questions are:

When I go to court my lawyer will…? If the jury finds me guilty, I…? While listening to witnesses testify against me, …? When the jury hears my case, they will…?

The *CAST-MR* was designed to test the competency of defendants who have already been diagnosed as intellectually disabled to assist in their own legal defense. It consists of 50 questions divided in three sections: the first section contains 25 written multiple choice questions that test defendants' understanding of basic legal terms; the second section contains 15 written multiple choice questions designed to test defendants' ability to assist in their own defense; the third section consists of 10 open-ended questions regarding the defendant's specific case and is asked orally by the examiner. The test, which requires a fourth-grade reading level, takes between 30 and 45 min to complete. Sample questions are: What does a judge do? (a) Defends you, (b) decides on the case, or (c) works for your attorney. What if the police ask you to sign something and you do not understand. What should you do? (a) Refuse to talk to them, (b) sign it anyway, or (c) ask to see your lawyer.

One important aspect that is often raised is the extent to which a defendant can successfully fake incompetence on these tests. Malingering is common among criminal defendants. Competence assessment instruments, including CAST-MR, have not been designed to measure response set and generally possess face validity, making them vulnerable to malingering (Stafford, 2003). Therefore, it is required that a competence to stand trial assessment includes a separate test for malingering. In the determination of ID and adjudicative competence, a stepwise approach is proposed to detect or minimize malingering and estimating the test taker's genuine abilities (Soliman and Resnick, 2010). The first step in the systematic process is when clinical suspicion arises, which is typically linked to signs such as uncooperativeness, inconsistencies in history or third-party accounts, the presence of atypical symptoms, or spontaneously offering symptoms. Once suspicion has been aroused, several sources are compared to confirm malingering: clinical interview, past clinical records, legal history, forensic evaluations, and police reports, as well as third-party accounts and screening tests such as Miller Forensic Assessment of Symptoms Test (M-FAST), used to assess the likelihood that a person is feigning a psychiatric condition. The third step after confirming that malingering is present is to ascertain whether it affects an adjudicative competence assessment (there may be other reasons for malingering). The fourth step is to determine the defendant's genuine abilities by further examining collateral data, inpatient observation, and a focused semistructured interview to explore underlying functional capacity. In the fifth and final step, a report is compiled, highlighting conclusions by considering four questions: (1) Is the defendant malingering? (2) What specific symptoms are being malingered? (3) Is the defendant attempting to feign incompetence to stand trial? (4) Even if he is feigning incompetence, is he genuinely incompetent?

By ensuring that a variety of measures are used, the defendant's competence to stand trial can be determined with acceptable accuracy under the standards of evidence and expert testimony. As malingering is estimated to occur up to 20% of the time in adjudicative competency evaluations, it should not be ignored and included in determinations of ID and competence to stand trial as a matter of standard protocol.

Restoring Adjudicative Competence

Restoration of an intellectually disabled defendant's competence to stand trial is a contentious issue. Not only is it costly and relatively ineffective, but there are ethical concerns as well. The main objective of a treating or clinical physician is to look after the interests of the client, ensuring that no harm is done. However, a successful effort to "restore" a client's competence to stand trial may result in the negative consequence of a conviction. Nevertheless, competency restoration inpatient treatment programs are used across the United States and typically include medication management, educational counseling, and multidisciplinary treatment (Watson, 2015). For intellectually disabled defendants, medication management and psychotherapy focuses on the alleviation of comorbid psychiatric conditions that may be present, while the educational component addresses criminal legal matters with the help of experiential approaches such as mock trials and courtroom scenarios. But, although there are programs that have demonstrated limited success, Hauser et al. (2014) argued that competence restoration is historically low among those with ID. The DSM-5 recently altered the definition of ID, moving from an IQ-oriented diagnosis system to a multifaceted approach, introducing more flexibility and nuance, which places a slightly different focus on restoration programs with more emphasis on cognitive and adaptive functioning. Watson (2015) warned that "special care must be taken with this population that the parroting of legal concepts alone does not pass for authentic competency-related skills" (p. 167). Therefore, restoration efforts mostly fail for individuals with "irremediable cognitive disorders" for whom indefinite inpatient hospitalization is in any case not possible or useful as, according to *Jackson v. Indiana* (1972), incompetent defendants cannot be held more than the reasonable time necessary without determining a substantial probability of attaining competence in the foreseeable future.

Rehabilitation of Intellectually Disabled Offenders

The clinical rehabilitation of intellectually disabled offenders is not within the scope of the current discussion, but it is suffice to say that such efforts focus on alleviating the symptoms of and dysfunctional behavior related to comorbid mental health conditions such as substance abuse, anger, anxiety, depression, etc. An intellectually disabled client is generally viewed as less amenable to both psychotherapy and medication, especially with a high level of comorbidity. There is often resistance to treatment, attention problems, and poor adherence to medication regimen that negatively influence treatment effectiveness and relapse. There have also been relatively few research studies to establish the validity and reliability of psychometric tests for this population, as well as evidence-based content and protocol for psychotherapy treatment programs (Flynn, 2012). Regrettably, intellectually disabled adults remain the most underserved mental health population of all.

References

American Association of Mental Retardation. 2002. *Mental Retardation: Definition, Classification, and Systems of Supports* (10th ed.). Washington, DC: American Association of Mental Retardation.

American Psychiatric Association. 2000. *Diagnostic and Statistical Manual of Mental Disorders* (4th ed., text rev.). Washington, DC: American Psychiatric Association.

American Psychiatric Association. 2013. *Diagnostic and Statistical Manual of Mental Disorders* (5th ed.). Washington, DC: American Psychiatric Association.

Atkins v. Virginia. 2002. 536 U.S. 304.

Baldwin, J. and McConville, M. 1980. *Confessions in Crown Court Trials*. Royal Commission on Criminal Procedure Research Study No. 5. London, UK: Her Majesty's Stationery Office.

Blume, J. H., Johnson, S. L., and Seeds, C. 2009. An empirical look at Atkins v. Virginia and its application in capital cases. *Tennessee Law Review, 76*, 625–639.

Brief for American Association on Intellectual and Developmental Disabilities (AAIDD) as Amicus Curiae supporting petitioner, *Wilson v. Thaler*, 450 Fed. Appx. 369 (CA5 2011).

Brief for American Psychological Association (APA) as Amicus Curiae supporting respondents, *Hall v. Florida*. 2014. 572 U.S.

Brief for National Association for the Advancement of Colored People (NAACP) as Amicus Curiae supporting petitioner-appellant, *Wilson v. Quarterman*. 2009. WL 900807 (ED Tex. 2009).

Camilleri, J. A. and Quinsey, V. L. 2011. Appraising the risk of sexual and violent recidivism among intellectually disabled offenders. *Psychology, Crime and Law, 17*(1), 59–74. DOI: 10.1080/10683160903392350.

Chaudry, M. and Ready, R. 2012. Differential effects of test anxiety and stress on the WAIS-IV. *Journal of Young Investigators, 24*(5), 60–66.

Cochrane, R. E., Grisso, T., and Frederick, R. I. 2001. The relationship between criminal charges, diagnoses, and psycholegal opinions among federal pretrial defendants. *Behavioral Sciences and the Law, 19*(4), 565–582. DOI: 10.1002/bsl.454.

DeMatteo, D., Murrie, D. C., Anumba, N. M., and Keesler, M. E. 2011. *Forensic Mental Health Assessments in Death Penalty Cases*. New York, NY: Oxford University Press.

Drizin, S. A. and Leo, R. A. 2004. The problem of false confessions in a post-DNA world. *North Carolina Law Review, 82*, 891–1004.

Dusky v. United States. 1960. 362 U.S. 402.

Duvall, J. C. and Morris, R. J. 2006. Assessing mental retardation in death penalty cases: Critical issues for psychology and psychological practice. *Professional Psychology: Research and Practice, 37*(6), 658–665. DOI: 10.1037/0735-7028.37.6.658.

Everington, C. and Luckasson, R. 1992. *Competence Assessment for Standing Trial for Defendants with Mental Retardation (CAST-MR)*. Worthington, OH: IDS Publishing.

Fabian, J. M., Thompson, W. W., and Lazarus, J. B. 2011. Life, death, and IQ, it's much more than just a score: Understanding and utilizing forensic psychological and neuropsychological evaluations in Atkins intellectual disability/mental retardation cases. *Cleveland State Law Review, 59*, 399–430.

Favole, R. J. 1983. Mental disability in the American criminal process: A four issue survey. In: J. Monahan and H. J. Steadman (Eds.), *Mentally Disordered Offenders: Perspectives from Law and Social Science*. New York, NY: Plenum, pp. 247–295.

Fazel, S., Singh, J. P., and Doll, H. 2012. Use of risk assessment instruments to predict violence and antisocial behavior in 73 samples involving 24,827 people: Systematic review and meta-analysis. *British Journal of Psychiatry, 345*, 1–12.

Firth, H., Balogh, R., Bretherton, K., Graham, S., and Whibley, S. 2001. Psychopathology of sexual abuse in young people with intellectual ability. *Journal of Disability Research, 45*(3), 244–252.

Fleisher, W. L. and Gordon, N. J. 2006. *Effective Interviewing and Interrogation Techniques* (2nd ed.). Burlington, MA: Academic Press.

Flynn, A. G. 2012. Fact or faith? On the evidence for psychotherapy for adults with intellectual disability and mental health needs. *Current Opinion in Psychiatry, 25*(5), 342–347.

Forth, A. E., Hart, S. D., and Hare, R. D. 1990. Assessment of psychopathy in male young offenders. *Psychological Assessment: A Journal of Consulting and Clinical Psychology, 2*, 342–344.

Gates, B. and Barr, O. 2009. *Oxford Handbook of Learning and Intellectual Disability Nursing*. New York, NY: Oxford University Press.

Girimaji, S. C. 2000. Comorbidity of mental retardation and affective disorders. *Journal of the Indian Medical Association, 98*(5), 248–249.

Gray, N. S., Fitzgerald, S., Taylor, J., MacCulloch, M. J., and Snowden, R. J. 2007. Predicting future reconviction in offenders with intellectual disabilities: The predictive efficacy of VRAG, PCL-SV, and the HCR-20. *Psychological Assessment, 19*(4), 474–479. DOI: 10.1037/1040–3590.19.4.474.

Grisso, T. 1986. *Evaluating Competencies: Forensic Assessments and Instruments*. New York, NY: Plenum.

Hall v. Florida. 2014. 572 U.S.

Hammack, L. 2010, September 11. Woman to be executed via lethal injection. *The Roanoke Times*. Retrieved from http://goo.gl/7AP5Us.

Hauser, M. J., Olson, E., and Drogin, E. Y. 2014. Psychiatric disorders in people with intellectual disability (intellectual developmental disorder): Forensic aspects. *Current Opinion in Psychiatry, 27*(2), 117–122. DOI: 1097/YCO.0000000000000036.

Hogue, T., Steptoe, L., Taylor, J. L., Lindsay, W. R., Mooney, P., Pinkney, L., …O'Brien, G. 2006. A comparison of offenders with intellectual disability across three levels of security. *Criminal Behavior and Mental Health, 16*(1), 13–28. DOI: 10.1002/cbm.52.

Holland, T., Clare, I. C., and Mukhophayay, T. 2002. Prevalence of offending by men and women with intellectual disability and the characteristics of offenders: Implications for research and service development. *Journal of Disability Research, 46*(1), 6–20. DOI: 10.1046/j.1365–2788.2002.00001.x.

In re Briseno, 135 S.W.3d 1 (Tex. Crim. App. 2004).

Jackson v. Indiana. 1972. 406 U.S. 715.

Jones, J. 2007. Persons with intellectual disabilities in the criminal justice system: Review of issues. *International Journal of Offender Therapy and Comparative Criminology, 51*(6), 723–733. DOI: 10.1177/0306624X07299343.

Lindsay, W. R., Hogue, T. E., Taylor, J. L., Steptoe, L., Mooney, P., O'Brien, G.,…Smith, A. H. W. 2008. Risk assessment in offenders with intellectual disability: A comparison across three levels of security. *International Journal of Offender Therapy and Comparative Criminology, 52*(1), 90–111. DOI: 10.1177/0306624X07308111.

Lipsitt, P. D., Lelos, D., and McGarry, A. L. 1971. Competency for trial: A screening instrument. *American Journal of Psychiatry, 128*(1), 105–109. DOI: 10.1176/ajp.128.1.105.

Lofthouse, R. E., Totsika, V., Hastings, R. P., Lindsay, W. R., Hogue, T. E., and Taylor, J. L. 2014. How do static and dynamic risk factors work together to predict violent behavior among offenders with an intellectual disability? *Journal of Intellectual Disability Research, 58*(2), 125–133. DOI: 10.111/j.1365-2788.2012.01645.x.

Morrissey, C. and Hollin, C. 2011. Antisocial and psychopathic personality disorders in forensic intellectual disability populations: What do we know so far? *Psychology, Crime and Law, 17*(2), 133–149. DOI: 10.1080/10683160903392442.

Norfolk, G. A. and Stark, M. M. 2011. Fitness to be interviewed. In: M. M. Stark (Ed.), *Clinical Forensic Medicine: A Physician's Guide* (3rd ed.). New York, NY: Humana Press, pp. 341–356.

Norko, M. A. and Baranoski, M. V. 2007. The prediction of violence; detection of dangerousness. *Brief Treatment and Crisis Intervention, 8*(1), 73–91. DOI: 10.1093/brief-treatment/mhm025.

Perrault, S. G. and Allan, C. 2010. *NPB Pre-Release Decision Sheet: Duane Edward Taylor*. Stony Mountain, MB: National Parole Board, Government of Canada.

Petersilia, J. 2000. *Doing Justice? Criminal Offenders with Developmental Disabilities*. Berkeley, CA: California Policy Research Center.

Petrella, R. C. 1992. Defendants with mental retardation in the forensic services system. In: R. W. Conley, R. Luckasson, and G. N. Bouthilet (Eds.), *The Criminal Justice System and Mental Retardation*. Baltimore, MD: Paul H. Brookes, pp. 79–96.

Quinsey, V. L., Harris, G. T., Rice, M. E., and Cormier, C. A. 1998. *Violent Offenders: Appraising and Managing Risk*. Washington, DC: American Psychological Association.

Roesch, R., Zapf, P. A., and Golding, S. L. 1999. Defining and assessing competency to stand trial. In: A. K. Hess and I. B. Weiner (Eds.), *The Handbook of Forensic Psychology* (2nd ed.). Hoboken, NJ: John Wiley & Sons, pp. 327–349.

Salekin, K. L., Olley, J. G., and Hedge, K. A. 2010. Offenders with intellectual disability: Characteristics, prevalence, and issues in forensic assessment. *Journal of Mental Health Research in Intellectual Disabilities, 3*(2), 97–116. DOI: 10.1080/19315861003695769.

Soliman, S. and Resnick, P. J. 2010. Feigning adjudicative competence evaluations. *Behavioral Sciences and the Law, 28*, 614–629. DOI: 10.1002/bsl.950.

Stafford, K. P. 2003. Assessment of competence to stand trial. In: A. M. Goldstein and I. B. Weiner (Eds.), *Handbook of Psychology, Volume 11: Forensic Psychology*. Hoboken, NJ: John Wiley & Sons, pp. 359–380.

Su, K. P., Yu, J. M., Yang, T. W., Tsai, S. Y., and Chen, C. C. 2000. Characteristics of mentally retarded criminal offenders in Northern Taiwan. *Journal of Forensic Sciences, 45*(6), 1207–1209.

Tassé, M. J. 2009. Adaptive behavior assessment and the diagnosis of mental retardation in capital cases. *Applied Neuropsychology, 16*(2), 114–123. DOI: 10.1080/09084280902864451.

Ventress, M. A., Rix, K. J. B., and Kent, J. H. 2008. Keeping PACE: Fitness to be interviewed by the police. *Advances in Psychiatric Treatment, 14*, 369–381. DOI: 10.1192/apt.bp.107.004093.

Wald, M., Ayres, R., Hess, D. W., Schantz, M., and Whitebread, C. H. 1967. Interrogations in New Haven: The impact of Miranda. *Yale Law Journal, 76*, 1519–1614.

Watson, C. 2015. Inpatient forensic psychiatry. In: R. L. Sadoff (Ed.), *The Evolution of Forensic Psychiatry: History, Current Developments Future Directions*. New York, NY: Oxford University Press, pp. 163–171.

Whitaker, S. 2012. The measurement of low IQ with the WAIS-IV: Critical review. *Clinical Psychology Forum, 231*, 45–48.

14 Intrapsychic Motivations in Stranger Homicides Involving Gay or Bisexual Males

Dallas S. Drake

Contents

Introduction 275
Offender Motives 276
Origins of Sexually Motivated Homicide 278
Victim Selection in Gay Male Homicides 279
  Opportunities for Prevention 288
References 288

Introduction

Many people are surprised to learn that homicides within the lesbian, gay, bisexual, or transgender (LGBT) population are dissimilar to other kinds of homicides.* Incidents occurring within this group present unusual challenges, such as recognition and investigation of cases, police–community cooperation which historically have been strained, and for creating and implementing creative, yet politically tolerable intervention and prevention strategies and techniques (Drake, 2004a, 2014). LGBT persons comprise a population demographic and include both LGBT victims and LGBT offenders (Drake, 2003). This group is unique for a number of differing characteristics, including cognitive motivations, incident behavioral characteristics, investigative interactions, and prosecutorial challenges. Perhaps the most important distinction is that these homicides, in contrast to the theoretical literature, are among the most frequent to be cleared by arrest when tested empirically (van Gemert, 1994; Riemann, 2004). Convictions, however, may be challenging as there exists a substantial history of varied legal defenses offered for these killings, as well as jurists who are biased against any nonheterosexual sexual orientation (Comstock, 1991; Brower, 2002; Young, 2011).

The overwhelming majority of LGBT homicides involve men killing men (van Gemert, 1994; Drake, 2014). These victims or offenders may comprise homosexual men who are identified as gay, or of homosexual men who are identified as straight. A third category includes bisexual men who are sexually attracted to either men and/or women and are identified in a heterogeneous manner. This chapter will address the murder of gay or bisexual men regardless of the sexual orientation of their killers—many of whom are homosexual or bisexual themselves (Adams et al., 1996; Drake, 2004a, 2014; Parrott and Zeichner, 2005). Colloquially, and because of its classification as a victim-type homicide based on its constitutive victim demographic, it will be referred to as gay or gay male homicide.

Prevalence of gay male homicide in the United States is less than would be statistically expected. It is overrepresented by certain types of homicides such as hate crime and intimate partner, but underrepresented

---

* Sometimes the letters within the acronym are reordered to create various renditions of the label depending on politics of the writer.

in other types such as armed robberies or child homicides.* The rate of homicide in the United States is much less, than perhaps in other countries, due to the disproportionate impact of drug, gang, and street killings on U.S. prevalence rates (Blumstein et al., 2000; Beeghley, 2003, 131). Best estimates, based on two data sources (the Minnesota Gay Homicide Study and the National LGBT Homicide Database), indicate a prevalence rate of approximately 3% of all U.S. homicides (Drake, 2014).[†] In stark contrast, lesbian victim homicide is extremely rare (Miller and Humphreys, 1980; Drake, 2004a, 2014). This owes, in large part, to the overwhelming involvement of men in homicides as either victim or offender (Lemert, 1951; Wolfgang, 1958; Silverman and Kennedy, 1987). There are also fewer lesbian women in the population compared to gay men at a ratio of 1:2 (Drake, 2004a, 2014, 2016).

Transsexual individuals are people whose self-perceived gender is different from the sex of their bodies. Many transition their bodies through the use of hormones and surgery to better approximate their gender (Beemyn and Rankin, 2011). Sexual orientation is generally determined by the gender of the individual and that individual's preferred partner(s). For example, if someone is born with a male body, but considers his gender to be female and then is attracted to males, he is considered heterosexual, whether or not his body has been fully modified to appear female (Coleman and Bockting, 1989). Thus, the killing of transgendered individuals is a complex area of investigation, dealing with the victim's mind as well as the body. Suffice it to say that these murders appear to be motivated more by perceived violation of gender or gender boundaries than by sexual orientation alone (Pharr, 1988; Herek, 1990; Koppelman, 1994; Stevenson and Medler, 1995; Meloy, 2000; Bartlett, 2007; Sanchez and Viain, 2009).[‡]

A census of transgender/transsexual homicides in the United States from 1969 to the present[§] indicates that most victims are heterosexual transwomen (whether or not their bodies are yet female in form) and the perpetrators are heterosexual males (Drake, 2004a, 2014, 2016). This could be one reason that transgender homicides tend to mirror the characteristics of heterosexual homicides. A conclusion that transgender homicides involve overkill (Davis, 2014; Teal, 2015) results mostly from two scenarios: (1) indoor killings that tend to be intimate partner homicides, which often involve overkill (Browne et al., 1999) and (2) outdoor killings that tend to result more from hate crimes (Comstock, 1991). Both types are overrepresented with intense emotional expression, leading to excessive injuring or overkill.

Offender Motives

There are often multiple motives for any crime scene action (Berk et al., 1992; Herek, 1992; Bushman and Anderson, 2001; Anderson and Bushman, 2002; Safarik et al., 2002; Drake, 2003; Arndt et al., 2004; Federal Bureau of Investigation, 2005; Gibson, 2010; Guminny, 2014). The range of offender motivations for killing homosexual or bisexual victims is as wide ranging as for that of nongay victims. Intimate partner homicide comprises a substantial, though declining proportion of the overall homicide rate (Dugan et al., 1999). Gay and bisexual males, as with all violence victims, come into conflict with those persons they spend the most time—their intimates. These account for 14.3% of gay or bisexual male homicides (National LGBT Homicide Database, 2014) compared to 11.2% of heterosexual homicides (Fox, 2000). Intimate partner homicide victimization is more prevalent among gay males than for heterosexual males, yet, lesbian women are less likely to be victims than their heterosexual counterparts (Block and Christakos, 1995). Most sexual killings occur between strangers or relative strangers (Meloy, 2000; Meloy and Felthous, 2004; Hickey, 2012). Intimate partner disputes among all couples rarely end in a sexual homicide (Meloy, 1996). However, Geberth (2003) includes intimate partner homicides as sex-related homicides (pp. 311–312).

A second, but related group, are the victims of intimate sexual homicides where there is little or no prior relationship (Chan et al., 2013). These couplings have been termed "casual" (Wentland and Reissing, 2011), "casual sexual encounters," or "intimate acquaintances" (Harris and Miller, 2000, 278, 280; Prestage et al.,

---

* The *National GLBT Homicide Database, 1969 to Present* is an incident-level database containing over 3000 cases of LGBT homicide. It is compiled by the Center for Homicide Research in Minneapolis, MN, using open-source data, police response and investigational reports, and court records.
† Prevalence estimates depend on population estimates. Murphy (1992) estimates that gays and lesbians account for 10% of the population (p. 230). Other studies provide higher or lower estimates.
‡ Special thank you to Thomas Wayne Johnson, MD for his expertise in suggesting edits for the portion of this manuscript on transgender homicides.
§ The "National LGBT Homicide Database, 1969 to Present" is an incident-level database containing over 3000 cases of LGBT homicide. It is compiled by the Center for Homicide Research in Minneapolis, MN, using open-source data, police response and investigational reports, and court records. The Center's Minnesota Gay Homicide Study, based on similar record types, conducted a census of all homosexual homicides from 1969 forward.

2001). They start as consensual, but may end in a homicide. In same sex relationships, the casual intimacy may be what leads 26.4% of gay male or bisexual homicides to being labeled explicitly sexual in nature. Offenders often lure victims with an offer of sex.

These sexual relations involve limited relationship-building efforts. While most interactions occur successfully, pairing with maladjusted individuals who ride the margins of society (Franklin, 1998) can lead the offender to experience a shame attack or identity implosion (Drake, 2014, 304, note 5). This occurs when view and understanding of the self crumbles following sex with nothing substantive to replace it. Shame attacks can be instigated via several intrapsychic dynamics.

Supposing the offender had sex with the victim, these killings have been attributed to an adverse reaction to the breaking of the homosexual taboo (Drake, 2004a, 2014, 304, note 4). Offenders, after withdrawing from the completed sex act, often feel devalued due to their own homosexual feelings. They begin to no longer see themselves as heterosexual, instead envisioning returning to their prior life having engaged in same sex behavior, but without the necessary coping tools. This produces dissonance for which the offender attempts to neutralize his shame and embarrassment. Offenders who project and transfer their shame outwardly may therefore attack and kill his sexual partner. In these instances, Abrahamsen (1973) says that victims and offenders are intertwined by a murderous impulse to neutralize psychic pain and diminishing self-esteem. He explains that "every homicide is unconsciously a suicide and every suicide is, in a sense, a psychological homicide" (p. 38). Shame attacks can result in an actual offender suicide if the shame is not resolved or transferred (Drake, 2004a). Shame attack homicides account for at least 23% of all gay male victims (Drake, 2014). The rate of resulting offender suicides is unknown.

The distinguishing feature between this shame response and an antihomosexual panic (Kempf, 1920; Lee, 2008) is that the shame attack comes following the sex, not before it, thus implying that the offender is himself homosexual or at least fearful of being viewed as homosexual (Rofes, 1978; Bagnall et al., 1984; Suffredini, 2001). Many potential offenders never progress into a shame attack or a panic, adjusting appropriately. It should be noted that excessive shame, whenever it occurs, should never be an excuse or a valid defense for murder.

At times these admittedly narcissistic interactions can involve sexually sadistic predation. One form is nonconsensual sexual sadism. While less severe forms of consensual sadism occur (Nitschke et al., 2009) and can be found in up to 11.4% of LGBT people (Goh, 2012), it rarely leads to death. Sexual sadism is a deviant paraphilia, where arousal or activity satisfies the sadist through "the pain, humiliation, or suffering" of others (Money, 1986; Nitschke et al., 2009; Fulkerson, 2010, 52). Male victims indicate a homosexual or bisexual offender because heterosexual sadists only engage with opposite sex victims. Female offenders are rarely sadistic (Brittain, 1970).

The sexual stigma that is felt in same sex homicides often leads offenders to steal items that can later support a nonsexual explanation of motive. This serves to protect the offender's projection of sexual normality (Douglas et al., 1992, 2013; van Gemert, 1994). There often is no sign of offender ejaculate (Podolsky, 1965).

Homosexual stigma is also sometimes embedded in an antihomosexual legal defense called the "homosexual advance defense" or "homosexual panic defense," wherein the offender responds in a hostile way to a sexual proposition or advance (Rofes, 1978; Bagnall et al., 1984; Slaby, 1994; Suffredini, 2001). In early explanations of this condition, it was made clear that it results not from a proposition but only from having actually had sexual intercourse. Slaby (1994) believes that shame attacks can occur in the absence of sexual activity if the "heterosexual" actor is combating same sex feelings or behavior. Thus far, defenses involving panic or shame have now been outlawed only in California (Ferguson, 2014). Although, "[c]ases involving the defense of homosexual panic which have reached the appellate level have never resulted in a defendant's acquittal by reason of insanity" (Bagnall et al., 1984, p. 501).

Another motive for killing gay men is rooted in the age difference often found between offenders and victims in gay male and bisexual victim homicides (van Gemert, 1994; Drake, 2004a, 2014). Offenders in these incidents are found to be younger than their victims 68% of the time. According to the National Database of LGBT Homicide (2014), offenders are on average 11 years younger than LGBT victims, with a median difference of 12 years. "The offender in a GLBT homicide is twice as likely to be younger than the victim, and nearly half of those offenders are more than 20 years younger than their victims" (Shulka and Drake, 2006, p. 1).

Age alone, however, cannot account for this animus. Resource jealousy, caused by "relative deprivation" between the offender and the victim, might however (Runciman, 1966, 9; Messner and South, 1981; Blau and Blau, 1982; South and Messner, 1986). The greater the inequality between the two, the more likely the crime will occur. Older more established men who pick up younger struggling men (for money or not) may lead an offender to feel psychologically antagonized (Visano, 1991; van Gemert, 1994).

The last homicide type worth of discussing is hate crime homicide, or what the Federal Bureau of Investigation (FBI) might label "group cause homicide" (Douglas et al., 1992, 2013). According to the National LGBT Homicide Database (2014), only 15.8% of LGBT homicides were judged to be hate motivated. Hate crime homicide is likely to be higher than is reported, since it is difficult to detect covert hatred or hatred caused by unconscious motives. Similar to sexual homicides, hate crimes are more likely to involve strangers (Berk et al., 1992).

Origins of Sexually Motivated Homicide

It is at this juncture, we turn to an unexpectedly problematic phenomenon—that of *homosexual* men who target and kill *Gay* men. This can happen within the context of individual or group motivation (i.e., sexual homicide or hate crime homicide). To better understand this, it is important to elucidate the distinction between the terms *homosexual* and *Gay*. Gay (capitalized) is a term used to describe persons who are politically affiliated with the Modern Gay Movement (Timmons, 1990; Weems, 2011). These are people whose worldview is shaped by their affectional orientation. They tend to go to gay places, read gay publications, and march in gay parades. Many authors do not capitalize this term.

Alternately, *homosexual* is a term describing the affectional and sexual orientation of a person. An individual can be homosexual, yet identified as heterosexual. This class of men is oftentimes referred to with the acronym *MSM*, meaning *men having sex with men* (Boellstorff, 2011). MSM often operate on the fringe of the gay community and only to the extent necessary to find a willing sexual partner (Franklin, 1998; Jarmon, 2013).

Fueling the need to maintain a heterosexual identity is a deep-seated fear of being personally linked to homosexuality. This fear is called *homophobia* and it can be experienced by anyone, heterosexual or homosexual (Kantor, 1998; Allen and Oleson, 1999). For homosexual men, however, fear of homosexuals can become internalized, leading to hatred of oneself as well as others (West, 1977; Adams et al., 1996). These men will typically refer to gay or homosexual men in the third person as a way of psychologically distancing themselves from homosexuality (Dong et al., 1997). The impact of this phenomenon can result in difficulty securing same sex sexual contact when desired, and a lack of emotional intimacy with male sexual partners. Couple this with intimate sexual contact, and you have the necessary ingredients for an outbreak of violence.

MSM are males who engage in same sex sexual activity but who do not see themselves as gay (Boellstorff, 2011), and therefore would avoid any stigmatizing behaviors. The MSM would only allow himself to *be serviced* during oral sex. During sex intercourse, the MSM seldom if ever would "bottom," or be the receptive sexual partner (Carter and Bridges, 2015). This is because of fear of becoming gay in what Herek (1992) refers to as "ego defensive violence" (p. 161). It is probable that there exists a range of homophobic intensity, and therefore of homophobic behavior. This may help explain the phenomenon of sexual substitution, wherein some object is substituted for the penis (Podolsky, 1965; Douglas et al., 1986; Holmes and Holmes, 1998, 2010, p. 116). One of the most common forms of sexual substitution is picquerism. In this behavior, the knife blade substitutes for the penis and the number of stab wounds is comparable to the number of pelvic thrusts during intercourse. Multiple stabbings are strongly correlated with sex-related homicides (Radojević et al., 2013).

A related injury involves a focus on cutting or stabbing of the neck (Bohnert et al., 2006), an erogenous region of the body. During oral sex, the neck can be viewed as a substitute vagina or anal opening. Strangulation homicides are considered very personal and strongly indicate a sexual motive. This motive may be linked to latent offender fantasies of asphyxiophilia, another form of paraphilia. If so, there may be repeated killings, especially if a ligature has been used. Stabbing or cutting of the neck is also considered sexual in origin (Ressler et al., 1986, 1988; Douglas et al., 1992, 2013; Geberth, 1996, 2014; Keppel and Birnes, 1997; Schlesinger and Revitch, 1997; Bohnert et al., 2004; Radojević et al., 2013). In particular, Radojević et al. (2013) found that 68.2% of stabbings correlated with sex (p. 503).

One hazard for the MSM is excessive bonding to a partner during sexual intimacy, and especially during sexual intercourse (Pedersen et al., 1992). Sex is a mutual interaction bringing participants as mentally and physically close and intimate as possible. This merging action is quite problematic for the homophobic MSM if it becomes too intense. Not unlike when a couple fights to break up, the MSM needs to disengage from his partner, and to do this, assaultive behavior is a possible result. Homicide is a much rarer outcome. One telltale sign of same sex behavior, however, is the resulting traces of the offender's semen in, on, or near the victim (Geberth, 1996, 2003, 2014).

Victim Selection in Gay Male Homicides

The selection of a victim is intimately associated with the offender's motive for killing (Mueller, 1992). Even such crimes as robbery (which often occurs to gay men) seems to be centered more on victim characteristics (Block, 1987; Comstock, 1991) rather than on monetary accessibility. Robbery is classified as a *crime against the person* rather than as a *property crime*. Punishments for robbery are therefore much more severe. It is a violent crime targeting particular victim groups, typically minorities. According to Lundrigan and Canter (2001), "The benefits of a criminal action are the net rewards of crime and include not only material gains, but also intangible benefits such as emotional satisfaction" (p. 597). Therefore, gay men are often targeted for robbery or other harassments or humiliations, usually on the street or in parks. Larcenies occurring after a killing (usually in an apartment) are termed thefts, not robberies (Becker et al., 2015).

The availability of identifiable gay men to any offender is an interesting and intriguing topic because, though stereotypes exist, homosexuality is an internal psychic trait. In the case of antigay killings, how does a heterosexual offender know how to locate members of a relatively rare and invisible target group? The answer is complex.

Commonly, offenders meet potential victims in *gay locations*. These include gay bars, clubs, or on prostitution strolls. The basis of an offender's knowledge of cruising or pickup sites is curious and perhaps even points toward veiled victim–offender motives and dynamics. The investigator should specifically question whether either the suspect or the victim has a history of prostitution or *hustling*,[*] as it may help explain victim access. Investigators should conduct a *forensic victimology* to better understand the points of possible victim–offender contact (Douglas et al., 1986; Turvey, 2011). This may also help position an offender in gay territory, thus linking an offender to motive and opportunity. Sometimes offenders are mistaken in their target selection because of location, thus resulting in the killing of a heterosexual male who only appears gay (Nardi and Bolton 1991; Berill, 1992; Broverman, 2010). This often is based on incorrect interpretation of external cues (Carter and Kolenc, 2005; Hughes and Bremme, 2011), including contact location.

Selection also relates to victim control and is impacted by victim availability (Turvey, 2011). Offenders typically target victims who, due to some vulnerability, are easy to control. African-American gay men may be victimized at higher rates due to their dual minority status (Lavers, 2011). Illicit behavior by victims can expose individuals to violence because offenders believe victims are reluctant to report crimes to the police for fear of being arrested themselves (Dong et al., 1997; Topalli et al., 2002). Homosexuality was at one time criminalized in the United States, and therefore animus between police and gay men is longstanding and entrenched (Shilts, 1988; Harry, 1992; Jay, 1992; Drake, 2014). This has provided offenders the perfect cover (and excuse) for targeting homosexual men.

Case Study 1

On the night of Wednesday, June 13, 1979, 31-year-old Leslie Benscoter had drinks at the Townhouse Bar in St. Paul, Minnesota. This is a longstanding, though poorly marked, gay and lesbian bar. The windowless gray-painted storefront easily blended in with the landscape of used car dealers and family-owned, largely minority businesses in a lower working class neighborhood. Later in the evening, around closing time, Benscoter bid his friends good night and stepped outside onto the well-lit thoroughfare of University Avenue (Stockton, 1979b), a four-lane business street, plus parking on either side. Benscoter began his mile long hike toward his apartment near University and Prior Avenues. A car soon pulled up aside him and the driver offered him a ride home, to which he agreed. Once at the two-story apartment building, Benscoter asked the would-be offender if he wanted to come up for drinks. The offender quickly agreed (Stockton, 1979h).

Benscoter did not show up for work over the next two days (Stockton, 1979b). On June 15, 1979 coworkers Kathleen Hansen and Roxanne Dahlstrom investigated his absence. They discovered his apartment door was locked and a clock alarm was sounding from inside. The women quickly located the manager and the decedent was discovered. Police and paramedics responded to the apartment at 7:46 a.m. (Stockton, 1979b). The body was found nude on his back on a bed (Stockton, 1979f) and was pronounced dead at the scene. Missing from the apartment were a stereo system, television set, men's wrist watch, and possibly a diamond ring. The words "fags will die" were spelled out with toothpaste on

---

[*] The term "hustling" sometimes refers to prostitution-like behaviors where no monetary exchange is involved.

the space where the stereo once sat (Stockton, 1979d). A key had been used to lock the apartment door, signaling there was no forced entry into the apartment (Leatham, 1979).

A forensic victimology of Benscoter reveals that he was a U.S. veteran, having served two tours in Vietnam. He was "one of six children" (Bissinger, 1979a, p. F5). According to his sister-in-law Bonnie, his brother Walter wanted nothing to do with him due to Walter's antihomosexual prejudice. Leslie Benscoter was raised in the Lutheran Church and was very kind to everyone he met (Drake, 1997).

At the time of his death, Benscoter was working at a nearby nursing home where he was employed for the last 4 years (Stockton, 1979b). All of the orderlies there were described as homosexual, except for one, Frank L. Jackson. Although he and Benscoter argued vigorously in their first week working together, Jackson quickly became a close friend in the 3 weeks preceding Benscoter's death (Stockton, 1979c). They apparently spent many off-duty hours together (Stockton, 1979c). After the death, Jackson sank into a "deep depression" (Stockton, 1979i, p. 2). Later he admitted he had developed "strong feelings (an affection)" for Benscoter (Stockton, 1979d, p. 1). Jackson was an early, but not the only, suspect. Around Christmas of 1978, Benscoter had a boyfriend named Mike (Merritt) who was eventually ruled out (Stockton, 1979f, 5, 1979g,j). Benscoter had numerous other intimate acquaintances (Stockton, 1979i).

Benscoter seemed to like straight or masculine men more than gay men, although he often frequented several Minneapolis area gay bars. Investigators also indicated that he had recently purchased a vehicle, but could not drive it due to lack of proper registration (Stockton, 1979b). Benscoter liked to drink and on occasion drank beer with the apartment manager (Stockton, 1979e). At one point, Benscoter attempted suicide for which he is alleged to have had scars on his neck from a rope. He signed himself in as a patient at the Hastings State Hospital for treatment for alcohol abuse (Stockton, 1979f). He later was released to a half-way house in Minneapolis (Stockton, 1979f). According to sister, Barbara Benscoter, he seemed happier "after he accepted his gayness" (Leatham, 1979, p. 1). Benscoter was known to hitchhike on University Avenue (Stockton, 1979j). Benscoter's coworker Kathleen Hanson described him as an "extremely clean" housekeeper (Stockton, 1979f, pp. 1–2).

As a victim, Benscoter may have been selected in part because of his having left a bar intoxicated. This might have altered his judgement and slowed his reactions, or it might have caused him to fit a profile that the offender was searching for. Benscoter also was vulnerable due to his practice of hitchhiking, which put him in proximity to various strangers, though perhaps he enjoyed the excitement it brought. Hitchhiking has long been held as a dangerous practice (United States of America, 1974; Keppel, 1989). Benscoter's habit of seeking out more masculine men, sometimes referred to as an attraction to "rough trade," is another somewhat dangerous occupation, even if sometimes successful (Richardson, 2005). The danger is increased by a victim's mistaken belief that it is safer to take someone to your own home where the would-be victim might have the advantage of environmental familiarity. What any potential victims fail to realize, however, is that this also makes body disposal easier. The offender can just leave it lie.

Meanwhile, on June 17, 1979, this case took an unexpected turn. The St. Paul Police were called at 7:46 p.m. to a car that crashed into a tree on West Como Lake Dr. at Horton Ave (Carlson and Seliski, 1979). The driver experienced "massive trauma" ending in death (p. 1). The crash victim was subsequently identified as Mark D. Miller, age 21. Miller was pronounced dead at 10:30 p.m. (Seliski and Carlson, 1979). Witnesses estimated the car was traveling at "70 mph and squealing its tires" (Younghans and Finnigan, 1979, p. 1). Investigators determined from scuff marks and experimental tests that Miller's car had been traveling just a little over 63 mph (Jyrkas, 1979b). Three watches were recovered from the car, along with four traffic tickets, and the title to the car. Several unopened cold cans of beer were found inside the car, along with one open can, crushed and spilled on the floorboards of the car (Groh, 1979). This was the same brand of beer as was found in Benscoter's apartment (Stockton, 1979h). One of these watches was later identified as Benscoter's, thus tying Miller to the murder (Stockton, 1979k).

Miller had been asked to move out of his parents' house. With no place to go, "he was living out of his car" (Winger, 1979a), which was uninsured (Winger, 1979b). Miller's license to drive was revoked at the time of the crash (Jyrkas, 1979a). He was a high school dropout (Bissinger, 1979b) who was working as a janitor at the Minneapolis–St. Paul International Airport (Winger, 1979a). Miller had a fiancée at that time, named Denise Mars, age 17, whom he had been seeing for 11/2 years (Stockton, 1979h, p. 1). A "past due" jewelry store notice was found in the car at the crash site (Seliski and Carlson, 1979, p. 2), perhaps indicating that Miller could not pay for his engagement ring. But curious reports emerged from Mark Miller's gay brother Steve that Mark had been picking up and beating gay hitchhikers since at least 1975 (Campbell, 1979). He may have been cruising and picking them up, but the beatings are an unverified account, perhaps used to veil his true motives for cruising. There is no evidence of Miller ever being injured in any purported attacks. Even his mother admitted that he liked to cruise and to pick up hitchhikers, usually out of kindness (Bissinger, 1979b; Webb, 1979a).

On the day of the crash, Miller was drinking. He first had a couple of beers with his fiancée and a couple later at a friend's house (Winger, 1979a). It was here that he confessed of the murder to an unnamed friend, and unsuccessfully tried to convince him to come and view the body (Webb, 1979a). He told his friend that he was going to drive around Lake Como until it was time to go to work (Winger, 1979a). According to interviews with his friends, police determined that Miller "was in a depressed state of mind due to his admission to friends of his being responsible for the homicide" (Jyrkas, 1979a, p. 3). It is not clear that this was remorse. Interestingly, none of his friends thought it important to turn Miller in to the police, even when several of them were mutually aware of the killing. This example of deindividuation illustrates how group norms and ideas take priority over the individual, further isolating homosexual or bisexual group members.

Police statements indicated that the crash "occurred on the southwest shore of Lake Como in an area which no prudent person would attempt to drive at 65 mph due to very sharp curves. There is a strong possibility that this act was deliberate" (Jyrkas, 1979a, p. 1). Miller had at one time been in a foster home. His foster mother indicated that Miller "could, no matter how intoxicated, could/would be able to drive a car" (Stockton, 1979a). Miller's mother, in a police interview, agreed that her son was in retrospect suicidal. She also excused Mark's murder of Benscoter as being motivated by theft (Webb, 1979a). It is well known, however, that a theft occurring during or just after a homicide is commonly for the purpose of covering up a sexual motive, thereby providing a psychological buffer (Drake, 2004a; Schlesinger, 2004; Douglas et al., 2013). In this instance, it also served to protect Mrs Miller's identity of having raised a "good boy" (Bissinger, 1979b, p. 1).

Mrs. Miller described her son as being protective of gay people. Mark Miller's brother Steve was homosexual and at that time lived in another state. She said that her son Mark had "often played cards with Steve and his friends" when he lived nearby. But according to his mother, he would get "violent when touched by a gay" (Stockton, 1979a, p. 1). In other words, he liked gay people so long as no one thought that *he* was gay. Mrs. Miller went on to describe two of her brothers who were sent to prison, "one for killing someone while robbing them." While in prison, "one of the brothers became a homosexual [sic*]." Once, when a friend made fun of his two uncles, Mark responded by saying, "he'd 'beat them [his friends] to death if they bother either one'." Mark's mother added that often Mark would step in to a conversation regarding either Steve or the uncle, defending their right to be "what he was" (Stockton, 1979a, p. 2). Mark Miller was against antigay prejudice when it felt safe to do so, and became quite excited to be engaged to a girl as a cover. His mother said it is the happiest she had ever seen him (Bissinger, 1979b).

Fiancée, Denise Mars, said that Mark Miller sold the TV "to a kid in St. Paul for $20.00" (Miels, 1979a, p. 1). The television set was later recovered from Tom Walters. Miller's best friend, along with Mars, helped orchestrate its recovery (Miels, 1979b, p. 1). Miller showed up as Mars got off work following the homicide and gave her the stereo and two speakers, saying, "This is something you always wanted," and that he had "strangled someone for it" (Stockton, 1979h, p. 1). He eventually "told her he had met a man hitchhiking on University [Ave.] and the man asked him to his apartment for a drink… While drinking and talking in the apartment the man tried to put his arm around Miller—and tried to get him into bed." Miller told Mars that "he then choked him with his hands on his neck." Mars said that "a friend told her that Miller put a cigarette pack in the man's mouth and a pillow on his face" (Stockton, 1979h, p. 2).

Miller told another friend, James Plasch, a similar, though different story. Miller said "that he had to use the bathroom and upon exiting this room he found the man on the bed without any clothing on" (Stockton, 1979g, p. 3). A lot of offender accounts of killing gay men begin with the offender indicating that the violent action started upon exiting the bathroom. The friend continued that Miller said he then "blew up" and started to choke the nude man (Stockton, 1979g, p. 3). Miller was 6 feet, 2 inches tall (Webb, 1979a). According to this friend, Miller "then put a cigarette pack in the man's [sic] mouth, his arm around the man's [sic] neck (from behind) and held him until he 'changed color'" (Stockton, 1979g, p. 3). There was, however, no mention of recovering a cigarette pack in any of the police or autopsy reports, thereby shedding doubt on Miller's account.

---

* Homosexual is an adjective rather than a noun. One can become homosexual, but not "a" homosexual. Furthermore, one does not really "become" homosexual, but instead "comes out" or becomes aware of one's own homosexuality.

The friend then revealed more of Miller's characterizations, recounting that Miller said "that the man did not offer any resistance that he almost wanted to die." When asked about writing at the crime scene, Miller said "he wrote something on a table with toothpaste—something with 'fags.' At this point [the friend] said Miller hated fags." Miller finished up at the murder scene by searching the victim's car (Stockton, 1979g, p. 3), apparently finding nothing to take. The car was 9 years old (Meyer, 1979) and about to be purchased by Benscoter for $175,[*] but he was low on cash and had to wait (Leatham, 1979). However, the car was in Benscoter's possession. One could argue that the car was not taken, as is common in many gay male homicides, because the offender already had a car, meaning he did not need to steal it to get away (Becker et al., 2015).

This homicide is a case of a shame attack resulting from an internalized self-loathing and subsequently projected homophobia (Herek, 1984; van Gemert, 1994; Kantor, 1998). Miller did have sex with the victim (Campbell, 1979). The police discovered semen in the victim's rectum, a sign that the offender was a "top" or the insertive sexual partner, indicating possibly a more homophobic actor (Carter and Bridges, 2015). It seems that Miller was the MSM who bonded too intensely with his sexual partner. This was compounded by immediate afterthoughts of his fiancée and unworkable impending promise to marry. Miller just wanted the problematic part of his own homosexuality to go away. His use of toothpaste as a writing medium seems spontaneously clownish at best.

Miller clearly had not thought through what he would do beforehand and was likely intoxicated at the time. The killing in this case appears to have been an unplanned act, with no weapon even brought to the scene. Considering crime scene behaviors, strangulation is a common kill method used in the commission of sexual homicides (Langevin et al., 1988). However, absence of a ligature in strangulation signals not only lack of preparation, but also lacking a need to control the rate of death, as would be necessary in sadistic serial sex killings. This offender did not appear sadistic.

Miller did attempt to stage the crime scene to imply an antigay killer, thus directing public attention away from himself. Privately among friends, however, Miller's claim that he inserted a cigarette pack in the victim's mouth was another unnecessary and fictitious bravadic embellishment designed to further dramatize his antigay machismo. For instance, although Miller used the phrase "blew up," police reported no signs of violence at the murder scene (Stockton, 1979h, p. 3). These characterizations appear only to be an effort to protect Mark Miller's heterosexual identity. Desecration of the corpse such as mutilation or dismemberment, common in antigay homicides, did not occur, nor were the remains posed or intentionally positioned. Interestingly, the Benscoter case is a good example of an age difference between the victim and the offender, with the offender being 10 years younger. Yet both came from roughly the same social class.

The crime was completed by stealing a few items. Although a theft occurred, it can easily be viewed by the offender as an inheritance from his newly bonded partner. But it also was an important cover for why Miller even had been inside the dead victim's apartment. It worked well for his mother who attributed Benscoter's killing as a way to access the victim's stolen items (Webb, 1979a). Consider that less than 0.02% of robberies end in death (Karmen, 1996, pp. 77–78). Though it occurs more frequently at homicide scenes, it is still quite rare with less than 11% of all homicides involving robbery (McNamara, 1994, p. 87). It is extremely unlikely that any robbery had occurred, however, a theft after-the-fact was part of the crime. Lastly, Benscoter's death did not involve any forced entry into the apartment, and his keys were missing afterward, with the apartment door having been relocked. In a sense, the offender was claiming ownership of the apartment, becoming the main key holder.

Benscoter's death was eventually ruled a homicide by the medical examiner and is documented by the St. Paul Police Department as having been "exceptionally cleared" (Stockton, 1979l; Scanlon and Johnson, 1979, p. A5). This means that, because the suspected offender was deceased, the case would be closed and listed as cleared, as is common in offender suicides.

It should be noted that all of this happened against a backdrop of another homicidal attack that happened on June 1—the very public baseball bat beating of Terry Knutson in downtown Minneapolis. This was a case that received considerable publicity. Although Knutson's death did not occur until the day Benscoter's body was discovered, the attack had already taken place, possibly triggering the Benscoter homicide (Webb, 1979b). Compounding this were the May 21st White Night Riots in San Francisco which followed the acquittal of Dan White. White murdered gay supervisor, Harvey Milk, and

---

[*] In 2015, according to the U.S. Inflation Calculator, that would be the equivalent of $575.27. See: http://www.usinflationcalculator.com/

supportive mayor, George Moscone, and was acquitted of first-degree murder charges. It seemed to be a series of cascading events.

In light of this, a curious thing is the lack of news coverage of the actual homicide incident. Police it seemed were trying to keep the lid on it. News of the Benscoter case only hit the newspapers on June 20, 5 days after his body was found. At first, the police worked hard to deny that a homicide had occurred. They speculated that Benscoter may have even killed himself. Then they seemed to make light of the death saying, "There seems to be a thief afoot" (Leatham, 1979, p. 1). One detective then followed up saying they needed to conduct more follow-up "if we only had the leisure time to do this" (p. 1), as if homicide investigations were some kind of recreational activity. Salt was then tossed on the wound when the police captain overseeing the Homicide Division reported that investigators "had no reason to believe Benscoter died violently…and haven't ruled out that Benscoter wrote" the message himself (Webb, 1979b, p. 1B).

The police response was to check the victim for toxicological signs of alcohol or drugs, as if the empty beer cans and wine glasses were not evidence enough. Rather they sought to *smear the queer*. Detective Stockton further theorized that "Benscoter died naturally and that 'an opportunist' entered his apartment, took his stereo and television set and wrote the message" (Webb, 1979b, p. 1B). Then Captain Kissling ramped it up a level higher telling the press "It's getting so that if a homosexual, Negro or Chicano gets killed, you hear all this stuff about cops not doing their job. When a WASP gets killed nobody says nothing. I'm getting pretty damn sick of all these pressure groups" (p. 4B).

Once Miller was implicated in the homicide, the police and county attorney repeatedly refused to release the offender's name in an effort "to protect the suspect's family." On July 11, the name finally appeared in news coverage (Scanlon and Johnson, 1979, p. A5). The historical mistrust of police by the gay community was cemented upon release of this news. The father of Miller's fiancée, Denise Mars, was a St. Paul Police Officer. Police uniforms in the car trunk of Miller's crashed car were given to Miller to use as automotive rags by her father. This is the same Donald Mars (then retired) who had worked for 6 years as a partner on the same squad as then patrol officer, and now Homicide Detective, Terrance J. Stockton (Stockton, 1979m, p. 1). It should be noted that Donald Mars did ask his daughter to turn in the stolen stereo. This did not happen until weeks following the homicide, even though the fiancée knew of the murder within about 24 h of the killing. The antigay animus of that period clearly helped prevent the rapid solving of this case. Considering the fragile state that this type of offender was in, it may also have contributed to the offender's own suicide. In a sense, Mark Miller was a second victim.

Law enforcement in Minnesota has come a long way since this homicide occurred. Many changes in professionalism and training may have helped reduce the antigay animus between police and the community. Agencies facing such a challenge must overcome the inertia that prevents change from occurring, confront attitudes that prevent the fair and impartial application of the law, and then support this change over time to rebuild the department's reputation.

Case Study 2

In the early morning hours of January 12, 1992, Earl Craig, Jr., a 52-year-old gay man cruised the streets of downtown Minneapolis searching for a male sexual liaison. This was something Craig did quite often. On a block bookended by a gaming arcade at one end and a gay bar at the other, Craig spotted a young man at "bar-closing time on Hennepin Av., a ritual known to gays as the 'sidewalk sale'" (Brunswick and Gendler, 1992, p. 9A). This is a custom whereby gay men, not already paired for the evening, would find their mate among the leftover bar crowd. It was near here that Craig pulled alongside him and after a short chat, 18-year-old Jayme Starkey climbed into the black jeep and they rode about a quarter mile to Craig's luxury condominium high-rise apartment that overlooks downtown Minneapolis.

Starkey claimed that he only went with Craig because he was offered an opportunity to "get stoned." He also said that he appreciated the ride (on a cold January night) where he hoped to travel to his home, a couple of miles away. This was curious because on other occasions he seemed to travel easily by bus, his normal mode of transportation (Trial Transcript, 1993, p. 145). Upon arrival at Craig's building, Starkey was then invited upstairs and into the condominium.

Once in the home, Starkey's account diverges from known facts, so the events of the evening are not easily discernable. Starkey made many conflicting statements (Starkey Statement, 1992; Trial Transcript, pp. 1539–1602) supporting the hypothesis that much of what he said from this point on was untrue. What *is* known though is that on January 14, Craig was discovered dead by friends, lying face up on his bed after he failed to show for work on the second day (Bonner and Rosario, 1992).

The crime scene was that of a classic gay male homicide. The "partially clothed" body of Craig was found (Rosario, 1992, p. 1C) lying on his back on a bed in the master bedroom, with what later proved to be a single stab wound to the neck, indicating a knife was the weapon used. According to police (and with similarity to the Benscoter case), "there was no sign of forced entry," however, his Cherokee brand Jeep was missing from the building's underground parking garage (Bonner and Rosario, 1992, p. 1A). This would indicate that the killer was someone Craig had invited into his own apartment. Police also reported seeing no signs of violence or of any struggle, at first thinking that Craig may have died naturally. This was not an entirely implausible scenario, because Craig was both African-American and overweight (Trial Transcript, p. 1065), two common risk factors of premature, though natural death (Stillion, 1995; Solomon and Manson, 1997; Snodgrass, 2011). And lastly, a delay had occurred in discovering the body and death scene* of more than 24 h—all common among homicides involving gay or bisexual males (Drake, 2004a,b, 2014, 2016).

Investigation of this death revealed several intriguing facts. First, while there "was blood on Craig's face and neck," the death was not initially ruled a homicide. The medical examiner said, "Finding blood on the mouth, face or above the neck is not rare or unusual in some cases of natural death." It was later explained that because of the advanced decomposition of the body, "the fatal stab wound to the neck was not readily visible, and investigators first thought that Craig might have died from a bleeding ulcer" (Rosario, 1992, p. 1C). It was determined at autopsy, though, that this knife wound had "severed the carotid artery and a jugular vein" (Complaint, 1992, p. 1), but with minimal "external bleeding" (State v. Starkey, 1994, p. 2).

A second intrigue is that the Cherokee Jeep was not the only item missing from the home. Craig's wallet, credit cards, and condominium keys were also missing. Later, a whole list of missing items was noted. This additionally included vodka (Trial Transcript, p. 347), "$160 in cash, a leather jacket, two autographed baseballs, … a half a case of beer, a bottle of champagne, gloves, three duffel bags, and a pouch containing credit cards." The offender also later claimed to have taken the knife (purportedly the victim's knife) and alleged he tossed it into the nearby Mississippi River (State v. Starkey, 1994, p. 4), although a folding knife was later found just below the balcony outside of his stepfather's apartment in Crystal, Minnesota (Trial Transcript, pp. 681–682). If this homicide were a case of self-defense, the perpetrator would be expected to call for help, render aid, and immediately surrender himself and his weapon to the police (Christopher, 2014). There is no shame associated with protecting one's own life from a life-threatening attack. But Starkey did not do any of that. Instead he stole some items and then drove away with the victim's Jeep. No life threat existed—except to Earl Craig.

A final detail surrounding this death is that, once inside the condominium, investigators discovered handwriting on a room wall. As investigators entered just inside the doorway of Craig's office area, they found written in large letters: "KKK Forever!" KKK was underscored, and the phrase was completed with an exclamation point (Trial Transcript, p. 599). Starkey admitted that he had "scribbled" this with a pen on his way out as a way to draw attention away from himself, because Starkey, too, was African-American (Trial Transcript, pp. 1494–1495). This act was not unlike that of the Benscoter case. Both were spur-of-the-moment acts. Starkey explained that the idea was lifted from having recently seen a segment on television that highlighted white supremacists (Trial Transcript, p. 1494).

Dr. Gary Alan Fine (2001) described a similarly spontaneous cognitive process as he investigated microinteractions at a game of little league baseball. In his study, players employed creativity. They did this by combining "novel combinations of previously familiar elements" of an existing knowledge base. Phrases, however, may be "given different meanings from that of their constitutive elements" which are "created spontaneously" (pp. 191–192). Exposure to previous knowledge can be thought of a sort of cognitive priming. According to Starkey, "I had recalled watching an episode of Jeraldo [sic: Geraldo Rivera] a day or so before where they had some white supremacists on there and that just popped into my head so I just wrote that on the wall" (Trial Transcript, p. 1494). The mechanism for which white supremacy had come to mind was Starkey's hatred of gays, which linked to the hatred of blacks by white supremacists. He was in the act of signaling hatred, not accidents or self-defense. Both Benscoter's and Craig's homicides offer instances of writing that provide insight into the mind of a killer as they attempt to direct attention away from themselves as suspects.

---

* Discovery of the Earl Craig, Jr., death scene occurred approximately 60 h afterward (Diaz, 1992).

The fabrication and use of crime scene writing indicates a communication need, not already apparent with the offender's demonstrated actions. It appears that many incidents of spray-painted threats (or crime scene writings) are instead indications that the scene has been either overtly or covertly staged or altered (McNamara et al., 2012). Actually, writing on walls is quite common among serial homicide offenders. It is said to fulfill both "psychological and rhetorical functions" and can provide clues to help solve the case (Gibson, 2004, p. 3). In the Craig case another psychological component was possibly that "KKK" expressed the offender's internalized racism. It inflamed hatred to the point that phone threats and written letters against black police officers, and black community leaders, following the homicide inspired an FBI investigation (Brunswick and Hodges, 1992). The harm was immediate and profound.

Despite all this, the crime scene itself was characterized by the medical examiner as "pretty tranquil" (Bonner and Rosario, 1992, p. 10A). "[W]hile Starkey contended the killing took place during a struggle, ample evidence indicated no struggle occurred before the stabbing. The fitted sheet on the bed remained neatly in place, Craig suffered no significant injury to his hands or arms, and the stab wound itself lacked any tearing that might have indicated a struggle" (Trial Transcript, p. 1061). Starkey also testified that after accidentally stabbing Craig, Craig held Starkey's arms for a moment, and then Starkey fell back to the bottom of the bed. However, this version of what took place is highly inconsistent with the internal accumulation of blood within Craig which, according to the medical examiner, was likely caused by pressure being applied to the stab wound, possibly by a hand or pillow.

Complicating prosecution of this case was that Earl Craig, Jr. was a well-known public figure—a leader in civil and human rights. He was "director of the Minneapolis Neighborhood Revitalization Program, a 20-year effort to pump $400 million into depressed urban neighborhoods" (Bonner and Rosario, 1992, p. 10A). His death was eulogized by a resolution of the Minnesota Senate. Yet, he maintained a distinction between his public and carefully veiled private life.

Earl Craig, Jr. was gay, a point which most all of his friends and political insiders knew. In public, this was less obvious (Campbell, 1992; Diaz, 1992). It might neither have been accepted in the mainstream of the black community nor by antiblack racists. So Craig kept his sexual orientation quiet (Spear, 1992). Craig had what is often described as a double stigma—being black and gay (Robles, 1992; Lavers, 2011), and this too apparently fed his need for secrecy.

With a hectic political schedule of working days in the office and of frequent after-hour meetings, there was little time for Craig to date. For this reason he was often observed cruising prostitution and pickup strolls. It should be pointed out, however, that "hustling" and "prostitution" are two preoccupations that tend to blur in gay life. One cannot easily be distinguished from the other. For instance, sex might be free, but one party might pay for dinner beforehand (Armstrong, 1981; Baumeister and Vohs, 2004). Participation of either Craig or Starkey in prostitution is neither known nor is it supported by the evidence in either case. Starkey, regardless of the media "innuendo," was never positively identified as a male prostitute (Trial Transcript, p. 111). Andrea LaForest, who rode around in the stolen Jeep with Starkey, testified that she knew Starkey was not gay because she had sex with him in the past (Trial Transcript, p. 395). Yet, it is well known and documented that many male prostitutes are heterosexual, with girlfriends on the side (Comstock, 1991; McNamara, 1994; van Gemert, 1994).

Starkey had an arrest record as a juvenile to include "truancy, curfew violations, and minor theft," but nothing serious (Brunswick and Gendler, 1992, p. 9A). He also "had been a client at Project Offstreets," a juvenile diversion program for runaway, or homeless[*] teenagers including the nearby Loring Park's young male prostitutes. No evidence ever surfaced to confirm Starkey's involvement in prostitution. He was not a runaway. He was instead in the process of moving to live in the suburb with his mother and stepfather at the time of the homicide (Brunswick and Gendler, 1992; Trial Transcript, p. 145).

A claim of prostitution (against the VICTIM, not the offender) (Trial Transcript, p. 1349) became a central smear in the defense of Jayme Starkey—that Craig picked up male prostitutes (Trial Transcript, p. 114), which was untrue (Decker Statement, 1992, p. 73; Trial Transcript, p. 663). Indeed, just as ludicrous was the prosecution's claim of theft as motive (Diaz, 1992; Schlesinger and Revitch, 1997; Trial Transcript, pp. 143–144). Many of the conferences in chambers with the judge occurred with the central theme of the defense trying to "dirty up" Mr Craig as a homosexual predator (Trial Transcript, p. 830). This claim was that he "cruised" for sex and because, as one defense witness stated, "all gays are predators" (Trial Transcript, p. 180, 562). The judge responded to this argument saying, "when there's an issue

---

[*] Somewhere between 6% and 35% of homeless teenagers are LGBT (Tenner et al., 1998). In many instances they are considered throwaway children because of rejection of their sexual orientation by their parents.

of self-defense…and the state inquires of a witness as to the victim's reputation for peacefulness, the only way in which the defense can impeach that testimony is by inquiring as to specific acts of violence" (Trial Transcript, pp. 181–182). In response to the defense team's claim of self-defense, the judge ruled that "the pertinent character trait is for peacefulness" or "quarrelsomeness" (Trial Transcript, p. 112, 122), not the social habit of "cruising," which he ruled as being irrelevant. Questioning about character or reputation is not allowed unless it is used to impeach the defendant, but it must be relevant to the crime.

The judge expounded on that, saying that if "we had on trial here a woman who had been involved in an incident with a man who she had met and they went back and the allegation was that he had tried to rape here [sic] and had picked up a knife, she took a knife and stabbed him, I can't imagine how the court would allow in evidence that this man had gone to parties to do so or gone to single bars or talked to women, things like that." The prosecution team cited several examples of case law for this including: "*State vs. Defannv, People vs. Lemus, State vs. Bland, State vs. Silverhus*" (Trial Transcript, p. 649).

The motive in this homicide case is that of a hate-motivated attack with possible underpinnings of internalized homophobia. Although Starkey's team argued self-defense, Starkey himself testified on the stand that the stab wound was "an accident" (Trial Transcript, p. 1572). The prosecutor questioning Starkey asked "Mr. Starkey, what is it? Was it an accident, or was it self-defense, which one?" Starkey responded that it was "an accident." Contrast this with what he said to his friends in the Jeep that night—that he "referred to the victim as a 'faggot,'" that they "were going to celebrate" and then said coarsely that he had "iced the fucker" (Trial Transcript, p. 386, 1585). Similar to the Benscoter case, this may have been interpreted as simple bravado, but then immediately following the killing of Craig, Starkey goes on to describe getting an "adrenaline rush" (Trial Transcript, p. 1603). With that descriptor, this case is elevated to the level of a thrill killing. He further expounded on this comment by describing a state of hyper arousal saying, "my heart was beating nonstop, my blood was racing nonstop, I was breathing hard nonstop" (Trial Transcript, p. 1604). Serial homicide offenders such as William Heirens, after having killed a young woman, "spent 2 h at the murder scene, wandering aimlessly from room to room as he enjoyed multiple orgasms." He too wrote a message on the wall (Newton, 2006, p. 115). It raises the question of whether Starkey is a sexual predator. A hallmark of the thrill killer is that satisfaction is sexually achieved from murdering the victim, rather than having sex with him (Holmes and Holmes, 1998). Thrill is a subtype of sexual predation. This is why the moniker of "erotic thrill killer" is frequently attached to this type of homicide.

What could all that arousal have led to? When the Jeep was recovered by the police, there was a pair of women's underwear inside the vehicle. The prosecutor suggested the panties belonged to one of the girls riding along with Starkey in the Jeep (Trial Transcript, p. 754, 828). These panties may have been kept as a sex trophy by which to remember that night (Dietz et al., 1990; Malmquist and Volavka, 2006; Woods, 2006; White, 2007; Warren et al., 2013; Meade, 2015). Earlier, Starkey had taken at least two of Craig's condoms from on the nightstand before leaving the crime scene (Trial Transcript, p. 1500), implying a sexual desire. It also was likely to have been an act of desecrating the gay-owned Jeep, as well as using the victim's own condoms. Frank van Gemert (1994) characterizing male prostitutes says that "to dispose of any doubts about his sexual preference and his virility, he starts seeing female colleagues…[t]his may happen right after…[t]his way he can prove to himself and other people that he still is heterosexual" (p. 165).

Forensic evidence revealed that Craig's death was neither accident nor was it self-defense. Starkey had held a pillow down over Craig's head and face after having stabbed him in the neck. Bloodstain pattern analysis conducted by the Minnesota Bureau of Criminal Apprehension assessed blood spatter and transfer marks. These showed how Craig's head moved back and forth "in a windshield wiper" pattern as he tried to get out from under the pillow being used to pin and possibly suffocate him. An imprint of Starkey's bracelet (that he wore the night of the attack) was found on both sides of Craig's pillow (State v. Starkey, 1994, p. 4). The forensic analyst also reported that blood spatter stains indicated the struggle had ensued *following* the injury, but not *before* it (Trial Transcript, p. 1278, 1283, 1690). And finally, the forensic evidence showed that the telephone nearest to Mr Craig had been unplugged so that no call for help could ever be placed, an act that Starkey admitted in court (Trial Transcript, p. 137).

The argument is not that Starkey is a homophobic heterosexual, but that for whatever reason he was homophobic, and feared or loathed people who were gay. He might be bisexual, or he might be completely heterosexual, lacking certitude of the fact. Starkey denied being homosexual, yet accepted an offer of a ride from a man he feared might be gay (Trial Transcript, p. 1439). Though he claimed it was too cold to walk home, he later (next night) called friends, waking them up in the deep of night to go driving in Craig's stolen Jeep. Starkey suspected Craig was gay because Craig tried to pick him up on at least one or the other occasions in the daytime about a month earlier (Trial Transcript, p. 1423, 1541). The media reported that Craig picked Starkey up by chance (Brunswick and Gendler, 1992), which is not entirely true. The story of Starkey leaving a nearby arcade located just several hundred feet from a gay bar, may have provided him a defense of plausible deniability of having targeted Craig, but their meeting also occurred coincidentally during bar-closing time when Starkey knew gay people would be looking to pick other men up.

Starkey also resented the upper class and Mr Craig was highly successful. Craig's condominium included a "huge chandelier, vaulted ceilings," and wood flooring (Drake Statement, 1992, p. 3). At one time, Craig employed a housekeeper (Trial Transcript, pp. 204–205). State Senator Alan Spear (a sitting senator) in eulogizing him made quite florid comments saying Craig had a penchant for "good food, good wine, [and] nice furniture" (Spear, 1992, p. 15A). Craig was commonly engaged in the development of public and foreign policy, and fit in with the city and state's political elites (Spear, 1992). According to Andrea LaForest, Starkey, while driving Craig's Jeep, described Craig saying he "probably was rich because he had a nice house, [and a] new truck" (Trial Transcript, p. 388). Interestingly, pages from Craig's banking statements were found near a dumpster at Starkey's suburban apartment building (Trial Transcript, p. 676).

In contrast, young Jayme Starkey, who had dropped out of school (Trial Transcript, p. 1414), was short on cash, hanging out on the streets of a major downtown city (Trial Transcript, p. 1546). In chambers, the defense attorney described trying to prove that Craig was a predator, saying while cruising, he was only "going through the low income areas, government projects, looking for young men, and exploiting young men." The defense finally conceded that no such youths were ever found (Trial Transcript, p. 647). But it showed that even Starkey's defense team recognized that Starkey's social class status was quite low. At the time of the murder, he was living with his stepfather in a rough area of the city (Trial Transcript, p. 1413), marked by poverty, high crime, and within a homicide cluster that has existed since at least the early 1960s (Drake, 2013). On the other side of the river was Mr Craig. The relative difference in age, wealth, and status was stark. Clearly, Starkey was jealous of Craig's social and financial status, but it did not end there however.

Starkey's actions indicated that he was also angry that Craig mirrored that part of himself of which he feared—his own latent homosexual (West, 1977) or bisexual thoughts or feelings. Coon (1957) describes such a situation saying, "Perhaps as the desire entered the periphery of consciousness, it was immediately projected and embodied in the stimulus object. Killing the stimulus object in this case could mean unconsciously the removal of both the stimulus and the desire" (p. 848). Craig was the stimulus object. Projection is not only of latent homosexuality but also of latent sadism. Starkey's anger projected his own aggression onto Craig as well (Kantor, 1998).

Theft of items was like the handwriting on the wall. It diverted attention away from sex-related motives, as was evidenced by the stabbing of the victim's neck. As stated earlier, injuries of the neck have a high correlation with other sexual activities and sex-related behaviors. For instance, cutting or stabbing (in a country widely known for its firearm homicides) is found in 28.5% of sexual assault murders (Greenfeld, 1997). Wounding of the neck (either by cutting, slashing, or stabbing) is believed to show latent sexual interest (De River, 1958; Hazelwood and Douglas, 1980; Hunt and Cowling, 1991; Douglas et al., 1992; Geberth, 1996, 2014; Schlesinger and Revitch, 1999; Drake, 2004a; Schlesinger, 2004). In the Craig case, the defense team was worried that the prosecution would emphasize an apparent "slashing" of the neck, although no such act occurred (Supplemental Affidavit, 1992, p. 4). Their concern was the possible appearance of a sexual assault on Craig (Trial Transcript, p. 953), as is commonly found with shame attack victims, such as Leslie Benscoter.

According to Dr. Eric Hickey (2012), an expert on serial homicide, "the process of sexual fantasy development may include stealing items from victims" (p. 177). In addition to the already mentioned stolen items, however, Starkey kept one unique item. He kept his jean jacket from the murder that night (Trial Transcript, p. 1385), which had the writing of several girls all over it. It also had Craig's blood on it. He admitted that he "never wore it after that night," nor did he launder it, or dispose of it (Trial Transcript, pp. 1474–1475). It was his personal souvenir, and the substance he stole was the victim's own blood.

A central risk factor for this homicide is that Starkey was part of a network of potentially delinquent or criminal associates with whom he surrounded himself (Andrews and Bonta, 2010). His friends immediately suspected the Jeep was stolen, and he eventually shared parts of what he had done. But similar to the Benscoter case, his associates never stepped forward to report it until prodded by law enforcement (LaForest Statement, 1992, p. 31; State v. Starkey, 1994, p. 3). Instead they lied to protect him, often leaving crucial details out of their statements or testimony (Trial Transcript, p. 368).

One unique component arising during the interview and statement of Starkey is how similar his lie was to that of Mark Miller's (in that Benscoter case). Both began with action emanating from the bathroom. While some features of his story may have been accurate up to that point, this "account"* referring to the bathroom was a pivotal point. It is here that the fabrication was anchored, to that one room, a room which is often associated with change—changing clothes, changing looks, or changing diapers, etc. Erving Goffman labels it the "backstage" area where "performance" is planned (Goffman, 1967, p. 112, 123). This fits nicely with Dr. Fine's (2001) "novel combinations of previously familiar elements." As the lie is spun, the offender draws creatively and spontaneously as he interprets his current actions "in terms of previous knowledge" (pp. 191–192). Starkey had a long history of constructing lies, and was quite adept at it (Court Transcript, pp. 1541–1542, 1552, 1583, 1588, 1598, and 1617).

Starkey was beaten while in county jail by several individuals, to the extent that the sentencing judge wrote the correctional officials to warn them that Starkey may need to be protected (Stanoch, 1992, p. 1). It is not known what prompted the beating. However, the victim in this case was inarguably one of the top African-American civil and human rights leaders in the state, and now he was dead.

Opportunities for Prevention

The preceding two case studies reveal several points at which to leverage preventative actions. An overall strategy must include reducing homophobia and heterosexism. This is necessary so that young homosexual and bisexual men can become better adjusted with fewer negative impacts on their overall health. Concealment of same sex attractions adversely impacts one's mental health (Schrimshaw et al., 2013).

Facilitators are externally controlled factors that exacerbate the risk, while protective factors typically have an internal locus of control. Rather than attack negative facilitators of homophobia, society should implement aggressive efforts to assist in development of sex-positive education as a protective factor, as well as positive sexual identity conceptualizations. In particular, this should include identity management education for youth as well as programs to increase socialization skills. Although athletics is a common vehicle for delivering such training, it should be noted that many people in this target risk group may be nonparticipants in sports and athletics. Additionally, socialization skills involve more than what is taught in most athletic programs. Identity development, outside of one-on-one counseling, is an uncommon curriculum.†

Sex education courses are another important part of changing the social and sexual health landscape. Some sexual education learning is now being made available outside of public school settings. This is important because the overwhelming focus in school-based sex education up to this point has been anything but sex positive (Fine, 1988). Furthermore, school-based programs will not likely address those at highest risk—young men who have dropped out of school. In many cities, alternative education environments exist where high school equivalencies are offered. Any plan must include this often neglected and difficult to reach group, and any program must address sexual differences within a sex-positive program.

References

Abrahamsen, D. 1973. *The Murdering Mind*. New York, NY: Harper and Row.
Adams, H. E., Wright, L. W., and Lohr, B. A. 1996. Is homophobia associated with homosexual arousal? *Journal of Abnormal Psychology*, 105(3), 440–445.
Allen, D. J. and Oleson, T. 1999. Shame and internalized homophobia in gay men. *Journal of Homosexuality*, 37(3), 33–43.
Anderson, C. A. and Bushman, B. J. 2002. Human aggression. *Psychology*, 53(1), 27.
Andrews, D. A. and Bonta, J. 2010. *The Psychology of Criminal Conduct*. New York, NY: Routledge.
Armstrong, E. G. 1981. The sociology of prostitution. *Sociological Spectrum*, 1(1), 91–102.
Arndt, W. B., Hietpas, T., and Kim, J. 2004. Critical characteristics of male serial murderers. *American Journal of Criminal Justice*, 29(1), 117–131.

---

* An "account" signals one possible version of a story, not necessarily true (often not true), or perhaps partially true. Criminals often provide several versions of accounts.
† Chicago Freedom School is one program that does focus on such development. One class they offer is called Identity, Power, and Oppression. Further information can be found at: http://chicagofreedomschool.org/what-we-do/training-and-organizing-3/

Bagnall, R. G., Gallagher, P. C., and Goldstein, J. L. 1984. Comment, burdens on gay litigants and bias in the court system: Homosexual panic, child custody, and anonymous parties. *Harvard Civil Rights-Civil Liberties Law Review, 19,* 497–515.

Bartlett, P. 2007. Killing gay men, 1976–2001. *British Journal of Criminology, 47*(4), 573–595.

Baumeister, R. F. and Vohs, K. D. 2004. Sexual economics: Sex as female resource for exchange in heterosexual interactions. *Personality and Social Psychology Review, 8,* 339–363.

Becker, M., H., Drake, D. S., Zhou, Y., and Telkova, I. 2015, June 12. Motor vehicle theft following homicide: Analysis of motivational undercurrents. Paper presented at the *Summer Meeting of the Homicide Research Working Group*, Clearwater, FL.

Beeghley, L. 2003. *Homicide: A Sociological Explanation.* Lanham, MA: Rowman and Littlefield.

Beemyn, B. G. and Rankin, S. 2011. *The Lives of Transgender People.* New York, NY: Columbia University Press.

Berill, K. T. 1992. Anti-gay violence and victimization in the United States: An overview. In: G. M. Herek and K. T. Berrill (Eds.), *Hate Crimes: Confronting Violence against Lesbians and Gay Men.* Newbury Park, CA: Sage, pp. 19–45.

Berk, R. A., Boyd, E. A., and Hamner, K. M. 1992. Thinking more clearly about hate-motivated crimes. In: G. M. Herek and K. T. Berrill (Eds.), *Hate Crimes: Confronting Violence against Lesbians and Gay Men.* Newbury Park, CA: Sage, pp. 123–143.

Bissinger, H. G. 1979a, July 11. *Murder 'Solved,' Suspect Is Dead.* St. Paul, MN: Pioneer Press, pp. 1, +5.

Bissinger, H. G. 1979b, July 12. *Miller Says Slayer Suffered, Too.* St. Paul, MN: Pioneer Press, pp. 1, +6.

Blau, J. and Blau, P. 1982. The cost of inequality: Metropolitan structure and violent crime. *American Sociological Review, 147,* 114–129.

Block, C. B. 1987. *Homicide in Chicago: Aggregate and Time Series Perspectives on Victim, Offender and Circumstance (1965–1981).* Chicago, IL: Center for Urban Policy.

Block, C. R. and Christakos, A. 1995. Intimate partner homicide in Chicago over 29 years. *Crime and Delinquency, 41,* 496–526.

Blumstein, A., Rivara, F. P., and Rosenfeld, R. 2000. The rise and decline of homicide—and why. *Annual Review of Public Health, 21,* 505–541.

Boellstorff, T. 2011. But do not identify as gay: A proleptic genealogy of the MSM category. *Cultural Anthropology, 26*(2), 287–312.

Bohnert, M., Hüttemann, H., and Schmidt, U. 2006. Homicides by sharp force. In: M. Tsokos (Ed.), *Forensic Pathology Reviews.* Valley Stream, NY: Springer/Humana Press, Vol. 4, pp. 65–89.

Bohnert, M., Müller, F. S., Perdekamp, M., and Thoma, R. 2004. Tötungsdelikt mit postmortaler Öffnung von Brust- und Bauchhöhle morphologische, kriminalistische und forensisch-psychiatrische Aspekte. *Archive Kriminologie, 214,* 37–47.

Bonner, B. and Rosario, R. 1992, January 16. Earl craig death was homicide. *St. Paul Pioneer Press.* St. Paul, MN, pp. 1A, +10A.

Brittain, R. P. 1970. The sadistic murderer. *Medicine, Science and the Law, 10*(4), 198–207.

Broverman, N. 2010, January 8. Gay-bashing just a bashing? *Advocate.* Retrieved from http://www.advocate.com/news/daily-news/2010/01/08/gay-bashing-just-bashing

Brower, T. 2002. Obstacle courts: Results of two studies on sexual orientation fairness in the California Courts. *American University Journal of* Gender, *Social Policy & the Law, 11,* 39–65.

Browne, A., Williams, K. R., and Dutton, D. G. 1999. Homicide between intimate partners. In: M. D. Smith and M. A. Zahn (Eds.), *Homicide: A Sourcebook of Social Research.* Thousand Oaks, CA: Sage, pp. 149–164.

Brunswick, M. and Gendler, N. 1992, January 18. Man, 18, charged with killing Craig. *Star Tribune.* Minneapolis, MN. pp. 1A, +9A.

Brunswick, M. and Hodges, J. 1992, January 28. FBI asked to look at letters to black police officers. *Star Tribune.* Minneapolis, MN. pp. 1B, +2B.

Bushman, B. J. and Anderson, C. A. 2001. Is it time to pull the plug on hostile versus instrumental aggression dichotomy? *Psychological Review, 108*(1), 273.

Campbell, T. 1979, August. Thank you, Barbara. *Positively Gay.* Minneapolis, MN. pp. 1, +3.

Campbell, T. 1992, February 3. *Earl Craig Defended. GLC Voice Newspaper.* Minneapolis, MN. p. 1.

Carlson, H. G. and Seliski, G. 1979. *Crimes against Persons Report,* June 17, 19:46 hrs. C.N.9065684. St. Paul Police Department, Patrol Division.

Carter, C. C. and Kolenc, A. B. 2005. Don't ask, don't tell: Has the policy met its goals. *University of Dayton Law Review, 31,* 1.

Carter, E. R. A. and Bridges, A. J. 2015. Who's on top? The mental health of men who have sex with men. *Inquiry*, *18*, 4–15.

Chan, H. C. O., Heide, K. M., and Myers, W. C. 2013. Juvenile and adult offenders arrested for sexual homicide: An analysis of victim–offender relationship and weapon used by race. *Journal of Forensic Sciences*, *58*(1), 85–89.

Christopher, R. 2014. Does attempted murder deserve greater punishment than murder: Moral luck and the duty to prevent harm. *Notre Dame Journal of Law, Ethics, and Public Policy*, *18*(2), 419–435.

Coleman, E. and Bockting, W. O. 1989. "Heterosexual" prior to sex reassignment-"homosexual" afterwards: A case study of a female-to-male transsexual. *Journal of Psychology & Human Sexuality*, *1*(2), 69–82.

Complaint. 1992. State of Minnesota v. Jayme Charles Fredrick Starkey. (Hennepin County District Court, No. 92–0189).

Comstock, G. D. 1991. *Violence against Lesbians and Gay Men*. New York, NY: Columbia University Press.

Coon, E. O. 1957. Homosexuality in the news. *Archives of Criminal Psychodynamics*, *2*(4), 843–865.

Davis, H. F. 2014. Sex-classification policies as transgender discrimination: An intersectional critique. *Perspectives on Politics*, *12*(01), 45–60.

Decker Statement. 1992. Statement of Douglas Alan Decker. (Minneapolis Police Department, CCN: MP9201011683; Supplement No. 27).

De River, J. P. 1958. *Crime and the Sexual Psychopath* (2nd ed.). Springfield, IL: Charles C Thomas.

Diaz, K. 1992, August 21. Earl Craig murder trial to feature political elite and painful allegations. *Star Tribune*. Minneapolis, MN: Metro Edition, p. 1A.

Dietz, P. E., Hazelwood, R. R., and Warren, J. 1990. The sexually sadistic criminal and his offenses. *Bulletin of the American Academy of Psychiatry Law*, *18*, 163–178.

Dong, A. E., Shephard, R., and Cutler, M. 1997. *Licensed to kill* [Film]. Los Angeles, CA: DeepFocus Productions.

Douglas, J., Burgess, A. W., Burgess, A. G., and Ressler, R. K. 2013. *Crime Classification Manual: A Standard System for Investigating and Classifying Violent Crime*. Hoboken, NJ: John Wiley & Sons.

Douglas, J. E., Burgess, A. W., Burgess, A. G., and Ressler, R. K. 1992. *Crime Classification Manual*. San Francisco, CA: Jossey-Bass.

Douglas, J. E., Ressler, R. K., Burgess, A. W., and Hartman, C. R. 1986. Criminal profiling from crime scene analysis. *Behavioral Sciences & the Law*, *4*(4), 401–421.

Drake, D. S. 2003. Data-set construction in homosexual homicide cases: Shedding the political issue of motive. In: M. D. Smith, P. H. Blackman, and J. P. Jarvis (Eds.), *New Directions in Homicide Research: Proceedings of the 2001 Annual Meeting of the Homicide Research Working Group*. Washington, DC: Federal Bureau of Investigation, pp. 197–204.

Drake, D. S. 2004a. Confronting and managing GLBT homicide and its associated phenomena. In: W. Swan (Ed.), *Handbook of Gay Lesbian, Bisexual, and Transgender Administration and Policy*. New York, NY: Marcel Dekker, pp. 311–348.

Drake, D. S. 2004b. *Recognizing Gay Homicide* (Research Brief). Minneapolis, MN: Center for Homicide Research.

Drake, D. S. 2013, November. Macro to micro: Exploring the birth of a homicide cluster. Paper presented at the *American Society of Criminology and Homicide Research Working Group*, Atlanta, GA.

Drake, D. S. 2014. Understanding Economic power dynamics as a method to combat LGBT Homicide. In: W. Swan (Ed.), *Gay, Lesbian, Bisexual, and Transgender Civil Rights: A Public Policy Agenda for Uniting a Divided America*. Boca Raton, FL: CRC Press, pp. 297–331.

Drake, D. S. 2016. LGBT homicide. In: R. Hough and K. Davies (Eds.), *American Homicide*. Thousand Oaks, CA: Sage.

Drake, D. S. (Interviewer) and Benscoter, B. (Interviewee). 1997. Telephone Interview with Bonnie Benscoter [Interview transcript]. St. Paul, MN.

Drake Statement. 1992. Statement of Bruce David Drake. (Minneapolis Police Department, CCN: MP9201011683; No. 31). [No relation to author].

Dugan, L., Nagin, D. S., and Rosenfeld, R. 1999. Explaining the decline in intimate partner homicide: The effects of changing domesticity, women's status, and domestic violence resources. *Homicide Studies*, *3*(3), 187–214.

Federal Bureau of Investigation. 2005. *Serial murder: Multi-disciplinary perspectives for investigators*. Retrieved from FBI.gov: http://www.fbi.gov/stats-services/publications/serial-murder/serial-murder-1#five

Ferguson, D. 2014, October 1. New California law eliminates 'gay panic' as a defense for attacks on LGBT people. *RawStory.com.* Retrieved from http://www.rawstory.com/2014/10/new-california-law-eliminates-gay-panic-as-a-defense-for-attacks-on-lgbt-people/

Fine, G. A. 2001. Culture creation and diffusion among preadolescents. In: S. E. Cahill (Ed.), *Inside Social Life: Readings in Sociological Psychology and Microsociology* (3rd ed.). Los Angeles, CA: Roxbury, pp. 191–192.

Fine, M. 1988. Sexuality, schooling, and adolescent females: The missing discourse of desire. *Harvard Educational Review*, 58(1), 29–54.

Fox, J. A. 2000. Uniform Crime Reports [United States]: Supplementary Homicide Reports, 1976–1997. ICPSR02832-v1. Ann Arbor, MI: Inter-university Consortium for Political and Social Research [distributor]. Retrieved from http://doi.org/10.3886/ICPSR02832.v1

Franklin, K. 1998, August 14–18. Psychosocial motivations of hate crimes perpetrators: Implications for educational intervention. Paper presented at the *106th Annual Convention of the American Psychological Association,* San Francisco, CA.

Fulkerson, A. 2010. *Bound by consent: concepts of consent within the leather and bondage, domination, sadomasochism (BDSM) communities* (Doctoral dissertation, Wichita State University).

Geberth, V. J. 1996. *Practical Homicide Investigation* (3rd ed.). Boca Raton, FL: CRC Press.

Geberth, V. J. 2003. *Sex-Related Homicide and Death Investigation: Practical and Clinical Perspectives.* Boca Raton, FL: CRC Press.

Geberth, V. J. 2014. *Sex-Related Homicide and Death Investigation: Practical and Clinical Perspectives.* Boca Raton, FL: CRC Press.

Gibson, D. C. 2004. *Clues from Killers: Serial Murder and Crime Scene Messages.* New York, NY: Barnes & Noble.

Gibson, D. C. 2010. *Serial Killing for Profit: Multiple Murder for Money.* Westport, CT: Praeger.

Goffman, E. 1967. On face-work: An analysis of ritual elements in social interaction. In: E. Goffman (Ed.), *Interaction Ritual.* New York, NY: Pantheon Books, pp. 5–45.

Goh, W. S. 2012. *Homicide Prevention Survey: Based on Intimate Relations* (Unpublished paper). Minneapolis, MN: Center for Homicide Research.

Greenfeld, L. A. 1997, February. Sex offenses and offenders: An analysis of data on rape and sexual assault. Washington, D.C.: Bureau of Justice Statistics (NCJ-163392).

Groh, S. 1979. *Supplementary Report,* June 17. C.N.9065684. St. Paul Police Department, Traffic Division.

Guminny, B. 2014. *Teenage serial homicide offenders: A typology* (Doctoral dissertation, University of Ontario Institute of Technology). Retrieved from https://ir.library.dc-uoit.ca/bitstream/10155/487/1/Guminny_Bailey.pdf

Harris, M. B. and Miller, K. C. 2000. Gender and perceptions of danger. *Sex Roles*, 43(11–12), 843–863.

Harry, J. 1992. Conceptualizing anti-gay violence. In: G. D. Comstock (Ed.), *Hate Crimes: Confronting Violence against Lesbians and Gay Men.* New York, NY: Columbia University Press, pp. 113–122.

Hazelwood, R. R. and Douglas, J. E. 1980. The lust murderer. *FBI Law Enforcement Bulletin*, 49(4), 18–22.

Herek, G. M. 1984. Beyond "homophobia": A social psychological perspective on attitudes toward lesbians and gay men. *Journal of Homosexuality*, 10(1–2), 1–21.

Herek, G. M. 1990. The context of anti-gay violence: Notes on cultural and psychological heterosexism. *Journal of Interpersonal Violence*, 5, 316–333.

Herek, G. M. 1992. Psychological heterosexism and anti-gay violence: The social psychology of bigotry and bashing. In: G. M. Herek and K. T. Berrill (Eds.), *Hate Crimes: Confronting Violence against Lesbians and Gay Men.* Newbury Park, CA: Sage, pp. 149–169.

Hickey, E. W. 2012. *Serial Murderers and Their Victims.* Boston, MA: Cengage Learning.

Holmes, R. M. and Holmes, S. T. 1998. *Contemporary Perspectives on Serial Murder.* Thousand Oaks, CA: Sage.

Holmes, R. M. and Holmes, S. T. 2010. *Serial Murder* (2nd ed.). Thousand Oaks, CA: Sage.

Hughes, S. M. and Bremme, R. 2011. The effects of facial symmetry and sexually-dimorphic facial proportions on assessments of sexual orientation. *Journal of Social, Evolutionary, and Cultural Psychology*, 5(4), 214.

Hunt, A. C. and Cowling, R. J. 1991. Murder by stabbing. *Forensic Science International*, 52(1), 107–112.

Jarmon, G. D. 2013. The African American church and HIV: A call to action using an Afrocentric approach. Retrieved from http://www.garlandjarmon.com/churchandhiv/

Jay, K. 1992. *Out of the Closets: Voices of Gay Liberation.* New York, NY: University Press.

Jyrkas, W. 1979a. *Supplementary Report,* June 17, 19:46 hrs. C.N.9065684. St. Paul Police Department, Traffic Division.

Jyrkas, W. 1979b. *Supplementary Report,* June 17, 16:30 hrs. C.N.9065684. St. Paul Police Department, Traffic Division.

Kantor, M. 1998. *Homophobia: Description, Development, and Dynamics of Gay Bashing.* Westport, CT: Praeger Publishers.

Karmen, A. 1996. *Crime Victims: An Introduction to Victimology* (3rd ed.). New York: Wadsworth.

Kempf, E. J. 1920. The psychopathology of the acute homosexual panic. Acute pernicious dissociation neuroses. In: E. J. Kempf (Ed.), *Psychopathology.* St Louis, MO: Mosby Co, pp. 477–515.

Keppel, R. and Birnes, W. 1997. *Signature Killers.* New York, NY: Pocket Books.

Keppel, R. D. 1989. *Serial Murder: Future Implications for Police Investigations.* Cincinnati, OH: Anderson.

Koppelman, A. 1994. Why discrimination against lesbians and gay men is sex discrimination. *New York University Law Review, 69,* 197.

LaForest Statement. 1992. Statement of Andrea Justine LaForest. (Minneapolis Police Department, CCN: MP9201011683; Supplement No. 6).

Langevin, R., Ben-Aron, M. H., Wright, P., Marchese, V., and Handy, L. 1988. The sex killer. *Annals of Sex Research, 1*(2), 263–301.

Lavers, M. 2011, July 18. 70 Percent of anti-LGBT murder victims are people of color. *Color Lines.* Retrieved from http://www.colorlines.com/articles/70-percent-anti-lgbt-murder-victims-are-people-color

Leatham, D. 1979, June 22. Death of gay man puzzles St. Paul Police. *Minnesota Daily.* pp. 1, +7.

Lee, C. 2008. The gay panic defense. *University of California Davis Law Review, 42,* 471–566.

Lemert, E. M. 1951. *Social Pathology; A Systematic Approach to the Theory of Sociopathic Behavior.* New York, NY: McGraw-Hill.

Lundrigan, S. and Canter, D. 2001. Spatial patterns of serial murder: An analysis of disposal site location choice. *Behavioral Sciences and the Law, 19,* 595–610.

Malmquist, C. P. and Volavka, J. 2006. *Homicide: A Psychiatric Perspective.* Washington, DC: American Psychiatric Publishing.

McNamara, J. J., McDonald, S., and Lawrence, J. M. 2012. Characteristics of false allegation adult crimes. *Journal of Forensic Sciences, 57*(3), 643–646.

McNamara, R. P. 1994. *The Times Square Hustler: Male Prostitution in New York City.* Westport, CT: Praeger Publishers.

Meade, E. 2015. *The Beast: Riding the Rails and Dodging Narcos on the Migrant Trail.* Ó. Martínez, D. M. Ugaz, and J. Washington (Translators), F. Goldman (Introduction). New York, NY: Verso.

Meloy, J. and Felthous, A. 2004. Introduction to this issue: Serial and mass homicide. *Behavioral Sciences and the Law, 22,* 289–290.

Meloy, J. R. 1996. Pseudonecrophilia following spousal homicide. *Journal of Forensic Sciences, 41,* 706–708.

Meloy, J. R. 2000. The nature and dynamics of sexual homicide: An integrative review. *Aggression and Violent Behavior, 5*(1), 1–22.

Messner, S. and South, S. 1981. Economic deprivation: Opportunity structure, and robbery victimization. *Social Forces, 64,* 975–91.

Meyer, G. 1979. *Supplementary Report,* July 2, 18:45 hrs. C.N.9064452. St. Paul Police Department, Homicide Division.

Miels, E. 1979a. *Supplementary Report,* July 5. C.N.9064452. St. Paul Police Department, Homicide Division.

Miels, E. 1979b. *Supplementary Report,* July 6. C.N.9064452. St. Paul Police Department, Homicide Division.

Miller, B. and Humphreys, L. 1980. Lifestyles and violence: Homosexual victims of assault and murder. *Qualitative Sociology, 3,* 169–185.

Money, J. 1986. *Lovemaps: Clinical Concepts of Sexual/Erotic Health and Pathology, Paraphilia, and Gender Transposition of Childhood, Adolescence, and Maturity.* New York, NY: Ardent Media.

Mueller, A. 1992. Can motive matter: A constitutional and criminal law analysis of motive in hate crime legislation. *University of Missouri-Kansas City Law Review, 61,* 619–805.

Murphy, B. C. 1992. Educating mental health professionals about gay and lesbian issues. *Journal of Homosexuality, 22*(3–4), 229–246.

Nardi, P. M. and Bolton, R. 1991. Gay-bashing: Violence and aggression against gay men and lesbians. In: R. Baenninger (Ed.), *Targets of Violence and Aggression.* Amsterdam: Elsevier/North Holland, pp. 349–400.

National LGBT Homicide Database. 2014. *National LGBT Homicide Database, 1969–2014* [Data file and code book], 1152-cases version. Minneapolis, MN: Center for Homicide Research.

Newton, M. 2006. *The Encyclopedia of Serial Killers.* New York, NY: Infobase Publishing.

Nitschke, J., Blendl, V., Ottermann, B., Osterheider, M., and Mokros, A. 2009. Severe sexual sadism—An underdiagnosed disorder? Evidence from a sample of forensic inpatients. *Journal of Forensic Sciences, 54*(3), 685–691.

Parrott, D. J. and Zeichner, A. 2005. Effects of sexual prejudice and anger on physical aggression toward gay and heterosexual men. *Psychology of Men & Masculinity, 6*(1), 3–17.

Pedersen, C. A., Caldwell, J. D., Jirikowski, G. F., and Insel, T. R. 1992. *Oxytocin in Maternal, Sexual, and Social Behaviors.* New York, NY: New York Academy of Sciences.

Pharr, S. 1988. *Homophobia as a Weapon of Sexism.* Little Rock, AR: The Women's Project.

Podolsky, E. 1965. The lust murderer. *Medico-legal Journal, 33*(4), 174–178.

Prestage, G., Ven, P. V. D., Grulich, A., Kippax, S., McInnes, D., and Hendry, O. 2001. Gay men's casual sex encounters: Discussing HIV and using condoms. *AIDS Care, 13*(3), 277–284.

Radojević, N., Radnić, B., Petković, S., Miljen, M., Čurović, I., Čukić, D., and Savić, S. 2013. Multiple stabbing in sex-related homicides. *Journal of Forensic and Legal Medicine, 20*(5), 502–507.

Ressler R. K., Burgess, A. W., and Douglas, J. E. 1988. *Sexual Homicide: Patterns and Motives.* New York, NY: The Free Press.

Ressler, R. K., Burgess, A. W., Douglas, J. E., Hartman, C., and D'Agostino, R. 1986. Sexual killers and their victims: Identifying patterns through crime scene analysis. *Journal of Interpersonal Violence, 1,* 288–308.

Richardson, N. 2005. Queering a gay cliché: The rough trade/sugar daddy relationship in Derek Jarman's Camvaggio. *Paragraph, 28*(3), 36–53.

Riemann, J. A. 2004. Gay homicide solvability: An analysis of gay homicide clearance rates for Minneapolis 1989–1999. In: V. P. Bunge, C. R. Block, and M. Lane (Eds.), *Linking Data to Practice in Violence and Homicide Prevention: Proceedings of the 2004 Meeting of the Homicide Research Working Group.* Chicago, IL: HRWG Publications, pp. 127–140.

Robles, J. J. 1992, January 24. As Craig knew, gay people of color carry a special burden. *Star Tribune.* Minneapolis, MN. pp. 15A.

Rofes, E. 1978, August 12. Queer bashing: The politics of violence against gay men. *Gay Community News.* Boston, MA. pp. 8–9, +11.

Rosario, R. 1992, January 26. Craig case still raises questions: Council member wants medical examiner probe. *St. Paul Pioneer Press*, p. 1C.

Runciman, W. G. 1966. *Relative Deprivation and Social Justice: A Study of Attitudes to Social Inequality in Twentieth-Century England.* Berkley, CA: University of California.

Safarik, M. E., Jarvis, J. P., and Nussbaum, K. E. 2002. Sexual homicide of elderly females: Linking offender characteristics to crime scene attributes. *Journal of Interpersonal Violence, 17,* 500–525.

Sanchez, F. J. and Viain, E. 2009. Collective self-esteem as a coping resource for male-to-female transsexuals. *Journal of Counseling Psychology, 56*(1), 202–209.

Scanlon, L. and Johnson, S. 1979, July 11. Suspect in gays's slaying died in crash. *Minneapolis Star.* Minneapolis, MN. p. A5.

Schlesinger. L. B. 2004. *Sexual Murder: Catathymic and Compulsive Homicides.* Boca Raton, FL: CRC Press.

Schlesinger, L. B. and Revitch, E. 1997. Sexual dynamics in homicide and assault. In *Sexual Dynamics of Antisocial Behavior* (2nd ed.), Springfield, IL: Charles C Thomas.

Schlesinger, L. B. and Revitch, E. 1999. Sexual burglaries and sexual homicide: Clinical, forensic, and investigative considerations. *Journal of the American Academy of Psychiatry and the Law Online, 27*(2), 227–238.

Schrimshaw, E. W., Siegel, K., Downing Jr, M. J., and Parsons, J. T. 2013. Disclosure and concealment of sexual orientation and the mental health of non-gay-identified, behaviorally bisexual men. *Journal of Consulting and Clinical Psychology, 81*(1), 141–153.

Seliski, G. and Carlson, H. G. 1979. *Supplementary Report,* June 17, 21:00 hrs. C.N.9065684. St. Paul Police Department, Patrol Division.

Shilts, R. 1988. *The Mayor of Castro Street.* New York, NY: St. Martin's Press.

Shulka, J. E. and Drake, D. S. 2006. *GLBT Homicide Analysis* [Research Brief]. Minneapolis, MN: Center for Homicide Research.

Silverman, R. A. and Kennedy, L. W. 1987. Relational distance and homicide: The role of the stranger. *Journal of Criminal Law and Criminology*, 78(2), 272–308.

Slaby, A. E. 1994. *Handbook of Psychiatric Emergencies* (4th ed.). East Norwalk, CT: Appleton and Lange.

Snodgrass, T. J. 2011, November. Obesity and premature death. *Epidemiology*, Retrieved from http://hearty-health.com/obesity/

Solomon, C. G. and Manson, J. E. 1997. Obesity and mortality: A review of the epidemiologic data. *The American Journal of Clinical Nutrition*, 66(4), 1044S–1050S.

South, S. and Messner, S. 1986. Structural determinants of intergroup association. *American Journal of Sociology*, 91, 1409–1430.

Spear, A. 1992, January 24. A defender of the poor and of fine food. *Star Tribune*. Minneapolis, MN. p. 15A.

Stanoch, J. M. 1992, September 28. *Letter to Frank Wood*. State of Minnesota, Fourth Judicial District Court.

Starkey Statement. 1992. Statement of Jayme Charles Frederick Starkey. (Minneapolis Police Department, CCN: MP9201011683; No. 33).

State v. Starkey, 516 N.W.2d 918; 1994 Minn. Lexis-Nexis 381.

Stevenson, M. R. and Medler, B. R. 1995. Is homophobia a weapon of sexism? *Journal of Men's Studies*, 4, 1–8.

Stillion, J. M. 1995. Premature death among males: Extending the bottom line of men's health. In: D. Sabo & D. F. Gordon (Eds.), *Men's Health and Illness*. Thousand Oaks, CA: Sage, pp. 46–67.

Stockton, T. J. 1979a. *Supplementary Report*, July 12, 10:10 hrs. C.N.9064452. St. Paul Police Department, Homicide Division.

Stockton, T. J. 1979b. *Supplementary Report*, June 18, 11:00 hrs. C.N.9064452. St. Paul Police Department, Homicide Division.

Stockton, T. J. 1979c. *Supplementary Report*, June 19, 1400 hrs. C.N.9064452. St. Paul Police Department, Homicide Division.

Stockton, T. J. 1979d. *Supplementary Report*, June 20, 10:30 hrs. C.N.9064452. St. Paul Police Department, Homicide Division.

Stockton, T. J. 1979e. *Supplementary Report*, June 21. C.N.9064452. St. Paul Police Department, Homicide Division.

Stockton, T. J. 1979f. *Supplementary Report*, June 22, 09:45 hrs. C.N.9064452. St. Paul Police Department, Homicide Division.

Stockton, T. J. 1979g. *Supplementary Report*, June 28, 09:00 hrs. C.N.9064452. St. Paul Police Department, Homicide Division.

Stockton, T. J. 1979h. *Supplementary Report*, July 2, 10:00 hrs. C.N.9064452. St. Paul Police Department, Homicide Division.

Stockton, T. J. 1979i. *Supplementary Report*, June 19, 08:30 hrs. C.N.9064452. St. Paul Police Department, Homicide Division.

Stockton, T. J. 1979j. *Supplementary Report*, June 22, 11:15 hrs. C.N.9064452. St. Paul Police Department, Homicide Division.

Stockton, T. J. 1979k. *Supplementary Report*, July 2, 15:30 hrs. C.N.9064452. St. Paul Police Department, Homicide Division.

Stockton, T. J. 1979l. *Supplementary Report*, July 16, 10:30 hrs. C.N.9064452. St. Paul Police Department, Homicide Division.

Stockton, T. J. 1979m. *Supplementary Report*, July 2, 10:00 hrs. C.N.9064452. St. Paul Police Department, Homicide Division.

Suffredini, K. S. 2001. Pride and prejudice: The homosexual panic defense. *Boston College Third World Law Journal*, 21, 279–314.

Supplemental Affidavit. 1992, March 2. Defendant's supplemental affidavit in support of ex parte application. (Defense Attorney, Ellis Olkon). (Sip No. 92004446).

Teal, J. L. 2015. *"Black trans bodies are under attack": Gender non-conforming homicide victims in the US 1995–2014* (Doctoral dissertation, Humboldt State University).

Tenner, A. D., Trevithick, L.A., Wagner, V., and Burch, R. 1998. Seattle YouthCare's prevention, intervention and education program: A model of care for HIV-positive, homeless, and at-risk youth. *Journal of Adolescent Health*, 23, 96–106.

Timmons, S. 1990. *The Trouble with Harry Hay: Founder of the Modern Gay Movement*. Los Angeles, CA: Alyson Publications.

Topalli, V., Wright, R., and Fornango, R. 2002. Drug dealers, robbery and retaliation: Vulnerability, deterrence and the contagion of violence. *British Journal of Criminology, 42,* 337–351.

Trial Transcript, 2–1758. 1993. State of Minnesota vs. Jayme Charles Fredrick Starkey. (Hennepin County District Court). (DC No. 92004446).

Turvey, B. E. 2011. *Criminal Profiling: An Introduction to Behavioral Evidence Analysis.* Boston, MA: Academic Press.

United States of America. 1974. *Thumbs Down-Hitchhiking* [Film]. Filmfare Communications.

van Gemert, D. F. 1994. Chicken kills hawk: Gay murders during the eighties in Amsterdam. *Journal of Homosexuality, 26*(4), 149–174.

Visano, L. A. 1991. The impact of age on paid sexual encounters. *Journal of Homosexuality, 20*(3–4), 207–226.

Warren, J. I., Dietz, P. E., and Hazelwood, R. R. 2013. The collectors: Serial sexual offenders who preserve evidence of their crimes. *Aggression and Violent Behavior, 18*(6), 666–672.

Webb, T. 1979a, July 13. Family bears pain of dead son being named in slaying. *Minneapolis Tribune.* Minneapolis, MN. pp. B1, +B16.

Webb, T. 1979b, July 20. St. Paul man's death questioned: Suspect held in death at Loring Park is freed. *Minneapolis Tribune.* Minneapolis, MN. pp. 1B.

Weems, M. 2011, January 1. Why I capitalize "Gay." [Blog]. Retrieved from http://www.mickeyweems.com/2011/01/01/coming-out-as-human/.

Wentland, J. J. and Reissing, E. D. 2011. Taking casual sex not too casually: Exploring definitions of casual sexual relationships. *The Canadian Journal of Human Sexuality, 20*(3), 75–91.

West, D. J. 1977. *Homosexuality Re-examined.* Minneapolis, MN: University of Minnesota Press.

White, J. H. 2007. Evidence of primary, secondary, and collateral paraphilias left at serial murder and sex offender crime scenes. *Journal of Forensic Sciences, 52*(5), 1194–1201.

Winger, K. G. 1979a. *Supplementary Report,* June 17, 19:46 hrs. C.N.9065684. St. Paul Police Department, Traffic Division.

Winger, K. G. 1979b. *Supplementary Report,* June 17, no time given. C.N.9065684. St. Paul Police Department, Traffic Division.

Wolfgang, M. E. 1958. *Patterns of Criminal Homicide.* Oxford, England: University of Pennsylvania Press.

Woods, D. D. Jr. 2006. Piquerism: The investigative challenge of serial murder. In: P. C. Shon and D. Milovanovic (Eds.), *Serial Killers: Understanding Lust Murder.* Durham, NC: Carolina Academic Press, pp. 113–120.

Young, K. M. 2011. Outing Batson: How the case of gay jurors reveals the shortcomings of modern voir dire. *Willamette Law Review, 48*(243), 12.

Younghans, J. and Finnigan, P. 1979. *Supplementary Report,* June 17. C.N.9065684. St. Paul Police Department, Traffic Division.

V
Epilogue
Investigative Considerations

15 Cold Case Homicides
Challenges and Opportunities

Michael Arntfield and Kenneth L. Mains

Contents

Introduction 299
Overview 300
Investigative and Analytical Challenges 301
    Inadequate or Missing Records 302
    Elderly Witnesses and Suspects 303
    Investigative Deficiencies 304
Investigative and Analytical Opportunities 307
    Criminal Investigative Analysis 307
    Media Stimuli 308
    Geographic Profiling and Psychogeography 309
Further Discussion 312
References 313

Introduction

Unsolved historical homicides, more commonly referred to as "cold cases," have become a matter of great sociolegal interest in recent years. Buoyed in large part by the geometric advances in deoxyribonucleic acid (DNA) evidence made in the late 1990s, coupled with increasingly standardized major case management protocols, cold cases—and the ability to both revisit and even solve these cases with comparable expediency—have rightfully seized the public's imagination. At the same time, they have evolved into a politically precarious issue for senior law enforcement officials who, for a variety of reasons cited here, have a contentious relationship with cold cases and the resources they demand. The subject of often romanticized depictions in film and television, viewers are frequently accustomed to seeing obsessively tireless criminal investigators, like in the HBO series *True Detective*, who remain haunted or obsessed with a given case for years and even decades, seeing it through to the end against all odds. Even factual or unscripted series such as the A&E Network's long-running *Cold Case Files*—arguably the first series to popularize the term—and which faithfully depicts the stark realities of initiating renewed investigations years after the fact—fail to accurately capture the time-consuming and costly nature of these momentous undertakings. The truth is that the day-to-day reality of cold cases is far less telegenic, and far more frustrating.

    Police officers, perhaps more so than most people, do not like to leave things unresolved—questions of fact unanswered. Beyond the nagging sense of unfinished business, there is of course the additional threat to public safety when murders go unsolved or uncleared, and the perpetrator remains indefinitely at large, free to offend again. As seen in so many cold cases, it is the apparent randomness of the crime—stranger on stranger sexual homicides in particular—that presents the greatest investigative challenge early on. Random cases of this nature, where no obvious suspects are immediately forthcoming, have the additional burden of ensuring the risk to the public is all the more significant, the need to expeditiously identify and apprehend the offender all the more necessary.

Yet, for all the meritorious reasons why cold cases should by this point be operational, public safety and public relations priorities for police departments at the local, state, and federal levels, it would seem that no two agencies see cold cases through the same lens—no two agencies seem to agree on how and when to go about reactivating these historical files. While larger law enforcement agencies frequently have the resources to fund and staff permanent open unsolved units, or at the very least have the means to equip ongoing task forces to which appropriately trained investigators can be seconded from the regular detective rotation, many agencies have neither the interest nor the wherewithal to prioritize such cases at all. Amidst today's fiscal realities for law enforcement, where corporate municipalities are declaring bankruptcy and police furloughs and layoffs are now a grim reality, many agencies are struggling to simply maintain basic adequacy standards and keep up with day-to-day operations, including new murders and the timely investigation of fresh cases. Such realities have unfortunately meant that once sizeable cold case squads and long-standing open unsolved units have been permanently shuttered in recent years.

When conducting a cost–benefit analysis of such units, the rationale for this aggressive downsizing by police managers runs the gamut. It has been known to include the supposition that because prime suspects or key witnesses in dated cases are either not locatable or believed dead, there is no reasonable prospect of laying charges or securing an indictment, much less a conviction. Other rationalizations include the fact that the families of victims are also dying off, or have simply moved on with their lives and grief to the extent that they are no longer in contact with investigators or police brass. They are thus unable or sometimes just unwilling to exercise the same type of political leverage and public pressure seen in more contemporary homicide investigations, and where cases remain in the public eye of the 24/7 news cycle until solved. The misplacement or outright destruction of original files and forensic exhibits, the retirement or death of original investigators whose institutional memory of these cases went with them, and the fact that many cold case units were from their outset misused as either dumping grounds for departmental malcontents or treated as cushy "sunset jobs" and sinecures for soon-to-be-retired investigators round out some of the more common reasons for their being collapsed, with many agencies no longer being able or willing to justify their expense. As some (Adams, 2003; Pettem, 2012; Arntfield, 2013) have already noted when looking at the currently underfunded and overlooked value of police cold case units, the climate is thus ideal for multidisciplinary collaboration, and for police to compensate by appropriately drawing on the good faith insights and forensic expertise of the academic and private sectors to make new investigative inroads in such cases. This can of course be done at no expense to taxpayers and without hemorrhaging a police department's own human or financial resources. As the successes of volunteer groups like the American Investigative Society of Cold Cases (AISOCC), a resource regularly drawn on by local and state law enforcement across the United States, and the Vidocq Society—recognized by the U.S. Justice Department as an approved investigative partner with respect to historical homicides (Walton, 2014)—as well as higher education think tanks like the Western University Cold Case Society in Canada have demonstrated, all evidences point to cold cases as being a highly specialized area of investigation whose sustainability will depend on scholarly and scientific collaboration as much as old fashioned detective work.

Overview

Unlike contemporary homicide investigations that are in most cases required to follow a clearly delineated command triangle and proscriptive set of procedures for the purposes of court disclosure, the investigative methodologies used in cold cases, and in fact the entire climate surrounding these investigations, have proven to be both uncertain and inconsistent. There is by extension also no consistent definition about when an unsolved investigation can officially be classified as "cold." A review of policies currently on the books among police departments in the United States, Canada, and the United Kingdom points to widely varying definitions, with many agencies opting out of assigning a definition altogether. For instance, the Los Angeles Police Department's Cold Case Homicide Special Section, a dedicated full-time unit devoted to open unsolved files, classifies cases that are 5 years old or more as being cold for the purposes of their mandate (Los Angeles Police Department, 2015). The New York Police Department, by way of comparison, and as revealed in a 2013 *Slate* magazine exposé, has no consistent definition or allocated resources for cold cases in spite of being an even larger agency and having a greater number of unsolved murders

(Peters, 2013). In the United Kingdom, the Bedfordshire Police created in a task force in 2014 that, rather than defining a cold case based its vintage, sought to examine all unsolved murders over a 40-year period, from 1974 to 2014 inclusive, classifying all cases falling within this range as cold. This step appears to have been motivated by the earlier strategy adopted by the Metropolitan London Police that did the same thing in 2012, focusing on unsolved murders committed between 1967 and 1980 inclusive (BBC, 2012). Meanwhile, the Toronto Police Service—one of the last municipal police departments in Canada to operate a full-time cold case unit—has no official definition of cold cases and does not limit its investigations to any specific period, allowing detectives to maintain a workflow of potentially solvable cold case files at their discretion.

A cursory examination of official organizational policies, or the lack thereof, across the English-speaking world and in locales with legal and police systems descended from British common law suggests that the Toronto Police model is the dominant trend, with what constitutes a cold case seeming to vary by location, circumstance, and available resources. The general consensus would appear to be that any case that remains unsolved for such a time that all initial investigative actions and forensic techniques have been exhausted—typically a year at the very least—is cold by default. In other words, unsolved or uncleared cases that remain officially "open" in the parlance of Uniform Crime Reporting but which are "inactive" might be said to constitute cold cases, meaning that the file is dormant and not necessarily assigned to any single detective's case load, but can be activated at any time based on the availability of new information. In this sense, "uncleared" would describe any case for which an offender has been identified but whose culpability cannot be established to the extent that they can be indicted or in some cases publicly named. This most frequently occurs when a suspect dies before being interviewed and where no DNA exists in the case to justify an exhumation, and where a definitive match between offender and crime scene cannot be made. In theory, such a case would remain on the books indefinitely in spite of investigators being satisfied they had identified the correct perpetrator, with such cases being less unsolved as much as they are just officially uncharged.

The ambiguity surrounding cold case intake, assessment, and reactivation procedures should be of particular interest to forensic experts—those in both private practice and employed by institutions of higher learning, as well as police criminalists and behavioral scientists—in that there now exist salient opportunities to impart subject matter expertise for the purposes of assisting law enforcement shortlist cases for review. This includes research and consulting in the area of cold case homicide investigation and the need for accredited experts to review and vet cases according to a consistent and professionally standardized solvability index. Such an index would in theory identify the strengths and weaknesses of a given file based on the current adequacy standards, forensic technologies, and body of knowledge with respect to victimology, suspectology, and related areas of criminal investigative analysis. The use of third-party subject matter experts as part of an intermittent cold case review process would equally ensure an independent and objective evaluation of cases that is scientific rather than ideological, with the reviewers having little to no existing knowledge or preconceptions of the crimes in question. The first step, as it is done now with groups like AISOCC already mentioned, would be to identify the strengths and weaknesses of a case as it currently exists based on the "four corners rule," or how the case reads in its present state, bearing in mind no prior assumptions, within the four corners of a hard copy case file or related compendium, sometimes referred to as a "murder book." From there, the forensic advisor—regardless of their home discipline and primary area of training—psychology, criminology, pathology, etc.—would develop a comprehensive list of known or suspected challenges a given case might present if reactivated, as well as a list of advantages that the current body of knowledge and array of available forensic techniques that might be brought to bear on a case would allow. In consultation with police managers and prosecutors, decisions would then need to be made about how to weigh the investigative potential of a case based on its current merits. In the sections that follow, we provide some examples, complete with recent case studies, about how such a review process might be undertaken and executed.

Investigative and Analytical Challenges

As mentioned, while homicide investigations unfolding in real time today are dynamic events that are carefully scrutinized, computerized, and managed by any number of stakeholders tasked with seeing an investigation through from inception to prosecution as part of a standardized concierge-style system, few if any cold cases offer the same degree of documentary completeness. This is especially the case in those investigations originally undertaken prior to 1990, when electronic records management in law enforcement began to become commonplace. In our experience, this is an almost universal reality, regardless of the size of the agency in question, the caliber and competence of the original detectives, or the breadth of the original resources devoted to a given investigation. Often, one of the first and most jarring observations that those tasked with auditing and assessing historical homicides make is the paltry state of the original file. This is also typically the biggest handicap faced by contemporary cold case investigators who open an old banker's box to find a disorganized assemblage of some basic handwritten notes and little else. Unfortunately, this is the rule rather than the exception.

Inadequate or Missing Records

Most contemporary police detectives find it difficult to conceptualize the conditions under which their earlier counterparts had to conduct homicide investigations. As time capsules that accurately reflect the investigative limitations with which police departments had to contend not so long ago, cold case files are often very scant in their detail. With no fingerprint database, ballistics identification network, or centralized repository of criminal records existing prior to the late 1980s in some jurisdictions—let alone anything remotely resembling a DNA database—records of cases dating to the 1960s and 1970s, or even earlier, not surprisingly reflect investigators operating largely in the dark and relying on field tactics that seem archaic by modern standards. Even in those cases where the original investigators conducted a fulsome and comprehensive investigation from the outset, documentary records from these earlier periods often reflect additional limitations placed on investigators in terms of the actual mechanical process of authoring and curating detailed reports. While the availability of computers and use of electronic records management systems are now commonplace in law enforcement, case files dating to earlier decades were typically relegated to handwritten field notes, many of which are found to have been mislaid over the years, or instead found to have been retained by the original investigators on into retirement. These notes are often written in a shorthand format for which the context has been lost with the passage of time, and which in many cases contain entries that are essentially inscrutable—a codex of no investigative value without their being translated by the original investigator(s).

In a rare handful of cases, field notes are supplemented by more detailed expository documents such as interim reports, case summaries, or investigative chronologies authored for review by commanding officers. In the majority of cases predating the 1990s, these documents were created using mechanical typewriters and only their original hard copy format exists. Notwithstanding the comparatively labor-intensive process of creating a report with the use of a typewriter—a process which naturally constrains the detail with which a report is written as a result of the cumbersome process of formatting a document and making corrections—the ephemeral nature of paper records has additionally led to problems of continuity and document integrity (Arntfield and Gorman, 2014). Whether damaged by mishandling, environmental conditions, or simply having become mislaid or misfiled during changes in storage location over the years, these reports are often illegible or impossible to procure in the first place. With no servers or hard disk storage to back up this information as would be the case today, records and reports not converted into a digital format and left under the control of a specific custodian of records are not likely to be consolidated in one place. Cold case files are thus frequently required to be cobbled together in piecemeal fashion, a process that only slows the reassessment and reactivation of a given file even further.

One strategy that cold case investigators and forensic reviewing consultants can employ to mitigate this deficiency in record completeness is to appropriately differentiate between *primary source documents* and *secondary source documents* comprising a file. This is one of the many points of convergence between cold case investigation and more conventional forms of historical or archival research conducted by academics. In brief, because both undertakings involve examining historical records and reconstructing past occurrences, a primary source is any record or person that can offer a firsthand account of an event, and a version that can be taken at face value without the need for additional corroboration. Conversely, a secondary source is any supporting set of materials that discusses, interprets, or analyzes the primary source material, or which can be used to complement and contextualize the primary source material. For instance, while an original investigator's report on the status of a particular homicide investigation would be a primary source document and would be the ideal starting point in examining a historical occurrence, the absence or incompleteness of such a report might be ameliorated by the ability to obtain secondary source materials to help fill in the blanks. These sources might range from period media reports or an accredited journalist's original notes to genealogical or land ownership records in the possession of a library or historical society. In fact, newspapers, libraries, hospitals, universities, historical societies, and similar institutions have generally proven to employ more conscientious and accountable storage practices and inventory controls than law enforcement agencies and are among the first places a cold case investigator should look when revisiting a case. For this same reason, the custodians of secondary source documents make logical stakeholders in the investigative process once a case is identified for review or reactivation.

Elderly Witnesses and Suspects

In recent years, in light of an aging population in North America and an increased awareness of how this shift in demographics will impact future criminal investigations, law enforcement agencies have sought to develop new protocols for the interview and interrogation of elderly subjects—including both witnesses and suspects. Standardized policies and specialized training with respect to the interviewing of children and minors have been in place among most law enforcement agencies for some time; however, as both mean and median ages have been gradually increasing in the Anglo-American world, the elderly have been amalgamated with children and similarly declared "vulnerable persons" for the purposes of structured police questioning. This includes special consideration being paid to their mental state, understanding of language, and stability of their faculties (Wright and Holliday, 2003). Implementing these special practices in the interview and interrogation of witnesses and suspects in cold case investigations thus presents a particular set of challenges for investigators. Unlike cases of fraud, elder abuse, and other crimes that occur in a contemporary context and which frequently involve elderly witnesses and victims, historical homicides present the additional challenge of interviewing persons who may be in a declining or compromised cognitive state about incidents that occurred many years—in some cases decades—prior to the actual interview. Factor in the reality that many of these same persons may have been interviewed repeatedly by police about the same incident over their life course, and additional issues arise with respect to the consistency and credibility of the information gleaned by contemporary investigators.

A significant shortcoming in the training modules encompassing police interview and interrogation techniques is that they have historically presupposed that all interview subjects are cognitively and emotionally healthy and stable, and will respond to stimuli and stressors in equally predictable fashion. This simply is not the case, and age of the interviewee has been widely recognized as primary factor impacting the effectiveness of conventional interview techniques (Wood and Aldridge, 1999). It was roughly 25 years ago, when child protection laws gained increased attention and previously unreported sexual offenses against children became the focus of specialized investigative units, that training in the special circumstances surrounding the interviewing of children first took speed. Today, elder abuse as the increasingly prevalent inverse of child abuse has underscored the fact that the investigative interviewing of persons over the age of 65 requires a similarly nuanced approach that departs from conventional tactics. Like children, there is neither a single "type" of elderly subject nor any single approach to conducting interviews; instead, investigators need to understand that there is a *range* of cognitive, physical, and emotional responses that the investigator will need to consider and account for in the planning and execution of effective interviews (Reid and Associates, 2015). A host of socioeconomic, physiological, and lifestyle characteristics such as education and previous occupations, marital status and family support, medications and existing medical conditions, residency status and independence, alcohol and drug use, general physical and mental fitness, and historical criminal activity should all be considered as factors when conducting interviews with elderly witnesses, and with an investigator having to continually reassess the effectiveness of his or her approach over the course of the interview. Studies in the United Kingdom involving interviewing subjects as young as 60 confirm that these types of individuating circumstances are often equated with a lack of witness credibility, and that police investigators lack confidence in their ability to obtain thorough and credible versions of events—and by extension admissible confessions—from elderly subjects as opposed to younger interviewees. Many police investigators also cite both a lack of training and lack of time to devote to these more complicated interviews (Wright and Holliday, 2005).

The process of interviewing elderly subjects in cold case investigations is further complicated by the following key variables as opposed to more recently occurring events:

1. Memories naturally fade with the passage of time, in some cases with new or alternate versions of events being artificially recalled due to either psychological trauma, cognitive degeneration, or prolonged coaching/influence. This can sometimes include false confessions or "deathbed" confessions that wrongly implicate persons still living.

2. Statements made may contradict earlier statements provided to police in previous interviews for any number of reasons, the ensuing differences complicating the timeline of events or raising issues of credibility.

3. Newly identified suspects may have made previous statements to police years or decades earlier as witnesses without being notified of their jeopardy or afforded the opportunity to consult with counsel. In these cases, admitting previous statements into evidence may be problematic.

4. Further to the previous, conventional and sometimes aggressive interrogation tools with which an investigator may be accustomed (Reid Technique, Wicklander-Zulawski interviewing, polygraph examination, tactical interviewing, etc.) have often been looked at with a jaundiced eye by the courts when applied to elderly suspects, even when apparently justified.

In summary, the process of interviewing elderly subjects in cold case homicides is fraught with legal, procedural, and ethical challenges, and is arguably the one area of a case over which the contemporary investigator has the least control. As with the other challenges cited in this chapter, police personnel may in turn wish to consider drawing on the expertise of third-party subject matter experts trained in elderly cognition, rather than going it alone and potentially compromising an investigation by failing to recognize that elderly witness–suspect interviews are an area of singular expertise to which conventional tactics do not necessarily apply.

Investigative Deficiencies

Lastly, cold cases, once reactivated or even just re-examined years later with fresh eyes, frequently offer sobering moments for contemporary investigators when they witness firsthand just how ad hoc major cases were investigated in previous generations. As with so many of the other variables that factor into a case going unsolved, such revelations also tend to vary greatly by jurisdiction. However, even in those cases for which larger, better-trained, and ostensibly more progressive agencies had carriage, one is bound to be frustrated by the investigative actions that would today be classified as procedural missteps—even instances of outright negligence or dereliction of duty. As discussed later, there are ways to remedy these missteps by bringing current forensic technologies to bear, but the real challenge in these circumstances is the need for modern investigators not to dwell on oversights or excessively critique the original investigation. The key in successfully reactivating cold cases and bringing them to closure is to understand that the original file is simply a starting point—a road map for where to go next.

The armchair quarterbacking of unsolved cases is, however, an unfortunately common practice among the police, the public, and especially the commercial press. Many investigators or others with access to primary source documents fall into the trap of investigating the *investigation* rather than more appropriately investigating the crime. For some of the reasons already mentioned, the original investigators in many cases were operating with few if any of the most basic resources to which investigators have access today, including now common training with respect to crime scene security, evidence integrity and continuity, and distinguishing the *modus operandi* of offenders. In our experience and based on an ongoing meta-analysis of still unsolved cases, some of the most common deficiencies seen in original homicide investigations include:

1. Purported alibis of persons of interest and even viable suspects taken at face value and never corroborated or followed-up.

2. Persons of interest and suspects never properly cleared of involvement or even formally interviewed.

3. Crime scene neighborhood canvass runs never completed, or haphazardly completed and not properly documented, including no list of persons spoken to or addresses attended.

4. No holdback evidence policy exercised, with details regarding motive, weapon, *modus operandi*, and offender signature all released to the public/media.

5. Offender blood and/or semen samples never blood typed before being destroyed/lost and/or offender hair not seized/preserved for (pre-DNA) medulla testing, despite the technology being widely available as early as the 1950s.

6. Victim's body moved/covered/compromised prior to crime scene photographs being taken or the body processed for evidence; crime scene generally trampled and treated as a curiosity with few if any access restrictions.

7. No understanding or associated training with respect to suspectology, psychological autopsies, or victimology, in spite of the seminal text in victimology and the taxonomic classification of victims having been published by Yale victimologist Hans von Hentig shortly after World War II, and its long having been a matter of interest to researchers.

8. Investigative "tunnel vision" leading investigators to prematurely focus on a specific individual or group to accommodate a theory or supposition with no basis in fact, and then reverse engineering the investigation accordingly. Most often seen in newly revealed cold cases arising from previous wrongful convictions.

These represent only a few of the prevailing issues one finds when conducting a meta-analysis of representative unsolved homicides from the previous 30–50 years. In noting these deficiencies, modern investigators tend to become either hypercritical of their forerunners, or—in many cases—actually fall into the trap of repeating and retreading the same missteps, taking the earlier investigative actions at face value and being reluctant to remedy them and potentially reveal the already compromised state of a given file. This is yet another justification for invoking objective and third-party oversight in cold case investigations, in part because the neutral observer—when properly trained to know what he or she should be looking for—can assist in shortlisting the deficiencies that can be immediately rectified based on current forensic standards.

Case Study: Missing and Presumed Dead—Team Killers

On or about October 24, 1992, 22-year-old Dawn Marie Miller was observed leaving the Academy Apartments in Bellefonte, Pennsylvania in the company of two men. That was the last time she was ever seen alive. Miller, who hailed from nearby Williamsport, had gone to the address to visit her boyfriend, Gregory Easton. The two men with whom she was seen leaving, sometime around 8:00 p.m., were later identified as Gregory and Gregory's nephew, a man named Joe Easton. Joe and Gregory Easton later returned to the apartment without Miller sometime between 11:30 p.m. and 2:00 a.m. As a result of incomplete records, when and by whom a missing person's report was first filed is today unclear, but on December 14, 1992—now nearly 2 months later—the Williamsport Bureau of Police initiated a criminal investigation. The case soon went cold.

By January 2008, Dawn Marie Miller was one of countless women in the United States flagged on the National Crime Information Center (NCIC) as missing and presumed dead, but with no active investigation being ongoing. Her biographical and biometric profile had, however, by then been uploaded to the Doe Network (doenetwork.org), an open-access online repository of missing persons intended for cross-reference to unidentified remains known as John Does (males) and Jane Does (females). Acting on the information gleaned from the Doe Network profile and the merits of the original missing person's file, Detective Kenneth Mains of the Williamsport Police reopened Miller's case in early 2008.

In assessing the original casework, the primary investigative shortcomings that Detective Mains identified involved both victimology and suspectology; in spite of the disappearance being deemed suspicious, it was not handled as a homicide. In applying modern techniques in forensic victimology, including his conducting a psychological workup of Miller, it was clear that the young woman was unduly trusting and naïve. Because the best indicator of future behavior is previous behavior, proper cognitive interviews conducted with Miller's friends and family that had not been done during the original investigation confirmed that she conformed to what—again returning to Hentig's foundational taxonomy—would be classified as a "lonely" victim type (von Hentig, 1948). This classification is not intended to be derisive in its nomenclature as much as it is an indicator of an enhanced predisposition to risk. It is a predisposition based on a lack of life experience, a preoccupation with pleasing others and being validated, and a willingness to self-bargain the merits being in compromising situations for their socially or sexually redeeming qualities—in this case, accompanying a new boyfriend and his much older domiciled uncle on a nighttime outing. Suspectology similarly requires that investigators use historical behaviors as a barometer for a suspect's baseline personality and own risk tolerance. In this case, with Joe and Gregory Easton being the last to see Miller alive and having never been properly cleared, the suspectology needed to begin with them.

Unlike in the case of victimology, where investigators are required to work backward from the time of death or disappearance, suspectology allows investigators to work backward *and* forward, with the activities, statements, and precise movements of a suspect or suspects following a homicide providing remarkable insight and helping blueprint themes and trigger points for future interviews. Ideally, suspectology will incorporate one or both physical and technical surveillance of a person or persons to verify statements made or locations attended, but with the passage of time such techniques have proven to be less fruitful as the murderer is able to return to a routine and avoid exhibiting telltale behaviors. In cold case investigations, absent the use of a specific stimulator to effectively return the suspect's state of mind to the time and place of the murder (a newspaper report on the anniversary of the crime, the use of an undercover operative to befriend the suspect, etc.), surveillance or wiretapping is a largely ineffective use of resources and the suspectology will need to be assembled through documentary records and interviews—secondary sources for the most part.

In the reinvestigation of Dawn Marie Miller's disappearance, the 16 years elapsed between 1992 and 2008 imparted a great deal of new information that assisted Detective Mains in cultivating new leads. Some of this information came from the actions of the prime suspects themselves, some from research conducted by forensic psychologists and criminologists who were by that time more readily available to law enforcement and actively contributing to a body of knowledge with respect to training and professional development.

In the years both before and after Miller's disappearance, Joe Easton had amassed a wide array of convictions that reflected both sexual sadism and pedophilic spectrum paraphilias such as blastolagnia (the sexual initiation of underage but postpubescent females), including indictments for statutory rape and indecent assault. His other convictions that ran the gamut from assault with a deadly weapon to corrupting minors similarly spoke to both a criminal versatility and a sense of grandiosity indicative of his possessing psychopathic tendencies, and with violence historically being prefigured by the use of alcohol and drugs as triggers and disinhibitors. Gregory Easton, while not a convicted felon or sex offender like his nephew, nonetheless had a history of acquaintance-stalking and self-destructive behaviors that reflected a lack of proper socialization, and he was described as living in constant fear of Joe who was both his criminal pedagogue and tormentor. Of note, the body of research assembled since this case first went cold confirms that team killers (consisting of two or more participants) are typically headed by a Caucasian male who as the more experienced criminal takes on a dominant role, and that Pennsylvania is also the state with the sixth highest prevalence of team killers since 1850 (Hickey, 2015). Further, the fact that Gregory was later reported to have typically brought Miller to a local lovers' lane at an isolated location, known as the Jacksonville Quarry, is probative given that such locations, "known vice areas" by definition, often factor in to the disposal pathways later used by offenders, serial or otherwise, who historically frequented such locations (Morton et al., 2014). With a victimology and suspectology complete, Detective Mains enlisted the assistance of the Pennsylvania State Police in effectively turning the clock back to October 24, 1992 and beginning the case anew. This included a reinterview of Academy Apartment residents—a neighborhood canvass run that was never properly completed during the original investigation.

In the coming months, Detective Mains and State Troopers, in the absence of a body or any biological evidence, were able to assemble various witnesses statements, as well as indirect utterances and admissions made by both Joe and Gregory Easton in the intervening 16 years, in order to create a cogent and compelling case that Miller had been lured from the apartment, murdered, and disposed of at an unknown location by both men. Leveraging this information with the assistance of modern investigative technologies—polygraph exams, tactical interviewing, the looming possibility of DNA being recovered at the disposal site, if located—by October 2008, just 10 months after reactivating the case, Detective Mains had in effect established the *corpus delicti*.

Corpus delicti is a Latin term for "body of crime"—the "body" in this case being the sum of facts and evidence indicating that a crime has actually occurred. Contrary to popular belief, in murder and missing person's cases, it does not indicate the actual recovery of a human body. Although the best evidence in such cases would be the physical presence of a body, the body of available evidence—circumstantial or otherwise—may be sufficient to convince a trier of fact beyond a reasonable doubt that someone is guilty of murder, even though no victim has been found. A frequently cited example would be the presence, at a missing person's home, of that person's identifiable blood in such a quantity that what is known as exsanguination (severe blood loss to the point of death) is the only reasonable inference to draw. The remaining facts and evidence in aggregate, *corpus delicti*, would subsequently determine, in light of such a find, if an indictment of a particular individual would be warranted. Although a rare occurrence, it is not without precedent to see a murder conviction registered without the remains of a victim or victims being recovered (DiBiase, 2014). The case of Dawn Marie Miller, it appeared during the early portion of the renewed investigation, might be one such case.

By the end of October 2008, however, Gregory Easton had committed suicide by hanging himself from a tree in rural Centre County, Pennsylvania. With his uncle dead, Joe Easton later implicated Gregory in the Miller murder, but admitted to being an accessory and helping bury the body following her death by a combination of strangling and bludgeoning for reasons that appear personally motivated, namely, that Miller was pregnant with Gregory's child. Cadaver dogs later failed to locate the body, with Miller's remains believed to have been later moved to Jacksonville Quarry from the wooded area where the girl was killed sometime prior to the original investigation commencing in late 1992. Despite the evidence and confession, Centre County prosecutors have never prosecuted Joe Easton for his role as an accessory in Miller's murder. The search for the body actively continues at the time of this writing.

Investigative and Analytical Opportunities

The Pennsylvania case study serves as an incisive example of how modern-day expertise can be used to troubleshoot and reinvigorate failed investigations. It demonstrates how retroactively adopting the scientific method and using verifiable, falsifiable, and demonstrably successful methods to find new inroads to historical homicides requires convergence between criminal investigative work and established research—as well as a willingness to both draw on and hare information from and with other agencies. In this case, Detective Mains began with a self-initiated investigation relying on public records and secondary source documents gleaned through the volunteer organization, the Doe Network. The information gathered was sufficient to justify, with the cooperation of the Pennsylvania State Police, a renewed and widened search of the area where Miller's body is believed to be located. While the remains were not recovered, this was carried out in concert with a number of applications of suspectology that ultimately drove the main suspect—later implicated by his nephew—to suicide. The case is also illustrative of investigations that are never perfect, and how having realistic expectations in cases of severely compromised or bungled investigations is a key competency among investigators. These are cases that, while perhaps remaining uncleared or uncharged, are not necessarily unsolved—partial victories for which current investigators can be satisfied have provided some sense of resolution, their, striking a balance between being homicide detectives and what is known as *disruptive innovators* advancing a larger cause.

Generally speaking, disruptive innovation describes any new technology or investigative technique—or set of techniques—that effectively overrides and disrupts the traditional law enforcement paradigm. The term also describes the process of leveraging new methods whose results and cost efficiencies force much needed change within established institutional models outside of policing and the criminal justice system. Some industries thrive on disruptive innovation, while some fear and even loathe it. With research on suspectology, criminal paraphilia, offender organization and weapon focus, and the interplay between psychology and geography in recent years all helping disrupt and modernize conventional investigative practices, unsolved historical homicides seem to be the one area where police leaders are most amenable to adopting forensic best practices developed in the private and academic sectors. In other words, it is the one area of criminal investigative praxis most primed for disruptive innovation. Some examples follow below, from most established to most recently emerging and experimental.

Criminal Investigative Analysis

Law enforcement outreach initiatives, and the willingness to consult civilian subject matter experts employed in academic, clinical, and forensic fields have become increasingly common during the brief history of criminal investigative analysis, more popularly—and sometimes erroneously—referred to as offender profiling. This type of interdisciplinary collaboration is especially common in unsolved serial cases. Notable examples include the profile of the unidentified murderer mythologized as Jack the Ripper, with forensic pathologist Dr. Thomas Bond having gleaned behavioral traits of the killer based on the nature of the wounds suffered by the victims on whom he performed autopsies (Petherick, 2014). Despite the fact that the Whitechapel murders of 1888 credited to the Ripper are likely not the work of a single offender, with the Ripper legend having been induced largely by a series of hoaxes and publicity stunts carried out by an unscrupulous reporter named Thomas Bulling, Dr. Bond's offender profile set the stage for the use of experts in unusually complicated, serial, or otherwise high-profile investigations. In later years, the New York City Police Department's (NYPD) use of Dr. James Brussel in helping profile and identifying "Mad Bomber" George Metesky and the creation of the interdisciplinary UNABOMB task force in the Federal Bureau of Investigation's (FBI) pursuit of serial letter bomber Ted Kaczynski helped legitimize criminal investigative analysis as a collaborative police–civilian undertaking.

While the FBI's Behavioral Analysis Unit (BAU) is generally regarded as the premier criminal investigative analysis resource in the United States, the evolution and maturation of "profiling" as both a practice and a theoretical discipline has led to the formation of similar units at the state level in many cases, and even the implementation of in-house analysis units among some larger municipal police forces. That said, the practice continues to be mired by issues of consistency and credibility. As an experiment in what is known as metacognition—the thought process relating to organization, planning, and self-evaluation—the Woodhouse Study, as it is known, has ultimately revealed that many self-proclaimed profilers are able to operate in a consistently incompetent and negligent fashion without ever knowing it, and without being properly identified as poor performers. This occurs in large part because their methods are neither immediately verifiable nor falsifiable (Petherick and Woodhouse, 2009). In other words, a profiler or analyst who is repeatedly mistaken can always default to the excuse that the information provided to help create the profile was erroneous or incomplete, or that the profile was misinterpreted and not acted on as intended. So long as a case remains unsolved and a perpetrator unidentified, the analyst cannot be officially discredited. The thought is that, in some cases, it is therefore in the interest of the profiler to provide intentionally vague, interpretative, or altogether inactionable information as a strategy of self-preservation. Alternatively, when the results are indeed actionable and lead to an arrest, the courts have very carefully scrutinized the methods and credentials of those conducting the associated analysis, often doing so with suspicion. In Canada, for instance, likely the most infamous incident—one that has had chilling effect on criminal investigative analysis in recent years—is the 2003 case of *R. v. Ranger*. At trial, it was revealed that the Behavioral Sciences and Analysis Unit of the Ontario Provincial Police had first identified a murder suspect based on little more than a hunch—textbook police tunnel vision—and then used their behavioral scientists to reverse engineer a profile to suit that same a priori theory. The judge in the case, while eventually convicting the accused of murder, nonetheless made a point of singling-out and rebuking the profilers involved, raising serious questions of fact about their competence, training, and ethics, in effect discrediting the entire unit wholesale (Petherick, 2014). The good news, however, is that these types of dubious cases provide a set of realistic guidelines, performance expectations, and best practices for forensic investigators to follow in creating offender profiles based on the available data and relying on a proper set of professional and ethical standards.

As with all undertakings involving data sets drawn from multiple sources, the key to effective and accountable criminal investigative analysis is—contrary to what was seen in the Ranger case—a process of blinded peer review. While a common and expected practice in the academic and scientific communities is to use a system of double blind peer review—a system where the reviewer is uncertain of who authored the report, and the author does not know who provided the review and related feedback—is one of several advances presently being either adopted or advocated in cold case investigations. The current climate surrounding both cold case investigations and criminal investigative analysis is consequently one where there is no shortage of resources for investigators to tap, both internally and externally to their own organizations, to maximize the attention an unsolved homicide receives. As with most or all investigative techniques, however, criminal investigative analysis with respect to suspectology should not be undertaken as the sole inroad to a historical case; it should be complemented with other methods, both emerging and established. The following two subsections highlight some proven methods that investigators may wish to consider in this respect.

Media Stimuli

As previously mentioned, crime beat reporters, staff writers, and editors working at traditional daily newspapers often make effective resources for cold case investigators with respect to secondary source material. Beyond the notes and files maintained by individual reporters, newspapers also keep archival collections that can be of use to investigators and help fill in the blanks with respect to data missing from the original case file. The same can be said regarding television news footage archived in a local or regional broadcaster's film library. In reviewing the media coverage of historical homicides, one will find a common theme in terms of how law enforcement agencies chose to circumspectly publicize the details of homicide cases. The media policies historically exercised by law enforcement reflected the journalistic realities of earlier generations; police investigators were generally able to keep information contained and release it in top-down fashion at their sole discretion. Today, things are obviously much different, and there are new opportunities for investigators to use the media as a conduit for reactivating cold case homicides and to engage them as stakeholders.

The rise of the second- and third-generation Internet—now known as the Semantic Web—as well as 24-hour news channels, social media, the blogosphere, and the ubiquity of smartphones has created an information-based society where technology drives the distribution of crime news and shifting opinions continuously shape content. The result is a dynamic news system where readers are also producers of that content, and where geographic distances are increasingly less important, both spatially and psychologically. This new reality is especially important with respect to cold cases, in that what is known as "time–space compression" in a wired world makes the passage of time as negligible as the distance between people (Harvey, 1990). Without getting overly academic about generational drift, nostalgia industries, and so forth, the key point is that investigators have seemingly endless options in terms of media outlet, format, and narrative style with which to either cultivate renewed public interest in a cold case and solicit tips, or to provoke or stimulate a suspect or person of interest for the purposes of criminal investigative analysis—up to and including the use of surveillance to record a predicted response. Some examples of how the current media climate offers cold case investigators remarkable new investigative and creative opportunities in terms of assessing, prioritizing, and reactivating cases—some of which have already been used successfully by law enforcement agencies—include some of the following:

1. Creating social media accounts, profiles, or pages committed to specific cases, and releasing photographs or portions of what was previously "holdback" information via social media on a daily or weekly basis as the case regains momentum.

2. Creating video files featuring pleas for information, original news footage, or crime re-enactments for upload to Internet file-sharing or streaming sites, or to a purpose-built site designed to be read on mobile devices in order to maximize distribution.

3. Strategically developing feature news pieces in cooperation with established and trustworthy reporters that detail the reactivation of a case or release of new information (increased reward, development of a DNA profile, impending exhumation of remains, etc.) for the purposes of provoking a suspect response. Ideally, the suspect will be under physical or technical surveillance contemporaneous with such pieces being published or otherwise released to the public.

These are but a few examples of how certain media strategies can stimulate a potential witness or a potential suspect. While a suspect may already be identified and revert to predictive behavior (moving away, changing routines, contacting old accessories, etc.), the reluctant witness is less predictable in their response to such stimuli. In many cases, witnesses who refused to provide information during the original investigation out of some misplaced loyalty or fear simply need a reminder—a stimulus of this type to come forward after earlier loyalties or vows of secrecy have caved under the weight of time.

Geographic Profiling and Psychogeography

Second only to DNA technology, arguably the most significant but still underrated forensic advance in recent years with respect to cold case investigations is the use of geographic profiling in helping investigators winnow people and locations of interest. Like the other investigative avenues cited here, geographic profiling is one of several tools that form part of a larger investigative toolbox—a suite of resources within the locus of criminal investigative analysis. Driven in large part by Canadian police officer-turned-researcher and innovator D. Kim Rossmo and British forensic psychologist David Canter, geographic profiling is a discursive term and concept that describes the physical and psychological intersections of space, time, and meaning in criminal offending. While Rossmo's work focuses largely on identifying and inferring an offender's movements across space and time relative to their "home base" (primary residence, workplace, safe house, etc.), his formula—using geometry to calculate a radially symmetric probability distribution based on the locations of offenses—does not discriminate between incidents or location types, and assigns no intrinsic or symbolic value to the locations used to plot the offender's probable movements (Rossmo, 2000). Conversely, Canter's work with the police in the United Kingdom and across Europe, primarily focusing on both serial rapists and serial murderers, lies at the crossroads of geography and psychology, and can be best described as a type of forensic pscyhogeography. The crux of psychogeography is that offenders willfully select locations for their attacks, confinements, kill sites, and dump sites that have some type of significance with respect to their inner narrative. It describes—and maps—how they mentally conceive, rehearse, and later replay their crimes (Canter and Gregory, 1994). In other words, Rossmo's method and the associated formula presuppose that offenders interact with their surrounding space and select offending locations somewhat arbitrarily and unconsciously based on the location of their home base. Canter's work, on the other hand, suggests that, in many cases, the locations and victims targeted by offenders reflect conscious and ego-driven decisions—the ensuing geographic profile being what Canter refers to as the Radex Model (Canter and Youngs, 2009). The key elements of each scholar's respective methods can be summarized as follows:

Rossmo's formula allows investigators to defer to a comprehensive taxonomy of four distinct offender types based on how those offenders interact with their surrounding space, and where crimes are committed relative to their home base.

1. *The Hunter:* An offender who targets a specific victim or type of victim in the immediate area of his home base, staying within the action space where he knows and can exploit the terrain.

2. *The Poacher:* The killer on the road, or an offender with a great degree of mobility who targets victims—usually a specific type—while away from his home base to exploit his anonymity as an outsider or passer-through.

3. *The Troller:* An opportunistic and impulsive offender—often disorganized—who will attack whenever and wherever opportunity strikes while going about his daily business, or when marauding around in search of such an opportunity.

4. *The Trapper:* Often associated with older and more organized offenders, it involves a death trap scenario in which the victim is lured to a specific location and into a premeditated situation or ruse.

Canter's Radex Model features a wider array of variables that are comparatively situational, and it to some extent consolidates Rossmo's four geographic offender types into two: the marauder offender and the commuter offender. The former denotes offenders who operate close to their home base while the latter, like Rossmo's "poacher," will travel to an area well outside their home base for the purposes of offending. In addition to these two offender types, Canter has espoused a *narrative theory* of crime that explains an offender's spatial decision-making process, in effect drawing a nexus between geography and psychopathology, up to and including the role of fantasy in the planning and execution of offenses. This is potentially one of the most incisive—yet still overlooked—developments in suspectology in recent years, and is supported by four distinct artistic styles that have emerged following a longitudinal analysis of hand drawn maps of crime scenes created by offenders. The map categories—varying in complexity, artistry, and point of view—reflect an inner narrative and perspective on the world indicative of four offender narrative types, all of which can be seen as complementing rather than competing with Rossmo's four geographic types:

1. *The Hero:* An offender who conceives violent crime as a quest and a righteous adventure, with his being an unlikely and embattled protagonist worthy of martyrdom.

2. *The Professional:* An offender who conceptualizes crime as a calling or a vocation, one in which he often holds grandiose delusions about being a master strategist. Dennis "BTK Strangler" Rader kept detailed operational notes and special "hit clothes" with respect to his murders, and is indicative of this narrative mindset.

3. *The Revenger:* An offender who rationalizes crime as a necessary response to the injustices of his own life, or the world in general, and who justifies offending as his righteously getting even with a specific victim, type of victim, or institution.

4. *The Tragedian:* An offender who defers responsibility and adopts a crime neutralization strategy through a fatalistic view of events, and who sees his crimes and self-destructive behaviors—and eventual downfall—as preordained, unavoidable, and irreversible.

These psychogeographic and narrative typologies help put the "hot zones" (probable home base locations) identified through Rossmo's method and the associated formula into greater context, and can provide invaluable insight into the patterns in movement and motivations of offenders. Known or suspected serial homicide investigations are especially predisposed to the use of geographic profiling as an investigative tool given that with the greater the number of data points that can be identified, the more detailed the ensuing map and profile.

Case Study: Multijurisdictional Child Murders—Serial Killer

In a 13-month span between February 1976 and March 1977, at least four children aged between 10 and 12 years—two boys and two girls—were abducted from public places around the metropolitan Detroit area, held captive for anywhere from 4 to 19 days, sexually assaulted and murdered, and then posed in public places outside the jurisdiction of the police department investigating the initial disappearances (Figure 15.1). Eventually, a total of eight municipalities across two counties served as crime scene locations, reflecting remarkable offender organization and mobility. Three of the victims—Mark Stebbins, Kristine Mihelich, and Timothy King—were suffocated or strangled, while 12-year-old Jill Robinson was killed by a single gunshot to the face. The crimes rightfully horrified the local communities and the whole of the nation, with the cases eventually becoming part of the largest multijurisdictional investigation undertaken in American history until that time. Despite the remarkable resources being brought to bear, however, the case of the Oakland County child killer went unsolved.

These murders can today be understood as reflecting a very specific offender narrative and engaging a wide array of paraphilias, as evidenced in part by the increasingly elaborate disposal methods that included Jill Robinson being posed across the street from a police station in the city of Troy. Kristine Milehich was similarly deposited in plain view of countless residential homes, being placed in a distinct funerary pose with legs neatly planked and arms folded across the chest. The final confirmed victim, 11-year-old Timothy King, was found to have had his clothes washed and pressed before being redressed by the killer who also fed the boy his favorite food, fried chicken, before being sexually assaulted with a foreign object and then suffocated to death.

The original investigation consisted of a task force headed by the Michigan State Police and focused on a number of key persons of interest either living in the Oakland County area or connected to a local pedophile ring that was uncovered incidental to the murder investigations. While forensic evidence was limited, in part due to the confinement and murder location(s) being unknown, all four victims were found with white dog hair of a common origin on their clothing. Witness reports of a blue AMC Gremlin near the abduction sites and a police composite drawing later led police to consider the involvement of a known sex offender named Christopher Busch, son of a Detroit automobile executive who some have

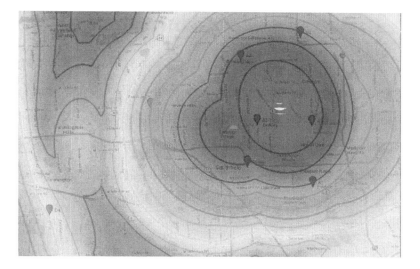

Figure 15.1 An *image file* (map) of the Oakland County, Michigan area with eight *image coordinates* (map pins) denoting the precise abduction and disposal sites of four child victims between 1976 and 1977. The *buffer distance* (a constant determined by the average distance between the coordinates) identifies a "hot zone" northwest of West Bloomfield Township, as indicated by the area furnishing the darkest shading as seen in black and white. As seen here, Rossmo's formula differentiates between hot zones (most likely offender home base) and cool zones (least likely home base) that through the use of specific software can be correspondingly color coded for best results. Mathematically and geometrically speaking, the hot zone corresponds with the location of maximal overlap between concentric circles representing the buffer distance. (From Western University Cold Case Society.)

alleged was able to leverage his police contacts to divert initial suspicion from his son. That was until 1978—the same year the Oakland County child killer task force disbanded—when Busch committed suicide by shooting himself in his parents' home. Conveniently located at the scene in plain view was rope thought to be consistent with the type used to bind the hands of the first victim, Mark Stebbins, as well as an unsettling sketch of a young boy consistent in appearance with Stebbins apparently screaming in pain. The origin of the sketch, found pinned to the wall in plain view in Busch's bedroom, and its creator were never determined. Thirty years later, white dog hair consistent with the type found on the children's bodies was also located in a locked cellar room that was never properly searched back in 1978.

In addition to Busch, a total of five other viable suspects were shortlisted, but no arrests were ever made. These suspects came to include a known pedophile living in suburban Detroit at the time named Theodore Lamborgine who turned down the offer of a reduced sentence on 15 sex-related charges in exchange to taking a polygraph exam in relation to the murders. Another area pedophile named Archibald "Ed" Sloan owned a blue Pontiac he would frequently lend to his sex offender associates. Scalp hair belonging to an unknown male was later found by police in that same vehicle—hair found to also match samples found on the bodies of Mark Stebbins and Timothy King, the first and final victims of the set.

Based on recent advances in mitochondrial DNA technology, the next logical course of action for investigators in this case would be to compare the dog hair from the children's bodies to the hair found in the Busch family home. Continuity issues aside, a potential match would of course not necessarily confirm Busch as the killer, or at least not as the lone perpetrator. In fact, given the possibility that more than one perpetrator may be involved, in part due to the fact that many of the suspects are known associates and all are documented pedophiles, geographic profiling would be an effective means of supplementing DNA tests of the animal hair in order to narrow the list of suspects and possible murder sites. Further, given that the Oakland County child murders involve so many discrete locations covering such a wide geographic area, it is ideally suited for the application of Rossmo's formula, the idea being that it provides investigators with a likely home base for one or more offenders.

Applied to the Oakland County case here for the first time, Rossmo's formula indicates a hot zone roughly 60 miles northwest of the mean center of the crime scenes. This area, to the north of West Bloomfield Township where the graphic treatment furnishes the most intense shade of red, encompasses the town of Fenton. A town of only 7 square miles in size that straddles Oakland and Genesee Counties, Fenton of all places is where Archibald Sloan happened to call home for much of the late 1970s. With geographic profiling and DNA technology now linking Sloan's vehicle and residence to the crimes through the still unidentified male donor of the hair in that same vehicle, we see the value of applying contemporary geoprofiling methods to historical cases—methods that for the most part remain in the domain of academe and have lamentably not yet been widely adopted by law enforcement.

Further Discussion

Despite the array of challenges that cold cases pose for criminal investigators and other forensic stakeholders—financial, procedural, and logistical challenges for the most part—as both police and civilian subject matter experts close ranks to revisit these cases based on the current body of knowledge, there are also new and unprecedented opportunities to clear the over 200,000 cold cases on the books in North America alone (Hargrove, 2015). While the implementation and increased sophistication of databases and registries housing fingerprints, violent crime linkages, firearm and ballistics data, criminal record and sex offender information, and DNA profiles have all proven momentous in both helping clear long-standing cold cases and also expedite the closure of new murder cases, the future of interdisciplinary cold case investigation will inevitably need to exploit other proprietary technologies not traditionally utilized in complex criminal investigations.

In recent years, for instance, the role of graphic design and 3D modeling software in advancing forensic art in cases of unidentified remains has proven to be remarkably effective. Similarly, the manner in which social media currently pervades society has allowed it to rival official police records management systems in terms of being able to efficiently locate people otherwise "not on file" with law enforcement, as well as to obtain valuable intelligence with respect to their movements, affiliations, and occupations—intelligence not historically available absent costly and time-consuming technical surveillance or through the use of paid informers. As technology has served to make the world smaller and expedite tasks that during the original investigations cited here would have usurped valuable time and human resources, the financial costs associated with cold cases have been somewhat defrayed by the ability of any enterprising individual—whether forensic expert of layperson—to serve as a contributor through what is known as open source investigation.

In this case, "open source" refers to the fact that the information available is in the public domain, as is the investigative actions of those accessing and acting on that information. Beyond some of the more popular and commercial social media platforms and their potential value to investigations, websites such as the Doe Network mentioned earlier, the Murder Accountability Project, Websleuths, Unsolved Canada, and others have been created and are curated specifically for the purpose of soliciting public input, proffering theories, and maintaining public interest in cold cases. While many law enforcement agencies have followed suit and operate their own scaled down versions of these sites—often by way of direct access from an agency's homepage—investigators would be remiss to not participate in, or at the very least monitor the chatter in the forums hosted by these private sites. Many of the contributors boast advanced credentials and conduct some very effective freelance research—at no cost to law enforcement—that is offered for public consumption. Such sites are presumably also visited and monitored by offenders or accessories to the crimes being discussed, with their no doubt expecting the related postings to serve as approximations of police interest in and knowledge of a particular case. Moving forward, as open source investigation and civilian interest—and inevitable involvement—in cold cases continues to intensify, law enforcement personnel would thus be wise to diversify their investigative tactics accordingly. By relying on accredited subject matter expertise and forensic guidance in some of the more esoteric areas of a given case on one hand, and at the same time recognizing the importance of open source investigations and layperson input as helping keep historical cases relevant on the other hand, investigators can ensure that all variables are being accounted for through a truly holistic approach. It is an approach that need not just apply to officially reactivated investigations, but *all* cold cases.

References

Adams, M. 2003. Cold case squad: Partnering with volunteers to solve old homicide cases. *Subject to Debate*. Washington, DC: Police Executive Research Forum.

Arntfield, M. 2013. Media forensics & fragmentary evidence: Locard's exchange principle in the era of new media. *The Canadian Journal of Media Studies*, *11*(1), 2–27.

Arntfield, M. and Gorman, K. A. 2014. *Introduction to Forensic Writing*. Toronto, ON: Carswell.

BBC News. 2012. Scotland Yard reviewing hundreds of unsolved murders. *BBC UK*. Retrieved from http://www.bbc.co.uk/news/uk-17240613.

Canter, D. and Gregory, A. 1994. Identifying the residential location of serial rapists. *Journal of the Forensic Science Society*, *34*(3), 169–175. DOI: 0.1016/S0015-7368(94)72910-8.

Canter, D. and Youngs, D. 2009. *Investigative Psychology: Offender Profiling and the Analysis of Criminal Action*. Hoboken, NJ: Wiley.

DiBiase, T. A. 2014. *No Body Homicide Cases: A Practical Guide to Investigating, Prosecuting, and Winning Cases When the Victim Is Missing*. Boca Raton, FL: CRC Press.

Hargrove, T. 2015. How many unsolved murders are there? It's greater than the population of Des Moines. *ABC News*. Retrieved from http://goo.gl/Ct0xUU.

Harvey, D. 1990. *The Condition of Postmodernity: An Enquiry into the Origins of Cultural Change*. Malden, MA: Blackwell.

Hickey, E. W. 2015. *Serial Murderers and Their Victims* (7th ed.). Belmont, CA: Cengage.

Los Angeles Police Department. 2015. Robbery-Homicide Division. *LAPD Online*. Retrieved from http://goo.gl/9BVpwW.

Morton, R. J., Tillman, J. M., and Gaines, S. J. 2014. *Serial Murder: Pathways for Investigation*. Quantico, VA: Federal Bureau of Investigation, Behavioral Analysis Unit.

Peters, J. 2013. Almost no one is working on New York's thousands of cold case murders. *Slate*. Retrieved from http://goo.gl/BKNsj6.

Petherick, W. 2014. *Profiling and Serial Crime: Theoretical and Practical Issues* (3rd ed.). Burlington, MA: Elsevier.

Petherick, W. and Woodhouse, B. 2009. Metacognition in criminal profiling. In: W. Petherick, (Ed.) *Serial Crime: Theoretical and Practical Issues in Behavioral Profiling* (2nd ed.). Burlington, MA: Elsevier, pp. 145–170.

Pettem, S. 2012. *Cold Case Resources for Unidentified, Missing, and Cold Homicide Cases*. Boca Raton, FL: CRC Press.

Reid, J. E. and Associates 2015. Interviewing elderly subjects. *Reid.com*. Retrieved from https://goo.gl/IICQmq.

Rossmo, D. K. 2000. *Geographic Profiling*. Boca Raton, FL: CRC Press.

Von Hentig, H. 1948. *The Criminal and His Victim: Studies in the Sociobiology of Crime*. New Haven, MA: Yale University Press.

Walton, R. H. 2014. *Practical Cold Case Homicide Investigations Procedural Manual*. Boca Raton, FL: CRC Press.

Wood, J. and Aldridge, M. 1999. *Interviewing Children: A Guide for Child Care and Forensic Practitioners*. Hoboken, NJ: Wiley.

Wright, A. M. and Holliday, R. 2003. Interviewing elderly witnesses and victims. *Forensic Update*, 73, 20–25.

Wright, A. M. and Holliday, R. 2005. Police officers' perceptions of older eyewitnesses. *Legal and Criminal Psychology*, *10*(2), 211–223. DOI: 10.1348/135532505X37001.

16 Piecing It Together

Using Crime Scene Reconstruction and Behavioral Profiling to Elucidate Homicide and Offender Characteristics

Laura G. Pettler and Joan Swart

Contents

Crime Analysis and Reconstruction 316
Bloom's Taxonomy 316
Victim-Centered Death Investigation Methodology 316
    Stage 1: Knowledge 317
    Stage 2: Comprehension 318
    Stage 3: Application 318
    Stage 4: Analysis 318
    Stage 5: Crime Synthesis 324
    Stage 6: Crime Evaluation 325
Behavioral Profiling and Analysis 325
    Process of Behavioral Profiling 325
    Method of Operation and Signature 326
    Victimology and Profiling 327
    Suspectology and Profiling 328
Final Words 329
References 329

In the preceding chapters, homicide and homicide offenders are explored by the principle type of each situation and perpetrator. Although it may seem to imply that such typologies are distinctive and nonoverlapping, in many, if not most, cases this is not the norm. For example, a domestic murderer can have a reactive personality too, and many sexual sadists are also psychopathic, as some of the case descriptions illustrated. Human behavior is an incredibly complex phenomenon, which requires multifaceted and multidisciplinary examinations of both theoretical and practical perspectives. We believe that this has been amply highlighted throughout this book as we journey the intricacies when personalities, needs, and desires clash in an activating context.

The book is concluded with a discussion of the application of crime scene reconstruction and behavioral profiling to gather and interpret all the relevant data and evidences: physical, contextual, and behavioral. These processes facilitate a deep understanding of the victim and offender, their relationship and interaction before and during the criminal event. It serves to not only construct a complete story line of events leading up to and during the crime based on scientific methods but also establish a credible profile of the perpetrator that can be used to guide investigative efforts. This is achieved by narrowing the suspect field and predicting the future behavior of the likely offender if he or she has not yet been identified. Alternatively, after the perpetrator has been identified and arrested, the evidence is used to guide decisions in the criminal justice system, including informing issues of mental capacity, legal accountability, crime series linkage, the risk of reoffending, the prognosis of rehabilitation, and aggravating and mitigating factors. Although the case studies presented throughout the book are retrospectively examined, the impact and importance of a thorough crime reconstruction and clinical assessment or profile processes should be obvious to ensure resolution in a manner of fair justice.

Crime Analysis and Reconstruction

Crime analysis and reconstruction are two of the most useful methods investigators can use to help learn more about what transpired between an offender and a victim during the course of a violent attack. *Crime analysis* is the analytical study of specific elements of a criminal event that includes the breaking apart of individual structures for individual study of specific components that lead to the determination of relevant interrelationships of the whole. Crime analysis specifically related to death investigation is a meticulous and tedious process that requires all aspects of a death case be separated, studied individually, compared and contrasted to one another, reorganized, and prepared for to be reassembled later into a newly understood whole. One of the ways in which these parts can be reorganized or restructured toward reassembly into a newly understood whole is through crime reconstruction. According to Chisum and Turvey (2011), *crime reconstruction* is the "determination of the actions and events surrounding the commission of a crime" (p. 652). It is through this process that all of the hard work investigators do during crime analysis pays off because reconstruction cannot take place before analysis is done.

Bloom's Taxonomy

In 1956, Benjamin Bloom created a set of six cognitive domains known collectively today as "Bloom's Taxonomy." Bloom's Taxonomy begins with *knowledge*. According to Bloom (1956), one must gain knowledge before he or she can do anything else. Bloom's second domain or category built upon the foundation of knowledge is *comprehension*. Bloom argued that one cannot understand or comprehend something until or unless he or she has actual knowledge of the subject. Third, Bloom argued that one must have knowledge and comprehend a subject before one can *apply* the premises of that subject. Next, Bloom argued that after one becomes proficient in the application of a practice, which of course is grounded by his or her comprehension of his original knowledge, he or she can then *analyze* the subject. Once an individual has grasped the concept of analyzing the complexities of each individual working part and their interrelationships, Bloom argued that then one can learn to *synthesize* all of those working parts into a newly understood whole. Bloom argued that after these five steps of cognitive process one can accurately *evaluate* the subject because he or she has started, at the beginning by first gaining knowledge, learning to understand that knowledge, then applying what he or she learned, after having moved through the analysis process, through synthesis, all the way up to evaluation where he or she assigned worth, value, or merit to the subject.

Bloom's Taxonomy is very helpful to investigators in a homicide investigation when organizing components of a case file for crime analysis and reconstruction. Pettler (2016) developed a method called *Victim-Centered Death Investigation Methodology* (VCDIM) that uses Bloom's Taxonomy as its "operating system," just like a computer uses an operating system for each program to flow in and out of respectively.

Victim-Centered Death Investigation Methodology

"Our system determines our outcome." Crime scene investigation (CSI) and reconstruction must be systematic and organized in nature. VCDIM is not only systematic and organized but also *victim centered*. That means that this methodology compares and contrasts everything to the victim in a death investigation. VCDIM is a death investigation methodology that can be used to help determine the events that resulted in the death of a victim. Sometimes that means the results reveal the victim was murdered. Sometimes the results are consistent with the victims having died as a result of an accident, suicide, natural death, and sometimes no answer can be determined. VDCIM is an objective method, free of emotion. It is a mixed method, research-based approach combined with traditional homicide investigation, CSI, and reconstruction methods. VCDIM consists of six stages: Knowledge, Comprehension, Application, Analysis, Synthesis, and Evaluation that are adaptive, flexible, and emergent in nature. Yet, it is also static as Bloom's taxonomic hierarchical arrangement of cognitive domains, which cannot be rearranged, are used in the VCDIM operating system (Figure 16.1).

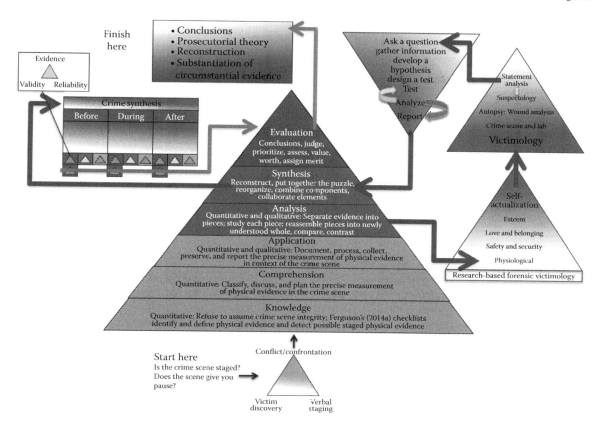

Figure 16.1 Victim-centered death investigation methodology (VCDIM). (Bloom, B. S. 1956. *Taxonomy of Educational Objectives, Book 1, Cognitive Domain*. White Plains, NY: Longman. Ferguson, C. 2014a. Detecting staged crime scenes: An empirically derived "how-to." In W. Petherick, *Applied Crime Analysis: A Social Science Approach to Understanding Crime, Criminals, and Victims*. New York, NY: Elsevier. Walter, R. Stein, S., and Adcock, J. M. 2011. Suspect identification using pre-, peri-, and post-offense behaviors. In: J. M. Adcock and S. L. Stein, *Cold Cases: An Evaluation Model with Follow-Up Strategies for Investigators*. Boca Raton, FL: CRC Press. With permission from Laura Pettler.)

Stage 1: Knowledge

Stage 1 of VCDIM begins with investigators arriving at the death scene. While it is true that not all crime scenes are staged, it is at this point that often the initial red flags of crime scene staging are revealed in a death investigation (Pettler, 2016). Crime scene staging as it relates to death investigation is anything an offender does to manipulate the physical and/or verbal evidence to misdirect an investigation toward making it look like a victim died or went missing due to a legitimate cause. Because it is critical that crime scene staging is detected early in an investigation to avoid catastrophic results when missed, the first step of VCDIM is to execute the Crime Scene Staging Trilogy before embarking further into the investigation. The Trilogy contains three parts in relation to three general questions:

1. Conflict: Who is in conflict with the victim? Is there someone in conflict with the victim?

2. Victim discovery: Who discovered the victim?

3. Verbal staging: Who reported the incident and/or what was said on the 911 call?

Conflict, victim discovery, and verbal staging are three of the most well-documented recurrent themes in empirical studies aimed specifically at studying crime scene staging (Eke, 2007; Ferguson, 2011; Pettler, 2011; Pettler, 2015). These three questions are best asked before entering the crime scene, but at no time is any information gleaned to bias the investigators in any way. Rather, when it comes to crime scene staging, empirical research has shown that crime scene stagers most often (a) are in conflict with their victims in some way prior to the death of the victim or before the victim goes missing, (b) they most often discover the victim dead or missing, and (c) they most often report the victim dead or missing to authorities (i.e., 911 call). By discovering the victim dead or missing and calling 911, the offender feels that he or she maintains the maximum amount of control over the situation, which makes him or her feel as though he or she is maximizing the potential to protect his or her identity from being implicated in the incident. Therefore, when investigators study crime scene staging, behavioral analysis, offender characteristics, coupled with experience of scholar–practitioners whose cases illustrate these concepts repeatedly, it is very helpful toward becoming proficient in identifying the behavioral red flags of what could be crime scene staging before investigators even walk the door of the crime scene. This is not to say that investigators should make any assumption about a witness, victim, suspect, crime, crime scene, or otherwise, this is simply to say that more information is better than a lack of information, and when it comes to crime scene staging, it is very clear that early identification often makes the case, while if staging is missed or detected late in an investigation, the results can lead to a case going cold or to monumental investigatory problems down the road in the crime analysis and reconstruction phases of the process.

After investigators gather the information related to the Crime Scene Staging Trilogy, which in some cases the Trilogy may be relevant and in many it may not, the next step is to enter the crime scene to gain *Knowledge*. In this phase, investigators are taking a cursory look at the crime scene, ascertaining what observable characteristics they see and what they can identify, define, and describe as evidence. Crime scene processing is only as good as the crime scene processor, so if the investigator is charged with the duty of investigating, the scene has a combination of education, training, and experience in balance with professional attributes, such as being detail-oriented, organized, systematic, etc. Chances are the investigator will know how to handle the situation the best way possible.

Stage 2: Comprehension

Stage 2 of VCDIM is Comprehension. In this stage, the CSI has already completed a cursory review of the crime scene and identified, defined, and described all of the physical evidence he or she is going to document, collect, and preserve. So at this point, the best way to proceed is to formulate a crime scene processing plan using a standardized agency Standard Operating Procedure (SOP) crime scene protocol, and to gather equipment needed to process the specific type of evidence identified during the cursory review and to prepare everything needed for proper execution.

Stage 3: Application

Stage 3 of VCDIM is Application. At this point, the investigator has gained knowledge of what is in the scene, understood the nature of the physical evidence, and therefore formulated a plan and gathered the necessary equipment. Now execution of the crime scene processing plan takes place and precise measurement of the evidence occurs. This step includes the documentation, collection, and preservation of all physical evidence in the scene. To note, in staged crime scenes, often it is during the Application stage when new evidence is discovered due to the fact that the crime scene stager has manipulated the crime scene by cleaning up, hiding evidence, moving the victim's body, or other behaviors consistent with offender behaviors. While the quantitative aspects of this step, such as the precise measurement of each piece of physical evidence, has to remain static, it is important that the overall stage stay qualitative in nature. This means that it is flexible, emergent, and allowed to flow as the crime scene develops. Accordingly, all opportunities to discover new identifiable and observable physical evidence in a crime scene are revealed.

Stage 4: Analysis

Upon completion of the CSI, Stage 4 Analysis begins. The Analysis stage of VCDIM contains several interrelated components: victimology, crime scene analysis and lab reports, wound pattern analysis, suspectology, statement analysis, and the scientific method. While it is important to complete each component in this order, it should be noted that there is some variance on a per case basis because there are many cases that warrant such flexibility in order to make it work properly.

Analysis means to break something apart and to study each individual piece toward understanding its interrelationships to other working parts. Essentially, all of the pieces of physical evidence collected from the crime scene are macrolevel working parts. But, before investigators do that, it is suggested in this method to complete victimology first.

Victimology: Studying the victim is the most important part of all death investigations. The more one knows about the victim, the more becomes known about the crime scene, and, by implication, the offender. This is especially helpful when there is not a known suspect in a case, and criminal profiling is employed toward the development of a suspect. Victimology is simply the analytical study of the victim. Studying a victim means studying everything there is to discover and learn about a victim from daily routine to the victim's most personal and private matters. Pettler (2016) developed a conceptual model called Research-Based Forensic Victimology, which studies victims systematically using Maslow's hierarchy of needs as a conceptual framework. Pettler argued that because the point of studying a victim is to determine why the victim became a victim, Maslow's hierarchy of needs provides the scaffolding that helps to identify strengths and weaknesses or areas of victims' lives that might have left them at greater risk to becoming a victim. When applying this concept to intimate partner homicide, for example, it is most often that observable victimological characteristics are revealed for why a victim became a victim in either (or both) the "Safety" or "Love and Belonging" levels of the hierarchy.

Pettler's Research-Based Forensic Victimology Outline (Pettler, 2015, pp. 357–360):

1. *Physiological:* Victim's Physical Demographics and Attributes

    a. Demographics

    b. Home

    c. Transportation

    d. Health and medical

2. *Safety:* Victim in Relation to Personal, Familial, Financial, and Occupational Safety

    a. Personal safety

    b. Family safety

    c. Financial situation and socioeconomic status

    d. Occupational safety

    e. Other resources related to safety

3. *Love and Belonging:* Victim in Relation to Relationships

    a. Marital status

    b. Intimate partners

    c. Friends

    d. Acquaintances

    e. Strangers

    f. Enemies

    g. Conflict

    h. Media and communication

4. *Esteem:* Victim in Relation to Personality, Cognition, Emotionality, Behavior, and Achievements

    a. Personality traits

    b. Cognition

    c. Emotionality

    d. Behavior

    e. Achievements

5. *Self-Actualization:* Victim in Relation to Relative Adoption of Worldly Concepts

    a. Envirosocioculturalism

        i. Environment

        ii. Society

        iii. Culture

    b. Victim risk

    c. Victim Routines and maps of routine activities

6. Appendices

    a. Live photos of the victim

    b. Family and friends organizational chart

    c. Timelines and calendars

Understanding the victim, including their behavior patterns, habits, demeanor, beliefs, emotional state, and movements, is a vital element in clarifying the victim–offender relationship and interaction, and developing an accurate profile of a known offender or most likely unknown suspect. This information is not only helpful to identify the perpetrator but also informs the criminal justice process to achieve the most appropriate outcome. Together with the total crime scene analysis and reconstruction, victimology provides the best modeling of the crime event and factors that determined its course.

Crime scene analysis and laboratory reports: VCDIM is a victim-centered model. That means everything is compared to the victim and to the other related parts. Again, the importance of studying the victim cannot be understated. Also, the more one knows about the victim, the more one knows about the crime scene. Consider this example: a woman's body is found in her home with an empty 16-oz plastic, Pepsi-Cola bottle beside her on the floor. The bottle is collected along with other pieces of physical evidence during the course of crime scene processing. Once victimology begins, the investigators gain insight into the victim's life through friends and family and learn that the victim loved pizza, her favorite color was red, and that if she drank soda she would only ever drink Coca-Cola from an aluminum can. Victimology concludes and the investigator begins to analyze the crime scene. As the investigator peruses through the crime scene photos, he all of a sudden comes to the first photo of the victim's body where the Pepsi-Cola bottle can be seen lying beside the victim's body. What did not give rise to an "Ah-ha" moment in the crime scene at the time of processing because the investigator did not yet know the victim, now upon having learned about the victim, the investigator now knows that the empty soda bottle could be of significance because it is highly unlikely it belonged to the victim. It is impossible for the investigator to recognize the significance of the bottle in the crime scene because he did not know the victim. But now, knowing the victim through victimology, it is clear that the bottle raises concern about how it ended up near a victim who would never drink that type of drink.

Crime scene analysis, generally speaking, is the breaking apart of the individual pieces of the crime scene and studying each one. This process is paramount to the outcome of all crime scene reconstruction work that might be conducted going forward, so considerable time and effort should be dedicated to this area. After pieces of physical evidence are collected from a crime scene, many of them might be sent to a crime laboratory for analysis. The crime laboratory then will furnish the submitting agency with a laboratory report. The results of the analysis should be interwoven into the pattern of the overall crime scene analysis, and it is during this process that investigators might discover that, when comparing the crime scene to the victimology, certain things match up and maybe some things do no not match up.

Wound pattern analysis: Assuming that in a death investigation there is a body that was autopsied, wound pattern analysis is the next component of the process. In partnership with the medical professional who conducted the autopsy, the investigator should study and learn everything he or she can about the nature of the wounds the victim suffered. Where the wounds are on the body is just as important as where the wounds are not, and wound location often alludes to behavioral characteristics and cognitive processes of the offender, so it is extremely important to understand how the offender wounded the victim, how the victim was attacked, how the victim was murdered so that the investigator has gained perspective about how the offender was behaving in the crime scene, how the victim was behaving the crime scene, and the dynamic or passive interaction in the victim–offender relationship before, during, and after the event. Once wound pattern analysis is complete, comparison to the crime scene, laboratory reports, and victimology is necessary. Investigators would be looking for how, for example, the bloodstain patterns in the crime scene photos interrelate to the wound types and patterns on the victim in relation to the DNA reports returned for the lab as to whose DNA was found in what locations in the crime scene, how many individuals were bleeding, and so forth. There are countless scenarios to consider. Thus, it is critical toward gaining perspective if a crime scene reconstruction effort is warranted going forward, all of this underpinning is necessary to substantiate any hypothesis in an upcoming phase. Wound pattern analysis is also an important aspect of the offender profile, together with blood pattern and ballistic analysis and any other forensic evidence, providing clues to his or her method of operation, signature, and possible motivation, including the victim–offender relationship and interaction during the event.

Suspectology: Like victimology, suspectology is the analytical study of the suspect. If there is a known suspect in the case, then a full suspectology is helpful in understanding the personality, cognition, emotionality, and behavior along with the *envirosocioculturalism* or the totality of how an individual's environment, societal structure, and culture influence his or her lifestyle, routine activities, occupation, belief system, traditions, etc. Human beings are creatures of habit. People often die the way they live and in turn, they often kill the way they live as well. Behavioral analysis is very helpful when conducting suspectology and learning about both the victim and the suspect because the victim–offender relationship is the most important relationship to consider in a death investigation. From the suspect perspective, past behavior is the best predictor of future behavior, so delving deep into a suspect's past sometimes is the only way to really understand underlying patterns of behavior that might not be overtly clear. In some cases, where crime scene reconstruction is not a possibility, these patterns of behavior might be some of the only illustrious evidence in a case that could be useful in bringing to light important elements that help move it forward. Suspectology is a broad topic, but overall, taking a systematic approach to studying a suspect is a viable method that can reveal information that is most often interrelated somehow.

As an effort to better understand the internal and external aspects of a known or unknown offender, suspectology considers victimology and crime scene evidence to construct a picture of the perpetrator. Together with the behavioral and psychological cues evident in the method of operation and signature, an accurate profile is formulated of the perpetrator. If he is unidentified, the profile is used to guide the investigation by narrowing the suspect pool and predicting future behavior. When the offender is arrested, the profile is applied to guide interrogation strategies, determine treatment and risk management requirements, and inform the trier of the fact during the criminal trial.

Statement analysis: Sometimes there are statements to analyze in a case. Sometimes there are not. Statement analysis is one of the components of the Stage 4 Analysis process that might be better to conduct before conducting suspectology in some cases. If the suspect in a case makes the 911 call, the 911 call should always be the first statement to be analyzed. Such a call should be formally analyzed during Stage 4, in part by listening to what is said on the 911 call before visiting the crime scene. Such an understanding can help reveal what the offender was thinking or trying to make investigators believe at the time the call was made. The author has experienced in the field that offenders who stage crime scenes often change their accounts from the time they call 911 to when the investigators arrive. It is critical that investigators have the first piece of the puzzle first…the 911 call…not 10 months later into the investigation…*but at the scene, at the time, in the moment, in the fluid investigation.* All suspect statements should be compared and contrasted toward identifying concepts for crime scene reconstruction hypothesis development. The information gleaned from this process should then be compared to the victim, the crime scene, laboratory reports, the wound pattern analysis, and the suspectology.

The scientific method: The scientific method is an organized series of steps that can help investigators reconstruct a crime scene. It is the last component of Stage 4 Analysis and can be used by investigators to help answer questions, such as:

1. What was the position of the victim at the time of the shot (in a shooting incident)?

2. What was the position of the shooter at the time of the shot?

3. What was the location of the victim at the time of the incident?

4. What was the location of the suspect at the time of the incident?

Crime scene reconstruction of this nature can only allude to a glimpse of the events that occurred and can possibly only provide an approximate estimation within an acceptable degree of scientific certainty of positions or locations of victims and suspects at best. It should never replace traditional homicide investigation or any other part of the process. Some of the ways crime scene reconstruction can be helpful is by identifying:

1. Is the scene staged or has it been manipulated with criminal intent

2. The estimated positions of the parties involved

3. The number of individuals involved in the incident

4. How the victim was killed

5. The sequence of events

6. Prosecutorial theory

And more specifically related to staged crime scenes in suspicious death cases:

1. Was it a homicide, specifically murder?

2. Was it suicide?

3. Was it an accident?

And what were both the victim's and suspect's approximate estimated actions or behaviors before, during, and after the incident grounded by the physical evidence in comparison to their statements? It is very important to be ultraconservative when conducting crime scene reconstruction because it is limited by several factors, such as:

1. Being an approximate estimate at best

2. Having no clear standard to compare to

3. Results that do not reveal the answer

4. Results yielding more than one way an incident occurred

The first step of the scientific method is to *ask a question*, such as one of the questions above. The second step is to *gather information*. This is where all of the hard work of investigators who invested their time conducting victimology, crime scene analysis, wound pattern analysis, suspectology, and statement analysis come in. Drawing from the results of all of these components, investigators can gather information related to the question. For example, a suspect might claim he or she was in a specific position and/or location at the time of the incident and additionally claims that the victim was also in a specific position and/or location. Using information gleaned during the Stage 4 Analysis process, investigators can gather information from victimology (i.e., medical history, physical ability, etc.), the crime scene, wound pattern analysis, suspectology, and statement analysis that will help them move into step 3, *develop a hypothesis*, or what do they expect to find. It is always best to develop several hypotheses during the reconstruction process because it helps investigators maintain objectivity about the many alternatives that could be possibilities. It is never a good idea to develop only one hypothesis in the crime scene reconstruction process because having only one idea to test is too narrow in scope when there could always be more than one way an event could happen.

The fourth step in the scientific method is to *design a test*. This means investigators will use disciplines of forensic science, such as bloodstain pattern analysis or trajectory analysis, commonly used in shooting incident reconstruction to design a test or several tests to test each of their hypotheses.

Bloodstain pattern analysis: Bloodstain pattern analysis is the study of the "size, shape, and distribution of bloodstains resulting from bloodshed events as a means of determining the types of activities and mechanisms that produced them" (James et al., 2005, p. 1). The scientific method can be used in conjunction with bloodstain pattern analysis to help investigators test hypotheses. A good working knowledge of how blood behaves according to specific scientific principles, such as certain laws of physics and how it is expressed in the language of mathematics, is fundamental to understanding for accuracy and success of bloodstain pattern analysis (MacDonell, 2005). Bloodstain pattern analysis is an objective process and grounded in scientific principle. Sometimes bloodstain pattern analysis can help determine approximate estimates of:

1. Where the victim was at the time of the assault

2. Where the assailant was at the time of the assault

3. What type of weapon was used

4. To locate evidence

5. The direction from which the blood originated

6. The area from which the blood originated

7. The number of offenders

8. Movements made during and after the assault by both the victim and offender

While this is a limited list, it is important to recognize that bloodstain pattern analysis is a useful scientific tool that can be used to help unravel the staged crime scene because it can help support or refute statements made by witnesses, victims, and suspects. A suspect might claim it happened one way, but the blood might tell a different story. Therefore, proper bloodstain pattern evidence documentation is very important during crime scene processing efforts because only well-documented scenes might be able to be reconstructed toward explaining in part what happened and the sequence of events. And again, bloodstain pattern evidence analysis helps investigators learn more about how each piece of the physical evidence interrelates to the totality of the evidence as a whole.

Shooting incident reconstruction: Shooting incident reconstruction is a multifaceted process. For the purpose of this discussion, the focus shall be solely on short-range bullet trajectory reconstruction, that is, shooting incidents that occur within 25 yards or less. First, it is important to recognize some of the elements taken into account when considering bullet trajectory reconstruction. According to Haag and Haag (2011) several components should be considered, such as:

1. How evidence is collected from the scene
2. Type of ammunition used
3. Projectile penetration and perforation in substrates
4. The type of firearm used
5. Determination of actual bullet holes or defects in the crime scene
6. Trace evidence and gunshot residue in relation to distance and orientation of the firearm
7. Ricochets
8. Wound track reconstruction in the victim
9. Falling bullets (i.e., in long-range shootings)
10. Cartridge case ejection patterns

This is only a sample of some of the considerations taken into account when conducting shooting reconstruction. According to Hueske (2006), "fired cartridge cases missing or out of place and bullet trajectories inconsistent with stated shooter positions" are two ways that can provide additional evidence to support or refute witness, the victim, and suspect statements (p. 251). It is important to recognize how shooting incident reconstruction using the scientific method can be instrumental in working toward resolving one small issue at a time in a case. As mentioned above, always working in partnership with the forensic pathologist and forensic laboratory analysts is essential because bullet trajectory and/or wound pattern and/or track analysis require various types of skill sets to complete the tasks. Additionally, using victimology as the litmus test is critical to understanding the whole situation and all of the evidence in totality. This is not to say the implementation of the scientific method should be qualitative in any way, in fact, it should not be at all. The scientific method is strictly quantitative.

Stage 5: Crime Synthesis

Once the analysis is complete in Stage 4, the next stage, Stage 5 Crime Synthesis can begin. In this stage of VCDIM, all of the relevant information revealed during the analytical process is plugged into a Crime Synthesis Matrix inspired by the original work of Walter et al. (2011). The Crime Synthesis Matrix contains three columns: Before the Death of the Victim, During the Death of the Victim, and After the Death of the Victim. Furthermore, a related idea that coincides with the Before-During-After concept is the Conflict-Resolution-Benefits model, which suggests that some types of murders follow this observable pattern before, during, and after the death of the victim. That is, the pre-existing (Before) conflict embedded in the victim–offender relationship prior to the victim's death gives rise to cognitive and emotional processes of the offender to resolve (During) the conflict with the act of murder in order to create a situation where the offender benefits (After) after the death of the victim. Take for instance the spouse who is having an affair and wants to move on with the new lover. The pre-existing conflict in the victim–offender relationship is the fact that the spouse needs to get rid of the spouse and for whatever reason divorce is not an option, so the cheating spouse resorts to the act of murder to resolve the conflict that his spouse merely exists and is in the way of his or her new life. Assuming the offender does not get caught, the cheating spouse benefits from the death of the victim in that he or she is then able to move on with the new lover.

So the synthesis process in Stage 5 of the VCDIM process follows the crime scene reconstruction efforts in Stage 4 by reviewing the victimology, crime analysis, wound pattern analysis, suspectology, statement analysis, and scientific method and listing all relevant information as it pertains to either Before, During, or After the victim's death. The next step is to then ask two questions about each item placed in each column: Is this piece of evidence valid? If so, what makes this piece of evidence reliable? Validity and reliability are the constructs by which the quality of empirical research must rest upon and when used in this investigatory manner, it can be helpful in identifying what pieces of evidence are valid and reliable, which items are only partially valid or partially reliable, and which might definitely be important, but are not valid or are reliable. The final step in the synthesis process is to try to "connect the dots" so to speak by comparing and contrasting the behaviors of the suspect before the death of the victim, during the death of the victim, and after the death of the victim to determine interrelationships even if only circumstantial relationships. Sometimes, during this stage, the "During" column can be discarded altogether when there is insufficient crime scene data or not enough information to do a reconstruction. Sometimes circumstantial cases can be built by synthesizing the interrelationships in the "Before" and "After" columns of the matrix.

Stage 6: Crime Evaluation

The final stage of VCDIM is Stage 6 Crime Evaluation. It is at this stage that investigators draw conclusions, prosecutors develop theory, and other plans are made for a case. It is also during this stage that staging might be confirmed or refuted. Sometimes a case that started out deemed a suicide turns out to have been a murder, accident, natural, or something else or the opposite. The possibilities are endless. This is the appropriate time to make judgments about the case. While working, the crime scene is not the right time to make judgments about the case, but it happens all the time, which is why cases go cold, irreversible errors are made, and crimes scenes are botched. "Our system determines our outcome." This also applies to the criminal profiling process, which, if correctly applied, can add significant value to the overall criminal investigation and legal decision-making.

Behavioral Profiling and Analysis

Rather than a stand-alone panacea to solve homicides quickly, especially serial murders, as is often portrayed in the popular media, profiling is a valuable addition to the traditional investigative and forensic toolbox. In a painstakingly thorough process, all the data from the crime scene reconstruction and available information about the victim and offender is synthesized to create a working understanding of the behavior of the offender. Cognitive science establishes a clear link between personal characteristics (e.g., thinking patterns, beliefs, fantasies, emotional state, motivations, and needs) and behavior patterns. Profiling utilizes these associations to develop a vivid personal "picture" of the likely offender to assist with pre- and postarrest strategies.

Process of Behavioral Profiling

Behavioral profiling, also sometimes referred to as criminal or offender profiling, and, more recently, investigative psychology, is most often associated with developing the most likely profile of an unknown offender. However, profiling a known offender by observational analysis and other accounts provides useful clinical and behavioral information to guide the investigative and legal processes. Although basic profiling principles have been studied and applied as an investigative technique and forensic for more than a decade, which involved cases such as Jack the Ripper and George Metesky, modern behavioral profiling was established at the Federal Bureau of Investigation (FBI) from the late 1970s under the leadership of John Douglas and Robert Ressler. Based on their interviews and analysis of 36 serial murderers between 1976 and 1979, they developed the organized–disorganized offender-type dichotomy.

This classification remains the basis of the traditional trait-based method of criminal profiling, which assumes that most offenders are specialized and distinctive in their offending behavior, which allows for reliable segregation into different offender types. Such deductive process emphasizes the reasons and motivations for an offender's behavior, from which personal characteristics are associated. The FBI approach relies on reasoning, experience, insight, and intuition of the profiler, and is, therefore, difficult to verify and formulate into a replicable scientific methodology.

Recognizing these potential pitfalls, British psychologist David Canter founded the field of investigative psychology in the 1990s. His studies also focused on the analysis and interpretation of behavioral crime scene evidence but found that organized behaviors typically co-occur in clusters, which he considered more meaningful to categorize and understand an offender. The FBI approach based the reconstruction of the crime scene and subsequent profile generation on a classification of the crime scene, primarily as organized or disorganized, from where they deduce even more traits and habits (e.g., age, race, occupation, living arrangements, transport, and social skills), often using an actuarial approach. Actuarial methods refer to the use of statistical and mathematical possibilities to establish likely parameters (Swart, 2015).

Proponents of the investigative psychology approach favored a clinical profiling philosophy instead that provides more individual and less generalized insight than deductive actuarial methods. Recognizing the complexity of human behavior, simplifications of real life that such processes apply are doomed to fail unexpectedly. As such, many experts view investigative psychology as a more inclusive and interactive process to quantify and qualify criminal behavior. By developing a structured and systematic profiling protocol, subjective reasoning, prejudice, and rater bias were minimized. This approach is often considered more interpretive, adaptive, flexible, and can be extended to postinvestigative forensic decisions such as risk assessment and treatment considerations. It was the objective throughout the book to illustrate the practical process of inductive-based profiling in various case studies and how it contributed (or could have contributed) to more appropriate investigative and legal decision-making. Two of the most important elements that form inputs into the profiling process are the offender's method of operation and signature.

Method of Operation and Signature

The *modus operandi*, or MO, as the offender's chosen or compelled method of operation, is one of the principal elements used to establish a criminal profile. MO describes the perpetrator's method of doing things that they deem necessary to commit the crime and escape detection. It is important to be aware that an MO is situational and tend to evolve over time as the offender gains experience and confidence and fine-tunes his operational parameters when repeated crimes are committed. More than a decade ago, Major Atcherley, a police officer in England, developed a 10-point system to describe an offender's MO. His technique was later adopted by Scotland Yard and examines the following factors (McElreath et al., 2013):

1. Location of the crime
2. Point of entry
3. Method of entry
4. Tools used in the crime
5. Types of objects removed from the crime scene
6. Time of day that the crime was committed
7. The perpetrator's alibi
8. The perpetrator's accomplices
9. Method of transportation to and from the crime scene
10. Unusual features of the crime

Another important element considered to develop an offender profile is a signature. Unlike the MO, the signature has no operational value to complete the crime or avoid detection. It is a behavior or object that is important to the perpetrator in some personal sense, offering psychological and/or physical satisfaction, which may be sexual gratification, a sense of power and control, or relief of distress. These behaviors are driven by deep-seated psychological needs and fantasies that a killer has often refined over many years. As such, when present, signature behavior reveals much about the psyche of an offender, and the depth and evolution of his or her needs and desires.

A signature is more often relevant with serial homicides and is useful to link such a series, in addition to gaining an understanding of the offender. However, the presence of a signature at an isolated crime event could indicate a higher risk of committing another homicide in the future or an undiscovered series. Torturing the victim, postmortem mutilation or posing, and the taking of souvenirs or trophies are signatures. Here, *posing* is distinguished from *staging* as the latter is a behavior that is considered a deliberate rearrangement of the crime scene to hide evidence or misdirect investigators. Overkill can be a signature if driven by the offender's psychological needs and fantasies, but it could also point to rage directed at someone else in a close personal relationship, or, as Schroeder (2016) has pointed out, indicate chronic rage or impulse control issues, psychosis, mind-altering substance, or projection.

It is mostly but not always true that signature behavior is fixed. Even the deepest psychological needs and fantasies may develop and refine over time. Also, the signature may be very subtle and indiscernible, or the perpetrator may not have had the opportunity to enact it, or the need was not activated by the desired victim response or another prompt (Brandl, 2014). Nonetheless, signature behaviors are unique as it evidences a specific psychological need or facilitates a fantasy that exists at the core of the offender's cumulative inner experiences that he or she has often cultivated for a long time before feeling compelled to act. As such, it is a presentation of an idealized scene, person, and/or program of activities that satisfy the particular emotional and psychological needs of an offender. These associations evolved over time to form a behavioral distinctiveness, which can be likened to John Money's "lovemap." He described a lovemap as "a developmental representation or template in the mind and in the brain depicting the idealized lover and the idealized program of sexual and erotic activity projected in imagery or actually engaged in with that lover." (Money, 1986, p. 290). This concept is of particular significance in sexual homicides.

As mentioned previously, the correct identification and interpretation of the MO and signature provides valuable information in the suspectology and, ultimately, the psychological profile of the perpetrator. It will likely point to his or her motivation, which is probably the most decisive aspect of forensic decision-making about accountability, mental capacity, rehabilitation prognosis, and risk of reoffending.

Victimology and Profiling

As mentioned previously, analysis of all aspects of the victim provides essential information to understand the circumstances of the homicide and formulate a complete profile of the offender, especially if his or her identity is unknown at the time of the investigation. Even if the offender or suspect(s) have been named, victimology is useful to determine the likely motive for the homicide, the situational risk of the victim, his or her state of mind, and interactions before and during the crime. As part of the larger crime analysis, victim profile determines subsequent focus and levels of investigation, jurisdiction, authority, and criminal justice process (Turvey, 2012). As such, it provides the context of the criminal acts and defines the suspect pool where the offender is unknown.

Turvey (2012) defines the explicit goals of victimology as the establishment of the context of the victim–offender relationship, and determination of the personal and environmental risks that the victim was subject to, which serves to define and narrow the suspect pool. Therefore, victimology defines the link between the victim and offender, helps with crime series linkage, and explains victim selection and/or victim and offender behavior. As a specific subset of the larger field of victimology that also considers victim advocacy, restoration, and empowerment of victims, forensic victimology systematically and scientifically examines, analyzes, and interprets victim evidence to answer investigative and forensic questions.

In addition to generating a better understanding of the victim–offender relationship and interaction, victim evidence assists to generate a time line of the crime, helps predict offender characteristics and behavior, confirms of contradict claims by the offender, and contributes to establishing offender motive and MO. Such information is valuable to the investigator, interrogator, and trier of the fact, while also useful to policy makers and those involved in crime prevention efforts and public safety responses.

Constructing a victim profile utilizes nomothetic methods (i.e., generalized knowledge about a victim group) and idiographic methods (i.e., examining the unique characteristics and functioning of the specific individual victim). The two types of methods are always used in a bottom-up approach where similarities and differences of idiographic data are compared with common and recurrent patterns and characteristics to provide meaning to different aspects of the crime and conclusions about the individual victim. Such an idiographic profile includes biophysical, intellectual, cognitive, clinical, educational, occupational, and personality descriptors, as well as behavioral patterns and habits.

Victimology is useful for investigative and forensic applications. The investigative goal is to collect and consider all the evidence, whereas forensic applications require the court to test its probative value to determine admissibility. This is decided based on the precedent, prejudice, and relevance in each case, whereby the reliability and validity of the scientific method and application and knowledge and expertise of the expert witness are considered. Therefore, evidences admitted in court are subjected to a more rigorous standard than evidence used to guide investigative efforts. Expert witnesses are also required to adhere to professional standards of practice and codes of conduct, which serves to ensure that their testimony is objective, ethical, and competent.

Collecting "data packages," which include descriptive, physical, social, and behavioral information, enables the investigator to build a comprehensive and unbiased picture of the victim that is required to consider and examine all theories of the crime. Data about the victim's appearance (i.e., clothing, jewelry, personal items, and grooming) and habits (e.g., routine activities and recent and upcoming events), and residential, relationship, employment, medical, and criminal justice information are included. Also, financial and digital data packages are put together. These include data from digital devices (e.g., mobile phone, computer, and Global Positioning System [GPS]), browser history, social networking activity, and financial transactions, benefits, and policies.

Using this information, together with witness accounts and forensic evidence (physical examination, toxicology, autopsy, etc.), an accurate timeline of at least the previous 24 hours is constructed and retraced, which highlights possible crime locations and method of approach and attack, if appropriate. Care must be taken to maintain an objective view of the victim and avoid deification or vilification based on aspects such as lifestyle and situational exposure, or psychological aspects. As we have seen in many cases, some of which have been highlighted in this volume, trauma can cause atypical or idiosyncratic behavior.

The victim's clinical profile is also valuable to establish consistency with having been traumatized, raped, or abused in the past, which helps inform patterns of their and others' behavior and exposure. This is particularly meaningful in cases where intimate violence played a role, such as described in the chapters covering domestic homicides and battered women offenders where theories of abuse and violence are applied to confirm whether the behavioral context is consistent with intimate partner violence. A psychological autopsy is done in equivocal death cases, such as unconfirmed suicides. The systematic protocol proposed to establish the victimology in homicide investigations is similar in which all available information on the victim is collected via structured interviews of family members, relatives or friends, health-care and psychiatric records, other documents, and forensic examinations. As a result, such a thorough interpretation is focused on highlighting subtle information that may have been overlooked, confirms the mode of death where questions existed, and provides a retrospective mental state of the victim where relevant.

Suspectology and Profiling

Suspectology is an approach that is applied to help identify the primary suspect in a homicide investigation. All precrime events, the facts of the crime, and postcrime behaviors of persons of interest are re-evaluated in the context of the crime type to formulate a working premise as to the most likely characteristics of the offender. The theory of the crime must withstand a test of any reconstruction effort using all evidence available and adjusted based on any new facts (Adcock and Chancellor, 2013). The old adage, "The theory must conform to the evidence; we do not conform the evidence to fit a theory" (p. 217) applies. A thorough and critical review is required. In cases where the perpetrator is unknown at first, the most likely suspect was often known to the police during the first 30 days of the investigation but has been overlooked or improperly eliminated as a suspect (Adcock and Chancellor, 2013).

Such a behavioral reconstruction often highlights disparities between a suspect's pre- and postcrime behaviors that guide further investigation and is more than psychological profiling alone. Criminology is the study of crime and criminals in social settings, whereas psychological inquiry is aimed at the study of the behavior and processes of the mind that can lead to predictions of future behavior. Specifically, criminology is "directed toward crime patterns, interview strategies, methods of operation, police work, and probabilities for crime subtypes" (Walter et al., 2015, p. 152).

Physical, direct, or circumstantial evidences that are either present or absent are reconciled with a recognized typology or pattern of crime, which we have attempted to demarcate by main distinctive features in the previous chapters. The data lead to refined probability factors about the who, what, where, when, why, and how of the criminal event. Walter et al. described the meaning of suspectology in offender profiling as follows:

> A profile is defined as a projective process of looking for probabilities related to the type of unknown individual who may commit this type of offense. Here, the focus is upon the offender's implied and probable behaviors, mental health status, character issues, motivations, and sexual paraphilia. Within this paradigm, the acquired data may infer information about the perpetrator's age, race, work, education, hobbies, and so on. Again, the profiler is concentrated upon the individual through the psychological continuum seeking individualized identity factors. (pp. 152–163).

As such, the offender profile is an expansion of the overall crime assessment process to provide an outline sketch of the offender to guide the investigation forward by providing potential leads. The projective and speculative nature of such a process requires properly trained, experienced, and qualified to conduct a behavioral analysis to prevent that a criminal investigation is derailed and resources wasted. Or worse, it can lead to wrongful arrests or convictions with tremendous injustice to the innocent and restitution cost to law enforcement.

Thus, crime assessment and offender profiling are not mutually exclusive. Victimology and suspectology are important pieces in crime reconstruction to help discover the overall "story" of what transpired before, during, and after the crime. Pre-, peri-, and postoffense behaviors are linked to identify the likely suspect(s). With an accurate psychological portrait of an offender, the link between crime and criminal becomes much more reliable. "By examining notification issues, scene issues (organized versus disorganized), body positions (staged versus natural), unusual findings or signatures, autopsy findings, and wound patterns, a perpetrator subtype can usually be identified" (Walter et al., 2015, p. 172). Such a structured profiling process targets the identification of persons of interest that are consistent with the resulting offender classification, thereby focusing further investigation in a narrower direction.

Final Words

Throughout the course of this book, we have illustrated that forensic psychology in the context of a homicide investigation is concerned with the application of psychological principles and concepts in all the steps necessary to identify and bring to justice the offender. The forensic psychologist assists the criminal investigation team by elucidating likely offender characteristics and behavior to narrow the suspect pool, provide potential behavioral leads, and contribute to an effective interrogation strategy. The forensic psychologist also consults as expert witness or trial strategist on behalf of the court, defense, or prosecution during different phases of the criminal trial.

One of the most important elements of these functions is to establish a clear cognitive and behavioral understanding of the known of unknown offender using all the evidence—forensic, suspectology, victimology, and crime scene reconstruction—at their disposal. Such an intimate clinical profile is used in the context of actuarial knowledge to strengthen the classification of the offender, and therefore insight into his or her behavioral patterns, motivations, thought processes, and personality beliefs, which are useful to determine the prognosis of treatment and rehabilitation and the likelihood of reoffending.

As has become abundantly clear in the many theoretical discussions and case studies presented in this book, establishing the typology of an offender is not an exact science but relies significantly on the expertise and knowledge of the forensic psychologist. Human behavior is incredibly complex and often not easy to delineate into definable and predictable categories as we may have suggested by the chapter divisions. Nevertheless, we have attempted to identify the primary characteristics, behavior patterns, and motivations of each of the types of crimes and offenders that we have selected. Thereby, we have illustrated common categories of homicide and perpetrators that represent the majority of cases a forensic psychologist, criminologist and criminal investigator, and legal professional can expect to become involved in.

References

Adcock, J. M. and Chancellor, A. S. 2013. *Death Investigations*. Burlington, MA: Jones & Bartlett Learning.

Bartol, C. R. and Bartol, A. M. 2013. Crime scene profiling. In: Bartol, C. R. and Bartol, A. M. (Eds.), *Criminal & Behavioral Profiling: Theory, Research and Practice*. Thousand Oaks, CA: Sage, pp. 21–56.

Bloom, B. S. 1956. *Taxonomy of Educational Objectives, Book 1, Cognitive Domain*. White Plains, NY: Longman.

Brandl, G. E. 2014. *Criminal Investigation* (3rd ed.). Thousand Oaks, CA: Sage.

Chisum, W. J. and Turvey, B. E. 2011. *Crime Reconstruction* (2nd ed.). San Diego, CA: Academic Press.

Douglas, J. E. and Munn, C. 1992. Violent crime scene analysis: Modus operandi, signature, and staging. *FBI Law Enforcement Bulletin*, 61(2), 1–9.

Eke, A. W. 2007. *Staging in Cases of Homicide: Offender, Victim, and Offense Characteristics* (Doctoral dissertation). Retrieved from Proquest (1390310091).

Ferguson, C. 2011. The defects of the situation: A typology of staged crime scenes. Gold Coast, Queensland: Bond University (Unpublished doctoral thesis).

Haag, M. G. and Haag, L. C. 2006. *Shooting Incident Reconstruction* (2nd ed.). Burlington, MA: Academic Press.

Hueske, E. E. 2006. *Practical Analysis and Reconstruction of Shooting Incidents*. Boca Raton, FL: CRC Press.

James, S. H., Kish, P. E., and Sutton, T. P. 2005. *Principles of Bloodstain Pattern Analysis: Theory and Practice*. Boca Raton, FL: CRC Press.

MacDonell, H. L. 2005. *Bloodstain Patterns* (2nd rev. ed.). Corning, NY: Laboratory of Forensic Science.

McElreath, D. H., Doss, D. A., Jensen, C. J., Wiggington, M., Kennedy, R., Winter, K. R., Mongue, R. E., and Estis-Sumerel, J. M. 2013. *Introduction to Law Enforcement*. Boca Raton, FL: CRC Press.

Money, J. 1986. *Lovemaps: Clinical Concepts of Sexual/Erotic Health and Pathology, Paraphilia, and Gender Transposition in Childhood, Adolescence, and Maturity*. New York, NY: Irvington Publishers.

Pettler, L. G. 2015. Crime scene staging: Victim-offender relationship, preceding, conflict, victim discovery, verbal staging, and murder scene location. *Journal of Cold Case Review*, *1*(1), 34–47.

Pettler, L. G. 2016. *Crime Scene Staging Dynamics in Homicide Cases*. Boca Raton, FL: CRC Press.

Schroeder, M. S. 2015. "Overkill" violence in a homicide: Is it always personal? *Journal of Cold Case Review*, *1*(2), 121–128.

Swart, J. 2015. *Criminal Profiling: Revealing the Science of Behavior*. Detroit, MI: Lilit Publishers.

Turvey, B. E. 2012. *Criminal Profiling: An Introduction to Behavioral Evidence Analysis* (4th ed.). Burlington, MA: Academic Press.

Turvey, B. E. 2014. *Forensic Victimology: Examining Violent Crimes in Investigative and Legal Contexts* (2nd ed.). Burlington, MA: Academic Press.

Walter, R., Stein, S., and Adcock, J. M. 2011. Suspect identification using pre-, peri-, and post-offense behaviors. In: J. M. Adcock and S. L. Stein, *Cold Cases: An Evaluation Model with Follow-Up Strategies for Investigators*. Boca Raton, FL: CRC Press.

Walter, R., Stein, S. L., and Adcock, J. M. 2015. Suspectology: The development of suspects using pre-, peri-, and post-offense behaviors. In: J. M. Adcock and S. L. Stein (Eds.), *Cold Cases: Evaluation Models with Follow-Up Strategies for Investigators* (2nd ed.). Boca Raton, FL: CRC Press, pp. 151–176.

Index

A

AA, *see* Alcoholics Anonymous (AA)
AAIDD, *see* American Association on Intellectual and Developmental Disabilities (AAIDD)
AAMR, *see* American Association of Mental Retardation (AAMR)
AB, *see* Antisocial behavior (AB)
Acceptance and Commitment Therapy (ACT), 230
ACT, *see* Acceptance and Commitment Therapy (ACT)
Acute embitterment, 20
Adaptive functioning, 2, 267–268
ADHD, *see* Attention deficit hyperactive disorder (ADHD)
Adjustment disorders, 2
Adolescent homicide, *see* Youth homicides
ADT, *see* Androgen deprivation therapy (ADT)
AEA, *see* Autoerotic asphyxiation (AEA)
Affective violence, 2
Aggression, 17–18; *see also* Proactive aggression; Reactive aggression
  subscale, 20
Aggression Replacement Training (ART), 181
AISOCC, *see* American Investigative Society of Cold Cases (AISOCC)
Alcoholics Anonymous (AA), 114
American Association of Mental Retardation (AAMR), 265
American Association on Intellectual and Developmental Disabilities (AAIDD), 257
American Investigative Society of Cold Cases (AISOCC), 300
American Psychiatric Association (APA), 19, 264
Amygdala, 238
Androgen deprivation therapy (ADT), 121
Anger excitation, 2
Anthropophagy, 3, *see* Cannibalism
Antidepressants, 30
Antisocial behavior (AB), 3, 167
Antisocial personality, 26–27; *see also* Personality dimension
  disorder, 3
Antisocial process screening device (APSD), 170

Anxiety, 3
APA, *see* American Psychiatric Association (APA)
APSD, *see* Antisocial process screening device (APSD)
ART, *see* Aggression Replacement Training (ART)
Asperger syndrome, 3
Asphyxiaphilia, 3
Attention deficit hyperactive disorder (ADHD), 3, 19, 250
Autism spectrum disorder (ASD), 3, 196–197, 240; *see also* Psychotic homicide offenders
Autoerotic asphyxiation (AEA), 3, 153

B

Barratt Impulsiveness Scale (BIS-11), 20
Battered woman syndrome (BWS), 3, 207, 213; *see also* Battered women homicide offenders
  abuse, 209, 212
  admissibility of evidence, 222–223
  assessment of, 213
  assessment protocols, 216–221
  batterer typology, 214–216
  BWSQ-3, 216
  case-specific vs. general expert testimony, 223
  case study, 219–220, 226–227
  criminal defenses utilizing, 221–222
  cycle theory of violence, 210–212
  DAPS, 217
  DISF, 216
  issue of imminence in self-defense, 224–225
  justification vs. excuse defenses, 223
  learned helplessness, 212–213
  MMPI-2, 217–218
  OBCS, 217
  problem of syndrome defenses, 225–227
  psychological trauma, 209
  PTSD assessment, 217
  RAAS, 216
  stages of, 209
  symptoms and victim beliefs, 213–214
  TSI, 217
Battered women homicide offenders, 207; *see also* Battered woman syndrome (BWS)
  clinical treatment, 230
  and crimes, 208

Battered women homicide offenders (*Continued*)
  criminal investigation, 228–229
  expert testimony, 229–230
  forensic psychological assessment, 229
  recommendations for handling cases of, 228
BAU, *see* Behavioral Analysis Unit (BAU)
BD, *see* Bondage and discipline (B&D)
B/D, *see* Bondage and discipline (B&D)
BDSM (bondage, discipline, sadism, masochism), 3, 129;
  see also Sexual sadism
Behavioral Analysis Unit (BAU), 308
Behavioral profiling, 325–326; *see also* Victim-centered
      death investigation methodology (VCDIM)
  operation method and signature, 326–327
  suspectology and, 328–329
  victimology and, 327–328
Biastophilia, 3
Bipolar disorder, 3
BIS-11, *see* Barratt Impulsiveness Scale (BIS-11)
Bloodstain pattern analysis, 323; *see also* Victim-centered
      death investigation methodology (VCDIM)
Bloom's taxonomy, 316; *see also* Victim-centered death
      investigation methodology (VCDIM)
Bondage and discipline (B&D), 129
Borderline personality, 27; *see also* Personality
      dimension
    disorder, 3
BPAQ, *see* Buss–Perry Aggression Questionnaire (BPAQ)
Brief Spousal Assault Form for the Evaluation of Risk
      (B-SAFER), 45
B-SAFER, *see* Brief Spousal Assault Form for the
      Evaluation of Risk (B-SAFER)
Buss–Perry Aggression Questionnaire (BPAQ), 20
BWS, *see* Battered woman syndrome (BWS)
BWSQ-3, 216

C

Callous–unemotional (CU), 167
Cannibalism, 103, 111
Canter's Radex Model, 310; *see also* Cold case homicides
Capital Offender Program (COP), 251
Catathymic crisis, 104
Catatonia, 3
Category D homicidal necrophile, 94; *see also* Paraphilia
Cathecol-*O*-methyltransferase (COMT), 167
CBT, *see* Cognitive behavioral therapy (CBT)
Child homicides, *see* Youth homicides
Coercive control, 3, 36; *see also* Domestic abuse nature
  case study, 38–40
  facets of, 37
Cognitive behavioral therapy (CBT), 28–29
Cognitive dissonance, 3
Cold case homicides, 299–301
  Canter's Radex Model, 310
  case study, 305–307, 311–312
  criminal investigative analysis, 307–308
  discussion, 312–313
  elderly witnesses and suspects, 303–304
  investigative challenges, 301, 304–305
  investigative opportunities, 307
  media stimuli, 308–309

  missing records, 302–303
  psychogeography, 309
  Rossmo's method, 310
  time–space compression, 309
Comorbidity, 3
Compliant victims of sexual sadist, 4
Compulsive, 4
COMT, *see* Cathecol-*O*-methyltransferase (COMT)
Conduct disorder, 4
Contingent paraphilia, 4
COP, *see* Capital Offender Program (COP)
Corpus delicti, 306
CPA, *see* Cyproterone acetate (CPA)
Crime, 2
  analysis, 4, 316
  reconstruction, 316
  scene analysis, 320–321
  scene reconstruction, 4
  Scene Staging Trilogy, 317
Crime scene investigation (CSI), 316; *see also* Victim-
      centered death investigation methodology
      (VCDIM)
Criminal profiling, *see* Profile
CSI, *see* Crime scene investigation (CSI)
CU, *see* Callous–unemotional (CU)
Cumulative strain theory, 58; *see also* Revenge killers
Cyproterone acetate (CPA), 158

D

DAPS, *see* Detailed Assessment of Posttraumatic
      Stress (DAPS)
DART, *see* Domestic Abuse and Stalking Reference Tool
      (DART)
DASH, *see* Domestic Abuse, Stalking and Honor-Based
      Violence (DASH)
DBE sex sadists, *see* Destructive/brief/elaborate sex
      sadist (DBE sex sadists)
DBS sex sadist, *see* Destructive/brief/simple sex sadist
      (DBS sex sadist)
DBT, *see* Dialectical Behavior Therapy (DBT)
Decapitation, 4
Defensive mutilation, 4
Dehumanization, 4; *see also* Depersonalization
Delusional disorder, 4
Dementia, 4
Dependency, 4
Dependent personality disorder, 4
Depersonalization, 4
Depression, 4
Derivative paraphilia, 4
Derogatis Interview for Sexual Functioning (DISF), 216
Destructive/brief/elaborate sex sadist (DBE
      sex sadists), 139
Destructive/brief/simple sex sadist (DBS sex sadist),
      138–139
Destructive/prolonged/elaborate sex sadist (DPE sex
      sadist), 138
Destructive/prolonged/simple sex sadist (DPS sex
      sadists), 138
Detailed Assessment of Posttraumatic Stress (DAPS), 217
DHRs, *see* Domestic homicide reviews (DHRs)

Diagnostic and Statistical Manual of Mental Disorders (DSM-5), 3, 4, 20
Dialectical Behavior Therapy (DBT), 230
Diminished capacity/responsibility, 4
Disembowel, *see* Evisceration
DISF, *see* Derogatis Interview for Sexual Functioning (DISF)
Disfigurement, 4
Disgruntled killers, *see* Revenge killers
Disinhibitors, 5
Dismemberment, 5
Disruptive innovators, 307
Dissociation, 5
Distortions, 188
Dizygotic (DZ), 167
DNA (Deoxyribonucleic acid), 107
Domestic abuse, 5
Domestic Abuse and Stalking Reference Tool (DART), 46
Domestic abuse nature, 36; *see also* Domestic homicide
    coercive control, 36–40
    Duluth model, 36
    power and control, 36, 37
Domestic Abuse, Stalking and Honor-Based Violence (DASH), 46
Domestic homicide, 35, 49; *see also* Domestic abuse nature; Intimate partner violence (IPV)
    cognitions of violent men, 41
    familicide, 43–45
    from IPV typologies to dimensional approach, 40
    recommendations for understanding of, 49–50
    risk factors for, 42–43
    role of emotion, 41–41
    understanding, 40–41
Domestic homicide reviews (DHRs), 49
Dominance and submission (D&s), 129
DPE sex sadist, *see* Destructive/prolonged/elaborate sex sadist (DPE sex sadist)
DPS sex sadists, *see* Destructive/prolonged/simple sex sadist (DPS sex sadists)
Drug-induced psychosis, 198; *see also* Psychotic homicide offenders
Ds, *see* Dominance and submission (D&s)
D/s, *see* Dominance and submission (D&s)
Duluth model, 36, 37; *see also* Domestic abuse nature
Dysphoria, 5
DZ, *see* Dizygotic (DZ)

E

Egodystonic, 5
Embitterment, 5, 62; *see also* Posttraumatic embitterment-type revenge killers
Emotional Problems Scales (EPS), 269
Empathy, 5
EPS, *see* Emotional Problems Scales (EPS)
Erotophonophilia, 5, 83; *see also* Paraphilia
Etiology, 5
Evisceration, 5
Excision, 5
Expressive/transformative behavior, 5
Exsanguination, 306

F

Fair trials, 225
Familicide, 5, 36, 43; *see also* Domestic homicide
    case study, 43–45
FBI, *see* Federal Bureau of Investigation (FBI)
Federal Bureau of Investigation (FBI), 67
Federal Rules of Evidence (FRE), 222
Fetish, 5
FFM, *see* Five-factor model of personality (FFM)
Filicide, 5, 67; *see also* Revenge killers
Five-factor model of personality (FFM), 171
Foreign object penetration, 5
FRE, *see* Federal Rules of Evidence (FRE)
Frotteurism, 5

G

GABA, *see* Gamma-aminobutyric acid (GABA)
GAM, *see* General aggression model (GAM)
Gamma-aminobutyric acid (GABA), 17
Gay, 278, 279; *see also* Intrapsychic motivations in stranger homicides
General aggression model (GAM), 40
Genuine necrophilia, 5
Geographic profiling, 309; *see also* Cold case homicides
Gerontophilic, 84; *see also* Paraphilia
Global Positioning System (GPS), 328
GPS, *see* Global Positioning System (GPS)
Green Ribbon Task Force (GRT), 132
Group contact theory, 75; *see also* Hate crime
GRT, *see* Green Ribbon Task Force (GRT)

H

Hallucinations, 5
Hate crime, 5
    in America, 71, 78–79
    against African-Americans, 74–75
    evolving otherness, 73–74
    examples, 78
    group contact theory, 75
    hate speech and impact, 75
    nativism, 76
    racist philosophy, 77
    slave patrols, 77
    slavery and discourse analysis, 72–73
    telishment, 78
    trauma, 77
HCR-20, *see* Historic Clinical Risk Management-20 (HCR-20)
Head-injury-induced psychosis, 197–198; *see also* Psychotic homicide offenders
Hematolagnia, 6
Her Majesty's Inspectorate of Constabulary (HMIC), 50
Hero, 310; *see also* Cold case homicides
Historic Clinical Risk Management-20 (HCR-20), 268
Histrionic personality disorder, 6
HMIC, *see* Her Majesty's Inspectorate of Constabulary (HMIC)
HNs, *see* Homicidal necrophiles (HNs)

Homicidal necrophiles (HNs), 97, 101, 109–110; *see also* Necrophilia
   Aggrawal's typology, 101
   building case against, 118
   case study, 105–109, 112–117, 119–120
   catathymic crisis, 104
   crime scenes, 110
   identifying and investigating, 110
   interviewing, 117–118
   legal aspects, 118
   linkage analysis and offender profiling, 110
   placophilia, 111
   psychopathic checklist-revised scores in, 109
   pygmalionism/agalmatophilia, 111
   recommendations for handling cases of, 117
   sarxenthymiophilia, 111
   somnophilia, 112
   taphophilia, 112
   thanatohierophilia, 112
   thanatophilia, 112
   typology of, 104
   victims of Sean Vincent Gillis, 111
   visceralagnia, 112
Homicidal sexual sadists (HSSs), 125, 127, 139–140, 152; *see also* Sexual sadism
   case study, 141–149
   cause of victim death, 142
   comorbid paraphilias, 153
   interviewing, 155–158
   investigating crime scenes, 140–149
   linkage analysis, 149–151
   Mellor's Typology of, 136
   offense characteristics, 141
   physical torture used by, 142
   profiling and investigation strategies, 151–153
   prosecuting, 153–155
   recommendations for handling cases of, 153
   treatment, 158
Homicide, 1
Homophobia, 278
Homosexual, 278; *see also* Intrapsychic motivations in stranger homicides
Hostile person, 16
Hostile world schemata, 16
HPA, *see* Hypothalamic-pituitary-adrenal (HPA)
HSSs, *see* Homicidal sexual sadists (HSSs)
Hunter, 310; *see also* Cold case homicides
Hyperactive, 6
Hypersexual, 6
Hypoactive, 6
Hyposexual, 6
Hypothalamic-pituitary-adrenal (HPA), 238

I

IAT, *see* Implicit association test (IAT)
ICD, *see* International Classification of Diseases (ICD)
IM-P, *see* Interpersonal Measure of Psychopathy (IM-P)
Implicit association test (IAT), 41
Inadequate personality, 27; *see also* Personality dimension
Incision, 6
Instrumental violence, 6

Integrated Model, 87; *see also* Paraphilia
Intellectual disability (ID), 6, 257; *see also* Intellectually disabled offenders
   comorbidity and criminal behavior, 260
   criteria of, 259
   susceptibility and external influence on, 260
Intellectual insanity, 188
Intellectually disabled offenders, 257; *see also* Intellectual disability (ID)
   adjudicative competence, 270–272
   assessing fitness to attend police interview, 262–263
   case study, 260–261, 262, 264–265, 269
   competence restoration, 270
   death penalty, 264, 265–266
   determination of functional impairment, 267–268
   factors contributing to mental health problems, 258–259
   interviewing, 261, 263–264
   IQ determination, 267
   law in Atkins v. Virginia, 264, 265–266
   law in Hall v. Florida, 266–267
   rehabilitation of, 272
   risk assessment of, 268–270
Intelligence quotient (IQ), 257
   determination of, 267
Intermittent explosive disorder (IED), 6, 15, 19; *see also* Reactive aggression
   aggression subscale, 20
   case study, 22–24
   DSM-5 Diagnostic Criteria of, 19
   as legal defense, 22
International Classification of Diseases (ICD), 207
   ICD-10, 25
Interpersonal Measure of Psychopathy (IM-P), 170
Intimate partner collateral murders, 43
Intimate partner homicide (IPH), 6, 35
Intimate partner violence (IPV), 6, 36; *see also* Domestic homicide
   at-the-scene risk assessments, 46
   forensic psychology in IPV perpetrator assessment, 45
   pathways to, 40
   predicting risk vs. predicting severity/potential lethality, 48–49
   risk assessment, 46–47
   victim risk appraisal, 47–48
Intrapsychic motivations in stranger homicides, 275
   case study, 279–288
   offender motives, 276–278
   origins of sexually motivated homicide, 278
   prevention, 288
   victim selection, 279
IQ, *see* Intelligence quotient (IQ)

J

JCI, *see* Juvenile correctional institutions (JCI)
Justifiable homicide, 6
Juvenile correctional institutions (JCI), 182
Juvenile homicides, *see* Youth homicides

K

Kleptomania, 6

L

Leakage, 26
Learned helplessness, 6
Legal insanity, 6
Lesbian, gay, bisexual, or transgender (LGBT), 1;
   see also Intrapsychic motivations in stranger homicides
   homicides, 275
Levenson Primary and Secondary Psychopathy Scale (LPSP), 170
LHA, see Life History of Aggression (LHA)
LHRH, see Luteinizing hormone-releasing hormone (LHRH)
Life History of Aggression (LHA), 20
Life without the possibility of parole (LWOP), 248
Limbic structures, 17
Linguistic Inquiry and Word Count software (LIWC), 67
Livor mortis, 103
LIWC, see Linguistic Inquiry and Word Count software (LIWC)
Lovemap, 6, 84, 327
LPSP, see Levenson Primary and Secondary Psychopathy Scale (LPSP)
5C lust murderer, 92; see also Paraphilia
Luteinizing hormone-releasing hormone (LHRH), 158
LWOP, see Life without the possibility of parole (LWOP)

M

Mania, 6
Manic depression, 6, 188
   disorders with psychosis, 195–196; see also Psychotic homicide offenders
Manie sans délire, 166; see also Psychopathy
Manslaughter, 6
MAOA, see Monoamine oxidase A (MAOA)
MARAC, see Multi-Agency Risk Assessment Conference (MARAC)
Mass murder, 6; see also Revenge killers
   classification of, 58
   conditions of, 57
MCBT, see Mindfulness-Based Cognitive Behavioral Therapy (MCBT)
Medroxyprogesterone acetate (MPA), 158
Mendota Juvenile Treatment Center (MJTC), 181, 240;
   see also Youth homicides
Men having sex with men (MSM), 278; see also Intrapsychic motivations in stranger homicides
Mentally ill, 187
MeRIT, see Merseyside Risk Identification Tool (MeRIT)
Merseyside Risk Identification Tool (MeRIT), 46
Metacognition, 308
M-FAST, see Miller Forensic Assessment of Symptoms Test (M-FAST)
Miller Forensic Assessment of Symptoms Test (M-FAST), 271
Mindfulness-Based Cognitive Behavioral Therapy (MCBT), 230
Mindfulness training, 29–30
Minnesota Multiphasic Personality Inventory (MMPI), 157, 216, 217–218
MJTC, see Mendota Juvenile Treatment Center (MJTC)
MMPI, see Minnesota Multiphasic Personality Inventory (MMPI)
Modus operandi (MO), 6, 326
MOMA, see Museum of Modern Art (MOMA)
Monoamine oxidase A (MAOA), 17, 167
Monozygotic (MZ), 167
Motivational Model, 85; see also Paraphilia
MPA, see Medroxyprogesterone acetate (MPA)
MSM, see Men having sex with men (MSM)
Multi-Agency Risk Assessment Conference (MARAC), 48
Murder, 7; see also Psychotic homicide offenders
   via bizarre acts, 194–195
   by proxy, 7
Museum of Modern Art (MOMA), 74
Mutilation, 7
Mutilophilia, 7, 92; see also Paraphilia
MZ, see Monozygotic (MZ)

N

NAACP, see National Association for the Advancement of Colored People (NAACP)
Narcissistic personality disorder, 7
National Association for the Advancement of Colored People (NAACP), 76
National Crime Information Center (NCIC), 305
National Institute of Mental Health (NIMH), 188
Nativism, 76; see also Hate crime
NCIC, see National Crime Information Center (NCIC)
Necrocoitolagnia, 7, 111; see also Necrophilia
Necroexteriolagnia, 7, 111; see also Necrophilia
Necrofellatiolagnia, 7, 111; see also Necrophilia
Necrofetishism, 7
Necromutilophilia, 7, 111, 127
Necropenetrolagnia, 7, 111; see also Necrophilia
Necrophilia, 7, 83, 97; see also Homicidal necrophiles (HNs); Paraphilia
   allure of, 110
   assessment of, 100
   case conceptualization, 120
   case study, 99
   categories A–D, 104
   crime scene analysis, 101
   destructiveness, 103
   diagnosis, 100
   etiology, 98
   genuine, 5
   prevalence, 100
   subclasses of class IX, 102
   treatment, 120–121
   typologies, 100
Necrophilic homicide offenders, 97, see Homicidal necrophiles (HNs)
Necrornopositophilia, 7, 111
Necrosadism, 7, see Necromutilophilia
Necrosodomolagnia, 111; see also Necrophilia
Negative emotionality, 7
New Mexico State Police (NMSP), 142
New York City Police Department (NYPD), 307
NGRI, see Not guilty by reason of insanity (NGRI)
NIMH, see National Institute of Mental Health (NIMH)

Index

NMSP, *see* New Mexico State Police (NMSP)
Not guilty by reason of insanity (NGRI), 119
NYPD, *see* New York City Police Department (NYPD)

O

OBCS, *see* Objectified Body Consciousness Scale (OBCS)
Objectified Body Consciousness Scale (OBCS), 217
Obsessive–compulsive disorder (OCD), 7
OCD, *see* Obsessive–compulsive disorder (OCD)
ODARA, *see* Ontario Domestic Assault Risk Assessment (ODARA)
Odaxelagnia, 7
ODD, *see* Oppositional defiant disorder (ODD)
Offender profiling, 307
Ontario Domestic Assault Risk Assessment (ODARA), 46
Oppositional defiant disorder (ODD), 7
Original paraphilia, 7
Ornophilia, 7
Overkill, 7

P

PACE, *see* Police and Criminal Evidence Act (PACE)
PAG, *see* Periaqueductal gray (PAG)
PAI, *see* Personality Assessment Inventory (PAI)
Paralagnia, 83; *see also* Paraphilia
Paranoia, 7
Paranoid personality, 27–28; *see also* Personality dimension
    disorder, 8
    Paranoid pseudo-community, 68–69
Paraphilia, 8, 83
    case study, 93–94
    counselling for specialists, 94–95
    crime investigation, 90
    criticism, 89–90
    disorder, 8
    etiology of, 84–89
    Integrated Model, 87
    Motivational Model, 85
    overlapping paraphilic crimes, 92
    paraphilic strokes, 90–91
    pathways, 8
    rape-slaying, 92
    signatures, 90
    Thematic-Derivative Model, 88
    Trauma-Control Model, 86–87
    wound interpretation and assessment of, 91–92
Parricide, 8
Partialist postmortem sex acts (PPSAs), 8, 103, 110
PBE sex sadist, *see* Preservative/brief/elaborate sex sadist (PBE sex sadist)
PBS sex sadist, *see* Preservative/brief/simple sex sadist (PBS sex sadist)
PCL, *see* Psychopathy Checklist (PCL)
PCL-R, *see* Psychopathy Checklist-Revised (PCL-R)
Pedophilia, 8, 84; *see also* Paraphilia
Perceptual Reasoning Index (PRI), 267
Periaqueductal gray (PAG), 17
Personality Assessment Inventory (PAI), 216
Personality dimension, 26; *see also* Reactive aggression
    antisocial dimension, 26–27
    borderline dimension, 27
    inadequate dimension, 27
    paranoid dimension, 27–28
Placophilia, 8, 111; *see also* Homicidal necrophiles (HNs)
PNC, *see* Police National Computer (PNC)
Poacher, 310; *see also* Cold case homicides
Police and Criminal Evidence Act (PACE), 262
Police National Computer (PNC), 39
Posing, 8
Postpartum depression, 8
Posttraumatic embitterment disorder (PTED), 8, 62–63; *see also* Posttraumatic embitterment-type revenge killers
Posttraumatic embitterment-type revenge killers, 58, 62; *see also* Revenge killers
    case study, 65
    core criteria of, 62
    Dorner's psychology, 65–66
    female, 66–67
    posttraumatic embitterment trajectory, 63–65
    PTED, 62–63
Post-traumatic stress disorder (PTSD), 8, 18
    assessment, 217
Power and control, 36; *see also* Domestic abuse nature
PPE sex sadist, *see* Preservative/prolonged/elaborate sex sadist (PPE sex sadist)
PPI-R, *see* Psychopathic Personality Inventory-Revised (PPI-R)
PPSAs, *see* Partialist postmortem sex acts (PPSAs)
PPS sex sadist, *see* Preservative/prolonged/simple sex sadist (PPS sex sadist)
PQS, *see* Psychopathy Q-sort (PQS)
Precipitants, 8
Predatory violence, *see* Instrumental violence
Predisposers, 8
Preservative/brief/elaborate sex sadist (PBE sex sadist), 139
Preservative/brief/simple sex sadist (PBS sex sadist), 139
Preservative/prolonged/elaborate sex sadist (PPE sex sadist), 138
Preservative/prolonged/simple sex sadist (PPS sex sadist), 138
PRI, *see* Perceptual Reasoning Index (PRI)
Proactive aggression, 16–17; *see also* Reactive aggression
    co-occurring reactive and, 18
    neurobiology of, 17–18
    style, 239
Processing Speed Index (PSI), 267
Professional, 310; *see also* Cold case homicides
Profile, 8, 328
Project CRAFT, 251; *see also* Youth homicides
Promiscuous Sexual Behavior, 175
Pseudonecrophile, 8, 104; *see also* Homicidal necrophiles (HNs)
PSI, *see* Processing Speed Index (PSI)
Psychogeography, 309; *see also* Cold case homicides
Psychological
    syndrome, 225
    torture, 8
Psychopathic homicide offenders, 165; *see also* Psychopathy
Psychopathic Personality Inventory-Revised (PPI-R), 170

Psychopathology, 9
Psychopathy, 9, 165, 169
    assessment of, 169
    case study, 173, 176–180
    diagnosis, 169–171
    environmental factors, 168–169
    etiology, 167
    genetics, 167–168
    homicide characteristics, 173–176
    interviewing psychopaths, 180–181
    observer measures for, 170
    recommendations for handling cases of, 180
    schizoid personality disorder criteria vs., 179
    treatment, 181–182
    typologies, 171–173
Psychopathy Checklist (PCL), 169
Psychopathy Checklist-Revised (PCL-R), 118
Psychopathy Q-sort (PQS), 171
Psychosis, 9; *see also* Psychotic homicide offenders
    not otherwise specified, 199
Psychotherapy, 9
Psychotic, 187
Psychotic homicide offenders, 187
    autism-spectrum disorder, 196–197
    discussion, 200–201
    drug-induced psychosis, 198
    head-injury-induced psychosis, 197–198
    manic-depressive disorders with psychosis, 195–196
    murder via bizarre acts, 194–195
    neurological risk factor, 190
    psychosis not otherwise specified, 199
    risk of violence in, 188–190
    schizophrenia, 190–194
    schizotypal personality with psychotic episodes, 199–200
PTED, *see* Posttraumatic embitterment disorder (PTED)
Pygmalionism, 9, 110
Pygmalionism/agalmatophilia, 111; *see also* Homicidal necrophiles (HNs)
Pyromania, 9
Pyrophilia, 9

R

RAAS, *see* Revised Adult Attachment Scale (RAAS)
Rape-slaying, 92; *see also* Paraphilia
Reactive aggression, 15, 16–17 30; *see also* Intermittent explosive disorder (IED)
    acute embitterment, 20
    case study, 21–22
    cognitive behavioral therapy, 28–29
    comorbid conditions, 20
    comorbid impacts, 25
    co-occurring proactive and, 18
    cross-examining defendant, 28
    extent of problem, 16
    heat of passion, 24–25
    and homicide-suicide, 20
    interviewing angry suspect, 26–28
    legal and forensic aspects of, 22
    and mental illness, 18
    mindfulness, 29–30
    neurobiology of, 17–18
    personality dimension, 26
    pharmacology, 30
    questioning suspect or defendant, 26
    treatment of pathological, 28
Reactive violence, 9
Recidivism, 9
Reflective interviewing, 262
Research-Based Forensic Victimology Outline, 319–320
Revenge killers, 5, 55, 69; *see also* Posttraumatic embitterment-type revenge killers
    aurora shooter, 61–62
    case study, 59–60
    chronic psychopathology trajectory of, 58
    classification of mass murder, 58
    conditions of mass murders, 57
    cumulative strain theory, 58
    defending, 68–69
    female, 60–61
    filicide as motive for spousal revenge, 67–68
    linguistic analysis comparison, 67
    mental health and social problems, 60
    paranoid pseudo-community, 68–69
    revenge fantasies, 57
    theory of revenge, 56–58
    types of, 56
Revenger, 310; *see also* Cold case homicides
Revised Adult Attachment Scale (RAAS), 216
Rigor mortis, 103
Risk–Need–Responsivity (RNR), 121
Ritual, 9
RNR, *see* Risk–Need–Responsivity (RNR)
Robbery, 279
Rossmo's method, 310; *see also* Cold case homicides

S

Sadism, 125–126; *see also* Sexual sadism
Sadism and masochism (S&M), 129
Sadistic cycle, 139
Sadistic personality disorder (SPD), 126; *see also* Sexual sadism
SARA, *see* Spousal Assault Risk Assessment (SARA)
Sarxenthymiophilia, 9, 111; *see also* Homicidal necrophiles (HNs)
Schizoaffective, 9
Schizoid personality disorder, 9; *see also* Psychopathy
    criteria, 179
Schizophrenia, 187, 190–194; *see also* Psychotic homicide offenders
    paranoid, 9
Schizotypal personality disorder, 9; *see also* Psychotic homicide offenders
    with psychotic episodes, 199–200
SCID-5, *see* Structured Clinical Interview for DSM-5 (SCID-5)
Scripting, 9
SDRS, *see* Short Dynamic Risk Scale (SDRS)
Selective serotonin reuptake inhibitors (SSRISs), 121
Self-report Psychopathy Scale (SRP-III), 170
Semantic Web, 308
Serial murder, 9

Sex Offender Risk Appraisal Guide (SORAG), 269
Sexual homicides, 83; *see also* Paraphilia
    desire for, 84
Sexually sadistic homicide offenders, *see* Homicidal sexual sadists (HSSs)
Sexual masochism, 9, 126
Sexual orientation, 276
Sexual sadism, 9, 83, 127; *see also* Homicidal sexual sadists (HSSs); Paraphilia
    case study, 129–135
    destructive vs. preservative, 137
    diagnosis, 127
    disorder, 126
    elaborate vs. simple, 137–138
    etiology, 135–136
    indicators, 128
    Marshall and Hucker's items of sadistic scale, 128
    prevalence, 127
    prolonged vs. brief, 137
    sadistic cycle, 139
    sexual sadists, 138–139
    torture, 9
    typology, 136
Shame attack, 9
Shooting incident reconstruction, 323–324; *see also* Victim-centered death investigation methodology (VCDIM)
Short Dynamic Risk Scale (SDRS), 268
Signature, 10, 90
Slave patrols, 77; *see also* Hate crime
SM, *see* Sadism and masochism (S&M)
S/M, *see* Sadism and masochism (S&M)
Sociopath, 166; *see also* Psychopathy
Somnophilia, 10, 110, 112; *see also* Homicidal necrophiles (HNs)
SOP, *see* Standard Operating Procedure (SOP)
SORAG, *see* Sex Offender Risk Appraisal Guide (SORAG)
Southern Poverty Law Center, 77
Souvenirs, 10, 103
SPD, *see* Sadistic personality disorder (SPD)
Spousal Assault Risk Assessment (SARA), 45
Spousal homicide, 42; *see also* Domestic homicide
SRP-III, *see* Self-report Psychopathy Scale (SRP-III)
SSRISs, *see* Selective serotonin reuptake inhibitors (SSRISs)
Staging, 10
Standard Operating Procedure (SOP), 318
Statement analysis, 321; *see also* Victim-centered death investigation methodology (VCDIM)
Stressor, 10
Strokes, 10
Structured Clinical Interview for DSM-5 (SCID-5), 217
Substance use disorder (SUD), 10
Substantially impaired, 25
SUD, *see* Substance use disorder (SUD)
Surrogate enactment, 10
Suspectology, 10, 321; *see also* Victim-centered death investigation methodology (VCDIM)
    and profiling, 328–329
Syndrome, 213

T

Taphophilia, 10, 112; *see also* Homicidal necrophiles (HNs)
TAU, *see* Treatment as usual (TAU)
TEDS, *see* Twins Early Development Study (TEDS)
Telishment, 78; *see also* Hate crime
Thanatohierophilia, 10, 112
Thanatophilia, 10, 112; *see also* Homicidal necrophiles (HNs)
Thematic-Derivative Model, 88; *see also* Paraphilia
Thematic paraphilia, 10
Thought disorder, 10
Tragedian, 310; *see also* Cold case homicides
Transsexual individuals, 276; *see also* Intrapsychic motivations in stranger homicides
Trapper, 310; *see also* Cold case homicides
Trauma-Control Model, 86–87; *see also* Paraphilia
Trauma events, 10
Trauma symptom inventory (TSI), 217
Treatment as usual (TAU), 182
Troller, 310; *see also* Cold case homicides
Trophies, 10, 103, *see* Partialist postmortem sex acts
TSI, *see* Trauma symptom inventory (TSI)
Twins Early Development Study (TEDS), 167

U

UAH, *see* University of Alabama in Huntsville (UAH)
UCSB, *see* University of California, Santa Barbara (UCSB)
UFOs, *see* Unidentified flying objects (UFOs)
Undoing, 10
Unidentified flying objects (UFOs), 188
University of Alabama in Huntsville (UAH), 66
University of California, Santa Barbara (UCSB), 59

V

Vampirism, 10, 103, 111
Vandalized lovemap, 84
VCDIM, *see* Victim-centered death investigation methodology (VCDIM)
VCI, *see* Verbal Comprehension Index (VCI)
Verbal Comprehension Index (VCI), 267
Victim-centered death investigation methodology (VCDIM), 316; *see also* Behavioral profiling
    analysis, 318–324
    application, 318
    bloodstain pattern analysis, 323
    comprehension, 318
    crime evaluation, 325
    crime scene analysis and laboratory reports, 320–321
    crime scene staging trilogy, 317
    crime synthesis, 324–325
    incident reconstruction, 323–324
    knowledge, 317–318
    research-based forensic victimology outline, 319–320
    scientific method, 322–323
    statement analysis, 321
    suspectology, 321
    victimology, 319–320
    wound pattern analysis, 321

Victimology, 10, 319–320; *see also* Victim-centered death investigation methodology (VCDIM)
and profiling, 327–328
Vincilagnia, 10
Violence, 2
Violence Risk Appraisal Guide (VRAG), 268
Visceralagnia, 10, 112; *see also* Homicidal necrophiles (HNs)
Voyeurism, 10
VRAG, *see* Violence Risk Appraisal Guide (VRAG)

W

WAIS, *see* Wechsler Adult Intelligence Scale (WAIS)
Wechsler Adult Intelligence Scale (WAIS), 216
-revised, 266
WAIS-III, 266
WMI, *see* Working Memory Index (WMI)
Working Memory Index (WMI), 267
Wound pattern analysis, 321; *see also* Victim-centered death investigation methodology (VCDIM)

Y

Youth homicides, 236
anger, 242
belonging, 243
case study, 244–245, 251–253
conviction of beliefs, 243
criminal justice system and, 246
depression, 243
developmental disorders, 240–241
domestic killer, 243
emerging psychopathy, 239–240
entitled/egoistic, 243
factors influencing child welfare, 248
fear, 242
investigating, 246–247
media and, 245–246
murderer relationship with victims, 237
neuropsychology and, 238–239
by numbers, 236–238
Project CRAFT, 251
punishment poll, 249
reactive aggression, 239, 243
reintegration into society, 250–253
resentment, 242
revenge killer, 243
risk factors, 241
school shooter, 244
sentencing youth, 247–249
thrill killer, 243
treatment and prevention of, 249
typology of homicidal youth, 242
in United States, 237

Z

Zoosadism, 10, 126